Haunted Bodies

The American South Series

Edward L. Ayers

Series Editor

Haunted Bodies

Gender and Southern Texts

Edited by
ANNE GOODWYN JONES
and
SUSAN V. DONALDSON

University Press of Virginia
Charlottesville and London

The University Press of Virginia
© 1997 by the Rector and Visitors of the University of Virginia
All rights reserved
Printed in the United States of America

First published 1997

⊗ The paper used in this publication meets the minimum
requirements of the American National Standard for Information
Sciences—Permanence of Paper for Printed Library Materials, ANSI
Z39.48-1984.

Library of Congress Cataloging-in-Publication Data
Haunted bodies : gender and southern texts / edited by Anne
Goodwyn Jones and Susan V. Donaldson.
    p.   cm. — (The American South series)
Includes bibliographical references and index.
ISBN 0-8139-1725-5 (cloth : alk. paper). — ISBN
0-8139-1726-3 (paper : alk. paper)
    1. American literature—Southern States—History and
criticism.   2. Literature and society—Southern States.
3. Southern States—Historiography.   4. Southern States—In
literature.   5. Gender identity in literature.   6. Southern States—
Civilization.   7. Body, Human, in literature.   8. Race in
literature.   9. Sex in literature.   I. Jones, Anne Goodwyn.
II. Donaldson, Susan Van D'Elden, 1951–   .   III. Series.
PS261.H34   1998
810.9'975—DC21   97-21472
                                                               CIP

Contents

v

PART THREE

Slavery and Southern Genders

Douglass and Jacobs, Jacobs and Douglass

PART FOUR

Where the Heart Is

Southern Strains of American Domesticity

PART FIVE

Bending Genders in the Modern South

Old Fears, New Desires

vii

Acknowledgments

Our heartfelt thanks go to Nancy Essig, director of the University Press of Virginia, for her endless patience with and enthusiastic support of this volume. Special thanks as well are due to Gerald Trett for his meticulous and herculean copyediting, to Noel Polk for making himself and his expertise available for a never-ending stream of queries, and to Mary MacNeil for her ceaseless yeoman labor. We would also like to express our gratitude to Ferdinand and Eleonore van Notten in the Netherlands and the staff of the Faculty of Letters at Chiba University in Japan for providing hospitality, fax access, and much-needed humor during the final stages of this project. Finally, we are grateful to the Virginia Center for the Humanities, the College of William and Mary, and the University of Florida College of Arts and Humanities for providing invaluable time and space at crucial moments.

We would like to thank the following for permission to reprint previously published essays: Lothar Hönnighausen, for a much expanded and revised version of Susan V. Donaldson's essay, originally published as "Gender and the Profession of Letters in the South," in *Rewriting the South: History and Fiction,* ed. Lothar Hönnighausen and Valeria Gennaro Lerda (Tübingen: Francke Verlag, 1993); Rutgers University Press, for Deborah E. McDowell's "Reading Family Matters," in *Changing Our Own Words,* ed. Cheryl A. Wall, copyright © 1989 by Rutgers, The State University, reprinted by permission of Rutgers University Press; Noel Polk, for "Around, behind, below, above Men: Ratliff's Buggies and the Homosocial in Yoknapatawpha," appearing originally in his *Children of the Dark House: Text and Context in Faulkner* (Jackson: Univ. Press of Mississippi, 1996); the *Southern Quarterly,* for a revised version of Mary Titus's "'Groaning tables' and 'Spit in the kettles': Food and Race in the Nineteenth Century South,"

Southern Quarterly (winter-spring 1992): 13–21; Bertram Wyatt-Brown, for his "The Mask of Obedience," published originally in the *American Historical Review;* and Cambridge University Press, for Richard Yarborough's "Race, Violence, and Manhood: The Masculine Ideal in Frederick Douglass's 'The Heroic Slave,'" in *Frederick Douglass: New and Literary Historical Essays,* ed. Eric J. Sundquist, © Cambridge University Press 1990, reprinted by permission of Cambridge University Press.

Haunted Bodies

Haunted Bodies

Rethinking the South through Gender

SUSAN V. DONALDSON
ANNE GOODWYN JONES

*Our conclusion must be that it is not sexuality which haunts society,
but society which haunts the body's sexuality.*
— MAURICE GODELIER

MAURICE GODELIER'S words, written for *New Left Review* in the early
1980s, ring with a peculiar resonance for students of sexuality and gender, especially in the American South.[1] Surely no bodies ever appeared
more haunted by society. From the body of the white southern lady,
praised for the absence of desire, to the body of the black lynching
victim, accused of excessive desire, southern sexuality has long been
haunted by stories designating hierarchical relationships among race,
class, and gender. But as the volume's subtitle, *Gender and Southern
Texts*, suggests, this collection goes further than Godelier to claim that
if "society . . . haunts the body's sexuality," it does so—at least in the
South—through cultural texts. During the Jim Crow era, for example,
a set of narratives portrayed the white South as a society under siege,
pressed by the imperative of protecting white women from black rapists
and thus driven to reenact lynching rituals over and over again. "Did
. . . [the "rape"] really happen?" asks a character in William Faulkner's
version of this narrative, "Dry September." When head lyncher McLendon responds, "Happen? What the hell difference does it make? Are
you going to let the black sons get away with it until one really does
it?" Faulkner suggests the power of sheer narrative, even when divorced
from fact.[2] Faulkner's more sympathetic character Quentin Compson
feels himself to be a barracks of garrulous ghosts, "his very body" an

"empty hall echoing with sonorous defeated names" and their stories.[3] A host of haunted southern bodies, black and white, male and female, could make the same complaint.

The stories of southern bodies have been structured in large part by the interlocking logics of dichotomy—masculine and feminine, white and black, master and slave, planter and "white trash," Cavalier and Yankee—that have characterized the dominant public written discourse of the South. Indeed, Eugene Genovese has observed that "slavery and all class stratification derived from the prior divine command that women submit to men—racial subordination derived from class subordination, which derived from gender subordination."[4] Certainly hierarchical and dichotomous gender constructions took a prominent place in antebellum proslavery ideology. Proslavery apologist George Fitzhugh, for example, shrewdly recognized in *A Sociology for the South* how crucial was the subordination of white women to the patriarchal authority of white slaveholding men. For Fitzhugh, "slave society . . . is a series of subordinations. . . . fathers, masters, husbands, wives, children, and slaves, not being equals, rivals, competitors and antagonists, best promote each other's selfish interests when they do most for those above or beneath them."[5] Another proslavery apologist, William Harper, linked the rigid boundaries of rank enforced by the system of slavery to the virtuousness of southern ladies: "The tendency of our institution [slavery] is to elevate the female character, as well as that of the other sex, and for similar reasons. In other states of society there is no well defined limit to separate virtue and vice. . . . Here, there is that certain and marked line, above which there is no toleration or allowance for any approach to license of manners or conduct, and she who falls below it, will fall far below even the slave."[6] In the South, then, gender construction—even at the relatively simple level of overt prescription—cannot historically be disentangled from constructions of race, class, and sexuality.

If gender prescriptions can be felt as fact—McLendon's question, "Are you going to let the black sons get away with it until one really does it?" produces a very material lynching—they can also be used as resistance. In her autobiography, abolitionist-feminist Harriet Jacobs writes that Linda Brent's rebellion against her master "Dr. Flint" (Dr. James Norcom) threatens his very sense of manhood. Apparently, the smallest assertion of freedom and defiance on the part of a slave woman had the power to shrivel a white slave-owning man's confidence in the power of his gender—because he believed his society's prescriptions requiring white male control.[7]

Indeed, the southern "subordinations" of which Genovese speaks can be deciphered, in their intricate linkages, in texts written from various positions of "stratification." Harriet Jacobs is by no means the only southern writer to locate a connection between slavery and gender. "There is no slave, after all, like a wife," South Carolinian Mary Chesnut caustically observes in her famous Civil War narrative.[8] Frederick Douglass exploits the slippage between slavery and gender in his 1845 account of the pivotal battle with the slave breaker Covey. Seeing the fight as the central turning point in his quest for freedom, Douglass declares in a celebrated passage: "You have seen how a man was made a slave; you shall see how a slave was made a man."[9] Even in modern fictional or nonfictional southern texts, references to manhood or womanhood shift surprisingly often to issues of slavery and race; conversely, language on race and slavery slips unexpectedly into discourse on gender. The very titles of Richard Wright's 1945 autobiography *Black Boy* and Ralph Ellison's 1952 novel *Invisible Man* underscore how white understandings of blackness exclude African-American males from any aspiration to visible manhood.

But sexuality and gender constructions in the South have also emerged from sources other than the official prescriptions of dominant southern ideology. The slave economy of the antebellum South depended—unlike emerging industrial capitalism in the North—on the home (or, in Elizabeth Fox-Genovese's more accurate term, household) as the site of production.[10] White men, whether rich or poor, did not typically leave home for long daily hours at a factory or a business. The South was, at least in comparison to the North and its commercial, urban, and industrial changes, still largely preindustrial and rural, even well into the twentieth century. Despite their escapes to the courthouse or tavern, men's "business" was typically at home. White men were still "lords and masters" at home in the South, regardless of class. White and black women's domestic power was deeply complicated by racial divisions of labor (including maternal labor) peculiar to the South. And black men's manhood was deeply compromised by an economy that not only made them, in Allen Tate's words, "liquid capital" but took from them parental and spousal legitimacy as well.[11] Furthermore, national as well as regional discursive needs to expand or contain, inflate or diminish, sentimentalize or denigrate the region, in short to represent the South as Other, have used gender as a tool, as writers from William R. Taylor to Nina Silber have observed.[12]

Despite gender's historical centrality to southern ideology and experience, it has been only since the early 1980s that students of southern culture have explicitly recognized the region's preoccupation with sexuality, bodies, and gender and focused on gender as an "analytic category," to use Joan Wallach Scott's useful term, in thinking about the American South.[13] Even so, some of the most innovative works in southern cultural studies of the 1980s repressed the realities of gender and sexuality, frequently effacing as a result links with class and race, with subordination and stratification. In *Tell about the South,* Fred Hobson writes that the "'representative' Southerner" is "conservative, religious, and suspicious of science and progress[;] he loves the land, has a sense of tradition and a sense of place, and he prefers the concrete to the abstract."[14] The assumption that a white man can represent a universal or "representative" southerner here uncritically extends Wilbur J. Cash's white male "Mind of the South," perpetuating a southern myth deliberately constructed by (among others) southern Agrarians like John Crowe Ransom, Allen Tate, and Robert Penn Warren.[15] Richard King in *A Southern Renaissance* dismisses southern white women (with the exception of Lillian Smith) from consideration because they "were not concerned primarily with the larger cultural, racial, and political themes that I take as my focus." (King omits blacks entirely "because for them the Southern family romance [King's paradigm] was hardly problematic. It could be and was rejected out of hand.")[16] Yet it is King's paradigm that forces women (and blacks) out of the "larger themes." "At the center of the [Freudian theory of the] family romance, in its patriarchal expression, was the father," King writes. "The family romance thus pitted son against father, and often joined grandson and grandfather."[17] Such a theory *cannot* explain women's writings, whether their themes are "large" or small, because it dictates the exclusion of women from the start. In *The War Within,* Daniel Singal develops the thesis that southern modernism involved the overturning of hierarchical Victorian dichotomies such as civilized/savage and human/animal. But he does not consider man/woman, and the sole woman he discusses is Ellen Glasgow.[18] Because Singal's theory of Victorian dichotomies omits the dichotomy of gender, neither the issue of gender nor actual women writers are available for analysis. It seems clear to us, then, that these exclusionary patterns emerge when their authors' theoretical assumptions are—perhaps unconsciously—homologous with dominant southern ideological patterns.

To take a more recent example, Jefferson Humphries's introduction to *Southern Literature and Literary Theory* develops a familiar rhetoric of dichotomies. Here the "we" is characterized primarily in opposition to "our elders," older southernists of the "[Louis D.] Rubin [Jr.] generation." (For "them," the Civil War was the predominant emotional fact; for "us" it is the civil rights movement. "We" believe in theory but not in old-fashioned "history as literary study.") Further, Humphries sees "the South" as finally "grounded in loss and defeat." But this is an old *white* story of the South. Southern slaves did not construct myths of the Old South or see its loss as a defeat, nor can the Old South in Toni Morrison's *Beloved* be explained using Humphries's eerily repetitive paradigm. In such ways, then, *Southern Literature and Literary Theory* repeats white southern ideology at the very moment it claims to defy and escape it, on the coattails of Paul de Man. Far from crossing "the threshold, beyond ideology," Humphries's key notions reimplant white southern ideology under the name of theory.[19]

Similarly, most southern historians until recently have ignored questions of gender in their primary focus on the history of men, slave and free, black and white. Although American women's history might have offered some hope, it developed—like the study of women's literature—out of a northeastern cradle. Southern women's history, with the exception of the work of Anne Firor Scott and her predecessors like Julia Cherry Spruill, remained unwritten until the last two decades.[20]

In the 1990s, though, southern women's history has established itself as a significant academic specialty. The Southern Association for Women Historians has hundreds of members and has sponsored major conferences on the subject of southern women and gender. To use Anne Firor Scott's words, historians are making southern women visible.[21] The early theoretical models that worked best in the Northeast, such as the assumption of a women's culture developing out of the bourgeois assignment of women to domesticity, have been helpfully complicated by more recent work. And now southern historians are taking up questions of manhood and masculinity. Southern literary study too has more fully engaged questions of gender for both sexes. Southern literary scholars regularly publish and present work on men, manhood, and masculinity, as well as on women, womanhood, and femininity, in journals from *American Literature* to the *Southern Quarterly* and at conferences from the Modern Language Association to the Society for the Study of Southern Literature. Courses in southern women writers and in new theoretical approaches to southern literature, such as southern cultural studies, attract students at a number of institutions.

Historians and literary critics find common ground in the new cultural approach to history. In Lloyd Kramer's words, this approach insists upon "the active role of language, texts, and narrative structures in the creation and description of historical reality."[22] Susan Mendus and Jane Rendall argue in their introduction to *Sexuality and Subordination* that any study of the historical reality of gender in particular must acknowledge "the importance that language and metaphor play in the depiction of sexuality."[23] The word *texts* in our volume's subtitle suggests our agreement with this approach. The essays this collection brings together reveal, to use Michel Foucault's phrase, "a multiplicity of discourses" about manhood and womanhood in the South, discourses that may have little to do with overtly prescribed gender. We discover a central preoccupation with gender in fields ranging from law to music. We also learn in careful detail how practices and narratives of southern masculinity and femininity have in fact been plural, unstable, and subject to bewildering shifts ever since the eighteenth century.

These insights may provoke surprise. Following the dominant southern and national stories' dichotomous logic, gender in the South has traditionally been seen as even more constrictively defined and polarized than elsewhere in American culture. Yet as scholars of gender have recently asserted, the very process of gender differentiation requires simplification through the suppression of anomalies and contradictions. Thus, seemingly stable categories of manhood and womanhood, invoked and repeated though they may be in numerous cultural texts, are everywhere inevitably susceptible to destabilization and alterity. Leftover areas of ambiguities always threaten to reassert themselves.[24] The assumption of a special clarity and permanence about *southern* gender evident in time-honored stories of white cavaliers and belles, of black Jezebels and rapacious Nat Turners, might well owe its origin and persistence, then, to general unease with the sometimes intense and always unending negotiations defining gender within the region. Such stories may have appeared all the more reassuring in a region where manhood and womanhood seemed so difficult to control. By the same token, such stories may have falsely reassured nonsoutherners that a simpler world existed elsewhere. "We need a refusal of [belief in] the fixed and permanent quality of the binary opposition," Joan Wallach Scott asserts, "a genuine historicization and deconstruction of the terms of sexual difference."[25] The writers in this volume heed Scott's caution, refusing to use in their own analyses a timeless, ahistorical model of fixed gender differences that replicates the ideology of its very object of study.

Mary Poovey asserts that texts make possible "the reproduction of ideology," including the ideology of gender.[26] But they are also the sites of ideology's failure, of the uncertainties, the ambiguities, and the constant changes in seemingly permanent and universal "nature"—in short, of the destabilization that constant gender negotiation implies and constructs. Cultural texts mark ideology's failures as well as its successes because they echo with the possibilities of alternative and opposite meanings, allude to language that has come before and will follow, and reverberate with discursive practices from a host of different discourses. Texts are marked by the same seismic tremors as is ideology itself—in Poovey's words, "fissured by competing emphases and interests"; texts echo, like Quentin Compson's haunted body, with conflicting names and stories.[27] In the American South, texts, like their writers and like the excessively gendered culture that speaks through them, are deeply riven. And if texts haunt bodies, bodies can nevertheless produce new texts that remember, dismember, and lay old ghosts to rest.

Our contributors, historians and literary critics alike, thus have produced new texts that explore southern gender arrangements as forms of representation, as southern texts. Recognizing the complex interactions between fiction and fact, literature and history, and striving to hear the multiple and divided ghosts haunting southern bodies, we have defined the title word *texts* in the broadest sense possible, to include diaries, blues lyrics, journals, letters, novels, poems, court records, petitions, short stories, rock songs, essays, autobiographies, transcriptions of African-American folk oral traditions, architectural plans, anthropological writings, and biographies. And we have brought together a wealth of interdisciplinary voices to this ongoing interdisciplinary endeavor. The cultural texts scrutinized in these essays on southern gender range from late eighteenth-century accounts of slavery to contemporary fiction by women. They include private diaries by white women—Mary Chesnut and Mary Henderson—and slave narratives by Harriet Jacobs and Frederick Douglass; anthropological research on African systems of honor and archives of government notaries and testamentary proceedings in eighteenth-century Spanish Florida; proslavery novels responding to *Uncle Tom's Cabin* and nineteenth-century accounts of southern dining customs; fictional representations by Edgar Allan Poe of the Virginia gentleman and lyrics of 1970s southern white rock music; critical and journalistic battles over black women's writing in the 1970s and 1980s and southern women's autobiographies. Also included in this range of texts are the canonical or conventional literary works one would expect in this sort of collection: plantation short stories, Zora Neale Hurston's *Their Eyes Were Watching God,* William Faulkner's *The Hamlet,* Eudora Welty's "A Memory," Allen Tate's essays and poetry, Toni Morrison's *Beloved,* and contemporary novels by Lee Smith, Alice Walker, and Dorothy Allison.

Passages: From Africa to the American South

We open the volume with two essays focusing on African, Spanish, and Caribbean cultural origins in the making of the American South and its black and white masculinities and femininities. Bertram Wyatt-Brown's essay, "The Mask of Obedience," builds on his well-known argument that the South retained an honor/shame ethic (as opposed to the emerging capitalist North's conscience/guilt ethic).[28] Studying available African anthropological and historical texts, he contends that Africans too were living in honor/shame cultures. In particular, Wyatt-Brown is concerned with understanding the probable psychological impact of the enormous status and cultural transitions African men were forced to undergo when they were renamed as American slaves. He suggests three modes of reaction: a deliberate, face-, honor-, and integrity-saving acceptance, marked by ritual deference; a more insidious internalization of the shame of being a slave, resulting in interior conflict between shame and self-esteem; and the enactment of shamelessness, an amoral, tricksterlike manipulation of masks outside the boundaries of honor and shame altogether.

"African-American Women and Their Pursuit of Rights through Eighteenth-Century Spanish Texts," Jane Landers's study of the texts generated by women of color in Spanish Florida, demonstrates in numerous ways the ingenuity and adaptiveness of African slave and free women. Because Spanish slavery offered certain rights to slaves that

English slavery did not (including, to lure them from the British enemy, freedom itself), a sizable number of slaves migrated south from Carolina. There they found the right to legal procedures providing protection against cruel masters, conjugal rights, the right to legal protection against the separation of children and parents, the right to hold and transfer property, and the right to initiate legal suits. Precisely because Spanish legal traditions viewed "society as an extension of family structures and connections," then, African-American women were able to make themselves heard and to assert their own agency within Spanish colonial courts in a way that was scarcely conceivable for slave women in the rest of the American South.

Victorian Southerners: Playing the Gentleman, Playing the Lady

Gender performance unites the three essays in part 2. In "Poe and Gentry Virginia," David Leverenz shifts the mask from African slave to free white poet to look at a different cultural boundary, between the forms of manhood enacted by traditional Virginia gentry and the forms of manhood emerging in the bourgeois Northeast. Poe, Leverenz argues, often assumes the mask of southern gentleman and Byronic poet but does so in an excessive manner that exposes the contradictions of gentry hierarchy. The poet, Leverenz suggests, even dares to substitute textuality itself as the true "source" of aristocracy. Moreover, Poe himself, mimicking "mastery in decline," serves as a trickster at the edge of the gentry he both emulated and interrogated.

As analyzed by Michael O'Brien in "The Flight down the Middle Walk," Mary Chesnut's textual labors have less to do with the politics of gender discourse than do Poe's but perhaps more to do with the gender of political discourse. Writing in her diary, rewriting, and then—in the 1880s—rewriting once again, Chesnut worked out innovations within a female tradition of literary form while she played the lady in her everyday life. Like Virginia Woolf, the modernist innovator whose story so uncannily replicates her own, Mary Chesnut exposed in her writing the signs both of her gender and of her postrealist temper. O'Brien argues that the fragmentary, elliptical style of the last version of her "narrative journal" bespeaks not a lack of control over her material but a deliberate representation of multiple voices in a world that for Chesnut—as a woman and a southerner—did not make sense in any of the old familiar ways. Chesnut, O'Brien asserts, was able to find in war and in her writing a way to break out of "the confined space of even a Senator's wife" through narrative experiments that questioned old certainties, disrupted familiar narrative traditions, and fragmented voices in a startlingly modern way, offering an early version of female modernism as a way to write political discourse.

If Chesnut, writing out her social voices, used the codes of women's writing in the 1880s to invent a modern sensibility, the writers discussed by Caroline Gebhard in "Reconstructing Southern Manhood" use the figures of the white southern colonel and his loyal black manservant to articulate contradictory and perhaps unconscious feelings about the codes of white manhood. These fictions both evoke and lay to rest the anxieties surrounding social and cultural threats to white masculine control. And the interracial homoeroticism that becomes almost explicit in James Lane Allen's fiction exposes the fragility of white male heterosexual control while confirming the overt homosocial bond relegating blacks to an ideologically inferior position. Thus, for Gebhard, the national popularity of plantation fiction after Reconstruction suggests a complex reworking of the national imaginary through these figures' capacity to evoke both sentimentality and camp humor.

Slavery and Southern Genders: Douglass and Jacobs, Jacobs and Douglass

While Poe explored the scripting and erasure of traditional white southern manhood, Frederick Douglass was engaged in rewriting African-American southern manhood. Examining Frederick Douglass's fictional depiction of a slave ship revolt, Richard Yarborough in "Race, Violence, and Manhood" uses the depictions of the same event by three other writers—William Wells Brown, Lydia Maria Child, and Pauline Hopkins—to foreground the degree to which Douglass wrote his version out of a sense of emerging dominant northern bourgeois understandings of manhood. Those understandings saw heroism not as collective but as isolated, not as a community but as an individual effort. The masculine ideal, for Douglass, requires leaving the South behind.

In "Santa Claus Ain't a Real Man," Anne Bradford Warner reads Harriet Jacobs's invention of Linda Brent in *Incidents in the Life of a Slave Girl* as a female trickster-narrator and emphasizes, as does Yarborough in his interpretation of Douglass, the subtlety and polyvocality of slave texts. Rather than Douglass's northern discourse of manhood, though, Warner finds strong African survivals such as the trickster figure that Jacobs frees from male exclusivity. For Warner, Jacobs (and Brent) can slip in and out of disguises and probe boundaries between white and black, male and female. Thus, Jacobs signifies on signification, creates a female carnival out of the all-male Johnkannau festival (itself a parody of white mastery), and thereby lays the groundwork for sites of African-American female resistance.

But what of Douglass's and Jacobs's actual lives in the South? Is there a southern cast to gender left to be deciphered in their lives and texts? In "Engendered in the South," Anne Goodwyn Jones uses the biographies of Douglass and Jacobs to reveal the differences between the specifically southern genders they learned as children and the narrative play with northern and African gender traditions that they inscribed as adults. Their lives should be read as texts no less than their writings, she claims, though their lives are texts over whose construction the two slave children had little control. Douglass's earliest sense of manhood was learned in intimate relations with southern white boys and men who served in part as objects of identification. Jacobs, too, grew up in a community in which class identifications determined gender in critical ways. Indeed, the life-texts of Jacobs and Douglass, as Jones reads them, suggest the intransigence of their early learning more than flexibility or amenability to signifying play, the focus of Yarborough and Warner. Such intransigence may be accounted for, Jones suggests, by the sense of privilege each former slave had learned could attend southern upper-class gendering.

Where the Heart Is: Southern Strains of American Domesticity

Southern white resistance to northern bourgeois gender paradigms—resistance with a conservative stamp—interests Lucinda H. MacKethan in "Domesticity in Dixie." Recognizing the power that Harriet Beecher Stowe had located in domestic ideology in *Uncle Tom's Cabin*, MacKethan turns to southern plantation novels to examine their response to domesticity in the South. In response to Stowe's condemnation of white southern men as betrayers of the home, white southern novelists, MacKethan suggests, tried to construct ideals of domesticity *within* their regional scheme of patriarchal order. But proslavery plantation novels found themselves straining against the limits imposed upon them by the domestic novel. The efforts of writers like John Pendleton Kennedy, Caroline Gilman, William Gilmore Simms, and Caroline Hentz show once again the fragility of apparently stable gender divisions in the face of more pressing political concerns. A patriarchal woman and a maternal man are only two of the inventions these writers develop as ways to reconcile domestic ideology with slavery.

Like Lucinda MacKethan, Mary Titus concentrates on the southern implications of domestic ideology—in particular, the preparation, serving, and eating of food. In the privileged homes in which domestic ideology would be most likely to take root, there was a fundamental problem: the kitchen, heart of the northern home, was an appendage to the plantation run by slaves. Taking off from this difference in "The Dining Room Door Swings Both Ways," Titus explores the meanings of southern architecture, food preparation and serving, and the etiquette of dining in a variety of texts, from abolitionist to proslavery to slave narratives, from cookbooks to memoirs and fiction by black and white women. Titus also shows the postbellum battle for discursive control of the meanings of the Old South, thereby suggesting the sources for today's *Southern Living*–style merging of southern food and southern hospitality.

In an attentive reading of North Carolinian Mary Henderson's antebellum diary recording the illnesses and deaths of her young children, Steven M. Stowe considers the patterns and processes that Henderson both recorded and produced through writing. Initially overwhelmed by grief and helplessness, Henderson used her diary to remember, rethink, and reshape the meanings of "home" in the context of the increasing professionalization of male doctors and of her increasing awareness of her home's vulnerability to the very dangers she felt bound to ward off. Stowe traces in "Writing Sickness" Henderson's emotional and intellectual changes as the diarist shifts from a world of women's and slaves' botanic medicines to a world of doctors' physicks, from confidence in herself as a mother to doubt, from confidence in men and doctors to doubt about them as well.

Bending Genders in the Modern South:
Old Fears, New Desires

Patricia Yaeger moves the volume into the twentieth century with an examination of texts revealing white women's anger and rebellion against rigidly defined roles of white southern femininity. In "Beyond the Hummingbird" Yaeger resurrects the old term *southern grotesque* to make sense of the huge, gargantuan bodies populating twentieth-century southern women's fiction. Noting that white southern women's bodies have traditionally served as texts upon which regional identity is inscribed, Yaeger argues that recent southern women's fiction rejects the image of the white southern lady by posing its antitype—the southern gargantua, the grotesque body rebelling against the "miniaturization and fragility" usually associated with southern women's bodies. Building on Peter Stallybrass's and Allon White's suggestion that discourses about the body become prominent when hierarchies start to change, Yaeger poses southern grotesque bodies as emblems both of the region's incarcerating ideologies of race, class, and gender and of the inevitable disruption and eventual dissolution of those ideologies.

In "Biting the Hand that Writes You" Catherine Gunther Kodat observes that the southern black folk oral tradition and a feminist quest can be at odds. Using Hurston's celebrated novel to construct a critique of Henry Louis Gates Jr.'s theory of African-American signifying, Kodat maintains that *Their Eyes Were Watching God* exposes the patriarchal traditions underlying the folk oral narratives Gates places on center stage and poses the possibility of another, more dialectically defined African-American voice. The result, Kodat concludes, is a novel that complicates monolithic critical assumptions about implicitly black male storytelling traditions.

Masculinity defined in terms of its fear of the feminine is the focus of Noel Polk's essay, "Around, behind, above, below Men." Polk reads William Faulkner's *The Hamlet* as an extended meditation on masculinity under siege. To be a man in Faulkner's world is to acquire ascendancy over other males but at the same time to retreat from the maternal into a homosocial world. Still, flight to the homosocial, Polk argues, is always compromised because Faulkner's men, such as the wandering sewing machine salesman Ratliff, carry around with them the reified images of the women they seek to flee—in Ratliff's case, the painted icon of a woman on his buckboard advertisement.

Contemporary Gender Wars: The 1970s, 1980s, and 1990s

Music lyrics and their rewriting of white masculinity constitute the focus of Ted Ownby's essay, "Freedom, Manhood, and White Male Tradition in 1970s Southern Rock Music." Ownby takes note of the preoccupation with manhood characterizing a slew of self-consciously identified white southern bands in the late 1960s and 1970s. Their lyrics, Ownby argues, suggest simultaneously an invocation, repudiation, and rewriting of traditional models of white southern manhood associated with paternalism, personal independence, honor, racism, and helluvafella violence and drinking. Often allying themselves with the African-American blues tradition, these white southern rock musicians ultimately celebrate a new form of white southern brotherhood—one lacking many of the more disturbing associations of traditional white southern manhood but also lacking a concrete place for women.

Deborah E. McDowell's essay, "Reading Family Matters," with its punning title, brings attention to "the literary battle royal" of the 1970s and 1980s between successful black women writers, Alice Walker in particular, and "resisting" black male reviewers and critics who protested the representation of black men in best-selling texts by women. Underlying that resistance, McDowell asserts, is an effort to retell and consolidate the traditional narrative of a unified black patriarchal family in order to repel the "intrusions" of black feminism. That effort, she adds, is ultimately underwritten by white control of language and representation, control dating back to "an older metanarrative written in the history of the slave master's hand." In both the historical and the contemporary narratives, the bodies and texts of black women serve as the terrain on which white and black men battle for masculine control.

This part concludes with Minrose Gwin's essay, "Nonfelicitous Space and Survivor Discourse." Reading novels by Lee Smith, Alice Walker, and Dorothy Allison, Gwin argues that southern women's fictional stories of father-daughter incest create a space for actual survival and resistance by interrogating the ideological construction of the southern patriarchal home and the identity that "home" and "place" impose upon southern daughters. These are stories, Gwin maintains, that rebel against the southern father's ownership of daughters' bodies and that insist upon the necessity of daughters writing their own cultural scripts.

The Past in the Present: Retelling Southern Histories

Three final essays each consider southern texts and gender over a larger historical and theoretical sweep. Peggy W. Prenshaw ponders the persistent patterns in southern women's autobiography, Elizabeth Fox-Genovese probes African-American women's troubled relations to southern history, and Susan V. Donaldson considers the history of southern literary history. Together these three essays suggest that rethinking the South through gender requires a reconfiguration of southern literary history.

Prenshaw argues in "The True Happenings of My Life" that southern women (and by implication southern men as well) must be understood as writing out of a regional subjectivity that differs from a national norm of individuation, separateness, and autonomy. When southern women write autobiography, the results fail to fit crucial theoretical claims about the genre precisely because they tend—from Mary Chesnut to Margaret Bolsterli over a century later—to focus on others, suppressing personal expression and self-reflection in the perhaps sacrificial interest of a relational self. Even anguished slave narratives like Jacobs's *Incidents in the Life of a Slave Girl,* Prenshaw argues, reveal the interwoven nature of women's identities with those that oppress them. As a genre, then, southern women's autobiography appears to make use of what Prenshaw calls a southern "female legacy of affiliation and shared identity with others."

Fox-Genovese, whose work on southern women's autobiographies influences Prenshaw, here moves into a more particular question: how does the history of black women in the South impinge upon the writing of black women's selves? Fox-Genovese argues in "Slavery, Race, and the Figure of the Tragic Mulatta" that the horrors of that history are at least twofold: what was done to black women, which evokes the writing of victimization, and what black women were forced to do to themselves and others, which evokes the writing of accountability. Either sort of story is painful, but the second is both more painful and more productive, as best seen in Toni Morrison's novel *Beloved,* the story of an escaped slave coming to terms with a past that includes killing her own daughter. The great achievement of Morrison's *Beloved* is that it can now speak what had been unspeakable for Jacobs and a host of other African-American women with southern roots and histories.

A rather different repression of history shapes the thesis of the final essay in the volume, "Gender, Race, and Allen Tate's Profession of Letters in the South." Like Prenshaw and Fox-Genovese, Susan V. Donaldson takes both nineteenth- and twentieth-century texts as her subject but sets her sights on masculinity. Starting from Allen Tate's famous essay "The Profession of Letters in the South," Donaldson moves back to look at *Russell's Magazine,* a mid-nineteenth-century Charleston publication whose contributors and editors felt some of the same gender anxieties as Tate. In both cases, there is an effort to construct a dominant southern literary tradition whose central figure is the white educated man. In both, the struggle for dominance must erase and efface the figures of women white and black and, in particular, African-American men. Donaldson shows in her look at writing from Paul Hamilton Hayne to Richard Wright and Ralph Ellison that black writers as well as whites have understood, and acted on, the threat that black men might be as culturally powerful as white men.

The essays collected in this volume thus suggest that gender in the end may be as important an analytic category for making sense of the South as race itself traditionally has been acknowledged to be. As these essays emphasize again and again, one can hardly tell, in fact, where the region's age-old worries about race and class end and its anxieties about gender begin. Whiteness and blackness, masculinity and femininity, domination and subordination have been inextricably intertwined in the South since the colonial period. One cannot account for the hypnotic power exerted by the image of the vulnerable white woman in the late nineteenth century, as Joel Williamson has argued in *The Crucible of Race,* without understanding the restlessness of black men and women in the aftermath of slavery or the economic and social losses of white men.[29] In the South gender and race haunt one another as they haunt the region's bodies.

Emerging from the composite picture of gender and southern texts drawn by these essays is a portrait of the region disconcertingly different from the monolithic images of the conservative, hide-bound, isolated South that we have inherited. First of all, looking at the region through the lens of gender reveals a South uneasily balancing polarized stereotypes of manhood and womanhood with the never-ending process of negotiating the boundaries between "femininity" and "masculinity" and between "whiteness" and "blackness." In this light the South, despite its fabled reputation for resisting change in all forms, reveals itself, oddly enough, as a radically unstable region, perhaps all too vulnerable to shifts in gender definitions originating within and without the region.

Secondly, these essays make us rethink what James C. Cobb has called in *The Most Southern Place on Earth* the notion of southern culture "as a free-standing set of exotic and immutable beliefs, rituals, and relationships mysteriously persisting in outright defiance of the powerful innovative influences of American mass society."[30] As essay after essay implies and sometimes asserts, manhood and womanhood in the South cannot be examined apart from general American notions of masculinity and femininity; American discourse on the family, households, race, class, and a host of other categories pertaining to daily life; or, for that matter, African, British, Spanish, Caribbean, and other international fictions of gender. Richard Yarborough, Caroline Gebhard, and Minrose Gwin in particular argue that the region's anxieties about gender point inevitably to the region's implication in national developments—in, for instance, the emerging antebellum bourgeois ideology of manhood, the late nineteenth-century obsession with reinforcing racial boundaries nationwide, and the contemporary emergence of incest survivor narratives. Bertram Wyatt-Brown, Anne Bradford Warner, Michael O'Brien, and Jane Landers are among those who call attention to the global web of meanings within which the meanings of the American colonies, the American South, and the United States have always been constructed.

There are, in the end, too many elaborately sexed and gendered bodies haunting the pages of southern texts not to pay heed to the region's preoccupation with manhood, womanhood, and their "proper" boundaries. Those bodies in turn bear too many inscriptions of age-old stories of masculinity and femininity for us to ignore. And while those inscribed bodies may well testify to the tragic incarceration of gender, they also bear witness both to the efforts of exorcism and to the freedoms of textuality that seem to mark one generation after another.

Notes

We would like to give special thanks here to Deborah Barker, David Leverenz, Noel Polk, and Bertram Wyatt-Brown for reading and commenting on earlier versions of the introduction. Susan V. Donaldson drafted the first version of the essay while a visiting professor at the University of Mississippi. With the assistance of a summer grant from the University of Florida, Anne Goodwyn Jones added sections to that version and revised the draft. A stay at the Virginia Center for the Humanities allowed Susan to work intensively on later versions, and the University of Florida Department of English rearranged Anne's teaching schedule to allow her to complete the final draft. We are grateful for all this assistance in the difficult but worthy project of co-authorship, and coeditorship, in the humanities.

1. Maurice Godelier, "The Origins of Male Domination," *New Left Review* no. 127 (1981): 17.

2. William Faulkner, "Dry September," *Collected Stories of William Faulkner* (New York: Random-Vintage, 1977), 171–72.

3. William Faulkner, *Absalom, Absalom!* corrected text, ed. Noel Polk (New York: Random-Vintage International, 1986), 7.

4. Eugene Genovese, "Our Family, White and Black," in *In Joy and Sorrow: Women, Family, and Marriage in the Victorian South, 1830–1900,* ed. Carol Bleser (New York: Oxford Univ. Press, 1991), 127.

5. George Fitzhugh, "Southern Thought," in *The Ideology of Slavery: Proslavery Thought in the Antebellum South, 1830–1860,* ed. Drew Gilpin Faust (Baton Rouge: Louisiana State Univ. Press, 1981), 291.

6. William Harper, "Memoir on Slavery," in *The Ideology of Slavery,* 119.

7. Harriet Jacobs, *Incidents in the Life of a Slave Girl, Written by Herself,* ed. Jean Fagan Yellin (Cambridge: Harvard Univ. Press, 1988).

8. "'Into the Black Cloud' / May 1861," *Mary Chesnut's Civil War,* ed. C. Vann Woodward (New Haven: Yale Univ. Press, 1981), 59.

9. Frederick Douglass, *Narrative of the Life of Frederick Douglass, an American Slave,* in *The Classic Slave Narratives,* ed. and introd. Henry Louis Gates Jr. (1845; rpt. New York: Penguin-Mentor, 1987), 294.

10. See Elizabeth Fox-Genovese, *Within the Plantation Household: Black and White Women in the Old South* (Chapel Hill: Univ. of North Carolina Press, 1988).

11. Allen Tate, *The Fathers and Other Fiction* (Baton Rouge: Louisiana State Univ. Press, 1977), 54.

12. William R. Taylor, *Cavalier and Yankee: The Old South and American National Character* (New York: Braziller, 1961); Nina Silber, *The Romance of Reunion: Northerners and the South, 1865–1900* (Chapel Hill: Univ. of North Carolina Press, 1993).

13. Joan W. Scott, *Gender and the Politics of History* (New York: Columbia Univ. Press, 1988), 28–50.

14. Fred Hobson, *Tell about the South: The Southern Rage to Explain* (Baton Rouge: Louisiana State Univ. Press, 1983), 13.

15. See Wilbur J. Cash, *The Mind of the South*, introd. Bertram Wyatt-Brown (New York: Vintage, 1991) and Twelve Southerners, *I'll Take My Stand: The South and the Agrarian Tradition*, introd. Louis D. Rubin Jr. (Baton Rouge: Louisiana State Univ. Press, 1977).

16. Richard King, *A Southern Renaissance: The Cultural Awakening of the American South, 1930–1955* (Oxford Univ. Press, 1980), 8–9.

17. Ibid., 34–35.

18. See Daniel Joseph Singal, *The War Within: From Victorian to Modernist Thought in the South, 1919–1945* (Chapel Hill: Univ. of North Carolina Press, 1982).

19. Jefferson Humphries, introduction, *Southern Literature and Literary Theory* (Athens: Univ. of Georgia Press, 1990), ix, viii, xvii, ix, xvi.

20. See Anne Firor Scott, *The Southern Lady: From Pedestal to Politics, 1830–1930* (Chicago: Univ. of Chicago Press, 1970); Julia Cherry Spruill, *Women's Life and Work in the Southern Colonies* (Chapel Hill: Univ. of North Carolina Press, 1938).

21. The allusion is to Anne Firor Scott, *Making the Invisible Woman Visible* (Urbana: Univ. of Illinois Press, 1984).

22. Lloyd Kramer, "Literature, Criticism, and Historical Imagination: The Literary Challenge of Hayden White and Dominick LaCapra," in *The New Cultural History*, ed. Lynn Hunt (Berkeley: Univ. of California Press, 1989), 97–98.

23. Susan Mendus and Jane Rendall, introduction, *Sexuality and Subordination: Interdisciplinary Studies of Gender in the Nineteenth Century*, ed. Mendus and Rendall (London: Routledge, 1989), 12.

24. Joan W. Scott, *Gender and the Politics of History*, 40–41.

25. Ibid.

26. Mary Poovey, *Uneven Developments: The Ideological Work of Gender in Mid-Victorian England* (Chicago: Univ. of Chicago Press, 1988), 17.

27. Ibid., 3.

28. See Bertram Wyatt-Brown, *Southern Honor: Ethics and Behavior in the Old South* (New York: Oxford Univ. Press, 1982) and idem, *Honor and Violence in the Old South* (New York: Oxford Univ. Press, 1986).

29. See Joel Williamson, *The Crucible of Race: Black/White Relations in the American South since Emancipation* (New York: Oxford Univ. Press, 1984).

30. James C. Cobb, *The Most Southern Place on Earth: The Mississippi Delta and the Roots of Regional Identity* (New York: Oxford Univ. Press, 1992), x.

PART ONE

Passages

From Africa to the American South

The Mask of Obedience

Male Slave Psychology in the Old South

BERTRAM WYATT-BROWN

Oppression driveth the wise man mad.
— BENJAMIN DREW, *The Refugee*

IN AUGUST 1788 Thomas Foster, a dirt farmer of Spanish Natchez, purchased for $930 two slaves—"dos negros brutos" the deed said, meaning that they were recent imports from Africa. One of the slaves was named Samba, meaning "second son" in the Fullah language of their native locale in the Futa Jallon country of modern Guinea. The other captive had a much more unusual name and finer pedigree: Abd-al-Rahman Ibrahima. He was the son of Sori, the *alimami,* or theocratic ruler, of the Fulani tribal group, whose capital was Timbo, an inland center that traded with distant Timbucktu, where Ibrahima had earlier received Islamic training.[1] Some months earlier, at the head of a cavalry detachment in his father's army, Ibrahima had been assigned to punish coastal tribesmen interfering with Fulani trade. He had been ambushed, captured, and sold to *slattees,* or native African slave traders.[2]

Through some means he conveyed to Foster the possibilities of ransom for himself in cattle and other valuables, perhaps including slaves, of which there was a great supply in Futa Jallon. But Foster had more immediate prospects in mind. The master dubbed his new prize "Prince" and at once had Ibrahima's long plaits of hair cut, though it took several men to restrain him. Intentionally or not, Foster had deeply shamed his black antagonist. In Ibrahima's eyes, he, a Fulbe warrior, had sunk to the level of a tribal youngster.[3]

Other and worse humiliations followed when Ibrahima refused to work. The Fulani were pastoral folk among whom even the lowliest

23

herdsman looked with disdain upon manual labor. Agricultural work was the task of the Jalunke, many of whom the Fulani had conquered and enslaved. After one of several whippings, Ibrahima ran off to the woods. Like most runaways, African or creole, he probably did not stray too far from the Fosters' five-acre clearing. Weeks passed and Ibrahima realized the hopelessness of his situation. Since suicide was a serious violation of the Qur'an, he had to assume that Allah had intended his predicament. According to a story long remembered in Natchez, he appeared in the doorway when Thomas Foster's wife Sarah was alone. Looking up, she saw the tall and ragged frame of the missing slave, eyes fierce and staring. But rather than recoil in terror, she smiled, according to the story, and offered her hand in greeting. Ibrahima took it, then knelt on the floor and placed her foot on his neck.[4]

Ibrahima's experience with bondage offers us clues about male slave psychology. The discussion is best limited, it should be added, to male slaves because they were considered the most troublesome and therefore upon them fell the greater demands for signals of servile habit. For newly acquired Africans, the requirement of docility and abject obedience, masters believed, had to replace traits associated with manly independence and self-direction. For those males born in slavery, dangerous signs of resentment or resistance were bound to meet prompt reprisal. In the struggle for control masters ordinarily had less reason to fear open rebellion from their female property: the women could be coerced with threats against their men or their young. Slaveholders expected that the wives would fall into line if the men were subdued and that mothers would raise their children with an understanding of the system and their circumscribed roles in it.

Few anecdotes—or even legends—explain how newly arrived Africans reacted to this regimen, which commanded not only their labor but also their change of behavior, even personality. We are accustomed to think in terms of more anonymous figures like Samba, the other slave with the stereotypical name and reputation that the New Orleans trader had sold to Foster. And yet there was a connection between the Timbo prince's ill-luck and the issue of what has come to be called "Samboism," the expression of complete servility.[5] Ibrahima's gesture can symbolize for us that process of learning the demands of servitude and what that meant for the millions once in bonds. Though they learned subservience, Ibrahima and countless other blacks retained independent judgment. As Erik Erikson has pointed out, "It takes a well established identity to tolerate radical change."[6] The Fulbe warrior had that kind of resiliency, pride, and dignity. His religion and former place in African society prepared him to make the best of things without losing a sense of who he was.

More important to our purposes is that in American slave culture, as in all societies, community life can be rendered unstable with differing effects upon the individual members, as circumstance, temperament, and the general situation shape their response. Under oppressive conditions, what traits are most affected may be subject to debate, but the issue of damage itself must be faced. We should not go on expounding about the riches of black culture without also examining the social and psychological tensions that slavery entailed.

Three approaches can help to explain slave psychology: the behaviorist position; the Freudian; and the cultural. None of them can be wholly separated from the others. The first involves role-playing, which can be oversimplified as a superficial performance without internal effect upon the actor. A more sophisticated reading suggests that role-playing does involve inner feelings. Pressure to conform to bondage, to recite the script as given, can lead to self-deprecation or even self-despising. Nor is the problem confined to slaves alone. In the eyes of others, "deviants" of one description or another must meet the obligations of their assigned stereotypes. According to Erving Goffman, the response of the victim to such requirements may be "hostile bravado," "defensive cowering," inarticulateness, or some other ineffectual reaction. Eugene Genovese finds the behavioral model inadequate in explaining slave behavior, but role-playing should not be denied: it is itself part of one's identity.[7] If we are brave or timid, confident or self-doubting, these traits will be registered to others. As Robert Park points out, "It is probably no mere historical accident that the word *person* [italics added], in its first meaning, is a mask." In all social circumstances, everyone plays a part. By these roles "we know each other," Park observes; "it is in these roles that we know ourselves."[8]

The second approach, the Freudian mode, has been somewhat discredited, owing to the disfavor into which Stanley Elkins's *Slavery*—and Freud himself—have fallen. The pioneer scholar of slave psychology, as it were, had adopted Harry Stack Sullivan's concept of the "significant other." As Elkins applied it, the Sullivanian theme was a variation on Freud's oedipal theory, which the historian used to describe the totalitarian relationship of white master and black slave. According to this analysis, the "Sambo" personality was derived from that loveless, brutal connection, one in which black culture, black family life, and white institutions of state or church played no major mitigating role.[9] Yet, for all its defects, which need not be recited here, Elkins's thesis was more Freudian than Eugene Genovese and Elizabeth Fox-Genovese have characterized it and is the stronger for that foundation.[10] Clearly, the slave in relationship with the master does not literally undergo the child's evolution from "object-choice" to identification with the master's superego as Sigmund Freud described the process. Yet in slavery the power as well as authority to demand dependency and total obedience was analogous to the impact of father upon child, as the proslavery "patriarchal" ideology emphasized.[11] Elkins recognized that subservience carried hidden psychic costs which, at the height of the controversy over *Slavery*, even his more discerning critics acknowledged as well.[12] Moreover, Elkins introduced a topic that almost receded from historiographical consciousness, a circumstance that does injustice to the complexity of the matter.[13] As the late Moses I. Finley, the Oxford University classicist, wisely observed, "Nothing is more elusive than the psychology of the slave."[14]

A third approach would combine elements of the first two but would in addition stress the cultural aspects of slave psychology. In such a strategy the focus is less upon the individual psyche and more upon the social character of the slave personality itself. As Bernard Meltzer reminds us, "The mind is social in both origin and function. It arises in the social process of communication. Through association with the members of his groups, the individual comes to internalize the definitions transmitted to him."[15] Moreover, such a characterization is particularly applicable to the small-scale, face-to-face community settings in which slaves and masters were placed. Under those circumstances there was less room for the kind of individualism that modern societies encourage, not only with regard to the slave but also the master as well. The combining of behavioral, psychoanalytic, and cultural factors provides a much sturdier foundation for understanding slave behavior and motivation than the adoption of one of them alone. In one of the few recent studies of the topic, Eugene D. Genovese and Elizabeth Fox-Genovese recognize the value of this strategy: "Historians need some sensitivity to personality structure and unconscious mental processes as well as to material conditions in order to understand the cultural patterns to which the newly enslaved clung, the ways in which they compromised with their enslavement, and the cultural order they forged for themselves." [16]

Africans transported to the Western world were already acquainted with the dictates of absolute rule and absolute servility, the latter a condition that encouraged a resignation severely inhibiting thought of rebellion. Slave rebellions were as rare in Africa itself as they were in North America, perhaps because Americans combined a familial bondage—the African mode—with commercial cropping on relatively small estates whereas purely commercial, impersonal, and large-scale plantations in the West Indies, for instance, resulted in much greater degrees of unrest. [17]

The African past and the servile present that Ibrahima symbolizes for us had in common a cultural pattern that both parties understood: the ethic of honor and shame. Indeed, the culture from which Ibrahima—and so many of the blacks enslaved in early America—came resembled much more the honor/shame paradigm I have proposed for the white South than the conscience/guilt model of the North. But the power exercised over the slaves complicated the situation for them. They were forced by circumstance to utilize the amoral posture of shamelessness, a pose that was intended to avoid the excesses of their victimization but that also resulted in both personal and social instability for the blacks themselves. [18]

In light of these factors, three major types of servility can be distinguished. The first is exemplified by Ibrahima—ritualized compliance in which self-regard is retained. The second is the socialization of subordination, a natural acceptance of circumstance that involved the incorporation of shame. The third type of subservience was the adoption of shamelessness. None of the forms of subservience is exclusive, for each was bound to merge into another with as much variation and contradictoriness as might be found in any individual. "Samboism," the third type may be called, was a disengagement from, a denial of, the conventional ethic though a part of the social order that both whites and blacks recognized. The strategy for dealing with whites did not in itself signify any sort of mental aberration or perversion. It did, however, involve an insensitivity to others and a dangerous selfishness. The untroubled Sambos served masters and themselves, sowing suspicion in the quarters and thus adding to the troubles of all. In other words, the slave who played Sambo did not suffer much psychic injury, because lacking morality at the time of taking the role, he lacked conflict. The real dilemma was what slaves of some sensitivity had to confront: how to maintain dignity in the face of shamelessness by masters and even by fellow slaves. In fact, both shame, as accepted by the slave, and shamelessness as sometimes adopted, were involved in community but not necessarily personal instability. Yet emotional confusion, misdirected violence or scapegoating out of repressed anger, severe or mild depression, self-contempt, and collective paranoia and mistrust could easily arise in poorly run or cruelly mismanaged plantation households.

First, a brief review of the chief aspects of honor-shame culture. It differs from the conscience-guilt style of conduct—the introspective, democratic, and individualized patterns that we like to think guide our own lives. "Whereas," says Gerhard Piers, "guilt is generated whenever a boundary . . . is touched or transgressed, shame occurs when a goal . . . is not being reached. It thus indicates a real 'short-coming.' Guilt anxiety accompanies transgression." [19] On the other hand, shame involves a total failure of the individual—the incapacity to do, think, and feel the right way because one despairs upon recognizing the low opinion and disrespect of oneself that others, who have respect and power, register. Thus, the excitation of shame involves a sense of defenselessness against the opinion, and, it may be, the physical threats of others who claim superiority. Still more serious, a person shamed also suffers, as Norbert Elias, the German sociologist, points out, an internal conflict "with the part of himself that represents this social opinion. It is a conflict within his own personality; he recognizes himself as inferior." [20] In the case of the slave, shame operates to affect his relations with other slaves whose good opinion of himself he wishes to have to enhance his own self-esteem, but to some extent it also conditions him to seek the good will of his master so that the master is less likely to shame him in front of his fellow slaves and the white world as well.

Just as shame and guilt are distinctive, so too are honor and conscience. Honor refers to the expression of power through the prism of reputation and rank based on gender, skin color, age, wealth, lineage, and other ascriptions rather than upon meritocratic criteria. Those who deviate from the accepted moral standards appropriate to their rank or who by their race, color, or lowly occupation are ineligible for membership and intermarriage are subject to the sanctions of shame.[21] Honor distinguishes between kin and alien, friend and enemy in very obvious terms. Group and personal esteem is tied to family and to friendship as well as to vengeance against betrayers of one or both. It follows that kinlessness and friendlessness are the marks of shame and disgrace in all honor cultures. For Africans like Ibrahima, the great fear was "unhappy solitude," the dread of being alone. The same was also characteristic of white southern life.[22]

Deference to illegitimate authority could not be countenanced by a man of honor. That was a principle that Ibrahima had come to live by. But if enslavement was one's fate, then the Fulani tribesman believed resignation the only response possible because divine forces ordained it. The gesture that Ibrahima employed was the traditional emblem of unconditional surrender in West Africa. Orlando Patterson has called enslavement "social death," a literal reprieve from its actuality.[23] By formalizing his subjection in this way, however, Ibrahima was not merely prolonging his life. He was helping to smooth out the hills and valleys of his emotions into a level plain. Rituals serve to inhibit and control wild feelings of total despair. Similar if less dramatic rituals of slave deference served that function for other slaves. Since honor was something that all whites shared in contrast to the shame of all blacks, acts of homage lent predictability—or were so intended—in a situation that offered no permanent security.

For Ibrahima the act of subjection was the beginning of unlearning his old self and teaching himself to present a new face of conformity. But he determined not to confess to dishonor, not to lose self-control. The Fulani people from whom he came were well versed in the connection between male honor and the ideal of emotional restraint—the stiff upper lip. To fail at that was to forfeit honor and authority, to acknowledge unmanliness. No doubt his success in maintaining dignity prompted his master to recognize his leadership qualities. Ibrahima became Thomas Foster's chief driver to whom other slaves, some of them also from Futa Jallon, had to defer. Upon that unequal collaboration between a former sandhiller and a former African nobleman, one of the most substantial fortunes in Mississippi was built.

The second category of subservience, the inculcation of shame, can also be illustrated by reference to the Fulani experience. In the Fulani areas, the condition of slavery, anthropologist Paul Riesman says, "most clearly expressed everything that is the opposite of Fulani." Slaves and captives belonging to that people were labeled "black, fat, coarse, naive, irresponsible, uncultivated, shameless, dominated by their needs and their emotions."[24] Slavery was a status given to strangers who were captured or bought; they remained kinless and subordinate, a traumatic experience in a society that was based on lineage and kinship networks.

More to our purposes are the slaves born into that condition in another Fulani corner of West Africa today. The anthropologist Bernd Baldus has recently studied the slave systems of Fulani herdsmen in the Bourgou region of northern Benin. The Batomba, agriculturalists, and the Fulani have lived side by side since the Fulani migrations began in the eighteenth century. Like other West Africans, the Batomba had long believed that if a child's teeth appeared first in the upper jaw, fearful disaster would afflict the kinspeople and tribe. Parents underwent rites of purification, but the babies were killed. After the Fulbe had settled, the Batomba gave or sold the infants as slaves to their new pastoral neighbors whose Islamic beliefs did not include the dental taboo.

Called *machube,* the stigmatized slaves and their descendants thereafter stood lower than those subject to three other forms of servitude in the area. As a result, when slaves of Bourgou were freed under French colonial rule about one hundred years ago, the machube continued in bondage more or less by force of custom alone. (Except briefly and ineffectively at the time of official abolition, they have never risen up against their masters.) The Fulani use neither physical nor legal means of coercion to enforce their will. When the anthropologist recently interviewed the slaves, he found that they had internalized their lowly status, ranking themselves below the Fulani and Batomba. Baldus discovered that the machube blamed themselves, not their superiors, for their plight. Their sense of humiliation was so powerful that, much abashed, they hesitated to account for their bondage until the anthropologist explained that he already knew. Somehow the machube were convinced that the Fulani provided them with special status. Whereas the Fulbe master assumes authority as a right, the machudo accepts slavery out of a mixture of awe for Fulani magic and sense of gratitude. Said one: "I work for the Pullo [another term for Fulbe] because he has taken me as a child from the Batomba. He has raised me, washed me, he has given me milk. . . . For this reason, as a sign of recognition, one carries out all his commands."[25] This mode of adaptation to an oppressive system very much resembles what Anna Freud called "identification with the aggressor" as a "potent" means for surviving danger.[26] According to Robert A. LeVine, an African anthropologist with particular interest in the Fulani and Hausa peoples of Nigeria, the incorporation of an individual's status into patterns of childrearing takes a generation or two. Eventually, though, the parent learns to shape the child's playing and acting to assure a match between the way the child perceives himself and the social and occupational position to be occupied in maturity. Those who adopt the strategy of imitative subserviency are by no means irrational or childish in some pejorative sense. In fact, in a patron-client society, such as that from which Ibrahima had come, "social incentives" tend to favor, LeVine argues, "the subservient follower" who understands human relations over the less politically minded "independent entrepreneur or occupational achiever."[27] Nor are their actions altogether selfish as the whole group may benefit from a greater sense of security.

Cosmic ideas also reinforce machudo docility. The slaves today adopt a fatalism similar to Ibrahima's Islamic faith of centuries ago but more intense. They find safety, protection, and even ultimate salvation by doing exactly as forefathers had done and Allah commanded. Asked why they obeyed so unquestioningly, the machube replied with such aphorisms as "'If you have a cock, then you do with the cock what you want, don't you?'"[28]

This identification with the owner's perspective rather than with their own suggests the mimetic feature of dependence: the desire to imitate the master's ways. By this means, something of the status of the Fulbe master is supposed to be accessible to the slaves. They want "to look like a Pullo," dress like him, talk like him, swagger like him. In error-ridden and inappropriate ways they adopt some of his exclusive customs despite the mockeries and derision of the Batomba and Fulani. The point is not to win favor from the masters. Instead, an acceptance of the master's power involves adaptation to his ways. As one former slave in America lamented, "The nigger during slavery was like the sheep. We have always had to follow the white folks and do what we saw them do."[29] Like the machube, they did so to raise their own low self-esteem and create a distance between themselves and others whose own position in society was not so lofty. When American slaves belonged to "quality folks," they often disdained the so-called "po' white trash."

This kind of behavior is part of the cultural order itself. Conventions of shame are part of the group's accepted wisdom, arising from necessity, not voluntary adoption. Just as whites in the Old South assumed their status over blacks and the sanctions and alleged superior worth that it conferred, so slaves, as a means of getting by day by day, accepted their position, only questioning it, consciously resenting it, when crises arose. Eugene Genovese claims that such slaves had adopted "a paternalistic pattern of thought."[30] With reference to the country slaves among whom he grew up, Frederick Douglass recognized the effects of ignorance and vulnerability. Alternatives to servitude were unimaginable because "life, to them, had been rough and thorny, as well as dark." Douglass, on the other hand, had had the experience of relative freedom as a slave in Baltimore, a circumstance that broadened his awareness of options and heightened his revulsion against bondage itself. Indeed, as whites well knew, any sort of individualistic skill or extraordinary status carried with it notions of self-esteem that whites sometimes found "impudent."[31] Likewise, Josiah Henson, a slave who eventually escaped to freedom, lamented that in his youth, he, like other country blacks, had long assumed the legitimacy of his own bondage. Moving his property before a sheriff's sale, his master had assigned him to guide some eighteen slaves from Virginia to Kentucky. "My pride was aroused in view of the importance of my responsibility, and heart and soul I became identified with my master's project of running off his negroes." Even though they floated past the wharves of Cincinnati where crowds of free blacks urged them to flee, Henson suppressed excited talk of freedom. As he sadly recalled, he "had a sentiment of honor on the subject." Accustomed to obedience and "too degraded and ignorant of the advantages of liberty to know what they were forfeiting," the crew heeded his orders, and the barge journeyed southward.[32] The incident was tragic, as Henson later realized in anguish, but most understandable. Plantation blacks who had little experience with autonomy were seldom quick to repudiate a humble conservatism that had so long served as a means of survival.

To return momentarily to the African experience with bondage, Baldus argues that our Western notions of corrective conflict, whereby the oppressed inevitably rise up in moral indignation as if by scientific or Marxian law, may simply not apply to the antique forms of socialization found in the northern Benin culture.[33] Indeed, other evidence from Africa supports his generalization. Observing "a prescribed code of conduct," T. J. Alldridge, an English trader, recounted how Mende slaves were accustomed to "cringe up and place their two hands one on each side of their master's hand and draw them back slowly . . . while the head is bowed." Similarly, on one occasion a recently imported African from Futa Jallon, possibly an enslaved Jalunke (a non-Fulbe black), met and recognized Ibrahima in Natchez. "Abduhl Rahahman [Ibrahima]!" he cried in wonder and fear. At once he prostrated himself on the ground before him.[34]

Although American bondage was different in purpose and context from that of the Bourgou tribes, Baldus's insights have pertinence to understanding servility in the Old South. Long acculturated American slaves whose concepts of liberty were far more sophisticated than those of slaves serving the Fulani held to a peasant caution with its own sanctions and rituals of allegiance. Even after emancipation, as Leon Litwack has observed, country blacks found it hard to break old habits of deference—much to the gratification of previous masters. South Carolinian Louis Manigault, Litwack records, was pleased that former slaves were still "showing respect by taking off their caps."[35] That attitude of mind was not just a casual matter: it was handed down from parent to child to prevent disaster. The trickster stories, which instructed as well as entertained, not only explained how shrewd and manipulative behavior could outsmart the powerful foe but also how sometimes the trickster's defiance led to trouble, defeat, even death. Recalling a ghost story from slavery days based on a real incident, ex-slave Silas Jackson, ninety years old, told how a slave, overheard praying for freedom, was killed by his master; "after that down in the swamp," he said, "you could hear the [murdered] man who prayed in his cabin praying."[36] As such tales and interpretations of events indicated, children of oppression had to learn the hard ways of the world. Said another oldtimer, interviewed in the 1930s: "I tells the young fry to give honor to the white folks and my [black] preacher tell 'em to obey the white folks, that they are our best friends, they is our dependence."[37]

It would be inappropriate to claim a universality of response from either such American examples or from the machudo's experience. The origin of the African slaves' fate is so particularized, the stigma so differentiating, that this form of slavery is unusual in its sole reliance on self-blame and on perpetual subjection. Undoubtedly, the American slave had access to different and more liberating values than did the machube. Even in Africa other forms of slavery flourished along different lines and provided for the slaves' more secure incorporation into the local society. Sometimes descendants were allowed to marry into the nonslave community. When told later that African and American slavery were much alike, Ibrahima disagreed, "No, no, I tell you, [a] man own slaves [at Timbo]—he join the religion—he very good. He [master] make he slaves work till noon, go to church, then till he sun go down, they work for themselves." Alas, as we have shown, Ibrahima exaggerated the benignity of his homeland institution, just as white masters did in America. As timocratic or honor-guided societies, the Fulani and other slaveholding tribes looked upon slavery as a means to procure "basic needs." Likewise, the southern ethic of honor upheld slavery just as slavery served honor.[38] Nonetheless, the African experience of bondage involved only the issue of caste or status, not race as well.

The first two forms of servility, the ceremonial type that Ibrahima epitomized and the more common pattern of cultural response to subordination, are somewhat different in character. The first involved less internalization than the second. Both, however, entailed outward demonstrations of fidelity beyond simply work faithfully performed. (Masters, for instance, liked to hear their slaves singing in the fields; silence was too ominous.) In keeping with that expectation, Ibrahima became what one of the Fosters' Pine Ridge neighbors described as "'a faithful, loyal servant.'" To please his American-born wife and Sarah Foster, his mistress, he even attended Baptist services on a regular basis after 1818. Nonetheless, he did not entirely forgo his Muslim religious practices.[39] Drab and demeaning though the role was, servility and its rituals were for him raiment to cover nakedness and vulnerability. By such means, one suspects, as his master's driver he remained an autocrat, never forgetting *pulaaku,* that is, the quality of character that identified the Fulbe warrior as virtuous and honor-proud. He expressed his feelings by never smiling, or so one white acquaintance who observed him for years reported. The withholding could well have signified his submission to Allah's will, not to man alone.[40] Ibrahima's style represented the requisite obedience to which all slaves had to conform in the presence of whites almost daily, a demeaning ritual but not requiring internalized self-abasement. The second, a pattern that began with childhood and formed part of the social order of the slaves themselves, was more deeply ingrained and did require a degree of low esteem.

The third ingredient in the framework of subservience is the traditional Sambo himself—one not so habitually deferential as the machudo example, not so reserved and dignified as Ibrahima. Elkins erred in defining this character as a whole personality when in fact Sambo was indeed a guise, adopted and cast aside as needed. When a slave took the role—some resorting to it more often than others—he made use of the third proposition in the system of honor and shame: namely, shamelessness.[41] As Elkins correctly argued, naked power, unchecked by any custom or institutional restraint, morally but not necessarily emotionally deforms both victimizer and victim. In other words, repudiation of ordinary and mediated ethics on the master's part could have induced an excessive servility and sense of unworthiness on the part of the slave. As a reaction, then, the Sambo repudiates internalization of shame but performs servility shamelessly. Anthony F. C. Wallace has noted, "Shame—awareness of incompetence in any sphere, whether growing from self-observation or information from others—may arouse so much anxiety as to inhibit further the person's competence."[42] Such individuals were probably rare in the slave quarters because most could find some skill or expertise to counteract the contempt of white men.

Even though Elkins failed to recognize the different responses that slavery could elicit, he was essentially right that Sambo behavior was authentic—but as ritual behavior, similar to but not identical with Ibrahima's alleged gesture. A reminder of how real this model of servility was appears in the diary of that remarkable South Carolinian Mary Chesnut, at the close of the war: "We had a wonderful scene here last Sunday—an old African—who heard he was free & did not at his helpless old age relish the idea. So he wept & prayed, kissed hands, rolled over on the floor until the boards of the piazza were drenched with his tears. He seemed to worship his master & evidently regarded the white race as some superior order of beings, he prostrated himself so humbly." The whites rewarded his gratifying performance with a blanket and other throwaways.[43] The observers knew how insincere he was, and all parties involved appreciated his immunity from moral responsibility in adopting the role.

The Samboism of the roguish, coarse, and deceitful slave describes only one role slaves might play, but in all honor-shame societies where slavery is a key institution, one finds the same ritualized and highly expressive phenomenon: in Muscovite Russia, Greece and Rome, Brazil, the West Indies, in fact nearly everywhere save parts of Asia. In all such societies, the slave was perceived as child and womanlike in character, only more so—violent (when spoiled), but usually passive, even affectionate.[44]

The source of the trickster mode lay in the unpredictability of a given master's behavior, a point that Elkins convincingly made. The slaveholder could be shameless in rule and the slave in protestations of dependency, driven by the emotions of the moment in a childish sort of way. The survivor was the conscienceless "chameleon" who adopted the coloration that the totalitarian slave regime—or the master's whim—imposed. The phenomenon in a contemporary society is well presented in Nien Cheng's *Life and Death in Shanghai*.[45] Both southern slaveowner and servant could act with a lack of decorous inhibition and yet not be mentally "damaged" or neurotic.[46]

In premodern societies, men and women lived in a very public style by which collective opinion reigned supreme.[47] The ancient Greeks, explains Sir Kenneth Dover, believed that to "be regarded as" virtuous was the moral equivalent of our more individualistic to *be* virtuous.[48] "I *wish* to be thought servile," says Sambo, in effect; not "I *am* servile." The shameless individual has no need to appear virtuous at all. As Patterson's study points out, those outside the circle of honor "aspire to no honor" and therefore "cannot be [made to feel] humiliated." In that freedom from the restraints and rules of dignity the slave exercised a mean autonomy in response to the willful and uncontrolled power of his owner. Probably the most eloquent form of shamelessness as a device for self-protection and enhancement was the wildly articulate lie. Mention has been made of the conscienceless trickster, Buh Rabbit and others, in black tales for children and even adults. According to the stories' moral lesson, the mouth and brain, not the arm and weapon, were the best protections available to the slave. As Charles Joyner observes, many of the tales provided a fantastic story of triumph in which the master-wolf is not only outdone by the weaker animal-slave but is thoroughly humiliated. In these little narratives victory for the slave lies in cunning and highly competitive action, but, as earlier remarked, sometimes the trickster is himself outwitted. The moral lesson was double: the necessity of subterfuge to win against the stronger party and the equally firm imperative to avoid being foolish and embarrassed oneself.[49]

Not surprisingly, black manhood was connected with the capacity to think, talk, and act fast. More significant than the moral lessons of folktales, acting out—"playing the dozens" as it is now called—taught by doing. In this children's game, one player insulted another's family so that the second party felt obliged "to defend his honor" (and that of his family). The challenges and replies escalate while the group eggs on the participants with laughter and groans. The game served a number of functions—as group fun; as an outlet for aggression that could not be directed toward whites; as a way to pick leaders for verbal agility; but also, most important of all, *as a device for making repression of deep feelings habitual.* A black psychologist explains it as the participants' experiment in keeping "cool and think[ing] fast under pressure, without saying what was really on their minds." Even if only half-believed, the elaborate alibi could reduce the chance of white revenge. Yet this kind of activity was amoral—shameless—defiantly so since the honor-shame nexus left no room for individual expression—aside from Ibrahima's singular strategy—except in the form of the dramatically deceptive self.[50]

Like honor and shame, sporting insult of this kind was another example of Afro-American cultural transference with modifications designed to meet the new circumstances. In Ibrahima's homeland, for instance, games of verbal abuse enable elders to discipline children and to vent tensions against others in a ritualized context, but the major objective is to teach and learn how to show restraint under provocation. Fear paralyzes the tongue, so worthiness to belong among peers can be achieved through the exchanged tauntings. One Africanist calls it "familiarity with a vengeance."[51]

An early and very instructive example of how the slave hid personal feelings and articulated in almost parodic fashion the opposite of insult can be found in recorded testimony before the Governor's Council in South Carolina, 1749. For reasons later revealed, a group of slaves, most of whom belonged to one James Akin, a Cooper River planter, had to testify before Council about an insurrectionary plot hatched by a former overseer on one of Akin's plantations a year or two before. The slaves' confessions before the dignitaries not only identified black conspirators on their own and on other plantations but also named some white transients as guilty of complicity. The whole group, they claimed, were preparing to canoe down river to Charleston, burn the city, blow up the magazine, and seize a ship to sail for Spanish St. Augustine.[52] Other planters, including Akin's brother Thomas, eventually informed the Council members that no such plot ever existed but was a concoction of Akin himself. Upon reexamination before the royal governor himself, one imprisoned slave named Cyrus recanted. He explained that before their first appearance before the council, Agrippa, another alleged conspirator, had told him and Scipio to leave the talking to him, as he "knew how to go before Gentlemen . . . had waited before on his Master in the Council Chamber, and was used to it." But, Agrippa had warned, keep Kent quiet because he "was a Fool and did not know how to Talk before White People." Indeed, Cyrus continued, if Agrippa had not "stood by and Pinched him, he would have told all & blown them." Scipio also said that Kent had been deeply afraid and that Scipio had "hunched him to make him speak as he ought to" before the governor. Some slaves could "jive," as the testimony shows, especially those who had frequent contact with the master class. Others were unable to do so and were thought in the slave quarters to be "fools."

When it became obvious during the hearings at Charleston that truth would prove more advantageous than falsehood, again the shameless Sambo type seemed the most articulate and credible. George, another slave, began his confession by saying: "Sir I am in your presence, my Master tells me that you are head of the Country. It is true I am not a white Man but I have a soul as well as others, and I believe there is a Heaven and a Devil." He claimed to be afraid that "God Almighty" would punish him if he continued to lie and he was "glad he was sent for, that he might tell all." [53] The ease with which the stories changed to fit the exigencies of the situation, the care with which the slaves shielded themselves from blaming any white, especially their master, the contrast between the articulate Sambos and the frightened mutes like Kent, and the unreliability that coercion had forced all of them to exhibit showed how smoothly slaves could function in the honor-shame context.

Nonetheless, the system of southern oppression was bound to have unhappy consequences for slave community and personal well-being. Black personality under bondage was partly dependent upon the sort of social climate that masters provided. Bitterness, hatred, or even a sense of well-being could be determined by a master's disposition. [54] Insofar as black honor under bondage is concerned, the true psychological limitation of slavery lay not in acceptance of honor-shame strictures but rather in the absence of rules and structure—anarchy, sometimes legalized anarchy. Plantation chaos and cruelty could place an emotional strain on the slave that is hard for us even to imagine. In other words, Ibrahima's maintenance of high character depended in part upon the reliability of his master. Had Thomas Foster been monstrous, his princely driver's actions might have been different.

Thus, a range of deferential modes and of inner acceptance existed with each slave adopting or, at times, rejecting servility as plantation environment, personal temperament, mood, and even unconscious motive allowed. A small number may well have fit Elkins's unhappy description and lived lives of self-deprecation and deception. At the other, more inspired extreme of Samboism, some slaves took positive delight in the jesting, roguish performance. Almost all varieties of servility involved some degree of shamelessness, for that signaled an inner contempt for the values of honor upon which the master rested his authority. But in dealing with their own feelings as opposed to the requirements of slavery, slaves avoided extremes for the most part. Some gave out contradictory or ambivalent signals. Such, for instance, was "Runaway Dennis," a slave belonging to Katharine Du Pre Lumpkin's grandfather in middle Georgia. Dennis so constantly quarreled with fellow slaves that they "'fought shy' of him," though treating him as a protected outcast, she recalled from family retellings. When called to account by the black driver, overseer, or owner, Dennis would vanish. Yet none of the slaves ever betrayed his whereabouts. He "shamefacedly" reappeared only when word reached him through the quarters that he had been promised amnesty, usually through the intercession of Lumpkin's grandmother, whom he revered. For a short time he was once more a model of conscientiousness and servile compliance. Even after freedom, the unreconstructed former slave showed loyalty to her by voting Democratic, being as "friendless" in the black community as he had been during slavery.[55]

Constantin Stanislavski, the great theatrical instructor, would have appreciated such attention to proper slavish behavior—the shuffling feet, hunched shoulders, downcast eyes, aimless gesturings of hand and body, along with shrewd or self-deprecating remarks to entertain overseer or master. As Stanislavski noted, "An actor lives, weeps, laughs on stage, but as he weeps and laughs he observes his own tears and mirth."[56] This "double existence" could make "art" out of Samboism. Unfortunately, the black, unlike the actor, had only one role to play before whites. No doubt that limitation had much to do with the rejection of shame that was part of the Sambo role itself. "He who is ashamed," says Erikson, "would like to force the world not to look at him, not to notice his exposure." But, he continues, "too much shaming does not lead to genuine propriety but to a secret determination to try to get away with things, unseen—if, indeed, it does not result in defiant shamelessness." [57] Slave thievery, breaking of tools, and other "subversions" should be seen in this light, not as rebellion exactly but as a covert way to gain advantage and also to stain the vaunted honor of the master. "I was never acquainted with a slave who believed, that he violated any rule of morality by appropriating to himself any thing that belonged to his master, if it was necessary for his comfort," declared Charles Ball, a fugitive slave.[58]

Caught like a child in the grip of a demanding, arbitrary father, the slave might react in open shamelessness. Richard Wright in *Black Boy* describes firsthand how an elevator operator named Shorty, playing the slavish clown, maneuvered a Memphis white man into giving him a quarter in exchange for a kick in the rear. Wright was disgusted with the triumphant Shorty. " 'But a quarter can't pay you for what he did to you.' 'Listen, nigger,' he said to me, 'my ass is tough and quarters is scarce.' " Anything goes so long as it means survival, as Elkins asserts. Ethically, however, the southern black lived in two worlds.[59] To please those in one sphere could well mean loss of respect in the other. Since ultimate power lay with the master, the temptation to rely on his largess and good favor was understandable.

To escape the dictates of shame and humiliation, then, male slaves had to repress emotions and exhibit nerveless behavior. But even so, the unpredictability of masters, the difficulty of avoiding white surveillance, the powerlessness of any slave in jeopardy could result in self-devaluation and doubt, "the brother," Erikson says, "of shame." [60] Charles Ball explained these feelings in his own family. Helpless to prevent the sale of his wife, Ball's father, once a man "of a gay social temper," turned "gloomy and morose . . . and spent nearly all his leisure time with my grandfather, who claimed kindred with some royal family in Africa." To avoid sale, Ball's father had to run away and only the grandfather remained to raise the boy, endowing Ball with a sense of selfhood, based, like Ibrahima's, upon the family lineage.[61]

Male abuse of women—sexual violence, desertion, insult—arose from feelings of personal dissatisfaction even as the aggression recapitulated white men's assaults on the black male ego.[62] These emotions of rage, depression, and stony resentment—often inwardly directed and involving alcoholism—are constantly emphasized in modern black autobiography and fiction, sources that put in artistic form some realities of black alienation.[63] The situation was the classic issue of neurotic conflict as Karen Horney portrayed it in *Neurosis and Human Growth*.[64] Though condemned for his unrealistic portrait of the historical Nat Turner, William Styron presents a picture of anarchic cruelty as the basis for such reactions that blacks adopted in whole or in part to protect selfhood.[65] The very pecking order of the plantation—mirror image in the quarters of the patriarchal, male-dominated, honor-obsessed rankings of the white society—encouraged shamelessness, disesteem of others, and self-abnegation. House servants were contemptuous of field hands, drivers of their underlings, lowly male slaves of their women, and women of the inferior members of their own kind. Accepting white standards of physical beauty, slaves often expressed a preference for light skin. Edward Wilmot Blyden, an early nationalist and advocate for Liberian settlement, declared, "We have been taught a cringing servility. We have been drilled into contentment with the most undignified circumstances." [66] White oppression stirred both compliance *and* fierce resentment, as Genovese explains in *Roll, Jordan, Roll*.

To make matters still worse, deep mistrust and rivalry rent the harmony of the slave quarters. Such problems had potentially tragic consequences. The darker side of "shamelessness," for instance, was that busy Sambos made untrustworthy companions. They might have been and probably were emotionally undamaged. The slave who acted the part but, unlike Ibrahima, had no memory of former rank was a likely victim of his own rage and conflict. But an imperviousness to moral self-control made the effective trickster dangerous to the stability of the slave community. As a novelist, W. E. B. Du Bois, for instance, created one such figure named Johnson, whom a Colonel Cresswell called " 'a faithful nigger.' He was one of those constitutionally timid creatures," Du Bois said, "into whom the servility of his fathers had sunk so deep that it had become second nature," but to the other Negroes, "he was a 'white folks' nigger,' to be despised and feared." [67] According to a recent scholar, Du Bois believed that the psychic damage of slavery was "an intense self-hatred" that made "racial solidarity an alien concept." Distrust and insecurity among blacks themselves multiplied as a result.[68] Needless to say, Sambo-like behavior—playing dumb, servile, or unconcerned—could well mask other designs or fool the white onlooker, to the satisfaction of the performer and his colleagues.[69] Nonetheless, how much effort, time, and emotional stress had to be directed toward self-protection alone, leaving less energy for more creative pursuit and self-development. What saved the situation from complete demoralization was the strength of family ties in a wide, extended-family kinship network characteristic of both American black and African culture. Though circumstances differed in both countries, sources of security outside the family were not available. In the American South, it did not pay to trust others even in the quarters.[70] Under such circumstances, Du Bois observed how blacks responded with a "double-consciousness," that is a "sense of always looking at one's self through the eyes of others, of measuring one's soul by the tape of a world that looks on in amused contempt and pity." How different that was from the studied and voluntary doubleness of which the stage director Stanislavski spoke, or from the sense of pride in personal reputation that southern white gentlemen so highly cherished.[71]

Equally serious was the sheer physical punishment that masters could inflict. The point is so obvious that one hesitates to belabor it, but even the most knowledgeable historians of slavery have underestimated its frequency and psychic effects.[72] The prospect of 150 lashes would make almost anyone a cringing coward. What is remarkable is the control that slaves exercised. Fortitude of this kind certainly had African roots. In some tribes thrashing ceremonies, called in northern Nigeria the *Sheriya,* tested stoic manhood. In any event the physical effects could be very severe even under law rather than simply under the arbitrary passion of an irate master. Corydon Fuller, a pious young bookseller traveling through Louisiana, recorded that in Claiborne Parish, Louisiana, 1858, a slave who had inadvertently struck his mistress in the face with a bridle was sentenced to "*one thousand* lashes to be inflicted 100 each day for ten days. Many think he will die."[73] Such punishments were scarcely everyday occurrences, but they also were not rare.[74]

From the psychological point of view, whippings had three major effects. They degraded the victim, shut down more normal communications, but, most important of all, compelled the victim to repress the inevitable anger felt toward those responsible for the pain and disgrace. As a result, even the merest hint of violence obliged the victim to retreat into as compliant a pose as could be managed.

In addition, less physically injurious cruelties abounded. We need not mention the threat of sale and separation from family and community, a sudden and often unpredictable event with sorrows hard to imagine. Moreover, masters sometimes used shaming rites, enlisting the other slaves to enjoy the spectacle and thereby doubling the misery while keeping the slaves disunited. Bennet Barrow, slaveholder of Louisiana, once threatened to put an offending slave on a scaffold in the yard, wearing a red flannel cap. In another example, a slave with an insatiable craving had stolen an enormous seed pumpkin from his master's patch. The other slaves told on him, and the master easily recovered the unconcealable object. So he made the slave eat a "big bowl of pumpkin sauce." The old slave who recalled the incident declared, "It am funny to see that colored gentleman with pumpkin smear on he face and tears running down he face. After that us children call him Master Pumpkin, and Master have no more trouble with stealing he seed pumpkins." [75]

With all the psychological, social, political, military, economic, and educational advantages that whites wielded, slaves could scarcely avoid feelings of oppression—and therefore of repression in a part of their social personality. To be sure, an essential self remained inviolable. Behind the mask of docility the slave was still himself and gave the lie to southern claims for "knowing" their blacks. As W. J. Cash pointed out, "Even the most unreflecting must sometimes feel suddenly, in dealing with him, that they were looking at a blank wall, that behind that grinning face a veil was drawn which no white man might certainly know he had penetrated." [76] And yet the cost of raising that impenetrable wall was high—less in playing the Sambo—than in repressing the hatred of the oppressors, the slave's own powerlessness, and the slavishness of other blacks. Male honor was richly prized in the slave quarters and defense of it established rank among fellow slaves. But slave honor was confined to the slave quarters, a restriction that may have made them all the more brutal out of frustration. Judge Nash of the North Carolina Supreme Court once declared that the slaves "sometimes kill each other in heat of blood, being sensible to the dishonor in their own caste of crouching in submission to one of themselves." Such behavior betokened a slave self-criticism, if not a self-despising, that sought a scapegoat in another person or possibly in an attempted identification with the master. For instance, Dan Josiah Lockhart, a fugitive in Canada but once a plantation driver, admitted, "I was harder on the servants than [my master] wanted I should be." From his account he was clearly taking out his resentment against his owner for selling his wife away to a farmer an unreachable eight miles away.[77] Whipping one's own children for the sake of discipline, whipping one's wife to keep her in line—these and other acts of violence in the quarters were often responses to the self-repressions that slaves could not avoid. Richard Wright explains that the reason why his mother, grandmother, and other family elders cuffed, slapped, and beat him was not only to vent their own miseries against a smaller creature but also to express a desperate love for him: without such treatment to curb his uncalculating independence, he would surely one day become, they thought, a white mob's victim.[78]

Another sign of self-hatred can be located in the examples of sabotage or apparent plantation "accidents" that historians have largely attributed to motives of subversion rather than to racist ideas of black "laziness" and irresponsibility. To take out disappointments on a hoe or horse would then be less politically calculated than an impulsive expression of anger against personal miseries in the quarters as well as in the slave system itself. We are unlikely ever to know.

Likewise we understand so little about how mothers raised their slave children. One suspects, though, that at some point early affection had to give way to stern and perhaps arbitrary discipline—a cuffing without explanation—to train the child to obedience and to staying out of trouble with the white man. "How many mothers and fathers had to punish severely children they loved so as to instill in them the do's and don'ts of a hideous power system in which a mistake could cost lives?" asks Eugene Genovese.[79] Male children more than female would have to be so trained.

Evidence of similar patterns in the experience of the Fulani slaves provides further insight. Anthropologist Bernd Baldus notes that the Fulani and Batomba superiors consider the machudo slave "'uncivilized'" or "'wild.'" The machube are demoralized to the point of extreme aggressiveness toward each other. Machube men never assault the mocking rulers but instead fall upon one another in often fierce violence. "Mistrust" and lack of internalized controls are "pervasive, covering even close social ties among neighbors, friends, or family members," the anthropologist explains. The experience of the machube is different from that of American slaves, who had the benefit of a Christian humanitarianism and more sophisticated attitudes with which to forge slave community bonds. But such unhappy conditions could well have existed on those plantations where masters sought to destroy a sense of black collectivity.[80]

In the last few years, the darker side of slave life has regained scholars' notice, but generally historians place the emphasis upon the remarkable endurance and even joyousness that slaves extracted from harsh conditions. Significant and valid though the brighter view is, the costs of honor and shame should not be ignored.[81] If repression and its manifestation in inappropriate ways was one of the chief emotional problems of bondage, the second was the related problem of communal mistrust and its effect upon the social personality of the slave.

Nat Turner's recurrent nightmare in William Styron's novel about the great Virginia slave revolt involves Nat seeing himself floating down a river. On a hill stands a white temple, familiar but closed to him. As he drifts by, all Nat can do is worship from afar the power of the whites' world which that edifice represents. The river takes him nowhere, just as the real Nat Turner's rebellion, for all its celebration in recent times, was futile.[82] Ibrahima, whose story introduced this paper, also dreamed of water and familiar distant places. After a lifetime of building the estate of his master into one of the great fortunes of Mississippi, Ibrahima hoped to die in his native land. Aged like his slave, Thomas Foster at last was willing to release him. But a final irony was that Ibrahima died at Monrovia on the coast, far from Timbo, with only his American kin to honor his memory.[83]

Notes

A shorter version of this paper was presented as the Commonwealth Fund Lecture at University College, London, on February 2, 1985. I wish to acknowledge the useful commentaries of the following participants at the seminar following the presentation: Howard Temperley, most especially; and also Hugh Brogan, Peter J. Parish, Owen Dudley Edwards, and Betty Wood. Also I thank these American critics for their helpful reviews of the document: Lawrence J. Friedman, Stanley L. Engerman, Timothy Huebner, and, above all, Anita Rutman.

    1. There are a number of terms by which the Fulani are known, but for the sake of clarity I chiefly use only two: Fulbe and Fulani.

2. This account is based on Terry Alford, *Prince among Slaves* (New York: Harcourt Brace Jovanovich, 1977), esp. 3–38. Charles S. Sydnor, "The Biography of a Slave," *South Atlantic Quarterly* 36 (1937): 59–73; "The Unfortunate Moor," *African Repository* 3 (February 1828): 364–67; and Thomas H. Gallaudet, *A Statement with Regard to the Moorish Prince, Abduhl Rahhahman* (New York: Daniel Fanshaw, 1828), 3–4 (there are inaccuracies, however, in these accounts so that Alford's careful researches are to be preferred). See also Paul E. Lovejoy, *Transformation in Slavery: A History of Slavery in West Africa* (Cambridge: Cambridge Univ. Press, 1983), 114–15; and entries for Mar. 9–12, 1794, in "Journal of James Watt in his expedition to and from Teembo in 1794 copied from the author's own hand," MSS Afr. 22, Rhodes House, Oxford University.

3. Alford, *Prince among Slaves*, 23, 44.

4. In Futa Jallon, Ibrahima's region, slaves constituted a majority of the population. See Paul E. Lovejoy, "The Characteristics of Plantations in the Nineteenth-Century Sokoto Caliphate (Islamic West Africa)," *American Historical Review* 84 (1979): 1273. Alford, *Prince among Slaves*, 45–47, and Major Steve Power, *The Memento: Old and New Natchez 1700 to 1897* (Natchez, Miss.: N.p., 1897), 13–14.

5. Joseph Boskin, *Sambo: The Rise and Demise of an American Jester* (New York: Oxford Univ. Press, 1986), 17–41.

6. Erik H. Erikson, *Insight and Responsibility: Lectures on the Ethical Implications of Psychoanalytic Insight* (New York: Norton, 1964), 96.

7. Erving Goffman, *Stigma: Notes on the Management of Spoiled Identity* (1963; rpt. New York: Jason Aronson, 1974), 17; Eugene D. Genovese, "Toward a Psychology of Slavery: An Assessment of the Contribution of *The Slave Community*," in Al-Tony Gilmore, ed., *Revisiting Blassingame's "The Slave Community": The Scholars Respond* (Westport, Conn.: Greenwood Press, 1978), 27–41.

8. Park, qtd. in Erving Goffman, *The Presentation of Self in Everyday Life* (New York, 1959), 19.

9. Stanley Elkins, *Slavery: A Problem in American Institutional and Intellectual Life* (Chicago: Univ. of Chicago Press, 1959); idem, "Slavery and Ideology," in Ann J. Lane, ed., *The Debate over "Slavery": Stanley Elkins and His Critics* (Urbana: Univ. of Illinois Press, 1971), 325–78; idem, "The Slavery Debate," *Commentary* 60 (Dec. 1975), 40–54.

10. Elizabeth Fox-Genovese and Eugene D. Genovese, *Fruits of Merchant Capital: Slavery and Bourgeois Property in the Rise and Expansion of Capitalism* (New York: Oxford Univ. Press, 1983), 91–135, esp. 102–5, 117–25.

11. See esp. Sidney Axelrad and Lottie M. Maury, "Identification as a Mechanism of Adaptation," in George B. Wilbur and Warner Muensterberger,

eds., *Psychoanalysis and Culture: Essays in Honor of Gèza Róheim* (New York: John Wiley & Sons, 1951), 168–84. Sigmund Freud, *New Introductory Lectures on Psychoanalysis* (New York: Carlton House, 1933), is briefly and lucidly explained in Peter Gay, *Freud: A Life for Our Time* (New York: Norton, 1988), 415–16.

12. See Kenneth M. Stampp, "Rebels and Sambos," in Allen Weinstein, Frank O. Gatell, and David Sarasohn, eds., *American Negro Slavery* (New York: Oxford Univ. Press, 1979), 240, 252 nn. 39 and 40, 241; James P. Comer, *Beyond Black and White* (New York: Quadrangle Books, 1972), 174–75.

13. Cf. Sterling Stuckey, *Slave Culture: Nationalist Theory and the Foundations of Black America* (New York: Oxford Univ. Press, 1987); Boskin, *Sambo: The Rise and Demise of an American Jester,* 17–41; Mary Frances Berry and John Blassingame, *Long Memory: The Black Experience in America* (New York: Oxford Univ. Press, 1982), 11; Robert Fogel and Stanley L. Engerman, *Time on the Cross: The Economics of American Negro Slavery* (Boston: Little, Brown, 1974), 228–32. For a more realistic appraisal of bondage and black reaction, see Willie Lee Rose, *Slavery and Freedom,* William F. Freehling, ed. (New York: Oxford Univ. Press, 1982), 164–76.

14. Moses I. Finley, *Economy and Society in Ancient Greece,* Brent D. Shaw and Richard P. Shaller, eds. (New York: Viking Press, 1983), 108.

15. Bernard N. Meltzer, "Mead's Social Psychology," in Jerome G. Main and Bernard N. Meltzer, eds., *Symbolic Interaction: A Reader in Social Psychology* (Boston: Allyn and Bacon, 1972), 13.

16. Genovese and Genovese, *Fruits of Merchant Capital,* 109.

17. James L. Watson, "Slavery as an Institution: Open and Closed Systems," in James L. Watson, ed., *Asian and African Systems of Slavery* (Berkeley: Univ. of California Press, 1980), 3–13; Allan G. B. Fisher and Humphrey J. Fisher, *Slavery and Muslim Society in Africa: The Institution in Saharan and Sudanic Africa and the Trans-Saharan Trade* (New York: Doubleday, 1971), 109.

18. See Bertram Wyatt-Brown, *Southern Honor: Ethics and Behavior in the Old South* (New York: Oxford Univ. Press, 1982); Orlando Patterson, *Slavery and Social Death: A Comparative Study* (Cambridge: Harvard Univ. Press, 1982).

19. Gerhard Piers, qtd. in Helen M. Lynd, *On Shame and the Search for Identity* (New York: Harcourt, Brace, 1958), 51.

20. Norbert Elias, *Power and Civility: The Civilizing Process: Volume II,* Edmund Jephcott, trans. (1939; rpt. New York: Pantheon, 1982), 292–93.

21. See Julian Pitt-Rivers, "Honor," in David L. Sills, ed., *International Encyclopedia of the Social Sciences* (New York: Macmillan, 1968).

22. Paul Riesman, *Freedom in Fulani Social Life: An Introspective Ethnography,* trans. Martha Fuller (1974 French ed.; Chicago: Univ. of Chicago Press, 1977), 67.

23. Riesman, *Freedom in Fulani Social Life,* 66, 68–69; Paul Riesman, "The Art of Life in a West African Community: Formality and Spontaneity in Fulani Interpersonal Relationships," *Journal of African Studies* 2 (spring 1975), 39–63; Allan Hoben, "Social Stratification in Traditional Amhara Society," in Arthur Tuden and Leonard Plotnicov, eds., *Social Stratification in Africa* (New York: Free Press, 1970), 195; Patterson, *Slavery and Social Death;* Alford, *Prince among Slaves,* 17, 47.

24. See Riesman, *Freedom in Fulani Social Life,* 117, 135. Although slavery was practiced by many tribes from whom transatlantic slaves were drawn—Wolof, Yoruba, Azande, Ibo, Congolese, and Angolan—there were great variations in household incorporation, intermarriage, and means to emancipation.

25. Bernd Baldus, "Responses to Dependence in a Servile Group: The Machube of Northern Benin," in Suzanne Miers and Igor Kopytoff, eds., *Slavery in Africa: Historical and Anthropological Perspectives* (Madison: Univ. of Wisconsin Press, 1977), 446; also 435–58.

26. Anna Freud, *The Ego and the Mechanisms of Defense* (New York: International Univ. Press, 1947), 117.

27. Robert A. LeVine, *Dreams and Deeds: Achievement Motivation in Nigeria* (Chicago: Univ. of Chicago Press, 1966), 41; also 19–22.

28. Baldus, "Responses to Dependence in a Servile Group," 447; also 446–58. The machube were Islamic in conviction as were their masters, a common identification of faith, as Max Weber first theorized regarding the nature of slave religious belief. So too does Weber's hypothesis apply in North American slavery. See Weber as discussed in John C. Gager, *Kingdom and Community: The Social World of Early Christianity* (Englewood Cliffs, N.J.: Prentice-Hall, 1975), 105–6.

29. B. A. Botkin, ed., *Lay My Burden Down: A Folk History of Slavery* (Chicago: Univ. of Chicago Press, 1945), 14–15.

30. Eugene D. Genovese, *Roll, Jordan, Roll: The World the Slaves Made* (New York: Pantheon, 1974), 143–44.

31. Frederick Douglass, *My Bondage and My Freedom,* William L. Andrews, ed. (1855; rpt. Urbana: Univ. of Illinois Press, 1987), 111. For examples of black identity arising from skills and social status, see the account of John Drayton, lumberjack, in Botkin, ed., *Lay My Burden Down,* 11–12; and of May, harpoonist, in Louis D. Rubin Jr., *William Elliott Shoots a Bear: Essays on the Southern Literary Tradition* (Baton Rouge: Louisiana State Univ. Press, 1975), 1–27.

32. Josiah Henson, *Father Henson's Story of His Own Life* (1858; rpt. Williamstown, Mass.: Corner House, 1973), 48, 53.

33. Baldus, "Responses to Dependence," 448; also 448–56.

34. Alldridge, qtd. in John J. Grace, "Slavery and Emancipation among the Mende in Sierra Leone, 1896–1928," in Miers and Kopytoff, *Slavery in Africa*, 419; Alford, *Prince among Slaves*, 61. Jacob Stroyer, a former slave of South Carolina, recalled that "the [slave] boys were required to bend the body forward with the head down and rest the body on the left foot, and scrape the right foot backwards on the ground while uttering the words, 'howdy Massa and Missie.'" Stroyer, qtd. in Thomas L. Webber, *Deep like the Rivers: Education in the Slave Quarter Community, 1831–1865* (New York: Norton, 1978), 33.

35. Leon Litwack, *Been in the Storm So Long: The Aftermath of Slavery* (New York: Knopf, 1979), 253.

36. Qtd. in Norman R. Yetman, ed., *Life under the "Peculiar Institution": Selections from the Slave Narrative Collection* (New York: Holt, Rinehart and Winston, 1970), 177.

37. Botkin, *Lay My Burden Down*, 35. Dependence of this kind by no means implies servile gratitude. The sentiment should arise from a balance of felt indebtedness and sense of independence. In a clientage or slave system in Africa, America, or anywhere dependency precludes gratitude because it leads directly to hostility when trust, ability or exigency to protect the client is snapped, a situation that occurred on a massive scale with Civil War emancipation. So-called slave ingratitude and hostility to former, often "kind" masters, especially by domestics and others well-treated, grew: from resentment of slavery (enforced dependence); from justifiable bitterness at abandonment; and from contempt for the once "superior" whites' loss of honor and power. Given the honor-shame ethos of bondage, white expectations of slave gratitude were ridiculous. See Dominique O. Mannoni, *Prospero and Caliban: The Psychology of Colonization,* trans. Pamela Powesland (New York: Praeger, 1956), 44–48; see also Daniel E. Sutherland, "A Special Kind of Problem: The Response of Household Slaves and Their Masters to Freedom," *Southern Studies* 20 (summer 1981), 151–66, which provides examples.

38. Alford, *Prince among Slaves*, 49, but see also 208 (note for p. 8); John Grace, *Domestic Slavery in West Africa with Particular Reference to the Sierra Leone Protectorate, 1896–1927* (New York: Barnes and Noble, 1975), 10, also 1–19. Introduction, Miers and Kopytoff, *Slavery in Africa*, 3–81, shows the diversity of African slavery, but stresses the severe marginality of the slaves' status. Watson, "Slavery as an Institution: Open and Closed Systems," 3–15, criticizes Miers and Kopytoff for underplaying the "closed" types and the "property" aspect of slavery in all societies. See also M. G. Smith, "Slavery and Emancipation in Two Societies," *Social and Economic Studies* 3 (Dec. 1954): 243.

39. Alford, *Prince among Slaves*, 48; also 17, 79–81. See also "Letter

from a Gentleman of Natchez to a Lady of Cincinnati . . . April 7th, 1828," in *National Intelligencer* (Washington, D.C.), May 8, 1828 (from Cincinnati *Republican*); *African Repository* 3 (Feb. 1828), 364–67; *African Repository* 4 (May 1828), 77, (Oct. 1828), 243, (Feb. 1829), 379; John W. Blassingame, ed., *Slave Testimony: Two Centuries of Letters, Speeches, Interviews, and Autobiographies* (Baton Rouge: Louisiana State Univ. Press, 1977), 682–86. In Blassingame, *Slave Testimony*, 40, 470–74, Omar Ibn Said, another formerly highly placed Fullah, enslaved in North Carolina, refused inquiries about returning to his homeland; he also submitted to Christian convictions after years of serving Allah in America.

40. In 1828, Prince claimed to be a loyal Muslim, but was "anxious" to have a Bible in Arabic. See *National Intelligencer* (Washington, D.C.), May 8, 1828; Alford, *Prince among Slaves,* 57. Thomas H. Gallaudet, *A Statement with Regard to the Moorish Prince, Abduhl Rahhahman* (New York: N.p., 1828), 3, asserted that Ibrahima's "wife, and eldest son have been baptized, and are in connexion with the Baptist Church." Anthropologist Paul Riesman, as quoted by Patterson, notes that like "chivalry," *pulaaku* signifies "at once certain moral qualities and a group of men possessing these qualities" (*Slavery and Social Death,* 84).

41. Julian Pitt-Rivers, "Honour and Social Status," in J. G. Peristiany, ed., *Honour and Shame: The Values of Mediterranean Society* (Chicago: Univ. of Chicago Press, 1966), 40–43; Charles Joyner, "The Trickster and the Fool: Folktales and Identity among Southern Plantation Slaves," *Plantation Society* 2 (Dec. 1986): 149–56.

42. Anthony F. C. Wallace, *Culture and Personality* (1961; rpt. New York: Random House, 1966), 182–83.

43. C. Vann Woodward and Elisabeth Muhlenfeld, eds., *The Private Mary Chesnut: The Unpublished Civil War Diaries* (New York: Oxford Univ. Press, 1984), June 4, 1865, 256.

44. See W. Thomas MacCary, "Menander's Slaves: The Names, Roles, and Masks," *Transactions and Proceedings of the American Philological Association* 100 (1969): 277–94; Philip Whaley Harsh, "The Intriguing Slave in Greek Comedy," *Transactions and Proceedings of the American Philological Association* 86 (1955): 135–42; George E. Duckworth, *The Nature of Roman Comedy* (Princeton: Princeton Univ. Press, 1952), 249–50. On slave tricksters in other slave societies, see Nerys W. Patterson, "Honour and Shame in Medieval Welsh Society: A Study of the Role of Burlesque in the Welsh Laws," *Studia Celtica* 16–17 (1981–82): 73–103, esp. 91–93; Keith Hopkins, *Conquerors and Slaves (Sociological Studies in Roman History volume 1)* (Cambridge: Cambridge Univ. Press, 1978), 121; Richard Hellie, *Slavery in Russia: 1400–1725* (Chicago: Univ. of Chicago Press, 1982), 313–17; Lionel Caplan, "Power and Status in South Asian Slavery," in Watson, *Asian and African Systems of*

Slavery, 169–94; James H. Vaughan, "Mafakur: A Limbic Institution of the Margi (Nigeria)," in Miers and Kopytoff, *Slavery in Africa,* 95–96.

45. Nien Cheng, *Life and Death in Shanghai* (New York: Grove Press, 1986), 363; *chameleon* is the Chinese term for those able to adjust quickly to authoritarian changes of policy.

46. Ebeneezer Hazard, a New Englander visiting Georgia in 1778, remarked, "The *Country Gentlemen* are . . . accustomed to tyrannize from their Infancy, they carry with them a Disposition to treat all Mankind in the same manner they have been used to treat their Negroes. If a man has not as many Slaves as they, he is esteemed by them their Inferior, even though he vastly exceeds them in every other Respect." Entry for February 25, 1778, in Fred Shelley, ed., "The Journal of Ebeneezer Hazard in Georgia, 1778," *Georgia Historical Quarterly* 41 (1957): 318–19 (citation kindly supplied by George Crawford). See also Solomon Northup, in Gilbert Osofsky, ed., *Puttin' on Ole Massa: The Slave Narratives of Henry Bibb, William Wells Brown, and Solomon Northup* (New York: Harper and Row, 1969), 338.

47. Norbert Elias, *The Civilizing Process: The History of Manners,* Edmund Jepthcott, trans. (1939; rpt. Oxford: Blackwell, 1978).

48. Sir Kenneth James Dover, *Greek Popular Morality in the Time of Plato and Aristotle* (Berkeley: Univ. of California Press, 1974), 226.

49. Patterson, *Slavery and Social Death,* 79, quoting from Julian Pitt-Rivers. See Pitt-Rivers, "Honour and Social Status," in Peristiany, *Honour and Shame,* 19–78, and idem, "Honor," in Sills, *International Encyclopedia of the Social Sciences.*

50. See Harry G. LeFever, " 'Playing the Dozens': A Mechanism for Social Control," *Phylon* 42 (spring 1981): 77; also 73–85; Lawrence Levine, *Black Culture and Black Consciousness* (New York: Oxford Univ. Press, 1977), 358.

51. Riesman, *Freedom in Fulani Social Life,* 124; also 76–79, 198; John Dollard, "The Dozens: The Dialect of Insult," *American Imago* 1 (Nov. 1939): 3–25; Roger Abrahams, "Playing the Dozens," *Journal of American Folklore* 75 (July-Sept. 1962): 209–20, esp. 213; Donald C. Simmons, "Possible West African Sources for the American Negro Dozens," *Journal of American Folklore* 76 (1963): 339–40; Millicent R. Ayoub and Stephen A. Barnett, "Ritualized Verbal Insult in White High School Culture," *Journal of American Folklore* 78 (1965): 337–44; William Labov, "Rules for Ritual Insults," in Thomas Kochman, ed., *Rappin' and Stylin' Out* (Urbana: Univ. of Illinois Press, 1972), 314; Amuzie Chimezie, "The Dozens: An African-Heritage Theory," *Journal of Black Studies* 6 (June 1976): 401–20; Walter F. Edwards, "Speech Acts in Guyana: Communicating Ritual and Personal Insults," *Journal of Black Studies* 10 (Sept. 1979): 20–39.

52. South Carolina Sessional Papers, Minutes of Council, December, 1748-December, 1749, Journal 17, Part 1, Public Record Office, British Manu-

scripts Project, Reel 34, I.C.O. 5/457, microfilm, January 27, 1749, pp. 55–120, South Carolina Department of Archives and History, Columbia.

53. Ibid., 64. Sambo, a witness, declared that they had collected no arms, at once a signal that no plot was underway. The head of the conspiracy was supposedly an overseer named James Springer who had left for a northern colony long before the hearings and therefore could not be made a material witness. See 73, 85. See also Philip D. Morgan and George D. Terry, "Slavery in Microcosm: A Conspiracy Scare in Colonial South Carolina," *Southern Studies* 21 (summer 1982): 122.

54. See, for instance, the story of Essex in John George Clinkscales, *On the Plantation: Reminiscences of His Childhood* (1916; rpt. New York: Negro Univ. Press, 1969), 12–36, a runaway slave who exhibited all these reactions in the course of a lifetime.

55. Katharine Du Pre Lumpkin, *The Making of a Southerner* (1948; rpt. Athens: Univ. of Georgia Press, 1974), 80; also 32.

56. Constantin Stanislavski, *Building a Character,* trans. Elizabeth Reynolds Hapgood (New York: Theatre Art Books, 1949), 167.

57. Erik H. Erikson, *Childhood and Society* (1950; rpt. New York: Norton, 1963), 252–53. Whereas guilt involves transgression of one's own moral sense, shame arises from loss of pride, fear of ridicule, and anxiety of failure to achieve self-set, often unrealistic goals. See Helen B. Lewis, *Shame and Guilt in Neurosis* (New York: International Universities Press, 1971), 18–23.

58. Ball, qtd. in Peter Kolchin, *Unfree Labor: American Slavery and Russian Serfdom* (Cambridge: Harvard Univ. Press, 1987), 242.

59. Richard Wright, *Black Boy: A Record of Childhood and Youth* (1945; rpt. New York: Harper and Row, 1966), 250.

60. Erikson, *Childhood and Society,* 253.

61. Charles Ball, *Fifty Years in Chains* (1858; rpt. New York: Dover, 1971), 12; also 12–13.

62. Robert Staples, *Black Masculinity: The Black Male's Role in American Society* (San Francisco: Black Scholar Press, 1982), 62–71; Ronald L. Braithwaite, "Interpersonal Relations between Black Males and Black Females," in Lawrence E. Gary, ed., *Black Men* (Beverly Hills, Calif.: Sage, 1981), 83–97.

63. Ralph Ellison, *Invisible Man* (New York: Random House, 1952); Richard Wright, *Native Son* (New York: Random House, 1940); Alice Walker, *The Third Life of Grange Copeland* (New York: Harcourt Brace Jovanovich, 1970) and *The Color Purple* (New York: Harcourt Brace Jovanovich, 1982); Ernest J. Gaines, *Bloodline* (New York: Dial, 1964), to name a few.

64. Karen Horney, *Neurosis and Human Growth: The Struggle toward Self-Realization* (New York: Norton, 1950).

65. William Styron, *The Confessions of Nat Turner* (New York: Random

House, 1967); John Henrik Clarke, ed., *William Styron's "Nat Turner": Ten Black Writers Respond* (Boston: Beacon Press, 1968); but see James R. Huffman, "A Psychological Redefinition of William Styron's *The Confessions of Nat Turner,*" *Literary Review* 24 (winter 1981): 279–307.

66. Blyden, qtd. in Wilson Jeremiah Moses, *Black Messiahs and Uncle Toms: Social and Literary Manipulations of a Religious Myth* (University Park: Pennsylvania State Univ. Press, 1982), 51.

67. James B. Stewart, "The Psychic Duality of Afro-Americans in the Novels of W. E. B. Du Bois," *Phylon* 44 (June 1983): 99. Du Bois expanded on this theme in *Dark Princess,* explaining that "the white always felt a Negro was watching him and he acted his assumed part . . . of strutting walk, loud talk, and swagger . . . accordingly. And the Negroes did watch from behind another veil. This was the veil of amusement or feigned, impudent humility" (Stewart, "Psychic Duality," 102).

68. Stewart, "Psychic Duality," 101. For a study of an analogous situation under colonial rule, see Leroy Vail and Landeg White, "Forms of Resistance: Songs and Perceptions of Power in Colonial Mozambique," *American Historical Review* 88 (1983): 883–919.

69. See, for instance, Walter L. Williams, "The 'Sambo' Deception: The Experience of John McElroy in Andersonville Prison," *Phylon* 39 (fall 1978): 261–63.

70. Herbert G. Gutman, *The Black Family in Slavery and Freedom, 1750–1925* (New York: Pantheon, 1976) and Mitchell A. Green, "Impact of Slavery on the Black Family: Social, Political, and Economic," in *Journal of Afro-American Issues,* 3 (summer/fall 1975), 343–56. On Afro-American family interconnections, see Raymond T. Smith, "The Nuclear Family in Afro-American Kinship," *Journal of Comparative Family Studies* 1 (autumn 1970): 55–70; Niara Sudarkasa, "African and Afro-American Family Structure: A Comparison," *Black Scholar* 11 (Nov./Dec. 1980): 37–60; and Herbert J. Foster, "African Patterns in the Afro-American Family," *Journal of Black Studies* 14 (Dec. 1983): 201–31, both of which essays argue for extended Afro-American kinship patterns.

71. Jean Lee argues that at least until the 1780s in the Chesapeake "no group of enslaved Afro-Americans was ever free from the threat of disruption," a circumstance that severely limited slave community development ("The Problem of Slave Community in the Eighteenth-Century Chesapeake," *William and Mary Quarterly* 43, 3d ser. [1986]: 341; also 333–61). Peter Kolchin extends the problem of stable community life into the antebellum period for slaves on small holdings. See his essay "Reevaluating the Antebellum Slave Community: A Comparative Perspective," *Journal of American History* 70 (1983): 584; Douglass, *The Narrative of the Life of Frederick Douglass* (1845), 92; W. E. B. Du Bois, *The Souls of Black Folk* (1918; rpt. New York: Fawcett, 1961), 16–

17. On the internalization of the deferential mode, see John Dollard, *Caste and Class in a Southern Town* (1937; rpt. New York: Harper and Row, 1949), 175–87, 286–313, which notes a diversity of reactions, including degrees of deference and hostility.

72. Herbert G. Gutman, *Slavery and the Numbers Game: A Critique of "Time on the Cross"* (Urbana: Univ. of Illinois Press, 1975).

73. See Pearce Gervis, *Of Emirs and Pagans: A View of Northern Nigeria* (London: Cassell, 1963), 183–84. Corydon Fuller Diary, June 21, 1858, in William L. Clements Library, Ann Arbor, Mich.

74. See, for instance, *State v. Dan* [Mrs. Letty Barrett's], Sept. 22, 1862, *State v. Sam* [Robert H. Todd's], Nov. 14, 1863, Magistrates and Freeholders Court, Anderson County, South Carolina Department of Archives and History, Columbia; Lawrence T. McDonnell, "The Whipping Post: Politics and Psychology of Punishment in the Slave South," unpublished paper, Social Science History Association, Toronto, October 26, 1984.

75. Edwin Adams Davis, ed., *Plantation Life in the Florida Parishes of Louisiana, 1836–1846, as Reflected in the Diary of Bennet H. Barrow* (New York: Columbia Univ. Press, 1945), entry for Dec. 24, 1839, 175; pumpkin story told in Botkin, *Lay My Burden Down*, 6. For a similar acceptance of white perceptions in labeling of deviant slaves, see Bessie Hough Williams, "Memoir of the King Family," William Rufus King Family Papers, Alabama State Department of Archives and History, Montgomery.

76. See John W. Cell, *The Highest Stage of White Supremacy: The Origins of Segregation in South Africa and the American South* (Cambridge: Cambridge Univ. Press, 1982), 241–43. Some planters were determined to insist upon dependence for food, denying their slaves garden plots, for fear of encouraging self-reliance, confidence, and laxness when working for master. See "Governor [James H.] Hammond's Instructions to His Overseer," in Willie Lee Rose, ed., *A Documentary History of Slavery in North America* (New York: Oxford Univ. Press, 1976), 348; Botkin, *Lay My Burden Down*, 25, 35, 93; W. J. Cash, *The Mind of the South* (New York: Knopf, 1941), 319.

77. Nash, qtd. in Genovese, *Roll, Jordan, Roll: A North-Side View of Slavery* (1855; rpt. Reading, Mass.: Addison-Wesley, 1969), 630; Lockhart, qtd. in Benjamin Drew, *The Refugee* 31.

78. Lockhart, qtd. in Drew, *The Refugee*, 31. Later he fled from another master because he had whipped his wife and children. "I don't want any man to meddle with my wife," he said, "I bothered her enough, and didn't want anybody else to trouble her at all" (34). See also Raymond Hedin, "Muffled Voices: The American Slave Narrative," *Clio* 10 (winter 1981): 129–42, a sensitive appraisal of the role that self-repression played in these accounts. Wright, *Black Boy*, see, for example, 94.

79. Genovese, "Toward a Psychology of Slavery," in Gilmore, *Revisiting Blassingame's "The Slave Community,"* 33.

80. Baldus, "Responses to Dependence," 450–58; Clyde W. Franklin II, "Black Male—Black Female Conflict Individually Caused and Culturally Nurtured," *Journal of Black Studies* 15 (Dec. 1984), 139–54; Robert Staples, "The Myth of Black Macho: A Response to Angry Black Feminists," *Black Scholar* 10 (Mar./Apr. 1979): 24–32.

81. See Bertram Wyatt-Brown, rev. of Patterson, *Slavery and Social Death,* in *Society* 21 (Mar./Apr. 1983): 92–94; Kolchin, "Reevaluating the Antebellum Slave Community," 579–601. See also Lawrence T. McDonnell, "Slave against Slave: Dynamics of Violence within the American Slave Community," American Historical Association Convention, Dec. 28, 1983, and "The Whipping Post," kindly lent by their author.

82. Styron, *Confessions of Nat Turner,* 3–5.

83. Alford, *Prince among Slaves,* 180–83.

African-American Women and Their Pursuit of Rights through Eighteenth-Century Spanish Texts

JANE LANDERS

EVEN WHEN free, women of African descent have long been thought to be "without voice" and doubly "victimized" by their race and gender in the Anglo South. If enslaved, they were legally oppressed as well. However, across the linguistic, political, and cultural divide that separated Florida from its northern neighbors, women of African descent found both voice and legal personality. Recent studies of Spanish "borderland" colonies such as Florida show that African and African-American women in Spanish communities, both free and enslaved, enjoyed legal protections and social opportunities significantly better than those of their counterparts in Anglo settlements and that they were assertive about pursuing both.[1]

Women in the Hispanic colonies of the South not only exercised gender rights traditionally observed in Spain but often acquired new and unexpected responsibilities and privileges and filled nontraditional roles with little social liability.[2] Until recently, however, the traditional male bias in history and the mistaken belief that women were "powerless" and therefore of minimal interest or consequence have excluded women from much of the historical literature of the borderlands South. The evidence upon which earlier borderland historians drew was generated primarily by male elites who were interested in great figures, mostly men, "high" politics, international and commercial intrigues, and battle strategies. Following the lead of the "major" figures they studied, these scholars pored over the most confidential levels of diplomatic correspondence and exhausted the records of government councils to write fine institutional, military, and political histories, but they usually ignored those aspects of the colonial experience that today attract social and cultural historians interested in the daily lives of women. Notably absent in the older borderland studies is any interest in domestic organization, women's economy, social networks, and sources of community, to name only a few of the topics engaging modern social historians.[3]

The neglect of women's colonial history in Hispanic regions is also due to the difficulty of the sources. Information is fragmentary and scarce. Much of the evidence is recorded in archaic Spanish and requires paleographic skills to decipher. Moreover, the records are widely dispersed in colonial archives in Spain and in the various colonies that shared jurisdiction for the southern tier of North America and the circum-Caribbean—Santo Domingo, Cuba, and Mexico, for example.

With determination and a different historical perspective, however, one can recover the overlooked and scattered bits and pieces of the unremarked lives of women even in this remote period and begin to reconstruct their meanings. While it is lamentably true that the lives of women are not as often visible in the documentary record as those of men and that the lives of women of color are perhaps even further obscured, a researcher in Spanish colonial materials actually enjoys a certain advantage, for the Spaniards were meticulous bureaucrats. Although the records for the earliest years of the sixteenth century are especially thin, they become more textured and rich by the seventeenth and eighteenth centuries.

Spaniards constructed particular political and social identities for women that drew on a variety of sources including Roman and Visigothic law, Aristotelian theories, theological principles of the Roman Catholic church, and centuries of customary law and practice in a racially and ethnically diverse Spain.[4] In the thirteenth century King Alfonso X (the Wise) codified Spain's varied legal traditions in the Siete Partidas. This code identified women along with children, invalids, and delinquents as in need of supervision but also deserving of familial and societal protection. Because Spain was a patriarchal society, a woman was, therefore, subject to the will of her father or brothers until either they died, or she reached twenty-five years of age or married.[5] Such juridical categorization obviously limited, at least temporarily, a woman's legal autonomy and economic power.

Behavioral prescriptions and normative rules also circumscribed women. By the fifteenth century popular works of a distinctly misogynist bent, such as *The Celestina,* parodied women as vain, deceitful, seductive, and greedy. Celestina is depicted as "a bewhiskered old dame . . . a witch, astute and wise in all evil things" whose specialty is repairing maidenheads. Women in general are described as "the limbs of Satan, the fountainhead of sin, and the destroyers of Paradise."[6] Later didactic works based in patristic exegesis of the Bible, such as Juan Luis Vives's *Instruction of a Christian Woman,* attempted to paint a kinder picture of women, but even as Vives argued that women should receive education the better to avoid sin, he warned that "women's thought is swift, and for the most part unstable, walking and wandering out from home and soon will slide by reason of its own slipperiness."[7] Another classic normative work, Fray Luis de León's *Perfect Wife,* reinforced societal views of appropriate feminine behavior as passive, virtuous, and focused on home and family.[8] At the same time the cult of Mary grew ever stronger and women were expected to emulate the long-suffering, pure, and devoted mother—a standard against which most women would be deviant. Thus, Spanish women were constrained in many ways.

Although their social and legal status was lower than that of males, women still might use the images of gender weakness and motherhood for their own benefit.[9] For women also enjoyed specific protections based in the same medieval Spanish law and custom that limited them. For example, women could inherit and hold property, and it could not be seized for the debt of their husbands. A husband could not alienate the dowry, or *arras* (the groom's marriage gift), of his wife, and with her husband's written license, or power of attorney, a woman could enter into a wide variety of legal transactions. Women could also testify in courts and seek redress for grievances.[10] These basic protections meant that over the course of their lives, even illiterate women might generate texts.

The Siete Partidas also guaranteed Spanish slaves a legal personality and voice. Drawing primarily on Roman law, which recognized slavery as an accident of fate and a violation of the laws of nature, the Siete Partidas detailed the rights as well as the obligations of slaves. In theory, their rights included personal security and legal mechanisms by which to escape a cruel master; conjugal rights and the right not to be separated from their children; and the right to hold and transfer property and initiate legal suits. Thus, slaves, as well as women, generated Spanish texts.[11]

Spanish legal institutions and customs were transferred to the Americas, where they underwent some modifications, codified as the Recopilación de Leyes de los Reynos de Las Indias, but their core principles remained remarkably durable. One of the most basic was the right to *buen gobierno,* or good government, and justice, which required access or a voice for all vassals within the vast Spanish empire, including women and slaves.[12]

The evidence for this essay is drawn from a diverse array of Spanish-language sources but will focus on memorials and petitions women filed in eighteenth-century Florida to report or respond to complaints to the court, to negotiate improvements in their condition, or to secure freedom. In St. Augustine the court or tribunal consisted of the governor, his legal counsel, and the royal notary. If the women who approached the court could not write, they could use the services of a friend or of the government notary. In those cases the women's X's would be accompanied by the signature of the person assisting and the notation "at the request of——who cannot write." But literate women of all races and ethnicities wrote and signed many of their own memorials and petitions. Because Florida has always been multicultural, women sometimes required the assistance of translators when they produced texts, and this fact, too, is duly noted in their documents. However, many women in colonial Florida were multilingual, especially women of African descent.

Many of the women's texts follow standard formulas and employ language that to the twentieth-century reader appears obsequious. The petitioners, both male and female, usually identify themselves by name, race, and legal condition and open with the phrase "with all due respect" or "with the utmost submission." The individual's complaint, charge, or request is then spelled out as well as the action they wish the court to take. A typical close to the petition might be "humbly trusting in the merciful charity and noted wisdom of the justice administered by Your Excellency." When rendered, such flowery and flattering phrases were considered a mark of civility, and in that context graceful language might conceivably improve the outcome of a petition. Although men and women employed the same formulaic openings and closings, women and slaves might also include within their memorials and petitions references to their weakness, poverty, or lack of other sources of assistance to elicit the proper sympathetic responses from the court. Women frequently referred to themselves as mothers and made references to their children. If they were sick, widowed, or abandoned, they made sure to mention it. The court was, then, held accountable for the same acts of charity and justice that a patriarch would be expected to render to family members or those of the "miserable classes."[13] Many documents in the official archives of Spanish Florida were not written or generated by women but nevertheless record significant aspects of women's lives. The parish registers of the Catholic Church in St. Augustine, dating to the sixteenth century, record marriages, baptisms, and burials and provide information on family structures, *compadrazgo*, or godparentage, networks, naming patterns, and data on fertility and mortality. Matrimonial licenses, required in the face of parental objections, for "mixed" marriages or for marriages involving persons of unequal legal or social status, also offer evidence about family networks, social mobility, and miscegenation. Letters between priests and the bishops in Cuba discuss public morals, social controls, ecclesiastical punishments, and more. Census records describe the women and their children, their property, their religious and ethnic affiliations, their legal and marital status. Civil and notarial records describe women's property holdings and business transactions—their indentures, dowries, bonds, mortgages, and manumissions. Testamentary proceedings include detailed inventories and appraisals of women's property, their debts and claims against their estates, and the inheritance patterns those proceedings show. Finally, criminal records indicate the crimes for which women are prosecuted and their treatment under the law, as well as crimes committed against women and the punishment meted out by the court.

There are a number of important collections of these archival materials for the southeastern borderlands, including the Stetson and Lockey collections gathered by archivists in Spain in the nineteenth century and the Papeles Procedentes de Cuba, all available in United States libraries. The collection known as the East Florida Papers, from which the memorials cited in this essay derive, is the most important of all, for it is the complete notarial archive of the Spanish government in Florida in the so-called second Spanish period (1784–1821). It contains both Spanish- and English-language records of historical significance for Florida, Louisiana, Georgia, and South Carolina.

It is at the notarial level where the voices of women can be heard most clearly. In these notarial texts women report their needs, complain against neighbors, ask for land grants, pensions, licenses, and passports, post bonds, mortgage, buy and sell properties, assume debt, and state their dying wishes. By examining a wide range of these records of daily life, one gets a better sense of the creativity of women, even within a patriarchal and conservative society. Although the documents confirm subordination, they also show the agency and initiative of women.

Agency, initiative, strength, and endurance were all requisite traits for the frontier life of Spanish Florida. When Spaniards first established St. Augustine in 1565, the men and women of the new settlement were surrounded and outnumbered by native peoples whom they alternately wooed and fought. The settlers also endured the hardships of hunger, disease, and ferocious weather. After 1670 the Spaniards faced another challenge when English planters from Barbados established Charles Town only two days to the north of St. Augustine. Shortly thereafter, the relative difference in English and Spanish slave systems prompted slaves of the English to flee southward from Carolina to Spanish Florida.[14] Among the first recorded runaways were two women, one of whom had a nursing child. Rather than return the fugitives, as English owners demanded, the Spaniards offered them religious sanctuary upon their conversion to Catholicism. In 1693 the Spanish king decreed "liberty to all . . . the men as well as the women . . . so that by their example and by my liberality . . . others will do the same."[15] The Spaniards recognized that each runaway was an economic loss for the enemy and a potential ally in what was to be more than a century-long struggle to control the Southeast. By the middle of the eighteenth century, hundreds of slave runaways from Carolina and Georgia had remade their lives as free people in Spanish Florida and many daring women were among them.[16]

In 1763 the Treaty of Paris required Spain to cede Florida to England, closing the escape hatch that was once available to fugitive slaves in the Southeast. Incoming Anglo planters soon established vast indigo, rice, sugar, and sea-island cotton plantations in Florida modeled after those in South Carolina and Georgia and imported large numbers of African slaves to work them. The British also imported into Florida their concepts of chattel slavery. They severely restricted free blacks, adopted a slave code based on that of South Carolina, and often subjected slaves to brutal punishments.[17]

At the conclusion of the American Revolution, the Treaty of Paris retroceded Florida to Spain, and many slaves took advantage of the chaos of war and the subsequent colonial transfer to flee British control.

Some escapees found a refuge among the Seminole nation, which had established flourishing villages in the central plains of North Florida. Several hundred, however, claimed refuge among the returning Spaniards on the basis of the 1693 religious sanctuary policy that was still in effect. These individuals formed the nucleus of the free black community in the second Spanish administration of Florida (1784–1821), and it is possible that having experienced a much more restrictive form of slavery, they were all the more motivated to test the limits of freedom among the Spaniards.[18]

Like their predecessors from the first Spanish tenure in Florida, the women among the runaways learned to manipulate Spanish law, customs, and gender conventions to their advantage. Free African-American women in Florida managed plantations, operated small businesses, litigated in the courts, and bought and sold property, including slaves.[19] Even enslaved women enjoyed certain rights not granted slaves in the Anglo colonies, including the right to hold property. In the Americas that right allowed them to purchase themselves or family members through an institution called *coartación*.[20] Slave women might also secure their freedom or that of their children through gratis manumission, which sometimes, but not always, involved a sexual relationship with their owners.

By the late eighteenth century, in fact, European-African unions were very common and accepted in Florida. Many of Florida's wealthiest ranchers, planters, government officials, and merchants had large mulatto families (sometimes in addition to white families) and recognized their mulatto children, educated them, and provided for them in their wills. Even in cases involving concubinage, the law and community consensus protected their widows and heirs, and the church often interceded "paternally" on behalf of women and mothers of African descent.[21]

One of the most common ways in which African-American slave women "worked" the Spanish legal system was in petitioning for manumission. If slave owner and slave amicably agreed upon a price, and the slave secured the money through wages earned in free time, gifts, or loans, the owner would appear before the government notary to have manumission papers prepared. However, if no agreement could be reached, or if an agreement broke down, slaves were quick to use the institutional structures available to them. By the mechanism of *coarta-*

ción (self-purchase) slaves could petition the courts to set their just purchase price.[22] Each party, owner and slave, then chose an assessor to evaluate the slave's value. If wide disagreement arose, the court appointed a third assessor and then made its decision. In cases involving children, a special advocate was appointed to protect the child's interests. Once the court established a slave's "just" price, owners had to honor it. If slaves could not afford their immediate freedom, they could make payments and move slowly out of slavery, or they could seek out new owners willing to pay the price and effect a change in their conditions that way.

Margarita Saunders was born and raised in the St. Augustine home of her owner, Juan Saunders. In 1794 Margarita asked the court to set her purchase price, alleging that Don Juan was trying to take her out of the city so that she could not earn a daily wage with which to buy her freedom. In St. Augustine, as in many other Spanish colonial cities, owners permitted slaves to work for themselves or for others in return for an agreed-upon return to the owner called a *jornal*. Any money earned above that amount was the slaves' to keep. This system gave slaves an autonomy that in some cases simulated freedom, but in reality it was a privilege the owner could easily revoke. In his required response Saunders stated that he could not afford to free Margarita, or all his other slaves would follow suit. Another mulatto woman had just fled his home, and he told the court resignedly that she would probably petition too. He refused to name his choice of assessor, but this tactic did not interrupt the process. The governor's tribunal ruled that Saunders's excuses were "insufficient reasons to impede her solicitation of liberty," and Margarita's price was set at 300 pesos (approximately equivalent to 300 dollars of the day). Saunders claimed he had been offered 600 pesos for her and argued that since he was being forced to free Margarita against his wishes, he should be paid at least 500 pesos. The governor refused this request, and after paying 300 pesos and court costs, Margarita obtained her certificate of freedom. As Saunders had predicted, another of his slaves, Lucia (also born and raised in his home), appeared before the court the following year petitioning for freedom. Saunders asked 350 pesos for her, but Lucia claimed this was an exorbitant price, and after three assessments, she was able to buy her freedom for 275 pesos. In telling the court that both women had been born and raised in his home, Don Juan made a sort of dual claim over them, as owner and "father." Ordinarily, both those images were powerful sources of authority, but Spanish justice recognized the women's natural right to "liberty" as even stronger.[23]

Manumission was not a common practice in St. Augustine in this period. From 1784 to 1800 only thirty-four manumission cases were considered although some of these involved more than one individual. Of those thirty-four cases, however, only one was denied. Most of the successful cases involved self-purchase; however, five husbands bought the freedom of their wives, and five parents bought their children's freedom.[24] Although the judicial system was effective and might even be regarded as sympathetic to the goal of liberty, slaves like Margarita knew that access to the cash economy of the city was almost a prerequisite for successful self-purchase. Even slaves who lived in the city would have found it an arduous process to save several hundred pesos when the average day's pay for a man was a half peso.[25]

Little is known about how slave women earned money to buy such a costly and precious commodity as freedom, but fascinating glimpses of their entrepreneurial activities occasionally surface in manumission suits. Filis and her husband, Edimboro, both Guinea-born, saved for many years before winning their freedom in a court battle against their wealthy and influential owner, Don Francisco Xavier Sánchez, the largest cattle rancher in Florida and a government creditor. While Edimboro used his free time to ply his trade as a butcher and gathered and sold firewood, Filis took in washing. (She was a laundress in the Sánchez household.) She also made and sold toys of unknown description and baked and sold "tortes of flour and honey, called *queques* [cakes?] which only blacks and poor boys eat." Filis and Edimboro also rented the top floor of a house in St. Augustine, where they hosted dances for the African-American community—a sort of colonial forerunner of the rent party. The attendants contributed money for the music and "refreshments," and Edimboro told the courts that he and Filis earned between one and a half to two pesos a night at these gatherings after paying for the rent of the place and the party fare. When they had saved enough money, Filis and Edimboro successfully worked their way through the courts to achieve freedom, despite the heated opposition of Sánchez.[26]

Sometimes women of African descent sought influential allies in their legal suits. Andaina, a literate slave woman originally from Baltimore, charged bad treatment by her owner, Catalina Acosta. In her handwritten petition, signed with a flourish, Andaina asked that she be given permission to seek another owner, a right commonly supported in St. Augustine, but she also wanted to pursue freedom. Andaina reported that over the previous three years she had been paying her mistress seven to ten pesos monthly from the income she earned on her own time. She estimated she had paid Catalina a total of 250 pesos and was nevertheless forced to buy her own clothing and that of her infant. "The few clothes with which I cover my flesh cost my said owner nothing, for what I earn from my labor I spend on my clothing and that of my little son." Andaina complained that Catalina continually castigated her and had on one occasion ripped her clothing. She asked the court to intervene because Catalina's asking price for her freedom (350 pesos) was too high, and at that rate she could find no other owner.[27]

Catalina, an illiterate shopkeeper of Minorcan descent, was unable to sign her required response to Andaina's petition and a government scribe recorded it for her verbatim. Catalina stated that she did not understand how a slave could complain. Denying any abuse, she admitted in colorful fashion that she yelled a lot, but added, "Shouts do not hurt anyone." Catalina portrayed herself to the court as a compassionate person who although "weighted down with small children and my husband absent," allowed Andaina to work as a wet nurse in the home of the widowed Don Domingo Reyes because he "begged with tears in his eyes." Catalina stated that she had pity on a "widowed father surrounded by little ones." Before long, Andaina became pregnant and was sent back to Catalina's home to deliver her baby, which was presumably also Don Domingo's since the widower tried to buy the mulatto child's freedom for twenty-five pesos. At first Catalina rejected the offer and refused to allow Andaina to return to Reyes's home, motivated, she said, by her desire to "end a scandalous connection." However, seeing that Don Domingo was unwilling to detach himself from Andaina and the child, Catalina agreed to the child's manumission for twenty-five pesos and let Andaina return to work for ten pesos monthly, rather than the seven she had previously charged Don Domingo.[28]

At that point Andaina took charge of the situation. According to Catalina, Andaina announced that she'd hang herself rather than work, so Catalina finally agreed her slave could be assessed and seek another owner. When Catalina agreed to this arrangement in another dictated document, she could not resist adding an extended comment on Andaina's unseemly behavior. She said that Andaina went to masked balls (hosted by Filis and Edimboro) in clothing so fancy her owner worried people would talk. When she challenged Andaina, Andaina retorted, "So what? Weren't the governor's own slaves there?" At that Catalina admitted she ripped Andaina's ruffles from her skirt, prompting Andaina, yet again, to threaten suicide and leave the house. Within moments Don Domingo stormed in "like a wild beast," shouting that Catalina had no rights to Andaina beyond the money she was due. In effect, Catalina did not, for once the court agreed to a just price, her slave moved inexorably toward freedom.[29] Catalina lost the dispute and her slave, but she closed with the final commentary that "passion blinds one" and discounted the statements of Don Domingo and of his friend, the magistrate of their barrio, because everyone knew they were "as close as fingernail and finger."[30]

From the safety of Don Domingo's household, it took Andaina four more years to accrue sufficient funds, but she finally secured her manumission papers, and within months of becoming totally free, Andaina was back in court with another handwritten petition. After describing how her former owner continued to abuse and insult her, events she stated were witnessed by many cited Dons, Andaina demanded that Catalina sell Andaina's two children, whose mistreatment was also witnessed. Catalina countered that Andaina repeatedly harbored her nine-year-old runaway son. Andaina denied that charge and specified which members of the community had sheltered the child until the priest finally took him in. Andaina used powerful imagery when she asked the court, "Do you think that even for hiding a son a mother deserves the martyrdom [and here she used the metaphor of being whipped by a lash] I continually suffer? . . . it is impossible to believe the inhumanity and rigor with which they treat my two children." Andaina reported her son had been beaten so badly his back bled and that he had been found almost dying of cold and hunger after running in the country-side. She also charged that her younger daughter was regularly beaten and that her body was covered in bruises as the neighbors could testify. When the governor's tribunal threatened a hearing to investigate the alleged mistreatment of Andaina's children, Catalina agreed to their sale. Once again, Andaina successfully employed a combination of personal connections, determined resistance, and traditionally accepted justifications, in this case, motherly grief and concern over witnessed mistreatment and neglect of her children, to work the system. Through that system's available legal texts, she won the freedom of her children.[31]

Not all slave women, of course, were as successful as these. Nancy McQueen, alias Ysabel McCully, went to court when she found that she, her husband, and her two children had been sold by John McQueen, of American Revolutionary War fame and one of East Florida's most prominent planters. Although unable to read or write, Nancy through the court notary claimed McQueen had no right to sell them since she and her family had been freed by their former owners in Charleston and she had written proof of this manumission. Nancy further claimed that her family members were *nuevo pobladores,* or homesteaders, not slaves. She challenged McQueen to show proof of their purchase.[32]

As required, McQueen answered Nancy's charge with his own memorial and told the court that following the British evacuation of Charleston during the American Revolution, the governor of South Carolina deposited with him a number of unclaimed slaves. McQueen cared for the slaves, including Nancy and her husband, for more than six months, during which time no one reclaimed them. In consideration of his services, expenses, and war losses, the governor rewarded McQueen with the remaining slaves. McQueen and other witnesses stated that they had read the paper Nancy believed was her manumission and that it seemed instead to be some sort of soldier's certification. McQueen stated that as he was preparing to move the slaves to St. Augustine, Nancy showed the papers to the magistrate on Sapelo Island, who also felt the paper was "useless." Nancy and her family were brought as slaves into St. Augustine, but there she resumed her quest for freedom.[33]

Informed by the court of McQueen's testimony, Nancy responded and verified that she and her husband had been deposited with McQueen but said they only agreed to stay because she was pregnant, sick, and starving. Had she better understood Spanish conventions about the protections due to women and mothers and those of the "miserable classes," Nancy might have phrased this information more powerfully to elicit sympathy from the court. Instead, her family's suffering is a minimal part of her statement, and she proceeds to what she considered important—legal property requirements. She asked the court how deceased owners could have reclaimed them. She charged that the overseers to whom she showed her paper must have altered it and discounted the testimony of these witnesses since they were all dependents of McQueen. Again she challenged McQueen or his representatives to show proof of ownership. She also asked that the court solicit testimony from Philadelphia, where her former owners had lived.[34]

Nancy first took her case to court in 1792 and fought for the next seven years to win freedom for herself and her husband, whose name, incidentally, never appears in the records. Although by this time McQueen had become even more prominent in the community, acquiring vast properties and military and judicial appointments from the Spaniards, he was repeatedly required, nevertheless, to respond to her petitions. Finally, a new governor ruled that it was unfair to McQueen to leave the case hanging and continually require him to appear in court. He said Nancy had repeatedly shown poor proofs of liberty and that she had fifteen days to produce better, or forever hold her peace.[35]

Although Nancy's determination equaled Andaina's, Nancy suffered many handicaps that contributed to her ultimate failure. She was an illiterate field hand, with apparently limited access to St. Augustine, and perhaps a flawed understanding of Spanish institutions. There is no evidence Nancy or her husband pursued the available option of *coartación,* for example. They may have had no way to earn extra money in the countryside. Instead, Nancy staked her claims on a piece of paper issued by a foreign government in a hand she could not read. Although Nancy understood the concepts of property and contract and repeatedly demanded written proof of sale and ownership, she seemed unable to grasp the important influence social relations had on determinations in the Spanish courts. Nancy had no important connections or allies in the community nor witnesses to any abuse from her owner. Furthermore, there is no evidence she sought the intercession of the church or any other legal representatives. Her case rested solely on her own testimony and on a text that ultimately betrayed her. Although Nancy ultimately lost her long battle, the fact that she was able to fight such a long delaying action against one of the court's own officers indicates the seriousness with which the Spanish court reviewed a claim to freedom. Her case also underscores Spanish commitment to the principle of access; even an illiterate slave woman could get repeated hearings and engage the court and her powerful and wealthy owner in a case lasting over seven years.

The cases described above, suits for freedom, could only have been litigated by African-American women, who were the only women enslaved. A brief review of the memorials and petitions submitted to the courts by women of other nationalities reflects some interesting differences. Women of Mediterranean or Spanish background, whose husbands were dependents of the Spanish government, went to court to enforce support payments for themselves and their children through payroll deductions. This option was not available to African-American women, whose husbands served in the local militias only during times of crisis. Nor do African-American women or their representatives appear in the courts to force a promised marriage. Only rarely do they report they've been slandered, as the Mediterranean and Spanish women frequently do. Such status complaints may have seemed impossible to win, or at least not worth the court costs. Although Spanish law held that slavery was an accident of fate and abhorrent to nature, there was nevertheless a societal stigma attached to having been descended from slaves. It was difficult for any African-American woman to win a case based on claims to virtue or honor or on appeals for protection traditionally due to women in Spanish society. One who tried, failed.

María Whiten (the former Judy Kenty, who had escaped slavery in South Carolina and been freed in Florida by claiming religious sanctuary) filed suit against one of the wealthiest Spanish families in the community who, she claimed, had insulted and physically mistreated her. In her petition she identifies herself as María Whiten, *vecina,* a term signifying a property-holding member of the community, but she makes no reference to her race or legal status. The omission is anomalous and seems a deliberate attempt to put herself on equal footing with those she is suing. María told the court that when she was waiting in a doorway for a young slave apprenticed to her the wife of Don José Sánchez queried her repeatedly about her business there. María told the court that on the third query she had responded, "Madam, I have not come to rob anyone of anything." Both María's failure to respond immediately to the elite woman and the sarcastic response she finally gave would have clearly been read as insolence, given María's lower socioeconomic status and her race. María told the court that on hearing the exchange Sánchez began to berate and beat her until her mouth and nose bled. She added that she was undeserving of such treatment since she was doing no harm and was in the neighborhood on business and asked the court to admonish her abusers. María was illiterate but her son, Francisco, who was educated in St. Augustine, produced the petition for her and signed by her X.[36]

Don José Sánchez responded to María's suit by admitting that he had beaten her, but he claimed that María had used English to say, "I'm not doing anything, you damned bitch." Although María had filed the suit and had her hearing, the governor found that "the latter statement having more verisimilitude . . . María should abstain in the future from lack of due respect to white persons." Spanish justice may have guaranteed access, but it was not class-blind and, as this example or others between persons of the same race might equally illustrate, courts deferred to the higher status of the elite Spanish woman.[37]

In another case, the widow and daughter of an African militiaman who had served in St. Augustine before the 1763 cession petitioned repeatedly to be granted the same government support enjoyed by other Spanish widows and orphans. Although church records established existence of a legitimate marriage and the two women had proof of the deceased's military service as a drummer, no woman of color from Florida had ever received such aid. Moreover, Spanish officials claimed military drummers were slaves salaried by their owners and so ineligible for government pay. In this case the drummer, Ignacio Rozo, was a free man, and so the women persisted for ten years while their petitions were dutifully routed through channels in Havana. Finally, Cuban officials referred the case to Aranjeuz, Spain, for royal review, but because Spanish law placed heavy emphasis on precedent, the women were ultimately denied "on the basis of their color" because no woman of color had ever before been granted military pensions.[38] However, Spanish law was not totally inflexible. After a later evacuation of Spain's black auxiliaries from Santo Domingo in 1796 (only four years after the negative ruling in the Rozo case), African-American women and children were finally granted government subsidies as military dependents. The difference may have been that the men who fought in Santo Domingo were clearly combat soldiers and therefore more deserving of honor and tribute than a drummer, a position associated with slavery.[39]

Several of the foregoing cases illustrate the conservative nature of Spanish law. Spanish society was also conservative and traditional when it could be, and this character sometimes worked to the advantage of African-American women. As noted at the outset of this essay, property rights of women had been protected in Spain since the Middle Ages.

The courts in Spanish Florida thus had no problem upholding the inheritance rights of African-American women and children if their relationship to the deceased was publicly acknowledged, even when the mothers were not legally married to the fathers of their children. For example, Juan Fernández left the free African-American Juana, "with whom he has lived many years and who has helped him to make his fortune," a half share in his estate, consisting of two houses, seven horses, a canoe, a cart, and a store of food and drink. His and Juana's six children inherited the other half of Juan's "fortune."[40]

Many of Florida's government officials and wealthy planters left even more substantial property to their common-law wives and natural children, and the community respected the desires of the deceased, as well as the rights of the bereaved. The institution of the extended kinship group (*parentela*), which included blood relations, fictive kin such as godparents, and sometimes household servants and slaves, and the institution of *clientela,* which bound powerful patrons and their personal dependents into a network of mutual obligations, were so deeply rooted in Spain that, according to one scholar, they might have been the "primary structure of Hispanic society."[41] Spaniards viewed society as an extension of family structures, and African-American women developed connections in the community through marriage, concubinage, and godparent choices that could produce tangible benefits.

Francisco Xavier Sánchez, who unsuccessfully opposed Filis and Edimboro's *coartación,* left two large families at his death, one African American and one Creole. Although Sánchez died intestate, he had expressed his wishes that his illegitimate children inherit, and his legitimate widow and children supported the inheritance of his first mulatto family in court. María del Carmen Hill wrote to the court, "It is well known . . . that my deceased husband always recognized them as his natural children . . . and as proof he provided for their food, education, and everything else necessary for their station." Moreover, María del Carmen stated that shortly before he died she had heard her husband say he wanted to give each of his natural children several slaves each for their support. She added, "I should not oppose their petition, on the contrary I wish them to receive what by law they are due." The two families were closely intertwined in multiple godparent relationships, and the legitimate family was bound by that obligation as well as by Sánchez's desires. The widow could afford to be generous. The court carefully inventoried Sánchez's five plantations, land holdings, and town properties before making the division in which the six natural children divided one-sixth of his estate. Sánchez's five mulatto daughters inherited a house, lots, and slaves worth about $7,000.[42] Before he died Sánchez also secured licenses for three of his mulatto daughters to marry Spanish army men, further enhancing their standing in the community.[43]

This is only a preliminary study, yet it clearly indicates that several important institutional, political, and social factors enabled African-American women successfully to pursue their rights in Spanish Florida. One was the observance of a legal code that upheld the property rights of women generally and supported their access to the courts. In this litigious society, all could generate texts and make their voices heard. Another was the particular political circumstance of Spanish Florida. Bordered by a competing nation that practiced chattel slavery, Florida sought to weaken the enemy by attracting and then freeing its slaves, and this policy worked to the advantage of women as well as men. Also important were the conservative and family-based religious and social systems and the gender conventions operating in Spanish Florida. Finally, after centuries of experience Spaniards were accustomed to Africans in their communities, and miscegenation was common in Florida. While racism was not absent, racial categorization was less rigid than in Anglo areas and became more a function of personal connections, wealth, and behavior. Much work remains to be done, but careful case studies in the rich Spanish records of borderland colonies such as Florida promise to tell us a great deal about the lives of African-American women and address issues of race and gender often more difficult to discern in Anglo-American colonial history.

Notes

1. Jane Landers, *African American Society in Spanish Florida* (Champaign-Urbana: Univ. of Illinois Press, forthcoming). For comparable findings in Louisiana, see Gwendolyn Midlo Hall, *Africans in Colonial Louisiana: The Development of Afro-Creole Culture in the Eighteenth Century* (Baton Rouge: Louisiana State Univ. Press, 1992); and Kimberly S. Hanger, " 'The Fortunes of Women': Spanish New Orleans' Free and Slave Women of African Descent," in *Discovering the Women in Slavery*, ed. Patricia Morton (Athens: Univ. of Georgia Press, 1996).

2. Landers, *African American Society;* Susan Parker, "In My Mother's House: Female Property Ownership in Spanish St. Augustine," paper delivered at the American Society for Ethnohistory, Salt Lake City, 1992.

3. Examples of this older tradition of borderland studies of the Southeast include Herbert E. Bolton and Mary Ross, *The Debatable Land: A Sketch of the Anglo-Spanish Contest for the Georgia Country* (New York: Russell and Russell, 1968) and Verner E. Crane, *The Southern Frontier, 1670–1732* (New York: Norton, 1981). Newer studies, such as David J. Weber's *The Spanish Frontier in North America* (New Haven: Yale Univ. Press, 1992), devote more attention to women.

4. On the legal and social position of women in Spain and the Spanish colonies, see Asunción Lavrin, Introduction and "In Search of the Colonial Woman in Mexico: The Seventeenth and Eighteenth Centuries," in *Latin American Women: Historical Perspectives,* ed. Asunción Lavrin (Westport, Conn.: Greenwood Press, 1978), 3–22, 23–59.

5. Unmarried women over the age of twenty-five and widows actually enjoyed even more freedom than their married counterparts in colonial Latin America (Lavrin, "In Search of the Colonial Woman," 30, 41). Others who have written insightfully on women and marriage in colonial Latin America are Patricia Seed, *To Love, Honor, and Obey in Colonial Mexico: Conflicts over Marriage Choice, 1574–1821* (Stanford: Stanford Univ. Press, 1988); Susan Migden Socolow, "Love and Marriage in Colonial Latin America," paper delivered at the Conference on Latin American History, December 1991; and Ramón A. Gutiérrez, "From Honor to Love: Transformations of the Meaning of Sexuality in Colonial New Mexico," in *Kinship Ideology and Practice in Latin America,* ed. Raymond T. Smith (Chapel Hill: Univ. of North Carolina Press, 1984), 237–63.

6. Fernando de Rojas, *La Celestina,* trans. Lesley Byrd Simpson (Berkeley: Univ. of California Press, 1955), 5–8. *La Celestina* draws heavily on the earlier classic by Alfonso Martínez de Toledo, *Little Sermons on Sin: The Archpriest of Talavera,* trans. Lesley Byrd Simpson (Berkeley: Univ. of California Press, 1959).

7. Gloria Kaufman, "Juan Luis Vives on the Education of Women," *Signs* 3 (1978): 891–96.

8. Fray Luis de León, *Obras Completas Castellanas de Fray Luis de León* (Madrid: Editorial Católica, 1951).

9. Mary Elizabeth Perry, *Gender and Disorder in Early Modern Seville* (Princeton: Princeton Univ. Press, 1990), 38–44, 56. For examples of the disadvantages faced by women in Latin America, see Asunción Lavrin, ed. *Sexuality and Marriage in Colonial Latin America* (Lincoln: Univ. of Nebraska Press, 1989).

10. Asunción Lavrin and Edith Couturier, "Dowries and Wills: A View

of Women's Socioeconomic Role in Colonial Guadalajara and Puebla, 1640–1790," *Hispanic American Historical Review* 59 (1979): 280–304; Edith Couturier, "Women and the Family in Eighteenth-Century Mexico: Law and Practice," *Journal of Family History* 10 (1985): 294–304.

11. William D. Phillips, *Slavery from Roman Times to the Early Transatlantic Trade* (Minneapolis: Univ. of Minnesota Press, 1985), 154–70; Ruth Pike, *Aristocrats and Traders: Sevillian Society in the Sixteenth Century* (Ithaca: Cornell Univ. Press, 1972), 170–92; Herbert S. Klein, *African Slavery in Latin America and the Caribbean* (New York: Oxford Univ. Press, 1986).

12. On the importance of justice and law for Spanish society, see Lyle N. McAlister, *Spain and Portugal in the New World, 1492–1700* (Minneapolis: Univ. of Minnesota Press, 1984), 24–26.

13. Another standard closing might be "The humble petitioner fully expects to be graced with the charity and justice for which your esteemed Majesty is well-known. I kiss your hand and pray that God grant you many years." On treatment of the "miserable classes" see Maureen Flynn, "Charitable Ritual in Late Medieval and Early Modern Spain," *Sixteenth-Century Journal* 16, no. 3 (1985): 1–30.

14. Frank Tannenbaum, *Slave and Citizen* (Boston: Beacon Press, 1992). Although he never examined the gender implications of his thesis, Tannenbaum pioneered comparative studies of slavery and argued that slavery was relatively less severe in Spanish America because it was moderated by legal and ecclesiastical institutions.

15. Royal Edict, November 7, 1693, SD 58–1-2/74 in the John B. Stetson Collection, P. K. Yonge Library of Florida History, University of Florida, Gainesville (hereinafter cited as PKY).

16. Jane Landers, "Spanish Sanctuary: Fugitives in Florida, 1687–1790," *Florida Historical Quarterly* 62 (1984): 296–313; "Gracia Real de Santa Teresa de Mose: A Free Black Town in Spanish Colonial Florida," *American Historical Review* 95 (1990): 9–30. Of a group of 251 claimants for sanctuary in the 1780s, 84 were women (Census Returns 1784–1814, East Florida Papers [hereinafter cited as EFP], microfilm reel 148, PKY).

17. Richard Oswald and his partner, Henry Laurens, imported hundreds of Africans from their operation in Bance Island, a major slave-shipping center in the middle of the Sierra Leone River. On their treatment see Daniel L. Schafer, " 'Yellow Silk Ferret Tied round Their Wrists': African Americans in British East Florida, 1763–1784," in *African American Heritage of Florida,* ed. David Colburn and Jane Landers (Gainesville: Univ. Press of Florida, 1995), 71–103.

18. Brent Richards Weisman, *Like Beads on a String: A Cultural History of the Seminole in North Peninsular Florida* (Tuscaloosa: Univ. of Alabama Press, 1989), 12, 75, 100–103, 174. Census Returns, microfilm reel 148, EFP, PKY; Jane Landers, "Spanish Sanctuary," 296–313.

19. Landers, *African American Society.*

20. Hubert H. S. Aimes, "Coartacíon: A Spanish Institution for the Advancement of Slaves into Freedmen," *Yale Review* 17 (1909): 412–31.

21. Tannenbaum, *Slave and Citizen* (Boston: Beacon Press, 1992). Landers, *Black Society,* 106–45; Daniel L. Schafer, *Anna Kingsley* (St. Augustine: St. Augustine Historical Society, 1994).

22. Rebecca J. Scott, *Slave Emancipation in Cuba: The Transition to Free Labor, 1860–1899* (Princeton: Princeton Univ. Press, 1985), 13–14.

23. Civil Proceedings, Petition of Margarita Saunders, 15 October 1794, EFP, microfilm reel 152, PKY; Civil Proceedings, Petition of Lucia Saunders, 5 Oct. 1795, EFP, microfilm reel 152, PKY.

24. Civil Proceedings, EFP, reels 152–69, PKY. The poverty of the colony made uncompensated manumissions a rarity in Florida. Most owners received reimbursements of between 200 and 300 pesos for the freedom of adult slaves, and usually less than 100 pesos for children.

25. Accounts of the Royal Treasury 1784–95, Payments to Antonio, 30 June, 29 Nov., 30 Dec., 1794, Santo Domingo, 2535, Archivo General de Indias, Sevilla, Spain (hereinafter cited as SD and AGI); Accounts of the Royal Treasury, 1796–1819, Payment to Juan Wright, 25 Nov. 1788, to Carlos Hall, 31 July 1797, and to Felipe Edimboro, 13 July 1818, SD 2536, AGI.

26. Civil Proceedings, Petition of Felipe Edimboro, 6 July 1794, EFP, microfilm reel 152, PKY. In order to improve their chances in the courts, Edimboro and Filis were baptized and married in the Catholic Church (Black Baptisms, Cathedral Parish Records, Diocese of St. Augustine Catholic Center, Jacksonville, Florida [hereinafter cited as CPR], microfilm reel 284J, PKY, and Black Marriages, CPR, microfilm reel 284L, PKY).

27. Memorials, Petition of Andaina, 13 Feb. 1793, EFP, microfilm reel 78, PKY.

28. Memorials, Response of Catalina Cantar (aka Acosta), 12 Dec. 1797, EFP, microfilm reel 79, PKY.

29. Memorials, Petition of Andaina, 13 Feb. 1793, EFP, microfilm reel 78, PKY.

30. Memorials, response of Catalina Cantar (aka Acosta), 12 Dec. 1797, EFP, microfilm reel 79, PKY.

31. Memorial of Andaina, 2 Dec. 1797, and response of Catalina Cantar (aka Acosta), 12 Dec. 1797, EFP, microfilm reel 79, PKY.

32. Civil Proceedings, Petition of Nancy, 19 Sept. 1792, EFP, microfilm reel 151, PKY. For more on John McQueen see *The Letters of Don Juan McQueen to His Family, Written from Spanish East Florida, 1791–1807,* ed. Walter Charlton Hartridge (Columbia, S.C.: Bostwick & Thornley, 1943).

33. Civil Proceedings, Petition of Nancy, 19 Sept. 1792, EFP, microfilm reel 151, PKY.

34. Ibid.

35. Ibid.

36. Memorial of María Whiten, 27 Aug. 1798, EFP, microfilm reel 79, PKY.

37. Ibid. and response by Dons José and Bernardino Sánchez. For a discussion of Spanish interrogatories and the relative weight assigned to witnesses of different status, see Alexandra Parma Cook and Noble David Cook, *Good Faith and Truthful Ignorance: A Case of Transatlantic Bigamy* (Durham: Duke Univ. Press, 1991), 87–89, 91–103, 112–14.

38. Petition of María Gertrudis Rozo, 25 Sept. 1792, SD 2577, AGI.

39. The Marques de Someruelos to the Governor of Florida, 21 Feb. 1801, EFP, microfilm reel 2, PKY.

40. Testament of Juan Fernández, 1821, EFP, microfilm reel 168, PKY.

41. McAlister, *Spain and Portugal in the New World,* 133–52. For an excellent look at how these systems actually operated, see Stephanie Blank, "Patrons, Clients and Kin in Seventeenth-Century Caracas: A Methodological Essay in Colonial Spanish American Social History," *Hispanic American Historical Review* 54 (1974): 260–82. An older but still useful study is by George M. Foster, "Cofradía and Compadrazgo in Spain and Spanish America," *Southwestern Journal of Anthropology* 9 (1953): 1–28.

42. Testamentary Proceedings ordered on the death of Don Francisco Xavier Sánchez, 1807, EFP, microfilm reel 118, PKY. Two unmarried daughters and their brother lived in the house. The other three sisters married Spaniards and had homes of their own.

43. Matrimonial licenses, EFP, microfilm reel 132, PKY.

PART TWO

Victorian Southerners

Playing the Gentleman, Playing the Lady

Poe and Gentry Virginia

Provincial Gentleman, Textual Aristocrat, Man of the Crowd

David Leverenz

Allen Tate's remarkable 1949 essay "Our Cousin, Mr. Poe," defines Poe as southern not only for his high sense of a writer's calling but because Poe understood better than anyone else that the modern world was going straight to hell, that is to say, the bourgeois, commodifying North. For Tate, a culture not controlled by leisured gentlemen means Dante's *Inferno*, which Poe rewrites as a disintegration from reason and community into machinelike, alienated egotisms of the will, vampiric women, and cravings for sensations. Tate mournfully concludes, however, that Poe lacked the stylistic and moral control to be a true southern gentleman. His "early classical education and a Christian upbringing" just didn't stick.[1]

Recent southern critics have been considerably more sensitive to the patriarchal and racist idealizations in such elegizing of gentry traditions. They tend to locate Poe's southernness paradoxically and peripherally in his marginality to gentry status. Louis Rubin links Poe's characteristic vitality of the "beleaguered intellect" to his less than legitimate status as an orphan in the home of John Allan, who himself felt alien to the Tidewater gentry and unappreciated by his wealthy uncle, William Galt. In the five years that Allan was trying to make his mark in England, for instance, Poe was boarded out from the age of seven. His guardian also made it clear that the boy was not to be treated as a member of the family. Others have made cases for Poe's southernness through his conservative, antidemocratic values. As Stuart Levine has summed them up, Poe was "a reactionary, a snob, and a racist."[2]

Yet Tate's sense of Poe as a kind of demonic, premodernist visionary, at best a marginal or negative or failed southerner, still holds. G. R.

Thompson puts the problem succinctly: Poe is the antebellum South's one original writer, and he is the one writer whose southernness is suspect. Except for three glancing allusions, Richard Gray leaves Poe out of *Writing the South,* a mute testimony to Poe's flight from regional entrapment. Resolutely antiprovincial in nearly every literary way, Poe spent most of his professional life moving from northern city to northern city, vainly seeking capital and cultural authority to edit an elite magazine for civilized gentlemen, in the spirit of Tate's ideal.[3]

The deconstructive and ideological turns of the last twenty years invite us to read Poe's southernness with more subtlety. This essay argues that Poe was more than an alienated visionary on the margins of the South because the southern ideal of the gentleman plays a crucial role in his writings as well as in his life. Yet the role of that ideal is far from simple. Poe's mix of claustrophobic Gothic, arcane reasoning, and cosmopolitan satire both exaggerates and undermines the gentry fictions of a postcolonial region doubly dependent on England and New England. As the site of raw materials for the emerging capitalist North, the South also grew tobacco and cotton for the world's capitalist center, in London. There John Allan came close to bankruptcy, much as William Byrd II had failed to make his London mark almost two hundred years earlier. Allan returned to inhabit the compensatory fiction that Byrd had helped to establish: a paradoxical self-image of the gentleman in the provinces, proud yet touchy, cool yet combative, masterful yet keenly defensive about any slights to his honor.

In *Imagined Communities,* an influential study of the interplay between colonialism and nationalism, Benedict Anderson suggests that metropolitan capital produces "tropical Gothic" as a postcolonial genre, and further, that racism is a way to "play aristocrat off center court." He goes so far as to say that colonialism invented racism as a fall-back strategy to establish and maintain dominance within provincial dependence. In *American Slavery, American Freedom,* Edmund S. Morgan anticipates Anderson by arguing that English emigrants used racism to displace and alleviate class tensions. Grounded in "fear and contempt . . . for the inarticulate lower classes" in England, their colonial and postcolonial rhetoric of liberty and equality depended on a binary opposition "lumping Indians, mulattoes, and Negroes in a single pariah class." This transformation of class divisions into racial dichotomies also "paved the way for a similar lumping of small and large planters in a single master class." Throughout the South, racism and slavery allowed white English emigrants to foster a social fiction of provincial aristocracy for squires and would-be squires, explicitly imitating and idealizing English gentry traditions. That Anglophilic fiction helped to preserve male status hierarchies in amber, warding off class and racial pressures for social change.[4]

William Byrd II helped to make Virginia the apex of the pseudoaristocracy's hegemonic arch. After his return from London in 1726, he turned his home at Westover into his ideal of what a planter's life in the provinces should be. Witty, urbane, civic-minded, he wrote his *History of the Dividing Line* in large part for his London friends—it was not published until 1841. Yet as Kenneth Lockridge suggests, Byrd also strove to fulfill "a rigid, almost unbending set of poses" defined in part by his struggles at the margins of London's high society. His coded diary became his secret "mirror" to reassure him that every day, in every way, he did what gentlemen do. Not only his 179,000 acres, from which Richmond and Petersburg were created, but also his public persona as the classic Virginia patriarch secured his position at the top of the provincial gentry hierarchy, despite enormous debts. When John Allan suddenly inherited his uncle's riches, which saved him from ruin, he also inherited three large estates: Lower Byrd, Little Byrd, and Big Byrd.[5]

Poe inhabits and undermines gentry fictions of mastery, not least by exposing the gentleman as a fiction that male characters struggle and fail to impersonate. Typically, he displays cultivated narrators unable to master themselves. An "imp" seems bent on their destruction, as if self-directed malevolence rather than socially virtuous benevolence constituted the "sixth sense" of Scottish moral philosophy. Or Poe celebrates masterful intellects, such as Dupin or himself, who keep resentments at bay with their powers to transcend revengeful emotions through mental mirroring. Poe's narratives also exaggerate gentry contradictions, especially the double imperatives of cool reasoning and impulsive bravado. His tales don't simply shame gentlemen of honor; he constructs, then deconstructs, their private life, by transgressing the great social divide between public displays of mastery and an inwardness felt as alien to oneself. Arabesques of public leisure become grotesque enslavements to obsession. Finally, Poe plays with gentry specters of a debased capitalist future to put his own indulgent yet satiric spin on nostalgia for idealized aristocracy. He is especially keen to make textuality itself the source for true aristocratic honor, a status to which only his genius can pretend.

To advance these arguments, I have divided my essay into four parts. The first discusses Poe's life in relation to gentry fictions and contradictions, with a look at reductive northern readings of Poe and the South. The second part considers Poe's playful textuality as his version of true aristocracy, whose distinction transcends the disintegration of the gentry's provincial gender codes. Here I touch on "Ligeia," "Usher," and Pierre Bourdieu. In the third part, I apply my reading of gentry hierarchy to "The Man of the Crowd." At the end, using "Hop-Frog," I consider Poe as a gentry trickster.

I

In the late fall and early winter of 1828–29, the Virginia legislature held a constitutional convention to consider the overrepresentation of Tidewater and Piedmont gentry in state politics. Resentful yeoman delegates from the west argued for representation based on the white male population, while plantation gentry delegates from the east argued that representation should also be based on property, including slaves. As the Tidewater delegates declared with special intensity, the gentry on larger plantations feared that more equal representation would slowly shift power westward. Then the great tradition of gentry leadership, symbolized by the presence of aged James Monroe as nominal presider and James Madison as chair of the key committee, would come to an end.

John Randolph, who probably served as one of the models for Roderick Usher, delivered the climactic gentry speech. Randolph, a delicate, even effeminate man who liked to ride in an old-fashioned English coach drawn by four English thoroughbreds, affirmed his class pride as clearly as the yeomen delegates voiced their class resentments. "I am an aristocrat," he liked to say. "I love liberty. I hate equality." Now, his speech warned, stripping the gentry of privileged property status would sound the "tocsin of civil war." Randolph meant class war, in Virginia.[6]

Despite Randolph's ominous invocations of Armageddon, the gentry's case for mixed-base representation lost, twice, 49–47. Finally, the gentry salvaged a compromise apportionment based on a favorable 1820 census, after a more progressive motion to use subsequent census reports had been defeated by a tie vote, 48–48. The final vote was still a cliff-hanger: 50–46.

In Alison Freehling's account of these debates, *Drift toward Disso-*

lution, the rhetoric of the convention delegates exposes three or perhaps four Virginias: the empowered eastern gentry from Tidewater and Piedmont; the resentful artisans, farmers, and mechanics of the west; and the more heterogeneous mix in the valley, spilling over into the Piedmont region, including Richmond, the capital, right on the fall line between Piedmont and Tidewater. In Richmond, Poe's home town and still not much more than a town, these political tensions were exacerbated by other tensions between two kinds of gentry: the old plantation elite and newer Scottish merchants such as John Allan, who were challenging the elite for economic dominance.

After Nat Turner's south Tidewater revolt in August of 1831, once again came a special legislative session. Surprisingly, a great many delegates—including Thomas Jefferson's (white) grandson and, behind the scenes, Governor John Floyd—favored "expedient abolition," though only to return slaves to Africa. Not one delegate declared slavery to be a positive good, though many eastern delegates proclaimed slavery indispensable to the gentry way of life. If the Virginia House had been apportioned on the 1830 census, Alison Freehling concludes, the overwhelming proabolition sentiment from the west would have brought the final tally within one vote of success. As it was, the vote was 73–58, east defeating west. Everyone agreed that abolition and the recolonization of free blacks and slaves to Liberia should be fully explored. When Jefferson's grandson was subsequently reelected, though only by 95 votes, this champion of abolition acknowledged that his support had come primarily from the "poorer" whites sympathetic to his unflinching position against slavery.[7]

In both legislative sessions, the eastern Virginia gentry seemed on the verge of losing a class war, yet they preserved their power handily. The dreams of colonization soon failed; the western part of the state eventually seceded in 1861 to become West Virginia. In *Southern Capitalists,* Laurence Shore argues that again and again the gentry found ways to absorb assaults and justify its right to rule. Part of the gentry's success came from its ability to subsume potential conflicts between men in a shared code that emphasized the manly display of honor. These ritualized performances both masked and helped to reconcile often conflicting merchant, plantation, and yeomen interests. A shared gender code of patriarchal honor preserved the economic and political power of perhaps one-twentieth of adult white men by encouraging other white men to proclaim mastery over women and African Americans. Slavery gave the gentry ample leisure to jockey for status, while racism gave status to every white nonslaveholder. In a still broader sense, slavery helped to preserve habits of stratification and deference against the growing pressures of class consciousness and entrepreneurial individualism.[8]

By 1830 the code was very clear. Any man who owned ten or more slaves and one hundred or more acres of land—the slaves were considerably more important to the title of "master"—could aspire to gentry status. Any man with more than twenty slaves had secured his position as a gentleman. To rise higher up the ladder built on that floor of natural and human property, a man had to display his status publicly, particularly through rituals of virility: "fighting, horse racing, gambling, swearing, drinking, and wenching," as Bertram Wyatt-Brown describes young men's mutual testing. When occasions required a more senatorial manner, a man had to embody cool, dispassionate, civic-minded reasoning.[9]

It was not simply a matter of conscious role-playing and masquerading, Wyatt-Brown argues, that made southerners so famously "touchy" about their virility. Southern men lived their code of honor as a constant test of manhood. In the North, normative middle- and upper-class families forsook the rod to internalize manly self-control through conscience and guilt. Virginia gentry families encouraged contentious acting out, with shame, not guilt, as the mediating agent for social control. It did not draw much comment when a professor at the University of Virginia was hit with a slingshot by a student who then tried to bite off the teacher's thumb. During one of the riots in the school's first year, 1825—Poe enrolled the next year—a student tossed a bottle filled with urine through a professor's window. Nose-pulling among adult males was an instantaneous invitation to a duel, though only among equals; a gentleman would lose status if he engaged in such ritualized conflict with an inferior. In Poe's short story "The Business Man," a shyster narrator signals his plunge toward dishonor by mentioning that he tried and failed to get a gentleman to pull his nose. The exceptionally large-nosed narrator of "Lionizing" loses his duel for prestige to a baron with no nose at all, so it cannot be pulled.[10]

This ideology of patriarchal, hierarchical honor not only fostered but featured contradictory dynamics: deference and strutting, dignified gentility and combative competitiveness. Steven M. Stowe details the intricate dance of decorum and insults that led to the death of Hawthorne's friend, Representative Jonathan Cilley, in an 1838 duel. It was a resolutely public decorum, as Stowe emphasizes, and a derivative one as well, since it explicitly upgraded the English squire to lordly status while appropriating a variety of classical models for civic conduct. George Washington invented himself as that remote, dollar-bill facade by emulating a literary text, Joseph Addison's *Cato*. Addison's play depicts a heroic Roman who mastered all personal passions to achieve lasting honor through dedication to public duty. Such assiduous self-fashioning to prepare a man for civic leadership depends on burying unperformable feelings *"living in the tomb"* of self-mastery, much as the social hierarchy stifled potential challenges from slaves, women, or creative imaginations.[11]

In his life, Poe frequently put on the poses of southern gentleman and his alienated intellectual double, the Byronic poet, often to near parodic excess. At the University of Virginia, the most expensive school in the nation, his extravagant aping of gentry manners ran up at least $2,000 in debts during just one year. As Kenneth Silverman's biography details, Poe also oscillated among the contradictory expectations of gentry roles. He could be charming and courtly with the ladies, including lady poets; a bantam cock in contending with his male literary peers; a dandy wearing abstruse learning on his fastidious sleeve; a heavy if intermittent drinker. Only in his seemingly asexual relations with women, including his sisterly wife Virginia, whom he married when she was thirteen, did Poe fail to comply with the basic model set by William Byrd so long ago, and present near at hand in John Allan's illegitimate twins. Otherwise Poe loved to brag about his physical prowess, emulating Byron's swimming feats and sometimes inflating to even greater lengths his remarkable running broad jump of 20' 6" at the university.[12]

Not infrequently, Poe conspicuously lost self-control. He prompted at least two fistfights, and launched a full-scale libel suit after the second one, when two men impugned his virility in print. One said Poe was an impotent coward, a forger, and a plagiarist who couldn't hold his liquor and reneged on his debts. The other published a parodic "Literati" sketch describing Poe as "'about 5 feet 1 or two inches, perhaps 2 inches and a half,'" instead of his actual 5' 8". For any man of honor, these were fighting words.[13]

In his reviewing Poe enacted the contradictions between English and provincial codes of the gentleman, while also responding to an emerging market for sensation. Poe used his "acquired Southern values and haughty temperament" as a key strategy to secure aristocratic status for gentleman poets. Poe's journalism also fed the market's avidity for fighting words. As Poe confidently told the first magazine publisher who employed him, Virginians thought they wanted "simplicity" but really enjoyed what the English magazines supplied: sensational subjects in a heightened style. Poe's Eurocentric role as a cosmopolitan man of letters rather than provincial apologist seemed grossly ungentlemanly, especially to the writers he gored. His "tomahawking" reviews lacked southern courtesy, tact, or generosity, William Gilmore Simms tried to tell Poe ten years after receiving one of the tomahawks. Yet gentry contradictions impelled his choice of weapons to fulfill his enormous desire for a high-status literary reputation. In creating "sensations" through his pugnacious reviews, Poe acted the adolescent Hotspur, while his otherworldly poems presented him as a Byronic southern Hamlet.[14]

From a distance, the contradictions and derivativeness in Poe's behavior seem less striking than the childishness. This too was conventional. One of Emerson's most supercilious journal entries records his response to a young "snippersnapper" from the South who "demolished me" in public. The southerner, he vengefully muses on October 8, 1837, is "a spoiled child . . . a mere parader. . . . They are mere bladders of conceit. . . . Their question respecting any man is like a Seminole's, How can he fight? In this country [!], we ask, What can he do? His pugnacity is all they prize, in man, dog, or turkey." Emerson's comparisons reduce the southerner to a child, an Indian, a turkey, or just hot air, filling "bladders of conceit."[15]

Venting his own conceits on southern heads restores Emerson's dignity. More subtly, his sense of North-South power relations emerges through clashing ideals of manliness, as Emerson's most telling phrase, "In this country," intimates. The phrase sets two postcolonial regions on a collision course. Yet New England, or "we," represents the only true country. "We" have men who do and talk, not children who fight and parade. New England has "civil educated . . . human" adults, Emerson says elsewhere in the entry; southerners act like Indian braves and barnyard brats. In later journal meditations, Emerson sometimes worries that the southern politician's "personality" and "fire" will dominate northerners in Washington. At bottom, however, he has the calm of an absentee landlord. As he writes to himself in May-June,

1846: if the southerner "is cool & insolent" while northerners "are so tame," "it is because we own you, and are very tender of our mortgages, which cover all your property." [16]

Emerson's presumption of his region's national mastery helps to explain Poe's vitriolic attacks on the Boston literati, especially Longfellow. Asserting his public "personality" with repeated "fire," Poe accused Longfellow of gross plagiarism as well as bad writing. When read in the context of Emerson's entry, the controversy dramatizes two regional codes for the gentleman. On the Virginia side, an ambitious, insecure provincial aggressively lords it over his Concord and Boston betters. On the Massachusetts side, both Emerson and Longfellow attempt to respond with a studied calm, at least in public. One of the most astonishing moments in Silverman's biography comes after Poe's death, when Longfellow actually visits Poe's beloved mother-in-law, "Muddy" Clemm. After telling her that Poe had been the greatest man living, Longfellow invites her to visit him in Cambridge, which she does. Such patrician generosity goes far beyond Emerson's public serenity and private snottiness.[17]

Emerson's South-baiting anticipates a recurrent note in Poe criticism: a thinly disguised critical disdain for the writer's poses and posturings. Most recently, Harold Bloom all but accuses Poe of being unmanly: he "fathered precisely nothing," and his criticism was right only about silly women writers, for whom he was "a true match." These innuendos buttress Bloom's claim that, like the South, Poe preferred "the Abyss" to the strong Emersonian self. These snide strictures about unmanly behavior and weak writing depend on a crudely sexualized anatomical dichotomy, probably borrowed from early Freud: the strong self has phallic power, while the weak self has fallen into a feminized Abyss. More surprisingly, Bloom's high New England seriousness about the self misses Poe's profoundly skeptical spirit of textual play. His narratives undecidably oscillate between exaggerating and parodying southern poses of gentry masculinity. What Bloom dismisses as the Abyss needs to be historicized as Poe's deconstructions of postcolonial gender codes.[18]

A complementary New England tradition searches for secret guilt in Poe's writings. Over thirty years ago, for instance, Harry Levin first suggested that Poe displaced concerns about slavery onto blackness, and that "The Fall of the House of Usher" can be read as an allegory of feudal plantation culture in its death throes. The latter still seems right. One could expand Levin's insight, using Rhys Isaac's *Transformation of Virginia*, since the webwork of fungi defining both Roderick's house and Roderick's hair parallels the gentry's fashionable display of twining vines on their plantations, imitating English country houses. Even so, the sociological allegory remains just what Daniel Hoffman says it is: a "ripple of meaning," more tangential than primary to the hyperliterary vortex that disorients the narrator's senses.[19]

Postabolitionist expectations of hidden gentry guilt about slavery continue to shape northern attitudes to the South as well as to Poe. I was first disabused of that expectation when reading a diary entry by a young Englishman who visited a Virginia plantation in the 1780s. Robert Hunter's day began with Montesquieu, then tea, then fun with friends. At the end of the day, "we supped en famille, played some tricks at cards, gave the Negroes an electrical shock, and went to bed at eleven."[20]

Faced with moments like that, modern democratic certainties about slavery and guilt falter. Critics who have read a great many southern diaries report with some wonder that slaves and free black people are rarely mentioned, even in passing. Various Poe writings reflect a pervasive gentry opinion that humans with black skins were less than human, though other tales, such as "The Man That Was Used Up" or "The Gold-Bug," can be read more ironically at the gentry's expense. And yet if Poe's scrabbling, marginal life intermittently imitates gentry codes of behavior, his narratives put his culture's greater fictions at risk.[21]

In *Life on the Mississippi*, Mark Twain inflates a cultural insight as well as the power of writers when he blames Sir Walter Scott for having caused the Civil War. Scott's model of medieval chivalry provided only one of many sources for the gentlemanly roles encouraged by the Anglophilic fiction of patriarchal honor. George Washington might read Cato, and James Madison might read Roman histories, but when the Virginia squires turned antisocial enough to read at all, they were most likely to pick up *Tom Jones*. Most gentry lived the fictions they rarely read. After learning to read his culture, Poe shifted the ground and raised the stakes for the game of being a provincial gentleman.[22]

II

Pierre Bourdieu's *Distinction* can help to situate Poe's writings in their cultural context of dependent, derivative pseudoaristocracy. Bourdieu's argument that court society persists in the Parisian haute bourgeoisie of the 1960s has considerably more applicability to antebellum Virginia than to the contemporary United States. In France's postaristocratic society, he argues, "cultural capital" secures and conveys the highest social status. The aesthetic aptitude "rigorously distinguishes the different classes" by dividing the naive from the sophisticated. Aesthetic detachment brings distinction: "a distant, self-assured relation to the world."[23]

Bourdieu's emphasis on the uses of cultural capital to gain social distinction seems to have almost nothing at all to say about the flagrantly anti-intellectual behavior of many antebellum southern gentry. As William Gilmore Simms memorably concluded, being a southern intellectual was as rewarding as "drawing water in a sieve." Despite the examples of Washington, Madison, Thomas Jefferson, and others, one gained cultural capital more from cockfighting than from poemwriting. Nonetheless, applying Bourdieu highlights the *pseudo-aristocratic* norms codifying the South's stratification of male status, with England as the idealized locus for gentry models. Beginning with his youthful pose as Byronic poet, Poe sought relatively conventional ways of aggrandizing his marginal status through cultural capital, or at least literary image-making, much as Simms and other intellectuals invoked Byronic genius to exaggerate or aggrandize their feelings of exile and dislocation. Only Poe, however, takes a decisive step beyond provincial conventions of cultural capital by making textuality itself the source of true aristocracy.[24]

In so doing, Poe gives an American twist to the mode that Michael McKeon has labeled "extreme skepticism." To simplify the neo-Marxist argument of McKeon's *Origins of the English Novel:* the rise of the novel mediates the rise to domination of class and individualism as new social categories of self-perception. Capitalist dynamics challenged traditions of status emphasizing deference, kinship, and lineage. Aristocracy itself, in McKeon's analysis, emerges as a simplifying "antithetical" abstraction to resist this massive social transformation.[25]

In an application of McKeon across the Atlantic one hundred years later, Poe expresses "the untenably negative midpoint between these two opposed positions." Poe negates a progressive ideology of individualism by emptying out the meaningfulness of the self as a coherent, independent entity. He exposes subjectivity as a collage of derivative literary conventions and a chaos of senseless, self-destructive desires. Simultaneously, Poe negates regressively prescriptive idealizations of the public man of honor—idealizations that animate Allen Tate's critique yet another century later.[26]

One of Bourdieu's most provocative passages illuminates the sheer sport and gamesmanship accompanying Poe's textual poses. "The petit bourgeois do not know how to play the game of culture as a game. They take culture too seriously to go in for bluff or imposture or even for the distance and casualness which show true familiarity." Because such people anxiously identify cultural capital with the accumulation of knowledge, Bourdieu continues, "they cannot suspect the irresponsible self-assurance, the insolent off-handedness and even the hidden dishonesty presupposed by the merest page of an inspired essay on philosophy, art or literature. Self-made men, they cannot have the familiar relation to culture which authorizes the liberties and audacities of those who are linked to it by birth."[27]

If we transpose these observations from fact to wish-fulfillment, we have the right context to explain a wide range of Poe's literary styles, from his plagiarisms to his critical panache to his fascination with style itself. His claims for beauty and aesthetic purity against the New England heresies of the didactic exalt intellectual abstractedness to invulnerably elite status, beyond any taint of subjectivity or bourgeois values. Poe's intellectual audacities and insolent irresponsibilities authorize his Family Romance rebirth, much as the narrator of "Ligeia" invokes "Romance" to preside over his first marriage, which gave him both upward mobility and the adoration of a learned, passionate parent-spouse. No longer born in Boston from disreputable theater parents, Poe displays his offhanded familiarities with European personages and texts as, to twist Veblen's phrase, conspicuous presumption. Such cultural capital enables Poe's leap beyond the Virginia squirearchy to a more cosmopolitan arena. More profoundly, he uses textuality to transform not only conventions of the southern gentleman but also his own mourning and marginality into cultural play. To turn felt insistencies and intensities of self and culture into a game, with what Bourdieu calls bluff, imposture, distance, and casualness, signifies the "true familiarity" of aristocratic breeding.

We see this quality, for instance, in Poe's intellectual strutting, the leisured glitter of thick high-culture allusions unmaking their meanings. From Mallarmé and Baudelaire to Derrida and Lacan, Poe has been cherished in France for just what normatively American readers—even expatriates such as James and Eliot—try to reduce to childish posturing: his Hoaxie-Poe trickeries, his melodramas of intellectual excess, the mind games. Poe fuses the bogus with the serious. His moments of maximum horror are also moments of maximum literary artifice. "MADMAN! I TELL YOU THAT SHE NOW STANDS WITHOUT THE DOOR!" Capital letters—a typographical *frisson* as well as a cry. "Madman"—a more startling surprise, since mad Roderick Usher now accuses the commonsensical narrator of having lost his senses. But "without the door"?[28]

The meanings surge in, to be sure. The "tottering of his lofty reason upon her throne" prefigured in Roderick's rhapsodic poem about "monarch Thought" culminates in a further confusion of "his" and "her," as Madeline "fell heavily inward upon the person of her brother." In their family, as in their house, being a (male) "person" depends not only on property and patriarchal lineage but also on internal doors that divide honor and reason from passions and the body. In Roderick's poem, a "throng" of forces imagined as lower class and chaotic overwhelms the house of the rational mind from within. Now the assault returns as the more intimately Gothic threat of a dead-undead sister who falls inward on the dichotomies that have constructed some persons and dispossessed others. Madeline's body, too, has lost its "door," suggesting both coffin and hymen, and implying incest. Yet "without" sounds ridiculously hyperliterary, as if Roderick had become spellbound by the "Mad Trist." The climactic moment's linguistic posturing undercuts its Hawthornean proliferation of meanings. The horror builds on a pun; the pun trumpets textuality; the textuality both inflates and undermines the horror.[29]

What Poe exposes in such moments, and they are legion, is a sudden Lacanian estrangement from words themselves. The reader's mind—like the narrator's—has been reduced to an infant's cribbed gazing, as if the endless incomprehensibility of big people's overly big words buzzes about a vacuum of staring. Poe doesn't make readers feel adult, the way Hawthorne and Emerson can do. Instead of offering narrators whose complex self-reflexiveness conveys maturity and understanding, Poe builds to a disorienting regression from the illusion of mastery to primal out-of-controlness, in which language itself becomes alien and theatrical.

Such baffling, fascinating textual moments suggest a paradox: that the seemingly ahistorical linguistic pleasures celebrated in Poe's long-running French connection illuminate his time and place—particularly the contradictions of southern white masculinity—more richly than do his explicitly southern themes. Not by accident has Poe's work become most honored in France, the most postaristocratic residuum in the Western world. As a self-made aristocrat, Poe uses textuality to aggrandize his status, while subverting the meanings of status stratification.

Poe's best tales invite an undecidable doubleness of interpretation. They point simultaneously to idealized gentry traditions of aristocratic contemplation and to demonized mass-market conditions for literary production. If the pleasure in aesthetic detachment consists of "refined games for refined players," as Bourdieu puts it, Poe's erudition ostensibly intensifies the sense of "membership and exclusion" on which distinction depends. Yet his texts grossly champion the vulgar and the shameful. His gentlemen come to look like apes and criminals. Contemporary opposition between "high" and "vulgar" uses of Poe can be historicized as a dynamic embedded in his own uses of aristocracy, toward the end of the long historical moment that challenged aristocracy's legitimacy.[30]

For Poe and the Virginia gentry, aristocracy signifies an idealized realm dislocated from specific social contexts. That idealization can be historicized. To invoke Michael McKeon again, the seemingly transcendent categories of aristocracy and romance function as antithetical simple abstractions, used to elevate high culture above history. If the romance of the gentleman displaces a yearning for metropolitan status, its theatricality signals self-consciousness about social conventions that were beginning to seem more alien than natural. Unlike the gentry's chivalric posturings, Poe's aristocratic textuality intimates not simply a muted inauthenticity but its own self-destruction. In Louis A. Renza's fine phrase, Poe's stories are "self-distracting artifacts."[31]

In the opening paragraph of "Ligeia," for instance, Poe flamboyantly transfers aristocratic status from property, lineage, and kinship to a world elsewhere in "that spirit which is entitled *Romance*." The narrator declares his transcendent mastery of cultural capital by not being able to remember any details that linked his adored first wife to the world, not even her paternal name. He recalls the full name, place, and kin of his despised second wife, "Lady Rowena Trevanion, of Tremaine," without effort. In subverting the traditional underpinnings of aristocracy, Poe exalts his narrator's conception of true aristocracy as abstractly textual. Like Roderick Usher, the world's first abstract expressionist painter, Poe's narrator locates the highest status in an art of aesthetic detachment, with no sordid connections to family, money, bodies, or social status. This narrator struggles toward an ideal: what Jonathan Auerbach nicely describes as Poe's characteristically disembodied first-person self that lacks a self.[32]

Yet "Ligeia" becomes a story about inheritance, property, and various kinds of "will": Ligeia's will to resist and conquer death; Ligeia's will bequeathing vast riches to a narrator seemingly above such concerns; the will of Rowena's family, who "permitted" their daughter to marry him "through thirst of gold." Most undecidably, the hidden will of the antipatrilineal narrator may have led him to the ultimate patriarchal act of killing one or both wives. Cynthia Jordan suggests that the narrator may have willed Ligeia's death and carried it out, hidden from his consciousness as well as his narrative.[33]

Or perhaps the narrator has an unconsciously racialized revulsion animating his passion. Joan Dayan suggests that Ligeia embodies a characteristic southern fascination with fictions of the tragic mulatta, or octoroon mistress, with eyes "far larger than the ordinary eyes of our own race." For that reason she could never tell the narrator her paternal name: the black wench inhabits the refined, even transcendent lady, as surely as her black eyes and hair bespeak her passionate loving. The narrator's presumption of transcendent whiteness, though transported from the South to vague European locations, depends on a very southern preoccupation with taints of blackness.[34]

By the end, the narrator has deconstructed as well as dishonored his own subjectivity. After exalting his childish dependency on textuality, personified as Mother Wisdom, he presents himself as several incompatible versions of possessed destructiveness: a drugged, hallucinating murderer, a medium for a demonic woman's will, or a witness to the return of the repressed black woman in the southern ideal of ladyhood. In any case, the narrator has been reduced to a craving for two black eyes.[35]

"The essential Poe fable," writes Michael Davitt Bell, "is a tale of compulsive self-murder." Placing Poe's dramas of self-murder in their gentry context highlights Poe's transgression of the southern elite's gendered border between public and private life. In the vortext of Poe's yearning skepticism about aristocratic status, female self-empowering becomes an alien signifier for contradictory psychological and social meanings: uncontrollable passions, uncontrollable patriarchal decay, and what Dayan calls "unspeakable slippages between men and women, humans and animals, life and death." Poe's tales of self-murder expose gentlemen in private, often doing and being done to by women, whose bodies if not voices struggle to be felt at the tales' destructive center. "Berenice" as well as "The Fall of the House of Usher" and "Ligeia" can be read not only as allegories of the male psyche's attempts to confront the inward female but as deconstructions of how antebellum gentry culture produced the categories of "gentleman" and "lady" along with its production of the more starkly binary oppositions, "black" and "white," slave and free.[36]

III

Several stories from the early 1840s illustrate Poe's making and unmaking of gentry meanings. Though this essay will focus only on "The Man of the Crowd" (1840), three other stories—"The Murders in the Rue Morgue" (1841), "The Purloined Letter" (1845), and "The Cask of Amontillado" (1846)—also feature a gentleman down on his luck who sees a modern urban world threatening the hierarchies on which he depends for social status. Each man tries to resurrect his sense of mastery, or self-respect, with what amounts to a solo duel. A displaced clash between northern and southern codes of masculinity frames the success or failure of each duel. Or rather, the stories present the northern future as versions of Allen Tate's myth of the Fall into an urban chaos of markets and mobilities, in which rootless masses hunger for sensations. Perhaps not surprisingly, most modern critics read these stories—especially "The Man of the Crowd"—forward into 42d Street, not backward into gentry Virginia.[37]

The first half of "The Man of the Crowd," as almost every critic has noted, presents what seems "a stable hierarchy" of descending social types, all "based on an aristocratic set of assumptions," in Jonathan Auerbach's words. The narrator begins as a conventional man of the Enlightenment, classifying "the tumultuous sea of human heads" outside his coffeehouse window with "abstract and generalizing" observations. Soon "I descended to details," in order to produce a hierarchy of types. His first two groups set the standard for "the decent," or what he later calls "gentility." Strangely, his details disorient the stability of the hierarchy he thinks he asserts.[38]

The first large group "had a satisfied business-like demeanor," the narrator summarizes. Yet "their brows were knit, and their eyes rolled quickly," whenever they feel pushed. Nevertheless, showing "no symptom of impatience," they "adjusted their clothes and hurried on." To say "symptom" rather than "sign" implies that any loss of self-control, even through "impatience," betokens disease and disorder. Even at the top of the social hierarchy, bodies betray what adjusted clothes conceal, while "business-like" belies gentility.

The second large group of "the decent" intensifies the tension between bodies and self-control. They seem "restless," with "flushed faces," "muttering" and redoubling "their gesticulations" when the crowd impedes them. They bow "profusely" when jostled, "and appeared overwhelmed with confusion." Having said all that, the narrator finds "nothing very distinctive about these two large classes." Their clothes enable him to blend "two classes" into one class: "Their habiliments belonged to that order which is pointedly termed the decent" (285).

Already contradictions abound. Two hierarchized groups, or classes, are really one class; men who have self-control also have bodies out of control; the narrator defines them as the standard, yet those who represent the standard have "nothing very distinctive"; decent clothes stabilize perception, yet behavior seems on the contradictory edge of hotheadedness and excessive deference. Moreover, the word *habiliments* implies a dressing up for public display, as if looking decent requires a facade.

Next he undermines even the bipartite division he has just tried to reestablish. "They were undoubtedly noblemen, merchants, attorneys, tradesmen, stock-jobbers—the Eupatrids and the commonplaces of society—men of leisure and men actively engaged in affairs of their own—conducting business upon their own responsibility. They did not greatly excite my attention" (285). A finely tuned, five-rank hierarchy briefly supplants the two groups. Clearly "noblemen" are at the top, while "stock-jobbers" and "tradesmen" are at the bottom. But where do "merchants" and "attorneys" go? Where did John Allan fit, in London? With "Eupatrids" or "commonplaces"?

If the border dividing that dichotomy becomes subtly contested, the dichotomy between "leisure" and "business" all but disappears. At the very least, the narrator forces a paradox: only leisured noblemen and Eupatrids truly exhibit "a satisfied business-like demeanor." The actual men of business, from merchants on down, look increasingly unsatisfied and anxious. On the other hand, even stock-jobbers threaten the edge of true gentility. No wonder all this bores him; to analyze it would be to expose gentility as both normative and nonexistent.

Earlier, the narrator has begun by describing himself in doubled terms, as a leisured gentleman at his coffeehouse, recovering from illness, on the edge between ennui and happiness, pain and pleasure, and describing the crowd as "two dense and continuous tides of population" (283, 285). Now he has come close to emptying out his simplifying dichotomies. Worse, he also implies that only clothes can be "read" without contradiction. His act of reading, and only his act of reading, makes gentility seem so stable and commanding. When he examines details at the top of the social order, not one person he sees inhabits the category of gentility without ambiguity, either between clothes and body movements or between business and leisure. The narrator's reading of types shows him not only imposing an uninhabited yet hegemonic social abstraction, the ideal gentleman, but reinventing the fiction with greater and greater assurance as his types deviate from his imagined norm.

Such ambiguities characterize a pseudoaristocrat, in terms very close to Richard Gray's history of the gentleman-planter ideal, in early Virginia. As "a compound of gracious feudal patriarch and bluff English squire," the planters were "always primarily businessmen" and "entrepreneurs" yet "anxious to assume the trappings of an aristocracy." In the early nineteenth century, those who sought to inhabit that contradictory, imported ideal were "a conscious and declining minority," as the two constitutional conventions in Richmond signify. The narrator's assessment of London's two standard-bearing groups expresses tensions in Virginia, not only between status ranking and class conflict but between hotheadedness and deference as well. Perhaps these tensions help to constitute provincial respectability.[39]

Two more Virginia-gentry tensions intensify as the narrator describes London's lower orders. First, he scorns the ungenteel yet relishes their attempts at upward mobility. Second, he shows inordinate contempt for men who work with their hands, while he defines women who work as prostitutes in the making. Significantly, the words *gentility, gentlemen,* and *gentry* don't appear except as stabilizing fictions of scheming aspiration for the hopelessly deviant. On "the scale of what is termed gentility" (286), various groups display "idiosyncratic" efforts to "be mistaken for gentlemen." Junior clerks who "wore the cast-off graces of the gentry" or senior clerks with the "affectation of respectability" (285–286) struggle without success to measure up. Further down the scale, the narrator comfortably calls pickpockets "these gentry" and gamblers "gentlemen who live by their wits." Their fraudulence licenses his mocking labels while subtly exposing the cultural fiction.

Then come "Jew pedlars," street beggars, invalids, and at last, women, all of whom work: "modest young girls returning from long and late labor" who shrink "more tearfully than indignantly" from presumably leering and lustful men. The girls' lack of anger signals their coerced, sexualized future in the world's oldest profession, already paraded by "women of the town . . . [their] interior filled with filth," and the "paint-begrimmed beldame," no better than an "utterly lost leper in rags" (286). Women who use their bodies for money—what worse violation of patriarchal protectiveness could there be?

Only one type is in fact lower on the narrator's scale: white men who work with their hands. Here Virginia gentry values become most manifest, diverging strikingly from urban class consciousness. Subhumans, that is to say, slaves or animals, should do physical labor. But the narrator sees a disorienting profusion of workers, none of whom seems to have the slightest regard for gentility: "pie-men, porters, coalheavers, sweeps; organ-grinders, monkey-exhibitors and ballad-mongers, those who vended with those who sang; ragged artizans and exhausted labourers of every description, and all full of a noisy and inordinate vivacity which jarred discordantly upon the ear, and gave an aching sensation to the eye." What would excite Walt Whitman, romantic "artizans" who sell and sing, makes the narrator feel depersonalized—"*the* ear," "*the* eye"—as well as "jarred" and aching, pushed against by the crowd for the first time, through his glass window. "As the night deepened," and the crowd's "harsher" features displace the "gentler" and "more orderly portion of the people," he feels almost enslaved by "wild" light upon blackness: "All was dark yet splendid—as that ebony" of Tertullian's; it all "enchained me . . . to the glass" (287).

"To work industriously and steadily, especially under directions from another man," writes Frederick Law Olmsted in *The Cotton Kingdom,* "is, in the Southern tongue, to 'work like a nigger.'" William Byrd II anticipated the danger of this attitude in a 1736 letter: slaves "blow up the pride and ruin the industry of our white people, who, seeing a rank of poor creatures below them, detest work for fear it should make them look like slaves." Not surprisingly, then, Poe's narrator brings closure to his social types by sliding from manual labor down to blackness. As Olmsted later points out, many of the Virginia gentry denied their emigrant origins as indentured servants, "tinker and tailor, poacher and pickpocket." Lacking true "manners" and "lineage," most wealthy planters struck him as more "ridiculously" pretentious than Fifth Avenue's "newly rich . . . absurdly ostentatious in entertainment, and extravagant in the purchase of notoriety." While Olmsted's assessment exudes an Emersonian scorn at the edges, Poe's narrator confirms the young traveler's sense of gentry inauthenticity.[40]

A progressive reading of "The Man of the Crowd" could build an incipient class conflict here. Of all the groups, only the workers reject upward mobility to the culture's hegemonic fiction of "the decent" as a mode of self-definition. Instead, they display not anxiously imitative posing but thronging "vivacity," whether selling or singing. The narrator strangely romanticizes them, even as his body recoils from the lowest of the low. Threatened into individuality and class consciousness by this working-class spectacle, so the argument could run, Poe's narrator experiences "a craving desire" to keep in view the strange old man who embodies the now "wild" extremes of the crowd, as if class conflict and self-consciousness could both be avoided by reading the man's compounded energy (287).[41]

By the end, however, the story has abandoned workers to their "temples of Intemperance" (289). As the narrator follows the old man hour by hour, the man of the crowd seems desperate to be part of a crowd, any crowd, as if in terror of being in solitude. Or is that the narrator's projection? The old man's unreadable idiosyncrasy prefigures urban anomie, not class war. Wearing dirty yet beautifully textured linen, hiding a diamond and a dagger, anomalous to all the narrator's hierarchic categories of status yet rushing from aloneness, the old man reduces a possible progressive reading of emerging self-reliance, individual mobility, and class consciousness to a spectacle of unresolvable contradictions. He, too, is a self without subjectivity.

To the narrator, the old man represents something much more unsettling than one of the urban homeless produced and abandoned by capitalist dynamics. As the narrator's double, the old man represents the contradictions already half-voiced at the metropolitan center of gentry hierarchy. In provincial Virginia, the display of face and clothes required not only a collective fiction of gentry honor and shaming rituals but also an envious group of white men below the elite, a petty bourgeoisie of men at the margins. Transposed from rural Virginia to urban London, from small farmers and shopkeepers to clerks, schemers, and frauds, this group displays an anxious, inept passion for imitating the more successful imitators. Their transparent failure paradoxically legitimates not only the gentry's success but also the narrator's ability to "read" social status. Otherwise the gentry's own pseudoaristocratic pretensions would lack cultural capital.

But the narrator's traditional status orientation blocks his ability to read "crime" in the modern way, as individual guilt. Rather, the narrator concludes, ironically implicating himself, crime begins in a flight from individuality. "This old man . . . is the type and the genius of deep crime. He refuses to be alone" (289). The old man's wild behavior continually animates yet empties out progressive and regressive readings of his motives because his mobility seems neither downward nor upward but simply and continuously *to belong* to a group, any group. At the interface between two comprehensive, antagonistic modes of social knowing, the old man comes to represent the narrator's fear of coming face to face with his own solitary individuality.

Trying to regain interpretive mastery, the narrator paradoxically erases the hierarchic differences on which mastery depends. Having decided to follow the old man, he leaves his club, not only putting on his overcoat but also "tying a handkerchief about my mouth," ostensibly because of the rain. Conspicuously masked, yet an inconspicuous shadow, the narrator begins to mirror the old man's contradictions. "Luckily I wore a pair of gum over-shoes, and could move about in perfect silence" (287–88). Conflating the old gentry role of duelist with the new lower-class role of gumshoe detective, the narrator unwittingly replicates the paradoxical mix of diamond and dagger in the old man's clothes. Self-stabilizing abstractions of gentility disappear in the narrator's own increasingly frenzied bodily behavior, just as his opening "details" anticipate. The two nameless men end as doubles, on opposite sides of the glass. Which one is the title figure?

Moreover, the narrator all but dares genteel readers to "read" either man of the crowd better than he can, by proclaiming at the beginning and the end that his story "does not permit itself to be read." As readers puzzle themselves about that, he tauntingly solicits their own craving desire to follow a doubled fiction that fends off their self-deconstruction.

IV

Poe fails at writing longer narratives, whether philosophical or fictional, especially in his arbitrary plotting of *The Narrative of Arthur Gordon Pym*—a story that only critics relish, for what they can do with it. His emptying out of "character" into detached intellectual mastery or passionate self-destruction cannot generate momentum in a longer genre. What can be riveting or shocking in the short story seems nihilistic and capricious in the novel. Faced with incipient bourgeois expectations for linear narratives about the social and moral education of complex selves, Poe presents a new aristocracy, intellects without subjectivity, or an old aristocracy using reason to be sensationally unreasonable. Teasing out the unstable fictionality in both modes of aristocratic self-construction, his narratives put any sustained subjectivity into linguistic difficulty.

In a prize-winning essay, Bertram Wyatt-Brown argues that the southern "Sambo" figure plays a role common to all honor-shame cultures: the shameless trickster. Sambo's mimicry of his unpredictable master acts as a signifying mirror for the "patriarchal, male-dominated, honor-obsessed" pecking order. To extend Wyatt-Brown's argument, such mirroring becomes a central mode in Poe's narratives, with a difference: he mimics mastery in decline. On the edge between northern journalist and southern gentleman, Poe exaggerates the honor and dishonor of the cultivated mind at leisure, a distinctive role enabled by slavery and urged by southern intellectual reformers as the height of social aspiration. Honoring and undermining gentry constructions of patriarchal identity, Poe's textuality also subverts its own aggrandized aristocratic status. In effect, he plays a trickster role at the alienated margin of gentry culture.[42]

In Poe's hypertextualized world, his fictions invite a skeptical indeterminacy collapsing southern past and northern future. More accessibly to us, he satirizes emerging mass-market culture, already filled with readers like the crass king in "Hop-Frog" (1849), who shouts to his trickster-jester, "'We want characters—*characters,* man—something novel—out of the way.'" "'Capital!'" roars King Audience, when Hop-Frog suggests a game that will turn them into chained Ourang-Outangs; "'I will make a man of you.'" Here Poe pointedly satirizes "capital," or capitalist, constructions of manliness, individuality, and the "novel." Simultaneously, Poe plays with gentry constructions of master-slave relations. By the end of the story, after Hop-Frog grinds his "fang-like teeth" above the masters he has tarred and torched, the trickster becomes a monstrous yet uninterpretable absence. His low-to-high exit through the roof leaves behind eight blackened bodies, whose undecidable identities fuse southern slave-masters with northern philistines.[43]

The ending's shocking indeterminacy bespeaks Poe's writerly rage, as if to say, "A plague on both your houses." It may well be, as Silverman surmises, that Poe's desperate last years drove his last stories into obsessive revenge plots, as if high literary status could be gained only through overkill. Yet Hop-Frog's trickster escape can stand as a metaphor for Poe's extreme skepticism. While upending idealized southern aristocracy, Poe's fictions depict a world without gentlemen as a descent into Allen Tate's rootless, urban hell. More precisely, trapped between gentry codes of pseudomanliness and the encroachments of urban capitalism, gentlemen-narrators discover that their own poses are as nightmarish as the prospect of vulgarian scrambling.[44]

"The glory of the Ancient Dominion is in a fainting—is in a dying condition," Poe wrote in 1835. By the mid-1840s, his fiction not only deconstructs idealized British models of the gentleman but dramatizes the clash of gentry hierarchy with capitalist dynamics in Virginia, the Old Dominion. On the margin of gentry culture, Poe plays with his culture's greater historical marginality. Once he has read the gentry as a beleaguered fiction, he mourns for the postcolonial dreams of aristocracy that he resurrects for himself with textuality. Sensing that his master has two masters, Old and New England, the white Sambo-trickster apes and empties out his pseudomaster's meanings.[45]

Notes

This essay is a revised and abbreviated version of "Poe and Gentry Virginia," in *The American Face of Edgar Allan Poe,* ed. Shawn Rosenheim and Stephen Rachman (Baltimore and London: Johns Hopkins Univ. Press, 1995), 210–36.

For helpful readings of earlier drafts, I am indebted to Frederick Crews, T. Walter Herbert, Linck Johnson, John Seelye, Bertram Wyatt-Brown, Shawn Rosenheim and Stephen Rachman, and the editors of this volume.

1. Allen Tate, "Our Cousin, Mr. Poe," rpt. in *Poe: A Collection of Critical Essays,* ed. Robert Regan (Englewood Cliffs, N.J.: Prentice-Hall, 1967; first delivered as lecture 1949), 38–50, quotation 49.

2. Stuart Levine, Introduction, *The Short Fiction of Edgar Allan Poe: An Annotated Edition,* ed. Stuart Levine and Susan Levine (Urbana and Chicago: Univ. of Illinois Press, 1990), xxx. On Allan and Galt, see Kenneth Silverman, *Edgar A. Poe: Mournful and Never-ending Remembrance* (New York: HarperCollins, 1991), 12, also 27–28, and 9–28 on Allan as foster father and businessman. On Poe's marginality, see Louis D. Rubin Jr., *The Edge of the Swamp: A Study in the Literature and Society of the Old South* (Baton Rouge: Louisiana State Univ. Press, 1989), 148–53, also 177–78 on Poe's Byronic poses.

3. G. R. Thompson, "Edgar Allan Poe and the Writers of the Old South," in *Columbia Literary History of the United States,* ed. Emory Elliott (New York: Columbia Univ. Press, 1988), 262–77, quotation 264; Richard Gray, *Writing the South: Ideas of an American Region* (Cambridge: Cambridge Univ. Press, 1986). Gray atones for the omission with "'I am a Virginian': Edgar Allan Poe and the South," in *Edgar Allan Poe: The Design of Order,* ed. A. Robert Lee (London: Vision Press, 1987), 182–201, arguing that Poe adopts various southern personae as well as expressing "profoundly conservative" southern values (190).

4. Benedict Anderson, *Imagined Communities: Reflections on the Origins and Spread of Nationalism* (London: Verso, 1983), 137, 139; Edmund S. Morgan, *American Slavery, American Freedom: The Ordeal of Colonial Virginia* (New York: Norton, 1975), 386.

5. On Allan, see Silverman, *Poe,* 20–22, 27–28; on Byrd, see Kenneth A. Lockridge, *The Diary, and Life, of William Byrd II of Virginia, 1674–1744* (Chapel Hill: Univ. of North Carolina Press, 1987), 46, 51; also Gray, *Writing the South,* ch. 1, on Byrd as the embodiment of the ideal gentleman.

6. Randolph, qtd. in Alison Goodyear Freehling, *Drift toward Dissolution: The Virginia Slavery Debate of 1831–1832* (Baton Rouge: Louisiana State Univ. Press, 1982), 63–64.

7. Ibid., 123–65, 201.

8. On West Virginia, see ibid., 260–62; Laurence Shore, *Southern Capitalists: The Ideological Leadership of an Elite, 1832–1865* (Chapel Hill: Univ. of North Carolina Press, 1986). Other useful studies on gentry leadership and contradictions in Virginia include T. H. Breen, *Puritans and Adventurers: Change and Persistence in Early America* (New York: Oxford Univ. Press, 1980), esp. ch. 8, on gentry uses of social rituals such as horse racing and gambling, and ch. 9, emphasizing the gentry's "hustler," or entrepreneurial, side. Rhys Isaac's *Transformation of Virginia, 1740–1790* (Chapel Hill: Univ.

of North Carolina Press, 1982) usefully highlights the gentry's attentiveness to rank and England but overstates the case for "transformation" by arguing that evangelicalism and individualism established a competing value system as early as the 1750s. Frederick F. Siegel's *Roots of Southern Distinctiveness: Tobacco and Society in Danville, Virginia, 1780–1865* (Chapel Hill: Univ. of North Carolina Press, 1987) similarly argues for the uneasy coexistence of self-made, bourgeois men with gentry paternalism, an Isaac-like dichotomy that most historians see as part of gentry social construction.

Allan Kulikoff, *Tobacco and Slaves: The Development of Southern Cultures in the Chesapeake, 1680–1800* (Chapel Hill: Univ. of North Carolina Press, 1986), defines gentry and yeomen through the relative numbers of their slaves as well as their property holdings (9–13, 262–63, 421–23). As he notes, "Perhaps a twentieth of the region's white men" were gentlemen, though one-half were yeomen, many owning a slave or two (262).

9. Bertram Wyatt-Brown, *Southern Honor: Ethics and Behavior in the Old South* (Oxford: Oxford Univ. Press, 1982), 164. See also Steven M. Stowe, *Intimacy and Power in the Old South: Ritual in the Lives of the Planters* (Baltimore: Johns Hopkins Univ. Press, 1987), esp. ch. 1 on the planter class's celebration of hierarchy, the close correspondence between self-esteem and social order, the public "showiness" in day-to-day life, and the divided gender worlds (5–49, also 251–54).

10. On "touchiness," see Wyatt-Brown, *Southern Honor*, 35. On nose pulling, see Kenneth S. Greenberg, "The Nose, the Lie, and the Duel in the Antebellum South," *American Historical Review* 95 (1990): 57–74. The nose was a "sacred object" (71), the most visible symbol of honor that a man could publicly display. To pull it was to accuse him of lying (68). On raucous student behavior, see Drew Gilpin Faust, *A Sacred Circle: The Dilemma of the Intellectual in the Old South, 1840–1860* (Philadelphia: Univ. of Pennsylvania Press, 1977), 9–10; also Silverman, *Poe*, 31.

11. On Cilley, see Stowe, *Intimacy and Power*, 38–49. On Washington and Cato, see Pauline Meier, "Good Show: George Washington Plays George Washington," *Reviews in American History* 17 (1989): 187–98, esp. 195–97. The Poe quotation comes at the climax of "The Fall of the House of Usher" (*Short Fiction*, 98). All further quotations from Poe's fiction will be taken from the Levines' edition.

12. Silverman, *Poe*, 30, 123, 197, 332, on Poe's pride in his broad jump. Silverman also says Poe's sexual relations with his wife were "uncertain," perhaps nonexistent (124), and that his flirtations with other women intimate not sexual desire but his need to be taken care of (282, 289–91, 371, 415). On Poe's student debts, see 32–34.

13. Ibid., 93, 289–91 (fistfights); and 307–15, 327–28, quotation 315, on the libel suit, which Poe won.

14. On Poe's southern values as literary strategy, see Michael Allen, *Poe*

and the British Magazine Tradition (New York: Oxford Univ. Press, 1969), 201. Allen stresses Poe's "desire for British recognition" at least through 1842 (155), especially in his emulation of John Wilson's critical style. After 1845, Allen suggests, Poe found "a sense of public identity" linked more to his American mass audience than to Wilson (157). On Poe's prescription for magazine sensationalism, see Silverman, *Poe,* 101. On Simms's response to Poe's reviewing, see Rubin, *Edge of the Swamp,* 131.

15. *Emerson in His Journals,* ed. Joel Porte (Cambridge: Harvard Univ. Press, 1982), 170. On October 5, 1837, Emerson notes how easily "little people . . . demolish me" while "a snippersnapper eats me whole" (170). His October 8 entry is probably his rejoinder to that experience. In *Mind and the American Civil War: A Meditation on Lost Causes* (Baton Rouge: Louisiana State Univ. Press, 1989), 48–69, Lewis P. Simpson reads Emerson's October 8 entry as a reflection of New England scorn for the anti-intellectual South, without noting the previous slight. Simpson's analysis of New England nationalism complements my emphasis on contrasting ideals of manliness.

16. *Emerson in His Journals,* 411, 358.

17. On Longfellow's solicitude, see Silverman, *Poe,* 438, 444; on Poe's attacks, see 234–37, also 145–46. Poe did praise Longfellow in a late public reading (385). For a fine analysis of the regional tensions in this controversy, see Kenneth Alan Hovey, "Critical Provincialism: Poe's Poetic Principle in Antebellum Context," *American Quarterly* 39 (1987): 341–54. Hovey argues that Poe's attempt to free the South from northern thought was at the root of his attempt to free poetry from truth (349). Hovey also notes that Longfellow may well have retaliated in his novel, *Kavanagh* (1849), by parodying Poe in the character of a poet who poses as " 'a pyramid of mind on the dark desert of despair' " (342).

18. Harold Bloom, Introduction, *Edgar Allan Poe,* ed. Bloom (New York: Chelsea House, 1985), 1–14, quotations 5, 12, 11.

19. Harry Levin, *The Power of Blackness: Hawthorne, Poe, Melville* (New York: Vintage Books, 1958), 160; Isaac, *Transformation of Virginia,* 35–39; Daniel Hoffman, *Poe Poe Poe Poe Poe Poe Poe* (Garden City, N.Y.: Anchor, 1973), 315–16.

20. Qtd. in Henry F. May, *The Enlightenment in America* (New York: Oxford Univ. Press, 1976), 136.

21. Stowe, *Intimacy and Power,* notes "the almost complete absence of black people in white accounts of ritual and daily routine" (253). In *Sacred Circle,* Faust discusses five Southern intellectuals, including Simms and James Hammond, who eventually turned to proslavery arguments to win recognition and respect after failing in other efforts to raise the status of intellectual work (116).

22. Mark Twain, *Life on the Mississippi* (1883; rpt. New York: Signet, 1980), chs. 40, 46, on Scott. Some years ago a Williamsburg tour guide men-

tioned that the book most frequently found on Virginia shelves during the late eighteenth century was Fielding's *Tom Jones*. That sharply contrasts with the equivalent secular primacy of *Pilgrim's Progress* and *Paradise Lost* on New England shelves.

23. Pierre Bourdieu, *Distinction: A Social Critique of the Judgement of Taste,* trans. Richard Nice (Cambridge: Harvard Univ. Press, 1984), 40, 56.

24. Simms, qtd. in Faust, *Sacred Circle,* 148.

25. Michael McKeon, *The Origins of the English Novel, 1600–1740* (Baltimore: Johns Hopkins Univ. Press, 1987), 162–69, 45–46.

26. Ibid., 118–19. McKeon's most prominent English example of extreme skepticism is the third earl of Shaftesbury. While others have found Shaftesbury more morally coherent than McKeon's analysis of his "indirect discourse of self-conscious and parodic impersonation" implies (118–19), McKeon's historicizing of indeterminacy applies not only to many elements in Swift but also to Poe. At the end, McKeon polemically asserts that extreme skepticism also characterizes contemporary poststructuralism, perhaps with similarly historicizable dynamics (420–21).

McKeon's argument that extreme skepticism parodically undermines both romance idealism and naive empiricism (63–64) suggests a way of historicizing what Joan Dayan, in *Fables of Mind: An Inquiry into Poe's Fiction* (New York: Oxford Univ. Press, 1987), has analyzed as Poe's linguistic despair, that his mind has nothing authentically in common with any order of empirical or fictional validation. Dayan emphasizes Poe's conversion of identity from a philosophic to a linguistic difficulty (201). Stanley Cavell suggests that Poe's skepticism betrays Poe's need for love and his fear of being loved; see "In Quest of the Ordinary," in *Romanticism and Contemporary Criticism,* ed. Morris Eaves and Michael Fischer (Ithaca: Cornell Univ. Press, 1986), 215.

27. Bourdieu, *Distinction,* 330–31. Culture as game recurs throughout *Distinction,* e.g., 12, and esp. 54 on "the games of culture" as part of the "aesthetic disposition" that "can only be constituted within an experience of the world freed from urgency." The value of culture, Bourdieu argues, is generated through the struggle between high and middlebrow, each dependent on the other (250–54 and passim).

28. Quotation from "The Fall of the House of Usher," Poe, *Short Fiction,* 98.

29. Ibid., 93, 98, 93. Linck Johnson suggests that "without" may seem more archaic now, since Noah Webster's 1828 dictionary gives "on the outside of" as one of its standard meanings, along with "unless," among others (personal communication). At the least, however, the word seems to call attention to Roderick's literary posing. See James Cox, "Edgar Poe: Style as Pose," *Virginia Quarterly Review* 44 (1968): 67–89, for a thoughtful account of Poe's emphasis on excessive impersonations and literary posings.

30. Bourdieu, *Distinction,* 499. This passage emphasizes the implied yet

denied aristocracy in the social game of taste: "The principle of the pleasure derived from those refined games for refined players lies, in the last analysis, in the denied experience of a social relationship of membership and exclusion. . . . the philosophical sense of distinction is another form of the visceral disgust at vulgarity which defines pure taste as an internalized social relationship" (499–500). My emphasis on textuality as Poe's passport to aristocracy is indebted to comments by Stephen Rachman and Shawn Rosenheim.

31. McKeon, *Origins*, 45–46, 168–69; Louis A. Renza, "Poe's Secret Autobiography," in *The American Renaissance Reconsidered*, ed. Walter Benn Michaels and Donald E. Pease (Baltimore: Johns Hopkins Univ. Press, 1985), 58–89, quotation 82.

32. Jonathan Auerbach, *The Romance of Failure: First-Person Fictions of Poe, Hawthorne, and James* (New York: Oxford Univ. Press, 1989), 21.

33. "Ligeia," Poe, *Short Fiction,* 84; Cynthia S. Jordan, *Second Stories: The Politics of Language, Form and Gender in Early American Fictions* (Chapel Hill: Univ. of North Carolina Press, 1989), 135–36.

34. "Ligeia," Poe, *Short Fiction,* 80; Joan Dayan, "Amorous Bondage: Poe, Ladies, and Slaves," *American Literature* 66 (1994): 239–73, rpt. in *The American Face of Edgar Allan Poe,* ed. Shawn Rosenheim and Stephen Rachman (Baltimore: Johns Hopkins Univ. Press, 1995), 179–209.

35. Jordan notes that the narrator cannot remember Ligeia's paternal name yet accepts her patrimony. She argues that the story is a fight for narrative authority, which the narrator wins only by silencing Ligeia's story with murderous patriarchal language. Leland Person, in *Aesthetic Headaches,* reads "Ligeia" similarly as the struggle of a man "to define and control a woman" through language, but comes to an opposite conclusion: the woman wins the "battle of wills," rendering the narrator's words impotent as "Ligeia resists objectification, death, and denial" (*Aesthetic Headaches: Women and a Masculine Poetics in Poe, Melville, and Hawthorne* [Athens: Univ. of Georgia Press, 1988], 30, 32).

36. Michael Davitt Bell, *The Development of American Romance: The Sacrifice of Relation* (Chicago: Univ. of Chicago Press, 1980), 99; Dayan, "Amorous Bondage," 244.

37. The longer version of this essay (see *American Face of Edgar Allan Poe,* 210–36) briefly discusses the Dupin stories and "Cask of Amontillado." In "Reading Poe's Mind: Politics, Mathematics, and the Association of Ideas in 'The Murders in the Rue Morgue,'" *American Literary History* 4 (1992): 187–206, John T. Irwin emphasizes that Dupin is a fallen aristocrat. More problematically, Irwin also calls Poe a "fallen Virginia gentleman" (205), overstating Poe's childhood status. In "Edgar Allan Poe and the Horrid Laws of Political Economy," *American Quarterly* 44 (1992): 381–417, Terence Whalen teases out Dupin's progress in the three stories from aristocrat to a professional who works for money (400).

38. "The Man of the Crowd," Poe, *Short Fiction,* 285. Subsequent references will be given parenthetically in the text. Auerbach, *Romance of Failure,* 27–34, quotation 28. Auerbach historicizes Poe primarily as a writer hostile to modernity and Jacksonian democracy (125–26, 55–56), as does Donald E. Pease in *Visionary Compacts: American Renaissance Writings in Cultural Context* (Madison: Univ. of Wisconsin Press, 1987), 168–75 (Poe vs. self-reliance), also 199–202 on Poe's taking self-reliance to an extreme of sensational immediacy without selfhood. See also Monika M. Elbert, " 'The Man of the Crowd' and the Man outside the Crowd: Poe's Narrator and the Democratic Reader," *Modern Language Studies* 21 (1991): 16–30, arguing that Poe's personae alternate between Whig and Democrat modes. Rubin, *Edge of the Swamp,* 138–39, citing Tate, also reads "Man of the Crowd" in relation to the deracinating modern city, as do many others.

39. Gray, *Writing the South,* 9–23, quotations 9 (feudal), 12–13 (entrepreneurs), 23 (minority).

40. Frederick Law Olmsted, *The Cotton Kingdom: A Traveller's Observations on Cotton and Slavery in the American Slave States,* ed. Arthur M. Schlesinger Sr. (1861; rpt. New York: Modern Library, 1984), 19, 562–63. Olmsted continues: "It is this habit of considering themselves of a privileged class, and of disdaining something which they think beneath them, that is deemed to be the chief blessing of slavery. It is termed 'high tone,' 'high spirit,' and is supposed to give great military advantages" (19). For Byrd's letter to the earl of Egmont, see Lewis P. Simpson, *The Dispossessed Garden: Pastoral and History in Southern Literature* (Athens: Univ. of Georgia Press, 1975), 20.

41. Three other progressive readings of "Man of the Crowd" are Robert H. Byer's "Mysteries of the City: A Reading of Poe's 'The Man of the Crowd,' " in *Ideology and Classic American Literature,* ed. Sacvan Bercovitch and Myra Jehlen (Cambridge: Cambridge Univ. Press, 1986), 221–46, a sophisticated neo-Marxist argument that the crowd is a "hieroglyph" for the modern city which conceals the social relations that produced it; Dana Brand, *The Spectator and the City in Nineteenth Century American Literature* (Cambridge: Cambridge Univ. Press, 1991), analyzing Poe's narrator as urban flaneur; and Whalen's "Horrid Laws," which analyzes various texts, including "Man of the Crowd" and the Dupin tales, in antagonistic relation to a literary marketplace "crisis of overproduction" (405, 410). In *Rudeness and Civility: Manners in Nineteenth Century America* (New York: Hill and Wang, 1990), John F. Kasson also discusses the narrator as a combination of flaneur and urban ethnographer.

42. Bertram Wyatt-Brown, "The Mask of Obedience: Male Slave Psychology in the Old South," *American Historical Review* 93 (1988), 1228–52; rpt. in this volume. As Michael Allen summarizes in *Poe and the British Magazine Tradition,* Poe grew up "in a South that was extending an aristocratic code from the original Virginia gentry to the whole region to consolidate it against

Northern pretensions" (133). British sources and models were crucial to the consolidation. See also Faust, *Sacred Circle*. Faust is especially interesting on the Usher-like depressions afflicting all five of the southern intellectuals she studies. Like Poe, each suffered the loss of a parent in his youth.

To my knowledge, Elizabeth Fox-Genovese is alone among recent southern historians in arguing that *patriarchy* as a term should be restricted to the Roman model, in which a husband could kill his wife, children, and slaves. See *Within the Plantation Household: Black and White Women of the Old South* (Chapel Hill: Univ. of North Carolina Press, 1988), 63–64. She suggests *paternalism* instead. See Isaac, *Transformation of Virginia,* 354–55, for an opposite argument that the role of gentleman "derived much of its content" as well as prestige "from the encompassing metaphor of patriarchy."

43. "Hop-Frog," Poe, *Short Fiction,* 264–65, 267. See Silverman, *Poe,* 405–7 on "Hop-Frog," also 316–18, and 515 on choosing to die. Dayan, in "Amorous Bondage," interprets "Hop-Frog" more simply as "Poe's envisioned revenge for the national sin of slavery" (258).

44. For this formulation I am indebted to T. Walter Herbert.

45. Qtd. in Hovey, "Critical Provincialism," 347.

The Flight down the Middle Walk

Mary Chesnut and the Forms
of Observance

Michael O'Brien

SHE KNEW the value of solitude for a writer, though she was very fond of society, whose brittle tensions were much of her subject matter. She liked to sit in her own room, designated and guarded as a retreat, that looked out on pleasant fields; there she would write, which she did with astonishing facility and speed, though she had trouble finishing things because she feared the world's opinion. She was very well read in the literature of the day, which offered confusing precedents, and she was prone to experimentation in matters of form; she was fastidious and a little cruel in the severity of her critical judgments. She had firm opinions that women needed an independent income. She herself was born to a comfortable estate, not quite the highest her society offered but close enough to give the opportunities of observing and mingling with the lofty and of becoming something of a snob. Yet she was troubled in the matter of parents and family. A father, in particular, later devastated with grief, was alternately charming and despotic towards her, which somehow hindered her growth into the prerogatives of adulthood; he became, for her, the symbol of an old order, whose destruction she survived and, intellectually, did much to subvert; she was to make him a central figure in her most important narrative. Her elder brother, to whom she was devoted, died young. As for her own marriage, it had satisfactions but many turbulences; her husband was involved in politics, mostly as an adviser to people more prominent than himself, and she liked in turn to advise him. Their sexual life was not a success: she had no children, which she regretted, and for this envied her sister, who was fecund. By the standards of her day, she was resistant to traditional gentilities and candid about the betrayals that characterized her contemporaries, while retaining a certain evasiveness about herself. She thought much about the relations between men and women, and amongst women, and had as much taste for female beauties as for male. She had many friends and few intimates. She lived through a great war that had a marked effect upon her sensibility and whose outcome destroyed the world into which she had been born. She kept a diary. She lived, for a while, in a place called Bloomsbury.

All the above statements are true of two women, Mary Boykin Chesnut and Virginia Woolf.[1] They are offered with some playfulness, since self-evidently there is very much that differed in their lives and sensibilities. Even these statements have had to be carefully phrased, sometimes to insinuate similarity when there is difference. Woolf finished many more literary ventures than Chesnut, who managed to publish very little in her lifetime, while Woolf feared critics far more than Chesnut, so much so that her bouts of illness were sometimes connected to trepidation about the reception of her books.[2] The literary precedents of 1880 in the American South and 1910 in England were different, though not abruptly so. Chesnut's critical judgments were privately expressed, while Woolf wrote abundantly for periodicals like the *Times Literary Supplement*. The father that troubled Woolf was her own father, Leslie Stephen, while Chesnut was bedeviled by her father-in-law, James Chesnut Sr. But Chesnut's father, Stephen Miller, did marry twice, like Leslie Stephen, and both Virginia Stephen and Mary Boykin Miller were daughters of the second wife. Dick Miller, Mary's elder brother, died when he was seventeen and she was nine, while Toby Stephen was twenty-six and Virginia was twenty-four. It is hard to know whether Woolf's husband offered more satisfactions than Chesnut's. It is doubtful that her marriage was as catastrophically asexual as Woolf's, yet Leonard Woolf offered an intellectual and spiritual comradeship of which James Chesnut was incapable. On the other hand, childlessness was a more scarring burden in Chesnut's society than in that of Woolf, many of whose contemporaries were childless; in fact, her sister Vanessa Bell was unusual in their set for having offspring. Lastly, trivially, though both lived in Bloomsbury, Mary Chesnut's Bloomsbury was a long walk from the British Museum; it was a small house bearing that name in Camden, South Carolina, where she lived briefly during the Civil War.

Yet I do not offer these parallels just for play. There is value in binding together the experiences of these two women writers. Woolf's position as a woman in the landscape of literature has been carefully plotted, but Chesnut's remains obscure. I intend this essay as a contribution towards locating the South Carolinian in more than her present position, which is the literature of southern history, and to suggest that literary critics might profit from considering where Chesnut's narrative techniques stand in the history of women and literature. To this end, it helps to begin with the matter of genre, a topic that has bemused the critical reception of Mary Chesnut.

As we now know from the edition of *Mary Chesnut's Civil War* published by C. Vann Woodward in 1981, the diary of Mary Chesnut is problematical. It is not, tidily, the diary that was published by, first, Isabella D. Martin and Myrta Lockett Avary in 1905 as *A Diary from Dixie*, then under the same title but revised by Ben Ames Williams in 1949. These editions claim it as a diary of contemporary events, straightforwardly set down during the Civil War, and under this impression historians for several generations used Mary Chesnut as a primary source. In fact, with varying degrees of incompetence, naïveté, and duplicity, these editors were cobbling together a diary from much more complicated and more interesting documents. As Woodward has explained, there are several sets of manuscripts. There is an original and incomplete Civil War diary, published as *The Private Mary Chesnut* by Woodward and Elisabeth Muhlenfeld in 1984.[3] There is a revised version of some sections, dated 1875, of about four hundred pages. There is a final, much longer version, dating from the early 1880s, which provided the copy text for *Mary Chesnut's Civil War*. There are fragments that offer differing versions of events. Virtually none of this was published during her lifetime.[4]

All this is confusing for those who like tidy and reliable evidence or those who like their literature to exist as finite texts, published at a definite time by intending authors; that is, for most historians. What, they are inclined to ask, is Mary Chesnut now good for? Much of *Mary Chesnut's Civil War* is of limited use as evidence for the direct experience of the Civil War because written two decades late. On the other hand, the mingling of the 1880s version and passages from earlier manuscripts mildly compromises its value as a specimen of American literature from the 1880s; whatever else *Mary Chesnut's Civil War* is, it is not quite what she would have published, if she had published.[5] As significantly, one can justly ask, what do we call this book, these manuscripts, this jumble? This is a practical matter as well as an intellectual one. One must call it something in one's own discussion. Woodward has defined our range of options, as far as it touches genre: "memoir, autobiography, fiction, chronicle, history," as well as diary. None of these is adequate. Both Woodward and Steven Stowe, suggestively, have called it a palimpsest.[6] But this is more elegant than practical. My own preference is, simply, to call it a narrative journal, which conflates her own terms.[7]

Critics have differed over the reasons for this apparent jumble. Elizabeth Fox-Genovese, who has used Chesnut as an inferior foil to Louisa McCord, inclines to think it resulted from intellectual inadequacies. "The tension between her historical and private selves accounts for much of the richness and fascination of her diary," she concedes. "Yet ultimately she lacked sufficient control of her material to forge it into a coherent story."[8] Chesnut's editors, surprisingly, are circumspect about her reasons. They stress her experiments in fiction and memoir, which were the prelude to the 1880s manuscripts, while being careful to insist on their failure. Woodward is most insistent that the palimpsest is a triumph, but does not say of what. It is not, one presumes, a triumph among palimpsests. On the whole, it seems to be argued that Chesnut blundered across her confusion of genres, because no one genre worked for her. I think this is only part of the truth.

It is my belief that Mary Chesnut knew what she was doing, which was partially to dissolve the principles of realism, that she understood her originality better than most of her critics have, and hence that a useful context for understanding her book is not only southern women's diaries like that of Sarah Morgan but also the transition from novels like *Vanity Fair* to those like *To the Lighthouse*.[9] But, it must be confessed from the onset, this belief rests much upon inference. In understanding Chesnut, we are peculiarly hampered by a lack of collateral evidence. Her surviving letters are few and mostly unilluminating; she made bonfires of much of her correspondence.[10] She wrote no literary manifestos, no prefaces, no afterwords. There are just the texts, which we must interpret, if we are to discern her meanings. So let me try to construct the pattern of inferences, which is made of several strands: her knowledge of modern fiction and history; the pressure of public events; the special consciousness of being a woman; her apprehension of instability; and her use of voices.

Like Virginia Woolf, Mary Chesnut mostly educated herself by omnivorous reading, though she did have some formal schooling, which

Woolf did not. In fact, one of her richest pieces of writing, her unpublished novella "Two Years—Or the Way We Lived Then," remembers Madame Talvande's school in Charleston. She became accomplished in modern languages, in French and German, but seems to have read the classics only in translation.[11] Woodward makes much of her Anglophile reading. Indeed, in "Two Years" she writes of herself as "intensely English in all my sympathies." She read the usual English authors, old and very new, and one, Jane Austen, seldom read in America.[12] Russian literature was largely unknown to her, though there is the odd fact that in 1880 she offered the editor of the Charleston *News and Courier* a translation of a "novelette" by Pushkin, presumably taken from the French (*MCCW*, xxiii).[13] The Germans feature more but did not matter much to her, with the usual exception of Goethe, and (a little) Schiller and Richter. These were fairly old-fashioned tastes, unlike those she had in French literature, which were more contemporary: Balzac, Sand, Dumas, Mérimée, and Sue, but no Baudelaire, Rimbaud, or Flaubert. Balzac was especially important; her narrative journal could be seen as a southern *comédie humaine*, swarming as it does with vignettes of character, sensitive as it is about social nuances. But it is important to remember her taste for older French authors like Montaigne, Molière, and above all, Pascal. She aspired to the epigrammatic, to distilled moments of wisdom or observation, that might help to comprehend life's hurly-burly; she scattered things like "In a revolution shy men are run over. No one stops to pick them up," or "Jealousy of the past is most women's hell" (*MCCW*, 271, 449).[14] In all this reading, she seems to have preferred narratives of social interaction with a marked edge, things that flirt with cynicism. This taste was summed up by Thackeray, her literary exemplar, to whom she gave a reverent eulogy:

> Thackeray is dead.
> I stumbled upon *Vanity Fair* for myself. I had never heard of Thackeray before. I think it was in 1850. I know I had been ill at the New York hotel. And when left alone I slipped downstairs and into a bookstore that I had noticed under the hotel for something to read.
> They gave me the first half. I can recall now the very kind of paper it was printed on—and the illustrations as they took effect upon me. And yet when I raved of it and was wild for the other half, there were people who said it was slow!! That he was evidently a coarse, dull, sneering writer, that he stripped human nature bare, made it repulsive, &c&c&c. (*MCCW*, 546)

This helps to explain her dislike of the usual feminine taste of the mid-nineteenth century, the literary domestic novel, which was for her too much the occasion for "piety and pie-making" and too little candid. Shakespeare, she once observed of *King Lear,* was good for "laying bare the seamy side—going behind the curtain of propriety. . . . He preceded Thackeray in that tearing off of shams. [Old] Mrs Chesnut set her face resolutely to see only the pleasant things of life and shut her eyes to wrong and said it was not there. The most devoted, unremitting reader of fiction I ever knew—everything French or English that came to hand—would not tolerate Thackeray. 'He is a very uncomfortable, disagreeable creature'" (*MCCW,* 65, 761–62). In this, Chesnut's mother-in-law agreed with Leslie Stephen, who married Thackeray's daughter. Virginia Woolf was to remember: "When my brothers had gone to school, he still went on reading to my sister and me, but chose more serious books. He read Carlyle's *French Revolution,* and stopped in the middle of *Vanity Fair,* because he said it was 'too terrible.'"[15] As Stephen explained elsewhere of Thackeray: "A man may be called a cynic not as disbelieving in the value of virtue, but as disbelieving in its frequency. He may hold that the tender emotions have a smaller influence in actual affairs than easy-going people maintain, and that a purely virtuous person is a very rare phenomenon indeed."[16]

Chesnut's narrative journal is written in this spirit of discomfort, of pulling "ostrich heads out of the sand," of a disillusion that stops short of cynicism because life is too interesting in its mayhem (*MCCW,* 762). She lays bare much: old Colonel Chesnut's mulatto children, Buck Preston's cruel and innocent flirtations, sexually frustrated soldiers grabbing at their nurses, the murder of an old woman by slaves, the beating of a pregnant slave by a mistress, a man mimicking the grins of the dead to amuse a dinner table, another gleefully fishing out a tumbled oyster from between a startled woman's breasts, the incessant human folly of society (*MCCW,* 31, 72, 414, 368, 189–227, 646–47, 626, 484). Few are spared, including herself. In this, she differed from Woolf, who usually omitted herself from her own fiction, often mistrusted self-representation, and could speak of "the dominance of the letter 'I' and the aridity, which, like the giant beech tree, it casts within its shade."[17] But Chesnut is a character in her own narrative, one who is mocked as "the Explainer General," full of foible and weakness, shown "spinning my own entrails," taking her opium, exercising her "power to hide trouble." Though Chesnut policed these self-revelations and toyed with omitting herself, with being merely "objective," she confessed all but the most intimate (*MCCW*, 172, 23, 29, quotation 23). She made it possible, for example, for us to understand the pain of her childlessness, though not its cause. Very early in her narrative, she writes: "I did Mrs. Browne a kindness. I told those women that she was childless now, but that she had lost three children. I hated to leave her all alone. Women have such a contempt for a childless wife." She confesses, baldly, "Of course, I know nothing of children. In point of fact am awfully afraid of them." And there is this: "Women need maternity to bring out their best and true loveliness," a commentary on herself, the belle who was never beautiful, but who admired feminine beauty extravagantly, even sensually. "Oh—I have been to see a delicious married beauty! So soft, so silly, so lovely, so kindly! Forbear!" Elsewhere, "Clear brunette she is, with the reddest lips, the whitest teeth, and glorious eyes—there is no other word for them" (28, 488, 105, 572, 146).

Fox-Genovese has argued that Chesnut's condemnations of slavery were untypical of her class and gender, which seems to me true, but also that they were untypical of her, which I doubt.[18] Mary Chesnut was often skeptical about her society and its ways; that is part of what her narrative journal is about, what her admiration of Thackeray meant. She poked fun at honor, for example: "The Hampton Legion all in a snarl about I forget what—standing on their dignity, I suppose. I have come to detest a man who says, 'My own personal dignity—self-respect requires'" (*MCCW*, 102). In "Two Years," she mocked the religious literalists: "Without a murmur, down on his knees went my late chatty interlocutor. I listened in amazement if I did not pray. / It was an eloquent appeal to the Almighty to keep his covenant. He had promised. We had his promise; he was a covenant God. There was his bond. We had it in black and white. Those exact followers of Calvin, they like documents legally executed—be the parties who they may."[19] Similarly, she incessantly made fun of the rituals of courtship, condemned beauty for its ruthless hardheartedness, amused herself at the feebleness of conventional oratory, and savaged southern integrity (*MCCW*, 229, 231, 638–39). The list could be easily extended. No doubt, these skepticisms did not form a consistent critique of her society, which is part of Fox-Genovese's point.

Nonetheless, one must confront the matter of Chesnut's attitude towards self and society. Like Thackeray, the historical novelist whose characters acted out their lives in real places and times, in colonial Virginia or near the battle of Waterloo, Chesnut acknowledged the reality of history, of things beyond the personal. The driving reality of the war that changed her life, destroyed her society, took away her ease, killed her friends, relatives, and enemies alike, was nonetheless exhilarating, what she struggled to call "objective." She started her original diary to do justice to its awful majesty.

At one level, she fashioned as good a book about the American Civil War as anyone—historian, novelist, poet—has produced. But its achievement is particular, and much shaped as literature by the dynamics of gender. Mary Chesnut was a woman who understood (no doubt conventionally) that war was about more than men and women or their relations. She wanted to touch that reality, to break out of the confined space of even a senator's wife, to realize "the very casques that did affright the air at Agincourt." She saw the war as her chance to be more than plain Mary Chesnut, the "childless wretch" who read modern novels (*MCCW*, 32).

But did she break out, definitively? It has been rightly stressed that the form that she chose freed her from many of the conventions of the novel. But all forms have their constrictions. A disadvantage of hers was that it tied the narration of events to her presence, drew them into the drawing rooms where she stood and sat, to the streets where she walked, into the words that she heard. She had to be there, even if only as the ear into which stories and gossip were poured. She is at the center of the war as she narrates it. As has been observed, she was in many important places—Charleston at the bombardment of Fort Sumter, Montgomery during the establishment of the Confederacy, Richmond while it was a national capital—but she was not everywhere. Manassas was a story, not a shell exploding next to her. So her narrative journal has few northerners in it; their nation is remote and unrealized. Lincoln appears because he is Jefferson Davis's rival, and she knew Davis. Sumner is there because her husband had berated the abolitionist in the Senate.[20] Ulysses S. Grant is a grim rumor, someone with whom those who vanish from her presence go to rendezvous. Hence, hers was more a book about women than about men, and usually only about men in the presence of women. She knew this. When Fort Sumter was being bombarded, she wrote of it: "We hear nothing, can listen to nothing. Boom, boom, goes the cannon—all the time. The nervous strain is awful, alone in this darkened room. . . . We were all in that iron balcony. Women—men we only see at a distance now" (*MCCW*, 48). She realized her ignorance of what men did away from women: "They [women] always decry and abuse men. Now the men praise women. But then, when twenty men are together without any women, I am not there. So I can't say they are not even with us." She saw the meaning of the war in a quarrel between the sexes: "We separated because of incompatibility of temper. We are divorced, North from South, because we hated each other so. If we could only separate—a 'séparation à l'a-gréable,' as the French say it, and not a horrid fight for divorce" (*MCCW*, 25).[21] But the North would not have it: "They hate us so and would clasp us—or hook us, as Polonius has it—to their bosoms with hooks of steel. We are an unwilling bride." This image flowed into her vision of slavery, a thing that violated marriage because it gave concu-bines to husbands, but also a thing that explained marriage: "There is no slave, after all, like a wife" (*MCCW*, 84, 59). Dissatisfied as a woman, as a wife, as a mistress, she was well prepared to comprehend the broken disillusionments of war, better perhaps than she might have understood success. Victory, it is true, might mean freedom for the South. But even this would be ashes: "After all, suppose we do all we hoped. Suppose we start up grand and free—a proud young republic. Think of all these young lives sacrificed! If three for one be killed, what comfort is that? What good will that do Mrs. Hayne or Mary DeSaus-sure? The best and bravest of our generation swept away! Henry De-Saussure has left four sons to honor their father's memory and emulate his example. But those poor boys of between 18 and 20 years of age— Haynes, Trezevants, Taylors, Rhetts, &c&c—they are washed away, lit-erally, in a tide of blood. There is nothing to show they were ever on earth" (*MCCW*, 412). Defeat, she certainly knew, meant entrapment. Few moments are more chilling than that when, at the end of things in 1865, she has her husband, her warden and warrior, express the sen-tence, "Camden for life" (*MCCW*, 792). A door slams, at that instant, between her drawing room and the world beyond. In that room, she wrote her book. It is not surprising that it is, to a large extent, about that room.

But she peopled her room extraordinarily. It teems "through the astonishing vividness and reality of the characters," to use Virginia Woolf's phrase about Thackeray's *Pendennis*.[22] Chesnut rushes around the room, listening, talking. She goes to the window—"We are forever at the windows"—and sees the men go away, turn the corner, come back with their stories and their wounds, or not come back. She scrutinizes them all, including the slaves: "I am always studying these creatures" (*MCCW*, 186). Above all, there are voices.

The thing that most distinguishes the original diary from the narrative journal are the voices. These were much of what she added and wanted to realize. They embody her quasi-modernist leanings par excellence because they are fragmentary, intentionally so, I believe. People say things. Often we do not know who is speaking. One quotation does not always follow logically from its predecessor. Voices are not always answered. The profound and the trivial lie next to one another, unreconciled. Contemporary voices sit next to literary quotations, Medea is adjacent to someone called Albert (*MCCW*, 302). Subject matters change abruptly. Consider this passage, long enough to give the flavor. It is February of 1865; she is in Lincolnton, North Carolina, and inter alia begins on the subject of Virginians.

These people are proud of their heroic dead and living soldiers—but are prepared to say with truth that [they] always preferred to remain in the Union and are ready to assure the first comers of Yankees that they have always hated South Carolina seceders and nullifiers as much as the Yankees do.

"You say Miss Giles is as clever as she is beautiful. Nonsense. Clever! She was out of the Confederacy and then came rushing in. Fool or mad, that was."

"Conduct of a fool. Most women atone for their sins when they marry."

"Spinsters and vestal virgins—how do you know? You have not tried it."

"We have ears to hear, eyes to see, and a heart to understand, all the same. Lookers-on see more of the game than players—&c&c."

F.F.'s have a dialect. Her cousin said "mighty little" for *very small*. She called a ball or a tea party "only a little company"—and another form of the simple word "very" was "right much." And she lived in the house where Mrs. Mat Singleton used English as pure as that of Victoria Regina.

"How I like to hear Mrs. John Singleton's clean-cut sentences, every word distinctly enunciated."

"I should say she was the delight of her friends, the terror of her foes. I am afraid of those words dropped one by one with such infinite precision—drops of vitriol, sometimes."

Remember that night as the train stopped—a ponderous bank president filled the door of the car.

"What was the use of bank presidents? We have no money."

"He says he paid himself his salary in gold, so there is money some-where for the stay-at-homes. He is a descendent-in-law of the pretender branch of the Stuarts."

"And he is as loud as a centaur."

"You mean *stentor*. He said, 'Miss ____, yes, yes—I come for yer—Huddy come 'long.' Now, this was only a slovenly habit of speech. He writes admirably."

What a look she gave me then.

"Worse, that 'right much'—eh?"

"What did you do?" "Nothing." Terebene lamps do not disclose blushes.

We had been bragging of South Carolina's purity of accent—Mrs. Mat's well of English undefiled, Mrs. Richardson Miles's sweetest and softest of voices, Miss Middleton's sweet low voice *and* wit *and* wisdom.

"Galore."

"Then came the rough boatswain's hoarse bawl." (*MCCW*, 743–44)

Who is Miss Giles? We are not told. She rushes late into the Confeder-acy, it seems, doubling for Virginia, foolishly marrying the Deep South, somehow unaware like a vestal virgin. The actions of Virginians bring up their speech, idiosyncratic and worthy of reproach. A bank president abruptly appears. Why? To point to fiscal dishonesty, partly. Mostly because, eventually, it is implied that he is a Virginian and his dialect is mimicked. Someone is offended. But who? Someone blushes. Why? For doing nothing. What required action? We do not know. South Caroli-na's linguistic purity is boasted of. But this is designated "bragging," so we know not to believe in it. "Mrs. Mat" is dangled before us in the words of Spenser's praise of Chaucer, Miss Middleton in Lear's com-mendation of Cordelia. Then a boatswain hoarsely bawls. Why? We are left to guess at the allusion. Throughout, the personal and the social are artfully interwoven, while she manages to convey the disjointed, crablike quality of conversation.

Chesnut's narrative journal everywhere speaks that she understood Woolf's complaint that the three-decker novel let the definition of hu-man character go unrecorded; out of evasion "spring those sleek, smooth novels, those portentous and ridiculous biographies, that milk and watery criticism, those poems melodiously celebrating the inno-cence of roses and sheep which pass so plausibly for literature at the present time."[23] This could pass for a description of most of the southern literature that came Mary Chesnut's way in Camden in 1880.[24] Chesnut was aware that her times were beginning to demand a different narrative technique and may even have been emboldened by the new vein of realist writing, though mainly by its starker subject matter, not its style.[25] Certainly she seems to have realized the shift more than, say, Augusta Jane Evans, whose novels, however much they dealt with subjects usually forbidden or inaccessible to women, held to a traditional narrative form. Chesnut knew that the matter of self was implicated in the sea change, though she found it awkward: "Those Tarleton memoirs, Lee's memoirs, Moultrie's, Lord Rawdon's letters—self is never brought to the front. I have been reading them over and admire their honesty and good taste as much as their courage and cleverness" (*MCCW*, 194). Should self be hidden? This was a practical matter. Should the original diary, should the narrative journal be locked away from curious eyes? Sometimes, yes. Sometimes, no.

Why did narrative break down for Chesnut? It was not—I cannot say this with more firmness—because she was incapable of coherence. Her narrative journal is full of stories, vignettes, anecdotes, that are as coherently fashioned and told as any traditional southern storyteller or Victorian novelist could wish. The tale of the "Witherspoon Murder Case," the old lady murdered in her bed by slaves, is a chillingly effective allegory that has stuck in the mind of generations of historians. The old patriarch, James Chesnut, is a character whom his daughter-in-law described and invented with stiletto care, a man more compelling by far than his counterpoint in Allen Tate's *The Fathers*, but serving the same purpose, to stand as the "last of the lordly planters who ruled this Southern world." Chesnut admires him, hates him, knows his passing is for the good even as she regrets it; she shows him in all his strength and weakness, "blind, deaf—apparently as strong as ever, certainly as resolute of will" (*MCCW*, 814–15). The following scene about his grief is, I would contend, one of the more remarkable in southern literature:

> Mrs. Chesnut was only a year younger than her husband—he is ninety-two or three. She was deaf. He retains his senses wonderfully for his great age.
>
> I have always been an early riser. Formerly I often saw him, sauntering slowly down the broad passage from his room to hers, in a flowing

flannel dressing gown when it was winter. In the spring he was apt to be in shirtsleeves, with suspenders hanging down his back. He had always a large hairbrush in his hand.

He would take his stand on the rug before the fire in her room, brushing scant locks which were shining fleecy white. Her maid would be doing hers, which were dead-leaf brown—not a white hair in her head. He had the voice of a stentor. And there he stood, roaring his morning compliments. The people who occupied the rooms above said he fairly shook the window glasses. This pleasant morning greeting and ceremony was never omitted.

Her voice was "low and sweet" (the oft quoted). Philadelphia seems to have lost the art of sending forth such now. Mrs. Binney, Mrs. Chesnut's sister, came among us with the same softly modulated, womanly, musical voice. Her clever and beautiful daughters were *criard*. Judge Hare said, "Philadelphia women scream like macaws."

This morning, as I passed Mrs. C's room, the door stood wide open. And I heard a pitiful sound. The old man was kneeling by her empty bedside, sobbing bitterly.

I fled down the middle walk—anywhere out of reach of what was never meant for me to hear. (*MCCW,* 610)

This is skill of a high order: the definition of time, the casualness of the opening ("I have always been an early riser," "sauntering"), the old ways observed by the young interloper, the man's vanity and indifference to all but his own ritual, his booming at his wife's deafness, their physical separation mitigated by the regularity of courtesy, the delaying paragraph (beginning "Her voice") so that we do not reach the climax too soon, the brevity with which the pitiful moment is portrayed, the anticlimax of Chesnut's recoil. There is a world of social history, and of character realized, in this story, which Chesnut perfectly understood.

One cannot convict Mary Chesnut of narrative inability. Her voices are artful, their incoherences intended. Why? Because she did not think that the world added up to a smooth story with an ordered moral. Rather, it was "full of strange vicissitudes, and in nothing more remarkable than the way people are reconciled, ignore the past, and start afresh in life, here to incur more disagreements and set to bickering again." In fact, Chesnut disbelieved for the reasons classically adduced to explain the onset of modernism. She had no faith in the old gods of Christianity, in the new ones of science, in the justice of her society, in

the goodness of human beings and the probability of happiness for
them. She did not even trust herself. But she knew that these skepticisms did not disavow the vitality of life—"so excited and confused—
worthy of me"—but made it more urgent, more necessary to be portrayed (*MCCW*, 29, 216).

The evidence of her antebellum beliefs is so scanty that one cannot
reliably date the onset of these beliefs; my guess is that the Civil War
deepened but did not create them, because they are not uncharacteristic
of her contemporaries, that odd truncated generation that was just
coming into possession of their world when the war came. Most appear
in her narrative journal: William Porcher Miles, Henry Timrod, Paul
Hamilton Hayne, Varina Howell Davis, Susan Petigru King, William
Henry Trescot, James Johnston Pettigrew, L. Q. C. Lamar. Many of
them were skeptical people, putting up with their privileged lot with a
half-smile, very interested in the salon and scandal (some of which they
occasioned), fashionable, witty, analytical, acting from necessity more
than hope, a little sad. They were very conscious of themselves as a
generation, at odds with but polite towards their elders, who in turn
noticed: "Mr. Petigru said of that brilliant Trescot, 'He is a man without indignation.' He and I laugh at everything" (*MCCW*, 36).[26] Above
all, they were clever. This was her favorite adjective. "Agreeable men,
clever and cultivated men, seem to spring up from the sands of the
sea." "We discussed clever women who help their husbands politically."
Trescot was "the very cleverest writer we have." Muscoe Garnett was
"the best and the cleverest Virginian I know." Lamar was "the most
original and the cleverest of our men." The word seems to have meant
force of mind, touched with irresponsibility and wit. Cleverness was a
social quality; it existed to be observed. Being assertive, it was usually
associated with being a man. For a woman like Mary Chesnut, there
was a price for laughing with Trescot: "Another personal defeat," she
wrote about an incident in 1862. "Little Kate: 'Oh, Cousin Mary, why
don't you cultivate heart? They say at Kirkwood that you had better let
your brains alone awhile and cultivate heart'" (*MCCW*, 358, 365, 568,
309, 393).

This burden of gender helps to make intelligible much of Chesnut's
sensibility and may explain her resorting to a changed form of observance, which most of her contemporaries did not. We have no comparable postbellum writings from Trescot or Hayne: on the contrary, the
effect of the war on men seems to have been to choke off the modest

experimentation of the 1850s, to make skepticism unseemly.[27] Less public, less responsible for the blood, tucked away in Camden, Mary Chesnut escaped the crippling burden of piety. But there may be another reason for this, which is gendered. Journals were a literary form in Chesnut's society that women used freely—not exclusively, for men wrote diaries too, but characteristically.[28] Chesnut poured all her genres, all her narratives into the form of the journal. In this she differed from Woolf, who kept genres distinct; the Englishwoman's diaries, letters, biography, essays, novels were then and are now all gathered between different endpapers, firmly labeled. More, Woolf tended to separate out her own styles into these genres; the voice of the novels is more lyrical and experimental than that of the diaries, which are in turn distinct from the letters, which are direct, even plain speaking. Chesnut put all these together in one place, defying purity of genre and style. One is tempted to say that this was more radical, more defiant of the rules. But the temptation should be resisted because one genre remained governing, the journal, suitable precisely because it had so few rules. The journal had long permitted authors, publicly or privately, to use history, memoir, autobiography, and fiction. It acknowledged only two imperatives: narrative must implicate self; the passages of time must be denoted.

For all this, one must stress that Mary Chesnut's achievement differs fundamentally from that of Woolf in *To the Lighthouse*. Chesnut dealt in articulated voices, Woolf in thoughts. "You have overheard scraps of talk that filled you with amazement," Woolf explained in 1924. "You have gone to bed at night bewildered by the complexity of your feelings. In one day thousands of ideas have coursed through your brains; thousands of emotions have met, collided, and disappeared in astonishing disorder."[29] Woolf's mature fiction seeks to capture this quality of internal character. But Chesnut kept disorder out of the mind because she feared it, as well she might. Chesnut may have understood the instability of reason and madness, but she certainly refused to confront it, sometimes escaping by means of the oblivion of opium:

> There was tragedy, too, on the way here. A mad woman, taken from her husband, and children. Of course she was mad—or she would not have given "her grief words" in that public place. Her keepers were along. What she said was rational enough—pathetic, at times heartrending.
> Then a highly intoxicated parson was trying to save the soul of

"a bereaved widow." So he addressed her always as "my bereaved friend and widow."

The devil himself could not have quoted Scripture more fluently.

<<It excited me so—I quickly took opium, and *that* I kept up. It enables me to retain every particle of mind or sense or brains I ever have and so quiets my nerves that I can calmly reason and take rational views of things otherwise maddening . . . <and have refused to accept overtures for peace and forgiveness. After my stormy youth I did so hope for peace and tranquil domestic happiness. There is none for me in this world.>[>] (*MCCW*, 29)[30]

So Chesnut kept her voices out in the world, attached to flesh and blood, where they were safer. Indeed, she seems even to have exported her own thoughts and attached them to others.[31] In this sense, Woolf was braver, in fracturing the line between the internal and external worlds, though she was to pay a terrible price for this courage.

Chesnut's flight down the middle walk, away from her particles of mind, reasonably disqualifies her from the modernist canon, as traditionally understood.[32] There are too many aspects of that movement to which Mary Chesnut would have been hostile. She had no notion of an avant-garde. There is no reason to believe that she would have looked on a Picasso painting or heard a Stravinsky score with equanimity. We are told, plausibly, that, "Modernist works frequently tend to be ordered, then, not on the sequence of historical time or the evolving sequence of character, from history or story, as in realism or naturalism; they tend to work spatially or through layers of consciousness, working towards a logic of metaphor or form. . . . synchronicity . . . [is] one of the staples of Modernist style."[33] Chesnut believed in history and studied character, as it happened in time. She would have recoiled from the proposition that older forms of mimesis were now irrelevant, even pernicious. She would not have thought it necessary to urge art as an ordering myth. She would have been too genteel to inhabit Henry Miller's tropics, though she might have managed an awkward laugh when Lytton Strachey pointed to that stain on Vanessa Stephen's white dress and asked, "Semen?"[34] On the other hand, she would have found Eliot's postbellum characterization of "the immense panorama of futility and anarchy which is contemporary history" intelligible. She would likewise have understood when Eliot argued that art is "not a turning loose of emotion, but an escape from emotion; it is not the expression of personality, but an escape from personality." [35] She would certainly have grasped the point when, in arguing for December 1910 as a turning point, Woolf explained, "All human relations have shifted—those between masters and servants, husbands and wives, parents and children." [36] But Chesnut could make her own case for an earlier turning point, a different social transformation. And she knew that literature responded to "fragmented utterances" and a "dislocation of parts." [37]

My argument is not that Chesnut is a modernist but that, on the subtle and confused continuum that leads from the Anglo-American literary culture of 1860 to that of 1930, she is closer to the latter end than we have thought. The inceptions of modernism were overlapping and uneven: many members of the Bloomsbury group other than Woolf, writers like Strachey, were less radical about form than Chesnut herself; it was Roger Fry who observed that they were "the last of the Victorians." [38] For one must remember that Chesnut's narrative journal was written in the early 1880s; because she brings to life the early 1860s, there is a marked temptation to annex her to the sensibility of the midcentury and to neglect the evident fact of her intellectual and aesthetic growth between 1865 and 1880. Chesnut is nearer to the fin de siècle than we usually realize.

Why was she so "advanced"? This is elusive. But it mattered that her starting point, Thackeray, was, of all the great Victorian writers, least committed to the principles of realism. It was Thackeray, after all, who understood that, whatever fiction did, it did not mimic real life. He was an author who began his career by writing parodies, one who debated genre and style: "We might have treated this subject in the genteel, or in the romantic, or in the facetious manner," he cheerfully explained to his readers in *Vanity Fair*.[39] Most importantly, Thackeray observed in *Pendennis:* "Ah sir—a distinct universe walks about under your hat and under mine. All things in Nature are different to each: the woman we look at has not the same features, the dish we eat from has not the same taste to the one and the other. You and I are but a pair of infinite isolations, with some fellow-islands a little more or less near to us." [40] Gregariousness in both Thackeray and Chesnut arose from this bleak insight; it was an attempt at island-hopping.[41] But Thackeray, like his admirer Anthony Trollope, had a strong sense of comity between author and reader that was alien to Chesnut. The men, with bluff clubbishness, talked to the reader over their port and cigars, even if they talked of isolation. Chesnut the woman never articulated a vision of her possible readers, was silent on their nature, was alone with her voices, and aspired to impersonality.

Hence much hinged on gender. Virginia Woolf, though she admired Thackeray, felt an unbridgeable gulf between herself and such as him. "It is useless to go to the great men writers for help, however much one may go to them for pleasure. Lamb, Browne, Thackeray, Newman, Sterne, Dickens, De Quincey—whoever it may be—never helped a woman yet, though she may have learned a few tricks of them and adapted them for her use," she wrote in 1929.[42] For men wrote assertively, with purpose and ambition. They commanded the genres of outwardness: history, political economy, travel writing, biography. Women were confined to fiction, the genre of enclosure, in "the common sitting-room," where they observed "human beings . . . in their relation to each other."[43] The mark of intellectual freedom for women would be the movement outward, out of the room, into the world. This is a beguiling interpretation that has been very influential upon modern opinion. It makes much seem intelligible, provides a historical explanation of the transit from Jane Austen to Margaret Thatcher, from Elizabeth Ruffin to Hillary Clinton.[44] It is useful for understanding Mary Chesnut, who moved towards the genres of outwardness, but by the half-step of importing a teeming world into her drawing room and mingling the techniques of fiction and "fact." Yet Woolf intended that the world should also be understood as thought and that the movement should be double, out into the world of facts, down into the realm of "myriad impressions—trivial, fantastic, evanescent, or engraved with the sharpness of steel."[45] Here too Chesnut took her half-step by admitting the disorder of voices but quarantining their chaos above the stream of consciousness. This was a humane compromise, however nervously accomplished. She once wrote, in her original diary in 1861: "Talked all night—*exhausted. & nervous & miserable today—raked up & dilated & harrowed up the bitterness of twenty long years—all to no purpose. This bitter world.*"[46] She died twenty-five years later, still writing, making sense of things, summoning vitality, transcending bitterness.

Notes

This essay was given, in an abbreviated form, to the seventh annual meeting of the Southern Intellectual History Circle, held at Coastal Carolina University,

Conway, S.C., in February 1994. There it benefited from the criticism of Elisabeth Muhlenfeld and David Moltke-Hansen, as well as a rigorous roundtable discussion. I want especially to thank Anne Goodwyn Jones and Steven Stowe for exceptionally thoughtful readings of its fuller version.

1. The standard biographies are Elisabeth Muhlenfeld, *Mary Boykin Chesnut: A Biography* (Baton Rouge: Louisiana State Univ. Press, 1981) and Quentin Bell, *Virginia Woolf: A Biography,* 2 vols (London: Hogarth Press, 1973).

2. But see Stephen Trombley, *"All That Summer She Was Mad": Virginia Woolf and Her Doctors* (London: Junction Books, 1981) for a convincing skepticism about the nature of Woolf's "madness."

3. C. Vann Woodward and Elisabeth Muhlenfeld, eds., *The Private Mary Chesnut: The Unpublished Civil War Diaries* (New York: Oxford Univ. Press, 1984).

4. C. Vann Woodward, ed., *Mary Chesnut's Civil War* (New Haven: Yale Univ. Press, 1981), xv–xxix (hereinafter cited as MCCW in text). See also Woodward, "What Is the Chesnut Diary?" in *South Carolina Women Writers,* ed. James B. Meriwether (Columbia, S.C.: Southern Studies Program, 1979), 193–209.

5. Woodward, of course, has scrupulously distinguished passages from the differing manuscripts; see "Editorial Problems and Principles," MCCW, liv–lviii.

6. C. Vann Woodward, "Mary Chesnut in Search of Her Genre" (1984) in *The Future of the Past* (New York: Oxford Univ. Press, 1989), 252, 260; Steven M. Stowe, "City, Country, and the Feminine Voice," in Michael O'Brien and David Moltke-Hansen, eds., *Intellectual Life in Antebellum Charleston* (Knoxville: Univ. of Tennessee Press, 1986), 314. It has been argued that the palimpsest is a characteristic form for female writers. Mary Lynn Broe has observed of Djuna Barnes that "her palimpsest texts, such as *Ryder* and *Ladies Almanack,* disrupt a masculine economy that would assign a single system of signification to each work" (Broe, "Djuna Barnes [1892–1982]," in *The Gender of Modernism: A Critical Anthology,* ed. Bonnie Kime Scott [Bloomington: Indiana Univ. Press, 1990], 19). Somewhat differently, Sandra Gilbert and Susan Gubar have written, "In short, like the twentieth-century American poet H. D., who declared her aesthetic strategy by entitling one of her novels *Palimpsest,* women from Jane Austen and Mary Shelley to Emily Brontë and Emily Dickinson produced literary works that are in some sense palimpsestic, works whose surface designs conceal or obscure deeper, less accessible (and less socially acceptable) levels of meaning. Thus these authors managed the difficult task of achieving true literary authority by simultaneously conforming to and subverting patriarchal literary standards" (*The Madwoman in the Attic: The Woman Writer and the Nineteenth-Century Literary Imagination* [New Haven: Yale Univ. Press, 1979], 73). Since Chesnut did not, in my opinion,

adopt a "surface design" that was patriarchal, I am unsure whether this analysis is directly relevant, though it is suggestive.

7. "Bloomsbury. So this is no longer a journal but a narrative of all I cannot bear in mind which has occurred since August 1862," entry for September 23, 1863 (*MCCW,* 425).

8. Elizabeth Fox-Genovese, *Within the Plantation Household: Black and White Women of the Old South* (Chapel Hill: Univ. of North Carolina Press, 1988), 371.

9. Charles East, ed., *The Civil War Diary of Sarah Morgan* (Athens: Univ. of Georgia Press, 1991). I should acknowledge that, though I wrote the first version of this piece before rereading her essay, part of my argument is anticipated in Elisabeth Muhlenfeld, "Literary Elements in Mary Chesnut's Journal," in *South Carolina Women Writers,* 245–61, a paper first delivered at the Reynolds Conference in 1975.

10. They barely support a master's thesis: see Allie Patricia Wall, ed., "The Letters of Mary Boykin Chesnut," M.A. thesis, Univ. of South Carolina, 1977.

11. She seems to have known her Seneca; see *MCCW,* 302, on Medea.

12. Mary Boykin Chesnut, "Two Years—Or the Way We Lived Then," the edited text that forms part 3 of Elisabeth S. Muhlenfeld, "Mary Boykin Chesnut: The Writer and Her Work," Ph.D. diss., Univ. of South Carolina, 1978, 84, 76.

13. Russian novelists like Turgenev and Tolstoy were barely making it into English by the time of Chesnut's death.

14. In Conway, David Moltke-Hansen suggested the *Memoires* of the duc de Saint-Simon (1675–1755) as a precedent for Chesnut. Although there were copies around in South Carolina—in 1826 the Charleston Library Society had a 1791 Strasbourg edition—references to Saint-Simon are surprisingly scarce in southern writing of the early or mid-nineteenth century, even in places where one might expect a reference, and there seem to be none in Chesnut's works. Among the few who did mention Saint-Simon are Francis Kinloch, *Letters from Geneva and France, Written During a Residence of Between Two and Three Years, in Different Parts of Those Countries, and Addressed to a Lady in Virginia. By Her Father,* 2 vols. (Boston: Wells and Lilly, 1819), 1:69; and Hugh Legaré, "D'Aguesseau," *Southern Review* 8 (1832): 399–443. See *A Catalogue of the Books Belonging to the Charleston Library Society* (Charleston, S.C.: A. E. Miller, 1826), 231.

15. "Impressions of Sir Leslie Stephen," in *The Essays of Virginia Woolf,* ed. Andrew McNeillie (San Diego: Harcourt Brace Jovanovich, 1986), 1:128.

16. Leslie Stephen, "The Writings of William M. Thackeray" (1878–79), in Geoffrey Tillotson and Donald Hawes, eds., *Thackeray: The Critical Heritage* (London: Routledge and Kegan Paul, 1968), 377. Doubtless because of

his family connection with the Thackerays, Stephen's essay is very guarded about Thackeray's moral shortcomings.

17. Virginia Woolf, *A Room of One's Own* (1929; rpt. London: Triad, 1977), 108, where admittedly she is speaking about a man's writing. In this critical work, unlike her fiction, Woolf does represent herself, though evasively, collectively: "Here then was I (call me Mary Beton, Mary Seton, Mary Carmichael or by any name you please—it is not a matter of importance) sitting on the banks of a river a week or two ago in fine October weather, lost in thought" (9).

18. Fox-Genovese, *Within the Plantation Household*, 335–65.

19. "Two Years," 103.

20. Nathaniel Russell Middleton to his son, undated fragment of autograph letter but perhaps the early summer of 1860, Nathaniel Russell Middleton Papers, Southern Historical Collection, University of North Carolina, Chapel Hill.

21. Divorce was illegal in South Carolina.

22. Virginia Woolf, "Mr Bennett and Mrs Brown" (1923), in *Essays of Virginia Woolf*, 3:385.

23. Virginia Woolf, "Character in Fiction" (1924) in *Essays of Virginia Woolf*, 3:436.

24. Consider this backhander: "In England Mr. Gregory and Mr. Lyndsay rise to say a good word for us. Heaven reward them. Shower down His choicest blessings on their devoted heads—as the fiction folks say" (*MCCW*, 72).

25. Both Anne Jones and Steven Stowe, after reading a preliminary version of this essay, suggested that Chesnut may have intended realism, that her fragmentary drafts may have been but preliminary to a more ordered final version. In the discussions at Myrtle Beach, Elisabeth Muhlenfeld helped me resist that interpretation by indicating how Chesnut, in revising her manuscripts, moved usually and deliberately to weaken coherence, not strengthen it. Even her punctuation, Muhlenfeld has argued, served this purpose: "A look at a holograph page of the Journal reveals that Mrs. Chesnut uses a unique system of punctuation, the effect of which is to reproduce as accurately as possible the mind casting back and forth over a day's events, stopping now and then to ponder, veering occasionally from the moment at hand to the associations it evokes. She punctuates almost exclusively with dashes of various lengths and with spaces which, on the manuscript page, give a very real feeling of spontaneous and unstructured thought" (Muhlenfeld, "Literary Elements in Mary Chesnut's Journal," 251). A better candidate as a realist is Susan Petigru King, as is argued by J. R. Scafidel, "Susan Petigru King: An Early South Carolina Realist," in *South Carolina Women Writers*, 101–15.

26. Of the names mentioned, all were born between 1822 and 1830.

27. Trescot's postwar eulogy for James Johnston Pettigrew, for example,

is lamentably gilded, uncharacteristic of the mind which Chesnut described as bristling with bayonets: see William Henry Trescot, *Memorial of the Life of J. Johnston Pettigrew, Brig. Gen. of the Confederate States Army* (Charleston, S.C.: John Russell, 1870); *MCCW*, 325.

28. I have discussed this elsewhere: see Michael O'Brien, ed., *An Evening When Alone: Four Journals of Single Women in the South, 1827–67* (Charlottesville: Univ. Press of Virginia, 1993), 2–4.

29. Woolf, "Character in Fiction," 436. One must remember, however, that Woolf was not contending against realism so much as locating reality at the level of consciousness. On this, see Astradur Eysteinsson, *The Concept of Modernism* (Ithaca: Cornell Univ. Press, 1990), 184.

30. The double angle brackets indicate material interpolated into the 1880s manuscript from the 1860s diary; single brackets mark words that Chesnut herself erased, but her editor thought it useful to restore. This passage shows clearly her reluctance to be too intimate, too introspective.

31. Muhlenfeld, "Literary Elements in Mary Chesnut's Journal," 257.

32. One must remember, however, that recent literary criticism has, by insisting upon consideration of female writers, begun to change our understanding of modernism. It remains unclear whether the effect of this will be to expand and reconfigure modernism or to end its usefulness as an analytical category of sufficiently broad application. On such issues, see Shari Benstock, "Beyond the Reaches of Feminist Criticism: A Letter from Paris," in *Feminist Issues in Literary Scholarship,* ed. Benstock (Bloomington: Indiana Univ. Press, 1987), 7–29; Gillian E. Hanscombe, *Writing for Their Lives: The Modernist Women, 1910–1940* (London: Women's Press, 1987); and Bonnie Kime Scott, ed., *The Gender of Modernism.*

33. Malcolm Bradbury and James McFarlane, "The Name and Nature of Modernism," in Bradbury and McFarlane, eds., *Modernism, 1890–1930* (Harmondsworth: Penguin Books, 1976), 50.

34. Bell, *Virginia Woolf,* 1:124.

35. "Ulysses, Order, and Myth" (1923), in *Selected Prose of T. S. Eliot,* ed. Frank Kermode (London: Faber, 1975), 177; Eliot, "Tradition and the Individual Talent" (1920) in *Selected Essays* (London: Faber, 1951), 21.

36. Woolf, "Character in Fiction," 422.

37. "Modernism," in M. H. Abrams, *A Glossary of Literary Terms,* 4th ed. (New York: Holt, Rinehart and Winston, 1981).

38. Qtd. in Ulysses L. D'Aquila, *Bloomsbury and Modernism* (New York: Peter Lang, 1989), 4.

39. William Makepeace Thackeray, *Vanity Fair: A Novel without a Hero* (1847–48; rpt. London: Thomas Nelson, 1901), 52.

40. Thackeray, *The History of Pendennis: His Fortune and Misfortunes, His Friends and His Greatest Enemy* (1848–50; rpt. London: Thomas Nelson,

1901), 176. On Thackeray and representation, see A. Savkar Altinel, *Thackeray and the Problem of Realism* (New York: Peter Lang, 1986) and J. Loofbourow, *Thackeray and the Form of Fiction* (Princeton: Princeton Univ. Press, 1964).

41. Many were surprised, because of his cynical reputation, to find that Thackeray was a sociable man. See, for example, John Esten Cooke, "An Hour with Thackeray" (1879), reprinted in Philip Collins, ed., *Thackeray: Interviews and Recollections,* 2 vols. (London: Macmillan, 1983), 2:256–64.

42. Woolf, *A Room of One's Own,* 83.

43. Ibid., 122–23.

44. On Ruffin, see O'Brien, ed., *An Evening When Alone,* 7–14, 57–106.

45. Woolf, "Modern Novels" (1919), in *Essays of Virginia Woolf,* 3:33.

46. Woodward and Muhlenfeld, eds., *Private Mary Chesnut,* 44.

Reconstructing Southern Manhood

Race, Sentimentality, and Camp in the Plantation Myth

CAROLINE GEBHARD

[Colonel Grangerford] was a gentleman all over. . . . His hands was long and thin, and every day of his life he put on a clean shirt and a full suit from head to foot made out of linen so white it hurt your eyes to look at it.

—MARK TWAIN, *Adventures of Huckleberry Finn*

He had been a colonel in the Confederate army, and still maintained, with the title, the military bearing which had always accompanied it. His hair and mustache were white and silky, emphasizing the rugged bronze of his face. He was tall and thin, and wore his coats padded, which gave a fictitious breadth and depth to his shoulders and chest. . . . Edna was glad to be rid of her father when he finally took himself off with . . . his padded shoulders, his Bible reading, his "toddies" and ponderous oaths.

—KATE CHOPIN, *The Awakening*

[Colonel Romulus Fields] represented a fair type of that social order which had existed in rank perfection over the blue-grass plains of Kentucky during the final decades of the old régime. . . . the inhabitants of that region had spent the most nearly idyllic life, on account of the beauty of the climate, the richness of the land, the spacious comfort of their homes, the efficiency of their Negroes, and the characteristic contentedness of their dispositions. Thus nature and history combined to make them a peculiar class, a cross between the aristocratic and the bucolic, being as simple as shepherds and as proud as kings.

—JAMES LANE ALLEN, "Two Gentlemen of Kentucky"

THE RANGE of my epigraphs is one index of the popularity of "the Colonel" as a postbellum reincarnation of the Cavalier or planter-aristocrat, the epitome of southern masculinity according to tradition.[1] With or without the white suit, he was ubiquitous in American fiction after the Civil War: in his ramrod posture, his integrity verging on absurdity, and above all in his unfailing sense of his own dignity, he embodied (white) southern male honor and pride, still intact despite Appomattox. Yet the postwar resurrection of this stock figure of antebellum legend does not in any simple way represent a reassertion of white supremacy or of the southern aristocratic values of masculine honor and valor bound up with race as well as class hierarchies. Indeed, what is striking about this figure of the Colonel is the excessive, overblown quality of so many representations of him, even in the work of the most sincere defenders of the Old South. For the unnatural stiffness that Twain burlesques in Colonel Grangerford and the padded authoritarianism that Chopin satirizes in Edna's Protestant patriarch of a father are clearly kin to the sentimental heroes of Thomas Nelson Page, James Lane Allen, and others.

Allen's Kentucky Colonel, for example, seems intended to be read "straight," that is, as a nonironic embodiment of the best in southern manhood, unlike Twain's or Chopin's Colonels. Yet Allen's figure, like so many others, is similarly marked by the extravagance, the posturing, that characterizes more ironic postwar literary representations of southern white men of the upper class. The glamour and pathos that surround these figures, especially dramatized through their sentimental relations with their manservants, I will argue, call into question any reductive reading of their appeal to the white mainstream, both North and South. The ideological work performed by such figures in late nineteenth-century American culture is neither simple nor trivial.[2]

In the guise of depicting the aging or sometimes deceased white master, still faithfully served or remembered by one devoted ex-slave, southern-identified male authors sought to renegotiate their generation's ideals of masculinity and patriotism in the aftermath of the Civil War and Radical Reconstruction. Slavery is repudiated, but not white supremacy, in narratives that both reveal and conceal white guilt, and allegiance to nation is refashioned along similarly unreconstructed lines. The result is often a paradoxically homoerotic as well as homophobic vindication of traditional southern male values, with southern white women put firmly back on the pedestal of an impossible purity.

Black women, too, when they appear, play the familiar roles of "mammy" or of willing sexual partners. However, in the now-familiar triangular structure of desire mapped by Eve Kosofsky Sedgwick, female bodies only exist to serve or to connect men; the important relationships celebrated in stories like "Two Gentlemen of Kentucky" are between men.[3] Yet these fictional pairings of master and slave in complex ways mediated not only southern but also national fantasies about race and power. Thus, reconstructing southern manhood becomes not merely a regional project but one with wider implications in an era, as Elaine Showalter has named it, of "sexual anarchy."[4]

In *The Epistemology of the Closet* Sedgwick locates a crisis in the figuration of gender and identity, beginning in the 1880s, marked by the displacement of an earlier mode of sentimental representation that foregrounded the female body. In the place of the feminine and the female body—one thinks inevitably of "Little Eva" on her deathbed in *Uncle Tom's Cabin*—the male body appears instead.[5] According to Sedgwick, these images of white men in pitiable postures signal an important historical shift: "What their persistence and proliferation dramatize is something new: a change of gears, occupying the period from the 1880s through the First World War, by which the exemplary instance of the sentimental ceases to be a woman per se, but instead becomes the body of a man who . . . physically dramatizes, *embodies* for an audience that both desires and cathartically identifies with him, a struggle of masculine identity with emotions or physical stigmata stereotyped as feminine." She even suggests that "antisentimentality" is often inextricably linked to the sentimental: "Nietzsche says, 'With hard men, intimacy is a thing of shame—and' (by implication: therefore) 'something precious.'"[6]

The postwar Reconstruction fiction that displays to the reader male figures like the Colonel, a once powerful white man brought low, a figure, moreover, with whom the reader is expected to identify, is also, I will argue, implicated in this nexus of sentimental/antisentimental relations analyzed by Sedgwick. Although Thomas Wentworth Higginson most likely did not literally cry over the story of the death of the young master in "Marse Chan," as has been claimed, he, like many in the 1880s, had come to believe that Page's narrative of slavery was closer to the truth than Harriet Beecher Stowe's.[7] That Higginson, once a militant abolitionist, commander of a black regiment, and an advocate of Radical Reconstruction, had come to sympathize with Page's sentimental renderings of master-slave relations does, however, indicate a great cultural shift.[8]

The spectacle of the white man's body in a scene designed to evoke tears and admiration placed readers in a sentimental relation to a site that had formerly been reserved for women and slaves; the "sentimental" pathos of these scenes, however, must have been not only pleasurable but also on some level troubling: men in such positions and such scenes evoked the threat of emasculation, destabilizing conventional understandings of gender and race differences. Segwick suggests that the new focus on the male body, part of a larger "modernist crisis of individual identity and figuration itself," brought into play a "relatively new problematics of kitsch, of camp, and of nationalist and imperialist definition."[9] I will tease out some implications of this modern problematics of representation, revisiting the Plantation Myth to argue that reconstructing white, southern masculinity is a project that must be understood as enmeshed in a fin-de-siècle crisis of sexual definition, postwar race relations, and the emergence of a modern American nationalism. Nevertheless, the masculinist "sentimental power" of such representations should not be underestimated; not until the 1960s was "the sentimentalist image of the plantation and slavery" probably tarnished "beyond recovery."[10]

> That the social life of the Old South had its faults I am far from denying. What civilization has not? But its virtues far outweighed them; its graces were never equalled. . . . It has maintained the supremacy of the Caucasian race, upon which all civilization seems now to depend.
>
> — THOMAS NELSON PAGE, *Social Life in Old Virginia before the War*

Critics have long remarked upon the surprising vitality of the Plantation Myth, in particular, its remarkable upsurge in popularity in the 1880s following the collapse of Radical Reconstruction. "The plantation underwent, then, in the ebullient writings of authors who never knew it or of those who remembered it in a passion of loyalty, a sea-change 'into something rich and strange,'" commented Francis Pendleton Gaines in 1924, perhaps the first to mark the excessive, phantasmagoric qualities of the postwar transformation of the favorite myth of the Old South.[11] The contradictions of the postwar craze for things southern in the North, mirrored by the contradictions of the

New South, have been accounted for most ably and influentially by C. Vann Woodward: "The deeper the involvements in commitments to the New Order, the louder the protests of loyalty to the Old." [12] Even the planter-aristocrat, seemingly the figure most resistant to fitting into a new, industrializing order, was nevertheless rehabilitated; according to Woodward, "The fabled Southern aristocracy, long on its last legs, was refurbished, its fancied virtues and vices, airs and attitudes exhumed and admired." [13] Most recently, Ritchie Devon Watson Jr., following Woodward, has argued in *Yeoman versus Cavalier* for what he calls "the abiding power of the Cavalier Myth," contending that well into the twentieth century white southerners were "unwilling to surrender the cherished conception of the South as a region inhabited by an aristocratic, honorable, and superior race of men." [14] Yet as astute as the analysis of the "divided South" proposed by Woodward and those who have followed him is, it does not fully account for the "rich and strange" character of the postwar Plantation Myth. And it does not explain the potency of what was so transparently a fantasy of white, male power. Yet it is precisely from the excessive, extravagant aspects that these fictions derive both their energy and their long-lived popularity.

These excesses, linked to the sentimental focus on the male body, make room for the fantasy both of mastery and of being forgiven for wielding power, yet not without courting melodrama and camp. Critics have often underscored the melodrama that marks so much post-Reconstruction writing. [15] What is less obvious is how writers employed humor to deflect the threat of emasculation that arises when men take the place of women and slaves as objects of sentimental identification. This humor, at odds with the sentimental scenario, functions like a Freudian slip, registering the text's unease at the spectacle of men behaving like, or asking the audience to relate to them as, women. The humor, as well as the extravagant sentimentality of these fictions, at times even veers toward camp.

Camp, as Susan Sontag has shown us, is a multifarious and elusive phenomenon. [16] Although she suggests that camp is usually associated with the urban, the self-conscious, and even the private code, features that seem incompatible with the work of writers like Page, Allen, and Smith, [17] camp also, she contends, may take a quite different form: "One must distinguish between naive and deliberate camp. . . . The pure examples of Camp are unintentional; they are dead serious." [18] Her analysis implies that the producer of this form of camp remains unaware of the mix of "the exaggerated, the fantastic, the passionate, and the naive" in his work.[19] From this perspective, the latent camp meanings of a work may have been invisible to its maker though nevertheless part of its appeal to contemporary, and especially later, audiences. In other words, men like Page and Allen did not set out to produce camp representations of southern masculinity; Page especially was "dead serious" about rewriting antebellum history.[20] Allen, however, I will suggest later, goes in the direction of deliberate camp. Whatever their intentions, by substituting male bodies for female ones—for example, in teary deathbed scenes—these writers inevitably became entangled in a crisis of representing masculine as well as national identity, whereby sentimentality in the late nineteenth century intersected not only with varieties of melodrama but also with those of camp.

The politics of camp, it is also worth noting, are as various as its diverse manifestations; David Bergman points out that writers usually argue "either for the disruptive potential of camp or for its ability to be co-opted by and integrated with oppressive forces."[21] Sontag sees camp as primarily apolitical; Philip Core wants to associate camp with a singular kind of heroism, those in the minority braving "the world's brutal laughter" with outrageous displays.[22] Nevertheless, he also sees that "nostalgia for a world its viewers can never know" provides the impulse for "a variety of mass camp," a form of camp that plays well to repressive, mainstream fantasies about "the beauty of a noble past" that give the lie to a less palatable history of oppression.[23] Camp, according to Andrew Ross, often marks the dethroning of an earlier mode of production that, though it "has lost its power to dominate cultural meanings," is freshly available to be refashioned to meet contemporary needs.[24] For a postwar South whose slave economy was forever broken, a South, moreover, determined to exploit its industrial potential, the planter or Colonel asserting his own honor to a fantastic degree was bound to function as an ambiguous symbol, dangerously close to camp. The excesses characterizing such postwar representations suggest that the desire to reassert an unblemished southern manhood was undermined by a tacit recognition that the Old South had truly lost its way.

The symbolic signs of emasculation often accompanying the figure of the old master—his age, frailty, incapacity to adapt to the new, or his blindness, figural or literal—are everywhere. In Page's "Marse Chan," for example, the "ole marster" is blinded trying to rescue a slave he had ordered into a burning barn, and Smith's *Colonel Carter of Cartersville* is so hopelessly inept at business and even paying his own bills that his body servant describes him as "nuffin' but a chile."[25] Intensifying these stereotypical signs of male impotence is often another kind of effeminacy: his dandyism. Allen notes that "a subtle evidence of deterioration in manliness" of his Colonel Fields is the way "he had taken to dress."[26] Even dapper dress—usually described in detail—becomes not only a marker of the aristocratic leisure of such a man, however shabby his surroundings, but also of his "feminine" separation from "normal" forms of masculine labor.

Although Ross reads the camp of the 1960s as self-consciously democratic, he points out that "the pseudoaristocratic patrilineage of camp can hardly be understated."[27] The "aristocratic affectations" of the intellectual who produces camp, he concludes, "are increasingly a sign of his *disqualification,* or remoteness from power, because they comfortably symbolize, to the bourgeoisie, the declining power of the foppish aristocracy, while they are equally removed from the threatening, embryonic power of the popular classes."[28] As I have suggested, the latent camp aspects of late nineteenth-century southern rewritings of the Plantation Myth were not the product of self-consciousness, nor were they a sign of a democratic politics. To men like Thomas Nelson Page and Francis Hopkinson Smith, "aristocratic" lineage was no joke; both men traced their ancestry to prominent old Virginia families. (The ancestor for whom Smith was named was a signer of the Declaration of Independence.)[29] James Lane Allen's claims to a noble heritage, like those of many Kentuckians, however, were based more on imagined than real connections to the legendary Virginia aristocracy.[30] Of course, any American's claim to be descended from English bluebloods was fundamentally paradoxical in a nation established on the proposition that all men are created equal, as even Page admitted, in attempting to explain the credo of a "Virginia gentleman": "He believed in a democracy, but understood that the absence of a titled aristocracy had to be supplied by a class more virtuous than he believed any aristocracy to be. He purposed in his own person to prove that this was practicable."[31] For men like Page and Allen, only boys during the Civil War, their identification with, as well as distance from, their Colonels must be grasped as a complex ideological performance. By clinging to outmoded figures of southern masculinity, these southern writers represented their distance from Yankee power and simultaneously registered their resentment. By flaunting the old, these writers also signaled their alienation from working-class southern white men as well as money-grubbing Yankees. Colonel Carter puts a New York grocer in his place by a sheer show of manners; the grocer is so "overawed" that he leaves without collecting the money the Colonel owes him (77). Allen's Colonel fails in business after the war because his "mind could not come down to the low level of such ignoble barter" (111). At the same time, these writers acknowledged, though perhaps not consciously, that this ideal of southern manhood had indeed become outmoded, if not obsolete, through the extravagant, even at moments bordering on camp, style in which his character is written.

The cultural anxieties raised by the specter of white southern manhood no longer relevant and possibly even ridiculous in the modern world, however, were quelled by another crucial figure, who makes possible the foregrounding of the white, male body as an object of sentimental desire. This figure, who supports these texts' insistent claims that white, southern men are members of an aristocratic, superior race, is the loyal body servant, the black man celebrated for staying on to serve his "master" long after emancipation. The peculiar sentimentality attached to keeping up this "brave pantomime" (119), in Allen's words, of master-slave relations, especially as sanctified by the tears of a black man, suggests that complex ideological work is going on: under the aegis of telling the "truth" about slavery, new ideological solutions to gender, race, and national identity are being put forward. The fact that these stories of faithful ex-slaves were popular with northern editors and readers also argues that postwar representations of homosocial bonding between white and black men cannot be dismissed as only the fantasies of would-be southern aristocrats bent on carrying on the Cause in a literary realm.[32] It is, then, to the "sentimental" portraits of relations between ex-masters and ex-slaves that we now turn.

> *The life about the place was amazing. There were . . . the boys of the family mingling with the little darkies as freely as any other young animals, and forming the associations which tempered slavery and made the relation one not to be understood save by those who saw it.*
> —THOMAS NELSON PAGE, *Social Life in Old Virginia before the War*

In almost every story about the special relation between a southern gentlemen and his manservant, there is a critical moment when a black man cries. Yet he cries, not for himself, but for his master. Near the end of Allen's "Two Gentlemen of Kentucky," when the old master, Colonel Fields, is on his deathbed, his manservant Peter weeps copiously: "'Oh, Marse Rom!' cried Peter, hiding his face, his whole form shaken by sobs" (130). Chad (short for "Nebuchadnezzar") sheds tears at the prospect of his old master's bankruptcy; he explains to the narrator of Smith's *Colonel Carter of Cartersville*: "I can't hab nuffin' happen to de fambly, Major. You know our folks is quality, an' always was, an' I dasent look my mistress in de face if anythin' teches Marsa George" (60). In "Marse Chan," often taken as the quintessential postwar plantation fiction, Sam—the black man assigned to serve his master almost from birth—tells how he cried when he brought his young master's body home from the war: "I couldn' see, I wuz cryin' so myse'f, an' ev'ybody wuz cryin'" (37). Although the tears here are provoked by the spectacle of the untimely as well as gallant death of the young man, Sam's self-confessed tears are often more generalized to represent his sincere mourning for the Old South. Perhaps the most widely quoted lines from Page's *In Ole Virginia* are these: "Dem wuz good ole times, marster—de bes' Sam ever see! Dey wuz, in fac! Niggers didn' hed nothin' 't all to do" (10).[33] Although in the narrative, the time to which they most directly refer is that of Sam's childhood, the tenor of the story invites us to read these lines, as they have so often been read, as evidence that slavery was not the evil institution that abolitionists said it was.

Of course, these tales made no secret of their desire to challenge the story of slavery told by Harriet Beecher Stowe and others. James Lane Allen had even originally written his "Two Gentlemen of Kentucky" to go with a nonfiction companion piece, "Mrs. Stowe's 'Uncle Tom' at Home in Kentucky," to correct the view that a true Kentucky gentlemen would have ever been capable of selling his slaves: "They were never sold by their Kentucky masters to the plantations of the South, but remained unsold down to the last day of slavery."[34] But the very terms of Allen's defense are riddled with contradiction; basing the "honor" of a Kentucky planter on his "incapability" to sell a slave like "Uncle Tom," almost a member of the family, vainly denied the obvious: slavery *was* traffic in human beings. "Unsold" as a description of a person testifies, in spite of Allen's claim, that slaves could be, and were, sold like chattel. In their representations of the past, these writers, then, were engaged in a convoluted act, not simply of denying the evil of slavery, but also wanting at the same time to be forgiven for the very evil that their texts steadfastly refuse to acknowledge. Thus, in Page's story, Sam's mourning for his young master should be read as a rather more complex projection of both white guilt and desire than it often has. The guilt over slavery—and possibly the continuing mistreatment of black people—is assuaged by the tears of a black man whose all-forgiving love and devotion absolve his former master. Significantly, Sam's tale seems to insinuate that for the sins of slaveholding the masters sacrificed their lives and their futures: the young master is cut down in his prime, a virgin, and the old master, already blinded, but alive to see his son die before him, is symbolically stripped of all of his power even before his actual death. The implication, then, of the tale that Sam tells is that the South's old masters have gone forever; no new ones can take their place.

On yet another level, however, master-slave relations are represented as far from obsolete; indeed, they are a model for race relations in the present. The clearly white, gentlemanly narrator of this tale stands in the place of the old master. Sam's "instinctive" deference to him enacts the subordination now demanded from all blacks by any white man: "Instantly, and as if by instinct, the darky stepped forward and took my bridle" (4). In a postwar America of labor unrest, increasing immigration, and growing support for female suffrage, the appeal of such a fantasy—the "instinctive" subordination of "inferiors"— may be measured by Page's popularity outside the South. Significantly, the only moment in the story that disrupts the fantasy of blacks willingly subjugating themselves to whites is a comic one; the story begins with Sam's grumbling as he searches for his dead master's lost dog: "Jes' like white folks—think 'cuz you's white and I's black, I got to wait on yo' all de time. Ne'm mine, I ain' gwi' do it!" (3). When Sam realizes he has been overheard by a white man, he explains, "He know I don' mean nothin' by what I sez. . . . He know I 'se jes' prodjickin' wid 'im" (3). But this game of "prodjickin" (projection?) in which Sam openly challenges the dog, who stands in the place of the absent master, embodies black resistance in a comic form, further suggesting that the white narrator's interruption of this game and his command to be told all about "Marse Chan" is not an accidental intrusion but driven by his fear of "masterless" blacks.

What is even more troubling than the implicit endorsement of the Jim Crow system—that is, the story's invitation to the (white) reader to inhabit the gaze of the master—is the way in which the romantic story the old "servant" tells reinforces its ideology of white supremacy through homosocial bonding. P. Gabrielle Foreman has recently analyzed what she calls the "homoerotics" displayed in Harriet Beecher Stowe's depiction of the relations between Augustine St. Clare and his male slaves, including "Uncle Tom" himself. She suggests that the violent death of the "good" master as well as the sadomasochistic overtones of Tom's being beaten to death are signs of "sexual transgression," of the "inconceivable realm of male homosocial desire." In her reading, Eva's "presence is superfluous," for she primarily functions as a link between men: she "is the expression of the desire over which Tom and St. Clare connect. . . . a classic example of the erotic triangular paradigm Sedgwick refigures, Eva (the ostensible beloved) occupies Tom ('rival'), as St. Clare ('rival,' father) looks on." She goes on to say: "When we figure only relations between female slaves and white men under slavery as a field of sexual violence and contestation, we allow ourselves to construct and maintain ideological gaps and representation silences. The ramifications of these lacunae fit into a broader set of regulations: the resistance to seeing the male body as penetrable. Dominant society's blinding desire of course perpetuates the erasure of gay identity and rights." As Foreman notes, the sexual vulnerability of black men to white men in white-dominated society, especially under slavery, is "one of those ornate silences"; she reminds us, however, that Harriet Jacobs offers one of the few nineteenth-century testimonies to the sexual victimization of black men. Foreman's analysis suggests new ways of reading the "sentimental" relations between ex-masters and ex-slaves foregrounded in late nineteenth-century America by writers such as Page, Smith, and Allen. A pattern emerges of men's exchanging of both black and white women, pointing always to the primacy of the connection between men. However, through the domestication of the black partner, who is pictured as willingly subordinating himself to the desires of his white master, a protomodern, dominant ideology of masculinity emerges, predicated upon the repression of the possibility of mutual, homosexual desire between men.[35]

In "Marse Chan," the young master arranges for Sam to buy his future wife, and in return Sam literally serves as a go-between, reconciling his master and his lady love. But the women's presence merely underlines the men's bond; it is the connection between these men—Sam and Chan have been inseparable since childhood—that proves deepest; Sam follows his master unquestioningly to war, on the most dangerous missions against Yankees, and finally holds himself responsible for his master's death in battle: "I 'specks dey done kill Marse Chan, an' I promised to tek care on him" (34). Earlier, his master promises, "Sam, we'se goin' to win in dis battle, an' den we'll go home an' git married" (33). The unintentional ambiguity of this statement points to the profound intimacy between these men: "Marse Chan" and Sam are already so joined that they will even consummate their marriages, in a sense, together. Their curious bond is thus another version of the "innocent marriage" between a white man and a racial Other first discussed by Leslie Fiedler.[36] In southern postwar fiction, however, it is significantly not the freedom of the wilderness that allows men to bond but slavery itself, which is why black men are so often imagined as willingly reentering the relation of servitude to their former masters. Slavery is thus rewritten under the sign of love.

If Foreman's analysis is correct, the violent death of the young master in Page's story may also be read as marking a sexual transgression: a repressed desire for a forbidden consummation. The end of the story, however, represents Sam anxiously hoping consummation awaits his master in heaven: " 'Dey tells me dat de Bible sey dyar won' be marryin' nor givin' in marriage in heaven, but I don' b'lieve it signifies dat—does you?' " (38). Yet Sam's concern borders on the excessive; the sentimental hope that lovers will consummate their relationship after death sounds odd when it originates not from the lovers themselves but from the black body servant who looks on. (Indeed, he constantly represents himself as an onlooker and eavesdropper.) The forbidden triangle obliquely figured here—a black man and a white man joined through the body of a white woman—suggests that the subordination of black people, especially black men, is naturalized through Sam's desire to serve; and although this desire is coded on the surface as innocent, the homoerotics of this representation of master-slave relations may be interpreted as part of the logic of a new racial order in which all blacks must "want" to cater to all whites. Such a logic of enforced desire also prefigures what will come to be the greatest symbolic threat to this new order—black men desiring not to serve white men but to possess white women. The epidemic of lynchings of black men for supposedly having violated white women in the postwar South is all too real a reminder of how horrifying the effects of such compulsory social desires can be.[37]

The same regulation of homosocial desire informs the postwar master-slave relations sentimentalized by Smith and Allen. In *Colonel*

Carter of Cartersville Chad and his master live in a cosy bachelor apartment in New York City after the war, even though Chad's wife, "Mammy Henny," is still living, back on the old place in Virginia. Chad, too, is another self-sacrificing black man, who once took a Yankee bullet in his leg in the rescue of his young master from a Union prison. And as in Page's "Marse Chan," women are exchanged between men; here Colonel Carter's father gives Chad his wife. The only woman of significance in this story, however, is Aunt Nancy, an antiquated southern belle whose perfume of sweet lavender is "the very smell that you remember came from your own mother's old-fashioned bureau drawer when she let you stand on tiptoe to see her pretty things" (82). The triangle in this tale is decidedly an oedipal one, with Chad and Colonel Carter sharing in Aunt Nancy a quasi-maternal figure to whom they are both devoted. Significantly, even heterosexual relationships do not figure in this text. Again, the bond between the men is primary. The "odd couple" comforts of their bachelor life together in New York repeat the theme of homosocial bonding although the erotic character of this male bond is almost rendered null because of their age. One man may wear another's clothes, show his caring in the daily acts of cooking for and tending to the needs of the other, yet this quasi-marital intimacy is not depicted as a homosexual relation, but as the "natural" subordination of a black man to a white one.

James Lane Allen's representation of a black man's intimate friendship with a white man in "Two Gentlemen of Kentucky," though, is the most remarkable of all; not only does its sentimentality almost collapse into camp, but its homoerotic character is also the most overt. In this, perhaps his most popular story, Allen also displays a protogay subjectivity.[38] It is important at the outset to mention two caveats. First, Allen's story is a projection by a white man of what a black man desires, and as such it tells us little, if anything, about black (homo)sexual desire; as Foreman points out, in a relation of power such as slavery where black men have been exploited by white men, their consent mattered little. And secondly, there is the danger, as Sedgwick has astutely warned, of damning a "homophobic masculinist culture . . . on the grounds of being *even more homosexual* than gay male culture."[39] In other words, there is a danger of finding Allen—figured as the "true homosexual"—to be more racist and more sentimental than his contemporaries. However, although Allen is *as* racist and as inclined to sentimentalize black and white men's relations as his contemporaries

are, his camp humor ultimately proves more destabilizing of those relations, and therefore more potentially subversive, than those imagined
by Page or Smith.

> *"Come closer!"*
> *Peter crept on his knees and buried his head on the colonel's thigh.*
> *"Come up here—closer;" and putting one arm around Peter's neck he*
> *laid the other hand softly on his head, and looked long and tenderly*
> *into his eyes. "I've got to leave you, Peter. Don't you feel sorry for*
> *me?" "Oh, Marse Rom!" cried Peter, hiding his face, his whole form*
> *shaken by sobs.*
>
> —JAMES LANE ALLEN, "Two Gentlemen of Kentucky"

Unlike Page, Allen did not come from a slaveholding family; his father
was an impoverished Kentucky farmer; in fact, one of his earliest memories is being overworked as a boy in the hemp fields.[40] Allen never
married and never seems to have been interested in women; Grant C.
Knight all but hints that he was gay although Knight does describe his
attachments to men in strictly Platonic terms: "It would take a shrewd
argument to establish his love for any woman other than a relative. . . .
His affectional history is feminine rather than masculine . . . and he felt
an almost sisterly attachment for a very few men whom he frankly
loved as men once loved in the days of big-hearted Dick Steele."[41] "Dick
Steele" refers to a piece Allen once wrote, "Always Bussing His
Friends," where he laments that the custom of men kissing and showing
affection openly, once possible in the London of Steele and Addison,
has no place in nineteenth-century America; the piece, which Allen
signed, "A Southerner (but not a Woman)," won the gratitude of Edmund Gosse because it obliquely took his part in the uproar over an
ungentlemanly attack on Gosse's literary scholarship by a friend.[42] Yet
the "literary" occasion seems inseparable from the passionate male
comradeship it imagines and regrets.

In "Always Bussing His Friends," Allen keeps conjuring up scenes
that mimic both homoerotic desire and the frustration or refusal of that
desire. He writes, "Up rushes Dick, his jolly round person resplendent
in scarlet and gold, takes the pale student of the bookstall in his arms,
hugs him, and starts to kiss him, only the other steps quickly backward
with a flush on his face" (140). Gosse, though happily married, was
attuned to such feelings; he later wrote to John Addington Symonds of

his own repressed feelings for a male friend, "The position of a young person so tormented is really that of a man buried alive and conscious, but deprived of speech." Later he predicted to André Gide, "No doubt, in fifty years, this particular subject will cease to surprise anyone, and how many people in the past might wish to have lived in 1974." [43]

When Knight wrote to Ellen Glasgow for information for his book *James Lane Allen and the Genteel Tradition,* she replied evasively, perhaps hinting at the familiar "open secret" of gay identity. She hopes she has been sufficiently "discreet"; she stresses that there were others who were much closer to him than she was but concludes, "The real trouble between us was that, try as hard as I could, it was impossible for me to admire his style of writing as ardently as all the sentimental young men of the nineties had admired it." [44] Of course, it is dangerous and finally impossible to construct from these few hints a writer's psychosexual identity without, on the one hand, recreating a stereotype, and on the other, underestimating his self-awareness. Whatever Allen's own sensibility, however, the homoerotically charged relationship that he represents in "Two Gentlemen of Kentucky" is the clearest working out of the fantasy of white southern aristocratic masculinity based on the sexual and social subordination of black men.

The above deathbed scene, with Peter embracing his master's thigh and sobbing at the prospect of his loss, serves as the climax to this story of "the last steady burning-down of that pure flame of love which can never again shine out in the future of the two races" (119). In Allen's narrative, women characters, black and white, function as ideals who are conveniently dead or absent: the white southern mother dies hearing of her other son's death; the loyal black wife dies, leaving the Colonel and Peter to a delicious male companionship untroubled by women. White women are associated with a deathly purity, black women with sexuality. The Colonel's long-ago failed romance, his guarantee of heterosexuality, appears in the tale as little more than a name—"Helen," the stereotypical belle dame sans merci. Although Peter tells his "love-story" to the Colonel (a guarantee of his heterosexuality?), the real love affair dramatized in the story is between ex-slave and ex-master. Peter, "the only one of the colonel's former slaves that had remained inseparable from his person and his altered fortunes," is first introduced as gazing at his master "with an expression of indescribable solicitude and love" (104).

The reader is invited to identify with both the gazer and the object of the gaze—the white man. Their exquisite intercourse is a symbol of the superiority of past race relations: "No one ever saw in their intercourse ought but the finest courtesy, the most delicate consideration. . . . To be near them was to be exorcised of evil passions" (119). An obvious political reading of the "evil passions" that Allen invokes here is the specter of race war used by whites to justify Klan violence as well as the need for racial segregation; the idea that *all* white men deserve an aristocratic, superior relation to black people, we should remember, made possible the birth of the Ku Klux Klan, which attracted not only poorer white men but also men of high station and social prominence throughout the South.[45] Allen's tale, then, is congruent with the literary as well as historical interpretation of Radical Reconstruction begun by writers such as Page and given academic respectability by the so-called Dunning school: Reconstruction was judged a total failure, a time of unparalleled political corruption when greedy carpetbaggers and ignorant blacks ruled over a defeated and demoralized South until the region was redeemed by its white men.[46]

But a reading that takes into account the curious excesses of this story must also explain why the tale so openly constructs a mutual, loving relation between men as a forbidden paradise. (Their tender relations are even called "a shadowy paradise" [119].) The camp humor threatening to disrupt the sentimental surface at every point only confirms that the gender and race identities that the tale seems to take for granted are at the same time revealed to be not so stable after all. To take just one example of the camp humor, their very names suggest something silly: "Romulus Fields" is bad enough, though relics of antebellum southern manhood are often equated with classical glory. Still, it is usually the ex-slave who is "Caesar" or "Pompey." But "Peter Cotton" is an even more ridiculous name, clearly linking the ex-slave to the "cottontail" rabbit. The emphasis on Peter's "tail," however, appears elsewhere in the story as well. Peter, once a slave preacher, had been the possessor of a miraculous blue-jeans coat, embroidered everywhere with scripture, such as "Servants, be obedient to them that are your masters according to the flesh." The seriousness of this already-too-much trope of Peter as text is further compromised by the word *Amen,* which appears in a very queer place: "But the only spot now left vacant was one of a few square inches, located just where the coat-tails hung over the end of Peter's spine; so that when any one stood full in Peter's rear, he could but marvel at the sight of so solemn a word emblazoned in so unusual a locality" (106). Noting the connection between a homosexual sensibility and camp, Sontag reads camp as "a gesture of self-legitimization" that "neutralizes moral indignation, sponsors playfulness."[47] In one way, Allen's tale is the story of the decline of the white master, which shows him in the unflattering but very human light of being reduced to powdering his face and leaning on his former servant for strength and support. From this angle, southern gentility as well as black inferiority are exposed as mutually dependent constructions. But, read another way, the lugubrious deaths of these two stage a sentimental climax that both inscribes a desire for as well as a fear of sexual transgression. Yet the overdone humor here leaves racist—and homophobic—paradigms intact. If the narrator's attention to Peter's anatomy comically invokes a forbidden place of male desire, the story nevertheless makes him the butt of the story's humor.

If white southerners as well as northerners long after the Civil War found solace in tales of tender affections between ex-slaves and ex-masters, we have reason to think such narratives provided versions of manhood as well as nation that satisfied mainstream tastes. In Showalter's study of the "myths, metaphors, and images of sexual crises and apocalypse" dominating late nineteenth-century English and American culture, she argues that the threat of a "revolution by women" received the most attention in England, where "the 'lower races' were safely distant in Africa and India, and the poor usually well out of sight."[48] Her analysis does not fit America nearly so well, where the freeing of the slaves after a bloody civil war, soon followed by wave upon wave of immigration, led to a different metaphorics of social breakdown. The special place of the South in the national imaginary, especially as embodied in the antebellum Plantation Myth, owes something to distinctly American fears and desires.

It is important to recognize that some writers resisted this homosocial fantasy of racial harmony. Nineteenth-century African-American male writers such as Charles W. Chesnutt and Paul Laurence Dunbar did not imagine ex-slaves mooning over their former masters. Indeed, "Uncle Julius" in "The Goophered Grapevine" frankly portrays his old master as a skinflint as well as a fool. Even Dunbar's figures who grieve for their plantation past, for example, the narrator of "The Deserted Plantation," mourn most for the community of black men and women that has been lost.[49] Yet their very need to resist indicates the "sentimental power" of this tale of interracial male bonding.

In *Imagined Communities,* Benedict Anderson suggests that one of the ways nationalist ideologies work is through what he calls "the reassurance of fratricide." Bloody and intractable race and class conflicts, he argues, are often retold and "explained" as essentially family feuds, thus creating the illusion of an unbroken national continuity through a complex process of selective remembering and forgetting: "A vast pedagogical industry works ceaselessly to oblige young Americans to remember/forget the hostilities of 1861–65 as a great 'civil' war between 'brothers' rather than between—as they briefly were—two sovereign nation-states." He adds that had the Confederacy won, "this 'civil war' would have been replaced in memory by something quite unbrotherly." Part of the story, then, of remembering/forgetting the Confederacy, and with it, slavery, the South's infamous peculiar institution, is the story of the happy slave, the slave woman or man—the "Mammy" or the "Uncle Tom"—who was supposedly part of the family. Slavery is remembered/forgotten not through the eyes of the field hand, but through the more reassuring ones of those who were almost "family." Anderson notes that "the first indelible image of black and white as American 'brothers'" is "Jim and Huck companionably adrift on the wide Mississippi," but "the setting is a remembered/forgotten antebellum in which the black is still a slave."[50]

Yet gender and race cannot be left out of an analysis of such "brotherly" constructions. As Sedgwick and Foreman remind us, the construction of white, heterosexual masculinity makes relations between men, especially between men of different skin colors, fraught with meaning. The postwar creation of the Colonel and his devoted ex-slave may be read as a complicated ideological renegotiation of masculine as well as national identity. If owning black people is no longer American and the southern white patriarch's power is correspondingly diminished, these narratives also reinscribe the necessity for blacks—especially black men—to subordinate themselves to whites; blacks can only become the "gentlemen" of Allen's and Smith's stories when they fully accept their status as social inferiors. By the same token, however, if owning black people is truly no longer American, if blacks potentially, like white women, are masterless, modern white masculine identity can no longer be constructed as a straightforward fable of mastery. This is why so many of these stories compare the Colonel to crumbling, ancient Greek temples, signs of patriarchal privilege under pressure. Thus, the excessive, the "too much" qualities of these stories, whether sentimental or bordering on camp, are especially ambiguous. They register the strain of the effort to recoup white male power, even as they admit that the terms of that power can never be the same.

Yet the hold of sentimental images such as the Colonel over America has proved strong; the staying power of the image may be measured in the millions made by Colonel Sanders, who recycled this figure once more to sell fast food.[51] Hence, fast food, that most democratic of American inventions, is repackaged as upper-class, genuine southern cooking through the figure of Colonel Sanders. If, because of Kentucky Fried Chicken, the figure of the Kentucky Colonel is now more kitsch than sentimental or even camp, that does not lessen the historical or mythic importance of this incarnation of white southern manhood.[52] James Lane Allen's exploration of this figure as half of a tender, interracial male couple suggests that the sentimental in the Plantation Myth could not be fully domesticated; even in the nineteenth century, it contained at least the camp potential to destabilize modern identities predicated upon white men being "naturally" superior and invariably heterosexual.[53]

Notes

I wish to thank Tracy Fessenden, James Goldstein, Pat Morrow, Paula V. Smith, and Rosemarie Thomson for their suggestions.

1. For the classic study of the masculine ideal as southern aristocrat, see William R. Taylor, *Cavalier and Yankee: The Old South and American National Character* (New York: Braziller, 1961). See also Bertram Wyatt-Brown, *Honor and Violence in the Old South* (New York: Oxford Univ. Press, 1986).

2. See Jane Tompkins, *Sensational Designs: The Cultural Work of American Fiction, 1790–1860* (New York: Oxford Univ. Press, 1985).

3. Eve Kosofsky Sedgwick, *Between Men: English Literature and Male Homosocial Desire* (New York: Columbia Univ. Press, 1985).

4. Elaine Showalter takes the phrase "sexual anarchy" from George Gissing for the title of her book *Sexual Anarchy: Gender and Culture at the Fin de Siècle* (New York: Viking, 1990).

5. Robyn R. Warhol notes that it is critics who have christened Stowe's hero "Little Eva," evoking "Little Nell," although the narrator calls her simply "Eva" or "Evangeline" (*Gendered Interventions: Narrative Discourse in the Victorian Novel* [New Brunswick: Rutgers Univ. Press, 1989], 215n).

6. Eve Kosofsky Sedgwick, *The Epistemology of the Closet* (Berkeley: Univ. of California Press, 1990), 146.

7. In his biography, Tilden G. Edelstein remarks that "it is very unlikely that the urbane Higginson literally shed tears, as Edward Channing mockingly claimed (and others have repeated) over the death of the slave owner in Thomas Nelson Page's portrayal of kindly master and loyal slave in 'Marse Chan,'" adding, "It is true, however, that he had come to give greater credence to Page's account of slavery than Theodore Weld's or Mrs. Stowe's" (*Strange Enthusiasm: A Life of Thomas Wentworth Higginson* [New Haven: Yale Univ. Press, 1968], 388).

8. Edelstein argues that this political evolution is less contradictory than it seems; acting in the tradition of his forefathers, Puritan ministers, Higginson condemned slavery but believed in the necessity of an educated elite to govern. According to Edelstein, "Higginson was remarkably consistent—history less so" (399). It is ironic, but wholly consistent with his views, that a man at the forefront of the antislavery fight should later doubt the wisdom of black suffrage and advise the nascent N.A.A.C.P. to "conciliate the more progressive class of southern white citizens" (392).

9. Sedgwick, *Epistemology of the Closet*, 132.

10. Jack Temple Kirby, *Media-Made Dixie: The South in the American Imagination*, rev. ed. (Athens: Univ. of Georgia Press, 1986), 165.

11. Francis Pendleton Gaines, *The Southern Plantation: A Study in the Development and the Accuracy of a Tradition* (1924; rpt. Gloucester, Mass.: Peter Smith, 1962), 63. However, Gaines's bias is toward the rosier view of the Old South. Despite admitting that many stock features of the Plantation Myth were "a dramatization of the lurid, the volatile, the sensational" (187) in plantation life, he swallows most of it whole: "It seems entirely probable that the average black on the Southern estate was, in moderate degree, happy and loyal" (224).

12. C. Vann Woodward, *Origins of the New South: 1877–1913* (Baton Rouge: Louisiana State Univ. Press, 1961), 155.

13. Ibid., 157.

14. Ritchie Devon Watson Jr., *Yeoman versus Cavalier: The Old Southwest's Fictional Road to Rebellion* (Baton Rouge: Louisiana State Univ. Press, 1993), 127.

15. See, for example, Susan Gillman, "The Mulatto, Tragic or Triumphant? The Nineteenth-Century American Race Melodrama," in *The Culture of Sentiment: Race, Gender, and Sentimentality in Nineteenth-Century America*, ed. Shirley Samuels (New York: Oxford Univ. Press, 1992), 221–43.

16. Susan Sontag, "Notes on Camp," *Against Interpretation and Other Essays* (New York: Dell, 1961), 285.

17. All three, however, preferred urban life: Allen never returned to the

Kentucky he celebrated, living most of his life in New York City as did Smith, and Page cut a fashionable figure in the nation's capital after his second marriage to a wealthy widow, Florence Lathrop Field.

18. Sontag, "Notes on Camp," 283.

19. Ibid., 285.

20. Page went so far as to claim that the South "owed her final defeat" to a "lack of a literature": "she was conquered by the pen rather than by the sword; and how unavailing against the resources of the world, which the North commanded through the sympathy it had enlisted, was the valiance of that heroic army, which, if courage could have availed, had withstood the universe" ("The Old South," *The Old South: Essays Social and Political* [New York: Scribners, 1908], 59–60). He devoted himself to a "career not less glorious: the true recording of that story, of that civilization whose history has never yet been written—the history of the Old South" (61).

21. David Bergman, Introduction, *Camp Grounds: Style and Homosexuality,* ed. David Bergman (Amherst: Univ. of Massachusetts Press, 1993), 9.

22. For an analysis critical of Sontag's desire to view camp as apolitical, see Marcie Frank, "The Critic as Performance Artist: Susan Sontag's Writing and Gay Culture," in Bergman, *Camp Grounds,* 173–84. Philip Core, *Camp: The Lie That Tells the Truth* (New York: Delilah Books, 1984), 9.

23. Core, *The Lie That Tells the Truth,* 41.

24. Andrew Ross, *No Respect: Intellectuals and Popular Culture* (New York: Routledge, 1989), 139.

25. Thomas Nelson Page, "Marse Chan," *In Ole Virginia; or, Marse Chan and Other Stories,* intro. Kimball King (1887; rpt. Chapel Hill: Univ. of North Carolina Press, 1969), 59; all subsequent page references are to this edition, a facsimile printing of the first edition of 1887, and appear parenthetically in the text. F. Hopkinson Smith, *Colonel Carter of Cartersville* (1895; rpt. Boston and New York: Houghton, Mifflin, 1919), 77; subsequent page references appear parenthetically in the text.

King focuses on the blindness of the old planter in Page's story as symbolic of his inability to see the flaws of slavery (xxii). In *Southern Writers and the New South Movement, 1865–1913* (Chapel Hill: Univ. of North Carolina Press, 1980), Wayne Mixon points out that F. Hopkinson Smith's Colonel Carter "is often little more than a buffoon" (45). Neither, however, explores the symbolic emasculation of these figures.

26. James Lane Allen, "Two Gentlemen of Kentucky," *Flute and Violin and Other Kentucky Tales and Romances* (1891; rpt. New York: Harper & Brothers, 1898), 113. Subsequent page references appear parenthetically in the text. The tale was first published as "Two Kentucky Gentlemen of the Old School" in *Century Magazine* 35 (1888): 945–57.

27. Ross, *No Respect,* 145.

28. Ibid., 147.

29. Mixon, *Southern Writers,* 32–33, 41–42.

30. According to Grant C. Knight, *James Lane Allen and the Genteel Tradition* (Chapel Hill: Univ. of North Carolina Press, 1935), the Allens liked to claim descent from English gentry through their Virginia ancestors (9). But he grew up not the son of a rich slaveholder but of a relatively poor farmer.

31. Thomas Nelson Page, *Social Life in Old Virginia* (New York: Scribners, 1897), 43.

32. Jay B. Hubbell was among the first to stress the "debt which the literature of the New South owes to the editors of Northern literary magazines" (*The South in American Literature, 1607–1900* [Durham: Duke Univ. Press, 1954], 730). For example, it was a northern editor who first directed Allen to write about Kentucky (John Wilson Townsend, *James Lane Allen: A Personal Note* [Louisville: Kentucky Courier-Journal Job Printing Co., 1928], 25–26).

33. Woodward, for example, comments upon the appreciation southerners lavished upon Page: "What bitter-sweet tears washed Nashville's grimy cheeks over Page's *In Ole Virginia!* 'Dem wuz good ole times, marster—de bes Sam ever see! Dey wuz in fac'! Niggers didn' hed nothin' 'tall to do'" (*Origins of the New South,* 167). Lucinda H. MacKethan singles out the same lines in *The Dream of Arcady: Place and Time in Southern Literature* (Baton Rouge: Louisiana State Univ. Press, 1980) as "the most important testament of all to the beneficent effect of the plantation setting on its inhabitants" (45).

34. James Lane Allen, "Mrs. Stowe's 'Uncle Tom' at Home in Kentucky," *Century Magazine* 34 (1887): 852–67, 853.

35. P. Gabrielle Forman, "'This Promiscuous Housekeeping': Death, Transgression, and Homoeroticism in *Uncle Tom's Cabin*," *Representations* 43 (summer 1993): 51–72; 52, 62, 67, and 71, n. 49).

36. See Leslie A. Fiedler's now classic *Love and Death in the American Novel,* rev. ed. (New York: Stein and Day, 1966). For his more recent assessment of his famous thesis, see his *What Was Literature? Class Culture and Mass Society* (New York: Simon and Schuster, 1982); in this book, he analyzes the sadomasochistic overtones of Uncle Tom's death as a kind of "connubial murder and rape" (175).

37. For an astute analysis of what rape means in American culture, see Susan Fraiman, "Geometries of Race and Gender: Eve Sedgwick, Spike Lee, Charlayne Hunter-Gault," *Feminist Studies* 20 (1994): 67–84. Fraiman contends that "one paradigm of American racism, available during slavery but crystallized in the period following Reconstruction and still influential today" is the one "in which white men's control of Black men is mediated by the always-about-to-be-violated bodies of white women" (70–71).

38. Roger Austen, *Playing the Game: The Homosexual Novel in America* (Indianapolis: Bobbs-Merrill, 1977), explores the late nineteenth-century roots

of explicitly gay fiction in the work of Bayard Taylor, Charles Warren Stoddard, and other writers of the period (1–20).

39. Sedgwick, *Epistemology of the Closet,* 154.

40. Allen remembers working with his father in the fields: "Backward and forward, backward and forward, across the soft brown earth he rode, sowing the hemp. I dropped corn, covered it, thinned it (an abominable business, I thought, working a boy's back as though he were a pair of sugar tongs)" (Townsend, *James Lane Allen,* 14).

41. Knight, *James Lane Allen and The Genteel Tradition,* 39–40.

42. James Allen, "Always Bussing His Friends," in Townsend, *James Lane Allen,* 140–42; Townsend reprints the piece from *The Critic* (3 March 1888). Subsequent references to the story are cited parenthetically within the essay. Townsend also reprints Gosse's enthusiastic letter to Joseph B. Gilder about Allen's essay (26–27). Ann Thwaite, *Edmund Gosse: A Literary Landscape 1849–1928* (London: Secker & Warburg, 1984), discusses the "scandal of the year" caused by the attack of John Churton Collins on Gosse (276–97).

43. In "Always Bussing His Friends," Allen comments, "Had I been his [Samuel Johnson's] contemporary and loved him as well as Boswell, I should never have offered to kiss Dr. Johnson, and I certainly should have resisted to the utmost limits of my strength every effort of the part of Dr. Johnson to kiss me. Nor would any earthly consideration have induced me to stoop to Pope" (141). Thwaite, *Edmund Gosse,* 320–21; she speculates that Gosse may have deliberately wanted his letters to Symonds, and their confession of his homosexual feelings, to survive.

44. *Letters of Ellen Glasgow,* ed. Blair Rouse (New York: Harcourt, Brace, 1958), 93–94.

45. See Eric Foner, *Reconstruction: America's Unfinished Revolution, 1863–1877* (New York: Harper & Row, 1988), 425–44.

46. Foner notes that the Dunning school's version of Reconstruction was influential even up until the 1960s, when W. E. B. Du Bois's earlier findings in *Black Reconstruction* that Reconstruction was not a total failure, but "an idealistic effort to construct a democratic, interracial political order," at last began to gain acceptance (xxi). Foner concludes that the effort to create a "democratic, interracial" order did not succeed but not because of incompetent black rulers or northern carpetbaggers; he suggests that freed blacks, together with northerners and southern unionists, failed to create an egalitarian social order out of the ruins of slavery for complex reasons, including the intransigence of the old southern ruling class but also the contradictory policies of the reformers themselves.

47. Sontag, "Notes on Camp," 292.

48. Showalter, *Sexual Anarchy,* 6.

49. Joanne B. Braxton, Introduction, *The Collected Poetry of Paul Lau-*

rence Dunbar (Charlottesville: Univ. Press of Virginia, 1993), also suggests that a poem like "The Deserted Plantation" must be read "from inside out": from this vantage, the narrator is not so simple, but imagined "in an Afrocentric environment" where black folks "enjoy each other's company and where they are self-identified rather than focused on the master" (xxvii).

50. Benedict Anderson, *Imagined Communities: Reflections on the Origin and Spread of Nationalism,* rev. ed. (London: Verso, 1991), 199, 201, and 203.

51. Lisa Howorth in her entry for the *Encyclopedia of Southern Culture,* ed. Charles Reagan Wilson and William Ferris (Chapel Hill: Univ. of North Carolina Press, 1989), notes that "to people all over the world the words 'It's finger lickin' good' evoke the image of a quintessential southerner, the Kentucky colonel, personified by Harland David Sanders" (750). She adds that Sanders was not a native southerner and became a colonel only through the commission of the governor, who traditionally bestows the title for community service or as a political favor. The company he popularized through this southern mythic figure, however, was worth $850 million when Pepsico bought it in 1986 (751).

52. Ross distinguishes between kitsch and camp; kitsch, from the German for pseudoart, is pretentious and usually "contains a range of references to high or legitimate culture which it apes in order to flatter its owner-consumer" (*No Respect,* 145).

53. See Chuck Kleinhaus, "Taking Out the Trash: Camp and the Politics of Parody," in *The Politics and Poetics of Camp,* ed. Moe Meyer (London: Routledge, 1994), 182–201, on camp's potential as an agent of liberating social transformation.

PART THREE

Slavery and Southern Genders

Douglass and Jacobs, Jacobs and Douglass

Race, Violence, and Manhood

The Masculine Ideal in Frederick Douglass's "The Heroic Slave"

Richard Yarborough

Sir, I want to alarm the slaveholders, and not to alarm them by mere declamation or by mere bold assertions, but to show them that there is really danger in persisting in the crime of continuing Slavery in this land. I want them to know that there are some Madison Washingtons in this land.

— Frederick Douglass

In 1877 the African-American author Albery A. Whitman published an epic poem called "Not a Man, and Yet a Man." At one level, his apparently contradictory title refers to the fact that although relegated to the category of chattel, of brute property, slaves possessed the ability to maintain their own humanity. At another level, Whitman's articulation of black heroism in male terms typifies a great deal of the discourse in nineteenth-century African America surrounding the slave experience. We encounter a more telling example of this tendency in Whitman's preface to a later work, *The Rape of Florida*:

> Amid the rugged hills, along the banks of Green River in Kentucky, I enjoyed the inestimable blessings of cabin life and hard work during the whole of my early days. I was in bondage,—I was never a slave,—the infamous laws of a savage despotism took my substance—what of that? Many a man has lost all he had, except his manhood.[1]

With its focus on "manhood," Whitman's proud self-representation recalls one of the most eloquent testaments to the slave's capacity to transcend attempts at dehumanization—*Narrative of the Life of Frederick Douglass, an American Slave, Written by Himself* (1845). In this text, Douglass first describes how he fell into the depths of slavery, becoming, in his words, "transformed into a brute"; then he makes one of the most often-quoted statements in African-American literature: "You have seen how a man was made a slave; you shall see how a slave was made a man."[2] The key step in this latter transformation involves Douglass's physical confrontation with a white slavebreaker:

> This battle with Mr. Covey was the turning-point in my career as a slave. It rekindled the few expiring embers of freedom, and revived within me a sense of my own manhood. It recalled the departed self-confidence, and inspired me again with a determination to be free. . . . It was a glorious resurrection, from the tomb of slavery, to the heaven of freedom. My long-crushed spirit rose, cowardice departed, bold defiance took its place; and I now resolved that, however long I might remain a slave in form, the day had passed forever when I could be a slave in fact. I did not hesitate to let it be known of me, that the white man who expected to succeed in whipping, must also succeed in killing me.[3]

These lines are replete with fascinating rhetorical turns, but I want to focus particularly on, first, the extent to which the term *manhood* comes to stand for the crucial spiritual commodity that one must maintain in the face of oppression in order to avoid losing a sense of self-worth and, second, the connection established between manhood and violent resistance.

One might argue that when writers like Douglass say "man" they mean "human," that when they say "manhood" they mean "humanity." It would follow then that David Walker, for instance, is addressing all blacks, regardless of gender, when he asks in 1829, "Are we MEN!!— I ask you, O my brethren! are we MEN? Did our creator make us to be slaves to dust and ashes like ourselves?"[4] Quite often, however, the broader rhetorical contexts of such statements reveal the gender-specific nature of the discourse. Thus Henry Highland Garnet's paraphrase of Walker's angry question in 1843 is prefaced by statements directed exclusively to his male listeners:

> You act as though you were made for the special use of these devils. You act as though your daughters were born to pamper the lusts of your mas-

ters and overseers. And worse than all, you tamely submit, while your lords tear your wives from your embraces, and defile them before your eyes. In the name of God we ask, are you *men?*[5]

Even a superficial survey of nineteenth-century writing and oratory reveals the extent to which African-American spokespersons like Whitman, Douglass, Walker, and Garnet saw the crucial test of black fitness to be whether or not black men were, in fact, what was conventionally considered "manly." As Calvin Hernton puts it,

> Historically, the battle line of the racial struggle in the United States has been drawn exclusively as a struggle between the men of the races. Everything having to do with the race has been defined and counter-defined by the men as a question of whether black people were or were not a race of Men. The central concept and the universal metaphor around which all aspects of the racial situation revolve is "Manhood."[6]

In this essay, I want to examine some of the complex ramifications of this obsession with manhood as manifested in early African-American fiction—in particular, in Frederick Douglass's "The Heroic Slave."

Contemporary scholars have focused on the obstacles that nineteenth-century black women encountered in convincing white society that they were little different from their middle-class white counterparts, that they embodied the attributes of True Womanhood with only slight adjustments.[7] Social scientists have noted for some time that black men have confronted related problems in meeting white society's criteria for male status. Indeed, one can identify a mythology of masculinity analogous to the Cult of True Womanhood and partially grounded, like the feminine ideal, in the nineteenth-century sentimental tradition. The Anglo-American bourgeois paradigms of both masculinity and femininity were equally imaginary in nature, essentially ideologically charged constructions serving, first, to bolster the self-image of privileged whites who endorsed and propagated them through their control of major acculturating institutions and, second, to keep marginalized those "others" who—on account of their appearance, speech, family background, class, religion, behavior, or values—did not measure up.

In striving to counter racist charges of inferiority, early African-

American authors understandably sought to shape their portrayal of black male heroes in accord with middle-class definitions of masculinity. Such definitions contained the following crucial ingredients: nobility, intelligence, strength, articulateness, loyalty, virtue, rationality, courage, self-control, courtliness, honesty, and physical attractiveness as defined in white Western European terms. Furthermore, as Robert Staples puts it, "Masculinity . . . has always implied a certain autonomy over and mastery of one's environment." [8] As if the need to have their black male protagonists embody these characteristics were not a daunting enough task, early African-American writers were also aware of the extent to which many of the white readers whom they wished to reach would have agreed with proslavery commentator John Campbell's characterization of blacks:

> The psychical attributes that peculiarly belong to man are adoration, benevolence, conscientiousness, intellectual appetite, fame, speech, prudence, admiration, and reason, or causality. In the Caucasian, these attributes are developed harmoniously, and he is *warlike,* but not cruel nor destructive. In the negro, on the contrary, these attributes are equally undeveloped: he is neither originative, inventive nor speculative; he is roving, revengeful and destructive, and he is *warlike,* predatory and sensual. [9]

Campbell's telling use of the term *warlike* here captures perfectly the dilemma confronting black authors. That is, whites were quite capable of viewing the same trait that signified heroism in whites as signifying degradation and inferiority in blacks.

African-American writers were fully aware of both the arbitrary way in which white middle-class standards of behavior were applied to blacks and also of how the environment in which most blacks lived prevented the full development of those very capacities that white readers appeared to value so highly. Accordingly, in 1860 the black abolitionist H. Ford Douglass qualified his claim for black manhood this way: "Now, I want to put this question to those who deny the equal manhood of the negro: What peculiar trait of character do the white men of this country possess, as a mark of superiority, either morally or mentally, that is not also manifested by the black man, *under similar circumstances?*" [10] His phrase "under similar circumstances" would appear to allow him to attribute any alleged lack of manhood among slaves to the oppressive conditions of servitude. At the same time, however, such a stance acceded to racist contentions that the masses of blacks were, in fact, inferior; as far as many whites were concerned, whether this inferiority resulted from heredity or environment constituted a rarely meaningful distinction. In an attempt to shore up this weakness in his racial defense, H. Ford Douglass takes his argument in a somewhat different direction: "After all, I say that the negro is a man, and has all the elements of manhood, like other men; and, by the way, I think that, in this country, he has the *highest* element of manhood." [11] By claiming the "*highest* element of manhood" for blacks, he turns his back on his environmentalist position and seems to welcome the application of the most exacting white bourgeois criteria in the evaluation of black abilities.

By hook or by crook (and occasionally through a disorienting wrenching of our credulity), mid-nineteenth-century African-American writers found ways to discover black male figures who could stand up to the most rigorous scrutiny and thereby substantiate H. Ford Douglass's lofty pronouncement. For example, in the 1853 edition of William Wells Brown's *Clotel,* currently recognized as the first novel published by an African-American, we have two heroic male slave characters, William and George Green. Brown describes the former as "a tall, full-bodied Negro, whose very countenance beamed with intelligence." [12] In speech and manner, he is hardly distinguishable from bourgeois whites, expressing himself in proper English for most of the novel. Brown's portrayal of George Green is even more striking. Like Harriet Beecher Stowe's George Harris in *Uncle Tom's Cabin,* he is virtually white in appearance: "His hair was straight, soft, fine, and light; his eyes blue, nose prominent, lips thin, his head well formed, forehead high and prominent." [13] Green resembles the typical middle-class Anglo-American male hero in terms of achievement as well, for Brown locates his ultimate fate firmly in what later became known as the Horatio Alger myth of success: having emigrated to England after escaping slavery, George works his way up to a clerkship and is eventually reunited with his ex-slave sweetheart.

Although Brown would seem to be giving ground to stereotypes and stock images here without much of a struggle, he and other black authors were often too committed to capturing in their writing the reality of the slave experience as they knew it to concede completely to convention. (Brown himself was an ex-slave.) That is, incongruities in their characterizations frequently reflect some degree of ambivalence on their part toward the social values and literary images they felt constrained to endorse in their fiction. Thus, although Brown's George Green is nearly white in appearance, William is clearly black. Even more revealing developments occur in the 1864 edition of *Clotel*—entitled *Clotelle; A Tale of the Southern States*—where we see significant differences in the appearances of both leading men. In the initial version of the novel, Brown describes William as "a tall, full-bodied Negro"; in *Clotelle,* however, he is "a tall, full-blooded African." [14] This change, although apparently minor, in fact manifests Brown's rejection of some of the racist ideological assumptions that supported popular white conceptions of blacks.

A more dramatic shift occurs in his recasting of George Green, now named Jerome Fletcher. In *Clotel* this character is "as white as most white persons"; in the 1864 edition, he is "of pure African origin, . . . perfectly black, very fine-looking, tall, slim, and erect as any one could possibly be." [15] Unfortunately, this flattering portrait is marred by Brown's inability to transcend all racist physical standards: "His features were not bad, lips thin, nose prominent, hands and feet small. . . . His hair which was nearly straight, hung in curls upon his lofty brow." [16] The significance of Brown's hasty qualification of this black image is brought home when we consider his depiction of another dark-skinned figure, Pompey, whose job is to disguise the ages of his master's slaves before they are put on the market. In sharp contrast to Jerome, Pompey is, in his own words, "de ginuine artikle." [17] Not only does he speak dialect, but his features are stereotypically "black." The differences between the two characters are directly related to their roles in the novel. The primary male lead in Brown's sentimental melodrama, Jerome must look the part; a partially comic embodiment of the degradation of slavery, Pompey is not intended to arouse our admiration or identification. Although Brown's emphasis upon Jerome's undiluted African heritage represents a small but significant move away from the nearly white male hero and thus an important step toward artistic self-determination, the problematic assumptions underlying Brown's strategy here are evident. Furthermore, he feels no need whatsoever to call into question the paradigms of male heroism that so inform his characterizations.

Perhaps the most pressing task confronting early African-American writers who sought to establish the manhood of their black slave heroes lay in determining how to depict their male protagonists' responses to slavery, especially given what Marian Musgrave calls the "interdiction, perhaps unconscious, perhaps deliberate, upon even mentioning the fearful possibility of black violence visited upon whites."[18] In the initial edition of *Clotel*, William Wells Brown attempts to solve this problem by locating George Green's bravery and militant resistance to slavery in both a black and a white context. Thus, immediately after Green is introduced, we learn that he is the sole surviving member of Nat Turner's group of rebels. Then, in a dramatic trial scene, this articulate and well-educated slave endorses armed resistance to injustice by invoking the ideals of the American War of Independence; at one point he declares, "Did not American revolutionists violate the laws when they struck for liberty? They were revolters, but their success made them patriots—we were revolters, and our failure makes us rebels."[19] In a quite calculated move, Brown links two violent acts of liberation—one that many of his white readers would instinctively reject and one that many of them would readily endorse. Brown cannot go much further than this lest the crucial link he is forging between the American Revolution on the one side and the Nat Turner rebellion on the other be broken.[20] Consequently, for all of his militant background and patriotic talk, George does not come close to committing a violent act in the novel. Even his freedom is won not through any assertion of force but rather through the intervention of his slave lover, Mary, who exchanges clothing and places with the imprisoned George in one of the novel's less credible plot twists.

In the final edition of the novel—entitled *Clotelle: or, the Colored Heroine* (1867)—history provides Brown with something of a way out of this conceptual cul-de-sac—the Civil War, an event that most black leaders saw as the opportunity to fulfill what David Blight terms the "quest for the irrevocable recognition of manhood and citizenship."[21] For possibly the only moment in United States history, black men were provided with a socially sanctioned opportunity to bear arms against their white American oppressors. It is hardly surprising, then, that Brown has his fictional hero, Jerome, return to the United States toward the end of the novel and eventually lose his life in the bloody engagement at Port Hudson. What is unexpected, however, is the fact that Jerome does not die in an attack upon Confederate forces; rather, he is decapitated by a shell while attempting to retrieve the corpse of a fallen (presumably white) officer. In one fell swoop, Brown skillfully identifies the male slave's militant struggle for freedom with the Union's struggle for survival and simultaneously strengthens his hero's claim upon the respect due one embodying the best of American manhood without forcing his readers to confront a dramatization of black violence against whites.

In November 1841, a slave named Madison Washington played a key role in a revolt aboard the American ship *Creole* while it was en route from Virginia to New Orleans. After commandeering the vessel, he and his fellow blacks sailed to Nassau, where they gained their freedom. Although Washington's story is relatively little known today, in antebellum circles his name was often mentioned in the same breath with those of other black heroes. Henry Highland Garnet, for example, extols Washington as "that bright star of freedom" and ranks him with the likes of Denmark Vesey, Nat Turner, and Cinque.[22] Thus, in 1853, when Douglass published a fictionalized version of the *Creole* revolt entitled "The Heroic Slave," his audience was probably already familiar with his protagonist and his remarkable story.[23] No nineteenth-century African-American thinker was more concerned with the issue of manhood than Frederick Douglass, and the manner in which he transforms Madison Washington from a historical personage into a fictional epitome of militant slave resistance vividly reveals the representational strategies he adopted in attempting to dramatize black male heroism.

Just as William Wells Brown does in depicting his protagonists, Douglass initially focuses upon Washington's attractive physical appearance:

> Madison was of manly form. Tall, symmetrical, round, and strong. In his movements he seemed to combine, with the strength of the lion, a lion's elasticity. His torn sleeves disclosed arms like polished iron. His face was "black, but comely." His eye, lit with emotion, kept guard under a brow as dark and as glossy as the raven's wing. His whole appearance betokened Herculean strength.[24]

In sharp contrast to Brown's relatively unadorned treatment of George and Jerome, however, Douglass conveys the superhuman stature of his hero through explicit allusions to both Greek legend ("Herculean strength") and the Old Testament ("black, but comely" from the Song of Solomon). Douglass is also quick to qualify Washington's seeming ferocity: "Yet there was nothing savage or forbidding in his aspect. A child might play in his arms, or dance on his shoulders."[25]

This elaborate description differs radically from Douglass's celebration of Madison Washington in a speech that he delivered in April 1849—four years before the publication of "The Heroic Slave":

> About twilight on the ninth day, Madison, it seems, reached his head above the hatchway, looked out on the swelling billows of the Atlantic, and feeling the breeze that coursed over its surface, was inspired with the spirit of freedom. He leapt from beneath the hatchway, gave a cry like an eagle to his comrades beneath, saying, *we must go through*. . . . Suiting the action to the word, in an instant his guilty master was prostrate on the deck, and in a very few minutes Madison Washington, a black man, with *woolly head, high cheek bones, protruding lip, distended nostril, and retreating forehead,* had the mastery of that ship.[26]

In a characteristic use of irony here, Douglass contrasts the racist connotation of certain black physical attributes with the fact that Washington has just taken control of both the *Creole* and his fate. In "The Heroic Slave," however, Douglass forgoes the sarcastic thrust at racist conceptions of black physiognomy so that his protagonist's appearance will fall more in line with conventional Anglo-American conceptions of ideal masculinity. Unfortunately, in so doing, Douglass retreats from his attack upon the racist stereotypes that he had earlier successfully undercut.

One year after the publication of "The Heroic Slave," Douglass indirectly reveals his tendency to link physical appearance with mental capacity as he describes Irish peasants whom he encountered on a trip to Europe:

> I say, with no wish to wound the feelings of any Irishman, that these people lacked only a black skin and woolly hair, to complete their likeness to the plantation negro. The open, uneducated mouth—the long, gaunt arm—the badly formed foot and ankle—the shuffling gait—the retreating forehead and vacant expression—and, their petty quarrels and fights—all reminded me of the plantation, and my own cruelly abused people. . . . The Irishman educated, is a model gentleman; the Irishman ignorant and degraded, compares in form and feature, with the negro![27]

Douglass then asks, "But what does it all prove? . . . It raises the inquiry—May not the condition of men explain their various appearances? Need we go behind the vicissitudes of barbarism for an explanation of the gaunt, wiry, ape like appearance of some of the genuine negroes?"[28] Douglass's argument here—what Waldo Martin terms "an ambiguous environmentalism"—is flawed in a number of ways, not the least of which is his tacit endorsement of the assumption that "form and feature" are accurate indications of psychological development.[29] As a result, he lets stand one of the fundamental assertions of the racist, proslavery position: that the appearance of most blacks signified inferiority. Thus, for Douglass, the heroic stature of his fictional Madison Washington is directly related to the fact that his protagonist is not a "genuine negro," despite his apparently undiluted black pedigree and harsh experiences as a slave. Madison's manner reinforces his uniqueness even further, for as soon as he opens his mouth, he reveals himself to be extremely articulate and formally educated—hardly the typical slave. A white sailor in the story later notes, "His words were well chosen, and his pronunciation equal to that of any schoolmaster. It was a mystery to us *where* he got his knowledge of the language." It is likewise a mystery to the reader, but one upon which Douglass offers no comment.[30]

Like William Wells Brown in *Clotel*, Douglass confronted an especially troublesome dilemma in depicting black violence. He had encountered a similar challenge several years earlier when he sought to trace his own evolving rebelliousness in his 1845 narrative. There, in describing his battle with Covey, he goes to extraordinary lengths to portray himself as having exhausted every reasonable alternative before resorting to force. And he makes it quite clear that when he at last turns to violence, he is not the aggressor; rather, he presents his goal as solely to keep Covey from beating him.[31] The emotionally controlled, rational, and physically restrained persona Douglass meticulously constructs serves both to establish his narrator's genteel, bourgeois credentials and to render his violence palatable to his white audience. Douglass's job would have been far simpler had the speaker in his *Narrative* been a white man, for most readers would have been quite prepared to endorse his use of force. In fact, they would likely have criticized the narrator for not vigorously resisting Covey from the outset. Simply put, blacks were not granted the same freedom of action as whites, and yet they were condemned for not meeting popularly held norms of behavior.

Black men were viewed as unmanly and otherwise inferior because they were enslaved; at the same time, they were often viewed as beasts and otherwise inferior if they rebelled violently. Moreover, black writers like Douglass must have realized at some level that to make their heroic figures too independent, too aggressive, might permit white readers to evade acknowledging that they themselves must intervene in order to end the horrors of slavery. Many African-American authors saw no easy way to make their black male characters deserving of sympathy and at the same time to celebrate their manhood.

Given Douglass's complex sculpting of his own violence in his auto-biography, it is hardly surprising that in his fiction he emphasizes not Madison Washington's use of physical force but rather his restraint after taking command of the vessel. In his 1849 comments on the *Creole* incident, Douglass makes it clear that Washington encouraged if not actively participated in the attack that resulted in the death of several whites. In contrast, because the white sailor through whose eyes we witness the revolt is conveniently knocked unconscious at the outset of the uprising, in "The Heroic Slave" we see Washington neither commit nor directly urge any acts of physical violence whatsoever. When the white man awakens, the fighting has ended, and Washington is doing his utmost to prevent further bloodshed.[32]

Despite Madison Washington's exemplary behavior during the insurrection, however, Douglass takes no chances and has his protagonist justify what violence has been used:

> You call me a *black murderer.* I am not a murderer. God is my witness that LIBERTY, not *malice,* is the motive for this night's work. I have done no more to those dead men yonder, than they would have done to me in like circumstances. We have struck for our freedom, and if a true man's heart be in you, you will honor us for the deed. We have done that which you applaud your fathers for doing, and if we are murderers, *so were they.*[33]

Washington's phrasing reflects Douglass's deliberate attempt to exploit the parallels between the rebellion on board the *Creole* and the American Revolution and thereby to gain reader approval of his protagonist's implied violence. Like William Wells Brown in *Clotel,* Douglass turns a backward glance to the early days of the American republic to find socially approved examples of violent male action, and the name of his chosen hero doubtless makes this tactic seem especially appropriate. As the white sailor who narrates the final chapter of the story puts it, the name "Madison Washington" was one "ominous of greatness."[34] Accordingly, Douglass from the outset emphasizes the links between Washington and two especially well-known white American political leaders—James Madison and George Washington.

If Douglass sensed that his white audience might experience some discomfort with the means adopted by his slave hero to win his freedom, his concern was well grounded. As Ronald Walters points out, a resolution put forward by one antislavery group in support of the *Creole* revolt manifests the ambivalence felt by many abolitionists:

> The society decided that while we would deprecate a resort to arms for the emancipation of the enslaved population of the south, yet we rejoice in the fact proved, by the recent strike for freedom of the slaves of the *Creole,* that slaves are not indifferent, as our opponents have often declared, to the inestimable blessings of civil liberty.[35]

That Douglass was struggling with his own mixed feelings regarding the appropriateness of violent resistance to slavery and his solidifying opposition to Garrisonian pacifism at the time he wrote "The Heroic Slave" also contributes to the tensions we find in the text surrounding this issue.[36]

Douglass's sensitivity to and absorption of the values and expectations of his target audience inform his depiction of Madison Washington in other important ways as well. For example, Douglass's fascination with self-reliance and heroic male individualism thoroughly shapes his conception of Madison as a leader.[37] Thus, although there were reportedly several key instigators of the *Creole* revolt, Douglass omits mention of all but Washington, thereby highlighting the individual nature of his protagonist's triumph as well as the man's superiority in comparison to his fellow blacks.[38] Furthermore, Douglass's celebration of solitary male heroism leaves little room for women. In his 1845 narrative, critics have noted, he downplays the role played by female slaves in his life. As David Leverenz points out, Douglass's wife, Anna, "seems an afterthought. He introduces her to his readers as a rather startling appendage to his escape and marries her almost in the same breath."[39] At first glance, Douglass's treatment of black women in "The

Heroic Slave" appears to differ considerably from that in his narrative. Not only does Madison allude frequently to his wife, Susan, but it is her support that enables him to hide in the wilderness for five years. In addition, he is recaptured after his successful flight from slavery because he decides to return to Virginia to rescue her. However, not only do we receive no description of Susan whatsoever but, more significantly, she is rendered voiceless in a text marked, as Henry Louis Gates notes, by "a major emphasis on the powers of the human voice," on the potency of speech acts.[40] Finally, Douglass has Susan murdered during her attempt to escape with her husband. Her disappearance from the text at this point simply reinforces Washington's heroic isolation.

One way to appreciate fully the strategies underlying the characterization of Madison Washington in "The Heroic Slave" is to compare the novella not just with Douglass's own comments in his 1849 speech but with three other literary dramatizations of the incident—by William Wells Brown in 1863, by Lydia Maria Child in 1866, and by Pauline E. Hopkins in 1901.[41] The most significant ways in which Brown, Child, and Hopkins revise Douglass's rendering of the *Creole* revolt involve the handling of violence in the story, the depiction of Susan, Madison's wife, and the role of whites.[42]

First, Brown, Child, and Hopkins all treat Madison Washington's violence more directly than does Douglass in "The Heroic Slave." In describing Washington's recapture, for example, Brown does not qualify the slave's fierce resistance:

> Observed by the overseer, . . . the fugitive [was] secured ere he could escape with his wife; but the heroic slave did not yield until he with a club had laid three of his assailants upon the ground with his manly blows; and not then until weakened by loss of blood.[43]

In depicting the revolt itself, both Brown and Douglass stress Washington's determination to shed no more blood than is absolutely necessary. However, Brown differs sharply from Douglass by locating his hero at the very center of the violence:

> Drawing his old horse pistol from under his coat, he [a white "negro-driver"] fired at one of the blacks and killed him. The next moment [he] lay dead upon the deck, for Madison had struck him with a capstan

bar. . . . The battle was Madison's element, and he plunged into it without any care for his own preservation or safety. He was an instrument of
enthusiasm, whose value and whose place was in his inspiration. "If the
fire of heaven was in my hands, I would throw it at these cowardly
whites," said he to his companions, before leaving their cabin. But in this
he did not mean revenge, only the possession of his freedom and that of
his fellow-slaves. Merritt and Gifford, the first and second mates of the
vessel, both attacked the heroic slave at the same time. Both were
stretched out upon the deck with a single blow each, but were merely
wounded; they were disabled, and that was all that Madison cared for
for the time being.[44]

Like Douglass in "The Heroic Slave," Brown, Child, and Hopkins all
portray Madison Washington as a superman, but their hero is one
whose strength, courage, and power find unmistakably violent outlet.

In their treatment of Susan, Madison's wife, Brown, Child, and
Hopkins again revise Douglass quite extensively. In contrast to the face-
less character we encounter in "The Heroic Slave," William Wells
Brown's Susan receives an even more elaborate description than does
Washington himself:

> In the other cabin, among the slave women, was one whose beauty at
> once attracted attention. Though not tall, she yet had a majestic figure.
> Her well-moulded shoulders, prominent bust, black hair which hung in
> ringlets, mild blue eyes, finely-chiselled mouth, with a splendid set of
> teeth, a turned and well-rounded chin, skin marbled with the animation
> of life, and veined by blood given to her by her master, she stood as the
> representative of two races. With only one eighth of African, she was
> what is called at the south an "octoroon." It was said that her grandfa-
> ther had served his country in the revolutionary war, as well as in both
> houses of Congress. This was Susan, the wife of Madison.[45]

Furthermore, Brown arranges for Susan to be among the freed blacks
when her husband takes over the *Creole*. Susan's death *before* the revolt
in "The Heroic Slave" reflects both Douglass's lack of interest in incorporating a sentimental reunion into his happy ending and his conception of Washington as an isolated male protagonist. In Brown's vision
of Washington's successful heroic action, liberation leads to a restora-

tion of the integrity of the domestic circle, the black family unit; in Douglass's, it does not.[46]

Although similar in phrasing to Brown's, Child's depiction of Susan manifests an added concern with the beautiful slave as the embodiment of endangered womanhood. Child describes Susan's peculiar plight this way: "[A] handsome woman, who is a slave, is constantly liable to insult and wrong, from which an enslaved husband has no power to protect her."[47] Hopkins, in turn, both corrects and elaborates on Child's comment not only by showing that Madison Monroe (as she calls her hero) *does,* in fact, save his wife from sexual assault but also by making Susan almost as much the protagonist of the story as Madison. In Hopkins's rendering, most of the drama on board the *Creole* centers not on the revolt but on the white captain's attempted rape of Susan, which coincidentally occurs on the same night that Madison has planned his uprising.[48] Even the syntax of the emotional reunion scene reinforces Hopkins's focus on Susan: "*She* was locked to his breast; *she* clung to him convulsively. Unnerved at last by the revulsion to more than relief and ecstasy, *she* broke into wild sobs, while the astonished company closed around them with loud hurrahs."[49] On the one hand, Hopkins implicitly rejects Douglass's obsession with masculine heroism as she gives Susan not only a voice in the text but also force—the first act of black violent resistance aboard the *Creole* is Susan's striking the white captain when he kisses her in her sleep. On the other hand, by having Madison fortuitously appear and interrupt the assault on Susan like some white knight rushing to the aid of his damsel, Hopkins ultimately falls back on the conventions of the sentimental romance. Hopkins does succeed in reinserting the black female into a field of action dominated, in Douglass's fiction, by the male. However, in claiming for Susan a conventional role generally denied black women, she necessarily endorses the accompanying male paradigm in her depiction of Madison, a paradigm drawn from the same set of gender constructions that provides Douglass with his heroic model.

Finally, of the four versions of the *Creole* incident under consideration here, Douglass places the greatest emphasis upon the role played by whites in the protagonist's life. Granted, for much of "The Heroic Slave," Madison Washington is the epitome of manly self-reliance. At key points in the text, however, Douglass qualifies the isolated nature of the protagonist's liberatory struggle not by creating ties between Madison and a black community but rather by developing a close relationship between Washington and a white northerner named Listwell. As Robert Stepto suggests, Douglass probably modeled Listwell on the abolitionist James Gurney.[50] Yet Douglass claims in his 1849 speech on the *Creole* incident that another abolitionist, Robert Purvis, also played an important role as Washington's friend and advisor. Douglass's decision to incorporate the white Gurney and not the black Purvis into his story reflects his desire to reach and move white readers. Like George Harris's former employer, Mr. Wilson, in *Uncle Tom's Cabin*, Listwell gives the white audience a figure with whom to identify; as Listwell comes to endorse Washington's behavior—to evolve literally before our eyes into an abolitionist—Douglass hopes that the white reader will too.

In none of the three later versions of the revolt do we encounter a white character who plays the central role that Listwell does in "The Heroic Slave." Brown, Child, and Hopkins all depict a sympathetic white named Dickson who employs Madison after he first escapes; but there is no great intimacy between the men. Furthermore, whereas Douglass has Listwell slip Washington the files and saws that he subsequently uses to free himself and his fellow slaves on board the *Creole,* Brown, Child, and Hopkins all tell us that Madison obtains these implements on his own, before he returns to Virginia in the ill-fated attempt to free his wife. By having Listwell provide Washington with the means of his escape, Douglass doubtless intends the white audience to see that they should not only sympathize with the slaves' plight but work actively to help them gain their freedom. As a result, however, he implies that even the most self-reliant and gifted black male slave needs white assistance.

In composing "The Heroic Slave," Frederick Douglass could have easily taken a strictly documentary approach. The unadorned story of Madison Washington's exploits certainly contained sufficient drama and courageous action to hold an audience. Moreover, Douglass's writing to that point had been primarily journalistic; the novella would hardly have seemed the form with which he would have felt most comfortable. In depicting Washington in fiction, however, Douglass ambitiously set out to do more than demonstrate the slave's determination to be free; he sought to transform his black male protagonist into a heroic exemplar who would both win white converts to the antislavery struggle and firmly establish the reality of black manhood. The route that Douglass chose in order to achieve these goals was to master the codes of Anglo-American bourgeois white masculinity, and his own internalization of the values informing mainstream masculine paradigms made this strategy relatively easy to adopt. In addition, as Robert Stepto observes, the act of fictionalizing this story of successful violent male resistance to slavery offered Douglass the opportunity not only to express his ideological independence from Garrison but also to present a potent alternative to the model of the black male hero as victim promoted so successfully in Stowe's *Uncle Tom's Cabin*.[51] Ultimately, however, Douglass's ambitious agenda was undermined by his intuitive sense that he could challenge white preconceptions regarding race only so far without alienating the audience that he sought to win and by problems inherent in the masculine ideal that he so eagerly endorsed.

Douglass's strategies for appealing to white readers in "The Heroic Slave" were flawed in at least three important ways. The first involves the extent to which his representation of Madison Washington as the embodiment of black manhood inevitably emphasizes the distance between his hero and the average slave. In celebrating this unusually self-aware, courageous, aggressive, conventionally educated, and charismatic figure, Douglass never explains his attractive capacities in terms that would encourage the reader to extrapolate a general sense of the black potential for heroic action from the extraordinarily endowed Washington. The gap between Douglass's protagonist and less gifted blacks is widened even further by the presence of Listwell. That the one character both emotionally and intellectually closest to Washington is white indicates the extent to which Madison's strengths and capabilities, training, and manner distinguish him from other slaves and thereby weaken his usefulness as a counterargument against claims that most blacks were inferior to whites.

A second problem derives from Douglass's attempt, in William Andrews's words, "to domesticate a violence that easily could have been judged as alien and threatening to everything from Christian morality to the law of the high seas."[52] Employing a common abolitionist gambit, Douglass works to establish a link between Washington's rebellion and the American War of Independence. However, doing so, Andrews contends, precipitates Douglass and other antislavery writers into a troublesome conceptual trap: "Even as they violate the ideals of Uncle Tom's pacifism and declare blacks free from bloodguiltiness for killing their masters, they justify such actions by an appeal to the authorizing mythology of an oppressive culture."[53] That is, the very figures whose patriotic heritage Douglass claims for his hero won their fame by working to establish a social order in which the enslavement of blacks like Madison was a crucial component.

In his careful packaging of Washington's manly heroism, Douglass also chooses not to dramatize a single act of physical violence performed by his protagonist. One might argue that this approach reinforces the statesmanlike quality that Douglass may have been striving to imbue in his portrayal of Washington—after all, how often do depictions (literary and otherwise) of George Washington fully convey the violent nature of his heroism? Ultimately, however, Douglass's caution here strips his fictional slave rebel of much of his radical, subversive force. As Douglass knew from personal experience, revolution usually entails violence, and black self-assertion in the face of racist attempts at dehumanization often necessitates a direct and forceful assault upon the very structures of social power that provide most whites (especially white males) with a sense of self-worth, security, and potency.

In his public statements regarding the *Creole* revolt both before and after he wrote "The Heroic Slave," Douglass apparently felt little need to undermine the implications of the black militancy that Madison Washington embodied. We have already examined his celebration of Washington's heroism in his 1847 speech. In commenting on West Indian emancipation ten years later, Douglass goes even further:

> Joseph Cinque on the deck of the Amistad, did that which should make his name dear to us. He bore nature's burning protest against slavery. Madison Washington who struck down his oppressor on the deck of the Creole, is more worthy to be remembered than the colored man who shot Pitcairn at Bunker Hill.[54]

Granted, the exhaustion of Douglass's patience with the limited efficacy of moral suasion as an antislavery tactic surely informs this quite remarkable repudiation of the popular appeal to an American patriotic past as a way to validate black slave violence. I would argue, however, that there was something about the mode of fiction itself (and possibly about autobiography as well) that stifled the radical nature of Douglass's anger. The "controlled aggression" that Donald Gibson sees as informing every aspect of Douglass's *Narrative* underlies the depiction of Madison Washington in "The Heroic Slave" as well.[55] The key may lie in what Houston Baker describes as the "task of transmuting an authentic, unwritten self—a self that exists outside the conventional literary discourse structure of a white reading public—into a literary representation." Baker continues: "The simplest, and perhaps the most effective, way of proceeding is for the narrator to represent his 'authentic' self as a figure embodying the public virtues and values esteemed by his intended audience."[56] Baker's argument applies with particular force to "The Heroic Slave," for it appears that the freer rein the form offered Douglass in his depiction of the exemplary black male hero paradoxically also confronted him more directly than possibly ever before with the restrictions imposed by the expectations of the whites to whom he was appealing.

The third weakness in his attempt to use fiction to shape his white reader's attitudes toward slavery is structural. That is, by rendering the *Creole* revolt through the recollections of a white sailor, Douglass cuts us off not just from Washington's heroic violence but from his emotional responses to the dramatic events in which he plays such a crucial part. William Wells Brown's straightforward depiction of Washington's rebellious behavior in his sketch dramatizes by contrast the extent to which Madison's role in "The Heroic Slave" is primarily catalytic, as Douglass emphasizes through shifts in point of view his impact upon the whites around him. Such elaborate formal manipulations result in what Raymond Hedin terms "an emphatically structured fiction," which serves to convey a sense of the writer's control and thus to permit a release of anger in a rational and somewhat unthreatening manner.[57] As one result of this strategy, at the end of the novella Washington stands not as the embodiment of expressive, forceful self-determination but as an object of white discourse, a figure whose self-assertive drive to tell his own story—to reclaim, in a sense, his own subjectivity—is ultimately subordinated by Douglass to a secondhand rendition by a white sailor who did not even witness the full range of Washington's heroic action. This decentering of the black voice in "The Heroic Slave" may be the greatest casualty of Douglass's polemical appeal to white sympathies.

Finally, like the majority of nineteenth-century black spokespersons, Douglass was unable or unwilling to call into question the white bourgeois paradigm of manhood itself. Consequently, his celebration of black heroism was subverted from the outset by the racist, sexist, and elitist assumptions upon which the Anglo-American male ideal was constructed and that so thoroughly permeated the patriarchal structure of slavery. As Valerie Smith points out, "Within his critique of American cultural practices, then, is an affirmation of its definitions of manhood and power." That is, "Douglass . . . attempts to articulate a radical position using the discourse he shares with those against whom he speaks. What begins as an indictment of mainstream practice actually authenticates one of its fundamental assumptions."[58] It should go without saying that one can scarcely imagine how Douglass might have extricated himself from the conceptual briar patch into which he had fallen, given both the political purposes to which he directed his fiction and the extent to which he sought validation in the most conventional, gender-specific terms for himself in particular and for black men in general from a white society unwilling to acknowledge the complex humanity of blacks in any unqualified way.

The dilemma so powerfully rendered in Douglass's attempt to dramatize the Madison Washington story in fiction is one that has plagued most African-American fiction writers—and, indeed, most African-American thinkers—over the past century and a half.[59] His failures do not qualify the boldness of his attempt, and one can argue that the short-term benefits of his approach must be taken into account in assessing the overall success of his enterprise. Ultimately, however, Douglass's "The Heroic Slave" may be most valuable insofar as it enables us to understand better the complex internal and external obstacles to a balanced, complex depiction of black men and women in African-American fiction. If nothing else, it leaves us wondering whether the tools of the master can ever be used to achieve the complete liberation of the slave.

Notes

I am grateful to a number of people whose comments and criticisms have been useful in my work in this essay. In particular, I want to thank King-Kok Cheung, Kimberle Crenshaw, and Mary Helen Washington.

1. Albery A. Whitman, *The Rape of Florida* (1885; rpt. Upper Saddle River, N.J.: Gregg, 1970), 8.

2. Frederick Douglass, *Narrative of the Life of Frederick Douglass, an American Slave, Written by Himself,* ed. Houston A. Baker Jr. (1845; rpt. New York: Penguin, 1982), 105, 107.

3. Ibid., 113.

4. David Walker, *Walker's Appeal* (1829; rpt. New York: Arno, 1969), 27.

5. Henry Highland Garnet, *An Address to the Slaves of the United States of America* (1848; rpt. New York: Arno, 1969), 96 (emphasis added). Garnet first delivered this speech in 1843; in 1848 he published it bound together in one volume with Walker's *Appeal*.

6. Calvin Hernton, *The Sexual Mountain and Black Women Writers: Adventures in Sex, Literature, and Real Life* (New York: Anchor/Doubleday, 1987), 38.

7. Barbara Welter, "The Cult of True Womanhood," *American Quarterly* 18 (Sept. 1966): 151–74. For more on nineteenth-century black women's ongoing engagement with this feminine ideal, see Paula Giddings, *When and Where I Enter . . . : The Impact of Black Women on Race and Sex in America* (New York: William Morrow, 1984). Also see the work of, among other scholars, Hazel V. Carby, Barbara Christian, Frances Smith Foster, Deborah McDowell, Valerie Smith, and Mary Helen Washington.

8. Robert Staples, *Black Masculinity: The Black Male's Role in American Society* (San Francisco: Black Scholar, 1982), 2.

9. Review of *Negro-Mania,* by John Campbell, *Southern Quarterly Review* (Jan. 1852): 163–66; emphasis added.

10. James M. McPherson, *The Negro's Civil War* (New York: Vintage, 1965), 101; emphasis added.

11. Ibid., 102.

12. William Wells Brown, *Clotel; or, The President's Daughter* (1853; rpt. New York: Citadel), 171.

13. Ibid., 224.

14. Ibid., 171; William Wells Brown, *Clotelle; A Tale of the Southern States* (1864), rpt. in *William Wells Brown and Clotelle,* by J. Noel Heermance (Hamden, Conn.: Archon, 1969), 46.

15. Brown, *Clotel,* 224; idem, *Clotelle,* 57.

16. Brown, *Clotelle,* 57–58.

17. Ibid., 11.

18. Marian E. Musgrave, "Patterns of Violence and Non-Violence in Pro-Slavery and Anti-Slavery Fiction," *College Language Association Journal* 17 (1973): 426–37. Also see John Demos, "The Antislavery Movement and the Problem of Violent 'Means,'" *New England Quarterly* 37 (1964): 501–26. The literary event before the Civil War that brought the issue of black heroism and violence to center stage was the publication and astounding success of Harriet Beecher Stowe's *Uncle Tom's Cabin.* For a survey of the diverse black literary responses to Stowe's novel, see Richard Yarborough, "Strategies of Black Characterization in *Uncle Tom's Cabin* and the Early Afro-American Novel," in *New Essays on Uncle Tom's Cabin,* ed. Eric J. Sundquist (New York: Cambridge Univ. Press, 1986), 45–84.

19. Brown, *Clotel,* 226.

20. This appeal was complicated by what Sundquist terms "the ambivalence that pre–Civil War generations felt and expressed toward the legacy of the founding fathers" (Eric J. Sundquist, "Slavery, Revolution, and the American Renaissance," in *The American Renaissance Reconsidered: Selected Papers from the English Institute, 1982–83,* ed. Walter Benn Michaels and Donald Pease [Baltimore: Johns Hopkins Univ. Press, 1985], 2).

21. David W. Blight, *Frederick Douglass's Civil War: Keeping Faith in Jubilee* (Baton Rouge: Louisiana State Univ. Press, 1989), 14. Douglass was an especially powerful spokesperson for this view of the war. See, for instance, his "Men of Color, To Arms!" *Frederick Douglass' Monthly* 5 (1863): 801; and "Another Word to Colored Men," *Frederick Douglass' Monthly* 5 (1863): 817–18. For a detailed look at black military involvement in the Civil War, see Mary Frances Berry, *Military Necessity and Civil Rights Policy: Black Citizenship and the Constitution, 1861–1868* (Port Washington, N.Y.: Kennikat, 1977).

22. Garnet, *Address,* 96.

23. Douglass's novella was serialized in his *North Star,* beginning in March 1853; Julia Griffiths also included it in her *Autographs for Freedom* of that year.

24. Frederick Douglass, "The Heroic Slave," in *Autographs for Freedom,* ed. Julia Griffiths (Boston: John P. Jewett, 1853), 179.

25. Douglass, "Slave," 179.

26. "Anti-Colonization Meeting," *North Star,* 2; second emphasis added.

27. Frederick Douglass, *The Claims of the Negro, Ethnologically Considered* (Rochester, N.Y.: Lee, Mann, 1854), 30.

28. Ibid., 31.

29. Waldo Martin, *The Mind of Frederick Douglass* (Chapel Hill: Univ. of North Carolina Press, 1984), 237. For a thorough discussion of Douglass's ethnological views, see 197–250. Much later in life, Douglass called this speech "a very defective production," but Martin argues that Douglass's ethnological views did not change substantially over time (Martin, *Mind,* 230).

30. Douglass, "Slave," 233. In the most thorough modern examination of the *Creole* revolt, Howard Jones reports that Washington was "the slaves' head cook" ("The Peculiar Institution and National Honor: The Case of the *Creole* Slave Revolt," *Civil War History* 21 [Mar. 1975]: 29). If Jones's information is correct, it is understandable that Douglass would refrain from mentioning this somewhat undignified aspect of his hero's life. It should be noted that Jones draws primarily upon testimony provided by white witnesses at an inquiry after the revolt. (See *Senate Documents,* 27th Cong., 2d sess., Jan. 21, 1842, no. 51, 1–46.) One must not take for granted the objectivity of such individuals, most of whom had reasons to create their own fictional versions of the *Creole* incident. For a southern proslavery reading of the event, see the article

"Mutiny and Murder" from the *New Orleans Daily Picayune* (Dec. 3, 1841), in which the author notes with admiration how the captain's dog "fought furiously against the negroes" until he was killed.

31. A number of scholars have examined the strategies that Douglass adopts in shaping the narrator's persona in his autobiographies in general and in this scene with Covey in particular. See, for example, William L. Andrews, *To Tell a Free Story: The First Century of Afro-American Autobiography, 1760–1865* (Urbana: Univ. of Illinois Press, 1986); Houston A. Baker Jr., *The Journey Back: Issues in Black Literature and Criticism* (Chicago: Univ. of Chicago Press, 1980); Frances Smith Foster, *Witnessing Slavery: The Development of Ante-bellum Slave Narratives* (Westport, Conn.: Greenwood, 1979); Donald B. Gibson, "Reconciling Public and Private in Frederick Douglass' *Narrative,*" *American Literature* 57 (1985): 549–69; David Leverenz, *Manhood and the American Renaissance* (Ithaca: Cornell Univ. Press, 1989); Valerie Smith, *Self-Discovery and Authority in Afro-American Narrative* (Cambridge: Harvard Univ. Press, 1987); Robert B. Stepto, *From behind the Veil: A Study of Afro-American Narrative* (Urbana: Univ. of Illinois Press, 1979); Peter F. Walker, *Moral Choices: Memory, Desire, and Imagination in Nineteenth-Century American Abolition* (Baton Rouge: Louisiana State Univ. Press, 1978).

32. Howard Jones notes, "Casualties were light on both sides because there was little resistance to the revolt and because Washington and another mutineer, Elijah Morris, restrained the others from killing the whites" (Jones, "Creole," 30).

33. Douglass, "Slave," 234–35.

34. Ibid., 232.

35. Ronald G. Walters, *The Antislavery Appeal: American Abolitionism after 1830* (Baltimore: Johns Hopkins Univ. Press, 1976). One also wonders if it is mere coincidence that the version of Douglass's speech published in the *Liberator* (run by the pacifist William Lloyd Garrison) matches that in the *North Star* exactly, except for the striking omission of Douglass's comments on the *Creole* episode ("Great Anti-Colonization Mass Meeting," *Liberator,* 11 May 1849, 74). This speech contains some of Douglass's most openly militant statements. Perhaps the best known is his prediction that "unless the American people shall break every yoke, and let the oppressed go free, that spirit in man which abhors chains . . . will lead those sable arms that have long been engaged in cultivating, beautifying and adorning the South to spread death and devastation there." This portion of Douglass's comment was, in fact, carried in the *Liberator* in full.

36. For Douglass's stance on violence as an antislavery weapon, see, among other studies, Allison Davis, *Leadership, Love, and Aggression* (New York: Harcourt Brace Jovanovich, 1983); Philip S. Foner, *Frederick Douglass* (1950; rpt. New York: Citadel, 1969); and Martin, *Mind.*

37. Douglass's speech "Self-Made Men" was one of his most often-delivered presentations. See Martin, *Mind,* 253–78.

38. See Jones, "*Creole,*" 30 n. 7.

39. Leverenz, *Manhood,* 128. Frances Smith Foster suggests that Douglass's withholding information regarding Anna enables him to suppress certain positive aspects of his slave experience (*Witnessing,* 113). Also see Gibson, "Public and Private," 551.

40. Henry Louis Gates Jr., *Figures in Black: Words, Signs, and the "Racial" Self* (New York: Oxford Univ. Press, 1987), 107. The closest we get to hearing Susan speak is Madison's explanation that in his extreme concern for her safety after his flight to Canada, he "could almost hear her voice, saying, 'O Madison! Madison! will you then leave me here? can you leave me here to die? No! no! you will come! you will come!'" (Douglass, "Slave," 219).

41. William Wells Brown, "Madison Washington," in *The Black Man, His Antecedents, His Genius, and His Achievements* (1863; rpt. New York: Arno, 1969), 75–83; Lydia Maria Child, "Madison Washington," in *The Freedmen's Book* (Boston: Ticknor and Fields, 1866), 147–54; and Pauline E. Hopkins, "A Dash for Liberty," *Colored American Magazine* 3 (Aug. 1901): 243–47.

42. Some of the minor distinctions among these four versions are revealing as well. For example, Brown's description of Washington is far more ethnically specific than Douglass's: "Born of African parentage, with no mixture in his blood, he was one of the handsomest of his race" ("Washington," 75). This emphasis on Washington's African background recalls Brown's treatment of Jerome in the 1864 *Clotelle,* published one year after *The Black Man* appeared. It must be noted that there are several instances where Brown, Child, and Hopkins employ remarkably similar phrasing. Brown had appropriated material from Child before, in the first edition of *Clotel.* There is evidence of extensive borrowing here as well—either by Brown from an earlier version of Child's sketch or by Child from Brown's in *The Black Man,* or by both Brown and Child from an earlier text by another writer. In a letter written in 1865, Child had this to say regarding the composition of *The Freedman's Book:*

> The reason my name appears so often in the Index is that I re-wrote all the Biographies. They are not only interspersed with remarks of my own, but are so completely and entirely told in my own way, that I cannot, with any propriety ascribe them to anyone else. . . .
>
> You will find William and Ellen Crafts the most interesting. I collected it from various sources; some of it verbal information. James Madison Washington is also very romantic, and every word of it true. (Child to James T. Fields, 27 Aug. 1865, *Lydia Maria Child: Selected Letters, 1817–1880,* ed. Milton Meltzer and Patricia G. Holland, assoc. ed. Francine Krasno [Amherst: Univ. of Massachusetts Press, 1982], 458–59.)

Pauline Hopkins was familiar with the work of both Brown (whom she had met personally) and Child, and thus would likely have encountered their versions of the *Creole* revolt. To complicate matters, Hopkins cites neither Brown nor Child as her primary source but rather an article by Thomas Wentworth Higginson.

43. Brown, "Washington," 80.

44. Ibid., 83.

45. Ibid., 81. Brown's portrayal of Susan closely resembles the sentimental depiction of his light-skinned heroines in *Clotel*.

46. We find what is perhaps the first suggestion that Madison Washington's wife may have been aboard the *Creole* in "Madison Washington: Another Chapter in his History," *Liberator,* June 10, 1842. In his recent article on "The Heroic Slave," William Andrews quite rightly suggests: "This effort by the *Liberator* to infer a romantic plot underlying the *Creole* incidents testifies to the strong desire of American abolitionism for a story, if not *the* story, about Washington that would realize him as a powerful symbol of black antislavery heroism" ("The Novelization of Voice in Early African American Narrative," *PMLA* 105 [1990]: 28).

47. Child, "Washington," 147.

48. Characteristically, Hopkins provides an extensive discussion of Susan's mixed racial pedigree. For a look at the role of ancestry in her most important fictional work, see Yarborough, introduction to *Contending Forces,* by Pauline E. Hopkins (1900; rpt. New York: Oxford Univ. Press, 1988), xxvii–xlviii.

49. Hopkins, "Liberty," 247; emphasis added.

50. Robert B. Stepto, "Storytelling in Early Afro-American Fiction: Frederick Douglass's "The Heroic Slave," *Georgia Review* 36 (summer 1982): 363 n. 8.

51. For a further discussion of what Robert B. Stepto calls the "antislavery textual conversation" between Stowe's *Uncle Tom's Cabin* and Douglass's "The Heroic Slave," see Stepto's "Sharing the Thunder: The Literary Exchanges of Harriet Beecher Stowe, Henry Bibb, and Frederick Douglass," in *New Essays on Uncle Tom's Cabin,* 135–53. Stepto contends that Washington's revolt also appealed to Douglass because it "in some measure revises his *own* story" ("Thunder," 359).

52. William L. Andrews, *To Tell a Free Story: The First Century of Afro-American Autobiography, 1760–1865* (Urbana: Univ. of Illinois Press, 1986), 186.

53. Ibid., 187.

54. Philip S. Foner, *The Life and Writings of Frederick Douglass,* vol. 2, *Pre–Civil War Decade, 1850–1860* (New York: International, 1950), 438.

55. Gibson, "Public and Private," 563. See also David Leverenz's discus-

sion of the tension between Douglass's "genteel self-control and his aggressiveness" in the 1855 edition of his narrative (*Manhood,* 114).

56. Baker, *Journey,* 39.

57. Raymond Hedin, "The Structuring of Emotion in Black American Fiction," *Novel* 16 (fall 1982): 37.

58. Smith, *Self-Discovery,* 20, 27. Also see Baker, *Journey,* 32–46; Leverenz, *Manhood,* 108–34; and Annette Niemtzow, "The Problematic of Self in Autobiography: The Example of the Slave Narrative," in *The Art of Slave Narrative,* ed. John Sekora and Darwin T. Turner (Macomb: Western Illinois Univ. Press, 1982), 96–109.

59. In "In the First Place: Making Frederick Douglass and the Afro-American Narrative Tradition," Deborah McDowell examines how the tendency to give Douglass's *Narrative,* with its uncritical inscription of sexist Anglo-American concepts of gender, a central position in constructing the African-American literary tradition marginalizes black women's texts (*Critical Essays on Frederick Douglass,* ed. William Andrews [Boston: G. K. Hall, 1991], 192–214).

Santa Claus Ain't a Real Man

Incidents and Gender

ANNE BRADFORD WARNER

We were rowed ashore, and went boldly through the streets, to my
grandmother's. I wore my sailor's clothes, and had blackened my
face with charcoal. I passed several people whom I knew. The father
of my children came so near that I brushed against his arm;
but he had no idea who it was.

— HARRIET JACOBS

IN THIS scene from *Incidents in the Life of a Slave Girl,* Harriet Jacobs
creates a moment that mines the ironies of an identity strangely empowered and doubled: a woman in a man's clothes brushes unrecognized
the man with whom she has experienced sexual intimacy; a familiar
and hunted African-American slave, "blackened" with charcoal, passes
as an unfamiliar sailor; the return home constitutes a stage in an escape.
Through this self-portrait of a dark-skinned male stranger, Jacobs conveys the powerful existence of a second and parallel history of African-
American female resistance, unrecognized by the official society.

Such passages, embedded in an apparently ingenuous and sentimental narration that is "strictly true," suggest the actual distance of a
female slave from the culturally constructed representations of her by
the dominant society.[1] This passage, in Jacobs's careful way of doing
things, may indicate not only hidden aspects of Brent's relationship with
Mr. Sands but also Jacobs's relation with her designated white readers
who must thus be careful not to "brush" past important "incidents"
in this intimate story of a woman's life. Frances Foster discusses Jacobs's
literary play around color and gender lines in her essay "Discourse of
Distrust";[2] such passages also suggest the greater diversity of readership

and the function of encoded messages Foster implies. White female readers can be brought to hear when Jacobs asserts directly that "the slave woman ought not to be judged by the same standard as others" (56), but such readers must work harder to hear how Jacobs tells in more covert ways the story of a female trickster, a transformer of the culture, a shape-shifting witness to an untold tale. Jacobs's project goes beyond the construction of a representative generic female hero. While Linda Brent fits Joanne Braxton's formulation of the "outraged mother" and Valerie Smith's "self-in-relation,"[3] neither of these interpretations fully describes the narrator. It seems, instead, that Jacobs herself undermines the very concept of a static character, even of a stable text. *Incidents* is a tale of possibilities, of shifting gender roles, mirrored figures, and doubling. Jacobs challenges old authorities and introduces new patterns, patterns of spiritual promise; she does this by reshaping the whole notion of a narrating persona—not as a static type in a stable text but as a trickster in a world of linguistic and cultural possibility.

It is on this female trickster—and the broadest possible implications of such a figure—that I wish to focus as a way of grasping a whole picture of the shifting, subversive, spiritual, and satiric narrative called *Incidents in the Life of a Slave Girl*. I propose that the very concept of a fragmented and shifting perspective is articulated in the title of the narrative, which makes repetitions and reversals, inversions and subversions, disguise and deceit—all kinds of doublings with a difference— the very fabric of its language. The trickster understands, above all, that language is not static, that no text is static, that interpretation is power because words may easily be turned upon themselves. Full of empowering repetitions and reversals, *Incidents* uses the techniques of the slave trickster tales but is not strictly about their sort of cunning power. Instead, the text partakes of the spirit of the folk festival described within its chapters and concerns the kind of spiritual rebirth out of brutality that such festivals produce and that Bakhtin describes in the medieval folk carnival of Rabelais.

The trickster motif in Jacobs's work may best be understood through an examination of how her "feminist" voice (so clearly rendered in criticism about Jacobs's revisionist treatment of sentimental discourse) interacts with her use of carnivalesque parody, her adaptations of tropes and themes from African-American animal trickster tales, and her active signifying along the lines described by Henry Louis

Gates. In such contexts Jacobs blends her female voice with African-American, male-identified ritual in order to expand the gender boundaries within the tradition and to locate the spiritual groundwork for slave resistance.

Both Joanne Braxton and William Andrews refer to Harriet Jacobs/ Linda Brent as trickster. Speaking of her "sass" to Dr. Flint, her concealment, and "the atmosphere of moral ambiguity that surrounds her," Braxton calls Brent "a feminine reflection of the trickster figure."[4] In his analysis of the dialogization of *Incidents* and Jacobs's warfare from her place of concealment, Andrews argues that her "first experiments in writing let her play the role of slave trickster lodged in the interstices of a social structure that she pries apart with her spying eyes and ventriloquistic voice."[5] It is my contention that these claims quite accurately reflect Jacobs's techniques and invite others to push such arguments further. Jacobs appropriates the trickster role throughout the text; it is a fixed feature, perhaps the only fixed feature, of her narrative empowerment. The subversions of sentimental literature and true womanhood convey the same reversals of situation that characterize the trickster tales. Jacobs speaks not only with the authority of her Christian faith but also with the cultural authority of the African-American folk context—frequently presented in terms of her affirmation of the slave community. This second context invites her to express a wide range of emotions and opens a new ground for female signifying upon restrictions within her own culture.

A brief look at the dynamic of the trickster tales will illuminate the central figure and its relation to the narrator of *Incidents*. Henry Louis Gates argues that African trickster figures, especially from the Yoruba and the Fon cultures, are "fundamental, divine terms of mediation: as tricksters they are mediators and their mediations are tricks"; they are male figures representing "generation and fecundity."[6] The trickster is a spiritual figure that serves to reshape the dynamics of power. In his study of African-American adaptations of these trickster tales, Lawrence Levine observes that the figure becomes thoroughly humanized, though the central figure may retain the form of an animal. In fact, the most recognizable survivals from African sources are the animal tales—those with the hare and the spider. The central figure of these stories is without apparent power and must outwit the stronger figure, reversing established power and status. Characteristically, these African-American tales carry on an "assault upon deeply ingrained and culturally sanctioned values."[7] The motive in such tales moves beyond survival to a kind of spiritual or material advancement, and often the central figure must find means that are "morally tainted." The plot of these tales conveys a world in anarchy, in moral chaos, a world without hope of justice. Levine argues that such tales supply "psychic relief from arbitrary authority."[8]

This list of qualities certainly suggests the Harriet Jacobs/Linda Brent figure and her situation—her apparent powerlessness, her assault on southern morality and the church, the moral ambiguity of her methods for resisting Flint, the failure of justice, her temporary empowerment through concealment enabling her to move beyond the goal of survival, the writing of letters and telling of the tale as "psychic relief." But her narrative extends beyond the worldview expressed in these trickster tales, appropriating other, more spiritual elements of the slave culture. Further, Jacobs alters the phallic competition both Levine and Gates cite as characteristic of trickster figures. Still, she claims the trickster's strategy to win through cunning and signifying, winning through reversal and ridicule of the competitor's method.

In his study of the trickster motif, Gates suggests that women can also signify, especially upon their male counterparts. His most famous example of signifying, Zora Neale Hurston's parody of a passage in Frederick Douglass's *Narrative,* concerns Douglass's apostrophe to the free sails on the Chesapeake.[9] Jacobs, in her time, echoes and reverses the gist of that apostrophe, as she sails to freedom: "And how shall I describe my sensations when we were fairly sailing on Chesapeake Bay. O, the beautiful sunshine! the exhilarating breeze? and I could enjoy them without fear or restraint" (158). Trickster signifying is certainly a part of her mid-nineteenth-century tradition.

Levine, though he explains that the great majority of African-American trickster tales feature males as their central figure, cites a significant female variation: tales of Anansi, the spider, took one special form in the Carolinas and Georgia, with the figure of Ann Nancy or Aunt Nancy. One such North Carolina story is told with phrasing that is echoed in Jacobs's own writing. Ann Nancy, caught stealing Buzzard's food, obtains her freedom through her wily humility, saying that Buzzard "sail in the clouds while she 'bliged to crawl in the dirt." But her sense of insult is so great that she deals Buzzard another trick, scalding and balding his head. In this tale, while Ann Nancy "spin her house she just study constant how she gwine get the best of every creeter."[10]

It seems less than an accident that Jacobs, as she writes of the tedious progress of her "poor Book," describes "its Chrysalis state" and claims, "though I can never make it a butterfly I am satisfied to have it creep meekly among some of the humbler bugs" (238). Without being too precise about entomology here, I speculate that Jacobs has seen the empowerment of these "humbler bugs" and chooses to work her own transformations on the spider trickster. But, instead of the self-spinning spider, Jacobs alludes to the shaping of a chrysalis, a spinning for re-birth.

Jacobs through Brent, with her "spying eyes and ventriloquistic voice," appropriates the role of male trickster to make her own revisions. Her years of invisibility, confinement, and even near paralysis invite the plot in which the weak figure wins through wit. Her literary assaults on Dr. Flint, long dead but not forgiven, are deeply colored by the energy of this folk tradition, its pragmatism and amorality, and its "latent yearning for structure, for justice, for reason . . . not to be had in this world." [11] But finally, from freedom, Jacobs modifies the trickster figure with more benign but equally empowering tricks and significations—with far more hope, perhaps, than the slave teller.

One modification, or rather extension, of the trickster strategies in Jacobs involves her dialogization of *Incidents* and finally her use of the carnivalesque.[12] In the "sass" of the dramatic encounters between Flint and Brent, the reader is a witness not only to the cunning of the trickster's revision of language but also to the competing worldviews of slave owner and resisting slave. However, Jacobs's propositions are not only voiced by Brent; the writer creates other dialogues that render a diversity of voiced values.

The spirit of revolution captured in Bakhtin's *Rabelais and His World* has significant kinship with Jacobs's own use of the "Johnkannau" festivities in chapter 22 of *Incidents*. Here the official society allows a temporary reversal of power—of the sort a trickster might arrange—but in this case a community of slaves, organized with costumes, music, lyrics, enacts a ritual older than their life in the New World to "uncrown" the established order. Bakhtin says of the medieval folk carnivals, "They were the second life of the people, who for a time entered the utopian realm of community, freedom, equality, and abundance." [13] Like the Johnkannau festivals, medieval carnivals often marked the end of the year, secular or religious, and the beginning of the new. Mocking both tyrants and time, as Bakhtin describes the festival, "the clown was first disguised as a king, but once his reign had come to an end his costume was changed, 'travestied,' to turn him once more into a clown." [14] Jacobs describes the Johnkannau leaders but does not tell the reader what other later commentators have included: that the leader or "king" along with others wore masks with distorted features, painted white "with something like buckram." And carnivalesque laughter ("the air of gruesome mirth") accompanies the revolutionary spirit of the occasion. [15] Thus, the official white society was rendered in parody. This festive laughter, Bakhtin maintains about medieval carnivals, "created no dogmas and could not become authoritarian; it did not convey fear but a feeling of strength. It was linked with the procreating act, with birth, renewal, fertility, abundance." [16]

In the central chapters of *Incidents*, Brent becomes a trickster giving voice and language to unrecognized figures of resistance: Mrs. Flint, Aunt Martha, Ben, Peter, Betty, Luke, the local militia, the captain of the ship on which Brent escapes—each speaks for a specific set of values. Their positions are set in play in relation to each other. Often, though not always, confrontations involve the philosophical oppositions between slave and free, between the folk and the official society. The narrator uses the subversive voices of others to mirror her own; she herself uses shifting authorities—the Bible, the Declaration of Independence, folk beliefs, traditions of resistance—in shaping responses to the arbitrary powers that so govern her life. This multiplicity of voices, these competing authorities, especially as they expose the sham morality of the slavocracy, move toward the carnivalesque, toward the dramatization of folk resistance.

Jacobs's strategy here reveals commitment to a war that must be fought for reversal of authoritarian uses of language. In chapter 22, "Christmas Festivities," her description of the Johnkannaus becomes a central trope for such resistance to authority. [17] Crossing boundaries of both the folk and the dominant community, she deliberately blends her narrating voice with an all-male raillery. Here the Jacobs/Brent narrator most clearly enacts a female appropriation of the African-American trickster figure—a character of many shapes, always diminutive and always acting from the margins. Jacobs's voice emphasizes the laughter and mock ritual that unmask the authority of the official society. This New World carnival provides the one day that slaves may be lawless, may capture "many a pig or turkey" and "regale [the] ears of any white man or child who refuses to give them a trifle." By describing the spectacle—the leaders "in calico wrappers" with a brightly striped net "thrown over them," with cow's tails and horns (118–19), Jacobs draws attention to the symbolic metamorphosis, the many forms that become a part of the celebration. She also conveys the order behind the raucous bands, the musicians keeping time and the carefully composed songs. Likewise, in her own composition, the apparent candor and spontaneity are carefully orchestrated.

Jacobs makes a point to describe this highly structured festival (performed within the U.S. only on the eastern coast of North Carolina). The patterns of the slave trade brought a concentration of Nigerians and Nigerian-influenced Dahomeans to these coastal plantations. The literature of that area indicates that "it was only because the original Kuners and their descendants in America were slaves that the women and children were able to congregate before them to be entertained." The ceremony, called John Canoe or John Kunering (or Johnkannau), closely resembles the Egungun harvest festival honoring the ancestors of the Yoruba in southern Nigeria. In that setting the men, who wear masks to embody the ancestral figure, take part in a night of prayer, a procession into the village, and a dance. Women were not allowed to participate in the ceremony. At the same time, there was a second form of Kunering with the addition of men masquerading as women, apparently a ritual influenced by the Dahomean presence.[18] Commentators on postbellum festivals in North Carolina note that all participants "were men, but a few wore the clothes and acted the parts of women. Both the leaders and the 'women' actors wore the white Kuner masks."[19] It is clear that the entire Edenton community gathered to see this festival, with companies of more than one hundred men pouring through the close streets of the small colonial town. The Christmas season and the gift giving of that Christian holiday were incorporated in the festival. Such an occasion must have embodied great spiritual—and political—power for those who understood its function as resistance.

With her description Harriet Jacobs blends her woman's voice with this all-male ritual, binding together male and female. With this act she also reshapes the Christian vision so prominent in the narrative. In this scene, as well as others, Jacobs lays African-retained and Christian practices side by side, shaping a spiritual coherence out of these dualities. Thus, Jacobs participates in what Frances Foster points out as "the ecumenism of early African American women's literature," its African and American "faith in the power of the Word," and the extraordinary tradition of spiritual autobiography and conversion narrative.[20] The integration of Christian and African spiritual beliefs occurs in the "Christmas Festivities" chapter of *Incidents* as well as elsewhere in the narrative. Kim Connor points out such a combination in the graveyard scene, which dramatizes the narrator's decision to seek her freedom. As Jacobs/Brent visited this sacred place, she observes "a black stump, at the head of [her] mother's grave . . . all that remained of a tree [her] father had planted." She heard her father's voice urging escape as she passed "the wreck of the old meeting house" (90–91). As Connor argues, the scene evokes both Christian and African spiritual traditions, combining the two: "Linda's response to this sacred place and the presence of spirits . . . indicates her faith went beyond the simple rudiments of Christianity as presented by the slaveholders to encompass an African concept of God as an indwelling spirit."[21]

Affirming the combination of several traditions are Jacobs's references to the "spirits" in her letters to Amy Post.[22] I speculate that the year or more that Jacobs spent in Rochester at the home of Quaker spiritualists increased her hope that Christian belief could reach beyond doctrinal limits, that women could be empowered by their gifts of vision, and that all might embrace the multiple concerns that so preoccupied the Rochester community—abolition, feminism, and spiritualism. It is clear that the African-American women's literary tradition also integrates such multiple perspectives. Jacobs's evocation of the Johnkannau festival with her trickster voice superimposed upon it also suggests her ability to deconstruct and, perhaps then, to reconcile a range of dichotomies, of false oppositions—of gender, race, religion, class. There is no doubt that Jacobs values interdependence and possesses a sense of the collective, but the fact is that her forms of collectivity radically alter all traditional boundaries between male and female, African traditional religion and Christianity, black and white.

Though Jacobs uses the carnival as a combining and regenerative force in her narrative, it also functions as a mode of disguise and empowerment for the trickster-narrator. I want to devote the remainder of this essay to two important forms of empowerment enabled by the narrator's trickster techniques. The first is her development of shifting gender roles and identities; the second involves the extensive use of doubles, of multiple and mirrored actors in the drama of resistance.

One important shift in gender identity takes place in the "Christmas Festivities" chapter in which the narrator has already claimed a female voice in a male ritual. This chapter begins with Brent's peeping through her loophole at her own children dressed in the Christmas suits she has sewn for them. As a part of her mockery against the official society, she presents a scene beneath her loophole: "I heard Benny ask a little playmate whether Santa Claus brought him anything. 'Yes,' replied the boy; 'but Santa Claus ain't a real man. It's the children's mothers that put things into the stockings.' 'No, that can't be,' replied Benny, 'for Santa Claus brought Ellen and me these new clothes, and my mother has been gone this long time'" (118). Indeed, Santa Claus "ain't a real man"; Brent's magical role as Santa and Benny's lie about her— for he later reveals that he knows his mother is hiding in the house— become a part of the raillery and the renewing energy of the "greatest attraction" of Christmas Day. Jacobs has encoded her own gender shift, debunking the Santa Claus myth and changing his gender while affirming an African ritual recreated in the hostile environment of slavery.

The same gender boundary is exposed and violated by the scene with Brent's sailor disguise—which itself suggests the androgyny of the narrating trickster. Her invisibility as a woman gains emphasis through the estranged description of Mr. Sands as "the father of my children." The phrasing suggests the peculiar circumstance of a slave woman whose children share their father's blood but are not his in the way they are hers.

Empowered by her disguise as an African-American sailor free to move about in a southern town, Jacobs/Brent mocks the ironies of skin color in the South—that she must darken her skin to be less clearly seen. A final element in Jacobs's parody here is her probable allusion to Frederick Douglass's escape as a sailor at the close of his first narrative. He made his way to the North through Anna Murray's financial support and a sailor disguise of her making, but Douglass's construction of the solitary male hero de-emphasized his ties to community and mandated silence about the support for his escape.[23] Unlike Douglass, this womanish sailor in *Incidents* makes a circular escape into a voluntary captivity, not to the North, in order to stay near her children. Her male disguise allows the narrator to address the critical pressures faced by slave women and the values with which they respond. Like Ellen Craft, Jacobs relied upon a male disguise, but unlike Ellen Craft, Jacobs also claimed the prerogative of telling her own story in her own voice. The story of the Crafts' escape, told often by William Craft on the abolitionist tour, reached publication at about the same time as *Incidents*. Yet in *Running a Thousand Miles for Freedom*, William Craft seemed to acknowledge and accommodate the discomfort of a white reader who perceived "a temporarily 'unsexed' woman artful and devious enough to pass for male as well as white."[24]

One more scene, rarely commented upon by critics, shapes a radical revision of representations of sexual exploitation, especially as they appear in other slave narratives and much antislavery polemic. The scene's introduction as one of Brent's "Southern reminiscences"—echoing the language of a travelogue title Jacobs's employer, N. P. Willis, might select—grows increasingly appalling as the reader encounters the background to Brent's chance encounter with an old friend. In the episode with the runaway Luke (chapter 40), the role of female sexual victim is dramatically reversed. Luke, himself, is the victim of a dissipated, "degraded wreck of [white] manhood." Before Luke's escape and his trickster theft of "money nuff to bring him to de Free States," Luke had been "chained to the bedside" of his invalided owner, and "was not allowed to wear any thing but his shirt, in order to be in readiness to be flogged" (192–93). As with much antislavery polemic addressing the victimization of slave women, where whips and cowhides stand for sexual assault as much as for physical beating, Jacobs has used those operative symbols but reversed the gender. Breaking a taboo far greater than that which forbids antebellum writers to address rape and miscegenation directly, Jacobs addresses the vulnerability of the male slave to sexual abuse: "Some of these freaks of nature," she writes, "were of a nature too filthy to be repeated" (192).

Without minimizing the acts of victimization located earlier in the narrative, Jacobs has already changed the representation of the female slave from victim to resister; in this later episode of abuse she has again captured the horror of sexual abuse without portraying Luke merely as passive victim. Like Jacobs/Brent, he is a trickster and a runaway. Presenting Luke as a double, she emphasizes their parallels and shows the strength of their kinship across the class line suggested by Luke's dialect as well. In this section Jacobs moves beyond the sexual doubleness of her narrator, which allows her access to a male domain, and draws our attention to the "feminine" vulnerability of the male slave. Jacobs's ostensible purpose in this episode is to present the problem of the slave's "moral sense": She asks, "When a man has his wages stolen from him, year after year, and the laws sanction and enforce the theft, how can he be expected to have more regard to honesty than has the man who robs him?" (193). This sleight-of-hand—the validity of the question notwithstanding—has Jacobs's signature, for her most radical attacks upon the slavocracy come in disguise. The slave's moral sense is actively outraged here, and the grim presence of this sexual abuse deepens the reader's sense of the degradation of slavery while it further undermines the distinctions of gender.

The second method of female empowerment, most intense in this middle section of the *Incidents,* involves Jacobs's creation of doubles for her narrator. The present writer and the past self, the historical Jacobs and her pseudonymous Brent, suffuse the narrative with a doubled presence. This doubled image of Jacobs in her Idlewild garret secretly writing out the life of Linda Brent in hiding creates a strong sense of the continuity of unseen resistance and of a double vision for transforming the world of slavery. Jacobs writes to Amy Post, "I sometimes wish that I could fall into a Rip Van Winkle sleep and awake with the blest belief of that little Witch Topsy that I never was born but you will say it is too late in the day I have outgrown the belief oh yes and outlived it too but you know that my bump of hope is large" (238). Having "outlived" and "outgrown" the wish never to have been born into the abused and victimized identity of a slave, Jacobs has the power to shape a text of rebirth, process, and possibility—a text that rips apart the moral posturing of the slavocracy. While these layered selves double the actors for resistance, Jacobs creates a text that refuses to let her daughter's life be a double of her own. In fact, it is Brent's sense that her daughter might duplicate the fate of concubinage and exploitation that finally brings her to choose escape or death. Thus, the daughter is a double who will be free.

During the ordeal of concealment and paralysis in *Incidents,* Jacobs dramatizes her power through doubling; she creates a fugitive double through the false letters she arranges to be sent from the North. In order to deflect Dr. Flint's local search, Jacobs/Brent writes two letters, one to her grandmother and one to Flint himself. In spite of her grandmother's uneasiness, the plan effectively dupes Flint, who himself fictionalizes statements in the letter he delivers to Aunt Martha. The war of fictions, like the war of language earlier, is waged between Flint's and Brent's false doubles, and Flint's unsuccessful deception makes Brent's northern twin all the more powerful. Andrews points out that Jacobs/Brent uses her writing "to project an alter ego in freedom up North, not a lunatic self raging in rebellion in a psychic attic." [25] The fictionalized northern fugitive—cast against the attic captivity, the lost power of speech, the fear of permanent crippling—does embody an alternative strength and freedom, a sort of spiritual extension of the captive Brent. The doubling is an effective trickster's device and something more; it suggests the imaginative, spiritual freedom that counterbalances Brent's physical debilitation.

Another instance of doubling has farther-reaching effects. As Brent lies in her garret near the end of her seven long years of concealment, she becomes aware of a similar fugitive in the little hut on her grand-mother's property. Jacobs draws the reader's attention more than once to the parallels in these captive situations. The fugitive Fanny sought the shelter of her mother's hut after she and her children had been sepa-rated and sold to pay her owner's debts. Jacobs/Brent comments, "My friend Fanny and I remained many weeks hidden within call of each other; but she was unconscious of the fact" (149). This passage suggests an unseen community of fugitives whose kinship develops at a level beyond their factual awareness: "[Fanny's mother] little dreamed that my grandmother knew where her daughter was concealed, and that the stooping form of her old neighbor was bending under a similar burden of anxiety and fear; but these dangerous secrets deepened the sympathy between the two old persecuted mothers" (149). This "unconscious" and dreamlike relation between the harbored fugitives and their "moth-ers" mirrors not only the long captive sleep of concealment but the potential for their awakening and shared resistance.

When Brent's faithful friend Peter offers his plan for her escape, the fugitive disguises and long-sustained secrecy are dramatically unrav-eled. Brent's decision to let Fanny go in her place, Fanny's long wait in the vessel for the wind to turn, Brent's sudden risk of exposure and resolution to flee—all these events lead to a moment when concealment and fear of betrayal are reversed into a double escape and a community of resistance. In Brent's escape, the captain of the departing vessel inter-prets Peter and the hired boatmen as "officers . . . pursuing his vessel in search of the runaway slave he had on board." When the chase is revealed as an effort to put another slave named Linda on board the escape ship, the captain comments, "That's the name of the woman already here. . . . I believe you mean to betray me" (153). There are two Lindas, doubled escapes. None of the anticipated betrayals takes place. Much betrayal is unmasked as loyalty that crosses boundaries of race, class, and gender. The doubling of fugitives develops into an expanding scene of successful resistance. The powerful dream of freedom, beneath the oppressive "sleep" of these women in the South, becomes a part of waking reality.

Jacobs's repeated use of doubling points to her assertion of forces of resistance, especially female resistance, lying beneath the observed surface of official society. One can speculate as well that such representations relate to the masquerades of African-retained ritual and the paired leaders of the Johnkannau procession. Along with Dougald Mac Millan, Sterling Stuckey suggests that in some of the American performances of the Johnkannau men dressed as women,[26] mirroring a modern day festival in Yorubaland, Southern Nigeria, called Gelede. This all-male ritual is performed to appease the spirits of powerful women and the elderly women of the village. In this spectacle, often danced in identical pairs, there is an important thematic emphasis on doubling and twins. The symbolism suggests the dual nature of the women, who are believed to have access to the domain of the spirits.[27] Even more, the Gelede offers a setting for the spirits to "intermingle with humans" and features pairs formed with "a strong spiritual dimension": "When two partners make a pact and adopt a secret name, they often choose to dress alike and may be mistaken for twins. By virtue of their pact, the friends mutually guard and protect each other, and it is implied that the two can communicate by mental telepathy. . . . This doubling seems to imply increased spiritual force and transcendency. Some informants believe that twins share one soul or that one twin is the spirit double of the other."[28] The concerns with powerful, possibly revengeful, female spirits whose fertility is signified in the magical properties of twins resonate with the text of *Incidents*—its African retentions, its unforgiving revenge upon Flint, its masquerades and disguises, its paired performers.[29] The association suggests the rich blend of spiritual resources in Jacobs—abolitionist, feminist, spiritualist, believer in folkways, a freed slave proudly a part of an African heritage.

This courageous and intelligent woman has, in *Incidents,* revealed the spiritual groundwork for her community's resistance. As trickster and Christian, African and American, even female and male, Jacobs marshals the spectrum of her experience to wage her relentless war against the slavocracy. Her trickster transformations capture that power she has discovered in the margins, reshaping the official world into a fool's paradise and a moral hell, but finding resources in her own experience for new combinations. Jacobs's large "bump of hope" makes her an experimenter and explorer. The reader is a witness to her seven years of suffering and renewal, of Bible reading, of dependency on folk wisdom and loyalty. We are aware through Jacobs's letters of another seven years of writing and soul-searching to bring her story to the world. Through these letters we understand that Jacobs became an active abolitionist and feminist, and she participated in the first phases of American spiritualism, attending séances at the Posts' house in Rochester.[30] *Incidents in the Life of a Slave Girl* conveys the fragmentation of this woman's experience in its title, but each incident in the life Jacobs/Brent orchestrates for us also hints at the encoded "second life of the people." It conveys the relentless principle and grace with which Jacobs asserted a spiritual will toward wholeness.

Notes

1. Harriet A. Jacobs, *Incidents in the Life of a Slave Girl,* ed. Jean Fagan Yellin (Cambridge: Harvard Univ. Press, 1987), 1. Subsequent references to this text are cited parenthetically within the essay.

2. In *Written by Herself: Literary Production by African American Women, 1746–1892* (Bloomington: Indiana Univ. Press, 1993), 107, Foster cites Robert Stepto's term for the strategy through which African-American writers bring "resistant" readers to a shared understanding. She explains that Jacobs makes a complex use of race and gender signifiers (83, 107). Along these lines, I believe Jacobs shapes very different types of encoded messages: some to bring the readers into the antislavery fold and some to reinforce or address the positions of readers already within the politics of antislavery. Of particular importance is her signifying on African-American male privilege within her cultural group. These messages are not for the designated white reader; they exist on another level for those who know the codes.

3. Joanne Braxton, *Black Women Writing Autobiography* (Philadelphia: Temple Univ. Press, 1989), 18–38; Valerie Smith, *Self-Discovery and Authority in Afro-American Narrative* (Cambridge: Harvard Univ. Press, 1987), 26–43.

4. Braxton, *Black Women Writing,* 30.

5. William L. Andrews, *To Tell a Free Story: The First Century of Afro-American Autobiography, 1760–1865* (Urbana: Univ. of Illinois Press, 1986), 259.

6. Henry Louis Gates Jr., *The Signifying Monkey: A Theory of African American Literary Criticism* (New York: Oxford Univ. Press, 1988), 6.

7. Lawrence Levine, *Black Culture and Black Consciousness: Afro-American Folk Thought from Slavery to Freedom* (New York: Oxford Univ. Press, 1977), 103–5.

8. Levine, *Black Culture,* 105–20.

9. Gates, *Signifying Monkey,* 54, 72, 196–98.

10. Levine, *Black Culture,* pp. 105, 117–18.

11. Ibid., 120.

12. See M. M. Bakhtin, *The Dialogic Imagination,* trans. Caryl Emerson and Michael Holquist (Austin: Univ. of Texas Press, 1981), and *Rabelais and His World,* trans. Helene Iswolsky (Cambridge: MIT Press, 1965). For the particular role of dialogization and novelization in slave narrative, see Andrews, *To Tell a Free Story,* 271–73, and "Novelization of Voice in Early African American Narrative," *PMLA* 105 (1990): 23–34.

13. Bakhtin, *Rabelais,* 9.

14. Ibid., 197.

15. Dougald Mac Millan, "John Kuners," *Journal of American Folklore* 39 (1926): 54; Ira De A. Reid, "The John Canoe Festival," *Phylon* 3 (1942): 349–50.

16. Bakhtin, *Rabelais,* 95.

17. This section of the essay is adapted from "Carnival Laughter: Resistance in *Incidents,*" in *New Essays on Harriet Jacobs,* ed. Deborah Garfield and Rafia Zafar (New York: Cambridge Univ. Press, 1996). For discussions of the Johnkannau Festivals in the New World, see Sylvia Wynter, "Jonkonnu in Jamaica," *Jamaica Journal* 4 (1970): 34–48; Dougald Mac Millan, "John Kuners," 53–57; Ira De A. Reid, "The John Canoe Festival," 349–70; Sterling Stuckey, *Slave Culture: Nationalist Theory and the Foundations of Black America* (New York: Oxford Univ. Press, 1987), 64–75. I am indebted to Professor Maureen Warner-Lewis at the University of the West Indies—Mona for insights into the carnival celebrations in the Caribbean.

Stephen Nissenbaum, in *The Battle for Christmas* (New York: Knopf, 1996) argues that, from earliest practices in modern Europe, Christmas was identified with popular, non-Christian seasonal celebrations—as a time of festivity and excess in "a world of scarcity." The celebration, censured in New England by the Puritans and, well into the nineteenth century in the United States, perceived as an unwarranted assumption of privilege by the lower classes, was tenaciously practiced by working classes and plantation slaves to let off steam (3–11). The holiday was domesticated in the mid-nineteenth century, largely through the impact of magazine publication. Jacobs, in Idlewild in the late 1850s, would have been a witness to the changing nature of Christmas observances.

18. Stuckey, *Slave Culture,* 68–70.

19. Mac Millan, "John Kuners," 54.

20. Foster, *Written by Herself,* 16, 20.

21. Kimberly Rae Connor, *Conversions and Visions in the Writings of African-American Women* (Knoxville: Univ. of Tennessee Press, 1994), 62.

22. These letters are located in the Isaac and Amy Post Family Papers in the Department of Rare Books and Special Collections, Rush Rhees Library, University of Rochester, and on microfilm for Black Abolitionist Papers. References to the "spirits" occur in four of these letters as I discussed in an unpublished paper delivered at Berry College, Southern Women Writers Conference, April 9, 1994, "Harriet Jacobs and the Rochester Rappers."

23. Houston Baker, Introduction, *Narrative of the Life of Frederick Douglass, an American Slave,* by Frederick Douglass (New York: Penguin, 1986), 18; *Invented Lives: Narratives of Black Women 1860–1960,* ed. Mary Helen Washington (Garden City, N.Y.: Anchor, 1987), 8. This example and other instances of Jacobs's signifying on Douglass and Stowe may be found in "Carnival Laughter."

24. Andrews, *To Tell a Free Story,* 213.

25. Ibid., 259.

26. Stuckey, *Slave Culture,* 69.

27. Henry John Drewal and Margaret Thompson Drewal, *Gelede: Art and Female Power Among the Yoruba* (Bloomington: Indiana Univ. Press, 1983), 10–11. I am indebted to Kimberly Wallace-Sanders for first drawing this resemblance between Jacobs's treatment of the Johnkannaus and the contemporary Gelede ritual to my attention.

28. Drewal, *Gelede,* 136.

29. Ibid., 10–11, 14.

30. Nancy Hewitt, "Amy Kirby Post," *University of Rochester Library Bulletin* 37 (1984): 13.

Engendered in the South

Blood and Irony in Douglass and Jacobs

ANNE GOODWYN JONES

IN 1845, the year of Frederick Douglass's first visit to Britain, another fugitive slave made a journey to England as well, though her visit evoked no fanfare then or now. A conference celebrating the 150th anniversary of Douglass's visit brought international scholars to Keele University in the Midlands of England in 1995; to my knowledge, there was no celebration of Harriet Jacobs's 150th.

Nor was there likely to be. Whereas Douglass arrived in Liverpool in the glow of fame—his *Narrative of the Life of Frederick Douglass* had sold 4,500 copies in the United States by fall 1845 (it had been published in June), and gone into three international editions—Jacobs's trip was hardly an antebellum book tour.[1] Her own slave narrative, *Incidents in the Life of a Slave Girl, Written by Herself,* would not appear in print until 1861.[2] Instead of a public figure, Jacobs was a domestic worker. She left her own children in America sometime after late March (Douglass was to leave in late fall) to sail for Liverpool as the nursemaid to three-year-old Imogen Willis, whose mother had just died. Imogen's father, Nathaniel Parker Willis, a New York magazine writer and brother of the writer Sara Payson Willis Parton, known to her readers as Fanny Fern, completed the party. Jacobs spent ten months in England on this trip, staying in London and in Steventon as the family visited relatives who survived Imogen's mother. She returned in the winter of 1845–46; Douglass stayed for a year longer, returning after Christmas 1846.[3]

It is fascinating to imagine that Harriet Jacobs's path crossed Frederick Douglass's—their stays in Britain coincided for at least four months in late 1845—but there seems to be no evidence to support such a fantasy; in fact, Douglass spent most of that time in Ireland.[4] Four years later, though, Jacobs was working in the same movement, the same town, and even the same building as Frederick Douglass, in the antislavery reading room above the offices of Douglass's abolitionist newspaper the *North Star* in Rochester, New York. She referred to Douglass almost casually by now. She wrote to Amy Post in 1849, for example, that "the Office go on as usual had a few here to meeting on Sunday. . . . I suppose we shall have Frederick and the Miss Griffiths here on Sunday to draw a full house   Rochester is looking very pretty   the trees are in full Bloom and the earth seems covered with a green mantle. . . . The Miss Griffiths has been here this afternoon   Frederick went with them to the falls   they seemed much pleased with the reading room."[5] But her slave narrative was not to appear for a dozen more years, in 1861, whereas Douglass's *Narrative of the Life of Frederick Douglass, an American Slave* had appeared of course before he set sail for Liverpool in 1845. And when Harriet embarked on a second journey to England in 1858, to find a British publisher for her book, her efforts failed. (In 1862 W. Tweedie was to publish it in London under the title *The Deeper Wrong: Incidents in the Life of a Slave Girl, Written by Herself.*)[6]

The coincidence of their 1845 visits to England and the tellingly different characters of those visits suggest rather predictable gender contrasts between the two fugitive slaves. Though both were managed and paid by whites, for example, Douglass had become a heroic figure in the public, predominantly male world, while Jacobs, despite an equally dramatic escape from slavery (and five years seniority to Douglass), remained in the female world of domesticity.[7] Indeed, their ways of telling their stories of the visit to England differ in predictably gendered ways. Douglass emphasizes the importance to him of the world of political connections. In *The Life and Times of Frederick Douglass* (1881, revised 1893), the last of the three versions of his autobiography, he wrote: "My visit to England did much for me every way. Not the least among the many advantages derived from it was the opportunity it afforded me of becoming acquainted with educated people and of seeing and hearing many of the most distinguished men of that country."[8] Such acquaintances made new links in a continuing *narrative* of linear progress, the story of a life that was moving from success to success as a public figure. By contrast, Jacobs began her story of her travel to England by telling her readers of her lodgings and supper. She then moved to the privacy of the bedroom she shared with little Imogen, in order to emphasize what for her was the major effect of being in England, a feeling that emerged when she was alone. "Ensconced in a pleasant room, with my dear little charge, I laid my head on my pillow, for the first time, with the delightful consciousness of pure, unadulterated freedom."[9] Such an *incident*, enclosed, interior, almost timeless, is not tied to a narrative of public accomplishment; on the contrary, its very accomplishment is, in a sense, privacy itself. Jacobs's title, of course, suggests her story's difference from Douglass's narrative. In the 1849 letter to Amy Post quoted above, Jacobs veered suddenly from a sentence about the forthcoming "full house" for a public meeting to a lyrical evocation of Rochester in the spring. Though it is not exactly a green thought in a green shade, a sort of outdoors version of her feelings in bed in Britain—Jacobs may well have been thinking of the effects of the setting on the conferees—neither is it a thought or a transition that Douglass would be likely to have made, at least in writing. He would have stayed focused on the narrative of the public event, at which, of course, he was front and center.

The forking path of gendered binary oppositions clearly lies ahead—after public/private, workplace/home, and culture/nature come the inevitable autonomous/interdependent, political/personal, rational/emotional. Although taking such a path is clearly useful, as is evident in the work of such critics as Richard Yarborough, David Leverenz, Stephanie Smith, Jenny Franchot, Valerie Smith, Anne Warner, Jean Fagan Yellin, Frances Foster, and Eric Sundquist, this essay will choose from the volume subtitle the path less taken.[10] Emphasizing the regional term in *Gender and* Southern *Texts*, it will raise questions about the historical and regional specificity of the gendered oppositions suggested above on which gender analysis has tended to rely.

I propose to argue against certain claims and implications of such analyses of Douglass's and Jacobs's lives and works on the grounds that these sets of gender oppositions are to an important extent effects of the culture and history of the American North and thus are useful only in a limited sense for understanding the complicated and polycultural lives and works of Douglass and Jacobs. I will speculate as to the gender implications of some of the differences between the slaveholding South and the rest of the nation; and I will suggest that there is a wider gap between the rhetoric of Douglass's and Jacobs's writing and the history of their lives than has been supposed. That gap, as I see it, can be understood as the effect of significantly differing gender systems. In one the two fugitive slaves and writers were raised; in the other they lived as adults; and it was to the latter—the gender system of the emerging industrial capitalist urbanizing North—that they addressed the rhetoric of their self-writing. More profoundly shaped by the South than was their writing, however, their lives as adults performed scripts—texts—of specifically southern manhood and womanhood. And manhood and womanhood in the South for black as well as white, slave as well as free, were deeply implicated with meanings of class.

Ellen Glasgow, the Virginia realist/modernist novelist, early in her career made the remark, itself an ironic revision of Bismarck's call for German "Blut und Eisen," blood and iron, that what southern literature needed was blood and irony.[11] Certainly Douglass's and Jacobs's narratives (and incidents) fill Glasgow's prescription. After trying to argue that southern gender meanings shaped Douglass's and Jacobs's lives, I'll try next to suggest ways in which their writings joined a rhetoric that appealed to northern gender norms with themes that emerged from southern gender experience. Thus Douglass's *Narrative* and Jacobs's *Incidents* can be read as progenitors of southern literary thematics, thematics of blood and irony and much more as well.

Analyses of gender in American studies have tended to assume that the contours of gender that developed in the first half of the nineteenth century in the American North can be successfully generalized elsewhere. For example, despite taking his data exclusively from the Northeast, Anthony Rotundo entitled his recent book *American Manhood* and argues that the key definition of American manhood during the first half of the nineteenth century was what he calls "self-made manhood," the product of a market economy, a burgeoning middle class, and "an economic and political life based on the free play of individual interests." A self-made man took his "identity and social status from his own achievements, not from the accident of his birth," according to Rotundo.[12] By the same token, the notion still prevails in many quarters that during the same period domesticity became the gender norm for American women, domesticity in a home that was no longer the man's place of work so now became the woman's center of power.[13]

Yet a moment's thought will make it clear that such gender assumptions could not work so smoothly for people in the American South, white or black, rich or poor, slave or free. For manhood, the notion of "the free play of individual interests" in a rigidly hierarchical and paternalistic society or of gaining social status through achievement rather than birth in a culture based on family lineage had to remain only a gleam in the eye for the southerner born with the wrong blood or condition of servitude and without a silver spoon in his mouth. Most southern men, that is to say, would not have had access to Rotundo's "American" manhood. And even those most likely to—the men of the master class—argued quite explicitly against such ideas, for example in the proslavery speeches, sermons, and essays.[14] Yet clearly genders existed and were quite sternly enforced in the South. To understand Douglass and Jacobs, then, in particular to understand their gender identifications as they played out through their lives, one must look at the ways in which these two were likely to have been originally engendered in the South. Northern gender ideals became their rhetoric and their hopes; such ideals shaped to a great extent their free and deliberate choices as adults; but southern gender realities shaped their first and irreducible sense of self, a sense that could never entirely be recognized or erased.[15]

Harriet Jacobs's slave youth and young womanhood in Edenton, North Carolina, and Douglass's, from Tuckahoe to Baltimore, were shaped by intimate interracial emotional bonds, bonds that slavery created in its invention of what plantation patriarchs tended to call "my family, white and black."[16] Jacobs records a life spent within town households, as a child loved and taught by her white mistress, as a young woman obsessively pursued by her white master, and as a fugitive slave hidden for a time in a white friend's house. She spent seven famous years holed up in her "loophole of retreat" in a garret in her grandmother's home a block from her white master's house and a few doors from her white lover's (and her children's father's) house. Jacobs's grandmother, Molly Horniblow, had been bought and freed by the sister of her former white mistress—a woman who, unlike the slave she freed, was illiterate. She signed the petition for emancipation with an X.[17]

Like Harriet Jacobs, Frederick Douglass lived in cross-racial households that produced complicated intimate relations as well: the Eastern Shore home of Aaron Anthony (possibly Douglass's father), assistant to the hugely wealthy planter Edward Lloyd; the Baltimore household of Hugh and Sophia Auld; and the Eastern Shore household of Thomas and Lucretia Auld, in particular. While he lived next to Lloyd's manorial Wye House, he was chosen (age six) as the constant companion for the youngest Lloyd son, Daniel (age twelve); they hunted, played, and explored the slave "city" together.[18] Later, living with the Baltimore

Aulds, he played with a group of boys both black and white in the streets of Fells Point. No doubt their closeness to free people and to white people underlined for both Jacobs and Douglass the horrific differences of slavery. I want to speculate that their intimacy with the master class went also into the construction of their original and fundamental sense of gender. For both slaves and their masters in the South, the identificatory processes that constructed gender were processes that were likely to involve multiple mothers and sometimes multiple fathers, complicated kin networks, cross-racial relationships, and a sense of class propriety. Indeed, class identity may have appeared to be more stable than even race, gender, or condition of servitude as a marker of one's "authentic" self. In the passage quoted earlier from Jacobs's chapter "A Visit to England," Jacobs tells us that "for the first time in my life I was in a place where I was treated according to my deportment, without reference to my complexion."[19] Her deportment signified her class, more precisely her classed gender; her color was, she thought, correctly read as irrelevant to her social identity. If for Douglass and Jacobs the distinction between slavery and freedom was more important than the distinction between white and black, as seemed to be the case, class divisions may have meant more to them than either. Because of their class identification, both Douglass and Jacobs, I submit, grew up feeling themselves to be in key respects more like than unlike their white privileged families.

Bertram Wyatt-Brown argues in his essay in this volume, "The Mask of Obedience," that male slave psychology emerged from the similarities between African and southern systems of honor. Both were systems of social order that depended on public shame and humiliation to organize behavior rather than on private conscience and guilt. In his analysis, Wyatt-Brown locates three plausible responses to the shame of enslavement: the dignified moral decision to abase oneself, producing self-respect; the internalizing of shame, producing self-blame; and the denial of shame, in an amoral, tricksterlike shamelessness. The majority of slaves responded by internalizing shame.

These categories may be less useful for Douglass and Jacobs. Wyatt-Brown's subject is more precisely the period of transition from Africa to America; Douglass and Jacobs both were born into families that took pride in tracing several generations in America. Furthermore, both chose a fourth alternative that Wyatt-Brown does not mention—escape into freedom. Yet they seem to have shared with Wyatt-Brown's first

group a psychology that allowed them to resist the Althusserian inter-
pellations of slavery and to make dignified moral decisions. That is,
both Frederick Douglass and Harriet Jacobs were able, to some extent
through their writing itself, to separate a sense of personal identity,
dignity, and worth from their identities as slaves by perceiving slave
identity as imposed rather than earned or essential and by focusing on
its exteriority. They were able to observe with vigilance slavery's efforts
to produce an internalized sense of shame and humiliation; their vulnerability to such feelings was contained by their strong sense of selfhood and by their capacity to think and act out of that center rather
than simply react to the system. Both recognized early on that the only
satisfactory response to the shaming designs of slavery for them was to
escape into freedom; presumably writing their own personal narratives,
both articulated and clarified the distance between their identities as
slaves and their identities as free Americans, man and woman. And
both found models and solace for their sense of self in identifications
with the white upper class with whom they shared "deportment."
Douglass deliberately learned to speak "perfect" white upper-class English (to the amazement of his later listeners), just as Jacobs learned
the rules of upper-class politeness to which she finally found a positive
response not in the rude North but in the white South's Anglophiliac
dream: mother England herself.

But when they constructed their lives after escaping to the North
and when they wrote their narratives for northern audiences, inevitably
they drew on gender assumptions they knew their new community
shared. Those assumptions differed from southern assumptions, and in
a sense they split the genders still more severely. Thus, as Leverenz has
argued, Douglass refashioned himself in *My Bondage and my Freedom*
in language and tone that fit a northern bourgeois man. His emphasis
on isolation, on individual "self-made" achievement, on literacy, on
professional success, on democracy and equality, shows his awareness
of the meanings of manhood in his new and permanent region.[20] And
Jacobs, knowing she spoke to an audience of northern women whose
primary value was married domesticity, addressed them as follows:
"Reader, my story ends with freedom; not in the usual way, with marriage. . . . The dream of my life is not yet realized. I do not sit with my
children in a home of my own. I still long for a hearthstone of my own,
however humble. . . . But God so orders circumstances as to keep me
with my friend Mrs. Bruce [the second Mrs. Willis]."[21]

How did these deliberate, adult gender constructions used in their public writing differ from those that shaped the writers when—as children—they were most vulnerable to social construction? In the South, the meanings of gender had been articulated through class and race and working condition to a much fuller extent than in the North. Gender-appropriate behavior changed with one's class, regardless of race; racially specific gender characteristics were ascribed in ways that easily contradicted the gender determined by class; and traditions of gender from British and African sources made contact, mixed, and produced new cross-cultural revisions that were not necessarily coherent with either class or race. A light-colored woman working as a house slave could differ more in her sense of womanhood from a field slave than she did from her own mistress. A white heir's personal slave could be a closer friend to the young master than other white boys. The young slave's sense of manhood surely would be inflected by his daily life, in the company of white men and boys.

In Jacobs's South, upper-class womanhood was shaped not by the turn to domesticity required when men left home to go to work, as in the North. Southern white privileged men may have left home during some of some days or for stretches of days at a time, but they did so on different, less predictable and systematic work schedules and for various and different reasons, including sport and play. "Dr. Flint" keeps such a "schedule." They remained patriarchs at home. So, rather than becoming the queens of the kitchen and the sole monarchs of domestic space, their wives submitted to their lords and masters (at least in the rhetoric, which many internalized) and shared authority over the household with female slaves. As Elizabeth Fox-Genovese has emphasized, the home was still the workplace, certainly on the plantations and, in Jacobs's narrative, in town as well. Northern domesticity, like northern urbanization, simply did not exist. Instead, upper-class womanhood, black and white, in reality and in ideology, was marked by a curious combination of power and powerlessness. Such a woman had the power of literacy and education, the power to speak her mind, to move through the town freely, to make independent judgments, even to support herself—Jacobs's grandmother was the town's classiest baker. Such a woman had the power to own, buy, sell, whip, or free slaves as well, though obviously her race and legal and marital status determined to some extent which powers she held when, and which would be invoked. Yet such a woman deferred to masculinity as a matter of habit.

Louisa McCord, one of the most articulate, argued that the pedestal was not only the smartest but the safest place for women to be in a culture infused with, and defined by, violence.[22]

And such a privileged woman, white or black, was constrained, albeit differently, in matters sexual. Although the white bride could choose her husband freely (within familial and social constraints), it seemed to writers like Jacobs and Mary Chesnut a given that her groom would almost inevitably betray her sexual trust and take a black mistress. Eventually, the ideal white lady would be culturally marked by her sexlessness. Moreover, the white woman's apparent privilege of having slave wet nurses and slaves care for her children resulted, as Lillian Smith put it most dramatically, in the distortion and failure of her maternal bonds.[23] Black women of Jacobs's class—women who could claim the appellation "lady"—shared with whites certain sexual constraints: if not the "double mother" system, they shared the injunction to purity, as Jacobs's representation of Linda Brent's grandmother shows.

Ultimately, both the black woman's and the white woman's power to control her actions was contingent upon the greater power of the white master or the husband, supported by the law. Fear of the white man's power, and ultimately of his violence, undergirds even the white intellectual Louisa McCord's otherwise complex argument against giving women the vote. Angelina Grimké, in her "Appeal to Christian Woman of the South," tries to convert her (white female) implied reader to antislavery by creating a wedge between her submission to her husband and her submission to God, suggesting by implication the southern identification of Lord (in every sense) and master. And the slave woman, whatever her class identification, was of course in every sense vulnerable to the various powers of the white master.

In Douglass's South, white manhood—the only manhood that was allowed?—was shaped not by competitive capitalist emphasis on individualism but by an honor-driven need to perform one's worthiness in the eyes of other men, at least if we accept Wyatt-Brown's argument. Homosocial bonds not only held; they were constantly in the process of being forged and reforged, through sometimes bloody rituals that entailed the construction and display of symbols of masculinity and femininity. Physical prowess, passionate self-expression, and violence affirmed and demonstrated manhood in the South to a degree that shocked northern observers. White manhood clearly must have meant sexual prowess as well, but texts that comment on women's and blacks' absent or dangerous sexuality are strangely silent on the sexuality of white men. Perhaps that silence is not only a function of gentlemanly circumspection but also in part to protect—to render circumspect— the practice of (re)producing two families, one acknowledged and legal, the other unspoken and illegal. Ultimately, in any case, white manhood meant mastery in a hierarchical system in which equality of the sexes and classes was as unthinkable as equality of the races or of the free and unfree. And it meant mastery of one's own domain, including one's family and slaves, a domain in which one's behavior was limited only by one's honor. The effects on black manhood are evident in Harriet Jacobs's brother John's comments on their father: "To be a man, and not to be a man—a father without authority—a husband and no pro- tector—is the darkest of fates." [24] Manhood as authority for children and protector for women, whatever its etiology from African sources, had come as a visible norm more immediately from southern planter ideals; even John Jacobs's imagery of light and dark, in a troubling irony, comes from white discourse.

The shapes that upper-class gender took in the South can be traced both in the writings and in the lives of Harriet Jacobs and Frederick Douglass. Linda Brent (as Harriet Jacobs calls herself in *Incidents*) rep- resents herself as a girl with an articulate voice and the courage to speak her mind from the outset. There is no drama of acquiring a voice, no struggle with silencing represented here, as we might expect. On the contrary, her capacity to address her northern female audience forth- rightly and directly appears to be far more limited than her capacity to address her masters and mistresses. We can infer that her southern courage emerged in part from the example of her strong and articulate grandmother, in part from the confidence instilled in her by her first mistress's affection and lessons in literacy, and in part by her class privi- lege as an adult. Her voice falters—or rather, she represents it as falter- ing—at the moments she tells her readers about her sexual dilemma and, especially, her sexual decision. Unable to escape through her own brave speech from the insistent sexual presence of Dr. Flint, from his unwanted words and gaze, she chooses to enter into an affair with an unmarried white man, "Mr. Sands," who lives near her grandmother, who will soon be elected to Congress, and who has no claim on her but, as she puts it, kindness. Linda tells us she believed this decision would serve both as revenge on and protection from Dr. Flint. (How true Jacobs's representation of her motives was to her experience we will perhaps know better when Jean Fagan Yellin completes the biography. There are implausibilities in the account as it stands, however, that suggest that Jacobs's choice may have been one of sexual desire as well; there is no explanation given, for example, of her continuing the relationship after it fails to discourage Dr. Flint. In any case, representations of an active sexual desire on Linda Brent's part, or a loving and sexual relationship between Sands and Linda, would have been entirely unfathomable to a northern white female audience.) Yet her anxiety over the decision appears in her fear of her grandmother's disappointment and ire. The crisis Linda faces, then, when her determined and intelligent will, whatever its motivations, confronts the cultural limitations on her sexual freedom embodied by her grandmother, differs in that respect from the crisis of a slave pursued by a master; such a conflict could happen to any southern woman, white or black, whose desire and will did not coincide with her class constraints, or whose "lord and master" exercised his legal rights against her will. Of course, a husband's or father's rights over a white woman's body did not approach the near totality of an owner's rights over that of a chattel slave; nevertheless, Linda's difficulties with her grandmother's sexual standards could have been experienced by a white woman.

Linda has named her son by Mr. Sands after her escaped brother and her daughter after the sister of her father's white mistress. The namings suggest in small the complexities of interracial relationships within her form of slavery, representing as they do objects of affection from both groups, slaves and enslavers. The desire to sustain maternal bonds with her children is evocatively presented in *Incidents,* through representations of tender and intimate moments that give still more impact to the awareness of slavery's power to sever those bonds. Whatever southern white women can lose of mothering to slavery and the double-mother system it encouraged, it is clear that slave women, despite class privilege, live in constant risk of losing the children themselves. The power of Jacobs's representation of the life of a woman in slavery is thus underscored by her identification with privileged southern white women, for the sole difference Jacobs continually returns to is the ever-present total and arbitrary power of slavery.

By the same token, the intimacy with white people in Douglass's early life, as the favored friend of Daniel Lloyd, then as a child loved by and loving Thomas Auld, in William McFeely's persuasive interpretation, then as part of the loving Hugh and Sophia Auld family in Balti-more, highlighted the differences that slavery made. These intimate relations must have meant also that his primary identification as a man was not as an idealized northern bourgeois but as a white southern master. Unlike Harriet, who had her grandmother to claim as kin and serve as mother, Douglass had no black man to claim as intimate kin or serve as father. The significant males in the plantation and town households in which he spent his early years, the years of learning what gender means, were for the most part white. His love-and-hate–filled long-term relationship with Thomas Auld must have been marked by many of the emotions and the identifications of father and son. And Frederick's relationship to Daniel Lloyd and his family put him in a position both to desire the great house and to recognize his exclusion from it.

With this in mind, certain pieces of the Douglass puzzle may fall into place. How could the great antislavery advocate bring articulate, politically active white women—possibly as lovers—to live in the house with his dark wife, who stayed in the kitchen while the guests were in the living room, and who remained illiterate—illiterate, Frederick Douglass's wife—all her life? How could he live later at Cedar Hill with a white wife in a big house apart from the black community? Why was he determined to make himself into a gentleman, his son into a violinist, and his daughter into a cultured lady? To me it seems plain that despite his deliberate and obvious self-refashioning into a northern man, using the rhetoric of self-made manhood, Douglass's primary gender identi-fications came out of his southern past. Even the points at which he explicitly sees himself becoming a man—fighting Covey or traveling through Britain as a young lion—even these points were arguably facets of a specifically southern manhood, a manhood whose honor is deter-mined by physical prowess and community approval.

It is misleading, then, for critics to assume that all gender possibili-ties were the same in nineteenth-century America and that Douglass's and Jacobs's rhetorics of gender—which appealed to the structures of northern gendering—should be taken as historically accurate and complete descriptions of their historical gender identifications. If we look carefully and imaginatively at the structures in which they grew up, structures that are really nowhere available to us to see today, we can speculate that for slaves in the South becoming a man and becoming a woman were both more complicated than has been thought, and more determined.

If Douglass and Jacobs were more southern than we might have thought, particularly in their gendered selves, can their texts—despite their northern audiences—be read as part of a southern literary tradition? Glasgow's desire for blood and irony in southern literature can be used as a way both to identify their texts as southern and to differentiate the texts by gender. Both are deeply concerned with blood, with the literal wounds of slavery and with the metaphoric implications of blood as a sign of bodily integrity, but also with bloodlines, genealogy. And both take full advantage of the numerous opportunities for irony that slavery offers in the land of the free. But Douglass's 1845 narrative is almost obsessively drawn to representations of blood—I count dozens—whereas Jacobs's is at pains to show the lacerations of language. These features can be read as markers of southern gender distinctions. Among southern white men especially, making another man's blood flow, whether in ritual fights within one's cohort or by lashing slaves, had become a sign of masculine dominance as clearly as controlling the passing and naming of one's own family "blood" was a sign of patriarchal power. Frederick Douglass remarked that "everybody, in the South, wants the privilege of whipping somebody else. . . . The whip is all in all. . . . Slaves, as well as slaveholders, use it with an unsparing hand."[25] To make another man's blood leave his body was, at least as I read it, a sign of relative effeminization; to keep it within one's own body, and metaphorically within the family or the race, was a sign of bodily and racial integrity. But for Linda Brent blood signifies *primarily* inheritance, and it is words not whips that wound. Her story of slavery, of the "deeper wound" that women experience, is the story of a master's insistent whispers, suggestions, and sexual demands. Her bodily integrity and unmarked beauty are precisely what is at issue now in the register of sex. Dr. Flint wants her to *agree* to allow him to penetrate her sexually; this would be more wounding than rape, for it would mean he had her body and soul. Irony thus becomes her weapon of choice, while blood is Douglass's; she resists Dr. Flint with language and fools him with letters, while Douglass fights Covey with his fists.

If Douglass and Jacobs both bring blood and irony to southern literature, as Glasgow urged, how else can their life stories be read as part of the southern tradition? I will conclude with a few speculations.

Did Charles Chesnutt write his short story "The Wife of His Youth" with Douglass in mind?[26] In that story, set in postwar Washington, we meet Ryder, a successful African American, as he is about to hold a party for the club to which he belongs. This club, derisively called the Blue Vein Society by darker blacks, is exclusive to light-skinned wealthy African Americans of free birth. The protagonist intends to announce his engagement to one of the members at the ball. But a knock on his door admits an ugly, poor, old, very black woman who tells him the story of losing her husband, a free man of color, during the war. She knows he is looking for her still, she says, for their love was deep and real. She is trudging her way north to find him again; and she asks if the protagonist has met a man by his name. Of course it is he, so changed as to be unrecognizable to her. Without acknowledging his identity, then, the protagonist holds the party and calls the group to attention to hear the story—names omitted—and to give their opinions on what such a man should do. Unanimously they say, claim the wife of his youth. The protagonist reveals himself, introduces his wife, and all is presumably well, perhaps because the rest of the story is left unnarrated.

Douglass never legally abandoned the wife of his youth, yet clearly his situation was far from well. Unlike Chesnutt's protagonist, Douglass found it impossible happily to join the two worlds he inhabited. Instead, he—like the southern masters he so despised yet loved—reversed the image of the white master, his white lady, and the slave mistress to create a black master, his "slave" wife, and his lady mistress. If Douglass was Chesnutt's subject in "The Wife of His Youth," the message Chesnutt sent had to be a critique. For Chesnutt, race solidarity, the solidarity of family and history, should clearly take precedence over white dreams, however deep in one's identity they may rest. Yet Douglass's identity had been shaped in a setting in which slavery and slavery's class system were the defining differences more than race or gender. Cross-race gender identifications naturally emerged within a given class and within a particular family structure that united people regardless of color in shared and intimate daily experience. By the time Chesnutt wrote, race, not slavery, was the defining difference; race loyalty, not class or gender loyalty, the political desideratum. The time for Douglass's and Jacobs's sorts of gender identity, their sense of what it meant to be a man and a woman, had passed, and race would become the issue for the future of the region and the nation.

With this in mind, a wider southern literary lineage can be speculated, one that crosses races to show similarities in class relations. If Frederick Douglass's story leads to Charles Chesnutt's "The Wife of his Youth," his longing for Wye also resembles Faulkner's story of a young boy, Sarty Snopes, entranced by the sight of a huge beautiful white mansion, and his father, who recognizes that "nigger sweat" and white trash sweat have built that house.[27] It bears even more resemblances to Faulkner's great novel *Absalom, Absalom!*[28] The novel, which many critics think to be Faulkner's best, tells the story of a man seduced by the image of a big house on the hill, a seduction that is clinched when he is rejected at the door and sent to the back by the black slave inside. Thomas Sutpen marries in Haiti; this wife of his youth bears him a son, Charles Bon. But Thomas sets aside this wife and son when he learns of her black blood: she is no longer incremental to his design, founding a patriarchal family to inherit the big house he builds in Yoknapataw-pha County. Sutpen's design is thwarted; the last surviving bearer of his blood is, ironically, a very black idiot, Jim Bond, whose speech is only a howl. But Faulkner chose to make the construction of a white southern patriarchy his character's passionate design, and here the similarities end. Frederick Douglass's passionate design was not to produce a white patriarchy: it was to end slavery and work against racism. Yet the power of his having been engendered in the South played itself out willy-nilly. His own family, like Sutpen's, seems to have collapsed under the weight of his desire. His racially and socially double relationships with women, his need for control and mastery at home, created resistances and dependencies in his wife and children that they were never able to work through. Unlike Sutpen, Douglass chose a design that allowed him to construct both a self and a career that meshed well with emerging northern norms of masculinity. But he carried his southern past into that northern story of success.

Harriet Jacobs, too, arguably played out for the rest of her life a narrative written for her as a woman in the slaveholding South. Though she worked for antislavery causes, and of course wrote, found a publisher for, and at times literally sold her *Incidents,* Jacobs was employed for much of her life as a domestic servant, a nursemaid and nanny for the growing number of Willis children. This was a role that emerged from slavery's division of maternal labor. Later in life she ran a boardinghouse in Cambridge, Massachusetts, a single woman turning domestic skills into a business for herself as her grandmother had done in Edenton.

If Charles Chesnutt and Faulkner can be seen at least tentatively as writing within a thematics set by Douglass, who rewrites Jacobs's story? For reasons about which it would be interesting to wonder, the story seems to have been taken up more by white writers than by African-American southern women like Alice Walker and Gloria Naylor. I am thinking of Katherine Anne Porter, for example, whose version of Harriet Jacobs in "The Old Order," Nanny, stays with her mistress after the war but finally transforms herself in a free and independent "aged Bantu woman";[29] of Willa Cather's *Sapphira and the Slave Girl,* another story of mastery, sexuality, and escape;[30] of Ellen Douglas in her remarkable work about contemporary white mistresses and black maids, *Can't Quit You, Baby.*[31]

Finally, if in reading Douglass and Jacobs we need to be cautious about assuming that northern gender arrangements determine the identities of people raised in the South, perhaps we need to be equally attentive to the differences between slavery and racism. Jacobs and Douglass, southern born and raised, slaves, then fugitive slaves, and, finally, free, wrote and lived their stories in opposition primarily to slavery; race was secondary, in part because they had learned in the South how gender and class can override to some degree the constraints of the color of one's skin. These days, though, to be called "slave" (or to be told "yo' mama was a slave") is an insult not for the reasons Jacobs and Douglass protested slavery, that is, for the humiliations produced on a people subject to the whims of totalitarian authority. Those were humiliations that antislavery workers believed could disappear with the erasure of such authority and such a system. Today it is an insult that is perhaps harder to resist because one's skin color, like one's sex, cannot be erased through legislation. Working against racism and sexism, as both Douglass and Jacobs were to learn in the free North, would pose different problems and require different strategies. Hence the paucity, perhaps, of a literature of narratives of successful fugitives from race and gender. Other literary forms would be required for other forms of freedom.

Notes

I am grateful to Martin Crawford, to Alan Rice, and to Richard Godden, for their commentary on an earlier version of this essay. Thank you as well to David Leverenz, a reader for all to envy, and to Susan Donaldson, Elizabeth

Fox-Genovese, Anne Warner, and Bertram Wyatt-Brown for their helpful comments on earlier versions of this essay.

1. William S. McFeely, *Frederick Douglass* (New York: Simon & Schuster, 1991), 116.

2. The standard edition is Harriet A. Jacobs, *Incidents in the Life of a Slave Girl, Written by Herself,* ed. and introd. Jean Fagan Yellin (Cambridge: Harvard Univ. Press, 1987).

3. Ibid., 224, 185, xvi; McFeely, *Douglass,* 145.

4. McFeely, *Douglass,* 199–227.

5. Harriet Jacobs to Amy Post, Rochester, May 1849, in Jacobs, *Incidents,* 230.

6. Ibid., 225.

7. In the case of Douglass, they were Maria Weston Chapman, William Lloyd Garrison, and Wendell Phillips, leaders of the American Anti-Slavery Society for whom Douglass worked (McFeely, *Douglass,* 117).

8. Frederick Douglass, *Autobiographies: Narrative of the Life of Frederick Douglass, an American Slave* (1845), *My Bondage and My Freedom* (1855), *Life and Times of Frederick Douglass* (1893) with notes by Henry Louis Gates Jr. (New York: Library of America, 1994), 679.

9. Jacobs, *Incidents,* 183.

10. See the essays in this volume by Richard Yarborough (on Douglass and manhood) and Anne Warner (on Jacobs on womanhood). See also David Leverenz, *Manhood and the American Renaissance* (Ithaca: Cornell Univ. Press, 1989), 108–34; Stephanie Smith, *Conceived by Liberty: Maternal Figures and Nineteenth Century American Literature* (Ithaca: Cornell Univ. Press, 1994); Jenny Franchot, "The Punishment of Esther: Frederick Douglass and the Construction of the Feminine," in *Frederick Douglass: New Literary and Historical Essays,* ed. Eric J. Sundquist (New York: Cambridge Univ. Press, 1990); Valerie Smith, *Self-Discovery and Authority in Afro-American Narrative* (Cambridge: Harvard Univ. Press, 1987); Jean Fagan Yellin, "Harriet Jacobs's Family History," *American Literature* 66 (1994): 765–67 and *Women and Sisters: The Antislavery Feminists in American Culture* (New Haven: Yale Univ. Press, 1989); Frances Smith Foster, *Witnessing Slavery: The Development of Ante-bellum Slave Narratives* (Westport, Conn.: Greenwood Press, 1979); and Eric J. Sundquist, *To Wake the Nations: Race in the Making of American Literature* (Cambridge: Harvard Univ. Press, 1993), 27–134.

11. Glasgow used the phrase in *A Certain Measure: An Interpretation of Prose Fiction* (New York: Harcourt, Brace, 1943), 28. C. Hugh Holman summarizes her claim as follows: "Blood . . . because Southern culture had strained too far away from its roots in the earth; . . . irony . . . [as] the safest antidote to sentimental decay" ("Ellen Glasgow and the Southern Literary Tradition," in *Southern Writers: Appraisals in Our Time,* ed. R. C. Simonini Jr.

[Charlottesville: Univ. Press of Virginia, 1984]), 104. See also *Southern Writing: 1585–1920,* ed. Richard Beale Davis, C. Hugh Holman, and Louis D. Rubin Jr. (New York: Odyssey Press, 1970), 934; and Frederick P. W. McDowell, *Ellen Glasgow and the Ironic Act of Fiction* (Madison: Univ. of Wisconsin Press, 1963), 231.

12. E. Anthony Rotundo, *American Manhood: Transformations in Masculinity from the Revolution to the Modern Era* (New York: Basic Books, 1993), 3.

13. But see the essays in this volume by Lucinda H. MacKethan, Steven M. Stowe, and Mary Titus. See also Elizabeth Fox-Genovese, *Within the Plantation Household: Black and White Women of the Old South* (Chapel Hill: Univ. of North Carolina Press, 1988) on antebellum southern women and Drew Gilpin Faust, *Mothers of Invention: Women of the Slaveholding South in the American Civil War* (Chapel Hill: Univ. of North Carolina Press, 1996) on southern women during the Civil War. Although differences among these and other thinkers about southern womanhood in the nineteenth century center on differing convictions as to the definitions and social meanings of the southern economy, all point out that womanhood in the South suffered strains if and when it was (and is) read under the rubric of northern domesticity.

14. See, for example, the excellent collection and introduction in *The Ideology of Slavery: Proslavery Thought in the Antebellum South, 1830–1860,* ed. and introd. Drew Gilpin Faust (Baton Rouge: Louisiana State Univ. Press, 1981).

15. Though I disagree with certain of her fundamental propositions, Elizabeth Fox-Genovese has gone a long way toward developing a theory of gender's meanings for southern white women that takes account of the blurring between public and private spheres and the hierarchical ideology on the slave plantation. Though less has been written about southern white manhood, arguably Bertram Wyatt-Brown's notion of honor as opposed to conscience is about masculinity in all but name, and sometimes by its name. See Fox-Genovese, *Within the Plantation Household,* and Bertram Wyatt-Brown, *Southern Honor: Ethics and Behavior in the Old South* (New York: Oxford Univ. Press, 1982).

16. See, for instance, Eugene Genovese, " 'Our Family, White and Black': Family and Household in the Southern Slaveholders' World View," in *In Joy and in Sorrow: Women, Family, and Marriage in the Victorian South, 1830–1900,* ed. Carol Bleser (New York: Oxford Univ. Press, 1991), 69–87.

17. Jacobs, *Incidents,* n. 6, 262.

18. Dickson J. Preston's *Young Frederick Douglass: The Maryland Years* (Baltimore: Johns Hopkins Univ. Press, 1980) is especially useful for showing the range and depth of interracial relationships in Douglass's childhood.

19. Jacobs, *Incidents,* 183.

20. Leverenz, *Manhood and the American Renaissance*, 108–34.

21. Jacobs, *Incidents*, 201.

22. See, for example, Louisa McCord's "On the Enfranchisement of Women," opposing the vote for women, in *All Clever Men, Who Make Their Way: Critical Discourse in the Old South,* ed. Michael O'Brien (Fayetteville: Univ. of Arkansas Press, 1982). See also the recent collection of McCord's writing, Louisa Susanna Cheves McCord, *Political and Social Essays*, ed. Richard C. Lounsbury (Charlottesville: Univ. Press of Virginia, 1995).

23. See Lillian Smith, *Killers of the Dream* (1949; rpt. New York: Norton, 1961).

24. Jacobs, *Incidents*, n. 3, 262.

25. Qtd. in Preston, *Young Frederick Douglass*, 60.

26. Charles Chesnutt, "The Wife of His Youth," in *The Wife of His Youth, and Other Stories of the Color Line* (Boston: Houghton-Mifflin, 1899). In the same year (1899) Chesnutt published his biography of Frederick Douglass. See Charles W. Chesnutt, *Frederick Douglass* (Boston: Small, Maynard, 1899).

27. William Faulkner, "Barn Burning," in *Collected Stories of William Faulkner* (New York: Vintage, 1977), 3–25.

28. William Faulkner, *Absalom, Absalom! The Corrected Text* (New York: Vintage, 1990).

29. Katherine Anne Porter, "The Old Order," in *The Collected Stories of Katherine Anne Porter* (New York: Harvest/Harcourt Brace Jovanovich, 1972), 321–68.

30. Willa Cather, *Sapphira and the Slave Girl* (New York: Vintage, 1975).

31. Ellen Douglas, *Can't Quit You, Baby* (New York: Penguin, 1989).

PART FOUR

Where the Heart Is

Southern Strains of American Domesticity

Domesticity in Dixie

The Plantation Novel and
Uncle Tom's Cabin

Lucinda H. MacKethan

When George Fitzhugh wrote his defense of slavery, *Cannibals All! or, Slaves without Masters,* in 1851, he drew upon imagery that became essential to the arguments of both sides of the national debate on the issue in the last decade before the Civil War: public opinion in the South, he said, "unites with self-interest, domestic affection, and municipal law to protect the slave. The man who maltreats the weak and dependent, who abuses his authority over wife, children, or slaves is universally detested."[1] Fitzhugh sought to connect domestic affection with public opinion, self-interest, and municipal law as governing forces of a slavocracy; still, wife and children were linked with slaves as dependents within a patriarchally structured family, over which "man" wields "authority," pure and simple.[2] What Fitzhugh was attempting to combine in his defense of slavery—patriarchal authority and domestic affection—involved images and ideologies that were, with the advent of capitalism, increasingly viewed as mutually exclusive. Certainly in the North, and I would argue, in the South as well, the concept of "domestic affection" belonged, by the 1850s, to the cultural ideal of domesticity, which separated matters of home and hearth (women and children) from matters of public opinion, self-interest, and law (men and marketplace).

Fitzhugh was one of many proslavery advocates who, historian Willie Lee Rose tells us, intended through their vision of slavery as domestic "to suggest a benign institution that encouraged between masters and slaves the qualities so much admired in the Victorian family: cheerful obedience and gratitude on the part of children (read slaves), and paternalistic wisdom, protection, and discipline on the part of the father (read master)."[3] Yet abolitionists were able to put their counterargument productively in domestic terms as well and to ask, How can the slave be both child, defined as member of a family united in domestic affection, *and* economic unit, defined instead by law and self-interest? Rose, who has traced the slavery apologists' increasing reliance on "this pleasant little word 'domestic'" in their depictions of slavery, tells us that "it is . . . a supreme irony that the phrase 'domestic slavery' should have become in the nineteenth century the most frequent designation of an institution that was supposed, then and now, to have had a particularly devastating effect on family life."[4]

The irony of conceiving of slavery as a domestically ordered institution is perhaps no more dramatically illustrated than in the plantation fiction of southerners writing into and through the 1850s. Both the popularity of the domestic literary genre and their own social agenda led southern writers into the attempt to render the plantation household as a vision of proper domesticity. In mid-nineteenth-century America, Beverly R. Voloshin tells us, "Victorian culture . . . glorified the role of woman as homemaker and idealized the moral influence of wives and mothers."[5] Any novel that wanted to display plantation home life in this period could hardly structure a vision of its society without somehow incorporating the values of home valorized by domestic ideology. However, to enlist domesticity's attractions in the service of the plantation meant invoking images of fatherhood, motherhood, and childhood that might easily collide with some of the harsh realities of a chattel system. Moreover, to try to narrate the slave into the domestic space of the home was a direct challenge to legal and market definitions naming the slave's very existence.[6] No one, of course, understood this better than Harriet Beecher Stowe when, in early 1851, she began writing a novel calculated to influence public opinion against slavery. *Uncle Tom's Cabin* thus stands jarringly alongside southern domestically framed plantation novels of the period.

In the discussion that follows I will look at four novels—Caroline Gilman's *Recollections of a Southern Matron* (1838, reissued 1852), John Pendleton Kennedy's *Swallow Barn* (1832, revised 1851), William Gilmore Simms's *Woodcraft* (1852), and Caroline Hentz's *The Planter's Northern Bride* (1854)—which adapted many trappings of the domestic mode of fiction, originating in the North, to portrayals of plantation life.[7] Clearly, they intended to domesticate the plantation, to place the woman-centered home viably at the center of patriarchal slave society, but in such a way that the ideology of home would not threaten the necessary assumption of absolute patriarchal power in the society. A preliminary look at Stowe's antislavery accomplishment in *Uncle Tom's Cabin,* however, serves to demonstrate that all of these proslavery southern writers were forced to distort cherished values of both literary form and social ideology when they appropriated for their fictions the "pleasant little word" that Stowe made into such a formidable weapon against them.

When Stowe made the domestic novel the weapon of choice for her crusade to end slavery, she picked a form embodying strategies and values that she understood very well. Her sister Catharine Beecher was a prominent spokeswoman for the idealization of home as the embodiment of stability and the natural dominion of women. In her essay *A Treatise on Domestic Economy* (1841), Beecher had proposed that women, removed from the public sphere of the marketplace, acted in the private space of the home as faithful adjuncts providing both refuge from the world and amelioration of the hardships connected to industrial capitalism with its specters of unbridled ambition and greed.[8] Home and marketplace are thus separate realms, yet within the home, women shape the values that sons, brothers, and husbands carry into the masculine domain: "The wife sways the heart whose energies may turn for good or evil the destinies of a nation," Beecher proclaimed.[9]

Catharine Beecher connected women's domestic sphere to men's marketplace sphere through the wife and mother's role as teacher. Stowe certainly worked this connection in *Uncle Tom's Cabin.* As Elizabeth Ammons writes, "Like her sister Catherine Beecher, Harriet Beecher Stowe displays in *Uncle Tom's Cabin* a facility for converting essentially repressive concepts of femininity into a positive (and activist) alternative system of values in which woman figures not merely as the moral superior of man, his inspirer, but as the model for him in the new millennium about to dawn."[10] Two other recent studies of Stowe's domesticity offer readings that complicate the idea that Stowe is pushing an "alternative" system to patriarchy. Myra Jehlen argues that *Uncle Tom's Cabin* "appropriates the patriarchal ideology only to force it to repossess itself," so that what is sought is "not autonomy but reconciliation" between the two spheres once patriarchy is "reformed."[11] Gillian Brown, on the other hand, sees Stowe's agenda as more revolutionary; Stowe "envisions the revolt of the mother" and "the advent of mother-rule" requiring "a feminized world and domestic economy, the post-patriarchy of Liberia or a reformed America. The consolidation of domestic hegemony relies on the acceptance of Stowe's proposition that patriarchy be replaced with matriarchy for the good of the family." [12] Whatever degree of activism these readings ascribe to Stowe's domesticity, all of them indicate that in her system, patriarchal authority survives, if at all, only in a reformed condition. Stowe's influential formulation of domesticity offered a difficult, finally insurmountable challenge to southerners attempting to forge an alliance leaving the patriarchal agenda ascendant.

Uncle Tom's Cabin names slavery "the patriarchal institution" in chapter 1, where Stowe loses no time in warning her readers of the error of making "anything beautiful or desirable" out of "the oft-fabled poetic legend of a patriarchal institution." [13] The early chapters of Uncle Tom's Cabin, set on the Shelby plantation in Kentucky, create a picture of plantation domesticity only to dramatize how patriarchy, synonymous with marketplace economics, is antithetical to the domestic organization of the family. Stowe opens this section with two gentlemen sitting in "a well-furnished dining parlor." The fact that the sale of Uncle Tom and Eliza's little Harry is arranged within Mrs. Shelby's well-kept home is the first sign of the incongruity inherent in the term domestic institution applied to slavery. The men bargain and conclude a deal that has as its immediate consequence the separation of members of a family; the mother of the child to be sold appears in the scene, and the "gentlemen" (Stowe uses the term sarcastically) actually discuss, but then dismiss, the "onpleasantness" of taking the boy from his mother. So much for Mrs. Shelby's exemplary attempt to make her plantation home an ideal of domesticity. She is completely powerless to stop the monetary transaction that will destroy families she has nurtured and protected.

Stowe constructs the Shelby drama along fixed gender lines—with white men playing the roles of betrayers of domestic ideals and women, along with Uncle Tom himself, playing the roles of potentially revolutionary matriarchs. [14] The true, though ironic, locus of plantation domesticity is the cabin of Uncle Tom, who as we meet him in chapter 4 sits at a table with Shelby's son George, learning his letters, while across the room his wife cooks and his children play. The cabin's organization is purely matriarchal, the kitchen at the center, as it will be later in the home of the Quaker Rachel Halliday. [15] The locus of power is completely opposite "in the halls of the master," the Shelbys' house, described at the end of chapter 4. Mrs. Shelby articulates the difference in her question, after her husband has concluded his trade at his dining room table: "How can I bear to have this open acknowledgment that we care for no tie, no duty, no relation, however sacred, compared with money?" (29). The sacred ties envisioned in Stowe's cabin scene are swept away by Master Shelby's debt and its resolution in the sale of slaves who have been nurtured as family; that is Stowe's answer to Mrs. Shelby's question and her challenge to proslavery novelists' need to present a thoroughly patriarchal institution as a domestically enlightened one.

The southern fictions examined below had to acknowledge and at the same time try to circumvent the implications of domesticity that Stowe appropriated for her abolitionist argument. Two of these works, written by men, have traditionally been categorized as plantation novels; the two written by women have consistently been placed under the heading of domestic fiction. For our purposes, there is little reason to distinguish between the two designations. In studying southern literature of the immediate pre–Civil War period particularly, we can gain important insights by bringing together novels usually separated purely on the basis of the gender of their authors.[16] White southern antebellum novelists' chief motivation—to set the record straight concerning the benevolent, familial nature of southern slavery—and the setting they depended upon—the agriculturally based world of the plantation— bring these male and female writers together in ways that are critical to their designs, both formal and political. By seeing the novels as inevitably and irrevocably "mixed," we can understand how the gender distinctions that have usually been used to categorize these works have little to do with matters of form and everything to do with the political bases of aesthetic judgments, a matter we will consider in more detail later.

In the analyses that follow, we will cross both gender and genre distinctions as we evaluate the strategies that four important antebellum southern novelists of plantation society devised in order to fix the ideals of domesticity within their society's patriarchal order. What we will witness in this investigation is the complex web within which southern writers, both men and women, found themselves caught by the plantation setting that determined both the limits of the genre they employed and the contradictions within their ideology. Two of the works, John Pendleton Kennedy's *Swallow Barn* and Caroline Gilman's

Recollections of a Southern Matron, were first published in the 1830s, *Swallow Barn* in 1832 and *Southern Matron* in 1838. Both were reissued in 1851 and 1852, respectively; the fact that these two works in some respects anticipate rather than react directly to *Uncle Tom's Cabin* indicates their authors' certainty that just such a phenomenon as Stowe, the "vile wretch in petticoats," as one reviewer so unkindly but tellingly put it, would be able to turn domesticity against their fictional territory. The other two novels that we will consider were conceived or completed in the immediate aftermath of *Uncle Tom's Cabin*. *Woodcraft* appeared serially in early 1852 at the time that Stowe's work was concluding its serial run in the *National Era*, where it had begun publication in June of 1851. While some controversy remains concerning ways that *Woodcraft* might have intentionally constituted a response to *Uncle Tom's Cabin*, Simms did write, after the fact, that his novel was "an answer to Mrs. Stowe."[17] *The Planter's Northern Bride*, published in 1854, was unequivocally a direct response to Stowe, written, as its author Caroline Hentz said, in order to correct "the unhappy consequences of that intolerant and fanatical spirit" (4) that she explicitly associated with *Uncle Tom's Cabin*.[18]

When Kennedy reissued *Swallow Barn* in 1851, his friend Simms wrote to him, less than a month before *Uncle Tom's Cabin* began appearing in the *National Era*, that "I am glad to hear that we are to have a new edition of *Swallow Barn*. Its genial and natural pictures of Virginia life, are equally true of Southern life . . . and are in fact the most conclusive answer to the abolitionists . . . that could be made."[19] Contemporary reviews of the novel echoed Simms's sentiment that the book functioned as an answer to the abolitionists. One reviewer even noted that "we were struck . . . to find how some of the speakers, though their remarks were written for them twenty years ago, anticipated, almost in their reality, the excitement which fanaticism has got up in this day, in the subject of domestic slavery."[20]

Modern assessments of *Swallow Barn* frequently see Kennedy's portrayals of slavery as countering Stowe's, especially if they emphasize his revision of the chapter entitled "The Quarter." The new material gives plantation owner Frank Meriwether's carefully considered defense of slavery in terms that reflect Kennedy's understanding of domestic politics. Meriwether, giving his sympathetic Yankee visitor a tour of the slave quarters, appears as pure patriarch, the royal ruler; the slaves become "petitioners," and Meriwether "has constituted himself into a high court of appeal" (1851 ed., 451). Yet an air of "kind family attachment" is also noted, as Mark Littleton, a northerner himself, comments that the slave "has the helplessness of a child" (1851 ed., 452–53). Meriwether promotes two reforms: the slaves' marriages and family arrangements should be legalized, and a kind of feudal class structure should be instituted that would elevate some slaves above others, giving them degrees of self-governance and a patriarchal sort of authority within certain jurisdictions. Kennedy, through Meriwether, thus attempts to combine the opposing values of family affection and patriarchal authority.

Another much less often noted revision that Kennedy made to *Swallow Barn* is even more important to consider in assessing how a plantation novelist might respond to antislavery attacks centered in domestic ideology. In this revision, Kennedy quite simply locks the southern white woman in a domesticated bower and throws away the key. Early in the novel Kennedy takes up the question of why southern girls should be educated at home. Frank Meriwether has two teenaged daughters, Lucy and Victorine, and Mark Littleton comments briefly in the 1832 edition that these two "family paragons" were "educated at home," where they were rather spoiled. Yet Littleton approves of this arrangement, because, he says, "there is nothing more lovely to my imagination than the picture of an artless girl, tranquilly gliding onwards to womanhood in the seclusion of the parent bower"; at home, he concludes, her rambles are "limited to 'her ancient neighborhood,' like the flights of a dove in its native valley."[21]

In 1851 Kennedy saw fit to elaborate considerably on this idyllic vision. The revision stresses that the girls "are educated *entirely* at home" (my italics). He then adds a commentary that reinforces the domestic emphasis on the split between home and world, stipulating through Littleton that the woman who remains at home will be kept in a necessary and total state of ignorance about the world beyond her "native valley." The new passage reads:

> No over-stimulated ambition is likely there to taint the mind with those vices of rivalry which, in schools, often render youth selfish and unamiable, and suggest thoughts of concealment and stratagem as aids in the race of preeminence. Home, to a young girl, is a world peopled with

kindly faces and filled only with virtues. She does not know, even by report, the impure things of life. She has heard and read of its miseries, for which her heart melts in charity, and she grows up in the faith that she was born to love the good and render kind offices to the wretched; but she conceives nothing of the wickedness of a world which she has never seen, and lives on to womanhood in a happy and guarded ignorance, which is not broken until her mind has acquired a strength sufficient to discern and repel whatever there may be dangerous in knowledge. (1851 ed., 45)

Kennedy's vision here clearly assumes a necessary separation between the plantation as "home" and the competitive outside world, a separation that attempts to affirm an ideology of domesticity.

Nina Baym has written that in *Swallow Barn* "Kennedy, like other antebellum writers [and she clearly means here *male* writers, from her context], was simply not interested in women; they did not form part of his myth of the patriarchal South."[22] And while much of the novel deals with Mark Littleton's rambles with other men of the plantation community, Kennedy sketches several southern women types, including a belle, a plantation mistress, old maid sisters, and the young girls who are the subject of his meditation on education. The 1851 revision of his thinking on this subject indicates that women did indeed form an important part of Kennedy's myth of the patriarchal South, updated for the traumatic era of the 1850s. His revision anticipates and attempts to refute the revolutionary idea of a purely matriarchal domestic ideology empowering women that Stowe was soon to present. Kennedy attempts to make his 1851 plantation both patriarchal and domestically pastoral; its program is to keep women ignorant and to insure that the men operate out of a right understanding of their duty. He asserts through Littleton's ideal for women's education that the plantation represents a reserve of purity where such marketplace crimes as ambition and competition cannot enter and where women must be kept safe, like slaves protected from a world their nature makes them unfit to enter. If the women are not kept in ignorance, they might become Mrs. Shelbys, Mrs. Birds, and Rachel Hallidays, the transformation that Stowe was working out close to the time that *Swallow Barn* reappeared. And if this transformation were to happen from within the plantation realm, then patriarchy, though not destroyed, would be radically reformed in a way that would make Kennedy's slavery-dependent domestic idyll impossible. As we have noted, Myra Jehlen argues that Stowe's plan was to force patriarchy to "repossess itself" along morally new lines through the agency of women.[23] Kennedy could hope to circumvent this process both by keeping the women in a domestic state of blissful ignorance and by reassuring his readers through Frank Meriwether's speech to Littleton that plantation patriarchy was sufficiently informed by enlightened self-interest. In any case, Kennedy's revision makes it impossible for southern women to interfere because it presents their place in the plantation as a feminized bower in which blinders are the order of the day.

Given Kennedy's several stratagems for securing what he called "domestic slavery" (*Swallow Barn* 1851 ed., 465) within an enlightened, but also totalitarian, patriarchy, a confusing turn for the novel is taken when he follows his chapter "The Quarter," and actually ends his novel, with a sentimental portrait of a black matriarch grieving for her lost son. In "A Negro Mother" Meriwether visits the cabin and tells the story of an old slave named Lucy, whose son Abe died at sea in a heroic attempt to save a sinking ship. Lucy is frozen in her grief for her child, who at an earlier time had been openly rebellious against his owners and the neighborhood in general. Meriwether sent the boy to sea in order to save him from prison for his misdeeds, and Abe eventually reformed, becoming an able seaman who volunteered for the rescue mission that ended in his death. Lucy remains on the plantation, driven crazy by the separation from her son, which she never clearly understands. Kennedy's intentions in offering this portrait are puzzling for many reasons. He has just concluded a strongly worded defense of slavery, which relies on a conception of slaves as helpless children; then he risks evoking, through his pathetic portrait of crazy Lucy defined *as mother*, the associations that his readers might make with other slave mothers whose separations from children were forced through much less kindly motives than Meriwether's. It does not help the general case of slavery to have Kennedy explain that Lucy's madness is caused by "a mother's instinctive love for her offspring" (1851 ed., 486). The vision of motherhood that ends the reader's tour of this plantation, while perhaps designed to pay respect to domestic affections, makes for an unsettling conclusion to Kennedy's pastoral idyll.

Recollections of a Southern Matron, Caroline Gilman's 1838 version of southern pastoral, in many ways strives to accomplish the same aim as Kennedy's work: to make, as it were, an air-tight case for the contrast between plantation home and market world. She accomplishes this aim perhaps more successfully than Kennedy because her narrator, Cornelia Wilton, is a country maiden who voluntarily chooses the pastoral confines of the plantation after an initiation into the life of a belle in the city. As Steven Stowe explains, in Gilman's geography "the plantation is Home and the city is the Other—not quite the same thing as a dichotomy between good and evil, but a sharp duality of values nonetheless." [24] In addition to creating a woman character who actively chooses the plantation for its moral superiority, Gilman also, unlike Kennedy, consigns her male hero to the same world. Arthur Marion, Cornelia's fiancé and then husband, is given a thoroughly domesticated vision of his lot that makes him for a time a more matriarchal than patriarchal character. Much more than Frank Meriwether does Arthur represent, in his training, a patriarch "repossessed."

Gilman creates her version of an ideal master in a domesticized, feminized mold without compromising his patriarchal right to superiority, yet she makes it clear that this superiority is based upon his thorough endorsement of matriarchal values. Gilman's description of Arthur Marion's preparations for becoming head of a plantation household is worth quoting at length: he was, we learn,

> preparing himself for usefulness. Inheriting a large estate, he did not feel authorized to enter on its duties without some personal discipline. He attended medical and surgical lectures . . . and interested himself in mechanics as a means of saving labor on his plantation. His fine person never looked more noble to me than when in his workman's jacket, with his tools in his hand, he superintended, and even aided, the works of his people. He felt the responsibility of his situation, and looked with a steady and inquiring eye on his duties, removing evil where it was practicable, and ameliorating what was inevitable. It was not gain only that he sought; he was aware that he controlled the happiness of a large family of his fellow-creatures. He neither permitted himself to exercise oppression, nor tolerated it in others. Happy human faces were his delight, and the blessings that followed his footsteps were like angel voices crowning his cares. He felt how much a planter has to answer to man and to God in the patriarchal relation he holds, and he shrank not indolently from the arduous demand. (234)

Here Gilman seeks to affirm Marion's right to patriarchal authority, but she shows that the basis upon which he earns that authority is his maternal care for his family. Indeed, he is in some ways a model for Stowe's young George Shelby, who would be molded not by the example of his failed and corrupted father but through the instruction of his determined, Christian mother.

Although Gilman did not revise *Recollections of a Southern Matron* when she republished it in 1852, she did refashion its context dramatically by including with it, in one volume, a shorter work, *Recollections of a New England Bride and Housekeeper,* which had been originally published in 1834, four years earlier than *Southern Matron.* In the 1852 edition, *Recollections of a Southern Matron* is placed first. Joined together, and readable as a possible reply to Stowe's reformulation of domesticity along antipatriarchal lines, the two works make a single point for Gilman, that the plantation, with slavery as a thoroughly domesticized institution, offers white women the best, perhaps even the only, environment within which to make the values of home supreme. Indeed, in the 1852 juxtaposition, Gilman shows by her contrasts that women's attempts to make a world for themselves beyond the nurturing organization of the plantation would be all but impossible. New England, in the companion text to *Southern Matron,* is synonymous with marketplace, and the young heroine in *New England Housekeeper* is only that, a struggling, ineffective "keeper" of a house that is constantly threatened by her husband's business problems, her servants' ambitions, the rivalries and sordid complications of urban existence generally. By contrast, in *Southern Matron* Cornelia Wilton can be just that, a "Matron," a woman organizing her world as intrinsically matriarchal.

In *Recollections of a Southern Matron,* Gilman wrote to offer a vision of woman's place as it ought to be and could be only by removal from the forces controlling the marketplace model that she embodied in the New England of her persecuted young northern bride. What Gilman stresses in her southern portrait is a perfectly domesticated version of the plantation, but she ties this vision to the qualifications of the plantation master as well as the mistress, both trained from youth onward to insure the stability of their world, which includes children, slaves, and even lower-class white neighbors, all as dependents. As Cornelia puts it, "We are as one" (105); there is what she calls a "system of attentions" that has replaced the system of competition that rules Gilman's New England setting. For Gilman, as Steven Stowe says, "the country was an analogue to the female domain."[25] After a brief visit to the city, Cornelia returns with relief to the domestic environment where woman belongs and where man will sustain her, since both fulfill themselves in a plantation organization that enshrines the matron in both sexes.

There is only one discordant note that mars Gilman's vision of the plantation as perfect female or feminized domain. Near the end of her novel, in a chapter entitled "The Planter's Bride," Cornelia Marion describes her life as a young wife on her husband's plantation, Bellevue, which she has envisioned before her arrival as "a quiet port in which I should rest with Arthur, after drifting so long on general society" (290). The reality that supplants this dream is startling, not only for Cornelia but for readers who have been led to expect that this plantation will confirm for woman the promise that the ideal of home has suggested throughout the novel. Instead of the completion of her ideal, Cornelia finds herself almost completely alone, abandoned by a husband whose talk and attentions begin to be taken up almost completely by "crops and politics, draining the fields and draining the revenue" (292). The plantation wife's only recourse, Gilman admits through her heroine, is "gentle submission," even if it "sometimes requires a struggle like life and death" (297). The good wife must let her husband know nothing of the struggle that follows "the first chill of the affections," a chill that is presented as inevitable; the reward will be "the star of domestic peace" (298), purchased dearly at the cost of any self-fulfillment on the part of the "planter's bride." Like Kennedy's late chapter, "A Negro Mother," this concluding commentary confuses the message and the motives that have governed the novel. The plantation becomes an isolated, lonely, boring prison; Arthur becomes "a sensible, independent married man, desirous of fulfilling all the relations of society," and Cornelia becomes the Angel of the House, consigned to one corner of society, called reverently, but also resignedly, "domestic peace." Another southern novel designed to promote domesticity, plantation-style, falls short of its goal.

William Gilmore Simms's *Woodcraft* and Caroline Hentz's *The Planter's Northern Bride,* written with their authors' full awareness of how effectively Stowe had revolutionized the functions of domesticity in her campaign against slavery, go to drastic lengths to provide some counterbalance. Kennedy and Gilman tried, albeit somewhat unsuccessfully, to adapt domestic values in a fairly straightforward way to the plantation scheme. In their turn, Simms and Hentz seem to have decided that images of traditional domestic ordering, with women *and* men encouraging the primacy of family and home, would not support the extra weight of slaves—not after Stowe's dramatic rendering of the failure of domestic space in the households of the Shelbys and St. Clares.

Simms in *Woodcraft* chooses to abandon the domestic ideal altogether in order to avoid making his plantation scene vulnerable to suggestions of the kind of overhaul Stowe proposed. It takes more than a third of the novel for Simms to get his hero, Porgy, with his faithful servant Tom, home to his plantation following the end of his service in the Revolutionary War. The chapter detailing their arrival is entitled "The Old Soldier Returns to a Ruined Homestead." It is almost as if Simms could see the future in a novel set in the distant past; as Porgy approaches his home, "it was the most dull, melancholy, dreary ride that any one could possibly take" (174), for the armies have destroyed nearly everything in their path, and while the house "had escaped the torch" (175), everything around it is a wasteland not unlike the scene that Confederate soldiers would find returning home in 1865. His plantation bears the name "Glen-Eberley," for "a goodly grandmother by whom it had been entailed on her brother's children" (175), but the maternal name is ironic, since the bachelor Porgy and his male companions become its only inhabitants. The housekeeping is all accomplished at Glen-Eberley by the faithful Tom, who runs *his* kitchen not like a gentle matron but like a "despot" enforcing army discipline.

Porgy is no Arthur Marion, schooled to maternally framed duties, yet he is also no Meriwether, an effective patriarch who promotes the image of father as well as businessman. Simms tries to meet Stowe's promotion of women as agents of change by creating his own powerful woman character in *Woodcraft*. The Widow Eveleigh manages to keep plantation order while Porgy flounders. She becomes the protector of the novel's plantation world, but not through gentle matriarchal nurturing. The twist Simms provides is that the Widow Eveleigh does not bring the world into accord with domestic values but instead herself masters the values of the marketplace. With courage, imagination, and efficiency that are entirely undomestic, the good widow opens the novel by going to departing British officials at the end of their Revolutionary War occupation of Charleston and demanding that they return her illegally confiscated slaves and those of her neighbor, the stalwart American soldier hero Porgy. There is no attempt to show slavery as familial in this scene; the slaves are called quite unequivocally "property." The widow engages in a battle of wits with British military officials, and as she ponders the ethics of stealing a document that will prove her case, she thinks, "Away with such childish scruples. It is war between us, perhaps, and I owe them no courtesies, no forbearance" (12). Widow Eveleigh is not the proponent of "domestic peace," like Cornelia Wilton, but instead takes the field, using men's language and men's arguments to fight for the first of all patriarchal values—her rightful ownership of property.

In a similarly patriarchal promotion, Simms makes the Widow Eveleigh stand for freedom, over marriage; she refuses marriage with Porgy because, as she says, "I have been too long my own mistress to submit to authority" (513). She also stands for individual will over obedience to husband; while her husband had been a tory, she was a colonist. Finally, she stands for law over feeling; while Porgy defies the sheriff in order to keep his land from a villainous creditor, using the argument of moral right not unlike Stowe's Mrs. Bird, Widow Eveleigh works within legal limits, turning to the right kind of authorities to effect necessary change within the system. For Simms, then, she is, as James Meriwether has noted, "the moral center of the novel";[26] the morality she upholds, however, is not the supremacy of the heart that Stowe's Mrs. Bird, for instance, proclaims, but a combination of head and heart, validating and upholding the dominance of patriarchal economy. Meriwether claims for Mrs. Eveleigh many masculine virtues: "She has the cooler head, the quicker wit, the better judgment. She is far-sighted and stable, a good administrator, and a good politician."[27] Charles S. Watson goes so far as to say that Simms makes Mrs. Eveleigh "the model planter."[28] Simms seems to have been aiming somehow to feminize the South's patriarchal scene without allowing the kinds of associations with domestic power, the power of woman *within* the home, that Stowe used so effectively to attack slavery as antifamily, antihome.

Caroline Hentz, like Simms, takes a path in *The Planter's Northern Bride* that affirms the South as patriarchy, and like Simms, she was at least partly motivated, we can assume, by her need to present an alternative to Stowe's vision of matriarchal domesticity as an organization that must triumph over both patriarchal slave economy and northern capitalism. Interestingly, while Simms the male writer turned a plantation mistress into a kind of ideal patriarch, Hentz the woman writer disallows the plantation mistress any effective agency, even or especially in the matriarchal functions of maintaining home and hearth.

Hentz gives to her planter hero, Russell Moreland, attributes of both genders that enable him to keep his plantation world intact. Unquestionably a patriarch, he is, moreover, a father who mothers his daughter, instructs his wife in housekeeping, puts down a slave insurrection, and politely but firmly refutes rude northern criticisms of his way of life. While many of Hentz's other novels contain strong, independent women characters, in *The Planter's Northern Bride* none of the women, southern or northern, has the strength of character to sustain a domestic order, much less reform one. Moreland, whose name links him with the extensive, idealized plantation he owns, makes all the decisions affecting life on his estate. In addition, he is divorced—his first wife, a woman of mysterious foreign birth brought up in a loving, wealthy southern home, lived only for licentious pleasures and had to be cast off. Moreland's sister is totally helpless, and his northern bride, the lovely Eulalia, is beautiful, sweet, eager to learn, and totally without adequate experience in homemaking—she cannot even play the piano. Only a southern man, schooled in duty, morally unshakable, physically invincible, can make the plantation world a safe haven in Hentz's scheme. Women are indeed on a level with children and slaves in respect to their abilities to handle affairs either within or beyond the plantation's confines.

Hentz's need to attack Stowe's domestic strategy leads her to include in her story of the plantation one plot element that seems particularly out of keeping, finally, with the overall point she wants to make about the superiority of southern life. Stowe, especially with Uncle Tom, but with her other slave characters as well, promoted a vision of the black race as docile and virtuous. At one point she speaks of Tom's "gentle, domestic heart," and she adds that this trait "has been a peculiar habit of his unhappy race!" (81). Stowe links northern white women and slaves in a gentleness and compassion that constitute a basis for power contrasting at every point with the authoritarian, aggressive means of the white patriarch. Hentz's slave characters, on the other hand, exhibit bestial physical power; unlike her passive, virtuous white women, her slaves are capable of violence and incapable of deep feeling or loyalty. Hentz was willing to include in her novel the threat of a slave uprising in order to give her readers an antidote to the long-suffering, nonviolent, sacrificial, and womanly Uncle Tom. In doing so, she threatened her own vision of secure plantation order with destruction. While the aborted uprising is blamed on ignorant, self-serving northern meddlers, the effect of placing even a potential for violent slave rebellion within plantation society undermines the southern claim that slavery was redeemed by domestic affections.

The southern novels that surrounded *Uncle Tom's Cabin* contain many of the standard features of both domestic and plantation fiction, yet they also present Kennedy's grief-crazed slave mother Lucy, Gilman's lonely and resigned Cornelia, Simms's ineffectual Porgy on his ruined and debt-ridden homestead, and, with Hentz, a whole host of helpless women and monstrous slaves. In all of these works, domesticity is given its due; the home is exalted as sacred and primary, yet never can these novels shake their awareness that the plantation depended, finally, on a patriarchal authority that could and often did sacrifice home to marketplace. The place of both women and slaves in this world is never secure. Kennedy's Swallow Barn, Gilman's Bellevue, Simms's Glen-Eberley, and Hentz's Moreland estate cannot, in the end, function as true domestic space any more than can Simon Legree's plantation. Images of maternal, familial nurturing fail to stand against incongruous yet inevitable insertions of images of patriarchal authority. With Stowe, a Senator Bird can capitulate in Indiana, and a young George Shelby can lead a reformation in Kentucky, both repossessed by the domestic vision of wife or mother. But a Meriwether, a Marion, a Porgy, and a Moreland have too much at stake to turn over the lines of power that sustain them.

In his 1853 review of Stowe's *Key to Uncle Tom's Cabin*, Simms shows how fidelity to gendered lines of power could entrap the novelist along with his characters in a web of contradictions. Simms complained that Stowe in her novel had created a "Mosaic monster" that did not conform to the conventions of any established literary genre.[29] Simms argued, as S. P. C. Duvall has summarized, that Stowe had used "the *structure* of the romance" but had undermined that genre by including social protest and so "had violated the formal canons, and her work was false to art."[30] Simms's interest in attacking Stowe in terms of her violation of genre is instructive of the way that genre becomes the vehicle of political power struggles. Genres become a way to restrict—a romance writer cannot enter the realm of social critique, just as in so much writing, even today, about domestic novels, it is assumed that domestic novels are narrowly concerned with women's concerns in the home. Simms also grounds his attack on Stowe in gender; he criticizes her ability to make her points logically, commenting that "she argues sensuously, from the woman nature."[31] It is not surprising to see Simms charging Stowe with violating rigid conventions of both genre and gender in his attempt to discredit a book whose ideology is what he really deplores. Interestingly, he never mentions the word *domestic* in his analysis of *Uncle Tom's Cabin*. It is a word, he might have understood, that he and other southern writers needed for their own campaign, as well as one giving a name to the particular ideological argument that Stowe had used so adeptly against them. Simms could neither acknowledge the source of *Uncle Tom's Cabin*'s persuasive power nor successfully transfer it to his own critical cause. He and other southern plantation novelists, both men and women, found themselves at the last undone by the moral confusion of their own ideology, which had to hold at all costs not only to the connection between patriarchy and domesticity but to the dominance of patriarchy within domesticity. The increasingly troubling distortions of acceptable male and female roles that this connection demanded in the end turned southern fictions of the plantation into a chaos of genres and genders. The label "mosaic monster" that Simms tried to attach to his northern literary nemesis became instead the epitaph of Domesticity in Dixie.

Notes

1. George Fitzhugh, *Cannibals All! or, Slaves without Masters* (1851; rpt. Cambridge: Harvard Univ. Press, 1960), 18.

2. Anne Firor Scott, in "Women's Perspective on the Patriarchy in the 1850's," *Journal of American History* 61 (1974): 52–64, discusses this and other statements by antebellum southerners who utilized "the image of a beautifully articulated patriarchal society in which every southerner, black or white, male or female, rich or poor, had an appropriate place and was happy in it" (52); other useful discussions of southern conceptions of patriarchy are Severn Duvall's "*Uncle Tom's Cabin*: The Sinister Side of the Patriarchy," *New England Quarterly* 36 (1963): 3–22, and Christina Zwarg's "Fathering and Blackface in *Uncle Tom's Cabin*," *Novel: A Forum* 22 (1990): 274–87. Elizabeth Fox-Genovese (*Within the Plantation Household: Black and White Women of the Old South* [Chapel Hill: Univ. of North Carolina Press, 1988]) prefers the word *paternalism* to describe the antebellum household's organization, "for paternalism invokes a specific metaphor of legitimate domination:

the protective domination of the father over his family" (64). However, Scott and Duvall show that there was widespread use of the word *patriarchy* to describe white male domination over the home. Elizabeth Ammons as well, in "Heroines in *Uncle Tom's Cabin,*" *American Literature* 49 (1977): 161–79, discusses how "the term 'patriarchal institution' as a synonym for slavery was common" (32). She is particularly interested in how Stowe "use[s] the words 'patriarch' and 'patriarchal' and . . . 'anti-patriarchal' in provocative ways" (174n).

3. Willie Lee Rose, "The Domestication of Domestic Slavery," in *Slavery and Freedom,* ed. William W. Freehling (New York: Oxford Univ. Press, 1982), 21.

4. Ibid.

5. Beverly R. Voloshin, "The Limits of Domesticity: The Female *Bildungsroman* in America, 1820–1870," *Women's Studies* 10 (1984): 284.

6. Elizabeth Fox-Genovese argues that white southerners, because they defined the household as the site of both "production and reproduction" (*Within the Plantation Household,* 61–66, 78–80), from the beginning did not accept an ideology of domesticity that separated home and marketplace. This ideology she sees as associated with a northern, urban, capitalist economy. Yet, as Kennedy and Gilman in particular show in their novels and as Willie Lee Rose's discussion supports, plantation slavery apologists often made use of the domestic concept of these "spheres" as separate, and they were committed to devising some means of connecting them, even if largely in order to support an ideal of slavery as a domestic (home-centered) institution operating safely within a white male-dominated power structure.

7. All quotations from these works, except as otherwise noted, are as follows: Caroline Howard Gilman, *Recollections of a Southern Matron* (New York: Putnam, 1852); John Pendleton Kennedy, *Swallow Barn; or, a Sojourn in the Old Dominion,* ed. Lucinda H. MacKethan (1851; rpt. Baton Rouge: Louisiana State Univ. Press, 1986); William Gilmore Simms, *Woodcraft; or, Hawks about the Dovecote,* rev. ed. (1856; rpt. Ridgewood, N.J.: Gregg Press, 1968); Caroline Lee Hentz, *The Planter's Northern Bride* (1854; rpt. Chapel Hill: Univ. of North Carolina Press, 1970).

8. Catharine Beecher, *A Treatise on Domestic Economy* (1841; rpt. New York: Shocken, 1977). The fullest discussion of Beecher's domestic program is Kathryn Kish Sklar's *Catharine Beecher: A Study in Domesticity* (New Haven: Yale Univ. Press, 1973).

9. Beecher, *Treatise,* 13.

10. Ammons, "Heroines," 163.

11. Myra Jehlen, "The Family Militant: Domesticity vs. Slavery," *Criticism* 31 (1989): 399.

12. Gillian Brown, "Getting into the Kitchen with Dinah: Domestic Politics in *Uncle Tom's Cabin*," *American Quarterly* 36 (1984): 522.

13. Harriet Beecher Stowe. *Uncle Tom's Cabin* (1852; rpt. New York: Norton, 1994), 8.

14. See Elizabeth Ammons's discussion of Tom as mother in her study of Stowe's "odd equation of mothers/Eva/Tom, an equation which, if followed through to its logical conclusion, argues the radical substitution of feminine and maternal for masculine values" ("Heroines," 163).

15. Jane Tompkins and Gillian Brown both discuss Stowe's kitchens, Brown emphasizing the disorder of Dinah's kitchen in the St. Clares' house as a sign of how political and domestic economies intersect and Tompkins reading Rachel Halliday's kitchen as "the symbol of maternal comfort" (Tompkins, "Sentimental Power: *Uncle Tom's Cabin* and the Politics of Literary History," *Glyph* 8 [1981]: 95).

16. The separation by gender of studies of antebellum novels is certainly the norm; thus, we have, for instance, Michael Kreyling treating only novels by males in his "The Hero in Antebellum Southern Narrative," *Southern Literary Journal* 9 (1984): 3–20, and Amy Thompson McCandless treating only novels by women in "Concepts of Patriarchy in the Popular Novels of Antebellum Southern Women," *Studies in Popular Culture* 10, no. 2 (1987): 1–16. Elizabeth Moss, in *Domestic Novelists in the Old South: Defenders of Southern Culture* (Baton Rouge: Louisiana State Univ. Press, 1992) places the antebellum southern women novelists she treats in the genre of "domestic fiction, a popular nineteenth-century literary form written exclusively by women for women" (3). This kind of categorizing can result in an oversimplifying of the goals and structures of both southern women's and men's novels.

17. James Meriwether argues against seeing *Woodcraft* as a deliberate answer by Simms to *Uncle Tom's Cabin*. In "The Theme of Freedom in Simms's *Woodcraft*" (*"Long Years of Neglect": The Work and Reputation of William Gilmore Simms,* ed. John Caldwell Guilds [Fayetteville: Univ. of Arkansas Press, 1988]), he reviews the evidence for and against reading *Woodcraft* as a response to Stowe. In "Simms's Answer to *Uncle Tom's Cabin:* Criticism of the South in *Woodcraft*" (*Southern Literary Journal* 9 [1976]: 78–90), Charles S. Watson maintains that Simms used *Woodcraft* not only to answer Stowe but to offer his own pointed criticism of the flaws of the South, especially the planter as represented by Porgy.

18. Elizabeth Moss, in *Domestic Novelists of the Old South,* reviews Hentz's reactions to *Uncle Tom's Cabin* and her haste to publish a reply that would counteract its effects (106–10).

19. Qtd. in Hugh W. Hetherington, ed., *Cavalier of Old South Carolina* (Chapel Hill: Univ. of North Carolina Press, 1966), 39.

20. Qtd. in William S. Osborne, ed., *Swallow Barn; or, a Sojourn in the Old Dominion* (New York: Hafner, 1962), xli.

21. John Pendleton Kennedy, *Swallow Barn; or, a Sojourn in the Old Dominion*, 2 vols. (Philadelphia: Cary and Lea, 1832), 1: 43.

22. Nina Baym, "The Myth of the Myth of Southern Womanhood," *Feminism and American Literary History* (New Brunswick: Rutgers Univ. Press, 1992), 187.

23. Jehlen, "Family Militant," 385.

24. Steven M. Stowe. "City, Country, and the Feminine Voice," in *Intellectual Life in Old Charleston,* ed. Michael O'Brien (Knoxville: Univ. of Tennessee Press, 1986), 304.

25. Ibid., 308.

26. Meriwether, "Theme of Freedom," 26.

27. Ibid., 27.

28. Watson, "Simms's Answer," 81.

29. William Gilmore Simms, "Stowe's Key to *Uncle Tom's Cabin,*" *Southern Quarterly Review* 24 (July 1853): 228.

30. S. P. C. Duvall, in his 1958 note, established Simms's authorship of this unsigned review and argues that Simms preferred to review Stowe's *Key*, rather than her novel, because the *Key* opened the way for Simms to base his attack on her artistic flaws rather than frontally on her ideology ("W. G. Simms's Review of Mrs. Stowe," *American Literature* 30 [1958]: 116).

31. Simms, "Stowe's Key," 218.

The Dining Room Door Swings Both Ways

Food, Race, and Domestic Space in the Nineteenth-Century South

MARY TITUS

> *Oaklands was famous for many things: its fine light-bread, its cinnamon cakes, its beat biscuit, its fricasseed chicken, its butter and cream, its wine-sauces, its plum-puddings, its fine horses, its beautiful meadows, its sloping green hills, and last, but not least, its refined and agreeable society.*
>
> —LETITIA BURWELL, *A Girl's Life in Virginia before the War*

LETITIA BURWELL'S easy movement from cuisine to company has not lost its appeal. One hundred years after the publication of her romantic memoir, it remains a characteristic gesture in descriptions of southern living. Yet the intimate confirming relations of cuisine and civility, rich food and hospitality, that have come to characterize the South have their roots deep in the region's farraginous history of race, gender, and social status and, like many cultural signs, serve in part to cover over their uncomfortable origins.

The groaning table of southern cuisine, heavily laden with baked, stewed, creamed, and beaten burdens, attests in cookbook, memoir, and fiction to the hospitality of the southern home. It is the triumphant image in a battle for popular representation of the southern home that took place in the second half of the nineteenth century, fought by former slaveholders, slaves, and abolitionists, writers of romantic memoirs, slave narratives, and plantation fictions—all striving for control of "the way it really was." Their accounts are ideologically influenced on every side, shaped by the dominant concerns of a period in which food preparation was intimately associated with a woman's social status and by the debate over the effects of slavery on domestic life.

This essay will suggest ways in which we can read conflicting postbellum representations of antebellum plantation life from the perspective of the dining room. First, I attempt to establish some of the meanings of dining—the ritualized consumption of food—in the mid to late nineteenth century. In the South these meanings burdened the threshold between the dining room and the kitchen with particular significance. I then turn to several literary texts from the second half of the nineteenth century, exploring the ways in which they employ representations of cooking and dining, kitchens and dining rooms, as part of their argument for "the way it was."

"Brutes feed. The best barbarian only eats. Only the cultured man can dine," announces a late nineteenth-century anthropologist. Dinner, properly prepared and consumed, indicates culture, achieved and enacted. The dining room, the table and sideboard, the linens, silver, and china, the courses, and the gestures appropriate to consuming each were all given special attention by nineteenth-century Americans. These eating rituals served as "protective symbolic covering" for a "primary bodily activity"; through them, as John Kasson notes, Americans expressed "their attitudes toward their physical bodies, their social relationships, and their sense of the larger social order."[1] By 1852, books of domestic architecture were giving significant space and detail to the dining room; "the possession of a well-furnished dining room indicated that the owner of a house had the wealth, the time, and the social knowledge to devote special effort to meal . . . consumption."[2] Elaborate meals served in elaborate rooms and eaten according to elaborate rituals had several confirming functions. In the North, particularly toward the end of the century, they served as the demarcations of social status in a society where newcomers could too easily voice a righteous egalitarianism. The importance of manners as a barricade against the aspiring is best evidenced in the numerous and popular books describing proper dinner table etiquette. "Social rituals . . . simultaneously offered a means for social mobility and for social discipline. . . . etiquette was to social interchange what civil laws were to society as a whole."[3] At the same time as dining room rituals functioned as signs of social status, they also participated in other cultural concerns. Attention to the dining room as the heart of the home accompanied the ideology of female domesticity. Descriptions of dining room furnishings in house-plan books make evident that the "room was to be part of the ideal Christian family home that was promoted by Catharine Beecher and other domestic reformers, a sacred space where the family could commune together."[4] After the table itself, with its careful setting, the most popular furnishing was an elaborate sideboard where a display of china and silver revealed the household's social position and devotion to domestic ritual.

In the South, where social institutions were shaped by slavery and racial institutions, food became a particularly complex cultural text. If in the North, table rituals demarcated social classes, in the South they confirmed white aristocracy. Thus, in both plantation fiction and romantic memoirs of the Old South we find numerous accounts of lavish dinners about heavily laden tables, equally graced by ornate tableware and the refined manners of a white southern woman. Accounts of the complex ritual of formal dinners at wealthy plantations function as symbolic descriptions of southern paternalism in action. The elegance and even extravagance of these meals testify to the aristocratic status of their host and hostess and suggest that nature blesses their social order. Ceremonial dining confirmed the white family's position in the hierarchical order of the plantation.

Yet the fact that the food on plantations was prepared by black slaves made the application of northern domestic ideology to southern family life less than perfect. Catharine Beecher might extol the well-designed, clean kitchen as the locus of family harmony, and her sister Harriet could represent the triumph of women's power to unite spiritual and temporal worlds in the Quaker Rachel's kitchen,[5] but for southern slaveholding women the actual cooking in the plantation kitchen was done by a black cook, most likely a woman as well. Delicious, exquisite dishes, beautiful china, elegant table rituals, even recipes equaled culture—but the labor of cooking itself generally did not. Thus, southern women like Mary Chesnut rejected the union of "piety and pie-making" that characterized the literature of domesticity.[6] Elizabeth Fox-Genovese points out that where "Northern bourgeois literature featured the kitchen as the heart of the household, the mother's empire . . . Southern literature, like Southern architecture, honored the kitchen by expelling it from the house."[7]

In the separation of kitchen and house, as well as the attention paid to elaborate dining, one can read symbolic separations between those who prepare the food and those who consume it. As Mary Douglas argues in *Purity and Danger,* "Some such break we would expect to find whenever the production of food is in the hands of the *relatively* impure."[8] Architectural readings of the layouts of famous plantations, such as Monticello or Shirley, note the elaborate spatial hierarchies of house and outbuildings, which relegate food preparation as well as disposal of wastes to buildings separate from the main house and invisible when that house is viewed from the front—the traditional viewpoint. Architectural historians William Alexander Lambeth and Warren H. Manning comment on Jefferson's Monticello: "Jefferson began by concealing all . . . the symbols which suggested service, veiling the materials of our lower activities . . . while preventing their overflow into, and their hard intrusion upon, the spirit of a home. Not only did Monticello do this, but it went further by obscuring those that performed the service."[9] The dining room in Monticello has dumbwaiters on either side of the fireplace and revolving shelves on the door so that wine and food could be invisibly served.[10]

No plantation had more elaborate arrangements than Monticello, perhaps because no other plantation owner gave as much intellectual time to the details of domesticity and their relation to his intellectual activity and symbolic role as did Jefferson. However, almost all large plantations—as studies of their layouts reveal—echoed master/slave, mind/body hierarchies in their location of offices, kitchens, and cabins and stables. As architect Carl Anthony notes, "The plantation system shaped the form of these mansions in important ways. The social distance between master and slave . . . required a special accommodation in domestic architecture,"[11] more special and careful because of the actual intimacy that exerted pressure on the symbolic distance. "The relationship between the master and the slave had a paradoxical quality: if the social and cultural distance between them was great, the physical distance was non-existent."[12]

Because of this physical proximity, evident in the movement of food from the black-dominated space of the kitchen to the white-dominated space of the dining room, the doorways of dining rooms and kitchens represent highly symbolic thresholds. As Mary Douglas reminds us in *Purity and Danger,* "The homely experience of going through a door is able to express so many kinds of entrance."[13] In her analysis, entrance has meanings that extend to the body, since the body functions "as a symbol of society," with the result that we can "see the powers and dangers credited to social structure reproduced in small on the human body." Her argument is of course highly applicable to the southern ideology of racial purity. But the mistake, Douglas argues, "is to treat bodily margins in isolation from all other margins."[14] The threshold between kitchen and dining room represents a crucial margin across which food passes; we could name this threshold the locus of the second most intimate possible relation between blacks and whites.

Reading back and forth from kitchen to dining room, dining room to kitchen in nineteenth-century texts, we can see how the position of each writer on the South's social institution shapes their representation of foodways. The antebellum accounts of slaveholding white women are significantly silent about food thresholds. As Elizabeth Fox-Genovese's research made evident, descriptions of kitchens appear more frequently in black- than in white-authored texts; it was a place "which mistresses almost never described before the war." In the letters and memoirs of these women, the kitchen threshold was the location of daily, often distressing responsibility. There they gave orders for the day's meals and often faced resistance to their authority. As Fox-Genovese notes, "Notoriously, cooks challenged their mistresses' greatest diplomacy in supervision. Commonly cooks would be older, as well as more experienced, than the mistress they 'served' . . . who could not run a proper household without their compliance."[15] In *Within the Plantation Household* she recounts two incidents from the memoirs of slaveholding women in which the young white mistress was denied entrance into the kitchen by the black cook, and told instead to keep to her sphere; as one cook is reported saying, "Jes' read yer book an' res' easy til I sens it ter de dining room."[16] The separation of kitchen from dining room, and the symbolic separation or "ritual break" between black food preparation and white consumption which that distance expressed, made the kitchen a marginalized location in the white household. Ironically, then, the kitchen became a place where black women could establish an authority that potentially threatened the white household at its very center—in the dining room and its rituals.

Abolitionists, who often perceived the power of slave owners over slaves as a sexualized relation and thus imagined the South as a locus of unrestrained licentiousness, saw the elevated culture and civilization that dinnertime rituals should confirm as corrupted by the presence of slaves waiting on the table. As one writer imagined the scene, "Not only in taverns, but in boarding houses and the dwellings of individuals, boys and girls verging on maturity altogether unclothed, wait upon ladies and gentlemen." [17] A similar perspective shapes Fanny Kemble's account of a dinner party, which occurs in the context of her critique of southern chivalry. Attacking the pretensions of "proud planters," Kemble exposes their real lack of civility through a description of their dining practices. Her account of "young gentlemen, in gay guard chains and fine attire, [who] played the gallants" and "filthy, barefooted, half-naked negro women [who] . . . stood all the while fanning the cake, and sweetmeats, and their young masters, as if they had been all the same sort of stuff," expresses her view that both the dignity and rank of the southern gentleman is compromised by his relations with slave women. "I felt ashamed for the lads," she concludes. [18]

Etiquette books promoted manners as the sign of the triumph of the civilized over the animal; as one manual noted, "Eating is so entirely a sensual, animal gratification, that unless it is conducted with much delicacy, it becomes unpleasant to others." [19] For Fanny Kemble, the proximity of uneducated slaves to whites meant the proximity of a degradation that compromised any construction of civilized life. Her description of the kitchen at her plantation forms part of her attack on slavery as an institution incompatible with civilization. Despite the fact that the "kitchen [is] detached from the dwelling," Kemble cannot separate production from consumption. The sight of the room "and its tenants," whom she describes as "a congregation of filthy negroes who lounge in and out . . . like hungry hounds at all hours of the day and night," makes the animal fact of eating too evident and is thus "enough to slacken the appetite of the hungriest hunter that ever lost all nice regards in the mere animal desire for food." [20]

Perhaps Stowe, writing from the perspective of northern domestic ideology, provides the most thorough condemnation of southern kitchens. In *Uncle Tom's Cabin*, the deeper south one travels, and the further one moves from abolitionist sympathy, the more disorderly the kitchen. The climax is of course Dinah's disorder; like the home of a "squirrel or magpie," it is made up of "hiding-holes," with a place for everything and everything out of place. [21] In Stowe's opinion, St. Clare's attitude toward this disorder is reprehensible, as reprehensible as his attitude toward the institution of slavery, which of course underlies the chaos in Dinah's kitchen. According to St. Clare, "Dinah gets you a capital dinner—soup, ragout, roast fowl, dessert, ice-creams, and all," but Stowe makes clear that his pleasure in the elaborate meal rests on his ability to ignore its origins. In fact, his reasons for avoiding the kitchen echo Fanny Kemble's: "Heavens bless us! if we are to go down there and view all the smoking and squatting about . . . we should never eat more!"[22] Unlike Kemble, however, St. Clare finds no argument against slavery in the chaos of Dinah's kitchen. Gillian Brown sums up the situation: "St. Clare prefers to ignore the problems of the state Dinah represents. Worrying about the details of slavery, he warns Ophelia, is 'like looking too close into the details of Dinah's kitchen. . . . St. Clare fails to recognize the intimacy between domestic and political issues" that is central to Stowe's argument.[23]

Slave narratives often brilliantly exploited the prevailing white ideological conceptions of dining and domestic space. In response to the visions of southern plantations as cornucopias of plenty for black and white alike, the narratives describe meager rations, parsimoniously distributed. Hunger, not plenty, labor, not leisure, characterize their accounts. Whereas abolitionist writers represented the intimate presence of uncivilized black slaves as undermining ideal domestic relations in the white household, writers of slave narratives revised this viewpoint by assigning uncivilized or bestial qualities and polluting behavior to whites, particularly white women, thereby rejecting the racism implicit in much abolitionist writing. Harriet Jacobs, for example, moves Stowe's connection between kitchen disorder and general social disorder one step further in her narrative. While Dinah's kitchen suggested a "squirrel's" or "magpie's" nest and Kemble saw her kitchen as a place of filth, where slaves, like "hounds," appeared at any hour, Jacobs relocates the animality in a slaveholding household in the white master and mistress. The Flints force their cook to eat the food they reject from the table, and then, more terribly, they demand that she prepare a dish for the dog and then eat the food it has slavered in and rejected.[24] Rather than nourishing, food is polluted and used for punishment in this kitchen, revealing the perversity of white domination. Two years earlier, Harriet E. Wilson had even more forcefully assigned bestiality to the white woman; in her 1859 novel *Our Nig*, Frado refuses to eat from her employer's dirty plate until the dog has licked it clean—rather the tongue of an honest animal.[25]

Likewise, writers of slave narratives associate the pollution of food, not its cleansing, with the white mistress. In one narrative included in John Blassingame's *Slave Testimony*, a black cook describes an "ole missus" who "looked like a witch" patting animal filth into butter the

cook had made "nice an' clean an' sweet" so that the slave would receive a punishment:

> She'd set dere an' dat look 'ud come into her eyes an' she'd study an'
> study what to whip me about. I 'member one mornin' she look at me an'
> she says to marster, "dat nigger needs a whipping." He don answer, but
> w'en out in de field. den she sent me to de churnery an' I made de butter
> nice an' clean an' sweet, an' I put it away. Pretty soon I saw she take it
> out an' pat it an' pat it. When marster come in to dinner he go to eat de
> butter, an', ugh, it smell, an' it look full er cows' hairs. Den he got up an'
> call me outside. Dat's de way my missus get me a whipping.[26]

Perhaps the most striking of such accounts of food pollution is Harriet
Jacobs's. If Sunday dinner was not on time, Mrs. Flint "would station
herself in the kitchen, and wait till it was dished, and then spit in all
the kettles and pans that had been used for cooking . . . to prevent the
cook and her children from eking out their meagre fare with the remains of the gravy and other scrapings." The Flints have so perverted
nourishment that they will lock their cook "away from her nursing
baby."[27] In a chapter titled "Sketches of Neighboring Planters," Jacobs
extends the connections between abuse and food throughout the white
slaveholding community. The chapter first describes a specific torture
in which "scalding drops of fat" from "a piece of fat pork" burn a
bound slave; it climaxes with the description of a young slave, trapped
in a cotton gin, "partly eaten by rats and vermin," the image suggesting
the horrific consumption of human beings at the heart of the southern
cotton economy.[28]

Thrift and order characterize households run by black women, not
white, in these slave narratives. Harriet Jacobs's grandmother makes
acclaimed crackers and preserves; her orderly household and her family's devotion locate the ideal of domesticity in the black, not the white,
home. In the chapter, "Fear of Insurrection," it is, in fact, crude, uneducated whites who enter and disrupt her grandmother's domestic harmony, and they have never been in so orderly and refined a household.
Likewise, Frederick Douglass's grandmother, lovingly described in *My
Bondage and My Freedom*, possesses great domestic wisdom and thrift.
Every winter, she carefully buries sweet potatoes in the warm earth near
her hearth: at the very heart of her home is the promise of family nourishment. Against the simple fare and happy community of his grand-

mother's house, Douglass sets the black children's starvation in the plantation kitchen and the white family's gluttony in the plantation dining room. When he describes the innumerable foods the Lloyds consume in their elaborate dinners, his prose becomes luxuriant, signifying on Edenic proslavery tracts in such elaborate terms that the plantation dinner becomes a scene of uncontrolled appetite rather than ordering ritual. The Lloyd family is transformed into a monster by Douglass, a "destined vortex," or "huge family net," that is slowly poisoned by what it consumes: "Lurking beneath all their dishes, are invisible spirits of evil, ready to feed the self-deluded gormandizers with aches, pains, fierce temper, uncontrolled passions." [29] Ultimately, the obscene appetites and unnatural practices that characterize white food use in Jacobs and Douglass point to the obscene, unnatural transformation of human beings into consumable slaves.

In the idealized plantation narratives increasingly popular through the course of the nineteenth century, the disruptive potential of the black cook is covered over by figures like the "mammy"; her power is reconstructed as a powerful devotion to the white family. The threatening threshold between kitchen and dining room becomes the setting for fictions of happy relation—the white woman's occasional ceremonial passage into the kitchen or the black woman's welcome into the dining room, both events suggesting that the separation of black and white takes second place to "family feeling." Susan Dabney Smedes's *Memorials of a Southern Planter* contains both events. Smedes places praise of the plantation life in the mouth of "Mammy Harriet," thus employing the black mammy figure in her characteristic role as paternalism's collaborator. Here, Smedes's mother, the white mistress, first opens the dining room to the slaves for a wedding, allowing Aunt Harriet full use of all the ritual items: "all de chany off de sideboard, cups an' saucers, de table, de white tablecloth." Then, during a harvest festival, the white woman enters the kitchen and in gestures richly suggesting her civilizing influence and the southern family romance she "cleanses" the slaves' food, throwing out spoiled meat and molasses infested with roaches. Although Smedes informs us that her mother never let "her own people eat what she would not eat," and wants us to know that Aunt Harriet's wedding food is cooked in the kitchen "same as for de gr'et folks," the mistress does not sit down with her slaves to share the meal. [30] The naming of similar foods is sufficient. "Eating together or eating similar foods in similar ways is an expression of equality," as food historians frequently note, "which is why integrating restaurants was so important in the Civil Rights movement in the United States."[31]

Writing in the last decade of the nineteenth century, Charles Chesnutt was acutely aware of the ways in which domestic landscape was deployed in ideologically burdened representations of antebellum life. In his conjure tales, which respond directly to such romanticized portrayals of plantation life as Smedes's *Memorials of a Southern Planter,* he joins his contemporaries in employing imagery of food and kitchens to express his position on life before the war. "Dave's Neckliss," for example, resembles Jacobs's narrative in its depiction of whites using food as an instrument of torture. In this disturbing tale, when Dave is wrongly accused of stealing from the smokehouse, his master punishes him by having a ham, attached to a collar, welded around his neck. Driven mad by the punishment, Dave comes to believe that he literally is a ham; eventually he commits suicide, hanging himself in the smokehouse. Like Jacobs, Chesnutt depicts unnatural, sadistic food use to comment on the unnaturalness of a social order in which human beings are transformed into commodities. Even more disturbing, however, is his suggestion that the abusive institution of slavery leads the slave himself to lose his humanity, to accept the view that he is a consumable object. As Richard Brodhead comments on Dave in his introduction to *The Conjure Woman and Other Conjure Tales,* "The man who says I AM a ham fiercely embraces the subhumanity an official degradation system assigns to him."[32]

As in Chesnutt's other conjure tales, "Dave's Neckliss" contains a narrative frame in which a white couple listen and respond to Uncle Julius's story of antebellum slave life. Yankees who have moved south in part to benefit from cheap land and labor, John and Annie bring with them the myths of antebellum life purveyed by popular plantation fiction. Offering them oblique views of slavery's reality, Julius encourages his listeners (and thus Chesnutt encourages his readers) to question romantic representations of plantation life and to reject rather than replicate the antebellum order in their domestic arrangements. His best success is with Annie. After hearing "Dave's Neckliss," for example, she cannot bear to eat the ham that evoked the narrative. In other words, what she has learned of the antebellum order nauseates her; she rejects the food that Julius's tale has made into a symbol of slavery, thereby at least for the moment rejecting any suggestion that she, like slaveholders, will sustain herself by commodifying or consuming another human being. Yet it must be noted that Annie's rejection of southern practices, past or present, is far from complete. She and John do invite Julius to enjoy a ham dinner at their table; however, they do not join him. Rather, John watches covertly from the piazza "to see how much he *could* eat."[33] As noted earlier, "eating together or eating similar foods in similar ways is an expression of equality";[34] through the simple details of this meal, Chesnutt reveals the limits of John's and Annie's northern liberalism.

In "Po' Sandy," Chesnutt uses Annie's desire for a new kitchen, "in the back yard, apart from the dwelling-house, after the usual Southern fashion," as inspiration for a conjure tale that again offers a corrective view of antebellum life.[35] Building the new kitchen, John hopes to recycle lumber from an abandoned schoolhouse; however, Julius's narrative reveals that those boards have a long history. Now a schoolhouse, they were formerly a plantation kitchen, and before that they were poor Sandy, a slave who sought escape from commodification by being transformed into a tree. Through this image of a plantation kitchen literally made out of Sandy's transformed body, Chesnutt figuratively represents the fact that the white slaveholder's home was built on and his family sustained by commodifying and consuming others. Floor, ceiling, and wall are cut from human suffering, anguish that the slaves recognize in the haunting cries of Sandy's spirit: "Dey could hear sump'n moanin' en groanin' 'bout de kitchen in de night-time, en w'en de win' would blow dey could hear sump'n a-hollerin' an sweekin' lack it wuz in great pain en sufferin'."[36] It is suitable that these boards instead become first a schoolhouse, and then a church; the present must not repeat the past, but neither must that legacy be forgotten. It is worth noting that Chesnutt's message moves beyond the domestic sphere in "Po' Sandy." Lumber, that material object representing the slave's body, is everywhere in the story, not just in the moaning walls of the plantation kitchen. John and Annie travel to the sawmill on first a plank and then a corduroy road; they do business in aptly named Lumberton. In short, Chesnutt tells the attentive reader, the present South, from home to highway, still relies on the domestic and economic arrangements of a past in which human beings were transformed into material objects.

In the battle waged through the second half of the nineteenth century for control over the representation of a remembered South, Charles Chesnutt wrote on the losing side. Romantic plantation fiction and memoir gained primary control of the popular images of southern hospitality for at least a century—*Southern Living* magazine provides endless variations on Letitia Burwell's "fine light-bread" and "refined and agreeable society." But one need only turn back to the horrors of "Dave's Neckliss" or the abusive use of food repeatedly depicted in slave narratives to recognize, in Frederick Douglass's words, that the laden plantation table "groans under [a] heavy and blood-bought" burden.[37]

Notes

1. John F. Kasson, "Rituals of Dining: Table Manners in Victorian America," in Kathryn Grove, ed., *Dining in America: 1850–1900* (Amherst: Univ. of Massachusetts Press, 1987), 114.

2. Clifford E. Clark, "The Vision of the Dining Room: Plan Book Dreams and Middle-Class Realities," in *Dining in America,* 148.

3. Kasson, "Rituals of Dining," 121.

4. Clark, "Vision of the Dining Room," 151.

5. See Catharine E. Beecher and Harriet Beecher Stowe, *The American Woman's Home; or, Principles of Domestic Science* (Hartford, Conn.: Stowe-Day Foundation, 1987).

6. Elizabeth Fox-Genovese, *Within the Plantation Household: Black and White Women of the Old South* (Chapel Hill: Univ. of North Carolina Press, 1988), 364–69.

7. Ibid., 98. The separation of the kitchen from the "Big House" certainly had practical purposes, keeping the house itself cool, clear of cooking odors, and less subject to fire. Yet it was also impractical, requiring often that foods be carried long distances before they reached the table. Consider the distance ham would have traveled at Monticello: "The kitchen was located beneath the right-angle turn of the South Terrace. . . . Food cooked for the family meals was carried by servants through the passageway underneath the house to the north side, and then it was taken up a small staircase into the narrow passageway that runs through the center of the north wing, and from there it was taken into the dining room" (William Howard Adams, *Jefferson's Monticello* [New York: Abbeville Press, 1983], p. 75).

8. Mary Douglas, *Purity and Danger: An Analysis of Concepts of Pollution and Taboo* (London: Routledge and Kegan Paul, 1966), 127.

9. William Alexander Lambeth and Warren H. Manning, *Thomas Jefferson as an Architect and a Designer of Landscapes* (New York: Houghton Mifflin, 1913), 15.

10. According to one account of his tenure at the White House, Jefferson

had serving so arranged that at intimate parties "by each individual was placed a dumbwaiter, containing everything necessary for the progress of the dinner from beginning to end" (Adams, *Jefferson's Monticello,* 210).

11. Carl Anthony, *The Big House and the Slave Quarter: Prelude to New World Architecture* (Univ. of California, Berkeley: Working Paper 3, 1975), 11.

12. Ibid., 36.

13. Douglas, *Purity and Danger,* 114.

14. Ibid., 115, 121.

15. Fox-Genovese, *Within the Plantation Household,* 160.

16. Caroline Merrick, *Old Times in Dixie Land,* qtd. ibid., 142. Fox-Genovese also quotes from Annie Laurie Broidrick's unpublished memoir, "Recollection of Thirty Years Ago" (162).

17. Qtd. in Ronald Walters, *The Antislavery Appeal: American Abolitionism after 1830* (Baltimore: Johns Hopkins Univ. Press, 1976), 74.

18. Fanny Kemble, *Journal of a Residence on a Georgian Plantation in 1838–1839* (New York: Harper, 1863), 296.

19. Kasson, "Rituals of Dining," 125.

20. Kemble, *Journal of a Residence,* 26.

21. Harriet Beecher Stowe, *Uncle Tom's Cabin; or, Life among the Lowly* (New York: Viking Penguin, 1981), 312.

22. Ibid., 317.

23. Gillian Brown, "Getting in the Kitchen with Dinah: Domestic Politics in *Uncle Tom's Cabin,*" *American Quarterly* 36 (1984): 504.

24. Harriet Jacobs, *Incidents in the Life of a Slave Girl* (New York: Oxford Univ. Press, 1988), 23.

25. Harriet Wilson, *Our Nig; or, Sketches from the Life of a Free Black* (New York: Vintage, 1983), 71.

26. John Blassingame, ed., *Slave Testimony: Two Centuries of Letters, Speeches, Interviews, and Autobiographies* (Baton Rouge: Louisiana State Univ. Press, 1977), 540.

27. Jacobs, *Incidents,* 22, 23.

28. Ibid., 49.

29. Frederick Douglass, *My Bondage and My Freedom* (New York: Dover, 1969), 110–11.

30. Susan Dabney Smedes, *Memorials of a Southern Planter* (New York: Knopf, 1965), 42–43.

31. Susan Kalcik, "Ethnic Foodways in America: Symbol and the Performance of Identity," in *Ethnic and Regional Foodways in the United States: The Performance of Group Identity,* ed. Linda Keller Brown and Kay Mussell (Knoxville: Univ. of Tennessee Press, 1984), 49.

32. Richard Brodhead, Introduction, Charles Chesnutt, *The Conjure Woman and Other Conjure Tales* (Durham: Duke Univ. Press, 1993), 18.

33. Ibid., 124.
34. Kalcik, "Ethnic Foodways," 49.
35. Chesnutt, *The Conjure Woman*, 45.
36. Ibid., 52.
37. Douglass, *My Bondage and My Freedom*, 107.

Writing Sickness

A Southern Woman's Diary of Cares

STEVEN M. STOWE

IN HER diary a few days before Christmas 1854, Mary Henderson, a planter-class woman living near Salisbury, North Carolina, looked back on a year of enclosing grief. Her feelings and the weather formed a single, cold climate of loss. "Since the first of April there has been nought for me but snow and crushing, heart consuming afflictions— At the beginning all was joy and brightness but ah how soon the sunshine of our household became overclouded." Two of her children had died in June: her only daughter, Anne, four months old, and a few days later, Edward, about five years old. Both had been ill since the early spring. Another young child had died less than a year earlier. The coming year would be as bleak, bringing the illness and death of Archibald, seven, called Baldy, the youngest of her three living sons.[1]

It is well known that antebellum women like Mary Henderson were the doctors of their households, facing dread disease as well as mending minor ailments. Women's historians have acknowledged this work as skillful and constant, yet we still know very little about how care-giving—especially in cases of serious or mortal illness—shaped women's thoughts and feelings. How did a woman come to terms with an experience at once so ordinary and yet so devastating? Especially in the South, how did a woman whose means included social prominence and slaves, define her care-giving resources in the context of the plantation community's rural isolation? And after she achieved some conceptual and emotional purchase on the experience, how did a woman's work against sickness illuminate her sense of herself as mother and wife?[2]

In what follows, the aim is to read one woman's account of the deaths of her children as casting light on women's experience of illness and the burdens of giving care. No woman is Everywoman, of course, and in her diary Mary Henderson speaks for herself and in her own way. She is unusually explicit about the details of her children's medication, for example, and somewhat less likely than many antebellum women to rely (or even reflect) on religion. But overall her journal is typical of women's vernacular writing in the way it fashions a "home plot," a story of domestic work and its meaning. Following one particular woman's writing permits a sense of the intricacy of these texts and raises questions about how other women in the same predicament also struggled to write their stories.[3]

Literate nineteenth-century women, learning from instruction, practice, and desire, chronicled their lives with great energy in their personal correspondence and diaries. Students of nineteenth-century women's lives have observed how their personal writings cut deeper channels of self-reflection than men's, even though women's stories might seem comparatively static. In contrast to men's tales of quest and conquest, the plots of women's vernacular writing typically involve a sense of home as a place where ordinary routine was at the heart of the story. It was a familiar story, beloved or merely endured, but never a simple one. A woman's household domain curiously mixed the humdrum and the profound; it was a place where "everything is . . . both foreordained and up in the air." It was the site of a thousand trivial tasks, but also the stage for the moral drama of the generations. All of these things made a woman's domestic story worth telling. Southern white women, like their counterparts elsewhere, engaged with this complexity by writing at length about its demands and satisfactions. Through their work, and in writing about their work, they literally authorized the rhythm of a family's daily life, making its ordinariness trustworthy. A woman worked for her family against surprise.[4]

Sickness threatened this world like nothing else. The intrusion of disease into the home was especially disruptive because it could be so subtle; its very nature was to hide mortality in the mundane. A child's sore throat seemed ordinary—but was it? A cough that (probably) was colic might be *something else,* something fiercely malign. This awful slide from the routine to the fatal happened to Mary Henderson, and in her diary she created a text that both reported and reconsidered the disaster. She haltingly and painfully rewrote a story of failure and grief into something else—a story of finding a way to know disease. Thus, as she wrote her way out from the shambles of her domestic world, she made it anew.[5]

To describe Henderson as "writing sickness" in this way, however, imparts an order and clarity to her diary that it does not have. The pages of her journal are feverish, at times darkly obsessive, driven by a rage for the physiological details of her children's sickness as well as the therapies that had failed to make a difference. In this sense, a "writing sickness" was something that possessed her. Throughout, the past overwhelms the diarist's present, filling the page. For instance, three months after Baldy's death, she recalled how he had "slept soundly at night and the symptoms would not have been discovered but for my anxious watchfulness, and in having him sleep with me—perhaps he ate too much fruit—but with the very first derangement of his bowels and as soon as he complained of the least pain I ought then to have given him a dose of Blue Mass—O how anxious my precious little boy was to get well and go off travelling—I can never forget his death bed—what a bright mind he had, was intelligent beyond his years. Mr. H—picked a water melon today, a fine looking one" (July 20).

Mr. Henderson and his watermelon are barely visible in the flood of the catastrophic past. Henderson's diary is made up of such passages, and the rushed, tumbling, circular quality of her writing reveals that much of what she achieved in the way of understanding illness was, at first, inadvertent. She simply wrote on and on, repeating, doubling back from one sick child to another.[6]

And yet understanding did begin to emerge from the act of covering the page with words. In her diary the painful memories slowly began to pass into new channels of thought, reconfiguring the meaning of illness. As I will seek to describe, Henderson moved from a close focus on the bodies of her sick children, and on her own guilt, to a deep interest in the chronology of their decline. In coming to focus on the timing of events, she adopted a wider angle of vision, writing more about others who peopled the social world of sickness and care-giving. She began to understand her home's vulnerability to catastrophe, not so much as a matter of blame or fate as a relation between a particular disease and the efforts of particular care-givers. Running through all of this, and tying it together, is Henderson's extraordinary interest in medicines. Especially compelling were those substances wielded by male physicians—healers called into the home from outside; men used to working with women, but tensely, and almost always at a certain remove. From these men, Henderson appropriated a way of looking at disease that pulled her from remorse toward understanding sickness.[7]

Although the emergence of Henderson's new understanding is the intellectual journey to be explored here, her growing awareness shares the pages of her diary with other expressions that give a context for her major preoccupation: explaining how and why her children died. One such expression is her vivid memory of her deceased children alive, especially Baldy, who had died most recently. The glimpses of the seven-year-old are striking for their image of him as both a boy and a man—both what he was and what he would have become. He was, on the one hand, a tender child who needed the protection and care of his mother's world. He had, she remembered, "a great passion for flowers and music" (June 30) and was a "real Mother's child and loved home above any other spot . . . very domestic in his feelings" (Sept. 22). On the other hand, she recalled Baldy already acting like a man of his place and class. He was, for instance, "quick tempered sometimes" (Oct. 27), and though affectionate, "rough with his affection and I was often impatient with him, particularly at the table when he was very careless, always wanted coffee and but rarely nice things" (July 7). More comfortably, Henderson admired his mature, "sterling principles" (July 12), and described him in language reserved for the ideal of planter-class manliness: "He was not quarrelsome and loved everybody, generous to a fault—impulsive—so noble in all his feelings" (Oct. 27).[8]

Combining images of Baldy as a homebody child and an adventurous little man allowed Henderson to express the magnitude of her loss and the difficulty she had realizing it. "My big, busy, happy child," she writes, "the most persevering and energetic little boy I ever knew—it seems so very strange that he should have died" (Oct. 19). Especially in the early weeks of her diary, expressions of her loss were almost invariably marked by an acid self-blame hardly diluted at all by the religious faith that should have consoled. "I *blame myself* yes, I erred erred erred terribly, fatally," she writes in an early entry. "My whole life seems to have been an error" (Dec. 21, 1854). Although she once or twice is able to imagine a "seraphic band" (July 8) of Baldy, Anne, and Edward waiting to embrace her in Heaven, she mostly fears that her former pride in her motherhood has brought her down, and that she deserves her fate. In fact, "it seems now to me that I almost wanted our children to take the disease, hoping it would not hurt them" (Oct. 22) and thus prove a sign of God's favor. Now she realizes that by "almost" having had such a desire, she had tempted God, and she begs that he "grant me strength to bear up and learn to kiss the rod which smites me so sorely" (Oct. 28).[9]

Brief passages of this kind, in which Henderson recalls her children at home, voices her self-blame, and, sometimes, hopes for God's grace, are a frame for her very different, primary focus on the particulars of her children's dying. Such passages at least suggest something about her life prior to the tragedies that push her to write. They remind us that she had a life apart from her driven recapitulations, shadowy though it is in the diary. At the same time, these glimpses of her wider life help us to appreciate the emotional and conceptual depths she manages to discover in writing sickness. What is so remarkable about her dense pages is how she compels herself to plumb the deep pool of events and remedies that her writing opens up.

She begins with the body, writing as a watcher of her children's bodies. She writes as one alone, concentrating on physical detail. As a mother, Henderson was used to watching her children at play or at rest. She was familiar with the profile of their bodies, the texture of their skin, the length of their limbs. She was aware, too, of the way in which the healthy body's invisible interior projects a kind of silence that is taken as evidence of the absence of disease: it is the sick body that calls out with symptom and sign. Advice to mothers—published or passed along by other mothers—told a woman to monitor this silence by watching what her children ate (never too much of one thing, especially too much fresh fruit) and what the body eliminated (stool should be looked at carefully morning and evening). And thus, although silent, the interior of her child's body was as much in a watchful mother's thoughts as the exterior.[10]

It is understandable, then, that Mary Henderson's initial way of writing about what befell her children was caught up with their bodies. In a typical passage, Henderson recalls the beginning of Edward's fatal illness in June 1854 in terms of a physical examination. She felt his forehead and found it "burning hot and his face very flushed." She immediately stripped him and examined his body: "His bowels were in good condition, hands and feet moderately cool, not hot, and his tongue perfectly clear" (Dec. 21, 1854). And yet he was feverish. These mixed signs puzzled her and continued to puzzle her a year later as she brought Edward's body back to her mind's eye, still looking for a clue.

With Baldy, too, she writes with a tight focus on a beloved body made strange by disease. Writing about one turning point in Baldy's illness, for instance, she believes that his unusually hot feet were the chief sign of the malady. Moreover, she recalls, he had begun kicking her in his sleep, strange "startings" (July 3, 4, 20) so violent that she had put him out of bed lest he injure her pregnancy. She tries to visualize the interior of his body, too, recording how his stool always had been "loose" in the morning, something that "I constantly watched but never dreamed was doing any lurking mischief" (Aug. 11). In fact, the condition of his stool had struck her as "perhaps salutary" (Oct. 28). But now she has doubts, recalling it as "too light colored and profuse not watery" (Oct. 28). From analyzing Baldy's stool, she ranges back over everything about his body, many times. Had she overlooked something? She records an episode of "panting hurried breathing" and then "about midday his nose and lips became icy cold" (June 30). She recalls a time when he "slept sweetly and perspired until midnight" (June 30). Most of his symptoms occurred at night, "and none but a very watchful parent would ever have detected them" (Sept. 6). She is not able to shake the thought that she had missed something, perhaps because she had watched the wrong things: "I was so much interested in watching the night persperations that I certainly forgot about his feet—he seemed to have so many points affected I did not know what to do and would forget the different symptoms" (Oct. 10).

Rehearsing this physical scrutiny, writing her way across the surface of her child's body, Henderson was, in one sense, searching for a key to the "cause" of her son's sickness. But her close descriptions did not lead her in any one direction or toward any particular end. She did not, as a physician might, work to locate and name a specific disease, for example. Rather, her recastings led her back into the round of shock and self-blame. She wrote as if her children's bodies had tricked her and feared that a good mother would not have been tricked. Gazing at her children's afflictions so intensely led her to fault herself for not seeing the "fatal" signs—a word suggesting not only her children's mortality but also her own life suspended in a fate that collapsed all of her skills at mothering into an effort to decipher the body. There was a further consequence, too. Writing in this tightly focused way about her children kept her from letting them go. In her imagination, she remained at the bedside, working with their bodies to keep them alive.[11]

Why Henderson changed her way of writing cannot be known for certain. The same plain-speaking, fluid consciousness that makes vernacular writing immediate and compelling also obscures the reasons why it changes. Unlike some diarists, Henderson does not comment on the text she is creating. She does not personify her diary as her "friend," nor, apparently, does she look back through her text and annotate it. She does not mention learning things about her character or mind from the act of diary-keeping. But perhaps because she wrote so much with such passion, she began to sense that her close focus on bodies alone would not lead her to the meaning she craved. Whatever helped bring it about, an important change in her writing did take place, one that transformed her diary from a repetitive record of physical symptoms to a narrative of sickness and care-giving. As if stepping back from the bedside, Henderson broadened her vision by turning to chronology: the underlying question *what* did I see? became *when* did I see it? She followed this by asking, in essence, what did I (and others) *do* about it? The effect on her writing was to transform detailed but airless passages of physical description—passages in which her "home plot" became lost in the revisioning of the body—into passages of narrative in which she reconfigures what has happened to her in terms of a story about care-giving.[12]

In particular, Henderson begins to depict herself and others engaged in the work of discovering and treating sickness, thereby opening up the social context of domestic care-giving. With regard to her daughter Anne's illness in the spring of 1854, for example, she gives an account in which there are three care-givers who mattered—first of all herself. The second was a young (and, she later decided, critically inexperienced) physician named Nesbitt, whom she called upon after her own efforts—including large doses of quinine and strong emetics—had failed to reduce Anne's fever. The doctor began by administering expectorants, apparently more concerned with the baby's labored breathing than with her fever. His work was watched over not only by Henderson but by Henderson's slave Eliza, who had been helping care for the child and who criticized the physician (after he had departed) for being too free with his medicines. Looking back, Henderson decided she agreed with her slave. Nesbitt "pronounces and prescribes . . . too hastily," Henderson concluded (Dec. 21, 1854). "I ought to have taken Eliza's advice, for she was experienced, and have all medicine withheld for a time, to see what nature would do" (Dec. 21, 1854).

Her story of Edward's illness, just a few days later, portrays a similar group of people. Fatigued and grief-stricken over Anne's death, Henderson was not the one who noticed Edward's first symptoms. Rather, as Henderson sat on the porch sewing buttons on the boy's clothing, her slave Polly "walked through the passage and [Edward] bothered her fretting very much. She said to him, 'I know you are going to be sick, babe, for it ain't natural for you to be so fretful'" (Dec. 21, 1854). Henderson suddenly felt shocked, seeing that her slave was right. She became "completely unnerved" (Dec. 21, 1854) and called for her sister to help; they administered a mustard plaster and an enema and sent for Mr. Henderson and a physician. Her slave messengers returned with the doctor (whom she does not name), but not her husband. Once again, the physician's prescriptions were piled on top of her own. Once again, either that night or the next day, her child died despite the efforts of family, slaves, and a doctor.

When Henderson tells about Edward and Anne early in her diary, she usually sees their deaths as encounters with fate. Her role as diarist is simply to record how one fatal step followed another. But a different theme begins to emerge, too, as she shifts her focus to a narrative of care-giving. It is a theme of *experience* as the quality of a good healer and the criterion for determining who among the many care-givers possesses the right measure of skill. She bitterly criticizes herself as the person who has failed to define the right experience and have it applied at the right time, but in doing so she takes responsibility for this role. At first, in Edward's case, Henderson tries to assign blame to the others. Polly, thought to be an experienced nurse, noticed the boy's symptoms but failed to give useful advice. Then Henderson decides that the physician's medicines were at fault: "The Dr. *did it all,* he gave the medicine ... *he* did it not I" (Dec. 21, 1854). But this does not suffice, either: "I ought to have known he was urging [the medicine] too far" (Dec. 21, 1854).

Thus, by opening up the social context of care-giving, Henderson begins to reflect on her responsibility—her work—compared to others' in a pluralistic medical world where the glut of therapies and opinions made responsibility difficult to affix. The several care-givers in her narrative did not represent a hierarchy of healers, each with a clear place and different brand of medicine. Rather, the group was a shifting one; each person's expertise was limited and shaded subtly into another's. As mother and mistress, Henderson was manager of this group; it was her place to direct care, to pull all of the prescriptions into a single therapy. What she strove to know as she wrote was how to do this—how to define "discharging my duty properly" (Dec. 21, 1854).[13]

Henderson's new narrative focus on the social context of care-giving also led her to a wider chronological quest for the origins of her children's illness, and through this to something even more telling—a conviction that the sickness that had ravaged her family was tied to a specific disease. With Baldy, especially, Henderson began to exchange her focus on his body for a search to recall exactly when she noticed something amiss and how it might have been related to some previous anomaly. She begins by writing, in June 1855, about Baldy's signal crisis a month earlier. She felt that this crisis, which followed a visit by a doctor and consisted of a "frantic crossness" developing into a "phrenzy [that] was heartrending to me," was the key to her son's decline (June 30). However, two months later, Henderson came to believe that the May crisis actually was rooted earlier, in March, when Baldy had suffered a fever and sore throat and had begun sweating and "starting" at night.[14]

Even as she recalled March 1855, she ranged back farther in time, to 1853, when Baldy was sick enough to be bedridden and, that same year, when he fell from a banister "which in some way injured him internally" with lasting effect (Oct. 22). Gradually, though, her attention centered on March 1854, when "whooping cough became epidemic and our two little boys took it at the school" (Oct. 28). She recalled the "brassy" coughing, her efforts to keep the children warm and nourished, and (she thought) their slow improvement. Baldy's tumble from the banister had predisposed him to whooping cough, she now was convinced, and Edward, too, had been weakened by it. But the whooping cough itself, she decided, "was the beginning of sorrows for us" (Oct. 28).

Thus, as Henderson turned toward this quest for the chronological origins of sickness, she reached for two related insights about sickness and the domestic world. This shift in her writing, characteristically, was messy and far from certain. She still slid backwards at times into a fixation on bodies and self-blame. But by the late summer of her diary-keeping, the shift is apparent. First, the new emphasis on a single, named disease as "the beginning" of the catastrophe is an important change because it implicates her family's downfall with a particular entity as well as a particular time. Because no one knew about whooping cough in its modern, bacteriological sense, it is important not to infer modern meanings from Henderson's use of the term. Most kinds of healers, including most physicians, perceived even firmly diagnosed diseases as far more protean and systemic than we do, capable of changing form and potency as they moved quickly through individuals and whole populations. Still, in seizing upon a particular disease as primary, Henderson took a significant step away from her sense of sickness as the eruption of fate. Like a physician, she discovered that settling upon a diagnosis cleared a conceptual place amid the suffering and loss. Giving an affliction a name was satisfying because it constructed a precise disease from the much larger, terrifying, existential realm of illness that could engulf the healer along with the sick. Reconfiguring suffering as a disease—a natural *thing*—held out at least the promise of being able to understand it as one would understand anything in the natural world.[15]

Henderson's second insight into sickness and the domestic world was more mixed in its meaning, but potentially even more radical. As she traced the origins of her children's sickness, she harshly illuminated an expansive array of worldly threats to children's health and—it now was obvious—to their survival. Because her writing took her on a search for "the beginning of our sorrows," Henderson saw with new clarity that sorrow was locked into the heart of childhood, its domestic routines, and the seemingly innocent necessities of making a home. It turned out that this world was full of signals and danger.

Even seemingly remote threats to a family's well-being were never so mild that they could not have some telling effect weeks or months later. Writing about all a mother needed to do, Henderson discovered a mortal lining to the happy thoughtlessness of normal routine. Reflecting more than a year later on the whooping cough of 1854, she recalled how some of her children's schoolmates were coughing. She had instructed her children to walk on the opposite side of the road from their friends. Did they do what she had told them? Should she have been more alarmed? She had to admit that she did not know. She regretted the two-mile walk to school in any case, especially in the cold weather. Perhaps she should have kept the children home from school, safe from contamination. For if they did not take the whooping cough from their fellow students, they certainly picked it up from the sickly infant of a slave woman who worked at the school. The slave children in the Henderson household also seemed part of a wider threat to the health of her own children. Her home was too open; Baldy was "so much with the bad little negros, it grieved and worried me" (July 3). She thought she should have done more to "estrange and separate" Baldy from one particular black child whom she thought especially dirty and rough (June 30).

As she recalled what she did, might have done, or could not have done, to make her home more secure from disease, she sifted through domestic details so fine that almost nothing was without significance. She searched her ways of mothering for the slight but crucial adjustment of the boundary between the world and her children, some redrawing of it that would have saved them. She thought about how she had sewed clothing for them, one of motherhood's most common tasks, but now, like other common things, no longer taken for granted. Clothes and sewing became symbols of a line that she struggled to draw between her home and the world. It was deeply disturbing for her to recall—though recall she did—mistakes she might have made in this fundamental work. Writing in July 1855, she remembers how she had put cotton socks on Baldy one day, "for I thought the woolen ones too oppressive. I hope that did not affect his bowels" (July 3). "My error," she had decided by October, "was in not putting flannel drawers on him *every winter*" (Oct. 13). Clothing became a trope for all she should have done against disease: "He should have worn a woolen roller over the abdomen—kept at home, from school, confined to the house, kept out of the sun" (Oct. 28). With all of her children, in fact, "I erred in not putting flannel next [to] their skin soon enough, allowing them to go barefooted and run too much in the sun and wind" (Oct. 17). All that a child did—having friends, playing in the sun, walking to school—seemed to her double faced and disease ridden. Home was not safe; it was shockingly vulnerable to the mortality that lay ready to break through the surface of daily life.

This realization was perhaps the most broadly significant one Henderson discovered as she wrote. In seeing that a woman's choice of socks for her children might bear directly on their survival, Henderson learned how brutal and exacting was the lesson repeated to midnineteenth-century mothers: what appears to be trivial actually is momentous and sufficient reason to absorb yourself completely in motherhood. This frightened her and, at times, led her through her memories into the cul-de-sac of self-blame. And yet, quite differently, her sense of the importance of understanding the timing of events also made these memories seem simply—and blamelessly—factual. She became notably less likely to express guilt over her home's permeability to disease. Instead, she wrote her pages as a kind of testimony to reality; her home's terrible vulnerability to disease and disaster became something definable—a plot—that required understanding, not remorse. Writing her narrative, therefore, became a means of discovering truths about home's place (and hers) in a wider, often deadly world.

By the early summer of 1855 there is a consistent element running through these themes that helped Henderson tie them together: her interest in therapy. She was fascinated with medicines and conversant in their powers. Her keen curiosity about therapy worked to join her new interest in the chronology and nature of disease to her sense that the key to sickness lay in the relationship between deadly world and fragile home. In terms of her writing, a focus on medicines and therapy lent itself easily to narrative: first we gave him this medicine, then we gave him that one, is the heart of a good story. Indeed, there is a clear parallel in the professional literature of physicians; the featured essay in medical journals of the time was the case narrative. These narratives did not highlight the "outcome" of the case with a clear diagnosis. Nineteenth-century medicine was too uncertain for general agreement on that. Rather, case narratives engaged readers by relating an often dramatic work-story, tied together by the sequence of medicines and their results. Diagnosis was uncertain, but recounting treatment was not. A therapeutic tale was a clear path for any healer's story.[16]

Reading Henderson, we can feel her seize upon the therapeutic story as a kind of drag on the rush of events, a way of slowing her plunge through retrospection. Recalling the details of therapy allows her, for instance, to bring her children's words into her story—a departure from her usual way of paraphrasing the remarks of others. Baldy had words about his own therapy that now seemed meaningful. She recalls his faith in her most basic care-giving, as when he asked her for "Irish potatoes mashed like Father always eats when an invalid" (July 3). When blistered on his abdomen, Baldy told his slave nurse, "I think, Aunty, this blister is doing me some good" (July 3), and he bravely urged on the physician who made an incision in order to cup him: "Cut again, Dr., cut again, Dr." (Sept. 12). As Baldy worsened, Henderson recalls him praying, "Lord, have mercy upon my poor little belly" (July 4). To her horror, after one bout with powerful medicines, he told her, "Mother I am so sick, I never can get well" (Aug. 17). Slowly, Henderson began to realize that except in her diary her children "had no voice to make known [their] sufferings" and that by reconstructing their therapies she was discovering some key link between the ailing bodies of her children and their thoughts and feelings (Aug. 17). As a physician might imagine a favorite medicine "operating" on the patient's whole "system," Henderson wrote about therapy as an occasion to tie her children's bodies and souls back together.[17]

And beyond these essentially writerly reasons for her attention to therapy was Henderson's sheer interest in the medicines themselves—seemingly inert substances that, ingested or applied, reacted with both body and disease to inscribe dramatic physical change, the supposed harbinger of recovery. Describing therapy, Henderson brings her writing to its sharpest focus. Medicines tried and abandoned—especially physicians' medicines—gave her a new, critical way to understand her family's tragedy.

Physicians of this era have been portrayed—rightly enough—as all too eager to jump in and do *something* when called to a case. Although by the 1850s increasing numbers of doctors recommended minimal medication, in order to see what nature might do, few rural physicians were able to wait for long, especially when urged to action by the patient's family. Indeed, many patients and domestic care-givers laid on hands and drugs as liberally as many physicians. Henderson certainly did not withhold medicines, and it is hard not to flinch at the many substances and procedures she and others wrought upon her children. Four-month-old Anne, for instance, was taken aggressively in hand: upon discovering Anne's fever, Henderson gave her frequent doses of quinine, enemas, and a blistering plaster of some kind, to which slave nurse Polly, at Henderson's direction, added a combination of molasses and castor oil, topped off with large (and Henderson came to believe excessive) amounts of her own remedies: "mint, catnip and hoarhound teas" (Dec. 21, 1854). Following upon all of this, Dr. Nesbitt arrived to pour in his belladonna and other expectorants. Henderson soundly physicked Baldy, too. In one quick succession, "I tried Port wine, Blackberry syrup, Essence of ginger, sweet gum tea, Sassafras tea, paregoric, Laudanum and starch enemas—I gave Dover's powder too which had been in the house two years" (July 3).[18]

The sheer number of different therapies did not come to interest (or alarm) Henderson nearly as much as the individual substances themselves, the amounts given, and, especially, the sequence in which they were administered. Her curiosity developed over time. In the earlier weeks, she was apt to note medicines without much comment, seeming to find almost talismanic power in running through their names. Sometimes she vented her frustration by dismissing medicines in general. Looking back on the treatment given Anne and Edward, she wrote, "I ought to have thrown the medicines into the fire" (Dec. 21, 1854). Gradually, though, she began to sift through the different kinds of prescriptions in a more systematic way. She notes not just the names of medicines but something about the timing of their prescription and administration. Sometimes she adopts an imperative present tense (for example, a certain medicine was "too stimulating—never give this without nitre in it") as if compiling notes for future reference (Oct. 28).

During the course of her diary-keeping, then, from the end of 1854 through the fall of 1855, we can see Henderson rethinking her children's therapy in terms of three different visions of medicine, involving both particular substances and the expectations tied to them. The reasons for the shifts in her view are typically inchoate, and her preferences sometimes overlap or are inconsistent. But the shifts are important nonetheless, because they coupled her changing sense of what was the best medicine to an increasingly critical view of physicians. Taken together, these were the precise means—a means born of her writing— of reconfiguring the significance of her work as a mother and her home.

In the early weeks of the diary, her favored therapy in retrospect— the therapy she wished she had relied upon more often—was, broadly speaking, botanic and strongly influenced by her slaves' remedies. Based on various cultivated medicinal plants and including items around the house used for nonmedicinal purposes as well (alcohol, for instance), this medicine was a part of Henderson's knowledge as a woman and mother. It is a knowledge that should not be sentimentalized. Not all botanic medicines were mild in their effects on the body, despite their now benign reputation. Nor should we picture slave and mistress always working in therapeutic harmony. Even so, in general, botanic therapies tended to be less harsh than the mineral-based drugs favored by physicians, as well as less damaging when taken over a long term. And, on the whole, free and slave women shared with each other what they knew. Henderson recalled with favor, for instance, a port wine and essence-of-ginger mixture she and her slave nurse had administered to Baldy, and she became convinced for a while that a "Burgundy pitch plaster between Baldy's shoulders when his cough returned in March [1855]" would have saved him (July 4). There is a sense, in these descriptions, of herself as a mother properly taking responsibility for sickness wholly within the close confines of the domestic remedies and female assistance at hand. Physicians were to be called upon only sparingly. They supplied iron tonics and a few other things not easily compounded at home, but they were best kept on the perimeter.[19]

Although it sounds straightforward enough, this view of physicians and therapy nevertheless was problematic. Holding doctors at arm's length did not prevent Henderson from criticizing them for their failures. Yet her criticism cut in two different directions, blunting its effect. On the one hand, she deeply respected doctors as learned men, with the emphasis on both their knowledge and their gender. When she called upon young Dr. Nesbitt to care for Edward and Anne, for example, she assumed that he possessed some precise therapeutic ways unknown to her domestic world. Even after she saw that his medicines were not working, the doctor's aura of expertise did not evaporate. "I ought to have begged the Dr. to discontinue his visits," she wrote, but she could not bring herself to challenge him (Dec. 21, 1854). On the other hand, she continued to embrace the ideal of woman's domestic realm as the key to health. When doctors failed her, she did not wish for a physician more skilled in his special knowledge and training. Rather, she longed for a doctor described by a domestic setting. She imagined an ideal doctor to be "an experienced old married man . . . who has children and prescribes carefully and cautiously for them" (Dec. 21, 1854).

Perhaps because it was conflicted, this vision of medicine and physicians began to change by the early summer of her diary, a change marked by a near-complete reversal of her preferred therapy. She began to believe, in retrospect, that a timely intervention with much harsher, mercury-based medicines would have healed Baldy's intestinal disorder. In particular, she now wished that she had given Baldy "a dose of Blue Mass that first day instead of [castor] oil. It is the course Mr. H— pursues with the servants" (July 11). The contrast between blue mass and castor oil is telling. Blue mass, a mercury compound, was a staple remedy of physicians—and slave owners who dosed their own slaves—in contrast to the relatively domestic castor oil. The more Henderson latched onto blue mass, regretting that she had not given it early and often to Baldy, the more woman's world of domestic medicines and slave nurses receded from view. Baldy became someone to be cleaned out with a powerful purgative, like her husband's slaves.

Wrapped up in her wish for a single-shot cure was a sense that her children would have done better under a man's care. She recalls certain advice she took from her husband and believes she should have called upon him more often for the small, particular things a man did well. Her husband carried a pocket watch, for instance, and so she felt she should have "begged him to watch [Baldy's] pulse for I am no judge of it" (Sept. 21). An ever-larger number of male physicians begin to appear in her pages. In addition to Nesbitt, Drs. Whitehead, Power, and Long made regular calls, as well as two other doctors who come at least once each. For a period of weeks, Henderson recounts in detail the therapies of these men, recalling her great hope that at least one combination of drugs would fell her family's sickness with one stroke. Expressing this hope, she wished to be free from crushing responsibility, declaring, "I cannot control events or disease," as if doctors could (Aug. 20). She watches their every move, tracks their medicines, for signs of success worthy of male protectors; she hoped to find a physician who, like a husband, would "watch over my family," and cherish it with "especial care" (July 3).

But her transition from keeping physicians and their medicines on the margins to hoping that they would fix everything was not Henderson's last shift in view. By August she had changed her favored therapy once again, and once again this signaled a key change in the themes that she constantly refashioned in her writing: her sense of loss, her responsibility, her home. She gradually moved away from both women's traditional, domestic drugs and the harsh, "male" purgatives. As she did so, she wrote in a dramatically different way about physicians, neither holding them at bay nor embracing them. Instead, she began to appraise them. She began to see doctors' therapies as made up of their assumptions and procedures as well as their powerful medicines. She slowly began to write about doctors' judgments as being as reactive and contingent as hers or any other healer's.

Because her diary itself is contingent—on the flow of memories loosened by her writing and on a style that is both fiercely retrospective and unselfconscious—Henderson once again gives no direct reason for this shift in her views. She rode her mixed and troubling narrative where it led her. A germ of her new appraisal of doctors and medicine— and what it implied about therapy and her role as mother—might be seen in the way she wrote of Baldy's May 1855 crisis, the "frantic crossness" and "phrenzy" that seemed to transform her son and prefigure his death. She alludes to this incident several times, and twice she writes about it more extensively than any other event in Baldy's decline. It is the closest she comes to a deathbed scene.

The steps in this pivotal three-day attempt to arrest Baldy's symptoms are easily told: the beginning was a Monday in May when she noticed blood in Baldy's morning stool. She was alarmed, gave him some sort of medicine, and alerted her husband. But she "could not get his Father's fears aroused. He [Baldy] being clear of fever and so playful he [her husband] thought he could not be much sick" (July 3). She remained worried, however, and began dosing Baldy with Port wine and anything else at hand, but "nothing I gave at all checked his bowels" (July 3). Her anxiety turning to alarm, she called in Dr. Whitehead on Thursday. Henderson does not relate her conversation with Whitehead, but it is clear that she felt she had done all she knew how to do. The doctor added his medicines, starting with a mixture of oil and laudanum. He followed this with something Henderson calls "the turpentine mixture" twice within a few hours, and shortly thereafter Baldy went into his frenzy (June 30, July 3).

Here the therapeutic tale pauses, indeed ends. It was this particular medicine, the turpentine mixture, she writes emphatically, "I have since thought operated too powerfully," bringing on Baldy's frenzy (June 30). The doctor, called in at last as both a hope and a sign of her own exhausted means, administered the fatal blow. Standing outside this scene, we do not find it easy to be so sure. After all, Henderson and Eliza had been drugging and purging the boy for three days before Whitehead arrived, and who can say which particular medicine in the long series was the irreversible one? The point is that Henderson believes she can. The turpentine mixture, she wrote in July, "I shall always believe . . . injured him" and brought on the frenzy (July 3). The physician thus occupies a special place in this narrative. It is not malpractice in the modern sense that Henderson sees—nothing so streamlined or litigious. Rather, the physician's failed therapy signals the collapse of the whole fabric of care-giving. In assigning Dr. Whitehead this role in her story, Henderson glimpsed the terrible, ironic mystery of care-giving: "There was something wrong done but at the time, it seemed as if all was being done right" (June 30).

Later, in her August diary, as she is shifting her view away from physicians and their favored store of drugs, this insight returns with new force. Physicians, who have populated her pages for weeks past,

become the focus for her new, critical understanding. More than anyone else, doctors make it seem as if "all was being done right," and yet
they, too, have failed her (Aug. 22). Especially painful is how they have
failed with her children in particular. When Fanny, a young slave girl,
was desperately ill, "Dr. Nesbitt . . . managed her case skillfully"; yet
"he attended my other children and *they all died*" (Aug. 22). Where
earlier Henderson would have seen this as fate, she now begins to see
it in terms of accountability—doctors' and, ultimately, her own. "I have
very little faith in Doctors for our own children," she writes. "They
either get scared or something, I can't tell what. Their *prescriptions do
no good*" (Aug. 12). But the problem is a deeper one. Whereas she feels
"*afraid of all*" doctors, she also realizes that she is unable to "rely upon
myself" (Aug. 20). Her mother's work as the manager of care was crippled not because she called upon physicians but because "I really do
not know how to oppose Physicians" (Aug. 16).[20]

Significantly, it is her fascination with medicines and other therapy
that seems to have been the key to finding a way "to oppose Physicians."
Her interest in therapy, growing from and supporting her urge to tell a
story, leads her by the late summer of her diary to look at procedures,
at step-by-step medicine: there was "something wrong done" and she
must discover it. As she comes to define the problem as one of process
and decision-making, she comes to see the solution in the same terms.

Thus, the specific therapeutic mode she adopts in her final shift of
views is one that steps away from internal medicine and favors procedures—primarily cupping—that manipulated the exterior of the body
in order to affect the interior. Physicians' failures, she comes to believe,
stem from their overuse of drugs. It would have been better to have
waited before jumping in with practically every available "physic"; a
good physician would have tried another means. "Ah, why was [Baldy]
not cupped more and physicked less? . . . We had two doctors but life
fled" (Sept. 11). Cupping, with its painful surgical incisions, was no
less drastic than medicine in its way; but it was comparatively precise.
As a procedure it could be controlled by the healer in a way that the
effect of internal drugs could not. Physicians professed to know a wide
range of drugs and their effects; but there was no way to tell exactly
how any drug would affect any particular patient. Once the medicine
entered the body and disappeared, everyone, including the physician,
could only wait to see what happened. Cupping and other surgical procedures kept a visible connection between therapeutic activity and the

hidden interior of the body. Everyone around the bedside, including the patient, could witness and have an opinion about the procedure, which was open for everyone to see.

Such therapy may also have appealed to Henderson because it allowed her to draw upon her own knowledge of Baldy's body, while at the same time adopting a procedure clearly identified with physicians and their knowledge. It thus combined her growing critique of doctors with a new willingness to take responsibility for understanding in a precise way what had been done to her children—to become, in effect, more like a physician herself. It is striking, therefore, when Henderson writes in September 1855, "from my reading I believe if *anything* could have availed, [cupping] would. . . . When the cough was so tight and violent I am convinced in *his particular* case it would have been better than all the medicines and expectorants in the world" (Sept. 11).

Here and elsewhere is evidence that she has been reading medical texts of some sort. Her phrasing of Baldy's illness as "his particular case" has a distinctly professional ring to it. She uses other textbook words here and there, as when she traces the "*three months* with Partussis (whooping cough) in his case" (Sept. 11). Her reading has given her more than a new vocabulary, though this is striking enough. Instead of worrying the question of why physicians were so inept, she advances a hypothesis, and it is a revealing one. She has been convinced by her reading that her "children's violent diseases have all been *symptomatic* but most unfortunately that was not considered in their treatment" (Sept. 11). That is, the signs of sickness seized upon by her physicians were just that: signs, and not the disease. Her physicians had been working "far too empirically" (Oct. 17), that is, by trial and error, missing the crucial fact that "dear little Baldy's [disease] was deeper seated" than the physical changes she and the doctors watched so carefully (Sept. 21).

Her new language signals that she has discovered something dramatic in her reading of medicine. She has learned that her community's physicians were making errors that other physicians (those whose books she has been reading) already had defined and warned against. These physicians had been attempting for years to reform the old orthodoxy of aggressive drugging. Henderson's observations mirror their argument precisely: too many drugs in too large doses only masked symptoms that the doctor needed to see in order to track down "deeper seated" disease. Like Henderson, reformist doctors used the term *em-*

pirics to denounce those backward practitioners who not only over-medicated patients but also indulged in what was criticized as "cookbook medicine"—that is, a therapeutic repertoire consisting of a few favorite remedies prescribed in a formulaic way. In contrast, reformers counseled a careful physical examination before settling on a therapy. Henderson, reading her medicine, echoed this critique when she wrote, "What a pity it is Docts. do not thoroughly examine *every organ* but especially the *lungs and liver* previous to prescribing" (Sept. 11).[21]

Observation, recollection, and reading—brought together in her diary—gave Mary Henderson a way to write sickness, to see it and see past it. Slowly, Henderson took hold of her loss and made it into a puzzle to be solved. As she wrote a story of disease and giving care, she released, so to say, the bodies of her children, examined and discarded various therapies, and, perhaps most strikingly, criticized physicians in terms she appropriated from this realm of men.

Seeing her do this leads us back to the urgent, swift quality of her writing, to the diary as a woman's way of inscribing medicine and care-giving. Henderson's new, critical insights gave her satisfaction, but challenged her, too, in their comparative breadth and in their implicit invitation to read and study further. Her diary does not reveal just how much further she went. Her insights were significant, and solidly phrased; but they were too raw to be more than partial. From an analytic frame of mind, her way of writing sickness remained messy and uncertain. But this may be what diaries most importantly teach about women's work. The blending of uncertainty and new knowledge in her pages, the sense of strain and urgency—but not indirection—reflect closely the work of care-giving itself. The homologic quality of her text and her work thus suggests that diaries and other vernacular texts make and reveal meaning not by arriving at an end but by being especially faithful to the means.

For Mary Henderson, the most important means to her family's well-being still were found in the home. In her ten-month struggle, we see the power of illness shake the ideal of home but not, finally, destroy it. Henderson once feared that her tragedy had made her "unfit . . . for every duty hereafter both conjugal and maternal," and yet she did not collapse or fade away (July 17). She was able to rewrite her "home plot" rather than abandon it. She had seen her home open wide to death despite all that she knew how to do. Even God proved oddly powerless when it came to therapy; it seemed worth pointing out that "He who sends disease could also have blessed the means" to end it, but did not (Sept. 12). Yet through the weeks of her struggle, she saw that the way out was not toward Heaven but toward the obscure, necessary plots of a woman's skills and understanding.

She took refuge in these. "Sewed industriously all day," she wrote, and resolved, "I must sew on lest other sickness and misfortune overtake me" (June 30). By fall, there was a newborn son, too, whom she kept out of her diary for a while, as if afraid to bring him bodily into her book of death. When we do see him, it is a relief and a promise: "Little Richard has very dark eyes and is a good babe" (Oct. 26). She began to back away somewhat from her pages, to see herself from the outside, as others did, and as she doubtless had before. "I will become, I fear, too careless even of my personal appearance," she worried. "I have good taste but not the spirit now to exert it" (Oct. 24). Home's mundane expectations would pull her to reclaim her spirit. These expectations might not have survived, save for the time she spent writing. And this seemed to be changing, too. "Time is passing," she observed in acknowledgment of how her writing had not only given her new understanding but also had been a kind of healing dream. "I must if possible arouse myself, for the past cannot be recalled and I am wasting precious time" (Sept. 21).

Notes

1. Mary Ferrand Henderson diary, December 21, 1854. Subsequent citations appear parenthetically in the text; all citations are for the year 1855 unless otherwise noted. The diary is part of the John Steele Henderson papers, Southern Historical Collection, University of North Carolina, Chapel Hill. Mary Henderson is about thirty-five years old when the extant diary begins with a long entry from which this quotation is taken. It then breaks off, resuming in June 1855, shortly after Baldy's death and a full year after the deaths of Edward and Anne. Thus there is no "eyewitness" account of any of these deaths. Regular entries continue through 1855, and the entire diary extends to 1861. Henderson sometimes did not place periods at the ends of sentences or capitalize the first words of new sentences. In a very few instances, I have added punctuation and capitalization for readability.

2. Domestic care-giving by southern women has received treatment in Sally G. McMillen, *Motherhood in the Old South: Pregnancy, Childbirth, and*

Infant Rearing (Baton Rouge: Louisiana State Univ. Press, 1990), esp. chs. 6 and 7; Catherine Clinton, *The Plantation Mistress: Woman's World in the Old South* (New York: Pantheon, 1982), ch. 8. See also Elizabeth Fox-Genovese, *Within the Plantation Household: Black and White Women of the Old South* (Chapel Hill: Univ. of North Carolina Press, 1988), ch. 3.

For works on sickness, medicine, and the South in general, see Ronald L. Numbers and Todd L. Savitt, eds., *Science and Medicine in the Old South* (Baton Rouge: Louisiana State Univ. Press, 1989); Todd L. Savitt and James Harvey Young, eds., *Disease and Distinctiveness in the American South* (Knoxville: Univ. of Tennessee Press, 1988). Todd L. Savitt, *Medicine and Slavery: The Diseases and Health Care of Blacks in Antebellum Virginia* (Urbana: Univ. of Illinois Press, 1978) is the pioneering work on health care in the plantation South.

Suggestive on the literary relation between women's moral character and giving care to the sick in this era are John Wiltshire, *Jane Austen and the Body: "The Picture of Health"* (Cambridge: Cambridge Univ. Press, 1992) and Diane Price-Herndl, *Invalid Women: Figuring Illness in American Fiction and Culture, 1840–1940* (Chapel Hill: Univ. of North Carolina Press, 1993).

3. I am borrowing the term *home plot* from Ann Romines. Although Romines uses the term with regard to women's writing of fiction, I have found her work useful for thinking about vernacular texts such as women's diaries and family letters and the way they attempt to capture the significance of everyday life. See Ann Romines, *The Home Plot: Women, Writing, and Domestic Ritual* (Amherst: Univ. of Massachusetts Press, 1992).

4. Ibid., 4. With regard to the peculiar nature of women's household work, Kathryn Allen Rabuzzi notes that if we think of plot only "as the arrangement of incidents . . . , we begin to understand the problem of storying women's experience. . . . what women do largely involves sameness without apparent differentiation" (*The Sacred and the Feminine: Toward a Theology of Housework* [New York: Seabury, 1982], 163–64). Elizabeth Hampsten, too, in her very suggestive interpretation of midwestern women's letters, points to the special qualities of vernacular writing. She observes that in order to understand what ordinary women have to say in their correspondence we should not look for the features of more formal literature. Instead, we should expect to confront "the very repetitive daily-ness" in women's writing "that both literature and history have schooled us away from" (*Read This Only to Yourself: The Private Writings of Midwestern Women, 1880–1910* [Bloomington: Indiana Univ. Press, 1982], 2).

On historical comparison of women's vernacular writing compared to men's, and the social context for both, see John Mack Faragher, *Women and Men on the Overland Trail* (New Haven: Yale Univ. Press, 1979); Joan E. Cashin, *A Family Venture: Men and Women on the Southern Frontier* (New York:

Oxford Univ. Press, 1991); G. J. Barker-Benfield, *The Culture of Sensibility: Sex and Society in Eighteenth-Century Britain* (Chicago: Univ. of Chicago Press, 1992), 161–62; Richard L. Bushman, *The Refinement of America: Persons, Houses, Cities* (New York: Knopf, 1992), ch. 2; Steven M. Stowe, *Intimacy and Power in the Old South: Ritual in the Lives of the Planters* (Baltimore: Johns Hopkins Univ. Press, 1987).

5. Southern women's letters and diaries abound with talk about sickness and health in this era, and any major collection of women's domestic or personal writing will include many references to who is sick and who is well. For particular comparison to Mary Henderson, see, for example, the manuscript diaries of Mahala P. Roach and Lucila A. McCorkle in the Southern Historical Collection, and that of Maria Dyer Davies in the Perkins Library, Duke University. Also see the journal of Ann Lewis Hardeman, in Michael O'Brien, ed., *An Evening When Alone: Four Journals of Single Women in the South, 1827–67* (Charlottesville: Univ. Press of Virginia, 1993).

6. The past in Henderson's writing is always the scrim through which the present is visible. It is visible, often, because illness punctuated the present, too, easily linking up to the past. In August 1855, as Henderson endured her last weeks of a pregnancy, five-year-old Fanny, the daughter of Henderson's slave Eliza, became gravely ill. Henderson's account of the two women's care for Eliza is the longest sustained departure from retrospection in the entire span of months covered here. Mary herself was violently sick for a week in late September, and in October the younger of her two surviving sons, Johnie, returned from a visit to kin in Asheville and was sick for a few days, causing Henderson great anxiety. Her other son, Len, occasionally makes an appearance, as does her husband Archibald. Even more visible are the slaves: Fanny, Eliza, Big Tom, Little Tom, Irene.

Apart from writing at some length about the care she gave to Fanny, Henderson writes succinctly about the present; her prose is spare and flatly descriptive. But her writing gathers a considerable power from this style. What Elizabeth Hampsten observes of her midwestern women holds true for Mary Henderson's prose: "There are virtually no figures of speech. . . . But this is not to say that women's writing lacks strong feeling, only that metaphor does not extend ordinary expression to another magnitude." When Henderson does turn a rare "literary" phrase—as when she refers to the irony of death coming to her family in "the leafy month of June"—it comes as something of a shock.

7. More will be said about Henderson and physicians, but for the general relation between nineteenth-century women and physicians, see Judith Walzer Leavitt, *Brought to Bed: Childbearing in America, 1750–1950* (New York: Oxford Univ. Press, 1986); Wendy Mitchinson, *The Nature of Their Bodies: Women and Their Doctors in Victorian Canada* (Toronto: Univ. of Toronto Press, 1991); Sylvia D. Hoffert, *Private Matters: American Attitudes toward*

Childbearing and Infant Nurture in the Urban North, 1800–1860 (Urbana: Univ. of Illinois Press, 1989); McMillen, *Motherhood in the Old South*. See also Steven M. Stowe, "Obstetrics and the Work of Doctoring in the Mid-Nineteenth-Century South," *Bulletin of the History of Medicine* 64 (1990): 540–66.

8. Historians have typically used similar language in describing southern manhood. Eugene D. Genovese, for example, observes that both critics and admirers saw planter class men as "tough, proud, and arrogant; liberal-spirited in all that did not touch their honor; gracious and courteous; generous and kind" (*Roll, Jordan, Roll: The World the Slaves Made* [New York: Vintage Books, 1976], 96). See also Bertram Wyatt-Brown, *Southern Honor: Ethics and Behavior in the Old South* (New York: Oxford Univ. Press, 1982); Drew Gilpin Faust, *James Henry Hammond and the Old South: A Design for Mastery* (Baton Rouge: Louisiana State Univ. Press, 1982).

9. On expressions of grief and guilt in private journals, see Paul C. Rosenblatt, *Bitter, Bitter Tears: Nineteenth-Century Diarists and Twentieth-Century Grief Theories* (Minneapolis: Univ. of Minnesota Press, 1983).

10. For typical advice books well circulated in the South, with much to say about diet, see Samuel K. Jennings, *A Compendium of Medical Science; or, Fifty Years' Experience in the Art of Healing* (Tuscaloosa, Ala.: M. J. Slade, 1847); John Hume Simons, *Planter's Guide and Family Book of Medicine: For the Instruction and Use of Planters, Families, Country People. . . .* (Charleston, S.C.: M'Carter & Allen, 1848). See also Elizabeth Barnaby Keeney, "Unless Powerful Sick: Domestic Medicine in the Old South," in Numbers and Savitt, *Science and Medicine,* 276–94.

In thinking about how illness makes the body "present" in a way the healthy body is not, I have been helped by Drew Leder, *The Absent Body* (Chicago: Univ. of Chicago Press, 1990), esp. 1–2, 39–45, 81; Elaine Scarry, *The Body in Pain: The Making and Unmaking of the World* (New York: Oxford Univ. Press, 1985), esp. chs. 1 and 3; Mary Rawlinson, "Medicine's Discourse and the Practice of Medicine," in Victor Kestenbaum, ed., *The Humanity of the Ill: Phenomenological Perspectives* (Knoxville: Univ. of Tennessee Press, 1982), 69–85.

11. Although by the 1850s physicians were more concerned than many other kinds of healers to give a name to an affliction, most care-givers searched the body for some sense of where an affliction originated. An intriguing view of the overlapping diagnostic visions and mutual influences of domestic healers and medical doctors is in Barbara Duden, *The Woman beneath the Skin: A Doctor's Patients in Eighteenth-Century Germany* (Cambridge: Harvard Univ. Press, 1991), esp. ch. 4.

12. Many women and men of the planter class considered diaries, commonplace books and the like, to be ways of building habits of self-

consciousness and good character. If Mary Henderson was taught this, as seems probable, her diary does not reflect it. For a collection of women's diaries that reveal varying degrees of self-consciousness about diary-keeping, see O'Brien, *An Evening When Alone*. For two women who looked back over their writing and criticized it as a prelude to further writing, see C. Vann Woodward, ed., *Mary Chesnut's Civil War* (New Haven: Yale Univ. Press, 1981); and Virginia Ingraham Burr, ed., *The Secret Eye: The Journal of Ella Gertrude Clanton Thomas, 1848–1889* (Chapel Hill: Univ. of North Carolina Press, 1990).

13. On the significance of the diverse medical worlds converging at the bedside of a nineteenth-century patient, see Leavitt, *Brought to Bed*, ch. 4, and her "'A Worrying Profession': The Domestic Environment of Medical Practice in Mid-Nineteenth-Century America," *Bulletin of the History of Medicine* 69 (1995): 1–29. For a healer's point of view, see Laurel Thatcher Ulrich, *A Midwife's Tale: The Life of Martha Ballard, Based on her Diary, 1785–1812* (New York: Knopf, 1990); Jacalyn Duffin, *Langstaff: A Nineteenth-Century Medical Life* (Toronto: Univ. of Toronto Press, 1993).

14. Diary, June 30. See entries for Aug. 22, Sept. 10, Oct. 21.

15. On physicians and the shift toward the idea of specific disease, see John Harley Warner, *The Therapeutic Perspective: Medical Practice, Knowledge, and Identity in America, 1820–1885* (Cambridge: Harvard Univ. Press, 1986), esp. ch. 3; W. F. Bynum, *Science and the Practice of Medicine in the Nineteenth Century* (Cambridge: Cambridge Univ. Press, 1994), esp. ch. 5. See also Charles E. Rosenberg, "Framing Disease: Illness, Society, and History," in his *Explaining Epidemics and Other Studies in the History of Medicine* (Cambridge: Cambridge Univ. Press, 1992), 305–18.

For a discussion of the significance of naming diseases, see Stephen J. Kunitz, "Classifications in Medicine," in Russell Maulitz and Diana E. Long, eds., *Grand Rounds: One Hundred Years of Internal Medicine* (Philadelphia: Univ. of Pennsylvania Press, 1988), 279–96, who views the act of assigning a name to a disease as furthering the patient's well-being by giving the patient a sense of "hard" knowledge. For a different view, one that stresses the mystification inherent in technical language, see Lawrence B. McCullough, "Particularism in Medicine," *Criticism* 32 (1990): 361–70.

16. In this way the actual practice of medicine—folk and orthodox—helped to make therapy far more dramatic than diagnosis. In the modern medical world, dominated by physicians' overall success, the story of diagnostic problem-solving and eventual outcome drives the story of the case. But in Mary Henderson's world, agreement on a diagnosis was difficult, even among M.D.s, because there was much disagreement about underlying pathological and physiological processes. Moreover, many nineteenth-century diagnoses were comparatively unspecific (e.g., "inflammation" or "congestion") and thus did not clearly indicate a single therapeutic course. In contrast, the therapeutic tale

was a rousing story of sleuthing and experiment, with dramatic physiological "operations" of medicines being taken for evidence of success. It was in the mid-nineteenth century that American physicians shifted over to a focus on systematic physical diagnosis before prescribing. But the change was slow and occurred much later in rural areas than in cities. On these matters, see Steven M. Stowe, "Seeing Themselves at Work: Physicians and the Case Narrative in the Mid-Nineteenth-Century American South," *American Historical Review* 101 (1996): 41–79.

For important historical accounts of this change, see Warner, *Therapeutic Perspective;* Charles E. Rosenberg, "The Therapeutic Revolution: Medicine, Meaning, and Social Change in Nineteenth-Century America," in *Explaining Epidemics,* 9–31. Guenter B. Risse and John Harley Warner, "Reconstructing Clinical Activities: Patient Records in Medical History," *Social History of Medicine* 5 (1992): 183–205. For suggestive comment on the ways in which the modern context shapes medical storytelling, see Howard Brody, *Stories of Sickness* (New Haven: Yale Univ. Press, 1987); Kathryn Montgomery Hunter, *Doctors' Stories: The Narrative Structure of Medical Knowledge* (Princeton: Princeton Univ. Press, 1991); Rita Charon, "To Build a Case: Medical Histories as Traditions in Conflict," *Literature and Medicine* 11 (1992): 115–32.

17. In blistering, a caustic substance was applied to the skin to raise a blister over an area deemed most affected by an internal ailment, and in cupping, an incision was made in the skin over the area and blood drawn out by suction. Both procedures aimed to draw toxic substances to the body's surface where they might be eliminated.

18. For a harsh view of aggressive physicians, see William G. Rothstein, *American Physicians in the Nineteenth Century: From Sects to Science* (Baltimore: Johns Hopkins Univ. Press, 1972). More balanced in their critique are Martin S. Pernick, *A Calculus of Suffering: Pain, Professionalism, and Anesthesia in Nineteenth-Century America* (New York: Columbia Univ. Press, 1985); Kenneth M. Ludmerer, *Learning to Heal: The Development of American Medical Education* (New York: Basic Books, 1985); Reginald Horsman, *Josiah Nott of Mobile: Southerner, Physician, and Racial Theorist* (Baton Rouge: Louisiana State Univ. Press, 1987); Warner, *Therapeutic Persuasion;* Leavitt, *Brought to Bed.*

Physicians did not simply dictate treatment to patients. As a profession, they did not yet have either the exclusiveness or the effectiveness that would give them the authority to do so. Moreover, physicians disagreed among themselves about how to achieve both bedside effectiveness and professional power. Many were increasingly likely to doubt the orthodox reliance on aggressive therapies. Nor were the terms of treatment—when and how a doctor obtained the patient's or family's consent—structured by a clear set of professional ethics or the law. Rather, the terms of treatment were negotiated through an uncertain process of reasoning and persuasion, often colored by fair amounts of mystification, bullying, and blind trust. On the growing skepticism of harsh drugs, see John Harley Warner, " 'The Nature-Trusting Heresy': American Physicians and the Concept of the Healing Power of Nature in the 1850s and 1860s," *Perspectives in American History* 11 (1977–78): 291–324.

19. See also July 7. Physicians and domestic care-givers did rely on significantly different approaches to healing, but the point here is that therapies also converged in the face of the necessities of rural practice. For a discussion of "eclectic" physicians as a kind of hybrid during this era, see John S. Haller, *Medical Protestants: The Eclectics in American Medicine, 1825–1939* (Carbondale: Southern Illinois Univ. Press, 1994). For an African-American tradition in healing, see Loudell F. Snow, *Walkin' over Medicine* (Boulder, Colo.: Westview Press, 1993).

20. As noted earlier (n. 6), Henderson's account of the way she and Fanny's mother Eliza cared for the five-year-old girl pulls Henderson out of her memories like no other event in the "present" of the diary. Or, rather, it is a current event that she can weave easily into her memories of her own children's illness. The account is interesting for the implication of race and slavery. Henderson praises Eliza's motherly work in nursing Fanny "most untiringly" and believes that "if she dies it will not be from neglect on [Eliza's] part" (Aug. 18). At the same time, Henderson faults other slaves for not helping enough—"I never saw such a selfish, indifferent set of servants" (Aug. 20). And while she writes tenderly about Fanny (a "nice, pretty, smart little girl . . . I should grieve to see her die") she draws the racial line: "It rends my heart to witness the sickness of even a little servant" (Aug. 16).

21. These reforms were much discussed in American medical periodicals beginning in the 1830s. But widespread change in actual practice took many years to filter into rural medicine in the United States. Reform involved a new emphasis on the specificity of disease and on the systematic physical diagnosis of each patient, each visit. It involved careful anatomical training in which students were encouraged to do autopsies in order to observe "lesions" left by disease and to classify their findings in an attempt to predict. It involved, too, a new interest in and reliance upon a specialized language, statistical measures, and a general respect for quantification. In short, reform encompassed many of the things that mark "modern" medicine. All of these aspects of reform were joined to changes in professional organization and, not surprisingly, show up earlier among urban physicians with European connections.

For discussion, see Bynum, *Science and the Practice of Medicine*, esp. ch. 2; Barbara Gutmann Rosenkrantz, "The Search for Professional Order in 19th-Century American Medicine," in Ronald L. Numbers and Judith Walzer Leavitt, eds., *Sickness and Health in America: Readings in the History of Medicine and Public Health*, 2d ed. (Madison: Univ. of Wisconsin Press, 1985), 219–32.

A particularly nuanced account of both theory and practice of reform is in John Harley Warner, *Therapeutic Perspective;* see also his "The Fall and Rise of Professional Mastery: Epistemology, Authority, and the Emergence of Laboratory Medicine in 19th Century America," in Andrew Cunningham and Perry Williams, eds., *The Laboratory Revolution in Medicine* (Cambridge: Cambridge Univ. Press, 1992), 110–41.

PART FIVE

Bending Genders in the Modern South

Old Fears, New Desires

Beyond the Hummingbird

Southern Women Writers and
the Southern Gargantua

PATRICIA YAEGER

Giant Bodies

THIS IS an essay with an agenda. I want to describe the political effects of the grotesque in southern women's fiction since it is my conviction that this fiction has a politics: a politics that can be read through southern women writers' amazing inventiveness—their daunting grotesques, their mingling of dirt and desire, their tragic invention of "old" southern children.

Despite its beauty and innovation, writing by southern women has for many years taken a back seat to writing by southern men. In 1980, when Richard King published *A Southern Renaissance: The Cultural Awakening of the American South, 1930–1955,* feminists were outraged at the race and gender bias of his study. Women were excluded from *A Southern Renaissance,* as were African Americans; their fictions may have been important, but they did not measure up to King's great themes: "I will generally focus on works which take the South and its tradition as problematic. For this reason I do not deal with black writers such as Richard Wright or Ralph Ellison or with women writers such as Eudora Welty, Carson McCullers, Flannery O'Connor, and Katherine Anne Porter." To "take the South and its tradition as problematic" meant to write about the southern family romance with its mythy fathers, pithy sons, its dim wives and daughters—as these characters were conceived by white males. According to King, southern women did not, for the most part, write with the same "historical consciousness" that inspired male writers. Even when their prose imitated the grandeur of a William Faulkner or a Robert Penn Warren, southern women seemed incapable of devoting themselves to "the tortuous process of dealing with the past of the region." [1]

Of course, King was neither an artless reader nor simple chauvinist. He argued that "all of these writers would demand extensive treatment in a complete history of the Renaissance. Black writers are not taken up because for them the southern family romance was hardly problematic. It could be and was rejected out of hand. . . . The case with the women writers is more difficult, but my reading of them indicates that whatever the merits of their work—and they are considerable—they were not concerned primarily with the larger cultural, racial, and political themes that I take as my focus." [2] It will be my argument that "the larger cultural, racial, and political themes" of southern life are precisely the issues that drive southern women's writing. If critics have been blind to these themes, it is because we have not yet learned to read this writing in all of its power and intricacy, nor have we discovered the ways in which this writing exposes the deforming effects of the southern political tradition upon women, men, and children of color, upon white women and children, and even upon white men. If we fail to acknowledge this "larger" dimension in southern women's writing, we are missing a great deal, indeed.

Surprisingly, the southern woman writer's lack of thematic, stylistic, or political "largeness" is a frequent reprise in criticism of southern fiction. In *The Faraway Country: Writers of the Modern South*, Louis Rubin admits a single woman into his book's southern pantheon, and while he intends his chapter on Eudora Welty to be an eloquent defense of her writing, he flavors this defense with odd diminutions of Welty's abilities. While Faulkner's Mississippi contains combatants "larger than life," Welty's Mississippi is a "tidy, protected little world." While Faulkner flings "whole dynasties of families" into space, while he writes tribal fugues about giant men who "rage at their human limitations," Welty proffers a smaller world "in which people go about their affairs, living, marrying, getting children, diverting themselves, dying, all in tranquil, pastoral fashion." For Rubin, Welty may possess a "muscularity" that pushes her beyond those mere "local colorists," Katherine Anne Porter and Marjorie Kinnan Rawlings, but she is not quite Faulkner, not so big, nor so bold: "I am not proposing that her work is *as* important as Faulkner's, but I am maintaining that in scope and insight her two novels deserve to be compared *with* Faulkner's. She is no lightweight; she is not merely picturesque; she is a serious writer."

And yet "the most startling quality of Eudora Welty's art is her style: shimmering, hovering, elusive, fanciful, fastening on little things. Entirely feminine, it moves lightly, capriciously, mirroring the bemused, diverted quality of the people whom it describes. Like the hummingbirds that appear frequently in her stories, it darts here and there, never quite coming to rest, tirelessly invoking light, color, the variety of experience." [3] In this essay I want to formulate new habits of reading that will take us beyond the hummingbird, beyond Faulkner's shadow, and into the hot southern day. My hope is to recover the political intrigue and bravura, the largeness and largesse, of fiction by southern women.

Let me start with a singular example from Eudora Welty's fiction. In her first collection of short stories, *A Curtain of Green,* we find a wonderful, puzzling story entitled "A Memory." The story seems to go nowhere—its plot line and its sense of character development are almost nil. And yet "A Memory" is Welty's own "spot of time"; the story seems entirely southern in setting and voice but resembles Wordsworthian autobiography in its side glances into the numinous terrors of the everyday. Although nothing happens, a little girl's secure southern world comes crashing down around her. In this moment the child's imaginative or writerly character is formed, and the results are the highly rebellious and political stories in Welty's first volume.

The focus of this story is a modest southern girl with a new obsession: she looks at everything through a frame made by her fingers. What she sees on the day of the story is a gargantuan woman, a ragged colossus in an old bathing suit. It is this gargantua who will inundate any notion that southern women writers are primarily concerned with "little things": "Fat hung upon her upper arms like an arrested earthslide on a hill. With the first motion she might make, I was afraid that she would slide down upon herself into a terrifying heap. Her breasts hung heavy and widening like pears into her bathing suit. Her legs lay prone one on the other like shadowed bulwarks, uneven and deserted, upon which, from the man's hand, the sand piled higher like the teasing threat of oblivion. A slow, repetitious sound I had been hearing for a long time unconsciously, I identified as a continuous laugh which came through the motionless open pouched mouth of the woman." [4] Her crossed legs "like shadowed bulwarks" among the sands, this is woman as Ozymandias; like Ozymandias, she is vulnerable to "the teasing threat of oblivion," to visions of horror and ruin. In surveying her vast, ungainly body, Welty refuses stereotypical portraits of southern women: she refuses to replicate southern women's preoccupation with "little things." How does this human earthquake initiate a new politics of southern women's writing?

The first thing to notice about Welty's earthquake woman is her gigantism. We know that giants—as opposed to the intensely private, palm-sized world of the miniature—are associated with history writ large, with governments as they rise and fall, with the sacerdotal moments of public life. In her marvelous book *On Longing: Narratives of the Miniature, the Gigantic, the Souvenir, the Collection*, Susan Stewart argues that gigantism may also augur change: "The giant is represented through movement, through being in time. Even in the ascription of the still landscape to the giant, it is the activities of the giant, his or her legendary actions, that have resulted in the observable trace. In contrast to the still and perfect universe of the miniature, the gigantic represents the order and disorder of historical forces. The consumerism of the miniature is the consumerism of the classic; it is only fitting that consumer culture appropriates the gigantic whenever change is desired." [5] Welty's giantess is the terrible harbinger of change for a demure southern girl. Why is her body so potent? How might it be political?

When Louis Rubin describes Welty's prose as "shimmering, hovering, elusive, fanciful, fastening on little things," he is touching upon a fragility and miniaturization that haunts southern women's bodies as well. In Katherine Anne Porter's "Old Mortality" Miranda's father insists that his female relatives were all slender as sylphs:

> He sometimes glanced at the photograph and said, "It's not very good. . . . She was much slimmer than that, too. There were never any fat women in the family, thank God."
>
> When they heard their father say things like that, Maria and Miranda simply wondered, without criticism, what he meant. . . . . What about great aunt Keziah, in Kentucky. Her husband, great-uncle John Jacob, had refused to allow her to ride his good horses after she had achieved two hundred and twenty pounds. . . . "Female vanity will recover," said great-uncle John Jacob, callously, "but what about my horses' backs? And if she had the proper female vanity in the first place, she would never have got into such shape." Well, great-aunt Keziah was famous for her heft, and wasn't she in the family? But something seemed to happen to their father's memory when he thought of the girls he had known in the family of his youth, and he declared steadfastly they had

all been, in every generation without exception, as slim as reeds and graceful as sylphs.[6]

This willful miniaturization of the female body may seem comical, but it is also quite dangerous. "What is, in fact, lost in this idealized miniaturization of the body," as Stewart says, "is . . . the danger of power."[7] We see this loss most poignantly in the confinement of Miranda's Aunt Amy, who is reduced to "a motionless image in her dark walnut frame." Estranged by a body that is caught "forever in the pose of being photographed," her nieces wonder "why every older person who looked at the picture said, 'How lovely.' . . . The whole affair was associated, in the minds of the little girls, with dead things. . . . The woman in the picture had been Aunt Amy, but she was only a ghost in a frame, and a sad, pretty story from old times. She had been beautiful, much loved, unhappy, and she had died young" (173). These young girls recognize implicitly that miniaturization insures loss of power and provides no protection against the process of time. And yet the need to miniaturize the southern female body also works paradoxically. It not only keeps some women off horseback and out of public life, but it also embroils them in southern history in the most contorted of ways. For the miniaturized female torso does not exist in simple opposition to gigantism and history—instead, the purified, rarefied, "transcendent" female body offers a site for political labor, a place for uncoding and recoding the epic disasters of the southern body politic.

How should we characterize this politicization of the intense privacy of white women's flesh? In "Identity: Skin Blood Heart," Minnie Bruce Pratt describes the ways in which public desires and private self-interest were flagrantly mapped onto her own girlish body. In the 1960s the white female body could still serve as a fulcrum for white power politics—becoming both its rallying cry and absurd rationale. At the height of the civil rights movement Pratt's father terrorized his children by lodging his own race-terrors—his flimsy beliefs in white supremacy—in his daughter's wayward, uncertain body:

> The entombment of the lady was my "protection": the physical, spiritual, sexual containment which men of my culture have used to keep "their women" pure. . . .

It was this protection that I felt one evening during the height of the civil rights demonstrations in Alabama, as the walls that had contained so many were cracking, when my father called me to his chair in the living room. He showed me a newspaper clipping . . . about Martin Luther King, Jr.; and told me that the article was about how King had sexually abused, used, young Black teen-aged girls. I believe he asked me what I thought of this; I can only guess that he wanted me to feel that my danger, my physical, sexual danger, would be the result of the release of others from containment. I felt frightened and profoundly endangered, by King, by my father: I could not answer him.[8]

It is crucial to examine the ways in which writing by modern southern women both adheres to and rebels against this ideological mask. As Anne Goodwyn Jones explains in *Tomorrow Is Another Day,* "The image wearing Dixie's Diadem" has offered, historically, a spectacular cartography for racist fears. This image

is not a human being but a marble statue, beautiful and silent, eternally inspiring and eternally still.

In that, southern womanhood is not alone. It has much in common with the ideas of the British Victorian lady and of American true womanhood. All deny to women authentic selfhood; all enjoin that women suffer and be still; all show women sexually pure, pious, deferent to external authority, and content with their place in the home. Yet southern womanhood differs in several ways from other nineteenth-century images of womanhood. Unlike them, the southern lady is at the core of a region's self-definition; the identity of the South is contingent in part upon the persistence of its tradition of the lady.[9]

We need to delve further into this tradition and what it might mean to have one's body "at the core" of the South's self-definition.

Bryan Turner suggests four different tasks that bodies create for the social systems trying to control them: "(1) the reproduction of populations in time, (2) the regulation of bodies in space, (3) the restraint of the 'interior' body through disciplines, and (4) the representation of the 'exterior' body in social space."[10] What's intriguing about this fourth category, the socially mandated miniaturization of the white southern woman's irregularly shaped frame, is that this reification of femininity—this representation of the white woman's exterior, racialized body in social space—also has stunning repercussions for the first three categories of public discipline. The racially pure and diminutive female body in need of protection becomes the motive force, the purported source for the taboo against race-mixing. As southern myth, this fragile white body helps to motivate (1) southern modes of population control reproducing black and white populations as separate, (2) the regulated segregation of these racial bodies in space, and (3) the need for deeply interiorized categories of racism that will do the work of segregation. In other words, the small compass of the ideal white woman's body is oddly at war with its epic stature in minds of white men; this fragile white body, slim as a reed and graceful as a sylph, becomes pivotal in each crucial task of bodily discipline.

What is most remarkable about southern women's fiction is the way in which it refuses such discipline. When the grotesque body marches onto the page, the ideology that controls southern bodies explodes in the most unexpected of ways. Southern women's writing is filled with bizarre somatic images that seem unnecessarily cruel or out of control, and yet this cruelty has a function: it tears at the social fabric and leaves it in shreds: "I have felt the destructive effects of personal race and class privilege first through [my mother's] life: her skin allergies that made her scratch her own white skin raw. The *her* in *me* feels the trap of that whiteness, the need to claw out. The times I have realized my own racism most, this image has come to mind: I am sitting in a white porcelain bathtub scraping my skin with Brillo pads; there is blood in rivulets in the tub." [11] This is from Mab Segrest's *My Mama's Dead Squirrel,* a text arguing that the grotesque is a neurotic, disreputable form for southern writers. And yet when Segrest wants to contemplate the terrible effects of racism—and the work of domination that the white female body performs on behalf of this racism—she resorts to a grotesque tropology. Her mother's bloody white body reveals the social agon hidden beneath the happy surfaces of feminine charisma and cleanliness. In Segrest's memoir women's open, wounded bodies become political intensifiers, spaces for mapping an entire region's social and psychic neuroses.

This is to argue that the bodies in southern women's fiction are intensely political; they are often concerned with "larger cultural, racial, and political themes" simply because southern bodies have had to endure such "themes" in daily life. As Lillian Smith recalls her childhood in *Killers of the Dream,* its lessons revolved around her body's sexual and racial markers: "Now . . . your body is a thing of shame and mystery, and curiosity about it is not good; your skin is your glory and the source of your strength and pride. It is white. And, as you have heard, whiteness is a symbol of purity and excellence. Remember this: your white skin proves that you are better than all other people on this earth. Yes, it does that. And does it simply because it is white—which, in a way, is a kind of miracle. But the Bible is full of miracles and it should not be too difficult for us to accept one more."[12] Southern women's fiction works with a similar irony; it abrades the surface of this body to bring the daily contradictions of "miraculous" whiteness to the surface. The stories we will examine work toward a massive category confusion in which the common classifications of southern life no longer make sense, in which the condensation and displacement of political contradictions onto the white female body no longer take place in secret but, instead, get held up for scrutiny.

To exemplify the female body's gargantuan labors, I want to tell the tale of another giant woman, Miss Eckhart, the foreign piano teacher in Welty's "June Recital," one of the stories in her 1949 collection *The Golden Apples*. We have already seen that Rubin's association of Welty with the miniature evokes a world of diminished associations in which Welty's style ("entirely feminine," moving "lightly, capriciously") mirrors the charming world that good southern white women were supposed to inhabit. But when we recast our image of Welty to reflect the awkward grandiosity of Miss Eckhart or the black musician Powerhouse in *A Curtain of Green*'s "Powerhouse" or the slovenly fat woman who stalks through "A Memory," these giant bodies invoke the messiness and hubris of history itself. While Miss Eckhart's body invokes a world of gender asymmetry and the gargantua in "A Memory" draws attention to southern fantasies about class, what gets magnified through Powerhouse's awkward frame is the great debacle of segregation itself. This stupendous man, "so monstrous he sends everybody into oblivion," entertains white audiences, but he is refused the right to congregate with them. During intermission Powerhouse turns his "African feet of the greatest size" and his mouth "vast and obscene," toward "Negrotown" to have a drink and then makes his way back through the pouring rain, "his mouth . . . nothing but a volcano."[13] When Welty's critics read Powerhouse as the epitome of Welty's improvisatory glee, her ability to write jazzy fiction that competes with the best boogie-woogie, they miss this story's hidden script: the fact that even the jazzman's fantasies and improvisations are restricted by segregation. Although Powerhouse mounts symbolic protests—avoiding his own sense of peril by telling thunderous tales about his wife's imagined infidelity and suicide—his powerful body still has to succumb to the illogic of Jim Crow. The merry misogyny of the stories he tells may carry the day, but they are also quite sad. His power and vastness contrast with his obsessive riffing on faithlessness and death; Powerhouse's huge frame and constricted fantasies emphasize the power and vastness of a system that still restricts this massive man's locomotion.

In Miss Eckhart we witness another kind of oppression: a great female pianist whose talent is denied because of her sex. On the thunderous summer day when she gives her concert in "June Recital," Miss Eckhart's body swells to enormous proportions; she represents new and frightening parameters for southern women's lives: "Miss Eckhart played as if it were Beethoven; she struck the music open midway and it was in soft yellow tatters like old satin. The thunder rolled and Miss Eckhart frowned and bent forward or she leaned back to play; at moments her solid body swayed from side to side like a tree trunk." [14] What is this burgeoning female body doing in the demure alcoves of southern women's fiction?

Mary Jacobus, Evelyn Fox Keller, and Sally Shuttleworth have argued that "the body, whether masculine or feminine, is imbricated in the matrices of power at all levels." [15] It is my contention that the bodies in southern women's fiction make this imbrication visible. The grotesque bodies occupying stories by Porter, Hurston, Welty, McCullers, O'Connor, Gilchrist, and Walker become premier sites for exploring the work of a southern polity in which women are barred from public power but become central players in its symbolic scripts. Miss Eckhart is a case in point. Her giant body becomes a symbol of female artistry and self-empowerment threatening beyond words; but her gigantism also becomes a battlefield for the social violence that is ordinarily scripted onto the body of the romantic white girl. When she sits down to play for her pupils, "the piece was so hard that she made mistakes and repeated to correct them, so long and stirring that it soon seemed longer than the day itself had been, and in playing it, Miss Eckhart assumed an entirely different face. Her skin flattened and drew across her cheeks, her lips changed. The face could have belonged to someone else—not even to a woman, necessarily. It was the face a mountain could have, or what might be seen behind the veil of a waterfall. There in the rainy light it was a sightless face, one for music only—though the fingers kept slipping and making mistakes they had to correct. And if the sonata had an origin in a place on earth, it was the place where Virgie, even, had never been and was not likely to go" (56). When Miss Eckhart's face blends with the huge forms of nature, she is usurping a power reserved for white males: her face changes, her music seems to come from some unearthly realm. To underline this transgressive power, Welty appropriates images from Shelley's "Mont Blanc" but with this difference.[16] While Shelley mourns—but then appropriates—Mont Blanc's grandeur and cruelty, the sublimity Shelley withholds from himself Welty gives to her heroine. Miss Eckhart *becomes* the mountain that stares back at Shelley and will not answer his call.

Ironically, it is Cassie Morrison, a child in need of giant reveries, who brings Miss Eckhart back to earth. She reimagines her piano teacher as a fallen woman, an untouchable, and reveals the policing mechanisms of the southern economy at its worst. Stunned by her piano teacher's arpeggios, Cassie protects herself by mapping communal stereotypes of race and rape onto Miss Eckhart's great body:

> She began to think of an incident that had happened to Miss Eckhart instead of about the music she was playing; that was one way.
>
> One time, at nine o'clock at night, a crazy nigger had jumped out of the school hedge and got Miss Eckhart, had pulled her down and threatened to kill her. That was long ago. She had been walking by herself after dark; nobody had told her any better. When Dr. Loomis made her well, people were surprised that she and her mother did not move away. They wished she had moved away, everybody but poor Miss Snowdie; then they wouldn't always have to remember that a terrible thing once happened to her. But Miss Eckhart stayed, as though she considered one thing not so much more terrifying than another. (57)

If Miss Eckhart gives us giant dreams, her listeners know how to resist them. Caught inside during an electrical storm, her pupils have listened to her music reluctantly—for like the storm itself, Miss Eckhart's playing is abusive and grand. Terrified of her newfound power and Miss Eckhart's refusal to bend her artistic talents toward the designated role of spinster-teacher, her pupils convert her harrowing body to its "proper" size.

Miss Eckhart's body is threatening because it becomes the locus for two different kinds of transgression. First, instead of a "hummingbird" style that fastens on "little things," her incredible music evokes all the elements of sublimity, transcendence, and violence that critics in search of "larger themes" could desire: "The music came with greater volume—with fewer halts—and Jinny Love tiptoed forward and began turning the music. Miss Eckhart did not even see her—her arm struck the child, making a run. Coming from Miss Eckhart, the music made all the pupils uneasy, almost alarmed; something had burst out, unwanted, exciting, from the wrong person's life. This was some brilliant thing too splendid for Miss Eckhart, piercing and striking the air around her the way a Christmas firework might almost jump out of the hand that was, each year, inexperienced anew" (56). Second, Miss Eckhart refuses the stereotypes of southern femininity. Her arm strikes a child; she wields too much creative power. But, as the editors of *Body/Politics* note, "the feminine body . . . is peculiarly the battlefield on which quite other struggles than women's own have been waged." [17] What "other" battle is raging in Miss Eckhart's body?

We have already seen the displacement of racial politics onto the white female frame in Minnie Bruce Pratt's frightened memories of Martin Luther King. What brings Pratt's and Miss Eckhart's stories together is not only an act of displacement in which white patriarchs and little white girls are so threatened by change (by the advent of black or female empowerment) that they regroup, recommit themselves to the white female's vulnerability. What's curious about this act of fetishism is that in each case the feminine body becomes prominent—turns into a battleground—when the social hierarchy is threatened, when the margins of power start to shift. As Peter Stallybrass and Allon White have suggested, "Discourses about the body have a privileged role, for transcodings between different levels and sectors of social and psychic reality are effected through the intensifying grid of the body. It is no accident . . . that transgressions and the attempt to control them obsessively return to somatic symbols, for these are the ultimate elements of social classification itself." [18] "The intensifying grid" of Miss Eckhart's body startles these children because her playing, with its brilliance and fireworks, escapes its classification and establishes a carnival moment, a temporary liberation from the established southern order. To diminish her body's grandeur, these children, well socialized by their habitus, go on the attack; they surround Miss Eckhart with a scary set of somatic symbols (their communal story about rape) to control her unwanted unruliness. When Miss Eckhart raises herself to great heights, revealing a musical brilliance reserved for great men, her pupils find a way to restore her abjection and lowliness.

Why do they impose this terrible discipline on her body? There is, of course, a regional pattern to this discipline. When Cassie converts her teacher's tempestuous playing into racial terror, she is rehearsing the perennial southern story that Jacquelyn Dowd Hall calls the "southern rape complex." Hall argues that this "complex," with its triumphant protection of white women, its calculated fear of black men, its ignorance of the abuses of black women, is an instrument of sexual and racial suppression scapegoating those players in the southern game who challenge the established order. Just as "lynching served to dramatize hierarchies among men," so stories of female victimization encourage white women to depend upon white men. Hall reminds us that the "southern rape complex" is extraindividual, a "dramatization of cultural themes, a story [white southerners] told themselves about the social arrangements and psychological strivings that lay beneath the surface of everyday life." "A woman who had just been raped, or who had been apprehended in a clandestine affair, or whose male relatives were pretending that she had been raped, stood on display before the whole community. Here was the quintessential Woman as Victim: polluted, 'ruined for life,' the object of fantasy and secret contempt. Humiliation, however, mingled with heightened worth as she played for a moment the role of Fair Maiden violated and avenged. For this privilege—if the alleged assault had in fact taken place—she might pay with suffering in the extreme. In any case, she would pay with a lifetime of subjugation to the men gathered in her behalf." [19] It is this culturally sanctioned form of "heightened worth" that Miss Eckhart tries to avoid. Even as scapegoat the pianist has maintained a public stance; she continues to teach, to take in pupils. To adapt to the trauma of rape when female honor is still a southern rallying cry means to challenge the political order at its grass roots—to acknowledge rape as an ordinary, terrible crime that should result in neither racial hysteria nor ostracism for its victims. And yet, like Powerhouse, Miss Eckhart is caught in her community's drama. Willy-nilly, her body becomes "the battleground on which quite other struggles" are waged. This means there is no need to rape this woman in fact to make her conform: she is raped repeatedly in the communal imagination. And this communal rape is not just the subject of adult brutality. In Welty's story Miss Eckhart is attacked, her rape reenacted, among the community's children, who have internalized a model of female powerlessness and continue to enforce this model upon each other and within themselves.

This is Miss Eckhart's designated story, and yet to end on this note could make us forget the scene in which she plays the piano and sways in treelike ecstasy. Miss Eckhart threatens her pupils because her body suggests a different world order in which women are allowed to be noisy and grand. The gargantuan body both maps its own limits and refuses to stay within boundaries, to serve asked-for ends. What resounds throughout this awkward female frame are the very power plays that the petite white female body tries to mask. If, as Louise Westling suggests, the southern white woman as "representative of Christian virtues was lauded in public to divert attention from the problems of slavery and racism," Westling also notes that this diversion has physical consequences: "The scope of her activities was severely limited."[20] The gargantuan body exceeds these limits and attests to the pleasures of inventing extraordinary human beings whose bodies don't follow the rules. The grotesque body is the focus for a "free play with the human body and with its organs" not permitted by southern conformity.

This giant female body offers itself as a totem, then, for our perusal of southern women's fiction: a totem that teaches two things. First, if the private bodies of white southern women are asked to become smooth public surfaces—if southern women have been compelled to inhabit pleasant, undifferentiated, fragile bodies in search of protection—Miss Eckhart's gigantism transgresses this role and renders it unstable.[21] She ushers a panoply of female giants into this study, from Carson McCullers's Amelia and Frankie to Flannery O'Connor's irate redneck matrons. We may even trace a ghostly gigantism in Kate Chopin's Edna Pontellier: "She turned her face seaward to gather in an impression of space and solitude, which the vast expanse of water, meeting and melting with the moonlit sky, conveyed to her excited fancy. As she swam she seemed to be reaching out for the unlimited in which to lose herself."[22]

At the same time, each of these giant bodies serves deliberate political ends; they give us hyperbolic visions of the systemic crises within each heroine's social milieu. By invoking the concept of systemic crisis, I want to expand upon the suggestion that female bodies are used as symbolic sites to cordon off or demarcate undesired social change. In addition, southern bodies are caught in a daily, formulaic round of hostility, tension, and emergency: a crisis that is ongoing, habitual, and monitored by white civilians and law enforcement alike. As Robin Kelley describes the pre–civil rights skirmishes that occurred on segregated southern buses in the 1940s and 1950s, "All oppositional and transgressive acts took place in a context of extreme repression. The occupants sitting in the rear who witnessed or were part of the daily guerrilla skirmishes learned that punishment was inevitable."[23] While white citizens were deputized to police the color boards, black men were denied citizenship on a daily basis. In "The Ritual of Survival" Robert Fleming testifies about this daily policing of southern race culture; he, too, describes an incessant round of racial and sexual emergency: "If a black man was to survive, he had to know his place, to step off the curb when a white person approached, and to lower his eyes whenever he spoke to a white woman. It seemed that daily lynchings of blacks were the meat-and-potatoes stories for the various Southern newspapers in those days, complete with graphic details of the grisly deed and the alleged crime for which the person of color lost his or her life."[24] Julius Lester summarizes these structural perversions, this state of perpetual emergency, in "Black and White Together." He remembers the terror of southern life during the protest movements of the 1960s when death became atmospheric: "To live in an atmosphere where the presence of death is as palpable as the smell of honeysuckle lacerated the soul in ways one dared not stop to know."[25] In the face of these repeated systematic assaults on African Americans' humanity, the fantasy of the gargantuan woman has not been limited to white women's fictions. Alice Walker's Feather Mae advances this story, as does Janie, in her reach for the horizon at the end of *Their Eyes Were Watching God:* "Then Tea Cake came prancing around her where she was and the song of the sigh flew out of the window and lit in the top of the pine trees. Tea Cake, with the sun for a shawl. Of course he wasn't dead. He could never be dead until she herself had finished feeling and thinking. The kiss of his memory made pictures of love and light against the wall. Here was peace. She pulled in her horizon like a great fishnet. Pulled it from around the waist of the world and draped it over her shoulder. So much of life in its meshes! She called in her soul to come and see."[26] The gargantuan Janie sends a promissory note. By throwing off her burdens, she refuses the boundaries of a racially constricted life, even as Tea Cake's lost, prancing body acknowledges the crises bred by racial hierarchy within a white-dominated culture all too careless of death.

In this context Miss Eckhart's refusal to be miniaturized, to fit within the confines of this system, should also remind us of the relative difficulty—for women, for people of color—of such public refusals. The stereotype of the "little woman" inheres so strictly in Miss Eckhart's habitus that it is always, already in circulation: the southern rape complex requires each woman's repeated miniaturization.[27] But southern women's fiction also contests the boundaries of these expectations, even when it gives in. When the gigantic, well-muscled Amelia, heroine of *The Ballad of the Sad Cafe,* starts winning the fight with Marvin Macy fair and square, her six-two frame is slick with body grease and the odor of victory, and we long for her success. But when Cousin Lymon comes to Macy's support, when he flies through the air and clutches "at her neck with his clawed little fingers" so that Amelia falls flat on her back, "her arms flung outward and motionless," her body also records a larger battle scene in which southern women submit to "higher" laws.[28] The exaggeration of her bodily boundaries reveals the exact location of these boundaries; the gargantuan woman becomes a political intensifier for mapping the gigantism of southern social derangements.

Miniature Bodies

In depicting the explosive body of a giant woman, Eudora Welty is exposing the southern power structure and its pervasive influence—the ways in which sexual and racial boundaries are enforced by white children as well as white men. Although King accuses southern women of writing without a sense of "historical consciousness," in "June Recital" this consciousness is all too acute. Miss Eckhart's lumbering frame exposes the quotidian social controls that keep blacks and women in their place.

It is this sense of the dailiness of history, this focus on diurnal politics, that I want to address in the second half of this essay. In reworking the image of the southern lady—in creating her grotesque or giant antitype—southern women writers do more than protest the burdens of ladyhood. Their grotesque heroines help bring the hard facts of southern racism and sexism into focus. At the same time, hard facts don't always operate through epic forms.

I've suggested that the giant body—in its outlandishness and strangeness—becomes a formal property of southern women's texts that gathers our attention and enlarges the scope of our vision so that the vagaries of southern politics (here, the southern rape complex) come to light in the sudden telescoping and shrinking of Miss Eckhart's body. We will see a similar pattern at work in "A Memory" when a fat woman's frightening body provides a moment of transformation for a staid southern child: "I saw the man lift his hand filled with crumbling sand, shaking it as the woman laughed, and pour it down inside her bathing suit between her bulbous descending breasts" (154). While the controlled body of the middle-class child promotes hierarchy, the grotesque body protests verticality. Against classicism and classism, this fat woman's sandy gigantism insists on the bodily equality of bowels, blood, and breasts. Her excess flesh will move us toward a rereading of class and gender hardship, toward an exploration of the excesses of a southern political system that inhabited little white girls as well as white men.

This suggests a turn in my argument: the giant female body relays these "larger" issues, but only insofar as she makes us pay attention to the miniature, the microcosmic, the quotidian. It is, after all, the quotidian details that express the hardest facts of southern life. Lillian Smith details this adversity in *Killers of the Dream* as she talks with one of her students about the daily struggles of the past:

> "Your parents and I lived our babyhood in those days of wrath. But always the violence was distant, the words vague and terrible for we were protected children. A lynching could happen in our county and we wouldn't know it. Yet we did know because of faces, whispers, a tightening of the whole town."
>
> I did not say more for I was caught in those old days, remembering: Sometimes it was your nurse who made you know. You loved her, and suddenly she was frightened, and you knew it. Her eyes saw things your eyes did not see. As the two of you sat in the sand playing your baby games, she'd whisper, "Lawd Jesus, when you going to help us!" And suddenly the play would leave the game and you would creep close to her begging her to shield you from her trouble. . . . Sometimes it would be your father, explaining a race incident to the older children. Even now I can feel that hush, the changed voices when they saw you listening, the

talking down to the little one in false and cheerful words, saying, "Sugar, what you been playing today?"[29]

Killers of the Dream was written in 1949 and describes the vanishing world of Jasper, Florida, at the turn of the century. And yet when Julius Lester describes the South of the 1940s and 1950s from the other side of the racial divide, the details are much the same: "It is almost impossible to describe that world the civil rights movement destroyed, that world of my childhood and adolescence ruled by signs decreeing where I was and was not allowed to go, what door I had to enter at the bus station and train station, where I had to sit on the bus. How do I explain what it is to live with the absurd and pretend to its ordinariness without becoming insane? How do I explain that I cannot be sure that my sanity was not hopelessly compromised because I grew up in a world where the insane was as ordinary as margarine?"[30] To say that the "large" issues of southern history come down to bus stations and baby games is not to trivialize these issues but to acknowledge the banality of history. Racism may be epic in reach and scope, but its horror lives on in the particular. In looking at "A Memory," I want to address the intersections between the giant female body and civic life, to explore the particularity of the gargantuan body as it becomes a site of transaction for the South's "ordinary" insanities.

Welty's "A Memory" is particularly eloquent about the politics of the everyday. Like Miss Eckhart, Welty's earthquake woman does not become a public colossus or politician. Instead, we watch a middle-class girl watching a lower-class family playing at the beach. The girl, an avatar for Welty herself, is a snob; she is offended by this unsavory family's "tasteless" hijinks. In mapping her own childish aversions and offering them as an index to an entire social milieu, Welty gives us politics of a different order from the male writers of the Southern Renaissance, but she gives us politics all the same.[31]

David Held has argued that political theory has a special purpose; it "aims to offer a systematic analysis of politics and of the ways in which it is always bounded by, among other things, unacknowledged conditions of action. It can, thereby, fracture existing forms of understanding and re-form the practically generated accounts of the political in everyday life."[32] Welty's fiction may not be exhausted by the limits of "political theory," but her stories do break new ground; they help us reformulate women's relation to "the practically generated accounts of the political" in everyday southern life.

This is worth stressing because studies of southern fiction focusing on political systems have, for the most part, limited their analyses to southern politics as monument and myth.[33] When Richard King gives his definition of the Southern Renaissance, he values the ways in which male writers deal with the three *p*'s of southern studies: plantations, patriarchy, and the past. "Put briefly: the writers and intellectuals of the South after the late 1920s were engaged in an attempt to come to terms not only with the inherited values of the Southern tradition but also with a certain way of perceiving and dealing with the past, what Nietzsche called "monumental" historical consciousness. It was vitally important for them to decide whether the past was of any use at all in the present. . . . The 'object' of their historical consciousness was a tradition whose essential figures were the father and the grandfather and whose essential structure was the literal and symbolic family. In sum, the Renaissance writers sought to come to terms with what I call the 'Southern family romance.'"[34] But there are other ways to come to terms with the legitimation crises of twentieth-century southern life. First, we need to recognize that any struggle with the use-value of the past must also be construed as a struggle within the present. It is this daily loss of legitimation, the inability of traditional or established patterns to make sense of the ebb and flow of everyday life, that southern women writers address in their obsession with the southern grotesque. We need not look to "monumental" historical consciousness—not to fathers or grandfathers or even large women—to understand the complexities that the weight of tradition brings to bear upon the diurnal round of southern life. Thus short stories, cookbooks, girlish fantasies, and personal vignettes can become sites for measuring a political crisis in the making. These private narrative forms have public dimensions implicated in the apportionment of power.[35] Welty's story also demonstrates that within a southern political schema, what a child thinks at the beach may be as telling as a trip to the statehouse; she may give us access to the ordinary dominations, the insane politics of everyday southern life.

In fact, it is just such frivolous techniques of the body that the earthquake woman engages in Welty's autobiographical story from *A Curtain of Green*. Like the little girls in "June Recital," the child who narrates "A Memory" is preoccupied with the apportionment of social space, with the division of the work of domination. All her energy goes into framing and judging her world. But as this frame breaks apart, what comes into the foreground are the "unacknowledged conditions of action" that dominate this child's caste-obsessed world, namely, her severe reliance on her position within a class that bases its Whiggish sense of superiority on warding off redneck threats to an established order.[36] The grotesque bodies in southern women's fiction give us special access to these barely acknowledged conditions of middle-class self-construction.

When "A Memory" opens, Welty's heroine is lying on the beach in the noonday sun, "looking at a rectangle brightly lit, actually glaring at me, with sun, sand, water, a little pavilion, a few solitary people in fixed attitudes, and around it all a border of dark rounded oak trees, like the engraved thunderclouds surrounding illustrations in the Bible" (147). The frame that she makes with her fingers mimics her social heritage; this child's middle-class southern Protestantism helps her frame judgments about the merits of those around her.[37] As she solemnly tells us, she sees no one at the lake but children, or "those older people whose lives are obscure, irregular, and consciously of no worth to anything" (147). What her frame offers is a system of stratification, a rectangle that designates who's in and who's out, who's valuable, and who is not.

For Welty's little girl these schemes are intricately tied up with romance. She is in love with love itself and dreams endlessly of a secret beau, meditating obsessively on the day she contrived to touch his wrist in the stairwell at school. "It was possible during that entire year for me to think endlessly on this minute and brief encounter which we endured on the stairs, until it would swell with a sudden and overwhelming beauty, like a rose forced into premature bloom for a great occasion" (149). Ironically, "A Memory" begins in the miniature world that Louis Rubin describes as typical of Welty's fiction. We see a sensitive child on her way to heterosexual stardom, preparing for the blinkered wisdom of middle-class courting where women relinquish their claim to the public world for summer cotillions and where every nerve strains toward the opposite sex.

The first hint that something is amiss in the southern romance plot is signaled with blood: "I remember with exact clarity the day in Latin class when the boy I loved (whom I watched constantly) bent suddenly over and brought his handkerchief to his face. I saw red—vermilion—blood flow over the handkerchief and his square-shaped hand; his nose had begun to bleed. I remember the very moment: several of the older girls laughed at the confusion and distraction" (150). The narrator's response is stereotypically feminine—she faints dead away. Her motive seems fairly clear; she is terrified at this splitting open of the male body, afraid of its dirtiness, its democratizing blood. Might the threat of menstruation and mortality inhere in a boy's body as well as a girl's? The older girls feel the incongruity of this reversal and laugh, but the young narrator finds her momentary superiority unbearable; when she faints, she restores her gender to its pristine passivity.

What this moment brings home is this culture's incredible anxiety about sexual difference; the heroine needs to believe that this boy is other, superior, remote from herself. But Welty also details a little girl's status anxiety in a way that is equally compelling; class hierarchy insinuates itself as another predatory worry exacerbating this child's sense of self. The narrator tells us that she knows nothing about her beau's family or background, and that "this occasioned during the year of my love a constant uneasiness in me. It was unbearable to think that his house might be slovenly and unpainted, hidden by tall trees, that his mother and father might be shabby—dishonest—crippled—dead. I speculated endlessly on the dangers of his home" (151).

The "danger" of other people's homes—the fact of class struggle—is the squalid little secret this story sets out to expose. As Pierre Bourdieu suggests, the bourgeois elite invent for themselves an "eternal sociodicy" in which "all forms of 'levelling,' 'trivialization,' or 'massification'" seem to threaten at once. The decline of modern society is associated with apocalyptic threats to the middle-class home. Welty's child, embroiled in this "sociodicy," seems particularly vulnerable to her caste's obsessive fears; she worries helplessly that her beau lives among the "undifferentiated hordes" of the underclass who threaten "to submerge the private spaces of bourgeois exclusiveness."[38]

Moreover, her obsession with squalor has the exaggerated overtone of a fairy tale or Gothic romance, and this suggests two of the gifts that Welty's story bestows. First, the romance plot is traditionally a place where class anxiety or turmoil can be repressed. The romance usually offers (as in *Jane Eyre*) a story of assimilation, or (as in most fairy tales) a discovery that the poor little goose girl is really a queen, or (as in *Mary Barton*) a genre where love scuttles class rebellion. "A Memory" refuses these terms. Romance becomes Welty's vehicle for exploring class consciousness; for her heroine an encounter with the Other generates real terror about the flimsiness of existing social boundaries. This breaking of boundaries is an enduring characteristic of southern women's fiction. Even a novella like *Member of the Wedding* questions the race and gender confines of the white heterosexual southern myths. Frankie may become "Frances," a budding belle, but only after Mc-Cullers asks us to mourn the sacrifice of her family's African-American housekeeper, Berenice, and the death of her androgynous cousin, John Henry.

Second, like McCullers, Welty explores the odd shapes of southern class consciousness by warping our vision of the southern child. At least since Rousseau the child has functioned to circumvent rumors of "sexuality and social inequality" in the West. According to Jacqueline Rose, the storybook child "is rendered innocent of all the contradictions which flaw our interaction with the world."[39] But Welty's preadolescent offers a social fulcrum, an entrance to cultural monstrosities as the grown-up Eudora Welty takes pleasure in staging scurrilous scenes for her own childish double. As her heroine lies on the beach, "squaring" the world with her fingers and dreaming about her bleeding beau, this girlish frame is disrupted by a family that acts out her worst social fears. This family's chief distinction is its slovenliness: "Sprawled close to where I was lying . . . appeared a group of loud, squirming, ill-assorted people who seemed thrown together only by the most confused accident, and who seemed driven by a foolish intent to insult each other, all of which they enjoyed with a hilarity which astonished my heart. . . . when I was a child such people were called 'common'" (152). Their "commonness" attracts and repels the little girl: "Lying in leglike confusion together were the rest of the group, the man and the two women. The man seemed completely given over to the heat and glare of the sun; his relaxed eyes sometimes squinted with faint amusement over the brilliant water and the hot sand. His arms were flabby and at rest. He lay turned on his side, now and then scooping sand in a loose pile about the legs of the older woman" (152–53). Bourdieu reminds us that our cognitive structures, the ways we divide up the world, are not innocent schema but "internalized, 'embodied' social structures" that are chaotic and culpable; they help to enforce the most unsavory oppositions between dominant and dominated: "All the agents in a given social formation share a set of basic perceptual schemes, which receive the beginnings of objectification in the pairs of antagonistic adjectives commonly used to classify and qualify persons or objects.

The network of oppositions between high . . . and low . . . fine . . . and coarse . . . unique . . . and common . . . is the matrix of all the common-places which find such ready acceptance because behind them lies the whole social order."[40] This is central to Welty's story. The oppositions between male and female, upper class and underclass, are the common-places, the building blocks of a southern class system that we may over-look because they are so ordinary. But beyond these prosaic categories of trashy white Others lies an entire social order. These distinctions are its foundations, and "A Memory" describes a child who is working hard to master these categories for herself.

This process is disrupted by an unsavory fat woman who will not take her place amidst these "antagonistic adjectives." Her body is filthy; it is covered with sand, but she refuses to accept a role of abjection: "Once when I looked up, the fat woman was standing opposite the smiling man. She bent over and in a condescending way pulled down the front of her bathing suit, turning it outward, so that the lumps of mashed and folded sand came emptying out. I felt a peak of horror, as though her breasts themselves had turned to sand, as though they were of no importance at all and she did not care" (156). This fat woman is bad taste incarnate, and her bad taste, her indecent exposure, her empty breasts have the exhilarating ability to wreck the child-narrator's de-limiting frame. As sand pours out of her body, we experience an empty-ing out of the little girl's romance plot as well. This woman's pearlike breasts are suddenly artifactual, lightened of female allure. Her anger matters; it shakes up a little girl's sense of privilege and hierarchy, as if Welty means to give notice that those class-and-sex dramas excluded from middle-class life can return in the most ungainly forms to haunt the power structure with its guilts and desires.[41]

Have I gone too far? Can a southern female child really represent "the power structure"? The little girl in Welty's story is obsessed with evaluating her social world. While the earthquake woman is, for her, an untouchable, a social pariah, this woman's body also works to dis-rupt this little girl's leisured superiority, her ease with the "work of domination" that these categorical modes of otherness instill. That is, this gargantuan southern body undoes the oppressive pleasantries of middle-class "taste" by imploding this child's hoped for conformities: "I felt a necessity for absolute conformity to my ideas in any happening I witnessed. As a result, all day long in school I sat perpetually alert, fearing for the untoward to happen. The dreariness and regularity of the school day were a protection for me" (149–50). This is an amazing statement from the childish avatar of one of the foremost inventors of the southern grotesque. Within this atmosphere of anxious conformity, the gargantuan female's "untoward" explosion of the child's precarious frame seems entirely just. At the same time, the child-narrator is herself a victim of her culture's fantasies, and in perusing her role in the story, we must come full circle, returning, via the child's diminutive and minoritized body, to the interactive politics of a gargantuan woman who can disrupt the miniature framework of a haunted little girl.

Children play a double role in southern women's writing. Marginal to mainstream culture but also caught up in its process of indoctrination, the child may question her society's values and provide a narrative space for challenging its beliefs. But children also become a tragic center for exploring the effects of the political in everyday life. As the focus of adult rules and regulations, the child is a victim and seismologist who registers the costs of a classist or a sexist ethic; she becomes a vivid, painful pressure point, a site of strain and unrest within an unjust social system. What the child is busy learning, along with fractions and table manners, is a system, a framework, a set of ideological desires and constraints. And ideologies carry their own political freight; they are symbolic systems that are continually "mobilized to sustain asymmetrical power relations in the interests of dominant or hegemonic groups."[42] The effect of the earthquake woman's family upon the young Welty is to break up this hegemonic assurance:

> It seemed to me that I could hear also the thud and the fat impact of all their ugly bodies upon one another. I tried to withdraw to my most inner dream, that of touching the wrist of the boy I loved on the stair . . . but the memory itself did not come to me.
>
> . . . I sank into familiarity; but the story of my love, the long narrative of the incident on the stairs, had vanished. I did not know, any longer, the meaning of my happiness; it held me unexplained. (155–56)

At this moment Welty's story offers us the specter of a southern legitimation crisis made flesh. As we watch a young child learning her culture's norms, trying to live inside them, we also see these norms breaking apart.[43] As she moves from the superiority of a romantic framework to an altered perceptual state that admits the grotesque body in all its "untoward" irregularity, she recognizes a world outside her habitus that remains "unexplained." That is, we see the glimmer of a child who is increasingly unable to inhabit the undemocratic certainties that both discipline and support her.

Unable to withdraw into her "most inner dream," this child is experiencing a diminutive version of a southern legitimation crisis. A culture comes to a crisis in legitimation when normative structures start to change and there is a gap, a dissonance, between the demands of the framework of the social apparatus and people's expectations and needs.[44] As old norms are pushed aside, new norms are invented that lack the force of motivation and belief. Louis Rubin has argued that this dissonance is a pivotal experience in the twentieth-century South, where old sources of certitude and belief remained entrenched but failed to offer "an adequate basis for daily experience." For Rubin this becomes a world "doomed" to fall apart. "In attempting to hold onto its traditional modes of thought and behavior so far as the Negro is concerned, the South seeks to retain a social structure doomed in and by time. In so doing, it fights a losing battle, in which racial segregation is but the immediate issue."[45] The dangerous potential inherent in angry women and their redneck consorts suggests another site of conflict. Welty's story reenacts the demise of a rose-tinted, romantic southern worldview that is no longer serviceable but seems quite irreplaceable. "A Memory" reenacts that catastrophic moment when a social formation starts to break down, and the cracks or gaps in its systems of classification seem more powerful than the system itself.

Welty has inscribed the miniature catastrophes of "A Memory" in the cusp of a full-blown southern crisis. Her story comes at the center of *A Curtain of Green,* a book set in the Great Depression that dramatizes the defamiliarization of the American Dream as it is mapped onto depressed southern bodies. The regional devastation of this depression, with its displacements of entire populations, its exaggeration of the already aggravated chasm between the North's (relative) wealth and the South's greater penury, its acceleration of the breakdown of a closed agrarian world, could only drive home the object lessons (and utter inadequacy) of an impoverished worldview whose demise is half-mourned and half-celebrated in "A Memory." Unlike most of the characters in *Curtain of Green* (mainly idiots, half-wits, deaf-mutes, sideshow or plantation relics, and con men), the heroine of "A Memory" seems out of place, for she is solidly middle class and hopelessly lyrical.

But by placing a formative moment from this white girl's uneventful past at the center of her story, Welty transforms the definition of an epic event; she insists that history is made by children, too. By suggesting that this story's narrator may be Welty herself, by dramatizing a moment from a southern female life when the rage for class demarcation and lyricism breaks down, Welty also suggests a mode of transformation. It is this child's youthful penchant for accurate vision, for seeing the socially unspeakable, that works to produce an adult writer who will not turn away from the grotesque but writes unflinchingly about Miss Eckhart or Powerhouse or the tenant farmers in "A Whistle." By questioning the values of a child who is at first repelled but finally feels eroticized by the grotesque world around her, "A Memory" offers the beginnings of an epistemic break, of a new era in one writer's consciousness: a suggestive description of that moment in Welty's own life when the feminine obsession with the romance ethos shatters, to be replaced with a passion for the ordinary power plays of southern life.

A similar crisis is played out in "The Power and the Glory," Robb Foreman Dew's autobiographical essay about Baton Rouge in the 1950s. As Dew describes the glory of inhabiting a white female body with the power to attract southern men—a body that also symbolizes women's supposed transcendence of class and race politics—she also describes a world where this symbolism inevitably breaks down:

> We worked so hard at being appealing! We had bedrooms that looked like beauty parlors, with storklike hair dryers, cosmetics of every variety, fashion magazines on our bedside tables. We slept miserably with enormous, bristly rollers wound into our hair and got up at six in the morning to unwind them so that we could painstakingly backcomb and construct our pageboys. . . . We applied makeupbase, eyeliner, mascara, lipstick, and a final dusting of loose powder. . . . This was in order for us to go to school! For me each day was like a premiere, and, in fact, I went to school as little as possible, because putting in an appearance required more energy than I could muster.
>
> One morning I couldn't find my eyelash curler, and so positive was I that without curled eyelashes I would be remarkable, that I would look grotesque, that I claimed illness and did not leave the house. . . . I no longer felt certain of my grasp of reality. If I was elected to one thing or another I began to suspect that it was because there was something terribly wrong with me—a physical deformity or perhaps some sort of

obvious mental illness . . . that elicited enormous sympathy from my
schoolmates. I could no longer manage all the secrets of my own life
in the face of the image I tried to sustain in public.

The fear of looking hideous, the description of southern charm as "a
crippling thing that entailed turning one's whole intelligence toward an
effort to be pleasing to other people," reinvokes the southern grotesque.[46] While Mab Segrest argues that southern "women who refuse
to stay in their place—who refuse to be grotesque, to stay fallen—upset
the whole shebang," my own thesis is exactly the opposite.[47] Following
Porter's and Welty's lead, southern women writers who appropriate the
grotesque are at work constructing a female tradition that refuses the
genteel obsession with writing (or inhabiting) the beautiful body in exchange for something more politically active and vehement: for the
angry sex- and class-conscious writing of the southern gargantua.

In Welty's story, the violence unfolding from the earthquake woman's grotesque body is threefold. First, this underclass woman possesses
a vitality that shatters the complacency of the prim southern girl narrating Welty's story; her body language is so squalid and damning that it
breaks the frame of the little girl's story altogether.[48] We encounter a
second variety of violence in the patriarchal hand that piles sand higher
and higher on this woman's body, "like the teasing threat of oblivion"
(153)—smashing this girl's delusions about an idealized division of labor. Here we confront the rigid divisions of labor and the work of domination that marks southern gender relations. But this woman responds
to her consort's violence with a violence of her own. ("A slow, repetitious sound I had been hearing for a long time unconsciously, I identified as a continuous laugh which came through the motionless open
pouched mouth of the woman" [153].) If her slovenly body, her sandy
disarray seems threatening, it is because she uncovers a world where
the beautiful body fails to keep at bay the heterogeneity and injustice
that southern manners are designed to hide.

Finally, Welty's story gathers new power from the fact that this
earthquake woman is not the ideal southern lady, but her antitype, her
mocking double. With a mirroring violence, this woman's daughter
hurls her body up and down the beach. Angry and wild, she is curled
in her "green bathing suit like a bottle from which she might, I felt,

burst in a rage of churning smoke" (153). When this young girl explodes, she comes "running toward the bench as though she would destroy it, and with a fierceness which took my breath away, she dragged herself through the air and jumped over the bench. But no one seemed to notice" (155). Welty invents the grotesque bodies in *A Curtain of Green* to expose the small, angry dramas of southern life that everyone experiences but no one notices. And smack in the center of this volume of stories, we encounter a new female vastness: the earthquake woman's excessive body opens up the excesses of a political system that inhabits little girls as well as great men.[49]

In story after story, Welty explores a southern world that fails to support its bodies; a comical culture whose comedy evaporates when its subjects wither, die, commit suicide, choose between the insane asylum and marriage, or endure crippling pain. This pain is not just the fate of a laboring class in the midst of national depression (the world Welty depicts in "The Whistle" or "Flowers for Marjorie" or "A Worn Path") but of a southern aristocratic class as well. Southern high culture, for all its seeming power, also lacks a working thesis, a mode of synthesis, a place to sustain the body. We feel this lack most sharply in the well-born Clytie, whose story ends when she sees a repulsive reflection of her face and drowns, her legs sticking out of the rainwater barrel "like a pair of tongs" (178). This is a frightening image of the body made mechanical and robbed of its being, an immobilized body that will fit neither the feminine nor the aristocratic frame invented by high southern culture.[50]

Bourdieu suggests that "the schemes of the habitus, the primary forms of classification, owe their specific efficacy to the fact that they function below the level of consciousness and language, beyond the reach of introspective scrutiny or control by the will."[51] Welty's framing metaphor in "A Memory" brings some of these "primary forms of classification" into prominence. I have suggested that her grotesque bodies have the uncanny ability to shift our focus even farther, so that the invisible schemes of the white southern habitus move closer to consciousness, become achingly visible. Perhaps it is no accident that Welty's earthquake woman is huge and ungainly. Her body has a great weight to bear, a weight made greater because southern women writers have worked so hard and so successfully to decode their region's political unconscious via the bodies of their southern gargantuas.

Notes

1. Richard H. King, *A Southern Renaissance: The Cultural Awakening of the American South, 1930–1955* (New York: Oxford Univ. Press, 1980), 8.

2. Ibid., 8–9.

3. Louis D. Rubin Jr., *The Faraway Country: Writers of the Modern South* (Seattle: Univ. of Washington Press, 1963), 131, 133, 133–34.

4. Eudora Welty, "A Memory," in *A Curtain of Green and Other Stories* (New York: Harcourt Brace Jovanovich, 1969), 153. Subsequent references to this text are cited parenthetically within the essay.

5. Susan Stewart, *On Longing: Narratives of the Miniature, the Gigantic, the Souvenir, the Collection* (Baltimore: Johns Hopkins Univ. Press, 1984), 86.

6. Katherine Anne Porter, *The Collected Stories of Katherine Anne Porter* (New York: Harcourt Brace Jovanovich, 1969), 174. Subsequent references to this text are cited parenthetically within the essay.

7. Stewart, *On Longing*, 124.

8. Minnie Bruce Pratt, "Identity: Blood Skin Bones," in *Yours in Struggle: Three Feminist Perspectives on Anti-Semitism and Racism*, by Elly Bulkin, Minnie Bruce Pratt, and Barbara Smith (Ithaca: Firebrand Books, 1984), 37.

9. Anne Goodwyn Jones, *Tomorrow Is Another Day: The Woman Writer in the South, 1859–1936* (Baton Rouge: Louisiana State Univ. Press, 1981), 4.

10. Bryan Turner, *The Body: Social Process and Cultural Theory*, ed. Mike Featherstone, Mike Hepworth, and Bryan Turner (London: Sage Publications, 1990), 133.

11. Mab Segrest, *My Mama's Dead Squirrel: Lesbian Essays on Southern Culture* (Ithaca: Firebrand Books, 1985), 167.

12. Lillian Smith, *Killers of the Dream* (New York: Norton, 1961), 89.

13. Eudora Welty, "Powerhouse," in *A Curtain of Green*, 254–55.

14. Eudora Welty, "June Recital," in *The Golden Apples* (New York: Harcourt, Brace & World, 1949), 56. Subsequent references to this text are cited parenthetically within the essay.

15. Mary Jacobus, Evelyn Fox Keller, and Sally Shuttleworth, Introduction, *Body/Politics: Women and the Discourses of Science*, ed. Jacobus, Keller, and Shuttleworth (New York: Routledge, 1990), 2.

16. "Thine earthly rainbows stretched across the sweep / Of the aethereal waterfall, whose veil / Robes some unsculptured image. . . . Thy caverns echoing to the Arve's commotion, / A loud, lone sound no other sound can tame; / Thou art the path of that unresting sound—Dizzy Ravine!" (Percy Bysshe Shelley, "Mont Blanc").

17. Jacobus, Keller, and Shuttleworth, *Body/Politics*, 2.

18. Peter Stallybrass and Allon White, *The Politics and Poetics of Transgression* (Ithaca: Cornell Univ. Press, 1986), 26.

19. Jacquelyn Dowd Hall, "'The Mind That Burns in Each Body': Women, Rape, and Racial Violence," in *Powers of Desire: The Politics of Sexuality*, ed. Ann Snitow, Christine Stansell, and Sharon Thompson (New York: Monthly Review Press, 1983), 332, 335.

20. Louise Westling, *Sacred Groves and Ravaged Gardens: The Fiction of Eudora Welty, Carson McCullers, and Flannery O'Connor* (Athens: Univ. of Georgia Press, 1985), 8.

21. Although Miss Eckhart is foreign, an outsider, she is still expected to conform to the community's norms. Although her rebellion is non-normative, it is not especially exceptional, except in its mode of aesthetic self-expression. As Robb Foreman Dew describes her own feminine cohort in "The Power and the Glory" (in *Portraits of Southern Childhood*, ed. Alex Harris [Chapel Hill: Univ. of North Carolina Press, 1987]), "The kind of charm we aimed for was counterfeit, because it had nothing to do with any one of us; we were only learning how to make someone else believe that he or she was enchanting. And it turned some of the brightest girls into incredibly manipulative and secretly angry women. I meet these people still, all the time; they are certainly not all southern, although they are all women, and there are no other social creatures of whom I'm as wary" (121).

22. Kate Chopin, *The Awakening* (New York: Norton, 1976), 29.

23. Robin D. G. Kelley, *Race Rebels: Culture, Politics, and the Black Working Class* (New York: Free Press, 1994), 72.

24. Robert Fleming, "The Ritual of Survival," in *Up South: Stories, Studies and Letters of This Century's African-American Migrations*, ed. Malaika Adero (New York: New Press, 1993), 33. Fleming is describing his grandfather's experiences in New Orleans in 1915.

25. Julius Lester, "Black and White Together: Teaching the 'Beloved Community' in Today's Racially Divided Classrooms," *Lingua Franca* 1 (1991): 30.

26. Zora Neale Hurston, *Their Eyes Were Watching God* (Urbana: Univ. of Illinois Press, 1978), 286.

27. We see the extent to which even Miss Eckhart has internalized this miniaturization in her response to Miss Snowdie: "What were you playing, though?" Miss Snowdie asks, "holding streams of bead curtains in both hands. 'I couldn't say,' Miss Eckhart said, rising. 'I have forgotten'" (Welty, "June Recital," 58).

28. Carson McCullers, *The Ballad of the Sad Cafe and Other Stories* (New York: Bantam, 1969), 68.

29. Smith, *Killers of the Dream*, 70.

30. Lester, "Black and White Together," 30.

31. It is generally accepted that "A Memory," the only story in *A Curtain of Green* narrated by a lyrical "I," functions as a memoir or fanciful redaction of Welty's own memories.

32. David Held, *Political Theory and the Modern State* (Stanford: Stanford Univ. Press, 1989), 4.

33. There are, of course, some wonderful exceptions, including Myra Jehlen's *Class and Character in Faulkner's South* (Secaucus, N.J.: Citadel Press, 1978) and Eric J. Sundquist's *Faulkner: The House Divided* (Baltimore: Johns Hopkins Univ. Press, 1983).

34. King, *A Southern Renaissance*, 7.

35. Although Cassie's automatic aversion to Miss Eckhart's playing can be described as part and parcel of a southern rape complex that refuses women autonomy and power, her autonomic remembrance of Miss Eckhart's rape could be described, with equal devastation, as a matter of condoned or appropriate "taste." As Pierre Bourdieu suggests, "The ultimate values, as they are called, are never anything other than the primary, primitive dispositions of the body, 'visceral' tastes and distastes, in which the group's most vital interests are embedded" (*Distinction: A Social Critique of the Judgement of Taste,* trans. Richard Nice [Cambridge: Harvard Univ. Press, 1984], 474).

36. See Jehlen's *Class and Character in Faulkner's South*, 137–51.

37. Jehlen describes the narrator's use of this framing device among the southwestern humorists: "Cultural historians who thought they were reading the other side of the Southern story in the work of the humorists, who found in it a way at last to raise 'the veil of smug respectability for a refreshing view of the real thing,' were . . . largely misled by formal differences. . . . Through the wise narrator whose commentary typically framed the action of the tale, the humorists projected precisely the plantation myth's image of a cultured aristocrat who was obviously meant to rule the South" (ibid., 138). Welty is reenacting this framing—first by literalizing her child narrator's reliance on a framework to stabilize her vision, and second by thrusting a set of 'rude mechanicals' into her line of sight. But when her narrator's frame gets interrupted or broken, Welty is also disrupting the political assumptions of a long-standing literary tradition. She refuses to repeat a simplified story of southern yokels as "uncouth, unclean, [and] lawless"—as poor whites with the ominous power of deranging the South's best traditions (ibid., 139), but instead asks the white trash at the center of her story to break—or call into question—the narrator's frame.

38. Bourdieu, *Distinction*, 469. As Jehlen points out, this anxiety takes on a particularly elitist patriarchal shape in the American South: "Walker Percy has explained the 'spectacular' change in the South as resulting from the defeat of 'the old moderate tradition of the planter-lawyer-statesman class' and 'the

consequent collapse of the alliance between the "good" white man and the Negro. . . . To use Faulkner's personae,' he writes succinctly, 'the Gavin Stevenses have disappeared and the Snopeses have won.' The dire prophecies of Hooper and Harris have been realized; Longstreet would have concurred, shuddering. The Whig Götterdämmerung has come and in its wake the 'uncouth, unclean, [and] lawless' poor whites have successfully taken over the ruined South" (*Class and Character,* 138–39).

39. Jacqueline Rose, *The Case of Peter Pan, or, the Impossibility of Children's Fiction* (London: Macmillan, 1984), 8–9.

40. Bourdieu, *Distinction,* 468–69.

41. This is also the subject of Peter Taylor's "The Old Forest," in which a working girl with an untold history breaks the careful framework of denial that upper-class Memphis society has constructed to maintain its wealth, security, and sense of history. The working girl's well-kept secret is that she is also working class and that her mother is the owner of a scurrilous bar (and is thoroughly frightening—a goiter-ridden, dragonlike, vestigial, but monstrous grotesque). The hero's romantic desire for this working-class heroine surfaces too late, and his new knowledge about this need to disassociate himself from his own class distorts his destined career path and underlines his alienation from the very traditions his well-bred marriage works so well to uphold (*The Old Forest and Other Stories* [New York: Ballantine, 1985], 22–82).

42. Held, *Political Theory,* 4.

43. Although the promise of heterosexual romance—of a world to be had for the marrying—offers this young girl some longed-for stability, Welty also insists upon its slenderness as a device for organizing the world.

44. Jürgen Habermas, *Legitimation Crisis,* trans. Thomas McCarthy (Boston: Beacon Press, 1975).

45. Louis D. Rubin Jr. and Robert D. Jacobs, Introduction, *South: Modern Southern Literature in Its Cultural Setting,* ed. Rubin and Jacobs (Garden City, N.Y.: Doubleday, 1961), 15.

46. Robb Foreman Dew, "The Power and the Glory," in *Portraits of Southern Childhood,* 122, 121.

47. Segrest, *My Mama's Dead Squirrel,* 29.

48. From the beginning of the story, this framework is, of course, already riven with contradictions: "I was at an age when I formed a judgment upon every person and every event which came under my eye, although I was easily frightened. When a person, or a happening, seemed to me not in keeping with my opinion, or even my hope or expectation, I was terrified by a vision of abandonment and wildness which tore my heart with a kind of sorrow" (Welty, "A Memory," 148).

49. Although this woman's body comments on the southern race-plot only indirectly (see David Roediger's *The Wages of Whiteness: Race and the*

Making of the American Working Class [New York: Verso, 1992]), Welty uses its violence to begin to expose the nightmarish underside of southern fantasies about race and class inferiority, fantasies that led to historic scenes of excess resembling the mob scenes Joel Williamson describes in his biography of Faulkner—scenes where grown-ups and children alike were participants in communal acts of predation: "The details of the Patton lynching were specific to Lafayette County, but the pattern was general. The justification was rape or attempted rape, the crowd numbered hundreds and thousands, an active cadre of several dozen men did the actual work, and the body would be mutilated, castrated, and displayed in a public, ritualistic, and dramatic way. Afterward, white people would feel a significant measure of relief. The Patton lynching was also true to the general pattern in that it was done not only by 'rednecks,' the lower orders of whites. It was done by everybody, and the white community found release in the event" (*William Faulkner and Southern History* [New York: Oxford Univ. Press, 1993], 159).

50. We have already seen that in *The Faraway Country* Rubin makes a more general suggestion about a southern world without synthesis. In the twentieth-century South "not only have towns become cities, and cities metropolises, but the moral order of the older South, the old notions of certainty and belief, have ceased to suffice as a sufficient explanation and an adequate basis for daily experience. I speak not only of religion, but of attitudes toward the values of the community, toward history, toward society. The future novelist or poet, growing up in the South in the 1900's and 1920's, did not find, as his father and grandfather had been able to find, sufficient emotional scope within the life of the community" (7). I am suggesting that Welty depicts a southern world in which this malaise has spread to the community at large. She intimates that when the upper classes forfeit the logic of their modus vivendi— their rationale for life at the top—the entire social structure is in danger of crumbling. In fact, the placement of "Clytie" in *A Curtain of Green* (it is the story following "A Memory") suggests that the traditionally gendered and elitist worldview that supports the heroine of "A Memory" has already declined past the point of use.

51. Bourdieu, *Distinction*, 466.

Biting the Hand That Writes You

Southern African-American Folk Narrative and the Place of Women in *Their Eyes Were Watching God*

Catherine Gunther Kodat

For me, the store porch was the most interesting place that I could think of. I was not allowed to sit around there, naturally. But I could and did drag my feet going in and out, whenever I was sent there for something, to allow whatever was being said to hang in my ear. I would hear an occasional scrap of gossip in what to me was adult double talk, but which I understood at times. There would be, for instance, sly references to the physical conditions of women, irregular love affairs, brags on male potency by the parties of the first part, and the like. It did not take me long to know what was meant when a girl was spoken of as "ruint" or "bigged."
—Zora Neale Hurston, *Dust Tracks on a Road*

At the tragic climax of *Their Eyes Were Watching God*, Janie Crawford is forced to kill the great love of her life, Vergible "Tea Cake" Woods, when, maddened by rabies, he attempts to kill her. This important event, while not completely ignored in contemporary criticism of the novel, has not received the same sort of scrutiny that has been lavished on, for example, Janie's deadly "signifying" on the manhood of Joe "Jody" Starks. But the scene introduces an important complication into the story of Janie's life, one that renders problematic whatever comforting closure is offered at the novel's end. For Janie does not escape the death of Tea Cake unscathed: "The pistol [Tea Cake's weapon] and the rifle [Janie's] rang out almost together. The pistol just enough after the rifle to seem its echo. Tea Cake crumpled as his bullet buried itself in the joist over Janie's head. Janie saw the look on his face and leaped forward as he crashed forward in her arms. She was trying to hover him as he closed his teeth in the flesh of her forearm. They came down heavily like that. Janie struggled to a sitting position and pried the dead Tea Cake's teeth from her arm." [1]

Since Tea Cake himself contracted rabies through a dog bite, readers cannot fail to draw the conclusion that Janie, too, is now infected. And though Hurston has prepared us to expect a medical rescue—Dr. Simmons has promised to arrive that morning with rabies serum in a last-ditch effort to save Tea Cake, and he does in fact appear at Janie and Tea Cake's cabin minutes after the shooting—she refuses to present us with any scene of, or allusion to, Janie's treatment. It seems likely that Hurston invites us to entertain the notion that, in fact, Janie was not treated; we are told only that she stays on the muck "a few weeks" after Tea Cake's death "to keep them [Tea Cake's friends] from feeling bad" (182). Further, Hurston withholds any word of Janie's condition at a moment in the text where it seems such information would easily have been introduced: during Dr. Simmons's testimony at Janie's murder trial, when the danger Janie faces becomes clear: "Dr. Simmons . . . told about Tea Cake's sickness *and how dangerous it was to Janie* and the whole town, *and how he was scared for her* and thought to have Tea Cake locked up in the jail, but seeing Janie's care he neglected to do it. And how *he found Janie all bit in the arm,* sitting on the floor and petting Tea Cake's head when he got there. And the pistol right by his hand on the floor. Then he stepped down" (177; emphasis added).

Of the many critics who have written on Hurston's novel in the past ten years, only one has remarked on these strange gaps in the text, and then only briefly.[2] By far the majority of recent critical work on *Their Eyes Were Watching God* has focused on Janie's assumption of a strong personal identity or voice and on Hurston's decision to render much of the novel in a southern African-American folk idiom. It is rightly assumed that Hurston intends these two most important aspects of the text to function together. Critics who posit a strong and self-aware Janie maintain that she comes into her voice through the language of the southern black folk; one thoughtful, carefully constructed example of this argument, which I will examine at some length here, is Henry Louis Gates Jr.'s chapter on the novel in his book *The Signifying Monkey*.[3] Those who are less certain of Janie's strength frequently lay the blame on what they see as Hurston's inability to make her folk material do orderly duty in a literary format (Lillie P. Howard, Bernard W. Bell, and Robert E. Hemenway all fault Hurston's skills in novelistic construction).[4] Adherents to this latter view maintain that Hurston's lack of control over her material is the problem. It is not usually argued that the southern black folk tradition *itself* somehow might render a feminist quest for independence problematic.

My aim here is to show that there is, in fact, considerable friction between the southern black oral narrative tradition as it is understood and presented in *Their Eyes Were Watching God* and the nascent feminist impulses attributed to the main character; Hurston's effort to represent that friction largely accounts for the novel's power.[5] Tea Cake's bite stands as a sign of the tensions Hurston admits into the novel, the moment where she renders the text as *wounded* by its own conflicting desires and ambitions. Far from representing a happy marriage of equals between the folk and the feminist, *Their Eyes Were Watching God* demonstrates the many impediments to such a marriage embedded in a largely patriarchal oral narrative tradition and the difficulty faced by women seeking to enter and find voice within that tradition. Janie Crawford does speak in *Their Eyes Were Watching God,* and she does construct a voice through southern African-American oral traditions, but her relation to those traditions remains a critical one. Gates has argued that Hurston makes use of the southern African-American rhetorical device called signifying—which he orthographically renders as Signifyin(g)—in order to create a uniquely black text.[6] Attention to the ways in which Hurston points out the gendered aspects of signifying, however, leads me to conclude that it would be more accurate to identify Hurston's technique as *meta*signifying: she shows her heroine speaking at a critical remove from the black male community in which she must continually negotiate her position as a speaking black woman. Thus Janie's speech does not make her free. Rather, her speech (as a character), as well as Hurston's (as novelist), is designed mainly to enable black women to speak again, in the hope of calling into being a productive union of black feminist consciousness and black folk consciousness. *Their Eyes Were Watching God,* however, may only gesture towards this utopia; Tea Cake's violent, contaminating bite, in which the touch of opposed values becomes an unresolved rupture in the novel itself, stands in signifying relation to that hope.

The first wave of contemporary criticism of *Their Eyes Were*

Watching God was very much shaped by the feminist movement of the late 1960s and early 1970s. In her foreword to the novel, Mary Helen Washington provides an excellent overview of this crucial period in literary study. As Washington makes clear, the rediscovery of *Their Eyes Were Watching God* (first published in 1937) served as something of a personal watershed for an emerging group of black women scholars: "I can still recall quite vividly my own discovery of *Their Eyes*. . . . What I loved immediately about this novel besides its high poetry and its female hero was its investment in black folk traditions. Here, finally, was a woman on a quest for her own identity and, unlike so many other questing figures in black literature, her journey would take her, not away from, but deeper and deeper into blackness, the descent into the Everglades with its rich black soil, wild cane, and communal life representing immersion into black traditions. But for most black women readers discovering *Their Eyes* for the first time, what was most compelling was the figure of Janie Crawford—powerful, articulate, self-reliant, and radically different from any woman character they had ever before encountered in literature."[7] This vision of Janie as a "powerful, articulate, self-reliant" black woman was soon questioned, however, and rather dramatically so in an event that also marked the arrival of Hurston's work on the academic scene. As Washington notes, it was during a 1979 MLA panel, "Traditions and Their Transformations in Afro-American Letters," that Robert B. Stepto "raised the issue that has become one of the most highly controversial and hotly contested aspects of the novel: whether or not Janie is able to achieve her voice in *Their Eyes*."[8] The introduction of this issue transformed the nature of scholarly study of *Their Eyes Were Watching God* from supportive appreciation of its romance/quest plot to more critical appraisals of its formal and stylistic strategies.

In his study of African-American literature, *From behind the Veil* (published the same year as the MLA panel), Stepto makes clear his reservations. "The one great flaw in *Their Eyes* involves not the framing dialogue, but Janie's tale itself," he writes. "Through the frame Hurston creates the essential illusion that Janie has achieved her voice (along with everything else), and that she has even wrested from menfolk some control of the tribal posture of the storyteller. But . . . Hurston's curious insistence on having Janie's tale—her personal history in and as a literary form—told by an omniscient third person, rather than by a first-person narrator, implies that Janie has not really won her voice and self after all—that her author (who is, quite likely, the omniscient narrating voice) cannot see her way clear to giving Janie her voice outright."[9]

Critical essays on *Their Eyes Were Watching God* continue to be published that dispute (or ignore) Stepto's assertions and praise the novel as a relatively unambiguous assertion of female power and independence that celebrates the southern black rural narrative folk tradition. For example, Claire Crabtree argues for a strong voice for Janie and further maintains that "folklore is . . . inextricably bound to the themes of feminism and Black self-determination."[10] A somewhat similar view is offered by Michael Awkward, who asserts that Janie's "life story—and its complex narration—suggest the manner in which the problematic state of Afro-American double consciousness (and its discursive corollary, double voicedness) can be resolved: by adherence to the communal principles of black culture"; Awkward casts Janie not only as a feminist heroine but also, in a sense, as a savior of the race.[11] However, Crabtree and Awkward both offer different versions of "essentialist" rhetorical readings, in which a specific type of African-American folk expression is posited as unified, timeless, and equally available to men and women speakers; they also ignore the textual difficulty presented by Janie's wound.[12] In fact, the problem raised by Stepto (articulated as an apparent disjunction of novelistic form and authorial intent) continues to haunt most critics of the novel, leading to some theoretically complex readings of the text and forcing a reappraisal of the move to cast *Their Eyes Were Watching God* as a triumphant feminist masterpiece. Indeed, despite the assertion in her foreword to the novel that the text's "unique contribution to black literature [is that] it affirms black cultural traditions while revising them to empower black women,"[13] Washington herself has admitted, in an essay written three years earlier, to becoming increasingly "disturbed by this text, particularly by two problematic relationships I see in the novel: women's relationship to the community and women's relationship to language." Washington finds here that "when the voice of the black oral tradition is summoned in *Their Eyes*, it is not used to represent the collective black community, but to invoke and valorize the voice of the black *male* community."[14]

An early, powerful (though somewhat indirect) effort to work through Stepto's critique of Hurston's manipulation of voice in *Their Eyes Were Watching God* appeared in Barbara Johnson's 1984 essay "Metaphor, Metonymy, and Voice in *Their Eyes Were Watching*

God.[15] Drawing on Roman Jakobson's famous essay "Two Aspects of Language and Two Types of Aphasic Disturbances," Johnson deconstructs the binary relationship of metaphor and metonymy—techniques of figurative language that turn on the substitution of one term for another[16]—in order to show how Hurston uses "a metaphorically grounded metonymy . . . a metonymically grounded metaphor" to dramatize Janie's attainment of personal voice during the waning years of her marriage to Joe Starks.[17] Johnson sees the scene in which Joe slaps Janie—prompting the realization that "her image of Jody [was] tumbled down and shattered. . . . She had an inside and an outside now and suddenly knew how not to mix them" (*Their Eyes,* 67–68)—as Janie's entry into figurative language, "where inside and outside are never the same." Johnson maintains that "it is from this point on in the novel that Janie, paradoxically, begins to speak. . . . Janie's increasing ability to speak grows out of her ability not to mix outside with inside, not to pretend that there is no difference, but to assume and articulate the incompatible forces involved in her own division. The sign of an authentic voice is thus not self-identity but self-difference."[18]

Gates has taken Johnson's work on rhetorical division and expanded it in his sophisticated, multilayered reading of *Their Eyes Were Watching God* in *The Signifying Monkey.*[19] Gates develops the notion of the split and thus speaking subject into a global theory of rhetorical division, in which, he writes, Hurston creates a "speakerly text" through her manipulation of two voices: "a profoundly lyrical, densely metaphorical, quasi-musical, privileged black oral tradition on the one hand, and a received but not yet fully appropriated standard English literary tradition on the other hand."[20] Hurston's use of free indirect discourse—a technique in which an author employs a narrative voice drawing on the qualities of both first- and third-person narration—mediates these two poles, Gates argues.[21] This technique thus becomes "the rhetorical analogue to the text's metaphors of inside and outside, so fundamental to the depiction of Janie's quest for consciousness, her very quest to become a speaking black subject."[22]

Early in his discussion of the novel Gates compares Hurston's fictional approach to Richard Wright's; the two authors held opposing views on the use of lyrical and naturalist styles and the literary worth of southern black rural culture.[23] In analyzing their dispute, Gates offers a reading of the dying mother scenes in Hurston's memoir, *Dust Tracks on a Road,* and Wright's *Black Boy.* Gates quotes the passage in which

Hurston recalls that her mother "looked at me, or so I felt, to speak for her. She depended on me for a voice." [24] Wright, on the other hand, begs his ailing mother to be silent and adds, "That night I ceased to react to my mother; my feelings were frozen." [25] Given that the feminist concern with *Their Eyes Were Watching God* is whether the female protagonist gains a voice, it is striking that Gates chooses to read these two scenes in terms only of the authors' ability to give voice to a larger, seemingly ungendered, African-American narrative tradition. Hurston, he writes, succeeds where Wright fails, by creating "a resonant and authentic narrative voice that echoes and aspires to the status of the impersonality, anonymity, and authority of the black vernacular tradition, a nameless, selfless tradition, at once collective and compelling, true somehow to the unwritten text of a common blackness. For Hurston, the search for a telling form of language, indeed the search for a black literary language itself, defines the search for the self." [26]

A search for language may certainly define a search for self; it is odd, however, that Gates bypasses questions of gender in his discussion, going so far as to choose language that strains to render the black vernacular as completely neuter: the mother's voice becomes "nameless, selfless," and anonymous. This lack of interest in the gendered aspects of Hurston's language reappears in Gates's discussion of the scene in which Janie gains a voice. While Johnson sees Janie's musing after Joe Starks's slap as the moment she realizes her self-division and thus her voice, Gates chooses a later event in the text: the scene in which Janie signifies upon Starks's manhood. Janie's successful participation in this African-American oral practice is crucial to the larger task Gates has set himself, which is "if not exactly to invent a black theory . . . , [then] to locate and identify how the 'black tradition' [has] theorized about itself." [27]

Gates presents signifying as something of a generic term for a host of African-American language games, including toasts, loud-talking, and playing the dozens. [28] For a contemporary example of signifying, Gates relates the story of a group of black high school students in Winston-Salem, North Carolina, who, frustrated by a series of standardized achievement tests, created their own test, "The In Your Face Test of No Certain Skills." The test, Gates explains, was designed to assess mastery of street language, and "one of the test's questions . . . is an example of Signifyin(g). The question reads, 'Who is buried in Grant's tomb?' The proper response to the question is, 'Your mama.' It is difficult to explain why this response is so funny and why it is an example of Signifyin(g). 'Your mama' jokes abound in black discourse."[29] Gates offers few further examples of such jokes—and no discussion of their gendered aspects.

Gates makes large claims for signifying: it is disruptive of binary opposition, inherently critical of established rhetorical systems, and therefore a sign for the rebellious, imaginative African-American literary tradition. Because signifying works within a frame of word play or semantic indeterminacy, it serves as a metaphor for a certain attention to style as well; as Gates puts it, "One does not Signify some thing; one Signifies in *some way*. . . . Signifyin(g), in other words, is synonymous with figuration. . . . in standard English signification denotes meaning and in the black tradition it denotes ways of meaning."[30] For Gates, signifying operates both intertextually and intratextually in the black literary tradition: writers may critically revise, or signify upon, their predecessors, as Gates sees Hurston's *Their Eyes Were Watching God* engaged in a signifying relationship with both Jean Toomer's *Cane* and Frederick Douglass's *Narrative*,[31] or there may be realized moments of signifying play within the text. In Gates's view, Janie's insulting of Joe Starks is just such a moment of signifying play. The scene is important to Gates not simply because it represents a transformative moment in the novel but because he identifies Hurston as "the first scholar to have defined the trope of Signifyin(g) . . . [and] the first to represent the ritual itself."[32]

Both definition and representation appear in a text published two years before *Their Eyes Were Watching God, Mules and Men*.[33] The signifying scene in *Mules and Men* (it appears on pages 124–25) shows a woman, Big Sweet, engaged in a signifying contest with her lover, Joe Willard; and though Gates never explicitly addresses the question of gender codes in signifying, it is clear that he finds it necessary—after all the jokes about mothers—to assert that women can signify, too, that the structure of signifying can somehow remain separate from its content and the gender of its users.

Gates takes pains at several points in the development of his theory to argue that signifying, as an activity, is gender-neutral, and points to the work of linguists Geneva Smitherman and Claudia Mitchell-Kernan, both of whom have discussed examples of women's signification, to bolster his claim.[34] And he expresses some disdain for those linguists "whose work suffers from an undue attention to the use of words such as *motherfucker,* to insults that turn on sexual assertions about someone's mama, and to supposed Oedipal complexes that arise in the literature only because the linguist is reading the figurative as a literal statement."[35] Gates freely admits that "intimations of sexual use, abuse, and violation constitute one well-known and commonly used mode of Signifyin(g),"[36] that is, the deeply male-centered verbal contest called the dozens. However, Gates argues that the dozens are simply a subset of the *genus* signification; this move enables him to present signifying as a black rhetorical device that, through its primary function as a racially unifying form of communication, transcends the mundane world of sexual politics. In fact, it is striking how frequently Gates appeals to the notion of transcendence in his descriptions of signifying. For example, a jazz musician's definition of signifying "is able to penetrate the content of this black verbal horseplay to analyze the significance of the rhetorical structures that *transcend* any fixed form of Signifyin(g), such as the verbal insult rituals called the dozens."[37] A few pages later, he argues that "the black person's capacity to create this rich poetry and to derive from these rituals a complex attitude toward attempts at domination, which can be *transcended* in and through language, is a sign of their originality, or their extreme consciousness of the metaphysical."[38] Though the notion of language's capacity to transcend racial oppression is appealing, Gates's decision to bypass questions of *gender* domination and even the issue of how signifying may or may not help indicate a "complex attitude" toward that form of oppression is disconcerting. In the last analysis, it is not enough to simply assert that women *can* signify—just as it is not enough to assert that women can be lawyers, doctors, or U.S. Senators. What needs to be examined is *how* women signify, as well as why and when they do so (or are allowed to do so).

Hurston specifically identifies the language game that Janie draws on in order to defeat Jody as the dozens and not, as Gates implies, a more gender-neutral form of signifying. This is the scene in which, according to Gates, Janie gains her voice, a scene that occurs nine years after the slap Johnson had identified as Janie's formative moment:

"I god almighty! A woman stay round uh store till she get old as
Methusalem and still can't cut a little thing like a plug of tobacco! Don't

stand dere rolling yo' pop eyes at me wid yo' rump hangin' nearly to yo' knees!"

A big laugh started off in the store but people got to thinking and stopped. It was funny if you looked at it right quick, but it got pitiful if you thought about it awhile. It was like somebody snatched off part of a woman's clothes while she wasn't looking and the streets were crowded. Then too, Janie took the middle of the floor to talk right into Jody's face, and that was something that hadn't been done before.

"Stop mixin' up mah doings wid mah looks, Jody. When you git through tellin' me how tuh cut uh plug uh tobacco, then you kin tell me whether mah behind is on straight or not."

"Wha—whut's dat you say, Janie? You must be out yo' head."

"Naw, Ah ain't outa mah head neither."

"You must be. Talkin' any such language as dat."

"You de one started talkin' under people's clothes. Not me."

"Whut's de matter wid you, nohow? You ain't no young girl to be gettin' all insulted 'bout yo' looks. You ain't no young courtin' gal. You'se uh ole woman, nearly forty."

"Yeah, Ah'm nearly forty and you'se already fifty. How come you can't talk about dat sometimes instead of always pointin' at me?"

"T'ain't no use in gettin' all mad, Janie, 'cause Ah mention you ain't no young gal no mo'. Nobody in heah ain't lookin' for no wife outa yuh. Old as you is."

"Naw, Ah ain't no young gal no mo' but den Ah ain't no old woman neither. Ah reckon Ah looks mah age too. But Ah'm uh woman every inch of me, and Ah know it. Dat's a whole lot more'n *you* kin say. You big-bellies round here and put out a lot of brag, but 'tain't nothin' to it but yo' big voice. Humph! Talkin' 'bout *me* lookin' old! When you pull down yo' britches, you look lak de change uh life."

"Great God from Zion!" Sam Watson gasped. "Y'all really playin' de dozens tuhnight." (74–75)

Gates concludes that Janie does find a voice here, a voice of power: "Jody, we well know, now thoroughly shattered by the force of Janie's voice, soon succumbs to acute humiliation and his displaced kidney disorder"—displaced because it is the figurative castration at Janie's hands that actually kills him.[39]

My discussion of Gates's reading of *Their Eyes Were Watching God* has been lengthy because it represents one of the most theoretically complex and thoughtful approaches to the novel currently available; it has played a crucial role in formulating my own view of the work. As I have suggested, however, the greatest strengths of Gates's approach—his belief that Hurston sought to forge a singularly (and single) black narrative expression and that the folk tradition of signifying was her chief tool—contain its greatest weaknesses, as he shies away from investigating the ways in which the southern black folk tradition in general, and signifying in particular, is a gendered, rather than a universal, structure. An investigation of the formation of "the" tradition that attends to its gendered aspects would force a reckoning with those characteristics of black speech that are marginalized and thus challenge the view that there is a "single" black tradition in the first place.

Gates's decision to make use of signifying theory to defend the rap group 2 Live Crew in its 1990 censorship case points up the problems with his model. While he is forced to admit that "more troubling than [2 Live Crew's] obscenity is the group's overt sexism," Gates seeks to blunt this admission by arguing that "their sexism is so flagrant . . . that it almost cancels itself out in a hyperbolic war between the sexes. In this, it recalls the inter-sexual jousting in Zora Neale Hurston's novels. Still, many of us look toward the emergence of more female rappers to redress sexual stereotypes."[40] Despite Gates's invocation of Hurston (or perhaps because of it), black feminists have found his defense of the group unconvincing.[41] And it is worth noting that the emergence of women rappers (for example, Queen Latifah, MC Lyte, and Salt-N-Pepa) has done little to change the sometimes violently misogynistic rhetoric of the wealthier, more famous male groups that dominate the market.[42] Rather, Gates's theory has proved a wildly successful fig leaf for sexist rap practice, seized upon by both rappers and popular music critics (the latter mostly white men) as a tidy way to give a respectable, intellectual gloss to the more sexist practitioners of the genre, allowing them to maintain that they are rhetoricians, not sexists.[43] Another example of the appropriation of Gates's theory to excuse sexist speech is Orlando Patterson's *New York Times* op-ed piece defending Clarence Thomas against Anita Hill's charges of sexual harassment. While Patterson does not quote Gates by name or use the term *signifying*, he does argue that Thomas spoke to Hill in the "down-home style of courting" common to the "Southern working-class backgrounds" they shared, and that Hill responded by construing those remarks in a white, "legalistic, neo-Puritan and elitist model of gender relations promoted by the dominant school of American feminists."[44] The implication here is that Hill became a "feminist" and betrayed her "blackness"; in Patterson's essay, black folk speech is construed in a matrix of power relations in which at least one type of call-and-response pattern is governed by rigid sexual protocol—breaking with that protocol is tantamount to breaking with the race. It was no secret to Zora Neale Hurston that much of folk speech was gendered in this way: as the opening epigraph to this essay shows, the *very first thing* the young Hurston learned about oral narrative traditions among the southern black rural folk was who gets to speak, and who is spoken about. ("There would be . . . sly references to the physical conditions of women . . . brags on male potency. . . . It did not take me long to know what was meant when a girl was spoken of as 'ruint' or 'bigged.' ")[45]

Some of the problems that arise from this neglect of the gender dynamics of southern black folk speech in *Their Eyes Were Watching God* have been outlined already by Washington, who sees the supposedly liberatory split between inside and outside operating on a narrative level that continues to objectify Janie and deny her voice. "Passages which are supposed to represent Janie's interior consciousness begin by marking some internal change in Janie, then gradually or abruptly shift so that a male character takes Janie's place as the subject of the discourse," Washington writes, adding that "even the much-celebrated description of Janie's discovery of her split selves . . . represents her internal life as divided between two men: her outside self exists for Joe and her inside self she is 'saving up' for 'some man she had never seen.' "[46] Washington's strongest complaint runs directly counter to Gates's reading of Janie's verbal attack on Starks as being somehow liberatory: "When Janie launches her most devastating attack on Jody in front of all the men in the store, she tells him not to talk about her looking old because 'When you pull down yo' britches you look lak de change uh life.' Since the 'change of life' ordinarily refers to a woman's menopause, Janie is *signifying* that Jody, like a woman, is subject to the humiliation of exposure. Now that he is the object of the gaze, Jody realizes that other men will 'look' on him with pity: 'Janie had robbed him of his illusion of irresistible maleness that all men cherish.' "[47]

The greatest harm that Janie can inflict upon Jody is to tell him that he resembles a woman—hardly a comforting gesture for a reader searching for a feminist method of signifying. In making this point, Hurston seems to want to underline how a male-dominated language game like the dozens is in fact *not* gender-neutral but so highly inflected by its provenance as to dictate the terms of its use. Hurston inserts a further complication into this scene when she compares Janie's insult to "the thing that Saul's daughter had done to David" (75). In 2 Samuel 6:16–23, Saul's daughter (and David's wife) Michal watches scornfully while David leaps and dances for joy as the Ark of the Covenant is returned to Jerusalem, and she berates him when he returns to his household: "How the king of Israel honored himself today, uncovering himself today before the eyes of his servants' maids, as one of the vulgar fellows shamelessly uncovers himself." Hurston leaves us to remember David's response: "And David said to Michal, 'It was before the Lord, who chose me above your father, and above all his house, to appoint me as prince over Israel, the people of the Lord—and I will make merry before the Lord. I will make myself yet more contemptible than this, and I will be abased in your eyes; but by the maids of whom you have spoken, by them I shall be held in honor.' And Michal the daughter of Saul had no child to the day of her death."[48]

The author of 2 Samuel clearly indicates who is in the right with a one-sentence pronouncement on the fate of Michal that takes the issue of power out of the realm of the verbal and into the world of the flesh. And though the now-feminized Jody is the one who suffers in *Their Eyes Were Watching God,* Hurston's use of the Old Testament reference hints that women choose to exercise their verbal power at considerable physical cost.[49] If Gates's analysis and terminology were retained to describe this altered reading of the scene, it could be said that Hurston shows how a black feminist signifying practice can work only by drawing attention to those patriarchal impulses, embedded within the signifying tradition itself, that necessarily circumscribe a woman's speech. In other words, a feminist does not simply signify; she *signifies on signifying itself* (that is, metasignifies), framing it with a critical discourse.

By contextualizing women's speech, Hurston reveals the ways in which that speech is encumbered or risky; this is especially true in the scene Gates selected as important to his theory of signifying, Hurston's first representation of the practice in *Mules and Men.* In chapter 7 the men at the Everglades Cypress Lumber Company in Loughman, Florida, decide to go fishing on an unexpected day off. Hurston accompanies them, along with two other women, Big Sweet and Lucy. The men pass the time telling animal fables and tales of John and Ol' Massa; the women rarely speak. Suddenly, Big Sweet enters the conversation:

> "And speakin' 'bout hams," cut in Big Sweet meaningly, "if Joe Willard don't stay out of dat bunk he was in last night, Ah'm gointer sprinkle some salt down his back and sugar-cure *his* hams."
>
> Joe snatched his pole out of the water with a jerk and glared at Big Sweet, who stood sideways looking at him most pointedly.
>
> "Aw, woman, quit tryin' to signify."
>
> "Ah kin signify all Ah please, Mr. Nappy-chin, so long as Ah know what Ah'm talkin' about."
>
> "See dat?" Joe appealed to the other men. "We git a day off and figger we kin ketch some fish and enjoy ourselves, but naw, some wimmins got to drag behind us, even to de lake."
>
> "You didn't figger Ah was draggin' behind you when you was bringin' dat Sears and Roebuck catalogue over to my house and beggin' me to choose my ruthers. Lemme tell *you* something, *any* time Ah shack up wid any man Ah gives myself de privilege to go wherever he might be, night or day. Ah got de law in my mouth." [50]

Here, Big Sweet wins the battle. However, she clearly loses the war when Jim Allen catches her in a bit of loud-talking in which he observes that "a man can cackerlate his life till he git mixed up wid a woman or git straddle of a cow" (124). When Big Sweet takes offense at being compared to a cow, Jim Allen replies that he wasn't talking about *her*, a classic maneuver in loud-talking.[51] His defense is bolstered by a second man in the group, who describes the "hidden meaning" of words—an embellishment that carries the discussion out of the realm of gender-inflected insult and into the "universal" region of explication:

> "Ah ain't called nobody no cow," Jim defended himself. "Dat's just an old time by-word 'bout no man kin tell what's gointer happen when he gits mixed up wid a woman or set straddle of a cow."
>
> "I done heard my gran'paw say dem very words many and many a time," chimed in Larkins. "There's a whole heap of them kinda by-words. Like for instance:
>
> "'Old coon for cunnin', young coon for runnin',' and 'Ah can't dance, but Ah know good moves.' They all got a hidden meanin', jus' like de Bible. Everybody can't understand what they mean. Most people

is thin-brained. They's born wid they feet under de moon. Some folks is born wid they feet on de sun and they kin seek out de inside meanin' of words." (125)

In this exchange Hurston reveals how an appeal to an overarching folk tradition successfully stifles protests from those who feel excluded from that tradition. Big Sweet is effectively silenced, not by a crude rebuff targeted against her sex but by a sophisticated appeal to a larger, special system of meanings to which she must defer (even as she reveals its gendered inner workings).[52]

In *Their Eyes Were Watching God,* Hurston contextualizes the appearance of female power and voice in ways that highlight the strategies necessary for its emergence. For example, the slap scene, which Johnson picks as the decisive moment in Janie's psychic development, is not, in fact, the first time that Hurston represents Janie as self-divided: much the same thing happens when she leaves Logan Killicks for Joe Starks. Killicks orders Janie to help him move a manure pile "befo' de sun gets hot" (30). When Janie refuses, and adds for good measure the complaint that "you ain't done me no favor by marryin' me" (30)—arguably an embryonic version of her later insult to Starks—Killicks takes a few threatening steps toward Janie, then contents himself with verbal abuse before returning to his work. In the next paragraph, Hurston tells us that "Janie turned from the door without answering, and stood still in the middle of the floor without knowing it. *She turned wrongside out just standing there and feeling.* When the throbbing calmed a little *she gave Logan's speech a hard thought and placed it beside other things she had seen and heard.* . . . What was she losing so much time for? A feeling of sudden newness and change came over her. Janie hurried out of the front gate and turned south. Even if Joe was not there waiting for her, the change was bound to do her good" (30–31; emphasis added).

Two of the aspects Johnson finds pivotal in the slap passage—Janie's awareness of her self as divided between inside and outside and her still, silent examination of her thoughts as if they were merchandise in a store—are anticipated in this section, in which Hurston shows us the progression of thought leading Janie to make a decision that, we come to realize, offers her a life of greater material comfort but not significantly greater personal independence. Reading the slap passage in light of this earlier one throws into doubt the view that Janie's later musings on self-division are sudden, new, or inherently liberatory; her self-examination after Joe slaps her thus gains a deeper, more thoughtful, less exhilarating hue. The fact that the later passage is immediately followed by Starks's interaction with Mrs. Robbins underlines the pessimistic mood: Mrs. Robbins's excruciating self-abasement, along with the assessment of the porch men that "if dat wuz *mah* wife . . . Ah'd kill her cemetery dead," does lead Janie to do "what she had never done before, that is, thrust herself into the conversation," but Hurston makes it clear that, at this point, Starks has no problem shutting her up and sending her off the porch (70).

Johnson's assertion that Janie "begins to speak" after Starks slaps her is correct in terms of textual time: Janie is slapped in chapter 6 and tells Joe off in chapter 7. But Hurston complicates this progression by pointedly noting the nine painful, silent years elapsed in "real" time, years that "took all the fight out of Janie's face. For a while she thought it was gone from her soul. *No matter what Jody did, she said nothing.* She was a rut in the road. Plenty of life beneath the surface but it was kept beaten down by the wheels" (72; emphasis added). This disjunction between "real" time and textual time highlights how strategies of representation can obscure as well as illuminate social reality. In the same vein, Hurston's own gloss on Janie's ability to separate her inner feelings from her outward actions is much less optimistic than Johnson's: "It was like a drug. In a way it was good because it reconciled her to things. She got so she received all things with the stolidness of the earth which soaks up urine and perfume with the same indifference" (73). The separation of inner and outer is thus *contextualized* (rather than essentialized—made virtuous by means of its very existence—as it is in Johnson's critique); whether it is productive of liberation or continued oppression is contingent upon the circumstances of its realization and not upon the simple fact of its appearance.

Hurston's move to contextualize the emergence of Janie's voice is compounded by her decision to draw attention to what she has elsewhere called the "rich metaphor and simile" of African-American language, a strategy that abets her larger scheme of metasignifying.[53] Janie's first expressed desire in the text is for a marriage "sweet . . . lak when you sit under a pear tree and think" (23). At many points in the text Janie is represented as a personification of the blooming pear tree that served as her introduction to sexual and romantic life (10–11); a corollary to this characterization is the move to describe Janie's search for a suitable husband as the need for "a bee for her bloom" (31). In this configuration, the man is the active, vocal searcher (the bees have an "alto chant" [10]), while the woman is still, silent, patiently waiting. Thus, while the plot shows Janie in movement (from Nanny's house to Logan Killicks's farm to Eatonville to Jacksonville to the Everglades and then back to Eatonville), actively searching for self-fulfillment, the metaphors Hurston draws upon to describe that search ground her in stasis, thereby setting up a disjunction between events and the words used to describe them. This disjunction is made explicit in a second metaphor Hurston introduces to describe Janie's life, the search for the horizon. This phrase first appears when Janie meets Joe Starks; Hurston tells us that she "pulled back a long time because he did not represent sun-up and pollen and blooming trees, but he spoke for far horizon" (28). An echo of the novel's opening lines,[54] this desire to move beyond boundaries adds further complications to Janie's life story: she seems to desire not simply a bee for her bloom but an arena for action. Janie wants to be a pear tree in bloom and on the move, a combination of ambitions rendered unimaginable by the language in which Hurston chooses to represent it. This deliberate overload of descriptive language—an overload highlighting the incompatibility of the images evoked—stands in a signifying relationship to those habits of African-American expression Hurston has praised elsewhere: the "will to adorn" and the ingenuity with which the African American had "made over a great part of the [standard English] tongue to his liking and . . . had his revision accepted by the ruling class."[55] By pressing this imaginative folk expression to its breaking point, Hurston shows how that expression breaks precisely over the issue of representing women's reality.

Hurston amplifies this point at three crucial junctures in Janie's development, where male-dominant modes of thinking and speaking are shown to be insufficient to represent her character's turmoil. When Janie leaves Logan Killicks for Joe Starks, Hurston notes that "new words would have to be made and said" (31). When Joe Starks moves out of the bedroom and begins to sleep downstairs after Janie feminizes him before the men at the store, Hurston writes that "new thoughts had to be thought and new words said" (77). Finally, as she tells Pheoby (in the narrative itself, not the frame) of her growing relationship with Tea Cake, Janie asserts: "If people thinks de same they can make it all right.

So in the beginnin' new thoughts had tuh be thought and new words said. After Ah got used tuh dat, we gits 'long jus' fine. He done taught me de maiden language all over" (109). Hurston's repeated use of this phrase—new thoughts thought, new words spoken—indicates an impatience and frustration with the thoughts and words available to her effort to represent a black woman's life in an African-American idiom (and the final use of the phrase further implies a strategic decision on Janie's part to let Tea Cake do her thinking and speaking for her). The repetition itself indicates that adequate new thoughts may never be found, new words never spoken; what Hurston must finally work for is a means of expression to express precisely that.

Hurston embeds this problem in a wider racial dynamic through a striking phrase describing the townsfolk's reaction to Joe Starks. When he moves into Eatonville, Starks immediately begins setting himself up as boss of the town, selecting those trappings of authority most reminiscent of white power: he builds a house that makes the rest of the town look "like servants' quarters" and paints it "a gloaty, sparkly white" (44). The residents of the town, who admire Starks's gumption and willingness to work hard, are nonplussed by this development. "It was bad enough for white people," Hurston writes, "but when one of your own color could be so different it put you in a wonder" (45). Hurston goes on to describe this feeling of discomfiture with an unusual simile: "It was like seeing your sister turn into a 'gator. A familiar strangeness. You keep seeing your sister in the 'gator and the 'gator in your sister, and you'd rather not" (45).

Economically knotted together in this expression are problematics of gender, race, and folk speech. A black man acting like a white man is like a sister (a word with both kinship and race connotations) turning into an alligator, a "familiar strangeness . . . you'd rather not" see. Racial power dynamics (black vs. white) are rendered, via a southern folk idiom (the use of the term *'gator*), into gender power dynamics, as the economy of the simile forces a series of translations: if the white man is like a 'gator, then the black man is like a sister. And if the black man is going to be a black *man* (i.e., not feminized in relation to the white man), then the sister had best remain a sister, that is, not avail herself of the "'gator" powers of the folk idiom.[56] Hurston's use of the phrase "familiar strangeness" here chimes with Freud's notion of the uncanny, that which is disturbing precisely because it is "homely" and familiar.

The passage thus reveals an uncanny relationship both within the story (Joe's strangeness in behaving like a white man is discomfiting precisely because it is so familiar) and throughout the text, as Hurston reveals her relationship to African-American folk idiom as one of powerful identification—to show the black man as a black man—and an equally powerful alienation—to show the 'gator in the sister.

Hurston does envision an ideal relationship between southern black folk idiom and black feminist consciousness, one in which the two terms are bound in a productive, mutually constitutive structure. Certainly, her decision to tell so much of Janie's story in the southern black folk idiom points to this hope. However, the most haunting image of this attempt to refigure the relationship is Tea Cake's bite. That Hurston chooses to represent a utopic (if unsettling) permeability as deadly, unresolved rupture sharpens the tactical nature of her appropriation of southern black idiomatic expression. As Janie has had to maneuver herself into a speaking position through a series of difficult trade-offs (Starks for Killicks, Tea Cake for Starks, a fatal wound for a voice with which to frame her narrative), so, too, is Hurston's text the product of a risky textual decision: to represent a woman's story in a man's language in such a way that the language would turn in upon itself. In *Their Eyes Were Watching God* Hurston makes the African-American practice of signifying both a way of meaning *and* the meaning itself, as we are made to see the need for an expanded horizon of what is deemed significant in African-American expression.

Notes

1. Zora Neale Hurston, *Their Eyes Were Watching God*, with a new foreword by Mary Helen Washington (1937; rpt. New York: Harper & Row, 1990), 175. All quotations are drawn from this edition; hereafter page numbers appear parenthetically in the text.

2. Bernard W. Bell, *The Afro-American Novel and Its Tradition* (Amherst: Univ. of Massachusetts Press, 1987), 127. Bell writes that "the tragic irony is that Janie is probably dying from Tea Cake's biting her as she cradled him in her arms after shooting him," but does not elaborate on the observation.

3. Henry Louis Gates Jr., *The Signifying Monkey: A Theory of African-American Literary Criticism* (New York: Oxford Univ. Press, 1988), 170–216.

4. Lillie P. Howard, *Zora Neale Hurston* (Boston: Twayne, 1980); Bell, *The Afro-American Novel;* and Robert E. Hemenway, *Zora Neale Hurston: A Literary Biography* (Urbana: Univ. of Illinois Press, 1980).

5. I would like to make it clear from the outset that I am in no way arguing that the southern African-American oral narrative tradition is somehow unique in its discomfort with women. It seems, in fact, that the *majority* of folk narratives and practices bear traces of hostility to women—or, as M. Z. Rosaldo puts it in her essay on feminism and anthropology, "human cultural and social forms have always been male dominated" ("The Use and Abuse of Anthropology: Reflections on Feminism and Cross-cultural Understanding," *Signs* 5 [1980]: 393). Rosaldo's essay is useful in considering Hurston's writings in general, as she shows how the anthropological search for origins most often replicates "biologically-based," or essentialist, arguments of gender relations: "To look for origins is, in the end, to think that what we are today is something other than the product of our history and . . . that our gender systems are primordial, transhistorical, and essentially unchanging in their roots" (392–93). This offers some insight into the source of the friction between feminism and folk expression in *Their Eyes Were Watching God* and other texts by Hurston, who trained as an anthropologist at Columbia University under Franz Boas.

6. Though most modern studies of black English focus on the oral practices of northern city dwellers, Gates maintains that "there can be little doubt that Signifyin(g) was found by linguists in the black urban neighborhoods in the fifties and sixties because black people from the South migrated there and passed the tradition along to subsequent generations" (71).

7. Washington, Foreword, *Their Eyes Were Watching God*, viii–ix.

8. Ibid., xi.

9. Robert B. Stepto, *From Behind the Veil: A Study of Afro-American Narrative* (1979; rpt. Urbana: Univ. of Illinois Press, 1991), 166.

10. Claire Crabtree, "The Confluence of Folklore, Feminism, and Black Self-Determination in Zora Neale Hurston's *Their Eyes Were Watching God*," *Southern Literary Journal* 17, no. 2 (1985): 55.

11. Michael Awkward, *Inspiriting Influences: Tradition, Revision, and Afro-American Women's Novels* (New York: Columbia Univ. Press, 1989), 56.

12. In her essay "The Politics of Fiction, Anthropology, and the Folk: Zora Neale Hurston" (*New Essays on* Their Eyes Were Watching God [New York: Cambridge Univ. Press, 1990]), Hazel Carby blames Hurston, rather than her readers, for this "representation of 'Negroness' as an unchanging, essential entity, an essence so distilled that it is an aesthetic position of blackness" (77). While I admire Carby's overall argument, which is to raise suspicion of the politics that have led *Their Eyes Were Watching God* to be so success-

fully resurrected in the academy ("Has *Their Eyes Were Watching God* become the most frequently taught black novel because it acts as a mode of assurance that, really, the black folk are happy and healthy?" [89–90]), I think that Hurston intends Janie's wounding to indicate that, in fact, the oral tale can *not* be taken as "a sign of a whole healthy culture" (83).

13. Washington, Foreword, x.

14. Mary Helen Washington, "'I Love the Way Janie Crawford Left Her Husbands': Zora Neale Hurston's Emergent Female Hero," in *Invented Lives: Narratives of Black Women, 1860–1960* (New York: Doubleday/Anchor, 1988), 237, 238.

15. Barbara Johnson, "Metaphor, Metonymy, and Voice in *Their Eyes Were Watching God*," in *A World of Difference* (Baltimore: Johns Hopkins Univ. Press, 1987), 155–71.

16. "In metaphor, the substitution is based on resemblance or analogy; in metonymy, it is based on a relation or association other than that of similarity (cause and effect, container and contained, proper name and qualities or works associated with it, place and event or institution, instrument and user, etc.)" (ibid., 155).

17. Ibid., 163.

18. Ibid., 163–64.

19. In fact, Gates and Johnson did extensive joint work on the novel before Gates's study appeared. See the coauthored essay "On Black and Idiomatic Free Indirect Discourse," in *Modern Critical Interpretations of Zora Neale Hurston's* Their Eyes Were Watching God (New York: Chelsea House, 1987).

20. Gates, *Signifying*, 174.

21. Gates offers an extended and wonderfully clear discussion of free indirect discourse in his chapter on Hurston's novel; see 207–15 in *The Signifying Monkey*.

22. Ibid., 181.

23. In his review of *Their Eyes Were Watching God*, Wright charged that "Miss Hurston voluntarily continues in her novel that tradition which was forced upon the Negro in the theater, that is, the minstrel technique that makes the 'white folks' laugh" ("Between Laughter and Tears," *New Masses*, 5 Oct. 1937, 23). For her part, Hurston (in "How It Feels to Be Colored Me") indirectly dismissed Wright as a member of "the sobbing school of Negrohood who hold that nature somehow has given them a lowdown dirty deal" ("How It Feels," in *I Love Myself When I Am Laughing . . . And Then Again When I Am Looking Mean and Impressive* [New York: Feminist Press, 1979], 153). Hurston's long-held disdain for the Communist party also fueled her dislike of Wright.

24. Zora Neale Hurston, *Dust Tracks on a Road* (1942; rpt. New York: HarperCollins, 1991), 63.

25. Richard Wright, *Black Boy* (1945; rpt. New York: Harper & Row, 1966), 111.

26. Gates, *Signifying*, 183.

27. Ibid., ix.

28. Ibid., 56–58.

29. Ibid., 66.

30. Ibid., 78, 80, 81.

31. Ibid., 171–72, 178–79.

32. Ibid., 198.

33. Zora Neale Hurston, *Mules and Men* (1935; rpt. New York: Harper & Row, 1990).

34. Geneva Smitherman, *Talkin and Testifyin: The Language of Black America* (Detroit: Wayne State Univ. Press, 1977), see especially 118–34; Claudia Mitchell-Kernan, "Signifying," in *Mother Wit from the Laughing Barrel: Readings in the Interpretation of Afro-American Folklore*, ed. Alan Dundes (Jackson: Univ. Press of Mississippi, 1973), 310–28.

35. Gates, *Signifying*, 80. However, one study Gates cites with approval—Roger D. Abrahams's *Deep Down in the Jungle: Negro Narrative Folklore from the Streets of Philadelphia* (New York: Aldine de Gruyter, 1970)—in fact devotes a good portion of one chapter to a psychosocial reading of the dozens that develops a theory of the ritual as a rejection of the feminine prompted by the extreme matrifocal nature of the African-American home (see the chapter "Neighbors and Relations," esp. 20–21, 24–29, 30–33). Indeed, the 1963 edition of Abrahams's work in many ways anticipates the infamous 1965 Moynihan report, which posits the "matriarchal" black family as pathological. Abrahams withdraws somewhat, but not completely, from this position in the 1970 revision. For an example of the earlier argument, see his 1962 essay "Playing the Dozens," reprinted in *Mother Wit from the Laughing Barrel*.

36. Gates, *Signifying*, 56.

37. Ibid., 69; emphasis added.

38. Ibid., 77; emphasis added.

39. Ibid., 202.

40. Henry Louis Gates Jr., "2 Live Crew Decoded," *New York Times*, 19 June, 1990, A23.

41. Belinda Edmondson dryly remarks that "Gates's intellectual virtuosity notwithstanding, this black listener could discern no finely veiled irony in 'make the pussy splat'" ("Black Aesthetics, Feminist Aesthetics, and the Problems of Oppositional Discourse," *Cultural Critique* 22 [1992]: 82).

42. In her study of rap, *Black Noise: Rap Music and Black Culture in Contemporary America* (Hanover: Univ. Press of New England, 1994), Tricia Rose maintains that "rap music and video have been wrongfully characterized as thoroughly sexist but rightfully lambasted for their sexism" and argues for

a view of rap that acknowledges its feminist aspects (15). Rose's discussion of feminist rap, however, is depressing; in her concluding chapter, "Bad Sistas: Black Women Rappers and Sexual Politics in Rap Music," one female rapper after another refuses to be characterized as a feminist (175–82). Rose sees this as a sign of white feminism's racist failure to include the problems faced by working-class women of color in its critique of patriarchy. This is undoubtedly true; however, bell hooks offers a different view in her essay "Black Students Who Reject Feminism" (*Chronicle of Higher Education,* 13 July, 1994): "Just as some black males hold on to macho stereotypes about maleness as a way of one-upping white men, whom they characterize as wimpy, some young black females feel that they finally can one-up white girls by insisting that they are already 'real' women, taking care of business, with no need of feminism" (A44). Hooks faults popular culture's pervasive sexism (as well as "a strand of Afrocentric thinking that incorporates rigid gender roles supposedly drawn from ancient Africa" [A44]). Rose, too, acknowledges the pernicious sexism of popular culture (15–16); however, she believes that subversive powers of rap enable it to transcend the more retrograde aspects of its pop roots.

43. In a recent essay—"Sexism and Misogyny: Who Takes the Rap?" *Z Magazine,* Feb. 1994—bell hooks argues that white racism and black sexism are linked phenomena. Thus, the misogyny of much gangsta rap is best read as "a reflection of the prevailing values in our society. . . . It is useful to think of misogyny as a field that must be labored in and maintained . . . to sustain patriarchy. . . . And what better group to labor on this 'plantation' than young black men" ("Sexism," 26).

44. Orlando Patterson, "Race, Gender, and Liberal Fallacies," in *Court of Appeal: The Black Community Speaks Out on the Racial and Sexual Politics of Thomas vs. Hill,* ed. Robert Chrisman and Robert L. Allen (New York: Ballantine, 1992), 163, 161, 160. Patterson's essay first appeared in the *New York Times,* Oct. 20, 1991.

45. Some authors have sought to trace a separate, more woman-centered tradition in black folk speech; see Paule Marshall's 1983 essay "From the Poets in the Kitchen" (in *Reena and Other Stories* [New York: Feminist Press, 1983]). It is tempting to speculate that Hurston places the framing discussion between Pheoby and Janie on the latter's *back* porch in an effort to represent, by difference of place, the difference a woman-centered southern black oral folk practice might offer. Tea Cake's bite, however, renders Hurston's final position on the emergence of a powerful woman-centered oral tradition more despairing than hopeful.

46. Washington, "'I Love the Way,'" 243–44.

47. Ibid., 241; emphasis added.

48. *The New Oxford Annotated Bible, with the Apocrypha* (New York: Oxford Univ. Press, 1977).

49. Janie's childlessness is frankly remarked upon earlier in the text ("She had no more blossomy openings dusting pollen over her man, neither any glistening young fruit where the petals used to be" [68]), though Hurston does not make it clear if the infertility lies with Janie or with her husbands.

50. Hurston, *Mules and Men*, 124. Hereafter page numbers for quotations will appear parenthetically in the text.

51. For an explanation of the mechanics of loud-talking, see Gates, *Signifying*, 82.

52. For an excellent discussion of Hurston's efforts to represent female speech as subversive and perpetually belittled by the male characters in *Mules and Men*, see Mary Katherine Wainwright's "Subversive Female Folk Tellers in *Mules and Men*," in *Zora in Florida*, ed. Steve Glassman and Kathryn Lee Seidel (Orlando: Univ. of Central Florida Press, 1991). My reading of women's speech in *Their Eyes Were Watching God* is less optimistic than Wainwright's, but in several ways quite similar.

53. Zora Neale Hurston, "Characteristics of Negro Expression," in *Negro: An Anthology*, ed. Nancy Cunard and Hugh Ford (1933; rpt. New York: Frederick Ungar, 1970), 24.

54. "Ships at a distance have every man's wish on board. For some they come in with the tide. For others they sail forever on the horizon" (1).

55. Hurston, "Characteristics," 24–25.

56. The most striking feature of the alligator, of course, is its huge mouth. See the many alligator stories in *Mules and Men*.

Around, behind, above, below Men

Ratliff's Buggies and the Homosocial in Yoknapatawpha

Noel Polk

WILLIAM FAULKNER'S 1940 novel, *The Hamlet,* begins with a blurring of geographical, temporal, and political boundaries. Though Frenchman's Bend lies "twenty miles southeast of Jefferson," it is "hill-cradled and remote, definite yet without boundaries, straddling into two counties and owning allegiance to neither"; the old Frenchman's mansion is still known as the Old Frenchman place, but "the original boundaries now existed only on old faded records in the Chancery Clerk's office in the county court house in Jefferson, and even some of the once-fertile fields had long since reverted to the cane-and-cypress jungle from which their first master had hewed them." But this "master" was only master for a time, and those who came after him have "almost obliterated all trace of his sojourn."[1] Even the old Frenchman's name has been forgotten; it now has "nothing to do with any once-living man at all"; his legend is "but the stubborn tale of the money he buried somewhere" (731, 732).

Presiding, omnipotent, over this cosmos is Will Varner,

the chief man of the country. He was the largest landholder and beat supervisor in one county and Justice of the Peace in the next and election commissioner in both, and hence the fountainhead if not of law at least of advice and suggestion to a countryside which would have repudiated the term constituency if they had ever heard it. . . . He owned most of the good land in the country and held mortgages on most of the rest. He owned the store and the cotton gin and the combined grist mill and blacksmith shop in the village proper and it was considered, to put it mildly, bad luck for a man of the neighborhood to do his trading or gin his cotton or grind his meal or shoe his stock anywhere else . . . ; he looked like a Methodist Sunday School superintendent who on week days conducted a railroad passenger train or vice versa and who owned the church or perhaps the railroad or perhaps both. (733)

Will Varner doesn't have to worry about boundaries: boundaries have to worry about him. In controlling *everything* in Frenchman's Bend so completely, he is as much a parody of white male power in Western culture as his daughter, Eula, is a parody of the Western idealization of female sexuality.

Eula is a parody of the male imaginary's idealization of all things female. Like her father, she, too, refuses boundaries.[2] But whereas he owns them, she simply disregards them. Nothing can contain her, not the perambulator that Will has made for her when she is a baby, not the undergarments her brother Jody insists that she wear, not the dresses that should cover her long legs as they dangle from behind Jody on the horse: she constantly spills over and out of whatever restrictions her brother and her father try to force upon her. But Will's disregard of boundaries for himself merely puts them more firmly in place for others: by his will he makes of himself central and singular head of the local hierarchate, patriarch, locus, and totem. Where all things move toward a center there is no need for outward boundary. Eula is a threat in Frenchman's Bend precisely because she is so completely indifferent to the patriarchal order that her father represents. At Labove's school, she is "neither at the head nor at the foot of her class, not because she declined to study on the one hand and not because she was Varner's daughter on the other and Varner ran the school, but because the class she was in ceased to have either head or foot twenty-four hours after she entered it. Within the year there even ceased to be any lower class for her to be promoted from, for the reason that she would never be at either end of anything in which blood ran. It would have but one point, like a swarm of bees, and she would be that point, that center, swarmed over and importuned yet serene and intact and apparently even oblivious, tranquilly abrogating the whole long sum of human thinking and suffering which is called knowledge, education, wisdom, at once supremely unchaste and inviolable: the queen, the matrix" (836–37). Eula's challenge to Will's centrality, then, lies not at all in ambition but rather precisely in her complete indifference to masculine hierarchy and tradition. Eula creates problems for all the males in Frenchman's Bend (except one, Flem Snopes, her future husband, who makes of her not a problem but an opportunity). On the one hand, she is supremely desirable; on the other, as we shall see, she is all that the men of Frenchman's Bend want to escape.

In appropriating the Old Frenchman place, Will possesses the classic Western tradition of male privilege and power. Not that he understands that tradition, of course. Though he kinglily sits in the flour-barrel throne, he does not have the imagination to conjure any sense of the Old Frenchman's "magnificence" (731); his primary response to the building is a puzzled sense of wonderment at "what it must have felt like to be the fool that would need all this . . . just to eat and sleep in" (734). The practical, nonidealistic Will completely misses the point of such a structure because he's thinking like the proletarian he believes himself to be and not like the bourgeois that he actually is. But of course it is not necessary to understand the tradition of power and privilege in order to inherit it or to exercise it or to cash in on it, and if anybody wanted to argue that one of the redeeming features of that tradition was the extent of the magnificence it created—the castles, the cathedrals, the mansions—it would follow that Will Varner, in trading the Old Frenchman place for his daughter's and his own good name, has debased that tradition even more completely than have the Frenchman's Bend folk who have been pulling it apart for years, using its lumber for firewood. But we cannot overlook the fact that the tradition's magnificence was based upon the ruthless exploitation of a laboring underclass, so that in eventually using the Old Frenchman place to purchase respectability for his family, Varner is not debasing the Old Frenchman place at all but rather in fact restoring that magnificence to its original debased use: the flashy exterior, the magnificence, was but the glamourous facade to hide a corrupt and corrupting system of white and male power and privilege.

The Old Frenchman place, then, aptly symbolizes the tradition Will has inherited and is so querulously trying to understand. It is a multilayered and complex symbol that each major male character in *The Hamlet*—Varner, Flem Snopes, and V. K. Ratliff—appropriates to his own meanings. For Will Varner, it is a puzzle of dimensions. For Flem, it is a means to an end. For Ratliff it is more complicated because for him, more complex and thoughtful, the Old Frenchman place's various meanings become fused with his more problematic responses to Eula Varner and to all things feminine.

House and domesticity, woman and economics, then, are inextricably linked in the symbolic structure of *The Hamlet*. Will Varner and the Old Frenchman place stand together at the center of the boundaryless economic and political unit called Frenchman's Bend, rooted and permanent. Ratliff is a roving vicar of Varner's economic tradition if not specifically of his empire. Moreover, though Ratliff insists upon mobility above all—he is constantly seen riding or sitting in his buckboard—he carries with him on his buckboard a reducto absurdum of the Old Frenchman place's many significations. By that symbol, Ratliff metaphorically tethers himself to Varner's economic center and he in effect moves Frenchman's Bend's very elastic boundaries with him wherever he goes. He is a sewing machine salesman, and he keeps a demonstrator model in the bed of his buckboard in a "dog-kennel . . . painted to resemble a house, in each painted window of which a painted woman's face simpered above a painted sewing-machine" (740). Ratliff's kennel-house, then, is an iconic crystallization of the economic and cultural traditions the Old Frenchman place represents; it is thus an apt and complex symbol of the economic relations between men, on the one hand, and between men and women, on the other—of the system's entrapment of women in the domestic: the painted simpering woman in the window of Ratliff's kennel-house makes one with the dozens of other women in Faulkner iconically framed in windows of the houses in which they are trapped.[3] Even the most dazzling mansion is little more than a social and economic prison for women, who both propel and are pulled along by the male economic vehicle. Indeed, powerful men might answer Will's question quite simply: we need all this room to keep it from looking like the prison it is. But it is a prison for the men, too, those who don't own such a mansion but who feel compelled by their own economic circumstances to desire the symbol of masculine power that owning it would invest them with, as though the symbol would bring with it the actual power.

For all of Eula Varner's overwhelming female presence, *The Hamlet* is preeminently a novel about relations among men: her alienage from both male and female in Frenchman's Bend and her value as a commodity in the male exchange system set the men's separation from the feminine into severe, if sometimes pathetic, sometimes tragic, sometimes comic, relief. It also confirms them in their relations with each other. Even those men who putatively compete for Eula's "hand" compete not at all for sexual pleasure or even for sexual conquest but rather for the sign of conquest, the reputation, the affirmation among their peers of sexual conquest, that "having"—owning—Eula or any other woman would produce. They calibrate their own worth in terms of how much of what they have other men want, and what other men will trade or do in order to get it. Even Labove, lacking the conquest itself, eagerly awaits the beating, the killing, he assumes Jody will give him as a public sign of his conquest. Ratliff understands that each of the young men who leaves Frenchman's Bend after Eula turns up pregnant is running mostly in the hope that everybody will think that he is the guilty party.

Men who run from the feminine usually run to each other, and in Frenchman's Bend they mostly congregate on the front porch of Varner's store, talking and ogling and staying away from home, where their wives are mostly doing privately the sort of backbreaking work that Mrs. Littlejohn, proprietor of Mrs. Littlejohn's Boarding House, does so publicly. The men's constant relationships with each other become sublimated into various forms of competition—horsetrading, for example—that galvanize them into a community that does not, cannot, admit women.

The Hamlet, then, defines masculinity as a retreat from the maternal, from that "rosy virginal mother of barricades," from the "supreme primal uterus" (835). Frenchman's Bend's retreat from the feminine may best be understood in the terms that Nancy Chodorow has used to describe the phenomenon in *The Reproduction of Mothering*.[4] In traditional family structures, the father is almost always nominally absent, so the mother becomes the familiar against which children's egos must function in order to define themselves.

> Because all children identify first with their mother, a girl's gender and gender role identification processes are continuous with her earliest identifications and a boy's are not. A girl's oedipal identification with her mother, for instance, is continuous with her earliest primary identification (and also in the context of her early dependence and attachment). The boy's oedipal crisis, however, is supposed to enable him to shift in favor of an identification with his father. He gives up, in addition to his oedipal and preoedipal attachment to his mother, his primary identification with her.
>
> What is true specifically for oedipal identification is equally true for more general gender identification and gender role learning. A boy, in order to feel himself adequately masculine, must distinguish and differentiate himself from others in a way that a girl need not—must categorize

himself as someone apart. Moreover, he defines masculinity negatively as that which is not feminine and/or connected to women, rather than positively. This is another way boys come to deny and repress relation and connection in the process of growing up.[5]

Because the father is nominally absent, or minimally present, masculinity is presented to boys as less available and therefore more desirable. Because it is more desirable, the culture idealizes the masculine; a boy therefore perforce "represses those qualities he takes to be feminine inside himself"—those qualities of connectedness—"and rejects and devalues women and whatever he considers to be feminine in the social world."[6] Yet Western culture assumes heterosexual domesticity, or at least its trappings, as its core value so that males must define masculinity in terms other than the domestic. According to Chodorow, "It becomes important for masculine identity that certain social activities are defined as masculine and superior, and that women are believed unable to do many of the things defined as socially important. It becomes important to think that women's economic and social contributions cannot equal men's. The secure possession of certain realms, and the insistence that these realms are superior to the maternal world of youth, become crucial both to the definition of masculinity and to a particular boy's own masculine gender identification."[7] These external, nondomestic, "realms" become the sites of what Eve Kosofsky Sedgwick calls the "homosocial," where protective bonding takes place and where relations between men, though putatively based in some form of competition, are structured to allow men both to dominate and to escape the domestic:

> The phrase "A man's home is his castle" offers a nicely condensed example of ideological construction [of the necessary relations between men and domesticity]. It reaches *back* to an emptied-out image of mastery and integration under feudalism in order to propel the male wage-earner *forward* to further feats of alienated labor, in the service of a now atomized and embattled, but all the more intensively idealized home. The man who has this home is a different person from the lord who has a castle; and the forms of property implied in the two possessives (his [mortgaged] home/his [inherited] castle) are not only different, but . . . mutually contradictory. The contradiction is assuaged and filled in by transferring the lord's political and economic control over the *environs*

of his castle to an image of the father's personal control over the *inmates* of his house.[8]

Men's deepest needs for self- and gender-identity lead them away from the feminine and toward each other, into the homosocial and, one might assume, easily into the overtly homosexual. But since the culture actively demands heterosexuality, it necessarily produces in homosocial men an intense and relentless homophobia that is at least as strong as the fear of the feminine. Thus men who cannot find comfort or ease in either homosexual or heterosexual worlds revert to the sexually neutered (but not neutral) world of the homosocial, from which vantage they can both escape and control the women, the domestic, that threaten them, and where they find acceptable, nonthreatening community in the company of other men. Women who encroach or even seem to encroach upon any of these "masculine" realms create anxiety in the men precisely because their attractiveness threatens their sense of self. At the same time that boys are developing a "dread" of the mother, they nevertheless still find her seductive and attractive, so that even the eventual substitution of a heterosexual partner for the mother does little to resolve the tense ambiguities, the complications, of a heterosexual life.

Not every bear hug or pat on the butt on the football field or in the locker room, perhaps not even many of them, is an overtly homosexual act, but each one is a publicly acceptable affirmation of gender solidarity and identity between the patter and the pattee and the surround of men who cheer them on in approval. The culture will not approve the next step, into homosexuality, but clearly that step is a logical extension of the range of possibilities that the homosocial allows and even encourages, but does not permit.

V. K. Ratliff is the most complex vehicle for understanding the homosocial in Frenchman's Bend. Ratliff's complex meditations on Eula and on domesticity, along with his attempts to connive the Old Frenchman place away from Flem, are the novel's central articulations of the problematics, for men, of heterosexuality and domesticity. His meditations—his running commentary on the developing saga of Flem and Eula, which he can interpret out of his own core experience of domesticity—provide us with the novel's, and Faulkner's, most profound anal-

ysis of the complexities of American gender structures. Ratliff is in all
ways tethered to the Old Frenchman place and to the cultural economy.
Though he owns a house in Jefferson, he is utterly mobile, economically
bound to his buckboard. But his load, his baggage—that simpering
face in the window of the dog kennel on the back of his buckboard—
is what interests us.

Ratliff ought to have made us more uncomfortable than he has
when we generalize about the novel's themes. If we condemn the materi-
alistic Snopeses, as earliest critics did, for leaving the land to become
merchants, we must ignore or explain away Ratliff's background, almost identical to Flem's, and his own defection from the plow to the
sewing machine business. If we want to make Ratliff the hero of a novel
that bemoans the failure of masculinity in Frenchman's Bend, we must
likewise ignore or explain away certain of Ratliff's essential characteristics—his occupation as sewing machine salesman, his preoccupation
with gossip, his sewing of his own shirts, his perennial bachelorhood—
that associate him more nearly with the women of Frenchman's Bend
than with any definition of masculinity the men of *The Hamlet* might
accept.[9] For all of Ratliff's contrapositions to Flem—his garrulity, his
neighborliness, his easy membership in and access to the community,
his general humanity, his manifest humanness—we in fact know very
little more about him than we do about Flem himself, and there are
ways in which he is as big an enigma as his arch rival.

Book 2 of *The Hamlet*, "Eula," is framed by the events of books 1
and 3. Book 1 chronicles the time from Flem's entrance into the community as a pauper to his accession to Will Varner's throne at the Old
Frenchman place, as virtual prince of the surrounding countryside. He
is in more ways than one Will's heir apparent. His rise is marked by
changes in his mode of transportation. Flem first walks to Varner's store
to work, then rides a mule. Before long he has taken Jody's place not
only in the store but also on his roan horse and at Will's side as they
make their daily rounds over Will's demesne. Very soon, too soon, Flem
moves into the Varner house, where he watches Eula's courtship by the
neighborhood boys; a month later Will buys a "new runabout buggy
with bright red wheels and a fringed parasol top" (814), to which are
harnessed Will's white horse and Jody's roan, and in which Will and
Flem drive their rounds, sitting "side by side in outrageous paradox"
(814). Months later Flem gives this runabout to Buck Hipps, after the
horse auction, for Buck to get back to Texas in. Buck is not so sure

about being seen in public in what he considers a sissified vehicle: "Only I ought to have a powder puff or at least a mandolin to ride it with," he objects. "I wouldn't get past the first Texas saloon without starting the vigilance committee," he says, and then wants to know "What's the short way to New York from here?" (1009).

This curious runabout poses some interesting and significant questions about Will's and Flem's relationship—about, if you will, the "vehicle" of Flem's rise up Varner's corporate ladder. Flem's advent into Frenchman's Bend is directly a result of Jody's temporizing with Ab Snopes. Flem's job in Varner's store is a form of "fire insurance," Jody's fearful effort to keep Flem's father from burning down the Varner barn. Jody, Will's son and presumptive heir to the Varner estates and privileges, ceases to be a major player after Eula's pregnancy. Flem completely supplants him.

Faulkner initially presents Jody as yet another of his male siblings, like Quentin Compson, who is overly concerned with a sister's virginity: he overreacts to Eula's long and casually displayed thighs as he rides behind her on the way to school and constantly gropes at her to see whether she's wearing her confining undergarments. Yet he cannot succeed his own father because he will not continue the Varner line: he is "not only unmarried," but he emanates "a quality of invincible and inviolable bachelordom," a "quality of invincible bachelorhood"; he is "the perennial and immortal Best Man, the apotheosis of the masculine Singular" (734, 735). Since he is not likely to continue the genetic Varner line and so its name, all he has as a claim on the Varner fortune is his economic competence, but he proves himself incompetent here too: even as a trader and merchant he is no worthy scion. The bad bargain he makes with Ab Snopes that permits Flem's entrance into the game is also the bargain by which he moves himself out. As Flem becomes more powerful, Jody gradually recedes in power and influence and, indeed, almost completely disappears from the novel as soon as Eula gets pregnant—a sure sign that he has also failed as protective brother and, more, failed to prove himself a worthy scion of the patriarchal tradition he stands to inherit. Faulkner suggests the degree of his failure later in the novel when he writes that Jody, perennial bachelor though he be, will one day be an old man "who at about sixty-five would be caught and married by a creature not yet seventeen probably, who would for the rest of his life continue to take revenge upon him for her whole sex" (1029).

That is, though Jody initially seems as thoroughly committed to the "tradition" of female purity as Quentin Compson and Horace Benbow are, Jody's story makes it clear that there's much more at stake in *The Hamlet*—and, reading backward, perhaps also in *The Sound and the Fury* and *Absalom, Absalom!*—than just the preservation of a sister's maidenhead. At issue is not at all its preservation but rather its appropriation by a male economy. All the obsession with incest in *The Sound and the Fury* and *Absalom, Absalom!* may be at least partially a scion's fantasy of despoiling the sexual merchandise—rendering her unmarketable by destroying that which makes her a valuable commodity—by which he fends off in advance his own preemption by a brother-in-law who might successfully compete not just for the father's affection but for his kingdom too. Thus, a sister's virginity is not just a commodity in the exogamic market; it is also, as the son sees it, a central value in the relationship between father and son, and therefore central to the maintenance of his own right to inherit. Flem does not claim Eula's maidenhead, but he certainly controls its value, so that he, and neither Jody nor Ratliff, is the rightful heir to Varner's position at the top of the totem pole.

Faulkner does not dwell on Jody, for in the larger, perhaps Darwinian, survival scheme, the patriarchy simply discards those who are not worthy of it. And, to be sure, Faulkner had already explored the inner workings of Jody's spiritual cousins in *The Sound and the Fury* and *Absalom, Absalom!* at considerable lengths and in *The Hamlet* moves deliberately away from such intensely internal, solipsistic explorations of sexual pathologies toward a more open, social view of such characters.

But even Jody's protuberant incompetence as son, protector, and trader does not explain why Will in effect adopts Flem, long before Eula gets pregnant, moves him not just into Jody's position in the store, at the gin, and by his own side as they make rounds but also, astonishingly, into his own house. Flem doesn't even have to usurp Jody's place: Will hands it to him on a platter—or on a sissy runabout, rather. But why? Fire insurance? I doubt it.

How does Flem come to own "some two hundred acres of land, with buildings"? (797). This is the portion of Jack Houston's land that Will has foreclosed on and that Flem, the new owner, has rented to his cousin Mink, who in turn now believes that Flem will be vulnerable to threats against his own barn. Perhaps Flem buys the property. But even if he does, there are more important questions: why does Will take up with Flem after Flem goes to work in the store, spending Sunday afternoons and evenings with him, in the wooden hammock, his Thomas Sutpen to Flem's Wash Jones, while Flem squats beside the tree and watches Eula being courted by the other young bucks in the county? (896). There is no evidence that Flem is a scintillating conversationalist, and none that Will himself needs somebody to talk to. If Flem must live in town, why not at Mrs. Littlejohn's boardinghouse? At whose invitation does Flem come to live in the Varner household? Will Varner is the only one who could have issued such an invitation. Further, why does Will agree to ride around the countryside with Flem in that sissified runabout? It may be easy to understand why Will marries Eula to Flem instead of to anybody else, but is it so easy to understand why Will gives him the Old Frenchman place to boot as dowry? Are we to understand that Flem refuses to take Eula unless Will includes the Old Frenchman place in the deal? What gives him such bargaining power? What, in short, is the relationship between Flem and Will Varner?

We have no direct answers to any of these questions, but we may approach an answer indirectly. Just after Flem has come to work at the store, Ratliff meets Varner at the Old Frenchman place. Varner, still riding his white horse at this point, proposes that he and Ratliff change places: "I want to sit down and ride," he says. Ratliff suggests they tie the horse behind and ride together in the buckboard, but Varner refuses: "You ride the horse," he says. "That's close as I want you right now. Sometimes you are a little too smart to suit me" (753). Though there's plenty of room for both of them to ride in the buckboard, Varner refuses to be so close to Ratliff—though he doesn't mind sitting with Flem in the runabout; perhaps it's just a whim, of course, and Will is certainly entitled to his whims. They proceed to town talking about the new employee and his family, Varner in the buckboard, Ratliff on the horse. The scene ends with Ratliff's proffered compliment to Will, that "there aint but two men I know can risk fooling with them folks. And just one of them is named Varner and his front name aint Jody" (755). Although Varner is polite enough to ask, and Ratliff shrewd enough not to answer, each knows who the one not named Varner is, and they part with this modest, muted, and mutual ratification of each other's skill as traders.

A related scene, at the beginning of book 3, occurs three years later, just after Flem and Eula have gone to Texas and, more specifically, just as Ratliff emerges from his fantasy about Flem in hell. Awaking and, as usual, "sitting in the halted buckboard" (875), Ratliff once again meets Varner, who is now, Ratliff observes, again riding the white horse "which, with the exception of the three-year runabout interval, [he] had bestridden it, the same saddle between them, for twenty-five years" (877). Ratliff continues thinking. "So he had to pay that too. Not only the deed to the land and the two-dollar wedding license and them two tickets to Texas and the cash, but"—and somehow this seems more important to Ratliff at the moment than the mere money and the land—"but the riding in that new buggy with somebody to do the driving, to get that patented necktie out of his store and out of his house." The seriousness with which Ratliff views *this* change, and Will's loss of the Old Frenchman place, is suggested by Faulkner's description of him as Varner approaches: Ratliff sits in the buckboard "neat, decorous, and grave like a caller in a house of death" (875).

Significantly, Ratliff is more upset about Varner's loss of the Old Frenchman place than about what nearly everybody in *The Hamlet* would call Eula's shame, at least partly because the loss involves Ratliff's disillusionment about Varner's invincibility as a trader. After a brief conversation, Varner rides off toward town, and Ratliff, from his buckboard, watches as Varner's horse begins to make his automatic turn toward the Old Frenchman place. Varner "haul[s] it roughly back" (878). The "roughly" suggests some agitation on Varner's part, some irritable reaction against his former castle, now that Flem owns it, which in turn implies that he too feels he is no longer the man Ratliff and others believe him to be. Losing the Old Frenchman place, he has lost status with Ratliff, with other men, and with himself. Moreover, the gesture makes it clear that he, and they, believe that he has gotten snookered in the deal, gotten beaten so badly that he has good reason to feel humiliated.

Again I ask: what are the terms of Will's and Flem's deal? What does Will get in exchange for his daughter and his ruined mansion? Ratliff's is a simple answer: fire insurance, an unburned barn. A considerably more complicated answer asks us to understand that Will has been beaten because Flem had a sight draft that he, but not Will, was willing to cash in.

Not to put too fine a point on it, I propose that there is some form of homosexual relationship, overt or latent, between Will and Flem. I grant, of course, that there is no proof of any sort of sexual liaison between Flem and Will, but the indicators are so numerous that we must at least see the possibility both as a logical extension of the extreme homosocial atmosphere in the novel and as an explanation of the more than curious external features of their developing relationship. The possibility also provides interesting resonances for other incidentals in the text. One cannot, for example, avoid Ratliff's vituperative speech early in book 3, in which he associates Will with Snopeses in a very curious way: "Snopes can come and Snopes can go, but Will Varner looks like he is fixing to snopes forever. Or Varner will Snopes forever—take your pick. What is it the fellow says? off with the old and on with the new; the old job at the old stand, maybe a new fellow doing the jobbing but it's the same old stern getting reamed out?" (879–80). One who gets beaten at a deal is said to get screwed; one beaten *very* badly is said to get screwed in the ass. Under the circumstances, then, we cannot help but wonder whether Will wants to ride in Ratliff's buggy instead of on his horse simply because, well, he is sore—and doesn't want to sit that close to Ratliff because of whatever of shame he feels, or the fear of being discovered somehow, perhaps by revealing himself in his physical or psychic discomfort. Of course what works on him is not any rational worry that he will reveal himself, but rather the quite irrational fear of what he knows about himself.

Flem's sight draft is not necessarily economic or social, then, but psychological: given his economic and social power, Will could dismiss any accusation of homosexuality as being simply unbelievable, and there is no reason to doubt that Will could survive a public confrontation over such issues. It is, then, the private confrontation that he cannot survive, the admission perhaps not even of overt homosexual acts but of the mere inclination toward them, and so he avoids the issue by yielding to Flem's threats, which may be only implied rather than real. In a novel so completely "about" compromised male sexuality in a homosocial world, a novel in which Flem regularly exploits the idealized masculinity of so many of Frenchman's Bend men, it should not be surprising to find homosexuality a significant part of the whole, as it is in many other of Faulkner's novels, or to find it a point upon which the novel's most overtly successful and "masculine" character should be vulnerable.

As Varner rides off, Ratliff's meditations move by fluid association from Varner's horse to his and Flem's sissified runabout to the wagons and buggies of the young bucks who had courted Eula to Eula herself to Eula's baby then to himself and to what he calls his own past's "tom-catting's heyday" (877), then to Flem and the waste that Eula's marriage to him represents. At precisely the point in Ratliff's meditations when he reaches Eula, Will reaches the lane going to the Old Frenchman place, jerks his horse "roughly" away from the turn, and Ratliff himself moves on. Ratliff's fantasy of Flem's negotiations with the Prince emerge directly out of Ratliff's meditations here, so that in effect Ratliff's single meditation on a variety of things connected with Eula and buggies is interrupted by his vision of Flem in hell, by the change from book 2 to book 3, and by his conversation with Will Varner. His elegiac cadenza on Eula tells us a good deal, I'd suggest, about himself and about the complex of reasons that govern men's homosocial retreat from women. These reasons are, I believe, here as in so many others of Faulkner's work, grounded in family structures that can best be understood in terms of Freudian oedipal theory.[10]

Book 2 is entitled "Eula," but like Caddy Compson in an earlier novel, Eula is primarily depicted in terms of the way men respond to her: those on the porch at her father's store; her erstwhile suitors; the drummer; her brother Jody; Labove; her father; Hoake McCarron; Flem. To this list I would add Ratliff, who makes his appearance in book 2 very late, just in time to watch Eula, Flem, and Varner in Jefferson going from Chancery Clerk to Circuit Clerk to bank. "He did not need" to see them married, so he goes straight ahead to the station "an hour before the train was due to wait to watch them board and depart"; at the station he sees her virtually in the same terms as the simpering woman in the window of the kennel on his buggy: he sees "the calm beautiful mask beneath the Sunday hat once more beyond a moving window, looking at nothing, and that was all" (867). His vision of that face "beyond a moving window" reminds us of *our* first vision of her, in the opening paragraph of book 2, as one who existed "in a teeming vacuum in which her days followed one another as though behind sound-proof glass, where she seemed to listen in sullen bemusement, with a weary wisdom heired of all mammalian maturity, to the enlarging of her own organs" (817). Now, as she leaves on her honeymoon, pregnant, her organs are enlarging indeed. Her face is wonder-full to Ratliff; it is all he sees, and his responses to that face suggest a range of things Ratliff associates with Eula and her environs. Frenchman's Bend is "a little lost village, nameless, without grace, forsaken, yet which wombed once by chance and accident one blind seed of the spendthrift Olympian ejaculation and did not even know it" (867). Like Labove, Ratliff knows how extraordinary Eula is. And that is the rub.

What follows is a magnificent, complicated passage, unlike anything else in Faulkner. After he places Eula in that "little lost village," Ratliff almost immediately notes the "three fairly well-horsed buggies" of the boys who courted her, buggies that disappeared after word spread that she was pregnant, and thinks of the gossip that flies "from cabin to cabin above the washing pots and the sewing, from wagon to horseman in roads and lanes or from rider to halted plow in field furrows." Among the gossipy men are "the young who only dreamed yet of the ruins they were still incapable of; the sick and the maimed sweating in sleepless beds, impotent for the harm they willed to do; the old, now-glandless earth-creeping, the very buds and blossoms, the garlands of whose yellowed triumphs had long fallen into the profitless dust, embalmed now and no more dead to the living world if they were sealed in buried vaults" (868). These "buried vaults" are, significantly, located "behind the impregnable matronly calico of others' grandchildren's grandmothers" (868). Hidden in that mouthful—"the impregnable matronly calico of others' grandchildren's grandmothers"—is the word "cuckold," the known fact of it in Flem's case and, I'd suggest, the fear of it in the minds and mouths of those men who talk about Flem and Eula.

The fear of being cuckolded, then, is the unspeakable terror at the heart of male heterosexuality. Though frequently invoked nervously as a topic of vulgar jokes, that terror always operates as an aggression, a sweeping indictment of all women, older than Chaucer, that admits all men's vulnerability to the cuckold's horns, which will publicly proclaim their own heterosexual insufficiency. This terror is especially real to the men of Frenchman's Bend, who know that Will Varner himself is very active in the bushes with other sharecroppers', and perhaps their own, wives. Even the proudly virile Mink Snopes can never rid himself of the phantoms of those bodies that had preceded him to his wife's bed (952–53).

From cuckoldry Ratliff abruptly moves back to Eula, or to the magnificence, the plenty, that Eula represents. "And which best," he wonders: "to have that word, that dream and hope for future, or to have had need to flee that word and dream, for past" (868). Ratliff wants to know whether it is better to have and hold the physical Eula from now on, to live with her in the give-and-take of domestic life, to watch her fade and grow old, to know that you will not be enough for her, that she *will be* unfaithful? or to have had her once, as Labove wants her, to have had the passion but not the problematics of possession, then to be free of her except as the grandest of perfect and unchanging memories? Ratliff answers his own question indirectly by thinking yet again about the buggies the boys courted Eula in: "Even one of the actual buggies remained. Ratliff was to see it, discovered a few months afterward, standing empty and with propped shafts in a stable shed a few miles from the village" (868). Ratliff then evokes, predicts, that buggy's future: no longer new and shining, it will gather dust; chickens will roost upon it and their droppings will streak and mar its once pristine finish. It will undergo a series of changes of ownership in a steady decline, "while its new owner married and began to get a family and then turn gray, spilling children, no longer glittering, its wheels wired upright in succession by crossed barrel staves until staves and delicate wheels both vanished, translated, apparently in motion at some point into stout, not new, slightly smaller wagon wheels, giving it a list, the list too interchangeable, ranging from quarter to quarter between two of its passing appearances behind a succession of spavined and bony horses and mules in wire- and rope-patched harness, as if its owner had horsed it ten minutes ago out of a secret boneyard for this particular final swansong's apotheosis which, woefully misinformed as to its own capacities, was each time not the last" (868–69).

This buggy's biography becomes, in Ratliff's imagination, an extended trope for marriage: the bright promise of youthful passion gradually destroyed by time and familiarity and use: domestication. For Ratliff, mutability casts its pall even over passion, and his answer to the question whether it is better to marry your goddess and have her reality or to forgo the reality in order to maintain her perfect memory is certainly suggested when, later in the trilogy, in *The Mansion*, we learn that he keeps a shrine to Eula in his house in Jefferson. Clearly, no less than Labove is Ratliff overwhelmed by Eula. But for the moment he evades that realization and focuses once more on "the calm beautiful mask seen once more beyond a moving pane of glass, then gone." But he jerks himself back from admitting what that face, that woman, means to him with the melancholy and unconvincing argument that it was "all right, it was just meat, just galmeat . . . and God knows there was a plenty of that, yesterday and tomorrow too. Of course," his other self counters, "there was the waste, not wasted on Snopes but on all of them, himself included—Except," he argues back, "was it waste?" Can anything that dangerous be worth having? Behind that face there lurks "only another mortal natural enemy of the masculine race. And beautiful: but then, so did the highwayman's daggers and pistols make a pretty shine on him" (869). And as he remembers Eula's unforgettable, dangerous, face moving off toward Texas behind the train's soundproof glass, he shifts gears a bit to imagine Flem in hell. Perhaps Ratliff's sympathies for Flem in this comic Faustian revery are stronger than critics have allowed: after all, in outtrading the Prince, what Flem gains is not heaven; in outtrading Will Varner, what he gains, by analogy, is, to the men of Frenchman's Bend, perhaps no different from hell itself: wife, mansion, domesticity.

As book 3 opens, Ratliff is still sitting in his buggy. Varner approaches, and the scene ensues that I noted a moment ago. As he watches Varner ride away, Ratliff thinks again about those courting buggies, which, as we now know, evoke in Ratliff all of youth's dangerous passion. He is fixated on those buggies. He imagines he sees them still tied to the fence around Varner's yard: "Those buggies were still there. He could see them, sense them. Something was [there]; it was too much to have vanished that quickly and completely." The air is "polluted and rich and fine which had flowed over and shaped that abundance and munificence." *Polluted* is the operative word here. It evokes the connection between sexuality and corruption that is as common as words in Faulkner's work. But the buggies, Ratliff finally understands, are "merely a part of the whole, a minor and trivial adjunct, like the buttons on her clothing," compared to Eula herself: "so why," he wonders, "should not that body at the last have been the unscalable sierra, the rosy virginal mother of barricades for no man to conquer scot-free or even to conquer at all, but on the contrary to be hurled back and down, leaving no scar, no mark of himself" (877). Ratliff almost reproaches himself for not having made his own desperate and futile cast on that height, even one time, at no matter what cost. But that—the passionate and injurious assault on such an "unscalable sierra"—*that*, he concludes, "would never have been for him," he admits, "not even in what he and Varner both would have called his tom-catting's heyday." The phrasing argues that Ratliff's "tom-catting heyday" wasn't, as he might put it, no great shakes of a heyday. "He knew," Faulkner tells us, "that without regret or grief, he would not have wanted it to be" for him to assail that height (877).

Ratliff has, then, simply opted out of sexual life. He tries to explain to himself his inadequacy before the likes of Eula—before Woman: "It would have been like giving me a pipe organ, that never had and never could know any more than how to wind up the second-hand music-box I had just swapped a mailbox for, he thought." He is not jealous of Flem, though, he thinks, because he knows that "regardless of whatever Snopes had expected or would have called what it was he now had, it would not be victory" (877). He is wrong, of course, as we shall see, because he thinks that Flem's relationship to Eula is based in the same sexual anxieties that plague him and the other Frenchman's Bend men. He thinks that Flem wants the same thing out of marriage that the men of the Bend do, but he clearly doesn't. From all we can tell from *The Hamlet* and *The Town*, Flem accepts his cuckolding as a part of Eula's exchange value: what he must pay to possess her, to have her long enough to trade her, as he trades the Old Frenchman place, for whatever he wants to own next.

Ratliff believes that even Eula will grow old and, growing old, fail to measure up to his and every other man's dream of her; at best Flem's marriage, like all others, will succumb to the ordinary; at worst, marriage will be for Flem the same domestic trap it is for every other man. So whatever Flem thinks he has won, Ratliff believes, Flem will soon know it as loss. But this thought, in its turn, prompts the admission from Ratliff, less self-deceptive than before, that Eula has indeed been wasted. But he is less concerned with how Eula is being wasted on Flem than with how she is being wasted on such a stinking, corrupt world as he lives in (877–78).

When Ratliff decides to buy the Old Frenchman place, he locates Flem on a drive in the country with his Varner family and invites him to drive with him back to Frenchman's Bend; he thus negotiates his "deal" to buy the Old Frenchman place while moving in his buckboard. As they negotiate, they pass the schoolhouse and Ratliff is reminded, as in a premonition of disaster, of the vanquished schoolmaster: "That fellow, that teacher you had three-four years ago. Labove. Did anybody ever hear what become of him?" (1063). Even if neither Ratliff nor Flem knows exactly why Labove left the country, Ratliff's question is Faulkner's reminder to the reader of Ratliff's kinship with Labove: the teacher already, and Ratliff about to be, vanquished by Eula.

Thus Ratliff is no less vanquished by Eula than Labove; he is so thoroughly unwomanned and unwomanable that we may well say that he has been prevanquished by all women. Faulkner tells us that though they share many similarities, Ratliff and Jody Varner have one "unbridgeable difference": Jody, as I noted a moment ago, will marry late and be unhappy. "Ratliff, never" (1029). Why? What quality of sexuality or domesticity impels Ratliff to abjure the womanned state? We do not know for sure, of course, because Ratliff is reticent. Neither do we know how Labove knows what love is—"That's it," he tells Eula when she resists him: "Fight it. Fight it. That's what it is: a man and a woman fighting each other. The hating" (842)—but we can reasonably suspect that some experience of his own parents' marriage is his inspiration: where else?

In Chodorow's terms, Ratliff can only define himself in terms of his resistance to, his separation from, his mother: hence his insistence upon mobility, unattachment. In Freudian terms, consistent with Chodorow's argument, Ratliff cannot separate himself from the oedipal attachments that have controlled him from the beginning of his life. In this he is like many, many of Faulkner's characters. As we have already noted, he seems to share Quentin Compson's sense that sexuality and corruption are inextricable. Like Horace Benbow in *Sanctuary* and *Flags in the Dust*, Ratliff owns a house in Jefferson in which he lives with his widowed sister and her children; like Horace, he brings into that home the prostitute wife of a man in that same Jefferson jail awaiting trial for murder; like Horace, he is fascinated by the hands of the accused as they grip the bars of the window of his jail cell.

On the back of his buckboard, as noted, Ratliff carries a "sheet-iron box the size and shape of a dog-kennel and painted to resemble a house, in each painted window of which a painted woman's face simpered above a painted sewing-machine" (740) in which he keeps his demonstrator sewing machine. These women smile at him in "fixed and sightless invitation" (797), though whether they are sirens or merely customers we do not know for sure. Those faces, however, are haunting vestiges from many of Faulkner's works, in which a face in the window invariably connotes some repression of the sexual life, some oedipal strife, and it seems reasonably clear that that miniature house on Ratliff's buggy represents some emotional baggage from his childhood that has made him a constantly moving refugee from the feminine.

When Ratliff and Varner part at the beginning of book 3, Ratliff drives directly to Varner's store, where, genial raconteur again, he begins a voyeuristic tale in which Flem and a Negro girl have sex against the back wall of Varner's store. Lump Snopes interrupts him when the word comes that Ike Snopes is about ready to perform with his paramour cow; all the real voyeurs rush across the street to the fence that Lump has prepared for viewing, and Ratliff finishes his story while walking with the men to the barn lot. Ratliff shuts the peep show down, but his initial response to what he sees is utterly astonishing: "He knew not only what he was going to see but that, like Bookwright, he did not want to see it, yet, unlike Bookwright, he was going to look." It may be easy to understand why he doesn't want to see it. It's not so easy to understand why is he determined nevertheless to look. "He did look, leaning his face in between two other heads, and it was as though it were himself inside the stall with the cow, himself looking out of the blasted tongueless face at the row of faces watching him who had been given the wordless passions but not the specious words" (913). Incredibly, Ratliff identifies with Isaac: he sees *himself* caught in the shameful act of stockdiddling. Why? His reaction to Isaac's activity is, *must be,* based in a sense of sex as something bestial and unclean.

Ratliff does not participate in the spotted horse auction, not even as a witness or commentator, and has contempt for those who do. But in one of the novel's funniest scenes, one of the ponies chases into Mrs. Littlejohn's boarding house and on into Ratliff's very room, where he stands in his nightshirt, preparing for bed; he and the pony see each other at the same time, each equally frightened of the other. The horse backs out the door, and Ratliff jumps out the window. Mrs. Littlejohn simply hits the unruly pony on the head with her washboard and tells him, as she might a husband, "Get out of here, you son of a bitch" (1014). Funny as the scene is, however, it leaves no doubt about Ratliff's sexual anxieties.

Amidst the swirling force of those ponies Buck Hipps is trying to sell, wagons and buckboards—not the courting buggies or sissy runabouts—represent a degree of security: the men run to the wagon when they feel threatened by the horses and find in the wagon bed a timid solidarity above that symbolically sexual and putatively masculine maelstrom, even if their security is as illusory and transient as the innocence that seems to protect Eck Snopes's son as he wanders about among the chaotic and dangerous ponies. One pony attacks Tull's wagon, which is loaded with himself and his womenfolks—Tull is, Faulkner tells us, so domesticated and tamed as to be "the eldest daughter" of his own wife (727)—and convulses the family as comically as Lucy Pate's stallion's attack upon her is tragic. Likewise, Tull's valiant but ineffective attempt to protect his family by standing up in the seat and beating the spotted pony with his whip also reminds us of Hoake McCarron's identical but more successful defense of his possession of Eula against his competition. It is therefore also worth noting that Hoake, too, for all his vaunted masculinity, is, like Tull, crippled during that attack, and that he, too, can consummate his sexual union only with Eula's active assistance: she must support him, actually hold him up, so that he can perform (860). It is, then, a serious question with me whether Hoake runs from Will and Jody Varner's wrath or from his fear at having touched the grandeur and terror that woman represents to the homosocial male.

Ratliff wants nothing to do with those wild if diminutive symbols of chaotic masculinity that simultaneously attract and elude the other men of Frenchman's Bend. He in effect already owns two: pulling his buckboard are not powerful stallions such as Jack Houston buys Lucy Pate, nor even a mismatched pair like Jody's roan and Will's white, which are yoked together to pull Flem's sissy runabout. His team is rather, in point of fact, a pair of "shaggy ponies as wild and active-looking as mountain goats and almost as small" (740). If they are not Texas spotted ponies, they are at least second or third cousins. Ratliff's ponies, then, are, to use Jack Houston's phrase, symbols of his own "bitted masculinity."

More specifically, like the spotted ponies, they symbolize heterosexual desire, the powerful and destructive oedipal impulse toward the seductive mother: toward domestication, toward entrapment, toward engulfment by the supreme primal uterus in any of its substitute or surrogate avatars. Indeed, what can the "supreme primal uterus," to which we are all prostrate, be, but Mama? This is why Faulkner's men want them and why they can't even catch them, much less handle them. For men, the unbearable paradox is that to get the prize, the public affirmation of their masculinity, is to be stuck forever with a constant challenge to it: to win is therefore not just to lose, but to be lost.

The men of Frenchman's Bend, then, are thus forever caught in suspension between heterosexuality and outright impotence. Their only safeplace is the economic shield of the homosocial provided by the dusty distance between the front porch of Varner's store and the barn lot where Buck Hipps auctions those forever elusive ponies.

Flem brings those ponies with him from Texas, along with Eula and Eula's baby; he is thus firmly in possession of all he needs to publicly establish his masculinity. He can afford, now, to discard, must get rid of, the sissified fringed runabout that symbolizes, even more than the Old Frenchman place, his victory over Will Varner, a victory he gains because he knows that sexuality, too, is rather a medium of exchange than an activity by which one defines oneself. He leaves Frenchman's Bend not in the runabout but in a buckboard much like Ratliff's, and drives three miles out of his way, Eula and baby in the wagon with him, in order to go past the Old Frenchman place, where the crazed Henry Armstid is still digging. For no other reason than to gloat, to proclaim his final victory over Ratliff himself, which is also a victory over Varner, over the symbolic order of things, of which he has now become master.

His victory over Varner and Ratliff is also a victory over the feminine that lies less in his having parlayed the Old Frenchman place into Ratliff's share of the Jefferson cafe where he and Eula will move than in his appropriating from all the Frenchman's Bend men the visible signs of the same mastery over the domestic that they have long admired in Will Varner. Flem and Eula and the baby are in their own wagon, transporting their load of "furniture and . . . trunks and . . . boxes . . . and small crocks and hermetic jars of fruit and vegetables . . . the dismantled bed, the dresser, the washstand with its flowered matching bowl and ewer and slop-jar and chamber-pot, the trunk which doubtless contained the wife's and the child's clothing, the wooden box which the women at least knew doubtless contained dishes and cutlery and cooking vessels" and the tent they will live in behind the cafe (1070, 1071): no shabby merchandizing symbol here of any sexual anxieties but rather a symbol, in all its domestic fullness, of Flem's absolute mastery of the patriarchal tradition.

Thus Ratliff is no worthier an heir of Varner's tradition than Jody, and he too is vanquished, not because he is more likeable and more human than anybody else in Frenchman's Bend—being *liked* has nothing to do with the tradition's maintenance of itself—but because, like Jody, he fails to demonstrate the necessary business acumen and to acquire the equally essential signs of mastery over a castle.

Ratliff prides himself on being a sharp trader, but there's in fact not much evidence of it in *The Hamlet*, certainly none in his dealings with Flem. Flem's entrance into the Frenchman's Bend economy and his growing reputation as a trader become a challenge that Ratliff cannot avoid but that he cannot win. In fact, though Ratliff makes one with the men on Varner's front porch, he doesn't do any business with them and has carefully staked out a market in which he doesn't even have to compete with Will Varner. As a sewing machine salesman, he naturally deals more often, and more safely, with their womenfolks, and he can be no less cold-blooded in dealing with women than Flem can be in dealing with either gender. To engineer the goat deal, recall, Ratliff "mistakenly" delivers a sewing machine to Mink Snopes's wife: he thus uses her to play upon Mink's desire for ownership as skillfully as Buck Hipps sells those worthless spotted ponies to the men, and she and Mink want the sewing machine for the same reason that the others want those spotted ponies.

Thus Ratliff's relationship to women is no less, perhaps even more, completely based in economics than Flem's is. For the most part he seems content to remain seated on his floating buckboard island, the reins of control always firmly in his hand, deliberately restraining his own sexual energies and fears, and carrying safely behind him a woman—any woman: all women: his mother, Eula—carefully locked away in a dog kennel on the back of his buckboard, a woman eternally simpering, eternally looking at him in "fixed and sightless invitation," though offering him no more of a challenge than the simper. These painted women, no less than Eula herself, no less than other women in Faulkner, are untouchable, unknowable, dangerous: the primal uterus's primal terror's very self, yet safe: harmless, voiceless, impotent: trapped in a vacuum behind a moving window made of soundproof glass, like Eula trapped and so contained at last not at all by man's strength; not by his sexual mastery but by his impotence; not by his love but by his economic power.

Notes

1. William Faulkner, *The Hamlet*, in *William Faulkner: Novels 1936–1940* (New York: Library of America, 1990), 727–1075. All citations are to this text and will be indicated by parentheses within the text.
2. See Dawn Trouard, "Eula's Plot: An Irigararian Reading of Faulkner's Snopes Trilogy," *Mississippi Quarterly* 42 (1989): 281–97.

3. See Noel Polk, "Children of the Dark House," in Polk, *Children of the Dark House: Text and Context in Faulkner* (Jackson: Univ. Press of Mississippi, 1996), 22–98.

4. Nancy Chodorow, *The Reproduction of Mothering: Psychoanalysis and the Sociology of Gender* (Berkeley: Univ. of California Press, 1978).

5. Ibid., 174.

6. Ibid., 181.

7. Ibid., 182.

8. Eve Kosofsky Sedgwick, *Between Men: English Literature and Male Homosocial Desire* (New York: Columbia Univ. Press, 1985), 14.

9. See Panthea Reid Broughton, "Masculinity and Menfolk in *The Hamlet*," *Mississippi Quarterly* 22 (1968): 181–89.

10. See Polk, "Children of the Dark House," 22–98.

PART SIX

Contemporary Gender Wars

The 1970s, 1980s, and 1990s

Freedom, Manhood, and White Male Tradition in 1970s Southern Rock Music

TED OWNBY

IN 1975 the Charlie Daniels Band recorded "The South's Gonna Do It Again," a song celebrating the music and musicians of the Southern Rock movement. This song points out the most important questions and tensions we can observe about those young white southern men in the late 1960s and 1970s. Daniels listed the names and home states of the major and not so major artists in what was called Southern Rock—Grinderswitch, the Marshall Tucker Band, Lynyrd Skynyrd, Richard Betts, Elvin Bishop, ZZ Top, Wet Willie, Barefoot Jerry, and the Charlie Daniels Band. There are two intriguing things about this song. First, the song that celebrates Southern Rock is not a rock song. Its rhythm is Texas swing in the tradition of the music Bob Wills and the Texas Playboys popularized in the 1930s and 1940s. Only at the end of the song does the sound vary, first with a guitar solo based in African-American blues, then with a piano solo based in New Orleans jazz, and finally with Daniels himself on a country fiddle solo. So the question becomes why Daniels used a decades-old musical tradition as the sound to celebrate a musical movement that was only six or seven years old?

The same desire to interpret a new musical movement as part of a long tradition showed in the very simple lyrics. After listing the leading groups in the movement, Daniels urged his listeners to "Get loud" and, perhaps as significantly, to "be proud" because "the South's gonna do it again."[1] Here is the difficult issue. What was it they wanted the South to do again? What traditions were worth upholding and reliving? Were they going to secede again? Fight again? Lose again? Most intriguing, how could they uphold traditions while they were at the same time, as young rock musicians, rebelling against authority? If, as Daniels urged, Southern Rock musicians took pride in being rebels, what was it they were rebelling against? Finally, why was the movement so exclusively and self-consciously male?

An important part of that effort to find or construct a heritage—if only, in some cases, to find a heritage against which to rebel—showed in the nearly constant references to the South or particular southern states and cities. Born mostly in the late 1940s and early 1950s, the musicians likely did not feel the South of their day offered many examples of whites in their region upholding admirable traditions. White southerners had not endured the Civil Rights movement with particular dignity. Nor did the dramatic economic gulf between rural poverty and hopefulness in Sun Belt cities suggest that the South offered antidotes to the problems of modern America. Whites of the Southern Rock generation had grown up hearing a great deal of criticism of the South. Just as national press criticism about the Scopes trial helped stimulate the Vanderbilt Agrarians to define their regional identity, it seems fair to assume that the intense criticism of white southerners would have set off similar desires among young white men coming of age in the 1960s.[2]

At the same time they were looking for a heritage, they were rebelling against numerous traditional ideals in both music and culture. Daniels's encouragement to "get loud" was one of many examples of breaking free from traditions. When Lynyrd Skynyrd said "Turn it up" at the beginning of their most aggressively prosouthern song,[3] they identified themselves against both the less raucous white musical traditions before them and all of the adults, especially parents, who may have told them to turn it down and assert themselves less. Not just in volume but in rhythm, in look and hair style, and in the themes in their lyrics, musicians in the Southern Rock movement identified themselves as rebels. The tension, then, was between being a rebel against southern traditions in the late 1960s and being a Rebel as part of the tradition of white southerners, and the challenge was to find ways to be rebels of both kinds.

Southern Rock was a men's movement. It was coincidence that the first group in the movement had the masculine name of the Allman Brothers Band, but it was very important that all of the musicians except a few backup singers were male. Thus, this essay is about fathers—musical predecessors as fathers, past cultural ideals for males handed down by fathers, and fathers in the lyrics of the songs. It is also about the absence of mothers and even wives from those ideals and lyrics. How did Southern Rock musicians rebel against their fathers, and how did they uphold virtues they associated with male ancestors, and what were the consequences of not seeing women as part of meaningful traditions?

Four of the traditional definitions of white southern manhood were important in Southern Rock. All of them depended on difference from women and either power over them or separation from them. First was the goal of personal independence. To many white southern men, working for someone else or depending on someone else for one's livelihood had long seemed to resemble the position of slaves, women, or men with no character. A second male tradition was the concept of honor. Men whose sense of esteem came not from themselves but from their communities had a repeated desire to prove themselves publicly and an extraordinary sensitivity to challenge.[4] Also important to the idea of honor was the notion of chivalry; a man of honor was supposed to protect a woman as an essential part of his household. A third meaning involved racism—especially the desire white men had long shown for physical power over African-American men and sexual power over African-American women. Finally, and most importantly for Southern Rock, the helluvafella tradition also suggested that violence could be necessary. W. J. Cash wrote that the primary goal of the helluvafella cut off from past social institutions was "to stand on his head in a bar, to toss down a pint of raw whiskey in a gulp, to fiddle and dance all night, to bite off the nose or gouge out the eye of a favorite enemy, to fight harder and love harder than the next man, to be known far and wide as a helluvafella."[5] The traditional meanings Southern Rock musicians were redefining had developed in an agricultural, white-supremacist society. What did personal independence, honor, racism, and especially the helluvafella tradition mean for young men long after small farming was a real possibility and shortly after the Civil Rights movement had overturned many of the meanings white supremacy had traditionally held?

The place to begin in discussing the heritage of the male perspective in Southern Rock is country music. Country songs have long tended to be nostalgic about life on the farm. An essential part of that nostalgia was the idealization of the traditional evangelical home. In *Subduing Satan,* I argued that white southern culture in the late nineteenth century displayed a profound tension between a hell-raising aggressiveness located wherever men gathered away from home and an evangelical culture centered in the home and church that stressed harmony, self-control, and the special religious virtues of women. This always shaky tension had grown very difficult to maintain by the early twentieth century, and the lyrics of country music showed men feeling guilty that they could no longer have it both ways. Thus, Hank Williams and his generation changed the home from what they considered an achievable ideal to an idyllic spot of rural purity that they could never reach.[6]

What was new about the helluvafella tradition in Southern Rock? Most of all, it did not exist in a balance with evangelical culture and the idea of a stable home life. Seventies musicians rejected some of the most important ideals of white southern culture. Born well after the period in which family farming was common or even a common memory, Southern Rock musicians did not see the old home as providing a balance for male behavior, or as an ideal to pursue or feel guilty about failing to achieve, or really as an important place at all in gender relations. One of the most dramatic contrasts between the lyrics of Southern Rock and country songs is that the younger musicians had virtually nothing to say about motherhood. Whereas older male country musicians sang endlessly about their mothers as exemplars and teachers of essential, often religious, virtues, Southern Rock musicians did not see southern motherhood as a significant burden or blessing.

One song stands out as such an extraordinary exception that it shows how little interest most Southern Rock musicians had in mothers. Lynyrd Skynyrd's "Simple Man" begins with the image of a child listening at his mother's knee. The mother tries to teach patience, endurance, and low expectations. She hopes her son will not "live too fast," assures him he will "find a woman," and urges him not to forget "There is someone up above." By pairing family and God in a message that came from Momma, the song upheld the old ideal of the religious significance of home life. And by connecting home life to the effort to endure troubles, the song recognized the religious ideals stated in the traditional marriage vow about the need to suffer patiently for the good of the household.

Restraint was not easy. The chorus, in which Momma urged, "And be a simple kind of man," contained some of the most strained singing by lead singer and songwriter Ronnie Van Zant, as he struggled to reach high notes that did not come easily. The strain indicated the gravity of the issues, but above all it suggested the difficulty of trying to be simple. "Simple Man" was an important song because the themes of respect for traditional understandings of simplicity, restraint, religion, home, and motherhood, all of them central to white cultural traditions and to country music, had virtually no other place in Southern Rock.[7]

If the songs of Southern Rock had almost no role for mothers, the musicians had great interest in fathers, both their presence and their absence. In describing their lack of roots, the Allman Brothers Band sang, "My father was a gambler down in Georgia" who, like Duane and Gregg Allman's actual father, "Wound up on the wrong end of a gun."[8] Black Oak Arkansas went even further in describing themselves as cut off from paternal traditions. Whimsically calling a narrator a "Son of a Gun" denied connections to a father and, given the sexual connotations guns carried in some Southern Rock songs, may have reduced a father to nothing more than an instrument of conception. Most importantly, the song announced that the narrator had plans that had nothing to do with the past. Not only did he intend to "whoop it up" outside community disapproval, but the narrator also asked, "Why should I settle down when I'm feeling so young?"[9]

It was Lynyrd Skynyrd whose songs most frequently discussed the lessons taught by fathers and the tensions those lessons caused. "Poison Whiskey" described a father as a street fightin' Cajun who died from the effects of "twenty years of rot gut whiskey." Continuing the theme of the unknown father, the narrator of this song only knew about his father from stories told by relatives. The narrator of "I Never Dreamed" began with the memory that his father always told him never to cry, to love pretty women, and, "Then you'll say good-bye." That lesson contradicted about as thoroughly as possible the lessons Momma taught about being a simple man. Strength meant a man's ability to leave a woman without sadness, the ability to go from woman to woman without worrying what they thought about it, and above all the ability to control his own life. Another Lynyrd Skynyrd song made a similar point about fatherhood. Since Lacy Van Zant, Ronnie's father, was a truck driver, "Truck Drivin' Man" took on particular importance. The song's title character found great freedom in a life characterized by flannel shirts, blue jeans, truck stops, and no supervision. Life on the road also gave the truck drivin' man the freedom to know women all over the country. In singing that "The only time he feels right is when he's rollin'," the song indicated again that the old ideal of home had little meaning.[10]

In 1978 and 1979 Molly Hatchet recorded albums very similar to Lynyrd Skynyrd in issues of fatherhood. In one song the narrator recalled the night his father initiated him into manhood at age seventeen by taking him to a joint called Jukin' City. United by ties to several white southern traditions, father and son got drunk on Jack Daniels, danced to country songs with "two fat mamas," and when the male friends of these women showed up, had to "fight to stay alive." The chorus that referred to going out with the father as "going there with a friend"[11] indicated as clearly as possible that the helluvafella tradition was the male tradition most meaningful in Southern Rock.

If the father in these songs was a whiskey-drinking, street-fighting, truck-driving, wife-betraying, woman-loving-and-leaving kind of southern man, how could the men of Southern Rock rebel against the heritage such a father represented? Rock music has generally rebelled against middle-class conformity, not against hard-drinking truck drivers. The answer seems to be that Southern Rock musicians located their rebellious pose in trying to live up to the helluvafella image and then, most importantly, to go beyond it. Since drunkenness was part of the helluvafella tradition, Southern Rock men giddily proclaimed themselves masters of that tradition. The narrator of a Lynyrd Skynyrd song, who claimed to have "drunk enough whiskey to turn a battleship around," proclaimed himself a "whiskey rock-a-roller" who understood nothing but "women, whiskey and miles of travelin'."[12] ZZ Top loved to announce themselves as "Beer Drinkers and Hell Raisers."[13] Molly Hatchet defined the good life as "wine, women, whiskey, and rock 'n roll," followed by plenty of sleep.[14] The Charlie Daniels Band sang the most outrageous song of all, titled "Whiskey," which began, "Tennessee Bootleg Moonshine Whiskey sure do make a man feel mighty frisky."[15] Album covers frequently depicted musicians celebrating and identifying with the pleasures of alcohol. Most revealing was the front cover of the 1974 *Way Down Yonder* album, which displayed the face of Charlie Daniels on a bottle of Jack Daniels Tennessee Sippin' Whiskey.[16]

Along with identifying with alcohol, Southern Rock musicians tried to build on the helluvafella tradition through numerous references to narcotics. In the mid-1970s marijuana was a frequent subject of humor. Charlie Daniels knew people thought he was crazy because "I get stoned in the afternoon." Daniels frequently joined alcohol and marijuana in joking and perhaps rebellious ways.[17] Far less whimsical were occasional references to heroin and cocaine. Lynyrd Skynyrd sang "The Needle and the Spoon," "Junkie," and "That Smell," all of which ended with messages about the drugs' potential for destruction.[18] Drama came in the suggestion that the singers had looked the worst effects of heroin and cocaine in the face and overcome them. The songs implied that only a strong man could survive such experiences.

The other element of the helluvafella legacy prominent in Southern Rock was the image of the fighter. While some musicians continued the fighting image of their male ancestors, others found ways to challenge or reject that tradition. A positive image of the violence of white southern men was difficult in light of violence against civil rights workers and widespread southern participation in an increasingly unpopular war. The image of the hell-raising drinker was therefore more common than that of the young man ready for a rumble.

It was possible, especially in the early 1970s, for Southern Rock musicians to adopt different forms of opposition to violence. Barefoot Jerry made two surprisingly straightforward statements of the need to modify old standards of combativeness. "Proud to be a redneck," they sang, "But I've changed." Announcing their unashamed identification with southern men, they put together two lines that have rarely been paired. They began, "We'll make peace and lots of love" but concluded that "The South's gonna rise again." They continued, "We don't have to be so doggone mean," choosing instead to be "just good ole country hicks." Here they rejected the fighting tradition for one of a peaceful rural community. It was not unusual for a song in the early 1970s to call for peace and love, but it was rare for such a song to be cast as part of a southern identity. A song by the same group that stated "Blood is not the answer" seemed to address the Vietnam War more than the Civil War.[19] Wet Willie explicitly connected the goal of peace to the legacy of the Civil War. "The war of the States left some scars on us," but southerners now lived in peaceful harmony.[20]

What may be more surprising was an antigun song by Lynyrd Skynyrd, normally one of the most belligerent of the groups. "Saturday Night Special" said that handguns were "made for killin'" and should be thrown "to the bottom of the sea." And if they questioned in one song the right to fight with the weapon of one's choice, in another they questioned conventional reasons for fighting. The narrator of "Gimme Three Steps" was dancing with Linda Lou when an armed and offended man came in "And he was lookin' for you know who." The frightened narrator asked one favor—that the offended man "gimme three steps toward the door." The song defied a long tradition of defending male honor, especially when a woman was involved, in favor of saving oneself. In fact, in the live version of the song, Ronnie Van Zant ad libbed, "I ain't gettin' shot over that cunt."[21] Perhaps running away from a confrontation constituted such a violation of manly traditions of honor and chivalry that the singer wanted to be particularly degrading to a woman in order to reclaim his control over the situation.

At least as strong as the impulse to rebel against the heritage of fighting, however, was the desire to live up to it and surpass it. Many Southern Rock songs rejected peace messages and announced their narrators ready to whip any enemies, especially northerners. Molly Hatchet took the lead in 1978 by challenging "your punks" from New York. "We're bad southern boys and don't you forget us."[22] Like Southern Rock musicians, punk rockers considered themselves angry and rebellious, so Molly Hatchet may have portrayed themselves as more menacing because, as southern white men, they were heirs to a tradition of violence. Such pride in the ability of white southern men to beat up New Yorkers constitutes one of the clearest attempts to uphold the Confederate heritage Charlie Daniels sang about in "The South's Gonna Do It Again."

Other songs, rather than depicting violence as an ideal, simply described the willingness to fight as a central aspect of male life. Lynyrd Skynyrd portrayed in a straightforward way the willingness to fight when challenged. In one combative song titled "You Got That Right," they sang of the need to keep moving, but, when challenged, "Not afraid to fight."[23] Others discussed living by such a code. A dark song by Molly Hatchet mentioned shooting a man in a poker argument. The narrator expressed no remorse, accepting his impending execution because "That's the price you pay."[24] The Charlie Daniels Band sang about escaping after a fight over cheating at cards and then took pride that it took so many policemen "Just to put one coon ass boy in jail."[25]

And if Lynyrd Skynyrd declined one tradition of honor in "Gimme Three Steps," they certainly tried to carry on another definition of honor in "Sweet Home Alabama." This well-known song began as a response to Canadian singer Neil Young's attacks on racism and violence in the South in two songs, "Alabama" and "Southern Man." What Lynyrd Skynyrd upheld instead was not clear, but what they resented was criticism by an outsider. When they reminded "ol' Neil" that "The southern man don't need him around anyhow," they were referring not merely to the title of Young's song but to the tradition of the southern white man who tolerated no challenge or criticism.[26]

Probably the clearest way Southern Rock musicians confronted issues of their heritage and tried to live up to its most confrontational side lay in their reshaping of the image of the cowboy. Historian Bill Malone has described the cowboy as an image both white southern country musicians and their national audience had long found appealing. Malone writes that both cowboys and mountaineers "valued, and presumably embodied, freedom and independence; both were heroic and fearless; both preserved those manly traits that had ensured survival on the frontier and that were distinctive and defining ingredients of American life."[27] Riding a horse would not seem a likely pastime for young men in Macon, Georgia, or Spartanburg, South Carolina, or Tampa, Florida. But becoming a cowboy helped tie Southern Rock musicians to a long tradition of southern musicians. In the cowboy image they could bring together the notion of personal independence with the notions of honor and willingness to fight that were so important in male traditions in the South.

Album covers again displayed the images the musicians wanted to project. Virtually all Southern Rock groups included members who wore cowboy hats. The Charlie Daniels Band repeatedly portrayed themselves as cowboys on the run, often with Charlie wearing the black hat. They rode horses, or they carried saddles, or they carried rifles. The Marshall Tucker Band consistently included on their album covers cowboys, some carrying guns, more of them playing fiddles.[28] While almost all Southern Rock musicians loved the cowboy image, most of them moved away from an older image of a smiling, singing cowboy and turned it in an aggressive, violent direction. Musicians from throughout the South put on long, sinister-looking dusters and became outlaws. One of the most important groups called themselves the Outlaws, and Molly Hatchet described themselves as "Outlaws on the loose runnin', runnin'." Always willing to sing about a fight, that group dwelled on the potential for violence among cowboys. The same song described a horseback cowboy armed with six-guns "Just gettin' back from a trip to hell."[29] Charlie Daniels wrote numerous cowboy songs, most of them involving violence of some kind. In "Billy the Kid," he told the story of the twenty-one-year-old destined to "go down shootin'."[30] Daniels tried to merge the helluvafella tradition with the cowboy heritage in a poem, "To Louis L'Amour and James Bama," that extolled the virtues of stories of "gut-rotting whiskey and Saturday night" along with "pistols and poker and hellacious fights." [31]

Why were gun-toting Texas cowboys so attractive to young white men in the modern South? Why was the cowboy era the only historical period with which the musicians identified? It seems fair to speculate that, beyond how the cowboy image connected them to country musicians, the violence represented by the cowboy was an appealingly safe form of violence for the late 1960s and 1970s. In their imaginations, the West represented a region where white men proved their worth to each other. By identifying with the cowboy, they could forget the most memorable recent scenes of white men doing state-sanctioned violence to African-American men, women, and children and replace them with images of noble white men protecting their honor through courageous individual action. The cowboy image also helped reconcile some of the potential tensions in the ideas Southern Rock musicians held about violence. While some songs embraced a good fight as part of the traditions of honor and the helluvafella and others rejected violence altogether or at least some of the traditional reasons for it, almost all of the groups could identify themselves as cowboys.

Along with their respect for supposedly noble violence, the musicians identified with the freedom that came from the mobility of the cowboy. Vital to the tradition white men in the South liked to claim as theirs was the notion that they controlled their lives far more than men in the urban and urbanizing Northeast. The cowboy seemed, as Bill Malone suggests, to embody this freedom extraordinarily well. Daniels's "Saddle Tramp" admired the cowboy who could come and go with "no strings on your bootheels or your heart." [32] The chorus of Molly Hatchet's "Gunsmoke" ended, "I grabbed my horse and run." [33] The Marshall Tucker Band described "This Ol' Cowboy" as a man ready to "hit the road again." [34]

Whether within the cowboy tradition or not, many of the songs that defined Southern Rock had to do with ramblin'. The most loved song of the movement was Lynyrd Skynyrd's "Free Bird," which described the need to keep moving because "There's too many places I've gotta see." [35] The Allman Brothers Band sang "Ramblin' Man," Black Oak Arkansas sang "Ramblin' Gamblin' Man," and the Marshall Tucker Band sang "Ramblin'." [36]

Is it possible that ramblin' was part of a southern male heritage?

Since so many white southerners had traditionally seen their identities as embedded in their homes and communities, were ramblin' men by necessity cut off from the influence of their fathers? It should be no surprise that Southern Rock musicians, like popular musicians from traveling minstrels to Bruce Springsteen, sang a great deal about moving. Country music had its share of ramblers, but they typically wanted to ramble back toward a home, and most road songs had a tragic quality. Hank Williams is the best example of a singer who believed his "life of sin" left him alone "On the lost highway." [37] Williams typically viewed the road as leading him away from the security and morality of home. He and most country musicians clung to an ideal of personal independence rooted in the household and the farm. White southerners' notions of freedom had derived from the combined effects of widespread availability of land with the freedom *not* to work as slaves and their descendants. By the time of the country music era, the independence of the landowning farmer was becoming a memory, and while some clung to it through nostalgia, others like Hank Williams blamed themselves for how far their lives away from the farm had taken them from the virtues they associated with home life.

The question for the young men of Southern Rock was how to reinterpret a tradition that already emphasized motion. If Ronnie Van Zant honored the mobility of his truck drivin' father, could he also rebel against that tradition? The musicians found their answer not in rejecting those traditions but in going beyond them. If other southern musicians had been mobile, Southern Rock musicians claimed they never stopped moving. They repeatedly sang that they were born into life on the road and, furthermore, that ramblin' was a central part of their identities. Personal independence lay not at the end of the road but on the road itself. Not cut off from rural and evangelical norms by ramblin', they were born ramblin', they could not help it, and perhaps most importantly, they liked it that way. The narrator of a ZZ Top song considered himself his "Papa's son" because "When I hit the ground I was on the run." [38] The Allman Brothers Band made the same point. The narrator, born in a Greyhound Bus, decides "Lord, I was born a ramblin' man." [39] Lynyrd Skynyrd continued the theme, "Guess I was born with a travelin' bone." [40] The Outlaws added an unusual twist in which the narrator first left home at age four.[41]

Most of the ramblin' of Southern Rock was not merely necessary; it was exciting. Life was best, a wide range of songs proclaimed, on the road. Southern Rock thus defied the old white southern fascination with traditions rooted in specific places; as the Outlaws asserted, "My home is on my back."[42] Being on the road, for Lynyrd Skynyrd, was "The only time that I'm satisfied."[43] The road that had represented a threat to security to earlier generations now represented chances for excitement. Molly Hatchet claimed they were proud to be "flirtin' with disaster" by "travelin' down the road." They liked being in charge of their lives no matter how much risk and surprise they encountered as ramblin' men.[44]

A definition of personal independence as free movement marked a dramatic break in the culture of white southerners. Home life or farm life was for the Southern Rock generation neither agrarian ideal nor country music idyll. Freedom meant the ability to hit the road.

Such a definition of freedom had enormous implications for the ideal Southern Rock held up for relations between men and women. In most country music, a good woman waited at the end of the road, but in Southern Rock, the women who mattered most were those the men met while ramblin'. The Outlaws played with that tradition in the line "I'll always love the girl next door" as long as "every place is home."[45] For Lynyrd Skynyrd, it was possible to have "100 women or more" only because "there's no place I call home."[46] If the definition of personal independence meant not only abandonment of the old home but also freedom from lasting commitments to women, Southern Rock had moved dramatically from the old belief that the household set standards for proper male behavior.

Ronnie Van Zant of Lynyrd Skynyrd wrote several songs that delighted in shunning traditional standards of male responsibilities to women. "What's Your Name" was the question he repeatedly asked a woman who spent the night with him in Boise, Idaho. He got her a taxi home and hoped to see her the next time the band came to town. "I Ain't the One" denied that he was the father of a child by telling his accuser he had never hurt her because he "Never pulled my gun." By equating sex with firing a pistol, this proudly misogynist metaphor suggested that the act of creating a child could in fact be an act of destruction. In another sexual metaphor about wanting freedom from ties to women, the narrator claimed to have a "travelin' bone"—a metaphor that suggested frequent sex with numerous women on the road. "Gimme Three Steps" took pleasure in dancing with a woman who had an angry boyfriend and living to tell about it.[47] In all of these ways the songs claimed that men on the road could get away with almost anything.

Many of the most memorable songs explained that since men were born to be ramblin', women should not be troubled when men left them. The Allman Brothers Band established this precedent when a narrator told a woman that he could not stay with her because "I was born a ramblin' man." [48] The Marshall Tucker Band made the same point. The narrator of "Heard it in a Love Song" said he loved a woman but simply had to leave her because "I was born a wrangler and a rounder" and expected he would always stay that way. In the eyes of the men of Southern Rock, women could not join men on the road. The narrator wished a woman could join him, "But I don't need a woman taggin' along." [49] In most of the songs it was impossible for a man to have a relationship with one woman and still consider himself free. In fact, a significant part of the definition of freedom was freedom from a permanent relationship.

It should come as little surprise that Southern Rock men did not offer women the same freedoms they expected to enjoy. When a woman rejected a man, a Lynyrd Skynyrd song suggested, a man should retaliate against her, possibly with violence. The narrator snarled about the "Cheatin' Woman" who "loved every man with pants on." He promised, "I'm gonna shoot you and end your world" so she would stop bothering "poor me." [50] Since white southern culture in general and country music in particular had long upheld a double standard for proper behavior for men and women, the song was most important in rejecting any suggestions of chivalry. One might have expected the narrator to see it as his duty to protect his household or even a cheatin' woman by killing male rivals, but the song instead took pride in rejecting the tradition of protecting women.

The most popular Southern Rock song, and the answer to the concert question, "What song is it you want to hear?" was "Free Bird" by Lynyrd Skynyrd. This 1973 song provided the most emphatic definition of freedom as the ability to ramble and not to stay with a particular woman. The narrator took the blame for leaving but once again simply had to leave to be true to his own nature. Not wanting to be cruel, he said they shared a "sweet love" and asked her, "please don't take it so badly." Above all, the song repeated its main theme that "This bird will never change." Freedom meant the freedom to avoid ties to home or, quite likely, to anything permanent except the unchanging desire to keep moving. The most memorable part of "Free Bird" consists of a long series of soaring solos by the group's three guitarists. By moving from a repetitive and mournful vocal section to a faster, trainlike rhythm with room for long paired solos, all building to a piano-and-guitar crescendo at the song's end, the structure of the song suggests a movement from structure and repetition to the freedom that was the theme of the song.[51]

To be sure, some Southern Rock songs claimed to long for a home at the end of the road—a home complete with a secure relationship with one woman. Not all women in Southern Rock songs were either passing partners for great sex or irritating drains on men's time. However, most of the musicians were reluctant to write and sing conventional love songs; more than any other song, it was "Free Bird" that defined Southern Rock's perspective on relations between men and women.

Much of the freedom these young men felt came in choosing which southern heritages they could consider meaningful. If Southern Rock musicians questioned and redefined many of the cultural ideals of country music, they found the blues tradition in some ways more meaningful and more appealing. Music historians have shown how thoroughly African musical traditions influenced the music of white southerners, and it is obvious that white musicians in the 1950s adapted or stole many of the rhythms or lyrical themes of African-American rhythm and blues. But Southern Rock showed the influence of African-American blues more directly and openly than previous forms of music created by white southerners. The Allman Brothers Band, the first group in the Southern Rock movement, was a blues band in both the songs it played and the way it played them. The Allman Brothers Band or Duane Allman in other settings recorded blues songs by Elmore James, Muddy Waters, Willie Dixon, B. B. King, and Sonny Boy Williamson. Their own songs showed a clear blues perspective as well, with the raspy vocals of Gregg Allman and the long blues improvisations of Duane Allman and Dickey Betts. White professional musicians in the South had played with black musicians in the past, but it was significant that a group calling themselves a band of brothers consisted of five white men and one black man, percussionist Jai Johanny Johanson.

The importance of the blues extended far beyond the Allman Brothers Band. The Allmans had profound effects on the groups that followed, possibly freeing many white southerners to attempt blues rhythms and long, wailing guitar solos and also to acknowledge the blues as part of a southern heritage they found meaningful. Most of the young musicians found ways to show their debt to blues players who influenced them. "Dixie Rock," a song Wet Willie recorded in 1975, described Southern Rock as having "a real good beat and a whole lotta soul" as well as "some blues on a black guitar." [52] ZZ Top recorded a song about southern music that mentioned Chicago, New Orleans, and Mississippi and placed themselves in a biracial tradition by paying tribute to both Muddy Waters and Elvis Presley. [53] In "The Ballad of Curtis Lowe," Lynyrd Skynyrd honored an old blues man who died poor and almost friendless, but the narrator was proud to have learned from "the greatest picker who ever played the blues." [54]

Embracing the blues had significant implications for ideas about manhood and gender relations. Whereas the country music perspective had traditionally stressed the ideal of harmony in the evangelical home even if it bemoaned the impossibility of satisfying that ideal, the blues perspective emphasized individual problems and pleasures without reference to any clear ideal. At their best, the blues stressed honest recognition of problems to endure and perhaps to overcome. At their worst, men's blues boasted about the ability to attract and have sexual and perhaps economic power over several women without having responsibilities to any of them. In his analysis of traditional blues lyrics, Lawrence Levine argues that blues songs recognized that male-female relations were usually difficult and painful, that pleasures were to be valued no matter how impermanent they were, that mobility was often both necessary and valuable, and that the individual and not the household was the basic unit of human experience and satisfaction. [55] That approach to gender relations sounds a good deal like the perspective of the Southern Rock movement, and the ramblin' blues man cut off from his community was an appealingly dramatic image to many young white men, including many in the South. This is not to attribute the misogynist tendencies of so many Southern Rock songs to the heritage of the blues. Rather, it points out that young white men who were finding freedom in ignoring or rejecting some of the traditions of white southern culture were sometimes looking instead to a tradition of African-American music.

It suggests as well that the young white men who played Southern Rock were finding ties of gender between white and black men more meaningful in some ways than ties of race between white men and women. One of Levine's most intriguing arguments shows how the often painful realism of the blues rejected the idealism of Tin Pan Alley love songs that held up a standard for romantic love that was too high for any couple to reach. Southern Rock showed the same distrust of the ideals of conventional love songs. As the Marshall Tucker Band sang, if they heard something in a love song, it "must be wrong." [56] Perhaps the clearest example of adopting a blues approach to the meanings of home showed in the Allman Brothers Band's "Leave My Blues at Home." [57] In the country tradition, depression and problems lurked on the road, but in Southern Rock, as in the blues, one could escape by leaving them at home.

In redefining male traditions, Southern Rock musicians cut themselves off from most of the community ties that had given those traditions meaning. The value of personal independence had traditionally referred to the ability of a man to keep his household free from depending on anyone else. The helluvafella had traditionally existed in counterbalance with the evangelical ideal; the man who raised hell away from home on Saturday night had generally respected the evangelical home and church on Sunday morning. The notion of honor depended on community approval and disapproval of a wide array of male activities and claimed it was manly to protect the family. The goal of racial control connected white men to a community of white men willing to use violence. In the culture of white southerners, fighting, most obviously in the Confederate army, carried the tradition of a community crusade to keep households independent, honors unchallenged, and black men in their place.

Southern Rock reformulated those meanings in very individualistic ways. Independence now meant the freedom to move around without answering to anyone—parents, employers, or especially women. The helluvafella tradition no longer existed in a balance with religious values. Nor did it cause significant guilt. Men claimed to drink more than ever and either to fight more than past men or to give up the fighting tradition altogether. The tradition of honor, no longer an elaborate code of behavior, meant only that individuals would not tolerate criticism, and the tradition of doing honor to women by protecting them and fighting to protect the integrity of the family meant nothing at all. And Southern Rock generally ignored the racist tradition except to claim that they admired the blues tradition and to suggest that the forms of violence they respected were distant in time and place from recent forms of violence.

With the old home carrying few positive meanings, the tradition of placing ultimate value in family life underwent dramatic transformation. But rather than discarding entirely the notion of family, the men of Southern Rock upheld the notion of brotherhood as an ideal worth celebrating.[58] In brotherhood they found an ideal that could continue the traditional fascinations with manhood and family but that did not raise the problems young men saw in many of those traditional meanings. Brotherhood showed in many ways, in album covers that lined up groups of five, six, or eight men in poses that suggested close friendship and defiance to authority, in the Allman Brothers Band's dedication of an album "To a brother," after the death of bass player Berry Oakley,[59] in an Allman Brothers Band album and song titled "Brothers of the Road,"[60] and in the concluding line of a Lynyrd Skynyrd song, "Cause your friend Lord is the most important thing."[61] The narrator of Lynyrd Skynyrd's "Don't Ask Me No Questions" returned home after weeks on the road and found irritating his old friends' desire to interrogate him about the life of a rock star. He told people to stay away unless they wanted "to talk fishin'."[62] Going home, then, offered not a hope for a reunion with a woman or larger family but, at its best, a reunion of male friends.

Probably the most important aspect of brotherhood the musicians celebrated lay in the nature of the music itself. Most of the bands were song-writing, creative units instead of groups of musicians playing behind a leader, and the Allman Brothers Band set a standard for extraordinarily long group improvisations new to white southerners. Men in the groups created their music together, and in that act of shared creation found an important sense of brotherhood. One of the most aggressively masculine displays of brotherhood showed in these shared improvisations during concerts. When all of a group's several guitar players lined up closely on stage, playing together with motions that suggested sexual bravado, with hips thrusting toward the audience or each other, and perhaps gunfire with their guitars pointing toward the audience, Southern Rock was managing to combine several of what the musicians considered the finest things about southern manhood—the possibility of sex and violence without consequences, loud, blues-inspired guitar improvisation, and close male friendship. For all of the musicians' desire to be part of a southern heritage, here was a new definition of family, along with older definitions of manhood.

Notes

1. Charlie Daniels Band, "The South's Gonna Do It Again," *Fire on the Mountain,* Kama Sutra KSBS-2603.

2. On efforts of recent white southerners to construct a regional identity, see George Brown Tindall, *The Ethnic Southerners* (Baton Rouge: Louisiana State Univ. Press, 1976); John Shelton Reed, *One South: An Ethnic Approach to Regional Culture* (Baton Rouge: Louisiana State Univ. Press, 1982).

3. Lynyrd Skynyrd, "Sweet Home Alabama," *Gold and Platinum,* MCA MCAD2-6898.

4. Bertram Wyatt-Brown, *Southern Honor: Ethics and Behavior in the Old South* (New York: Oxford Univ. Press, 1982); Steven M. Stowe, *Intimacy and Power in the Old South: Ritual in the Lives of the Planters* (Baltimore: Johns Hopkins Univ. Press, 1987); Kenneth S. Greenberg, *Honor and Slavery: Lies, Duels, Noses, Masks, Dressing as a Woman, Gifts, Strangers, Death, Humanitarianism, Slave Rebellions, the Proslavery Argument, Baseball, Hunting, and Gambling in the Old South* (Princeton: Princeton Univ. Press, 1996).

5. W. J. Cash, *The Mind of the South* (New York: Vintage, 1941), 52. See also Elliott J. Gorn, " 'Gouge and Bite, Pull Hair and Scratch': The Social Significance of Fighting in the Southern Backcountry," *American Historical Review* 90 (1985): 18–43.

6. Ted Ownby, *Subduing Satan: Religion, Recreation, and Manhood in the Rural South, 1865–1920* (Chapel Hill: Univ. of North Carolina Press, 1990). On the country music perspective, see Bill C. Malone, *Country Music U.S.A.,* rev. ed. (Austin: Univ. of Texas Press, 1985); Cecilia Tichi, *High Lonesome: The American Culture of Country Music* (Chapel Hill: Univ. of North Carolina Press, 1994).

7. Lynyrd Skynyrd, "Simple Man," *Gold and Platinum.*

8. Allman Brothers Band, "Ramblin' Man," *Brothers and Sisters,* Polydor CPN-0111.

9. Black Oak Arkansas, "Son of a Gun," *Best of Black Oak Arkansas,* ATCO SO36-150.

10. Lynyrd Skynyrd, "Poison Whiskey," *Gold and Platinum;* "I Never Dreamed," *Lynyrd Skynyrd,* MCAC 10790; "Truck Drivin' Man," *Lynyrd Skynyrd's Greatest Hits,* MCA D-42293.

11. Molly Hatchet, "Jukin' City," *Flirtin' with Disaster,* Epic JE 36110.

12. Lynyrd Skynyrd, "Gimme Back My Bullets" and "Whiskey Rock-a-Roller," *Gold and Platinum.*

13. ZZ Top, "Beer Drinkers & Hell Raisers," *Tres Hombres,* London XPS 631.

14. Molly Hatchet, "Let the Good Times Roll," *Flirtin' with Disaster.*

15. Charlie Daniels Band, "Whiskey," *Way Down Yonder,* Kama Sutra KSBS-2076.

16. Charlie Daniels Band, *Way Down Yonder.* Other albums with alcohol on the covers include *Dickey Betts and Great Southern,* Arista AL 4123; *The Outlaws,* Arista AL 4042; Wet Willie, *Keep On Smilin',* CP-0128.

17. Charlie Daniels Band, "Long Haired Country Boy," *Fire on the Mountain,* Kama Sutra KSBS 2603. For other examples see Daniels, "Texas," *Nightrider,* Kama Sutra 0698; "Whiskey" and "Looking for Mary Jane," *Way Down Yonder.*

18. Lynyrd Skynyrd, "The Needle and the Spoon," "Junkie," and "That Smell," *Lynyrd Skynyrd.*

19. Barefoot Jerry, "I'm Proud to be a Redneck" and "Blood Is Not the Answer," *Barefoot Jerry's Grocery,* Monument AL 33910.

20. Wet Willie, "Spanish Moss," *Keep On Smilin'.*

21. Lynyrd Skynyrd, "Saturday Night Special" and "Gimme Three Steps," *Gold and Platinum.*

22. Molly Hatchet, "Big Apple," *Molly Hatchet,* Epic PET 35347.

23. Lynyrd Skynyrd, "You Got That Right," *Gold and Platinum.*

24. Molly Hatchet, "The Price You Pay," *Molly Hatchet.*

25. Charlie Daniels Band, "Trudy," *Fire on the Mountain.* A "coon ass" is a slang expression for a Cajun.

26. Lynyrd Skynyrd, "Sweet Home Alabama," *Gold and Platinum.*

27. Bill C. Malone, *Singing Cowboys and Musical Mountaineers: Southern Culture and the Roots of Country Music* (Athens: Univ. of Georgia Press, 1993), 73–74.

28. Albums include Charlie Daniels Band, *Nightrider, Saddle Tramp,* Epic PE 34150, and *High Lonesome;* Marshall Tucker Band, *Long Hard Ride,* Capricorn CP 0170; *The Marshall Tucker Band,* Capricorn CPN-0112; *Searchin' for a Rainbow,* Capricorn CP-0161.

29. Molly Hatchet, "Bounty Hunter," *Molly Hatchet;* "Gunsmoke," *Flirtin' with Disaster.*

30. Charlie Daniels Band, "Billy the Kid," *High Lonesome.*

31. Charlie Daniels, "To Louis L'Amour and James Bama," poem on album cover of *High Lonesome.*

32. Charlie Daniels Band, "Saddle Tramp," *Saddle Tramp.*

33. Molly Hatchet, "Gunsmoke," *Flirtin' with Disaster.*

34. Marshall Tucker Band, "This Ol' Cowboy," *Where We All Belong,* Capricorn 2C-0145.

35. Lynyrd Skynyrd, "Free Bird," *Gold and Platinum.*

36. Allman Brothers Band, "Ramblin' Man," *Brothers and Sisters;* Black Oak Arkansas, "Ramblin' Gamblin' Man," *Balls o' Fire;* Marshall Tucker Band, "Ramblin'," *Where We All Belong.*

37. Hank Williams, "Lost Highway," *40 Greatest Hits,* Polydor 821 233-2.

38. ZZ Top, "Just Got Paid," *Rio Grande Mud,* Warner Brothers BSK 3269.

39. Allman Brothers Band, "Ramblin' Man," *Brothers and Sisters.*

40. Lynyrd Skynyrd, "You Got That Right," *Gold and Platinum.*

41. The Outlaws, "Freeborn Man," *Bring It Back Alive,* Arista AL8300.

42. Ibid.

43. Lynyrd Skynyrd, "Whiskey Rock-a-Roller," *Gold and Platinum.*

44. Molly Hatchet, "Flirtin' with Disaster," *Flirtin' with Disaster.*

45. The Outlaws, "Freeborn Man," *Bring It Back Alive.*

46. Lynyrd Skynyrd, "Whiskey Rock-a-Roller," *Gold and Platinum.*

47. Lynyrd Skynyrd, "What's Your Name," "I Ain't the One," "You Got That Right," and "Gimme Three Steps," *Gold and Platinum.*

48. Allman Brothers Band, "Ramblin' Man," *Brothers and Sisters.*

49. Marshall Tucker Band, "Heard It in a Love Song," *Carolina Dreams,* AJK Music, A 780–4.

50. Lynyrd Skynyrd, "Cheatin' Woman," *Nuthin' Fancy,* MCA-37069.

51. Lynyrd Skynyrd, "Free Bird," *Gold and Platinum.*

52. Wet Willie, "Dixie Rock," *Dixie Rock,* Capricorn CP-0149.

53. ZZ Top, "Jesus Just Left Chicago," *Tres Hombres.*

54. Lynyrd Skynyrd, "The Ballad of Curtis Lowe," *Lynyrd Skynyrd.*

55. Lawrence W. Levine, *Black Culture and Black Consciousness: Afro-American Folk Thought from Slavery to Freedom* (New York: Oxford Univ. Press, 1977), 190–297.

56. Marshall Tucker Band, "Heard It in a Love Song," *Carolina Dreams.*

57. Allman Brothers Band, "Leave My Blues at Home," *Brothers and Sisters.*

58. For recent scholarship on friendships among men, see Peter Nardi, ed., *Men's Friendships* (Newbury Park, Calif.: Sage, 1992).

59. Liner notes to Allman Brothers Band, *Brothers and Sisters.*

60. Allman Brothers Band, "Brothers of the Road," *Brothers of the Road,* Arista AL 9564.

61. Lynyrd Skynyrd, "Am I Losin'," *Nuthin' Fancy.*

62. Lynyrd Skynyrd, "Don't Ask Me No Questions," *Lynyrd Skynyrd.*

Reading Family Matters

Deborah E. McDowell

*Possibly the real determinants of interpretation are the literary and
cultural assumptions of particular communities in history.*
— Wallace Martin, *Recent Theories of Narrative*

They were a family somehow and he was not the head of it.
— Toni Morrison, *Beloved*

It is not late-breaking news that literary criticism is another form of
storytelling, of mythmaking. Nor is it news that literary texts take
shape in the minds of readers and critics who form disparate interpretive communities.[1] These communities are held together by shared assumptions, values, and desires that influence if not determine *what* they
see when they read and *how* they receive and represent what they read.
Or, to borrow from Mary Louise Pratt, reading and reception are "socially and ideologically-determined process[es]."[2] I use these commonplace insights as departure points in a brief meditation on one
interpretive community—primarily male—and its reading and reception of a group of contemporary black female writers, those published
since the 1970s. More specifically, I focus on the controversial and adhesive charge surrounding their work—that it portrays black males in
an "unflinchingly candid and often negative manner" as "thieves, sadists, rapists, and ne'er-do-wells."[3]

Let me start with some preliminary observations. First, this debate
has been waged primarily in the popular, white, East Coast literary
media—the *New York Times Book Review, New York Review of
Books, New York Times Magazine*—though it has also spread to academic journals and scholarly collections. Second, for all its intensity,

the debate has centered primarily on a very small sample of writers: Toni Morrison, Gayl Jones, Ntozake Shange, and, most frequently, Alice Walker. Finally, but perhaps most importantly, it has tended to polarize (though not neatly) along gender lines. With few exceptions, female readers see an implicit affirmation of *black women,* while males see a programmatic assault on black men, though I grant that these two responses are not mutually exclusive.[4] This tendency has been reflected especially in responses to and reviews of Alice Walker's *The Color Purple,* though most have centered disproportionately and inappropriately on Steven Spielberg's film adaptation of the novel.[5]

Why focus on a debate that seems to have outlived its interest and usefulness? Why focus, especially, since the controversy has in no way affected the reputations of the writers in question? Why spend time picking apart straw men whose arguments are so easily discredited? Why? Because for all their questionable arguments, from the perspective of readers more informed, these are men whose judgments help to influence the masses of readers largely untutored in African-American literature, who take their cues of what and how to read from the *New York Times Book Review, New York Review of Books,* and other organs of the literary establishment. As Richard Ohmann notes, the *Times Book Review* has "several times the audience of any other literary periodical" in the United States, a circulation that grants it a powerful and prestigious role in mediating the terms by which the writers and writings it selects will be received and understood. Further, such periodicals work with their counterparts—the college classroom and academic journal—and together they become, Ohmann adds, "the final arbiters of literary merit and even of survival."[6] The route Ohmann traces from prestigious literary journal to academic journal to college classroom to literary survival is surely not so direct, but it is useful nonetheless for mapping some of the salient points and problems of this debate. Finally, to borrow from Cathy Davidson, there is an "unequal distribution of story time" in this debate.[7] Mainly we see men telling *their* stories about the writings of black women, but we seldom get a counterresponse from a woman. While I do not presume to resolve the tensions on either side, I think that the debate over contemporary writings by black women might profit from an attempt to uncover and suggest something of what is fundamentally at issue and at stake here.

Lest what follows be read as the critical companion of the alleged fictional attack on black men, let me rush to point out that what fol-

lows is no composite portrait of *the* black male reader. Because all readers experience and express complex and often contradictory positions,
it is naive to suggest that any readership, male or female, can be so
simply abstracted. It is possible and necessary, however, even despite
dangers and limitations of a different order, to historicize readers, to
refer, after Paul Smith, "to specific modes of production, to definite
societies at historically specific moments and conjunctures."[8] That is
my modest attempt here.

I leave aside for the moment speculations about why the most influential literary publications tend mainly to employ black men to review and comment on the literature of black women and speculations
about whose interests are served in this debate. While I am interested
in these critical questions, I am equally interested in what this debate
illuminates about the inflections of gendered ideologies in the reading
process.[9] As Maureen Quilligan rightly argues, "To pose questions
about the gender of the reader is to pose questions that open the texts'
relations to the political arrangements of their audiences."[10] The relation between this specific group of readers and the texts they review
might be seen as the product of certain political arrangements. One
could argue, for example, that the shifting power relations between
black men and women in the literary sphere inform and partly explain
the terms of this controversy, terms defined mainly by black men.

If this debate is but part of the design of a larger pattern, it is useful to
trace it, if only telescopically. Actually, this is the second round of a
debate sparked in 1976 by the blockbuster success of Ntozake Shange's
choreopoem *for colored girls who have considered suicide when the
rainbow is enuf.* It spread with the publication of Michele Wallace's
Black Macho and the Myth of the Superwoman (1980).[11] These two
works were the subject of widespread and acrimonious debate from
many sectors of the black community. Vernon Jarret of the *Chicago
Defender* likened *for colored girls* to the pro–Ku Klux Klan film *Birth
of a Nation* and dismissed it as "a degrading treatment of the black
male" and "a mockery of the black family."[12] Perhaps the most controversial statement about Shange and Wallace, however, was an article by
Robert Staples, "The Myth of Black Macho: A Response to Angry
Black Feminists," published in the *Black Scholar* in 1979. Identified
significantly as "the noted *sociologist* on black sex roles," Staples reflects in his essay a tendency in the current debate (as in most discus-

sions of African-American literature) to read literature in terms that are overwhelmingly sociological.[13]

Staples argues that Shange and Wallace were rewarded for their "diatribes against black men," charging *for colored girls* with whetting black women's "collective appetite for black male blood." He attributes their rage, which "happily married women" lack, to "pent up frustrations which need release." And he sympathizes with the black male need for power in the only two institutions left to black control: the church and the family. During the 1960s, Staples continues, "there was a general consensus—among men and women—that black men would hold the leadership positions in the movement." Because "black women had held up their men far too long, it was time for the men to take charge." But as those like Shange and Wallace came under the powerful sway of the white feminist movement, he continues, they unleashed the anger black women had always borne silently. For witnessing this anger, he concludes, they were promoted and rewarded by the white media.[14]

A la Freud, I categorize this story that Staples tells as a family romance, defined by Janet Beizer as the "attempt to rewrite origins, to replace the unsatisfactory fragments of a . . . past by a totalizing fiction" that recuperates loss and fulfills desire.[15] This family romance is deromanticized in writings by the greater majority of black women. Text meets countertext, and the "confrontation" might be described, to borrow from Christine Froula, as between the "daughter's story and the father's law." Froula argues compellingly that "the relations of literary daughters and fathers resemble . . . the model . . . describ[ing] the family situation of incest victims: a dominating, authoritarian father; an absent, ill, or complicitous mother; and a daughter who [is] prohibited by her father from speaking about abuse."[16] Not surprisingly, it is for narrating, for representing male abuses within "the family," that contemporary black women are most roundly criticized in the family plots that follow. Though this narrative of the family romance inserted itself most aggressively in the discourse of the 1960s, this story of the Black Family, cum Black Community headed by the Black Male who does battle with an oppressive White world, continues to be told, though in ever more subtle variations. In Staples's version, as in the other essays discussed here, the rupture in the unified community, the haven against white racism, is the result of the white woman offering the fruit of feminist knowledge.[17]

While his story has a subtlety that Staples's lacks, David Bradley's enlists the same rhetoric of family to argue that "Alice Walker has a high level of enmity toward black men." In "Telling the Black Woman's Story," published in the *New York Times Magazine* in 1984, Bradley sets out to explain this enmity through pop psychobiography, tracing Walker's antagonism toward black men to a childhood accident when her brother shot her with a BB gun. "After that accident," Bradley explains, "she felt her family had failed her," specifically her father.[18]

Philip Royster goes Bradley one better to argue, in an obvious riff on her famous essay, that Walker "may be in search of not so much our mother's gardens as our fathers' protecting arms." Royster reads all of her fiction as an example of Walker's desire "to be the darling of older men and her bitterness toward younger ones." He compares her work to Morrison's in which "if a woman learns to be a daughter, then she will be able to be a wife to a black man and a mother to black children and a nurturer and preserver of black people."[19] Just what work by Morrison he has in mind I am not sure, since so much of Morrison's work features what Susan Willis calls "three-women households" that do not permit "male domination to be the determining principle for living and working relationships of the group."[20] The epigraph from *Beloved* alludes to another of these three-women households: "They were a family somehow and he was not the head of it."

Apart from their attempt to psychoanalyze Walker, using the language of family, the essays by Bradley and Royster reach a common conclusion and judgment: Walker's involvement with feminism has placed her outside the family of the larger black "community." In Bradley's essay there are repeated references to Gloria Steinem, feminism, and *Ms.* magazine, a world he describes as a "steam-driven meat grinder, and [Walker] the tenderest of meat."[21] Royster would like to see her escape the meat grinder, would like to welcome Walker back to what he calls "the extended family," the "unity of the tribe," but on one condition: she, along with other black women, "may have to feel a greater loyalty towards black men . . . than towards women throughout the world."[22]

Mel Watkins offers another variety of a domestic story transplanted in critical soil. His much-discussed "Sexism, Racism, and Black Women Writers" appeared in the June 1986 issue of the *New York Times Book Review.* He continues the charge that black women writers "have chosen black men as a target" of attack. In so doing, they "have set themselves outside a tradition that is nearly as old as black American literature itself." They have broken an "unspoken but almost universally accepted covenant among black writers" "to present positive images of blacks."[23]

In Watkins's version of the family romance, African-American literary history is written in a way that emphasizes family unity. Here we have a family of *writers* who were unified until contemporary black women decided, in Watkins's words, that "sexism is more oppressive than racism." In his abridged new literary history the ancestral keepers of the tradition are William Wells Brown, W. E. B. Du Bois, James Weldon Johnson, and Richard Wright, all of whom shared a commitment to "establishing humane, positive images of blacks." Though a negative character, according to Watkins, even Bigger Thomas "is presented within a context," absent in black women's writings, that "elucidates the social or psychological circumstances that motivate" Bigger.[24] Partially agreed. How else could the reader of any gender absorb Bigger's enjoyment of the "agony" he inflicts on his girlfriend Bessie? He enjoys "seeing and feeling the worth of himself in her bewildered desperation." And after he bludgeons her to death with a brick and throws her body down the airshaft, it occurs to him that he has done a "dumb thing"—"throwing her away with all that money in her pocket."[25]

I cite this passage not to take the cheap route of tit for tat but to suggest something about the critical double standard that glosses over the representation of violence, rape, and battering in Richard Wright's work and installs him in a "family portrait" of black writers but highlights that representation in *The Bluest Eye, The Third Life of Grange Copeland,* and *The Color Purple* to justify "disinheritance." Watkins's literary history conforms strikingly to what Marilyn Butler describes in her essay "Against Tradition: The Case for a Particularized Literary Method." Butler argues forcefully that "traditions are features of all regularized practices in all societies, for they are a basic tool of selecting and ordering the past in order to validate activities and people in the present. The literary critic calls on tradition when he draws up a genealogy or family tree of writers. . . . Transmission down the line is usually described as easy and harmonious, though there is often a gap, which tends to occur near to the present day."[26] The gap in Watkins's family tree of writers is created by the contemporary black *feminist* writers who are the subject of his essay.

Watkins's rhetoric of boundaries, of public speech about private matters, figures as well in Darryl Pinckney's essay "Black Victims, Black

Villains," which appeared in 1987 in the *New York Review of Books*. Following its appearance, I concluded that Pinckney's essay was the winter season's family narrative and Watkins's the summer season's, in this open season on contemporary black women writers in the establishment literary media.

Pinckney attempts a joint review of Walker's *The Color Purple*, Spielberg's film adaptation, and Ishmael Reed's novel *Reckless Eyeballing*. Why it was published in the first place is unclear, since *The Color Purple* had already been reviewed in *NYRB* along with Reed's novel *The Terrible Twos*.[27] Pinckney repeats this media match featuring Reed and Walker, but with a new twist on the family plot. This time it is the black male locked outside the family fold, and, borrowing from Morrison's *The Bluest Eye*, "his own kin had done it."

The first part of the three-part essay reads *The Color Purple*, book and film, as stories of excessive violence that present black women as the helpless victims of brutal black men. Part 2 briefly reviews *Reckless Eyeballing*, after a disproportionately long preface anatomizing the deterioration of the civil rights movement and the simultaneous rise of U.S. feminism. This shift "had a strong effect on Afro-American literature," Pinckney argues. "Black women writers seemed to find their voices and audiences," while "black men seemed to lose theirs." One such loser is Ishmael Reed, a thinly disguised Ian Ball in *Reckless Eyeballing*. Ball, a black playwright, has been "sexlisted" for not writing according to the feminist line and may well be the Flower Phantom who shaves the heads of black women whom he believes to be "collaborating with the enemies of black men."[28] Pinckney calls this subplot "a little nasty" and rushes to quote a long passage from the novel describing such a collaboration.

In part 3 Pinckney returns to *The Color Purple* and the Walker-Spielberg connection and links the work with other "highly insular stories" told by Hurston, Morrison, and Gayl Jones in which the white world has disappeared and with it the reason for the "struggling black families" whose stories these novels tell. This structuring should not go unnoticed, for it cleverly and subtly replicates Pinckney's argument. His review of Reed has been compressed and eclipsed, veritably sandwiched between Walker and Spielberg. The victims and villains of part 1 trade places in part 2, as black males become the victims of a partnership between Alice Walker and Steven Spielberg, a black woman and a white man. Their power to eliminate the publishing options of the black male is made pointedly and metaphorically clear by part 3, in which Reed has been erased altogether. An old folk expression reasserts itself here— "the freest people on earth are a black woman and a white man"—to explain the vagaries of the literary marketplace.[29]

Haki Madhubuti's reading of the U.S. publishing industry centers not on how and why it has excluded black men but rather on how it has neglected some black women. In two essays on Sonia Sanchez and Lucille Clifton, Madhubuti explains their critical neglect in terms of "the exchange nature of the game played daily in the publishing world; the only business more ruthless and corrupted is Congress." Clifton is neglected because she "does not live in New York, may not have 'connections' with reviewers nor possess Madison Avenue visibility."[30] Likewise, Sanchez "does not have the national celebrity that her work and seriousness demand" because "she does not compromise her values, her art, or her people for fame or gold."[31] In these two essays Madhubuti relies on archetypal distinctions between "good" and "bad" women, accordingly reserving condemnations for some (Alice Walker, Toni Morrison, and Ntozake Shange) and commendations for others (Lucille Clifton, Sonia Sanchez, Mari Evans, and Gwendolyn Brooks). And one does not have to search for the real basis for the distinctions: attitudes about family. He praises Sonia Sanchez and Lucille Clifton for being "cultural workers" who refuse to "become literary and physical prostitutes" in order to "make it." He takes care to note that for Sanchez, writing poetry is combined with "raising . . . her children, maintaining a home, [and] working fourteen-hour days." Her poetry, he continues, "highlights Black women as mothers, sisters, lovers, wives, workers, and warriors" committed to the "Black family and the Black woman's role in building a better world." "In a real fight," he concludes, Sanchez is "the type of black woman you would want at your side."[32]

In his essay on Clifton, the references to family proliferate. Madhubuti begins by describing Clifton as a "full-time wife, overtime mother, part-time street activist and writer of small treasures" whose focus is "the children, the family." He even speculates that she suffers neglect because "the major body of her work is directed toward children." He commends Clifton for her "unusually significant and sensitive" treatment of black male characters, ascribing it to "her relationship with her father, brothers, husband, and sons. Generally, positive relationships produce positive results." In his closing passages, Madhubuti tellingly quotes Clifton's poem "to a dark moses," demonstrating unambiguously the ideological basis of his critique: "You are the one I am lit for / come with your rod that twists and is a serpent / I am the bush / I am burning / I am not consumed." Not surprisingly, Madhubuti concludes, "I am excited about [Clifton's] work because she reflects me; she tells my story."[33]

What is the legible subtext of these male readings of black women writers? Let me make a direct and certainly predictable claim: this debate over black women writers' portrayal of black males is not principally about *this* issue (if it is at all). Rather, what lies behind this smoke screen is an unacknowledged jostling for space in the literary market-place (certainly apparent in the essays by Haki Madhubuti mentioned above) that brings to mind Hawthorne's famous complaint about the "damn'd mob of scribbling women" of the 1850s. Furthermore, to enlist Judith Fetterley's remarks from a different context, this debate is a lament for "the sense of power derived from the experience of perceiving one's self central, as subject, as literally because literarily the point of view from which the world is seen." This community of male readers brings to the reading of black women's texts a complex of powerful assumptions, not the least of which is "the equation of textuality with masculine subjectivity and masculine point of view."[34] This equation has operated historically in discourses about blackness. Calvin Hernton does well to note that "historically, the battle line of racial struggle in the U.S. has been drawn exclusively as a struggle between the men of the races. Everything having to do with race has been defined and counterdefined by the men as a question of whether black people were or were not a race of Men. The central concept and the universal metaphor around which all aspects of the racial situation revolve is 'Manhood.'"[35]

It should not go unnoticed that critics leading the debate have lumped all black women writers together and have focused on one tiny aspect of their immensely complex and diverse project—the image of black men—despite the fact that, if we can claim a center for these texts, it is located in the complexities of black female subjectivity and experience. In other words, though black women writers have made black women the subjects of their own family stories, these male readers/critics are attempting to usurp that place for themselves and place it at the center of critical inquiry.

The desire of these black male readers to see themselves reflected favorably back to themselves is aggressively unfulfilled in the work of contemporary black women's literature. And the ideas and ideals of masculinity and femininity upheld by the nuclear family deeply entangled in this desire are actively opposed in black women's literature. This emphatic desire for the family's recuperation and the father's restitution to his "rightful" place within it surges ironically at the very moment that this vision and version of family seem forever out of reach. In other words, as the fabric of the nuclear family progressively frays, the desire to be enfolded in it gathers force. Of course this ancient, urgent longing for the family's healing hold is not intrinsically masculine, nor does it always mask a naked will to power.

While this "regressive longing for the stem family of their nostalgic imagination" must be seen as part of a much wider cultural trend,[36] the frequency with which it has appeared in a variety of recent work by black men is suggestive. To choose a few random examples: In his moving autobiography *Brothers and Keepers,* John Wideman implies that the power of the family as a social unit could secure foundations badly shaken by the criminal activities of a brother. On the front jacket of the first edition is a jailed man in shadow, but on the back is a portrait of Wideman's family harmoniously gathered in front of the house: mother *and* father, children and grandchildren lined up in neat and orderly rows, faces smiling at each other, their bodies erect and composed. The family becomes the framing rhetoric and logic of Houston Baker's suggestive monograph *Modernism and the Harlem Renaissance.* Baker writes below a block of family photographs beginning with a picture of his wife's father, "the family signature is always a renewing renaissancism that ensures generation, generations." [37]

Finally, in *The Truly Disadvantaged: The Inner City, the Underclass, and Public Policy,* William Julius Wilson, a black sociologist, attributes the problem of an ineradicable underclass to intergenerational female-headed households. His solution, as Adolph Reed astutely notes, is not to appeal for "pay equity, universal day care and other initiatives to buttress women's capacities for living independently in the world" but rather to increase the pool of black "marriageable" men.[38]

Wilson too narrates a family romance with a sociological twist. He recalls nostalgically the time when "lower-class, working-class, and middle-class black families all lived more or less in the same communities . . . sent their children to the same schools, availed themselves of the same recreational facilities, and shopped at the same stores." [39] So powerful is the desire to recuperate the family and a safe and uncomplicated black community that Wilson ignores, according to Reed, the fact that the "glue" holding these earlier communities together "was not so much nuclear, 'intact' families as the imperatives of racial segregation." Reed continues pointedly that "the new concern with the black family—like the old concern with the black family . . . is a moralistic ideology that . . . enforce[s] patriarchal institutions by appealing to a past that may have been largely mythical . . . and one that was certainly predicated on the subordination of women."[40]

This narrative of a fantasy family is unfulfilled in the majority of writings by contemporary black women. Much of their work exposes black women's subordination within the nuclear family, rethinks and configures its structures, and places utterance outside the father's preserve and control. But while this work refuses to offer comforting and idealized fantasies of family life, it understands their origins and the needs they fill. To cite just one example, in her first novel, *The Third Life of Grange Copeland*, Alice Walker captures poignantly the origins of Brownfield's daydream family in his childhood observations of his father's numbing life as a sharecropper. As Brownfield waits with his father for the truck to come, he sees "his father's face [freeze] into an unnaturally bland mask. . . . It was as if his father became a stone or robot . . . an object, a cipher." And when the white Mr. Shipley appears, Brownfield is "filled with terror of this man who could, by his presence alone, turn his father into something that might as well have been a pebble or a post or a piece of dirt, except for the sharp bitter odor of something whose source was forcibly contained in flesh." Brownfield's only way to cope with this dehumanization is to retreat to the comfort of a daydream that comforts him throughout his childhood: "He saw himself grown-up, twenty-one or so, arriving home at sunset in the snow. . . . He pulled up to his house, a stately mansion with cherry-red brick chimneys . . . in a chauffeur-driven car. . . . Brownfield's wife and children . . . a girl and a boy—waited anxiously for him just inside the door. . . . They jumped all over him, showering him with kisses. While he told his wife of the big deals he'd pushed through that day, she fixed him a mint julep."[41] The text understands, then, this desire for the father's presence in the sanctity of the home, but it frustrates that desire and exposes this domestic space as the privileged site of women's exploitation.[42] It is telling, for example, that in Brownfield's idyllic fantasy, his wife and the cook are "constantly interchanged so that his wife was first black and glistening from cooking and then white and powdery to his touch." [43]

In the view of these reviews and essays, the possibilities for wholeness within the black family have been fractured by black women's consumption of the fruit of feminist knowledge, but more, by their affiliations with white women. Even signs of embattled reconciliation between them after long estrangement and distrust have made the black male a stranger in his own home, an outcast in his own family.

The scene in *Reckless Eyeballing* in which Becky French, a white woman, and Treemonisha Smarts, a black woman, decide the fate of Ball's play, *No Good Man,* captures the cross-racial reconciliation that demands the black male's sacrifice. As the two women exchange stares, Ball thinks

> of them in the same households all over the Americas while the men were away on long trips to the international centers of the cotton or sugar markets. The secrets they exchanged in the night when there were no men around, during the Civil War in America when the men were in the battlefield and the women were in the house. Black and white, sisters and half-sisters. Mistresses and wives. There was something going on here that made him, a man, an outsider, a spectator, like someone who'd stumbled into a country where people talked in sign language and he didn't know the signs. [44]

Quoting this passage in his review, Pinckney describes it as "a paranoid update" on a conspiratorial theme, and with that I can agree, but the passage suggests much more that bears directly on issues of gender and reading. The male readers of this debate, whose gazes are fixed on themselves, seem to have entered a fictional territory marked by unreadable signs. Pinckney refers to this territory as the kitchen. He remembers when "Black women's concerns had belonged to what was considered *the private,* rather than the public, as if the kitchen range could not adequately represent the struggle. But it turned out that the concerns of the kitchen were big enough to encompass the lore of struggle and survival." [45]

Pinckney's distinction between public and private space is a distinction repeatedly deconstructed in the writings of the black women under review, for they understand the operations of power within intimate domains, operations captured in that now familiar axiom "The personal is political." But more to the point, Pinckney's metaphor of the kitchen calls to mind Susan Glaspell's short story "A Jury of Her Peers." Feminist critics have read this story of a different form of family violence as a model of the workings of gender in the reading process. As the men of the story search for clues that will suggest a motive for Minnie's murder of her husband, they bypass the inside of the house and search its surroundings. They dismiss what one of them terms "the insignificance of kitchen things" and are consequently unable to "interpret this farm wife's world."[46]

While the story does not "exclude the male as reader," it attempts to educate him "to become a better reader."[47] In terms of our debate, that process of reeducation begins with questioning and adjusting the categories and constructs, the values and assumptions that we bring to bear *when* reading that have almost always been formed *before* reading. Put another way, that process begins with questioning what Fredric Jameson calls "the always-already-read," the "sedimented layers of previous *interpretations*."[48]

Alice Walker's story "Source," from her collection *You Can't Keep a Good Woman Down,* offers a different model of reading.[49] Choosing "Source" as a model seems especially appropriate because, of all the black women writers under critique in this debate, Walker has been the object of the most savage, sustained, and partisan attack (primarily for *The Color Purple*) and the lightning rod for these reviewers' hostility to feminism. It is notably ironic, then, that well before that controversial novel was published, Walker had, perhaps in an uncanny moment of prescience, staged in "Source" many general concerns and assumptions—both literary and cultural—at work in this debate.

The title announces the story's concern with origins, beginnings, with questions of male subjectivity and its relation to language and representation. Repeated references to Mt. McKinley function as figures of masculine potency and transcendence. In its parallel plots—one involving reading matters, the other family matters—the story stages competing words and conflicting discourses framed as a secular myth of origins. Further, it engages and complicates the salient and interlocking assumptions inherent in this controversy. For example, the story confronts head-on the twin beliefs inherent in these reviews: the belief in the text as *rejection* rather than *production* of self and world; the belief in a pregiven positive masculine identity. In the process, it poses questions about the nature of identification and recognition in the reading process.

> Source: from Latin surgere to raise, rise; the point of origin;
> a generative force or stimulus; genealogical lineage.

A veritable reference work, "Source" alludes to a number of books, song titles, films, and historical figures, including "Eleanor Rigby," *Steppenwolf, Imitation of Life, Autobiography of an Ex-Coloured Man, Confessions of Nat Turner, Birth of a Nation,* and *Louisa Picquet, the Octoroon: A Tale of Southern Slave Life.* These titles are suggestive and instructive, for they cast into bold relief the status of the story as *story,* as text. But more importantly, most of these titles comment on the constructed (not found) and contingent nature of identity and subjectivity. These allusions establish and announce the narrative's self-conscious insistence on its own *fictionality,* its own textuality, in a way that compares to Shari Benstock's reading of footnotes in the literary text. I agree with her that footnotes (and here I would substitute Alice Walker's various allusions to artistic works) "belong to a fictional universe, stem from a creative act . . . and direct themselves toward the fiction and never toward an external construct, even when they cite 'real' works in the world outside the particular fiction." [50]

The "real" works of Walker's story, the sources behind her "Source," instruct the reader about the disguises of identity, about identity as disguise. From the opening allusion to "Eleanor Rigby" (who keeps her face in a jar by the door) to *The Autobiography of an Ex-Coloured Man* to *Steppenwolf* to *Louisa Picquet, the Octoroon,* the underlying issue is the same: identity is textually constructed, not pregiven or found. The "real" persons function similarly: "once 'inside' the fiction, both fictional characters and real personages exist at the same fictive level." [51]

While Walker liberally incorporates references to historical personages throughout her fiction, she seems fully aware of both their fictive status in her work *and* their "fictive" status in the world. She compounds the story's many ironies and self-complications by suggesting that such *actual* historical figures may even have *made up* their identities. The reference to Kathleen Cleaver is a case in point. Although readers familiar with the Black Panther party recognize her as one of its leaders, the narrative stresses that identity is assumed, is made, is produced by the contingencies of time and place.

Anastasia's memory of her first meeting with Kathleen Cleaver "before *she* was Kathleen Cleaver" is suggestive. Male-identified, like Anastasia, Cleaver "sat in a corner all evening without saying a word. . . . Men did all the talking" (153). However, after the men are dead or jailed, Cleaver is forced to change; that change figures in her dress: in "boots and sunglasses and black clothes" she "poses for photographers [while] holding a gun" (153).

This dynamic, ever-changing historically and spatially situated nature of identity is counterposed to the static conception of identity embodied in Source, the title character, the only stationary figure in the text. While all move around him, Source sits on a bed and receives those who come to hear his static message: "The universe is unchangeable" (153). His name evokes the "original," "pregiven," positive racial self, historically and paradigmatically male. It is this conception of self that is demanded by these reviewers. Although the story's title leads the reader to expect a story *about* this guru/teacher/father figure, Source is not the work's center of reference. Rather, the nominal "center" is relocated to the margins of the text. His presence is deferred until the narrative action is well under way. And even at that, his appearance is brief and clearly subordinated to the narrative's dramatization of the reunion between Irene and Anastasia.

The narrative of this reunion brings to a head conflicting discourses about family and identity, discourses the story figures through its controlling metaphor of teaching. It juxtaposes Source's methods requiring passive and unquestioning acceptance and transcription of his authority to Irene's, requiring that her students "take an active part in their own instruction" (142).

These conflicting methodologies come to rest in Anastasia, who must negotiate between them and, in effect, between Irene and Source. As flower child and sometime mistress of Source, Anastasia finds unacceptable Irene's critique and rejection of Source's authority. In a section that dramatizes the family's site as production and construction of identity, especially the daughter's identity, Anastasia defends Source to a suspicious and judgmental Irene. Always painfully confused about her racial identity (she looks white but is considered black), Anastasia has spent much of her life drifting, changing identities as she changes "personal fashion" (143). After several such changes—"Southern Innocent," "New York Super Vamp," "Kathleen Cleaver type"—she meets Source, who hastens her along to her next change to flower child. Significantly, Source describes their first meeting by remembering that Anastasia looked like Kathleen Cleaver, her "hair like an angry, wild animal bush." He tames her, substituting her "militancy" for calm, and renames her Tranquillity.

Further, he helps her accept that "[she] is nothing," that "nobody's anything." More importantly, Source arranges the reunion between Anastasia and her family—arranges, more precisely, her reunion with her father, who "now wrote of God's love, God's grace, God's assured forgiveness, and of his own happiness that his daughter, always at heart 'a good girl,' had at last embarked on the path of obedience . . . [which] alone led to peace everlasting in the new and coming system of the world" (148). It is this "new and coming system" that Irene's questioning presence threatens. She sits with "a clenched fist resting" on the letters from Anastasia's father and poses a challenge to the universal negatives of Source's teaching: "Nobody's anything." "You can't change anything." Ensuring the continued circulation of his words, Source has his daughter write them down.

Reading this new and coming system accurately as an age-old sanction for the daughter's seduction and submission, Irene is invited to leave. Irene's life work is teaching students to respect and inscribe "their own personal histories and their own experience" (142), not to reinscribe themselves in another's "universal truths." Structured into Irene's method of teaching "Advanced Reading and Writing" is a provision for students to write their own books, which effectively contravenes the assumption that "bearing a father's word," as Source's daughter does, is "women's only acceptable role with respect to language".[52] Source's daughter is literally and figuratively bearing his word, as she is pregnant with his child. Here Margaret Homans's observations about women who "act as amanuenses . . . usually for men," are pertinent. "Like the mother of the Word, the woman who carries language from one place or state of being to another does not herself originate or even touch it, and she gets nothing for her labor, which she performs for others."[53] In addition, Irene's students are required to shift any identity constructs that lock them into a single reading persona or type.

"Source" incorporates various categories of readers and scenes of instruction. And while each characterizes a woman reader, the implications are more broadly applicable. Fania represents one category. Like many of the men sustaining this debate, Fania is a "resisting reader," to borrow from Judith Fetterley, refusing to learn to read anything that hurts (145) or in which she fails to recognize herself. While the narrative clearly sympathizes with Fania's reading strategies, it challenges her to move beyond her resistance to explore her "undeveloped comprehension of [self and] world" (153). For Fania, that expansion begins with the slave narratives of black women. Significantly, Fania, "a stout, walnut-colored woman," identifies with the narrative of *Louisa Picquet, the Octoroon,* though she does not *recognize* Picquet as identical with herself.

While Irene succeeds in teaching Fania a way to read that effectively displaces the recognizable and the familiar as privileged conventions of reading, she is in like need of instruction. And in an interesting narrative twist, as readers witness her instruction, they are taught themselves. The narrative sets the reader up for the familiar and "recognizable" story of a deprived but socially committed black woman and an indulged, confused, and irresponsible mulatto with a "lack of commitment to anything . . . useful" (166); but happily the story swerves from such banalities, for while Irene casts herself in the role of Anastasia's teacher, their roles reverse in the course of the narrative and teacher becomes learner and learner teacher. This reversal captures the very issues of constructed identities and idealized self-definition with which the story wrestles and which are most pertinent to the controversy about black women writers.

Though Irene is partly represented as an idealist with a knowledge of self that qualifies her to represent the race, she falls far short of that carefully constructed and controlled ideal. (Walker clearly intends a parallel with Nella Larsen's similarly deluded narrator Irene in *Passing,* the seeming foil to Clare.) Correlatively, Anastasia, who changes identities as she "changed fashion," helps Irene to "unmask her own confusion" about self and race.

The productive tension between Irene and Anastasia and the symbolic role reversals they undergo can only occur away from Source's watchful gaze and the influence of his teachings. Anastasia has bought these teachings uncritically, crediting them with reuniting her with her family. (Interestingly, while Anastasia accepts Source's teachings, which coincide with her father's words, she "never read the newsletter that Irene and her [students] published" [142].) But Anastasia pays for the family reunion, arranged on Source's terms and turf, with her own psychic and physical health. Her recovery requires that she review Source's teachings and unmask their repressive aims.

While Source would teach that "the good of life is indifference" (suggesting undifferentiation, nondifference) and that "nobody's anything," Anastasia progressively distances herself from his rhetoric and his universalization of stasis. Arguing that "only a fascist would say nobody's anything," Anastasia changes Source's words and substitutes her own, emphatically: "Everybody's something. Some*body*." In rejecting Source's positivization of the negative, Anastasia begins the process of unnaming and the recognition of the arbitrary relation between the name and the thing that necessarily calls into question any confident claims about positive black male identity. With "a permanent tremor under [her] eye," "constant colds, diarrhea, loose teeth and skin eruptions," Anastasia asks pointedly, "If I was tranquil, why was this happening?" Implicitly renouncing the name that Source has given her—Tranquillity—she has learned, to paraphrase a passage from *Invisible Man*, that "to call a thing by name is [not] to make it so." Similarly, Source, despite his name, is not the absolute source, the self-present origin, the namer, the author whose authority is unchallengeable.

Much the same might be said about Alice Walker as the source, the author, the originator of "Source"—suggestions not lost on Walker. The multiple listing of textual sources in the story might be read as Walker's commentary on the process of authorship, which implies a distance from received notions of a single author and the concept of single, self-identity it implies. Although, with that said, one cannot then take Walker's own words as Truth, it is nonetheless pertinent and useful to note that Walker's response to her critics takes the form of a discussion of self-identity. In "In the Closet of the Soul" she writes: "crucial to our development . . . is an acceptance of our actual as opposed to our mythical selves. We are the mestizos of North America. We are black, yes, but we are 'white,' tan, and we are red. To attempt to function as only one, when you are really two or three, leads, I believe, to psychic illness. Regardless of who will or will not accept us, including perhaps, our 'established' self, we must be completely (to the extent it is possible) who we are." [54]

It is precisely this question about self-identity that is thematized in

"Source." Like *Sula,* the narrative exploits, complicates, and affirms a dynamic conception of identity that resists any notion of a single identity to be "positively" represented in fiction. More, both through its figuration of Anastasia's "identity changes" and through its unmasking of Irene's "self-saving vanity" (141), the text reveals the workings of desire in the construction of identity. In this richly textured story, then, Shoshana Felman's words come directly to mind: "Indeed it is not so much the critic [reader/reviewer] who comprehends the text, as the text that comprehends the critic."[55] The narrative understands the critics who would charge Walker and her black female contemporaries with shattering the "established" image, the positive identity. More to the point, the text understands what their rhetoric of family reveals and conceals.

Whether or not one agrees that the text comprehends the critics of African-American women novelists, it is certain that these reviewers have had a constraining influence on the writers they attack. Since this controversy began, certain black women writers have expressed their fear and concern about how their depictions of black men would be received, and, more sobering, others might even be said to have adjusted their aesthetic vision because of the pressures of negative publicity. To take just one example, Gloria Naylor admits to being "self-conscious" about her first novel. "I bent over backwards," she says, "not to have a negative message come through about the men. . . . I worried about whether or not the problems that were being caused by the men in the women's lives would be interpreted as some bitter statement I had to make about black men."[56]

Similarly, in a 1987 interview Ntozake Shange agreed with Brenda Lyons's perception that between the controversial *for colored girls* and her most recent novel *Betsey Brown* (1985) there was "a movement away from radical feminist politics . . . toward what seems a return to family-centered values."[57] There is of course no necessary causal connection between the controversy and Shange's aesthetic shift, but it should not go unnoticed that Shange moves aesthetically toward representing the very value system espoused in these reviews. And while family- and female-centered writing need not be seen as incompatible, it is significant that Shange dedicates *Betsey Brown* to her family. And the back flap of the first edition features a photograph of her beaming down admiringly at her daughter. Completing the portrait is Ishmael Reed's lone blurb, which praises Shange for her "uncanny gift for immersing herself within the situations and points of view of so many different types of women." By delimiting her audience to women, he continues, "she has achieved an almost oracular status among her female readers." Although a "writer of many masks," he concludes, "the masks come off" with *Betsey Brown.*

I leave it to the reader to speculate about what Reed might mean by Shange's masks, but what his description of her as a writer for *female* readers suggests is unambiguous. His comments that give, then take away, represent a shift, however feeble, to a more sanguine response to a black woman writer. But it is only a momentary shift, for he resurrects his venom in his roman à clef *Reckless Eyeballing.* Ian Ball's is a clear self-portrait whose story allegorizes Reed's now well-known and predictable perception that the work of talented black men is being eclipsed by the power bloc of black women writers midwifed and promoted by white feminists.

"Sex-listed" in a feminist publication suggestively titled *Lilith's Gang,* Ball goes on to experience a positive reversal of literary fortune. But the more interesting development is a parallel "reversal" for Treemonisha Smarts, a thinly disguised Ntozake Shange. At novel's end, drunk with what the narrative describes as the "skull and crossbones" of literary success, Treemonisha has abandoned her successful career, moved to Yuba City, California, with a recovering drug addict and failed musician, renounced her involvement with voyeuristic white feminists, and resolved to "get fat, have babies, and write, write." [58] Reed's fantasy, no doubt. In this scenario, writing for a woman is preceded by getting fat and having babies and is best not followed by the "skull and cross-bones" of literary success, although achieving that same success has been Ian Ball's driving ambition. With *Reckless Eyeballing,* we might say, Reed's "masks come off," revealing plainly to this reader that reading family matters.

But this controversy is clearly not reducible simply to conflictual interaction between the texts of contemporary black women and a group of resisting male readers. Thus, its resolution is no simple matter of "adjusting" identity constructs and altering reading strategies at the finite level of the text, for, in the language of "Source," always "up there" is the Higher Power, the metastructure, which has not only already textualized "identity" but has also already determined whether there will be "reading" at all.

"Source" is sharply alert to the political economy of reading and writing, and it understands the inextricable relation between the source of funding and the source of words. In talking to Anastasia about how federal cuts ended the Advanced Reading and Writing course she was teaching to poor women in the rural South, Irene explains, "In the beginning there was no funding" and "the two women could not help grinning in recognition of the somehow *familiar* sound of this" (143–44; emphasis in text). But Irene, like Walker, defamiliarizes the familiar (familial) and secularizes the sacred origins of the myth of creation. She understands the twin relation of church to state and underscores the vulnerability of women's reading and writing to the power of their entwined control.

Walker uses references to Mt. McKinley to allegorize white male dominance over language and representation and to illustrate how, through the erasure of difference, that power is institutionalized. The highest peak in North America, Mt. McKinley, was renamed for President William McKinley in 1896, replacing the Indian name Denali (The Highest One). And while it is clear that Walker associates the "great elusive" Mt. McKinley with a power wielded mainly by white men, she knows that black men are also inescapably the agents of that hegemony in many respects. The narrative establishes an equivalent relation between Source's "bare feet," which he "cover[s] and uncover[s]" with a "white robe" (150), and another mountain, in Seattle, mentioned, but unnamed, at story's end. Tourists pointing in the distance "thought they were finally seeing the great elusive [Mt. McKinley], a hundred miles away. They were not. It was yet another, nearer, mountain's very large feet, its massive ankles wreathed in clouds" (167).

While these male gazes are fixed on the texts of black women in which they seek to find idealized reflections of themselves, they fail to see the highest mountain, the metastructure that has the naming power and in whose name and interests that power is secured. It is this looming, distant structure that orchestrates and dominates this literary battle royal, this already fixed match between black men and black women.[59] And one could argue that this fixed match reproduces an older metanarrative written in the history of the slave master's hand. In that narrative, as in this, the bodies/texts of black women have become the "battlefield on and over which men, black and white, [fight] to establish actual and symbolic political dominance and to demonstrate masculine" control.[60] This attempt to control both black women's written *bodies* and their *written* bodies must be read and its service to the family plot interpreted, for that plot makes women permanent daughters content merely to transcribe their father's words.[61]

Notes

I thank Susan Fraiman, Janice Knight, Cheryl Wall, and Richard Yarborough for their very helpful comments on an earlier draft of this essay.

1. See Wolfgang Iser, *The Act of Reading: A Theory of Aesthetic Response* (Baltimore: Johns Hopkins Univ. Press, 1978); Susan Suleiman and Inge Crosman, eds., *The Reader in the Text: Essays on Audience and Interpretation* (Princeton: Princeton Univ. Press, 1980); and Jane Tompkins, ed., *Reader-Response Criticism: From Formalism to Post-Structuralism* (Baltimore: Johns Hopkins Univ. Press, 1980).

2. Mary Louise Pratt, "Interpretive Strategies/Strategic Interpretations," in Jonathan Arac, ed., *Postmodernism and Politics* (Minneapolis: Univ. of Minnesota Press, 1986).

3. Mel Watkins, "Sexism, Racism, and Black Women Writers," *New York Times Book Review,* June 15, 1986, 1, 35.

4. A significant and controversial exception from a woman is Trudier Harris, "On the Color Purple, Stereotypes, and Silence," *Black American Literature Forum* 18 (winter 1984): 155–61. Though Harris focuses on *The Color Purple,* her assertions are echoed more broadly in readings of other novels by black women. She argues that *The Color Purple* satisfies white "spectator readers" by presenting stereotypical "black fathers and father-figures" who are "immoral [and] sexually unrestrained." See also Sondra O'Neale, "Inhibiting Midwives, Usurping Creators: The Struggling Emergence of Black Women in Fiction," in Teresa de Lauretis, ed., *Feminist Studies/Critical Studies* (Bloomington: Indiana Univ. Press, 1986), 139–56. Male exceptions include Calvin Hernton's *The Sexual Mountain and Black Women Writers* (New York: Anchor/Doubleday, 1987), 37–58, and Richard Wesley's "'The Color Purple' Debate: Reading between the Lines," *Ms.,* Sept. 1986, 62, 90–92.

5. Jack White, chief of the Chicago bureau of *Time* magazine, compresses this oppositional tendency in his question: "Why were so many black women moved by *The Color Purple* and so many black activists/artists/militants [presumed to be male?] revulsed by the film—and the novel?" And, not surprisingly, in his second question, White links these polar responses regressively to Shange's controversial choreopoem. He asks, "Why did so many black women walk out of *for colored girls* . . . shouting 'Amen' while so many black men denounced the 'bitch' who wrote it?" ("The Black Person in Art: How Should S/he Be Portrayed?" *Black American Literature Forum* 21 [spring/summer

1987]: 22). Theologian Delores Williams's reading can be regarded as a response to Smith's question. She sees *The Color Purple* as "feminist theology" affirming the belief that "women's liberation is the key to the redemption of our society. This social redemption depends upon . . . changing our consciousness about the maleness of God, about divine validation of heterosexuality and about authority as it relates to the masculine and feminine dimensions of culture." For these reasons, she adds, "we black feminists leave the cinema knowing we have seen something painfully significant about ourselves, men, God and redemption" ("Examining Two Shades of 'Purple,'" *Los Angeles Times,* Mar. 15, 1986). See also Williams's essay "What Was Missed: 'The Color Purple,'" *Christianity and Crisis,* July 14, 1986.

6. Richard Ohmann, "The Shaping of a Canon: U.S. Fiction, 1960–1975," in *Politics of Letters* (Middletown, Conn.: Wesleyan Univ. Press, 1987), 71, 75.

7. Cathy Davidson, *Revolution and the Word* (New York: Oxford Univ. Press, 1986), iii.

8. In Paul Smith, *Discerning the Subject* (Minneapolis: Univ. of Minnesota Press, 1988), 34.

9. For discussions of gender and reading, see Elizabeth A. Flynn and Patrocinio P. Schweickart, eds., *Gender and Reading: Essays on Readers, Texts, and Contexts* (Baltimore: Johns Hopkins Univ. Press, 1986).

10. Maureen Quilligan, *Milton's Spenser: The Politics of Reading* (Ithaca: Cornell Univ. Press, 1983), 178.

11. Excerpts of Wallace's book were published in *Ms.* magazine in December 1979.

12. Qtd. in Hemton, *The Sexual Mountain,* 44.

13. Among the most useful recent critiques of this tendency are Henry Louis Gates Jr., "Preface to Blackness: Text and Pretext," in Dexter Fisher and Robert Stepto, eds., *Afro-American Literature: The Reconstruction of Instruction* (New York: Modern Language Association of America, 1979), 44–69, and idem, "Criticism in the Jungle," in Gates, ed., *Black Literature and Literary Theory* (New York: Methuen, 1984), 1–24.

14. Robert Staples, "The Myth of Black Macho: A Response to Angry Black Feminists," *Black Scholar,* Mar./Apr. 1979, 26–27.

15. Janet Beizer, *Family Plots* (New Haven: Yale Univ. Press, 1986), 7. I confine my comments to the few essays, the rhetoric of which is most insistently "pro-family." To these could be added the following essays and newspaper and magazine features that protest the treatment of black men in the literature of black women. Some of them object specifically to the film version of *The Color Purple* but make no distinctions between film and novel: Gerald Early, "The Color Purple as Everybody's Protest Art," *Antioch Review* 44 (1986): 261–75; Richard Barksdale, "Castration Symbolism in Recent Black

American Fiction," *College Language Association Journal* 29 (1986): 400–413; E. R. Shipp, "Blacks in Heated Debate over 'The Color Purple,'" *New York Times,* Jan. 27, 1986; "Seeing Red over Purple," *People Magazine,* March 1986; Abdul Waii Muhammad, "Purple Poison Pulses," *Final Call,* Jan. 27, 1986; Lynn Norment, "The Color Purple," *Ebony,* Feb. 1986.

16. Christine Froula, "The Daughter's Seduction: Sexual Violence and Literary History," *Signs* 11 (1986): 621–44.

17. Despite abundant evidence that black women's "feminist" consciousness generally emerged organically from the material circumstances of their lives and can be documented well in advance of the second wave of the women's movement of the 1960s, this analysis continues to be perpetuated by black men. See bell hooks, *Feminist Theory: From Margin to Center* (Boston: South End Press, 1984), and Beverly Guy-Sheftall, "Remembering Sojourner Truth: On Black Feminism," in Pearl Cleage, ed., *Catalyst* (Atlanta: N.p., n.d.), 54–57.

18. David Bradley, "Telling the Black Woman's Story," *New York Times Magazine,* Jan. 1984, 34.

19. Philip M. Royster, "In Search of Our Fathers' Arms: Alice Walker's Persona of the Alienated Darling," *Black American Literature Forum* 20 (winter 1986): 3–57, 361. Royster keeps Walker's roles as daughter, wife, and mother clearly before the reader's eye, noting that she is a failed wife and an inadequate mother; see 353, especially.

20. Susan Willis, *Specifying: Black Women Writing the American Experience* (Madison: Univ. of Wisconsin Press, 1987), 106.

21. Bradley, "Black Woman's Story," 30.

22. Royster, "Our Fathers' Arms," 363.

23. Watkins, "Sexism, Racism, and Black Women Writers," 36.

24. Ibid., 37, 36.

25. Richard Wright, *Native Son* (New York: Harper & Row, 1940), 140, 224.

26. Marilyn Butler, "Against Tradition: The Case for a Particularized Historical Method," in Jerome J. McGann, ed., *Historical Studies and Literary Criticism* (Madison: Univ. of Wisconsin Press, 1985), 37. See also J. P. Stern, "From Family Album to Literary History," *Critical Inquiry* 7 (1975): 113–31. After Wittgenstein, Stern describes writing literary history as analogous to "pictures from a family album, not as scenes from a single story or drama" with sufficient continuity.

27. The novel was reviewed by Robert Towers in the Aug. 12, 1982, issue under the heading "Good Men Are Hard to Find," though Towers admitted then that "the two books have about as much in common . . . as one of Roy Lichtenstein's comic-strip blowups and a WPA painting of cotton pickers in the field." Reed's public conflicts with black women writers are well known, which piques my curiosity about this pattern of pairing his work with Alice Walker's

in literary reviews. See also Darwin Turner, "A Spectrum of Blackness," *Parnassus* 4 (1976): 202–18. For Reed's comments on this practice of pairing him with Walker, see Mel Watkins, "An Interview with Ishmael Reed," *Southern Review* 21 (1985): 603–14. There Reed talks about his belief, captured in the title of a symposium which he sponsored, that "Third World Men [are] the Scapegoats of Feminist Writers."

28. Ishmael Reed, *Reckless Eyeballing* (New York: St. Martin's, 1986), 4.

29. See, as just one example, the courtroom scene near the end of Hurston's *Their Eyes Were Watching God* in which Janie is acquitted of murdering Tea Cake. One of the group of black men outraged at the verdict says, "Well, you know whut dey say 'uh white man and uh nigger woman is de freest thing on earth.' Dey do as dey please" (1937; rpt. Urbana: Univ. of Illinois Press, 1978), 280.

30. Haki Madhubuti, "Lucille Clifton: Warm Water, Greased Legs, and Dangerous Poetry," in Mari Evans, ed., *Black Women Writers: A Critical Evaluation* (New York: Anchor/Doubleday, 1983), 159.

31. Haki Madhubuti, "Sonia Sanchez: The Bringer of Memories," in Evans, *Black Women Writers*, 419–20.

32. Ibid., 159, 432.

33. Madhubuti, "Lucille Clifton," 150–51, 159, 156. With this gesture Madhubuti reveals unwittingly a central tendency and irony in this debate. In the name of the black family and the survival of the larger black community, there is a thinly disguised desire for personal, individual gratification and reflection.

34. Judith Fetterley, "Reading about Reading: 'A Jury of Her Peers,' 'The Murders in the Rue Morgue,' and 'The Yellow Wallpaper,'" in Flynn and Schweickart, *Gender and Reading*, 150, 147.

35. Hernton, *Sexual Mountain and Black Women Writers*, 38.

36. Peter Gay, *Education of the Senses* (New York: Oxford Univ. Press, 1984), 436.

37. Houston Baker, *Modernism and the Harlem Renaissance* (Chicago: Univ. of Chicago Press, 1987), 106.

38. Adolph Reed, "The Liberal Technocrat," *Nation*, Feb. 6, 1988, 168.

39. William Julius Wilson, *The Truly Disadvantaged: The Inner City, the Underclass, and Public Policy* (Chicago: Univ. of Chicago Press, 1987), 7.

40. Adolph Reed, "Liberal Technocrat," 168.

41. Alice Walker, *The Third Life of Grange Copeland* (New York: Harcourt Brace Jovanovich, 1970), 9, 18.

42. All too little has been written about what black women experience within the family, a void partly created by the ideological discussions of the black family since the controversial Moynihan report *The Black Family: The Case for National Action*. Moynihan's "black matriarchy" thesis is well known

and need not be rehearsed here. It is enough to say that the flood of liberal repudiations it elicited, however well intentioned and sharply articulated, has done little to illuminate black women's subordination within the family. So strong have been the design and desire to refute with a mountain of "normalizing" data Moynihan's description of black families as "tangles of pathology" that black women's experiences, thought, and feelings have been buried. In his monumental *The Black Family in Slavery and Freedom* (New York: Random House, 1981), Herbert Gutman acknowledged that his study was "stimulated by the bitter public and academic controversy surrounding" the Moynihan report. He traces the development of the slave family and enlarged kin networks from 1750 to 1925, describing long-lasting slave marriages. But, as Angela Davis notes in *Women, Race, and Class* (New York: Random House, 1981), Gutman's "observations about slave women are generally confined to their wifely propensities." Similarly, in *Labor of Love, Labor of Sorrow: Black Women, Work, and the Family from Slavery to the Present* (New York: Basic Books, 1985), Jacquelyn Jones is at pains to prove that the "two-parent, nuclear family was the typical cohabitation" in slavery and freedom that protected the community at large from racial oppression. Only briefly does Jones, in an otherwise commendable study, indicate that, while racial oppression "could bind a family tightly together," "it could also heighten tensions among people who had few outlets for their rage and frustrations" (32, 34, 103).

43. Walker, *Grange Copeland*, 18.

44. Reed, *Reckless Eyeballing*, 77.

45. Darryl Pinckney, "Black Victims, Black Villains," *New York Review of Books*, Jan. 29, 1987, 81.

46. Judith Fetterley, "Reading about Reading," and Annette Kolodny, "A Map for Misreading: Gender and the Interpretation of Literary Texts," in Elaine Showalter, ed., *The New Feminist Criticism* (New York: Pantheon, 1985), 46–62.

47. Kolodny, "Map for Misreading," 57.

48. Fredric Jameson, *The Political Unconscious* (Ithaca: Cornell Univ. Press, 1981), 9. For a discussion of the extent to which what happens during reading has been "already limited by decisions made before the book is ever begun," see Peter Rabinowitz, *Before Reading: Narrative Conventions and the Politics of Interpretation* (Ithaca: Cornell Univ. Press, 1987), 2 ff.

49. Alice Walker, "Source," in *You Can't Keep a Good Woman Down* (New York: Harcourt Brace Jovanovich, 1981). Subsequent page references are given in the text.

50. Shari Benstock, "At the Margin of Discourse: Footnotes in the Fictional Text," *PMLA* 98 (1983): 205.

51. Ibid., 221.

52. Margaret Homans, *Bearing the Word* (Chicago: Univ. of Chicago Press, 1986), 160.

53. Ibid., 31.

54. Alice Walker, "In the Closet of the Soul," in *Living by the Word* (New York: Harcourt Brace Jovanovich, 1988), 82.

55. Shoshana Felman, *Writing and Madness* (Ithaca: Cornell Univ. Press, 1985), 161.

56. Gloria Naylor and Toni Morrison, "A Conversation," *Southern Review* 21 (1985): 579.

57. *Massachusetts Review* 28 (1987): 688.

58. Reed, *Reckless Eyeballing*, 130.

59. There are striking parallels between the reception of contemporary black women novelists and that of their counterparts, black feminist critics in the academy. In a very insightful and refreshing article, Theodore Mason discusses the controversial issue of *New Literary History* featuring essays by Joyce Joyce, Houston Baker, and Henry Louis Gates. Mason invokes Ralph Ellison's *Invisible Man* to explain this controversy between two black men and a black woman, arranged by the white male editor of the journal who watches his orchestrated combat with amusement. See "Between the Populist and the Scientist: Ideology and Power in Recent Afro-American Literary Criticism, or 'The Dozens' as Scholarship," *Callaloo* 36 (1988): 606–15.

60. Anthony Barthelemy, "Mother, Sister, Wife: A Dramatic Perspective," *Southern Review* 21 (1985): 787.

61. I borrow this phrasing from Alice Jardine, *Gynesis: Configurations of Woman and Modernity* (Ithaca: Cornell Univ. Press, 1985), 37.

Nonfelicitous Space and Survivor Discourse

Reading the Incest Story in Southern Women's Fiction

Minrose Gwin

In this essay I will be attempting to trace the convergences of material, textual, and cultural spaces in southern women's contemporary fiction about father-daughter incest.[1] This is not to imply that I see these three kinds of spaces as being distinct or noncontiguous. By *material space* I mean actual physical structures, landscapes, geographies, spatial locations that are represented within a text—the places in which a story or part of it happens (for example, the parlor in Lee Smith's *Black Mountain Breakdown*). Linked to the material spaces represented in a narrative are certain textual spaces, which I see as the intangible configurations, the openings and closures constructed by and within language, narrative, and silence. These textual spaces often fall between words that are hard to say and within stories that are hard to tell; they are formed by absence as well as presence. It is difficult to map such spaces (for instance, the mother's withdrawal from the abused daughter in Dorothy Allison's *Bastard Out of Carolina*) because they are evasive, slippery, difficult to retrieve. Of course, cultural space, with its permutations of the dynamic and incessant workings of ideology, layers all narrative. As Susan Stanford Friedman points out, cultural space comprises the "political resonances that traverse the text." These are the "stories, in other words, that reproduce, subvert, and otherwise engage with the dominant and marginalized cultural scripts of the social order." Cultural space within a text, Friedman adds, may include "certain interlocking narratives of race, gender, class, ethnicity, sexuality, religion, and so forth."[2] As I hope to show here, region is also an important component of cultural space, leaving ubiquitous traces of distinctive interactions of race, class, and gender in these women's stories of incestuous abuse in southern families.

Together, these three kinds of spaces in the novels I will be reading produce what I would call a fictional form of "survivor discourse," that is, "the discourse of those who have survived rape, incest, and sexual assault."[3] The survivor discourse of these stories, like that of the contemporary outpouring of autobiographical narratives about incestuous abuse (such as Maya Angelou's *I Know Why the Caged Bird Sings* or collections like *She Who Was Lost Is Remembered: Healing from Incest through Creativity*), reflects and refracts the cultural prohibitions that shape the volatile act of speaking out about incest.[4] What is the meaning of fiction in a discourse so heavily invested in "fact"? The effect of such stories, whether they be fictional or autobiographical (and I don't want to draw too fine a distinction between the two), is to create a fourth kind of space—a psychic space that forces the reader into a unsettling consideration of, on the one hand, patriarchal power carried to its most egregious form, and, on the other, the daughter's submission or resistance to that power. Like autobiographical narratives, then, the fictional incest story speaks a previously unspoken truth about the patriarchal family. Because it is not laden with exigencies of literal and specific "truth" claims, one might argue that such fiction is better equipped to tell the *cultural* story of father-daughter sexual abuse. I believe that this is nowhere more true than in southern stories of incest, which reveal how the white father's power in the southern patriarchal family is produced within and itself reproduces a cultural space that has historically emphasized property ownership and built up an institutionalized system of the containment and usage of women's bodies to that end. Historian Bertram Wyatt-Brown and legal scholar Patricia Williams, among many others, have pointed to the relation of white male dominance, property ownership, and the control of women's bodies (of all kinds) in the economy of the Old South—and particularly to the presence or threat of violence undergirding that economy.[5] This is certainly not to conflate the effects of such a system on black women (and men) and white women, or on women of planter and laboring classes. It is to say, though, that the white patriarchal family and its containment of female bodies for the purpose of holding and expanding property claims has had far-reaching repercussions, *as a specifically institutionalized ideology of dominance,* for familial dynamics and father-daughter relations in southern culture.

To further complicate this admixture of gender, race, and class, the South was and is a culture built upon a shared knowledge of male dis-empowerment at the hands of other men, whether through class and race privilege or through the loss of a war and a way of life. As Toni Morrison shows in *The Bluest Eye,* a novel set in the North but with its roots of violence still implanted in southern soil, the white man's violence against the black man can be reproduced with devastating ef-fects by the black man upon the black man's family, as in the case of Cholly Breedlove, whose sexual disempowerment as a young black man at the hands of white men is directly related to his rape of his eleven-year-old daughter many years later. Similarly, the narrator-survivor of Dorothy Allison's *Bastard Out of Carolina* is most in danger when her stepfather loses a job and thrusts the family into economic crisis (which he does frequently). This essay, then, will be an effort not only to locate the story of father-daughter incest within the material and textual spaces of these novels and mark its place on the cultural maps of both southern history and contemporary survivor discourse but also to trace dimensions of the nexus at which all of these spaces converge and overlay.

Like other forms of survivor discourse, these texts expose in a gen-eral sense what Christine Froula has called "the hysterical cultural script: the cultural text that dictates to males and females alike the ne-cessity of silencing woman's speech when it threatens the father's power." This silencing, which, Froula argues, has configurations similar to those surrounding the daughter's silence about incestuous abuse, "in-sures that the cultural daughter remains a daughter, her power sup-pressed and muted; while the father, his power protected, makes culture and history in his own image." [6] This uneven power dynamic works its way through multiple levels of discourse. Jane Gallop, Shoshana Fel-man, and Luce Irigaray have charted its course in the daughterly rela-tion of feminist theory and practice to Freudian and Lacanian psychoanalysis and argued in varying ways the necessity of excavating the patriarchal underpinnings of psychoanalytic theories of gender rela-tions. Similarly, I see each of the three novels I will discuss—Smith's *Black Mountain Breakdown,* Alice Walker's *The Color Purple,* and Al-lison's *Bastard Out of Carolina*—breaking the daughter's silence by exposing the exploitative power of the father. In each narrative the for-mation of the victim's/survivor's identity occurs in relation to the material spaces of incest and the cultural space encircling and forming that materiality.

In general, women's writing and life experiences, so often vexed with a sense of constricted material and cultural spaces because of gender and perhaps class, race, and sexuality as well, share certain borders with southern culture and literature, with their attention to place and the evocative nature of place in the formation of identity. As Lewis P. Simpson puts it, the South has traditionally been "both an emotional entity and a geographical place"[7]—a relation between identity and place that continues to be reflected in the writing of southerners. Within a dominant ideology that has historically emphasized the importance of property (owned place) and has manipulated women's bodies to that end, these southern women's stories trace the workings of patriarchal power within the father's house, explore the ideological construction of "home" (both as the material space of the house and the cultural space of the patriarchal family) as a space of female entrapment, and sometimes (not always) suggest that "home" can be reconstructed as a site of empowerment and survivorship for women.

Several feminist scholars recently have turned their attentions to the empowering retrieval of "home" in women's writing. Helen Levy has shown how the creation of "home place" by many women writers of the South and other regions of the United States has subverted masculinist systems and insisted upon neglected female power, and Ann Romines argues that in some American women's writing "the story of housekeeping, the 'home plot,' has generated forms and continuities very different from those of the patriarchal American canon."[8] I want to suggest here that, in incest narratives written by southern women— also stories of home space—the disruption of father-rule carries a particular insistence. This disruption, it seems to me, occurs in part because of the connection in southern culture between place (in these novels, the father's house—which may not be the father's but the landlord's) and identity (in these novels, the female's identity as daughter in the father's house). For the southern daughter in the patriarchal house, place and identity become compounded and conflicted because place/ identity equal(s) powerlessness.

This conflictual association of place and identity is multiply complicated in these narratives of father-daughter incest in that such a link is played out upon ideological networks of race, class, and gender in southern culture. These networks are located in the material spaces of rural geography as well as in cultural space. Narratives of incest have long circulated in southern popular culture and in popular culture about the South. Such narratives have been especially directed toward poor white Appalachian culture and other sparsely populated areas of the South (for example: the joke about the only ten-year-old virgin in Redneck/Hillbilly County; she's the one who can run fast [or the one whose daddy and brothers are in wheelchairs]. Or stories about *Deliverance*-style retarded offspring from the sexual relations of relatives).[9] The theme of incest from the point of view of the white male also has been the subject of southern male writers, particularly Faulkner, whose white male characters have had incestuous relations with a black daughter (*Go Down, Moses*) or desired a sister (*Flags in the Dust, The Sound and the Fury,* and *Absalom, Absalom!*). What Allison, Smith, and Walker do that Faulkner does not is to reveal and dramatize the effects of incestuous abuse on the female victim/survivor *from her perspective.*[10] (In *Go Down, Moses* the slave Tomasina, pregnant by her white father, never speaks.) These women's narratives of incest are intensely disturbing. They turn around unerringly to read the ideologies of patriarchal power and dominance that would seem to make father-daughter incest culturally inevitable. At the same time these stories, no matter what else they are (often they are also stories of great courage and insight), present the specter of female powerlessness under patriarchy.

I want to situate these three texts in yet another cultural space. Ranging in publication dates from 1980 to 1992, these novels span a period in recent history that has experienced an explosion of women's writing and speaking about incestuous abuse, particularly father-daughter incest. In this period of little more than a decade a whole discursive system has been built upon breaking what Sandra Butler called in 1978 "a conspiracy of silence" surrounding the issue of incestuous abuse, "a vastly elaborated intellectual tradition which served the purpose of suppressing the truth about incest."[11] As Judith Herman points out, this is a tradition of silencing the victim: "a tenacious prejudice, still shared by professionals and laymen alike, that children lie about sexual abuse." Herman argues that in the twentieth century this suppression of the reality of father-daughter incest originates in the work of Freud, who first acknowledged "seduction by the father" as the "essential point" in hysteria and then later repudiated his seduction theory. This silence about father-daughter incestuous abuse continues to configure a variety of psychiatric and legal studies and texts from Freud to the 1970s.[12] For incest survivors themselves who are part of an otherwise oppressed group, breaking silence may be translated as being disloyal to the family and community. In her introduction to *Crossing the Boundary: Black Women Surviving Incest*, Melba Wilson writes that telling about her sexual relationship with her father will be frowned upon and misconstrued by "many in our black communities," some of whom "may feel that I have breached an even greater taboo, crossed a bigger boundary (in their eyes) than incest." [13] The opening of survivor discourse, both in this country and abroad, has in fact largely been the work of feminism, rather than communal or clinical activism on behalf of victims/survivors; as Diane Russell notes, "It is a terrible indictment of both researchers and clinicians that credit for the public attention now focused on these serious and longstanding societal problems must be given not to themselves but to a political movement that was willing to provide validation and support for victims with the courage to tell the truth about their experiences." [14]

As Linda Alcoff and Laura Gray discuss at great length, however, there are other troubling issues surrounding survivor discourse and the way it functions within the discursive parameters set by dominant ideology. Themselves both survivors of incest, Alcoff and Gray argue that, although survival speech "has great transgressive potential" to disrupt dominant discourses that protect and enhance male power, those dominant discourses can and often do "subsume survivor speech in such a way as to disempower it and diminish its disruptive appeal." [15] Although it is to be hoped that survivor speech educates society and empowers victims, in reality "the speaking out of survivors has been sensationalized and exploited by the mass media" such as TV talk shows and programs with news-as-entertainment formats. Survivors are often eroticized, and discussions of sexual violence are used to titillate and expand audiences;[16] moreover, the confessional structure of survivor speech and its mediation by "experts," in addition to the speaker's own internalization of dominant ideas ("It was my fault"), often force such speech into conformity with dominant ideology. Alcoff and Gray argue that the transgressive challenge posed by survivor speech to dominant ideology is lost or greatly diminished when such speech about incestuous abuse, speech that has been and still is taboo, becomes a titillating media commodity objectifying the survivor, stripping her of authority and agency, and thereby deflecting attention away from the perpetrator and from societal responsibility for child abuse. Numerous "Geraldo" and "Oprah Winfrey" shows—among others—produce such effects. Furthermore, mediation of those experiences by "experts" whose theories or therapies position themselves as dominant over a survivor discourse conceptualized as "nontheoretical" displaces survivors as authorities on the subject of incest. What is needed, Alcoff and Gray insist, is a survivor discourse that is both experiential and theoretical, which "do[es] not retreat from bringing sexual violence into discourse, but, rather, . . . create[s] new discursive forms and spaces in which to gain autonomy within this process." [17]

Alcoff and Gray urge survivors to seize control of survivor discourse and make that discourse transgressive in every sense of the word. Interestingly, then, the issue of control of survivor discourse parallels the issue of control of the daughter's body. In terms of cultural narrative, Froula argues that the daughter in a literary text is much like the woman reader and writer in that she is "daughter of her culture"—a culture that inscribes mental and physical violence against women. [18] My project here is to suggest that more attention needs to be paid to southern women's fiction about incest for what it can tell us about master narratives of gender in the South and for its important contributions to the contemporary discursive network about incest in this country. Spatial strategies of the sorts I have discussed, of reading such texts, and particularly texts of southern women writers for whom place is such an essential and conflictual element, not only can set these texts into discursive circulation in new cultural contexts but also reveal the extent to which silence about incest still holds us hostage, as writers and as readers. My intention is not to become an outside "expert" who validates or theorizes from this fiction. I suggest instead that traveling the material, textual, and cultural spaces of these women's fictional narratives about the sexual abuse of girls by fathers can be part of a politics of transgressiveness creating more space for incest to be spoken, and heard.

> *And always in our daydreams, the house is a large cradle. . . .*
> *Life begins well, it begins enclosed, protected, all warm in the*
> *bosom of the house.*
>
> —GASTON BACHELARD, *The Poetics of Space*

Gaston Bachelard argues that we do not know ourselves in time but rather in space. Houses contain our memories of ourselves at certain times and these memories are quickened by material images of familiar spaces that return us to ourselves again and again. These images are of what Bachelard calls *felicitous space*[19]—space that is protective and maternal, "the space that we love." "The house," he says, "constitutes a body of images that give mankind proofs or illusions of stability." The "normal unconscious" is "well and happily housed, in the space of its happiness" and "knows how to make itself at home everywhere."[20] Bachelard constructs the felicitous space of the house as a stable order that protects, and the unconscious as therefore happy, healthy, and secure in its right to belong anywhere. Absent from this analysis is the question of power and gender. Who owns "the house"? Who rules the roost? And who offers that stability, security, and protection? What if the house is not a home?

Bachelard's notion of "the house" as a conflation of felicitous material and psychic spaces also parallels the ideological construction of "home" as a place of comfort and safety. Survivor discourse subverts and challenges such a construction of "home." Alcoff and Gray believe that "the notion that the 'home' signals safety and protection is a claim that is not only wrong but complicitous with sexual violence."[21] Its implicit reinforcement of the patriarchal construction of home space as felicitous for everyone makes it more difficult for women and children to name their fathers or father figures as attackers and thereby diminishes the credibility of survivor speech. Assigning "the house" the characteristics of maternal nurturance (as he puts it, "the maternal features of the house") makes Bachelard's claims for the efficacy of felicitous (home) space even more suspect from a feminist perspective, particularly when he also defines inhabited space as "the non-I [gendered female?] that protects the I [gendered male?]."[22] Given such a frame, it isn't surprising that Bachelard does not explore the dark corners of "the house," the silent spaces in which the father may exert his power.

What happens when the space of "home" becomes nonfelicitous? The space of the unspeakable? What happens when the unspeakable is spoken?

On the covers of my editions of these three novels, the words *incest, rape, sexual abuse* or similar terms do not appear. Although incest is by no means the central focus of one of the novels (*The Color Purple*), each novel does have incest as a significant topic. I wonder what this particular form of silence in marketing these books has to tell us about the cultural enclosure of survivor discourse and the ideological terrain these books inhabit. Unlike marketing strategies that Alcoff and Gray describe as manipulating survivor discourse for entertainment purposes, the omitted information and the tone of the cover descriptions of these books keep what Herman calls "the incest secret" secret.[23] These silences are particularly interesting in regard to *Black Mountain Breakdown* and *Bastard Out of Carolina,* both of which, in different ways, focus on the dangers to the victim of silence about incest and violence within the family. This is not to say that there are not important differences in how each text handles these topics. The incestuous abuse in *The Color Purple* is relegated to few actual words in the texts though these are indeed quite explicit, and the results of Celie's sexual abuse are multifarious. Situated in one claustrophobic space after another, *Bastard Out of Carolina* moves in excruciating fashion *toward* the particularly brutal rape, which looms larger and larger as it becomes inevitable. *Black Mountain Breakdown* is a study of the devastating effect of a rape that cannot be remembered until many years later. *The Color Purple* and *Bastard Out of Carolina* are primarily about survivorship though each depicts scenes of brutality. *Black Mountain Breakdown,* the only one of these books not to be told from the victim/survivor's point of view, is about Crystal's inability to survive victimization because of a failure to create her own survivor discourse. Interestingly, *The Color Purple* and *Bastard Out of Carolina* are primarily about poor rural people—black and white—whereas Smith's novel focuses on a family of white, middle-class, small-town Virginians. None of the fathers in these three texts is biological. Celie's father turns out not to be her father after all but her stepfather. Bone's attacker in *Bastard Out of Carolina* is her stepfather "Daddy Glen." Crystal's rapist is her mentally disabled uncle Devere, who, I will argue, carries out her father's incestuous desire. As in contemporary autobiographical narratives of survivors, the spaces of father-daughter incestuous abuse in these fictional texts, then, obviously have their own silent textual spaces, their own blank spots, and, at the same time, their own transgressive politics.

In part, their transgressiveness has to do with reversing the play of power between father and daughter through the act of telling the story of incest and thus revising a dominant cultural narrative of the father's power and the daughter's obeisance. This master narrative, as Lynda Zwinger has observed, has represented "normative" heterosexual desire within fiction that sentimentalizes women as desiring daughters whose fathers are innocent of any but culturally sanctioned designs upon them. These representations "ground the system of cultural constructs and prescriptions that we have learned to think of as heterosexual desire." Such stories, Zwinger points out, are always about power, and often the coercion of the father's "seduction" of the daughter is veiled: "The daughter's need for love and approval is glossed as complicity or even mutuality, while her vulnerability increases the titillation always encoded by virtue in distress." [24] As Jane Gallop shows in *The Daughter's Seduction: Feminism and Psychoanalysis,* unveiling the father's seductive power requires interrogating and sabotaging dominant narratives of gender identity and relations. [25]

These three narratives of father-daughter incest undertake this task variously, through confrontation and indirection, by "home" breaking and "home" making. In conflating the seductive father with his "retarded" rapist brother who "looks so much like [her father] that it sometimes makes Crystal cry to see him," [26] the first of these novels, Lee Smith's *Black Mountain Breakdown,* both masks and unmasks the father's power. The openly sinister space inhabited by her father Grant's double, his brother Devere, overlays what appears to be the innocent attachment of an ailing alcoholic father to his loving and obedient daughter. Grant is a father who has withdrawn from the world and, at the beginning of the novel, inhabits what was his wife Lorene's front parlor, which now "smells like old smoke, like liquor, like Grant himself, yet the combination is not unpleasant really and Crystal loves it" (14). Within this fatherspace, Grant reads to his adoring twelve-year-old daughter. He particularly likes to read poetry or stories that are either about death ("Little Boy Blue") and reduce Crystal to "huge racking sobs" (17), or are very frightening, such as "The Spider and the Fly":

> Grant makes his voice deep and full of cunning malice as he begins,
> " 'Will you walk into my parlor?' said the spider
> to the fly;
> " 'Tis the prettiest little parlor that ever you did
> spy.' "
> When the fly answers, Grant's voice is high and innocent.

" 'O no, no,' said the little fly, 'for I've often heard
    it said
They *never never wake* again, who sleep upon your bed.' "
Unconscious of what she's doing, Crystal twists the hem of her father's
    robe into a hard tight ball and bites it. (17)

During this seductive reading of a story of dangerous seduction, "Crystal sits close to [her father] on the floor, holding on to his knee under the old blue silk robe he always wears." Earlier she is both horrified and titillated by his reading of "Little Boy Blue," the poem about a child's death; "it's hard to tell by the tone of her voice whether she's delighted or upset. . . . her usually dreaming face is wholly alive." As Grant finishes "The Spider and the Fly," Crystal "shivers and lets all her breath out in one long shuddering sigh" at the same moment that her mother flings open the door and exclaims to her husband, "You ought to be ashamed of yourself!" (15–19). There are obvious erotic implications to this scene—the seductive story, the father's seductive reading, the daughter's fear and pleasure, the mother's outrage of discovery. As the novel progresses, Grant demands Crystal's presence in the parlor more and more often. We are told that when he calls "honey?" it isn't clear whether he is calling his wife, from whom he has withdrawn almost completely, or his daughter: "Maybe her but more likely Crystal; he wants Crystal all the time now. Lorene shuts the door before he has a chance to see her" (24). (The "her" here is left ambiguous; we are not certain whether Lorene doesn't want Grant to see her or their daughter.)

Parks Lanier Jr. has argued that after Crystal's rape by her uncle and the death of her father (which occur within a twenty-four hour period), the image of the dreadful parlor becomes Crystal's psychic space, a space from which she never escapes.[27] I want to suggest instead that Smith succeeds in bringing about a narrative enclosure of Crystal, which operates textually at the level of plot and character. (At the end of the novel, twenty years later, she is back in the family house, hysterically paralyzed and enclosed in her own room.) This incremental enclosure also operates within the reader's relation to Crystal. (During much of the novel, we don't know what is going on in Crystal's mind; and by the end of the novel, we, like the characters of the novel, are completely outside her mind while she, at age thirty-two, lies unmoving in her bed and staring at nothing "as outside her window the seasons come and go and the colors change on the mountain" [240].) Ultimately, we are failures at reading her story. There are too many silences. Just as Crystal's memory encloses and blanks out the actual rape for many years, in the end the space of the victim becomes a frozen, silent, uninhabitable terrain—a psychic space in which the reader remains as helpless as anyone else in the face of such silence, such blankness.

Crystal's enclosure also may be read in terms of the daughter's cultural space, which requires her, as Zwinger points out, "to want what she doesn't want," that is, to succumb to the desire of the father—in this case a failed southern father—and embed that desire with her own.[28] This is precisely Crystal's situation, as her father "reads" the patriarchal story to her. As Zwinger observes, "The production of a daughter with the right (that is, sympathetic to and complicitous with the father) reading perspective is an urgent patriarchal necessity. The one in the daughter's place is asked to agree to incite the very activity and instability she is constructed to disavow and also to repress any knowledge of the contradictions of her position. Essentially, this is the hysterical position."[29] Except for short periods in her life, Crystal essentially remains in the hysterical position, which reaches its culmination at the end of the novel as she lies in bed, not speaking and not moving—not even looking out the window. Similarly, Froula believes that the woman reader of a literary tradition that inscribes violence against women is an abused daughter and that, like physical abuse, "literary violence against women works to privilege the cultural father's voice and story over those of women, the cultural daughters, and indeed to silence women's voices."[30] Smith's project in *Black Mountain Breakdown*, it seems to me, is to expose the exploitative nature of the father's voice and his story as violent and destructive to the daughter.

The actual rape of Crystal by her uncle, which takes place in the material space of the toolshed at her father's family home, is textually enclosed between two scenes in the parlor with her father. In one he tells her gruesome stories of murder and hanging, including a story about a man killing his own son. In the other she finds her father dead and has to be dragged away from his body and tranquilized. She also refuses to leave her father's graveside, feeling "there's no ground at all, nothing but empty space beneath her feet" (66–67, 83). The night of her rape, remembering nothing, she sleeps in the bed in her father's childhood room "with her father's initials on the windowsill, W.G.S., the room where she always stays, and she does not dream" (69). Thus the textual space of the rape by Crystal's blank-looking uncle in relation to the material space of parlor indicates that the rape in the toolshed is the acting out of Grant's incestuous desire for his daughter, the desire that stays in the parlor (that remains seduction instead of rape) and is dissolved in death.

In the years that follow, Crystal the good daughter continues to want what she does not want. She wins beauty contests. She becomes promiscuous. She tries to be saved. She becomes involved with an angst-filled man who eventually hangs himself, leaving her to find his body. Finally, after being hospitalized with a breakdown, Crystal as an adult comes back to Black Rock and begins to teach. For the first time in her life she feels content and fulfilled. She is happier than she ever thought possible. She busies herself with her students and community activities. Then her former high school boyfriend Roger Lee Combs, who is married to another former classmate, appears at her door, declares his undying love for her, and persuades her to run off to Florida with him. When he kisses her breasts, "a feeling she has almost forgotten sweeps over her, closing her in" (209). The phrase "closing her in"—echoing the space of her rape and the claustrophobic parlor—is particularly apt here, for after Crystal runs off with Roger, her sense of well-being and purpose dissolves. As Anne Goodwyn Jones points out, she returns to passivity, to a state in which choices are made for her, rather than by her.[31] When Roger becomes more successful and runs for Congress, she finds she has nothing to do. She is campaigning for him by visiting a mental institution when one of the patients, a moon-faced man who reaches from his hospital bed for her hand, reminds her of Devere and triggers the memory of the rape. This encounter leads to a downward spiral back to her father and the enclosure of fatherspace ("the way daddy said it was" [235]). In the end, she goes home, lies down, and "paralyzes herself," becoming an uncanny double of her invalid withdrawn father and locating herself within the more narrow psychic space of the daughter-victim. To compound the father's seduction and the rape by her uncle, Crystal has been taught by her mother to embrace femininity, to "want what she doesn't want"—frosted hair, a boyfriend at an early age, beauty contests. Her eventual enclosure of self in hysteria, then, is "simultaneously what a woman can do both to be feminine and to refuse femininity, within patriarchal discourse."[32] It is a last resort.

Who speaks the survivor discourse in this novel? In *The Bluest Eye,*

Claudia speaks of "the damage done" and theorizes from a deep sense of what that damage is, both to Pecola and to the community. There is no character in *Black Mountain Breakdown* to serve such a function. Crystal's jealous friend Agnes is actually enjoying Crystal's paralysis and enclosure; Crystal's mother Lorene takes what comes and doesn't ask hard questions. The narrator's difference from and sympathy with Crystal's position is everywhere apparent, yet the narrator's position does not move into the arena of transgressive speech, except by indirection and implication. Material space (the parlor), textual space (the blankness and silence of Crystal's hysteria), and cultural space (the southern belle/failed father configuration) all move to enclose and silence the daughter. At the close of this novel I find myself as feminist reader drawn into a silent psychic space created by the narrator yet from which I am led to create a form of transgressive speech. Crystal herself gives me no clues but "just lies up there in that room every day, with her bed turned catty-corner so she could look out the window and see Lorene's climbing rambler rose in full bloom on the trellis and the mountain all green beyond the railroad track if she would turn her head" (238).

Look, I say, look outside your daddy's house. Look beyond your mama's roses. See the mountain all green.

Crystal, of course, does not answer.

> *Oh, Nettie, us have a house! A house big enough for us and*
> *our children, for your husband and Shug. Now you can come*
> *home cause you have a home to come to!*
> *Your loving sister,*
> *Celie*
>
> — ALICE WALKER, *The Color Purple*

In *Black Mountain Breakdown*, Crystal's victimization is figured in final enclosure within her father's house. Conversely, it is the redefinition of home space in *The Color Purple*—the recovery/renovation of "home" and its attendant restructuring of "family"—that makes female survivorship possible. For Celie, the renovated cultural space is the material space of the house, first Shug's house and then finally her own. Toward the end of the book Celie receives a telephone call from her stepfather's wife, Daisy. On the phone Daisy tells Celie that her stepfather, Alphonso, has died and the house in which he lived, along with the land and a dry goods store adjacent to it, actually belonged to Celie's biological father and so now was to be handed down to Celie and her sister Nettie. Alphonso, known to Celie as "Pa" and thought to be her father for many years, is the father of her two children through repeated rapes when she was fourteen and fifteen; he also bartered her off to Mr. —— (Albert) before she turned twenty. Celie's initial reaction is to say, "Anything coming from him, I don't want it."[33] However, with urging from Shug, she decides to take the property and make it her own.

This reconfiguration of material space—the house—is a process that occurs over time through concrete actions—a kind of "housekeeping"/"homemaking." It begins with Shug's smoking the house from attic to basement with cedar sticks, "chasing out all the evil and making a place for good" (217). "Making a place for good," in both of its meanings, soon thereafter becomes psychologically demanding when Shug leaves Celie for a young man named Germaine and Celie receives what turns out to be erroneous news that the ship carrying her sister Nettie and her family has been sunk off Gibraltar by the Germans. "Being alive," Celie writes, "begin to seem like an awful strain" (225). At the same time, though, Celie settles into her house and into what has been a gradual transformation of identity into someone who is in charge of "home" and self. She hires Sofia to help in the dry goods store. She realizes that she is at peace with herself and "can live content without Shug." She accepts her own lesbianism and rejects a second marriage offer by Albert, saying, "Naw, I still don't like frogs, but let's us be friends" (247). For hours, she and Albert sit on the porch and talk about the meaning of life. He makes shirts to go with her pants and even makes her a little purple frog perch for her mantelpiece—an implicit acceptance of her lesbianism. When Shug arrives, Celie shows her the pink room she has selected for her, and then her own room: "purple and red cept the floor, that painted bright yellow" (248). Celie has remade "home" (material and cultural spaces) as a place in which and through which she can reclaim her own identity—a reclamation that has been ongoing from the first pages in the book when she is raped by her stepfather and then, in a scene patterned on the model of southern slavery, is sold by him to Mr. —— for a cow. In the final scene, when Nettie and her family are dropped off at the edge of the drive and begin to walk slowly up the walk to Celie's house, it is for Celie a doubly resonant moment. She has a home to offer her sister, and she herself is at home in her own house.

Unlike Crystal, who, as Jones points out, is "beyond the healing capacity of language,"[34] Celie's recovery of material and cultural space is made possible by her creation of a textual space to gather and protect herself as a victim and to recreate herself as a survivor. Her letters mark on the page a material shape that has borders, margins, and substance. They trace and map her reembodiment as a woman, a lesbian, a mother, and a sister. For Celie, whose physical and psychic boundaries have been invaded again and again in the early part of her life, making a textual "home" to dwell within is an essential act of survival, one that remains crucial even at the end of the book when Shug and Nettie return. It is also critical, however, that Celie empowers herself to move across the borders of "home"—material, cultural, and textual spaces— to invite others inside. The remarkable openness with which she offers herself and her "home," her house and her text, creates a shared psychic space, not only with Albert, Shug, and her sister's family, but also with the readers of her story.

Although this is clearly a story of survivorship, there is, however, a disquieting convergence of cultural spaces in the novel. The obvious similarities in structure, narrative, point of view, and theme to women's slave narratives of the nineteenth-century South insinuate that a dominant ideology of white patriarchal privilege, with its linkages to property, can become a pattern for the relations of father and daughter in the African-American family.[35] These convergences reveal the production and reproduction of patriarchal ideology, as do certain readings (or censorship) of such spaces. In this sense, *The Color Purple* very clearly inhabits the terrain of contemporary survivor discourse which, through disclosure of father-daughter incest, unmasks the production of patriarchal power at its very site, the home, and in its most extreme form: "in the history of most incest survivors—eyes averted, voices unheard."[36] At the same time, the act of father-daughter incest in the novel is tied to the institution of slavery in a highly disturbing way because it renders the black father not only as "father" but also as master. Celie speaks the unspeakable—"Then he push his thing inside my pussy" (11). This is a story of the father's invasion of the daughter's physical and psychic space that also may be read as a cultural narrative whose story of incestuous abuse interlocks with the racial dynamics of historical intervention, the white invasion of African-American homespace, whose "survivor discourse" became the slave narrative and its literary antecedents. The fact that *The Color Purple,* vexingly enough, resembles a slave narrative suggests the incessant workings of power and domination that intersect and overlap the spatial dimensions to which we often confine them.

Some readers have strenuously resisted the novel's unveiling of patriarchal incestuous abuse in this southern African-American family and the transgressive feminist message of Celie's survivor discourse. When incest is reported, often the family breaks apart and the child is removed from the family and placed with other relatives or in foster care. Often the child is not adequately protected from recrimination from the father or father figure, and often she feels her removal from the family as punishment.[37] Vicious attacks on *The Color Purple* and its author from various "families," both from within the black community and outside it, have reproduced this pattern of blaming and dislocating the victim. The controversies involving the book have included widespread efforts to ban it from certain schools, libraries, and specific sites of reading. Responses from some members of the African-American community to Walker's portrayal of Alphonso and the early Albert, and their relations to Celie as father and husband, may also be related to the taboo described by Margaret Randall as "the speaking out, the telling,"[38] a taboo punishable (by the family or by society, or both) by putting the one who speaks "outside." To some members of the African-American community, as Melba Wilson points out, disclosure of "the dirty linen" may be construed as a disloyalty carrying more reprobation than incest itself.[39] A particularly egregious example of such "punishment" can be found in Philip R. Royster's "In Search of Our Fathers' Arms: Alice Walker's Persona of the Alienated Darling," in which he accuses Walker's fiction of portraying "women with frustrated psychosexual attitudes towards men (Ruth toward Grange, Meridian towards both Eddie and Truman, and Celie towards both Alfonso [sic] and Albert)." Walker's "alienation from black men [that] influences her portrayal of them in fiction" is described as the result of a childhood accident in which her brother shot her in the eye with a BB gun. Royster's essay attempts to uproot Walker's narrative of male-female relations from its home in the black community by portraying her as antimale, antiblack, and a bundle of childhood neuroses. (Interestingly, he does not mention her somewhat affectionate portrait of her own father in her essay "Father.") Royster also critically reproduces the all too familiar "blame the victim" syndrome by chiding Celie for being "too stupid to protect herself from Alfonso" and playing "the same game" with Albert.[40]

Transgressing an ideological terrain in which patriarchal power is maintained by silencing the female victim (or displacing her), *The Color Purple* thus occupies a dual position, as a text that tells Celie's story and as a textual configuration that certain critical communities have told stories *about.* Yet these positions elide, disclosing and denaturalizing the workings of the patriarchal "family," whether it be fictional or critical. So poised, Walker's novel, as narrative and as artifact, establishes, at once, the necessity, and the cost, of speaking out about incest.

> *My shoulder hit the doorjamb as he pushed me ahead of him into the bathroom. . . . He kept one hand on me while he pulled his belt out of its loops with the other. "Don't you dare say a word," he hissed at me. "Don't you dare."*
> *No, I thought. I won't. Not a word, not a scream, nothing this time. He pinned me between his hip and the sink, lifting me slightly and bending me over. I reached out and caught hold of the porcelain, trying not to grab at him, not to touch him. No. No. No. He was raging, spitting, the blows hitting the wall as often as they hit me. Beyond the door, Mama was screaming. Daddy Glen was grunting. I hated him. I hated him. The belt went up and came down. Fire along my thighs. Pain. . . . I would not scream. I would not, would not, would not scream.*
>
> —DOROTHY ALLISON, *Bastard Out of Carolina*

The space is the bathroom, the house, the fatherspace. In *Bastard Out of Carolina*, Allison draws it around us like a net. We as readers are being pulled into the material and cultural spaces of victimization in which a young girl named Bone lives with a violent and sexually abusive stepfather in a poor white southern family; as Bone puts it, "There was something icy in Daddy Glen's houses that melted out of us when we were over at our aunts."[41] Bone's mother tries to make meals of "flour-and-water biscuits with bacon-fat gravy" or crackers with ketchup (72). As Daddy Glen loses job after job, the net woven by poverty and violence pulls tighter and tighter. Bone and her sister Reese tiptoe around, stand in dark corners, know that the wrong gesture, the wrong word, the wrong silence will set him off. (Bone says, "There was no way I could be careful enough, no way to keep Daddy Glen from exploding into rage" [108].) Reading on becomes a claustrophobic experience in itself because we as readers are placed in the space of the object. We become Bone. Because the actual rape does not occur until the end of the novel, we, like her, stay on edge, each time expecting it to happen. Produced within this constricted space are the ideological workings of a dominant culture of white, middle-class health professionals indifferent to the victim's suffering and her fear of speaking and contemptuous of her mother's inability to stop the cycle of violence. In the end, when Bone is taken into the hospital (not for the first time) with multiple injuries from the rape, the sheriff reminds her of "Daddy Glen in a uniform. The world was full of Daddy Glens" (296). On an earlier trip to the hospital, Bone remembers, the doctor "looked angry, and impatient, and disgusted. He glared at Mama with no pity at all. I could feel Mama's fingers gripping the palm of my free hand, hear her breathing like she was going to be sick" (114).

I can attempt to extricate myself from this space, step back, and report: *Bastard Out of Carolina* is a brilliant meditation on the interactions of class and gender oppression in southern culture and the violence that erupts as a result. As Allison reminds us again and again, these are poor "white trash" people we are reading about. Like Grant Spangler in *Black Mountain Breakdown*, Daddy Glen is another failed southern father. Not only does he own no property; he cannot even hold a job to keep his family in shabby rental property for more than a few months at a time. His story draws us into the interlocking spaces of those interactions. It tells us what can happen when a man such as Daddy Glen, like Cholly Breedlove, transforms despair into violence against a daughter.

Yes, but. The truth is: I can choose not to read this book. But if I do read it, I am not outside looking into that bathroom. Nor am I really inside. But I am inside a textual space that reproduces material female space under patriarchy—a space that will be violated by rape by the end of the novel. A tiny bathroom. Locked door. Sweaty cursing man with belt. Cold porcelain. Slap of the belt. Things can only get worse.

And they do. As nearly all experts in child abuse point out, abuse inevitably escalates, and the child feels responsible. Then the discovery of violence and/or incestuous abuse often destroys the family unit and makes the victim feel guilt once again, this time for the family's dissolution. When an accidental discovery of Bone's injuries by her aunt results in a breakup of the family and sends her mother into a depression so severe that she cannot speak to her daughters or her extended family, Bone believes she is responsible for her mother's unhappiness: "It was my fault, everything. . . . I kept trying to figure out how I could have prevented it all from happening" (249).

Although she cannot prevent the abuse, Bone resists it. She will not scream. Her resistance seeps out under the bathroom door and through the cracks of the wall. In the end her resistance produces new spaces of survival and female connection that not only keep her alive but contain the potential of reproducing themselves again and again. Although her mother has left her, she sees herself, not yet thirteen years old, in relation to her mother and her mother's struggle. She wonders, "Who had Mama been, what had she wanted to be or do before I was born? . . . Her life had folded into mine. What would I be like when I was fifteen, twenty, thirty? Would I be as strong as she had been, as hungry for love, as desperate, determined, and ashamed?" (309). In the final scene of the book, Bone is sitting on the front porch with her aunt Raylene. In her pocket is the birth certificate her mother gave her before leaving. Having defended her own physical space so many times in her young life, she now opens herself up to allow her aunt to enter that space: "When Raylene came to me, I let her touch my shoulder, let my head tilt to lean against her, trusting her arm and her love. I was who I was going to be, someone like her, like Mama, a Boatwright woman. I wrapped my fingers in Raylene's and watched the night close in around us" (309).

It is tempting to conclude here and not discuss what I find most difficult to address about this novel: the disturbing link between pleasure and violence, not only for the perpetrator but also for the victim. (Angelou and Wilson both address this issue in discussions of their own abuse.) From early in her life when her mother first marries her stepfather, Bone is eroticized through violence. Her stepfather is continually snatching her up and rubbing her against him violently. Her beatings are obviously a sexual experience for him. It is more disturbing that she masturbates to fantasies of the violence that has made her victim and that she feels disgusted with herself. ("I lived in a world of shame," she says [113].) This is not an uncommon experience. As psychologist Karin C. Meiselman points out, for many victims "the humiliation and helplessness of their incest experience, along with premature sexual stimulation, can lead to attempts at mastery and reassertion of personal power in sexual ways."[42] Bone imagines herself being beaten by Daddy Glen with groups of acquaintances watching: "In my imagination I was proud and defiant. I'd stare back at him with my teeth set, making no sound at all, no shameful scream, no begging. Those who watched admired me and hated him. I pictured it that way and put my hands between my legs. It was scary, but it was thrilling too." These fantasies contrast with the reality of Bone's beatings: "There was no heroism possible in the real beatings. There was just being beaten until I was covered with snot and misery" (112–13).

In its unrelenting representations of incestuous violence far exceeding those of other such novels, including nonsouthern texts such as *The Bluest Eye* and Jane Smiley's *A Thousand Acres* and southern fiction not discussed here such as Kaye Gibbons's *Ellen Foster,* Allison's novel walks the tightrope of survivor discourse: the necessity of breaking silence and telling the story of abuse in specific detail without having that detail misused as Alcoff and Gray have shown it has been in popular culture, and thereby actually *contributing to* the ideology that perpetuates the father's power and violence in the first place. As Roseann Lloyd, one survivor writing in the anthology *She Who Was Lost Is Remembered,* acknowledges, this is not an easy balancing act: "The sexual details of abuse may seem to be a turn-on to the reader. Yet some explicit details *have to* be used . . . because the denial of abuse is so strong in our culture."[43] Allison herself has denounced "the pornography of victimization," commenting that "half of the incest books sell on sexual voyeurism. . . . It's very hard not to titillate when you're working with this kind of material, because American culture is consumed with it."[44]

This tightrope becomes even more perilous in a fictional text that itself is a commodified object—in the case of *Bastard Out of Carolina,* one both deeply disturbing in its subject matter and highly provocative in its ability to draw readers into its narrative space. This text, it seems to me, derives its very considerable power from its ability not only to reveal the horror of incestuous violence but also to make us keep reading by sustaining narrative suspense about the act of rape, which seems imminent at almost every turn of the page. In doing so, it may be read as a troubling commentary on the relation between pleasure and violence. It may also be read as a manipulation of that relation.

Anthropologist Henrietta Moore has suggested that a "text," be it a book or a living space, is not *representative* of ideology but is a *product* and *producer of* ideology, "of the 'lived' conditions of social reality."[45] The textual spaces of these women's stories of incest reveal the dynamic and incessant productions of ideology, as do my feminist readings of them. To read these stories with this awareness is to experience the process of ideology at work, to participate in the workings of this production and reproduction. Southerners have always maintained that place makes us who we are and that the stories we tell ourselves about "home"—the places we come from—are the means through which we negotiate identity. As I hope I have shown, the produced representation of the material and cultural spaces of father-daughter incestuous abuse in these three southern women's fictional texts interrogates the ideological construction of "home" and its felicity for girls and women when the father is in the house. That interrogation exposes the blank spaces in the cultural script and suggests that, for some daughters, "home" may not be grounded in place but in the *re*placement of the self elsewhere. What women's writing and feminist reading can do is to point to that other space, that "elsewhere," as Linda Abbandonato has described it,[46] in which the daughter can begin to write her own cultural story, create her own felicity. Call it home.

Notes

Susan Donaldson and Anne Goodwyn Jones have been of immeasurable help in the conceptualization of this essay.

1. I use the term *father* to refer to any male character who functions in the paternal role, such as a stepfather or uncle.

2. Susan Stanford Friedman, "Spatialization: A Strategy for Reading Narrative," *Narrative* 1, no. 1 (1993): 17.

3. Linda Alcoff and Laura Gray, "Survivor Discourse: Transgression or Recuperation?" *Signs* 18 (1993): 261.

4. Maya Angelou, *I Know Why the Caged Bird Sings* (New York: Bantam Books, 1970) and Louise M. Wisechild, *She Who Is Lost Is Remembered: Healing from Incest through Creativity* (Seattle: Seal Press, 1991).

5. Bertram Wyatt-Brown, *Southern Honor: Ethics and Behavior in the Old South* (New York: Oxford Univ. Press, 1982) and Patricia J. Williams, *The*

Alchemy of Race and Rights: Diary of a Law Professor (Cambridge: Harvard Univ. Press, 1991).

6. Christine Froula, "The Daughter's Seduction: Sexual Violence and Literary History," *Signs* 11 (1986): 632.

7. Lewis P. Simpson, Introduction to part 1, *The History of Southern Literature*, ed. Louis D. Rubin et al. (Baton Rouge: Louisiana State Univ. Press, 1985), 9.

8. Helen Levy, *Fiction of the Home Place* (Jackson: Univ. of Mississippi Press, 1992), 24; Ann Romines, *The Home Plot: Women, Writing and Domestic Ritual* (Amherst: Univ. of Massachusetts Press, 1992), 17.

9. Interestingly, *The Encyclopedia of Southern Culture* is silent on the subject of incest. There are no entries in either the table of contents or the subject index for either *incest* or *sexual violence,* nor is there a discussion of sexual violence, except for a brief discussion about the rapes of African-American women during slavery (*Encyclopedia of Southern Culture,* ed. Charles Reagan Wilson and William Ferris [Chapel Hill: Univ. of North Carolina Press, 1989]).

10. This is not to say that each of these three narratives is told from the point of view of the victim/survivor. In *Black Mountain Breakdown,* it is, in fact, often difficult to know what Crystal Spangler is thinking.

11. Sandra Butler, *Conspiracy of Silence* (San Francisco: Volcano Press, 1985), 9.

12. Judith Herman, with Lisa Hirschman, *Father-Daughter Incest* (Cambridge: Harvard Univ. Press, 1981), 9–18.

13. Melba Wilson, *Crossing the Boundary: Black Women Surviving Incest* (Seattle: Seal Press, 1994), 1.

14. Diane Russell, *The Secret Trauma: Incest in the Lives of Girls and Women* (New York: Basic Books, 1986), 5.

15. Alcoff and Gray, "Survivor Discourse," 270.

16. Ibid., 262.

17. Ibid., 273–80, 287.

18. Froula, "The Daughter's Seduction," 633.

19. Judith Fryer has taken this term as the title of her 1986 book *Felicitous Space: The Imaginative Structures of Edith Wharton and Willa Cather* (Chapel Hill: Univ. of North Carolina Press, 1986).

20. Gaston Bachelard, *The Poetics of Space* (Boston: Beacon Press, 1969), xxxi, 17, 10. Bachelard's theories of space and place have obvious implications for southern literature, as evidenced by the volume *The Poetics of Appalachian Space,* ed. Parks Lanier (Knoxville: Univ. of Tennessee Press, 1991).

21. Alcoff and Gray, "Survivor Discourse," 276.

22. Bachelard, *Poetics,* 7, 5.

23. Herman, with Hirschman, *Father-Daughter Incest,* 12.

24. Lynda Zwinger, *Daughters, Fathers, and the Novel: The Sentimental Romance of Heterosexuality* (Madison: Univ. of Wisconsin Press, 1991), 5, 9.

25. Jane Gallop, *The Daughter's Seduction: Feminism and Psychoanalysis* (Ithaca: Cornell Univ. Press, 1982), 46.

26. Lee Smith, *Black Mountain Breakdown* (New York: Ballantine, 1980), 29. Subsequent page references appear parenthetically in text.

27. Parks Lanier Jr., "Psychic Space in Lee Smith's *Black Mountain Breakdown*," in *The Poetics of Appalachian Space*, 63.

28. Zwinger, *Daughters, Fathers, and the Novel*, 120. (Zwinger generalizes this argument to women writers as well.)

29. Ibid., 122.

30. Froula, "The Daughter's Seduction," 633.

31. Anne Goodwyn Jones, "The World of Lee Smith," in *Women Writers of the Contemporary South*, ed. Peggy Whitman Prenshaw (Jackson: Univ. Press of Mississippi, 1984), 262.

32. Juliet Mitchell, *Women: The Longest Revolution* (London: Virago, 1984), 289.

33. Alice Walker, *The Color Purple* (New York: Pocket Books, 1982), 215. Subsequent page references appear parenthetically in text.

34. Jones, "The World of Lee Smith," 263.

35. In "'The Permanent Obliquity of an In(pha)llibly Straight': In the Time of Daughters," Hortense Spillers has argued that, to the contrary, both "father" and "daughter" are terms contingent upon patriarchal privilege and hence do not "suffice for occupied or captive persons and communities in which the rites and rights of gender function have been exploded historically into gender neutralities" (in *Changing Our Own Words*, ed. Cheryl A. Wall [New Brunswick: Rutgers Univ. Press, 1991], 129).

36. Toni A. McNaron and Yarrow Morgan, *Voices in the Night: Women Speaking about Incest* (San Francisco: Cleis, 1982), 11.

37. Herman with Hirschman, *Father-Daughter Incest*, 129–43.

38. Margaret Randall, Preface, in *She Who Was Lost Is Remembered: Healing from Incest through Creativity*, ed. Louise M. Wisechild (Seattle: Seal Press, 1991), xi.

39. Wilson, *Crossing*, 1.

40. Philip M. Royster, "In Search of Our Fathers' Arms: Alice Walker's Persona of the Alienated Darling," *Black American Literature Forum* 20 (winter 1986): 349, 362, 367. See Deborah E. McDowell's "Reading Family Matters," in this volume for further discussion of this and other attacks on Walker's depictions of black males and the black family.

41. Dorothy Allison, *Bastard Out of Carolina* (New York: Penguin, 1992), 80. Subsequent references appear parenthetically in text.

42. Karin C. Meiselman, *Resolving the Trauma of Incest* (San Francisco: Jossey-Bass, 1990), 49.

43. Roseann Lloyd, "Writing My Self into Existence" in *She Who Is Lost,* 72.

44. Dorothy Allison, interview, qtd. in Michael Bronski, "Dorothy Allison," *The Gay and Lesbian Literary Companion,* ed. Sharon Malinowski and Christa Brelin (Detroit: Visible Ink Press, 1995), 3.

45. Henrietta L. Moore, *Space, Text and Gender: Anthropological Study of the Marakwet of Kenya* (Cambridge: Cambridge Univ. Press, 1986), 87.

46. Linda Abbandonato, "A View from 'Elsewhere': Subversive Sexuality and the Rewriting of the Heroine's Story in *The Color Purple,*" *PMLA* 106 (1991): 1108.

PART SEVEN

The Past in the Present

Retelling Southern Histories

The True Happenings of My Life

Reading Southern Women Autobiographers

PEGGY W. PRENSHAW

IN SEPTEMBER 1932 Helen Dick Davis, a thirty-two-year-old writer living at the time in the little sawmill town of Philipp, Mississippi, received an extraordinary letter from Mary Hamilton, a woman from the backwoods of the Mississippi Delta. Davis had come to know the frail Mrs. Hamilton, who was then sixty-five, as the mother of her friend Edris and, more importantly, as a rich repository of stories of the clearing and settling of the Delta over the half-century span of her life there. Convinced that Hamilton's vivid tales of floods and cyclones, escaped convicts, and "feuds to the death" should be preserved, Davis urged her to write them down, "if only," she said, "as a record for her children and grandchildren."[1] Mary Hamilton complied with a few short sketches written with pencil on tablet paper. These were enough, however, to intensify Davis's determination to urge upon her the writing of a book-long personal narrative. Understandably, Mary Hamilton resisted. Unlike her young friend, who had a degree in journalism from the University of Wisconsin, Hamilton was neither a writer nor an educated woman. In addition to the sketches she had done to please Helen Davis, she had otherwise in a lifetime written only a few letters. Nonetheless, in early fall 1932 she wrote Davis that she would undertake the project. She begins her letter: "This is the first day I have sat up and I am going to write you the very first one, my best friend. I am convinced I am a selfish old lady, and it was a dream I had yesterday morning convinced me." She goes on to describe a remarkable vision. In the dream she is with Helen Davis's two children, picking lilies, handing all the flowers to them until she tires, telling them: "You get no more, children. This last is mine." Punishment for her "selfishness" comes immediately in the figure of a black snake's head, but she is spared and the children are returned to laughter. She concludes her letter with her interpretation of the vision: "I can't help believing that my little friend Nick, himself so lately from the Beyond, by coming to me in my dream and laughing at my selfishness, has given me courage to work on to the end of the trail. I believe that I have been spared to gather for myself that last and largest white lily, the writing down in a book the memories of a lifetime.

"So I will write down for you the true happenings of my life, and if I succeed all honor goes to Nick. I can hardly wait till I get home to start work and to see you."[2]

Hamilton's elaborate rationale—or rationalization—for the writing of her memoirs, published at last in 1992 as *Trials of the Earth*, is a clear indication of her resistance to the self-aggrandizement, or "selfishness," that autobiographical writing represents in her early twentieth-century world. Even when the writing is focused not upon the self but the self's surround—the family, the neighbors, the workaday world—as Mary Hamilton's book is, the southern woman writing autobiography is ever mindful of the risk she incurs in asserting a self in print. The double bind that constrained nineteenth-century European and American women generally was especially intense in the American South. For women, honor and good name and "selfhood," such as might be confirmed by one's society, were attendant largely upon a woman's acceptance of a private—not public—domain. The act of expressing herself in public in writing, of intruding the female self upon the male-dominated turf, meant risking her standing in her family and acceptance by her neighbors, her church, by the whole wide world, as far as she could tell. Even a backwoods woman like Mary Hamilton had to invoke a divine revelation and offer a confession of selfish transgression to justify to herself her "right" to tell the story of her life.

Southern women autobiographers present an especially complex problem for readers who approach personal narratives with questions about the "true happenings" supposedly represented and about the autonomy or self-possession signified in the narrators' personal pronouns—the I's and me's in the life writings, the "my" in Hamilton's assertion that she will write "my life." To read texts by southern women autobiographers with understanding, one faces the necessity not only of comprehending the shaping influences of gender ("women's writing") and the problematical literary-linguistic context of the form (the "mixed genre" of autobiography), but also their sociohistorical and regional context (their "southernness"). Doing so, one finds that a major barrier to a reader's direct engagement with the autobiographical self in these texts is the southern woman's indirection and obliquity in her revelations of self. The socialization that has constrained overt expressions of a public identity has also produced, not surprisingly, life writings that efface, or repress, or reconfigure a separate self in favor of subjectivity formed by a web of relationships, a subjectivity most fully approachable by means of inference. Although one may argue for an exception in the case of professional writers such as Ellen Glasgow, Zora Neale Hurston, or Eudora Welty—autobiographers whose work I will consider briefly later—one may fairly ask whether such women as Mary Hamilton even write of the self. And if they do, wherein is this southern female self? Is it expressed as the protagonist of the story? the narrator who recollects and relates it to the reader? or the woman with the pencil and tablet in hand, the one fashioning the narrator and protagonist? If we find that neither the narrator nor the reflective author is the self foregrounded, but rather the protagonist, a southern female figure who acts and reacts but reveals little of a self-reflecting consciousness, should the text then be called an autobiography?

Of course, these are also the very questions that form the center of debate of the past several decades about the theoretical underpinnings of autobiographical writing. And indeed, the questions or tensions between the truth claims (the "true happenings" domain) of speakers and writers and the instability and fluidity of language, whether that used by the writer or that read by the reader, have been subjected to steady, mainstream theorizing for a century. This scholarly debate about the problematic nature of autobiography comprises many useful insights one may productively apply to a reading of the texts and textual intentions of southern women autobiographers, writers who employ many strategies for simultaneously masking and revealing the self. When Mary Hamilton writes that she had a vision of two children, white lilies, and a black serpent's head, one puzzles over what she is *telling* Helen Davis and then turns to linguistic and psychological theories for help in interpreting her verbalization of the vision. Is her account "true"? How is one ever to know? And if posited as true by her and us, then what does Hamilton's account of the dream reveal?

Certainly one meaning revealed in this short passage from Hamilton's letter is the assertion of a creator self, even if a self cloaked in the rags of apology and denial, one who holds the power to create the past in her own present perception and words. Mary Hamilton the letterwriter reminds us that the referentiality of the text always hangs upon the writing self. Here is how she relates her recalling and interpreting the dream: "I woke with a start. Was I going to die? Was that snake head that just grazed my finger, Death? . . . I lay awake thinking about my dream, and when the late mail that day brought your letter to Edris I felt sure that my dream meant something and I had been spared for some purpose." [3]

On the face of it, Hamilton's story is not written for the purpose of self-reflection, for an understanding and analysis of how the life she had led has produced the person she is at the time of her writing. And above all, it is not a meditation upon the nature of that writing self, that crippled sixty-five-year-old woman facing death directly. Typifying many personal narratives by women, especially those by women who are not professional writers, her book issues from a construction of the self that lies between individualism and community, to invoke a paradigm that Elizabeth Fox-Genovese has most widely employed in articles and monographs about the female autograph. [4] Hamilton's account is filled with accounts of lumbering camps, her hard work of cooking for as many as eighty men, her work in the field, her piloting a ferry boat, keeping a rough backwoods home for an English-born husband who refused to be served the pork and corn foods of the Mississippi Delta, supporting siblings and neighbors, above all, bearing children—nine children, four of whom would die in infancy or childhood. Her story is presented to her reader as a recollected narrative of what happened *to* her, and decidedly not as the active recollecting of a dominating consciousness. In so writing her story, she reminds one of predecessors and contemporaries who likewise recounted life narratives with their female selves firmly effaced. Such texts have raised many questions for literary scholars and historians about genre placement—what do you call such texts?—the naming or categorizing by genre mattering because it greatly determines how we read the texts.

To understand more fully the issues at stake in the affixing or withholding of the designation *autobiography* in describing personal or life writing, one may consider one of the best known and most widely analyzed cases among nineteenth-century texts by southern women, the journal of Mary Chesnut. In 1982 Yale University Press published C. Vann Woodward's 886-page edition of *Mary Chesnut's Civil War*. Two earlier, shorter editions published in 1905 and 1949 with the title *A Diary from Dixie* had made portions of the Chesnut journal widely available—and widely admired. Edmund Wilson wrote of the journal in his 1962 study of the literature of the Civil War, *Patriotic Gore,* that it "is an extraordinary document—in its informal department, a masterpiece." He notes that "the very rhythm of her opening pages at once puts us under the spell of a writer who is not merely jotting down her days but establishing, as a novelist does, an atmosphere." In fact, he finds the Chesnut journal "much more imaginative and revealing than most of the fiction inspired by the war."[5]

With the more recent research of Woodward, Elisabeth Muhlenfeld, and other Chesnut scholars, we now have an expanded understanding of Chesnut's composition of the journal. To begin with, the journal, or diary, as it was known to the public in the 1905 and 1949 versions, was composed twenty years after the recorded events actually took place. Chesnut did keep a diary during the Civil War years, but the wartime diary differs greatly from the revised version of 1881–84. Woodward acknowledges that "the dating of the manuscript will inevitably raise questions among historians about the use of her writings and the way historians have used them extensively in the past. The bare fact of date of composition," writes Woodward, "certainly changes the prevalent conception of the work and removes it from the conventional category of 'diary.'"[6]

Indeed, threading throughout Woodward's introduction to this impressive, fascinating book is his puzzlement over what exactly *is* its nature and how to assess and understand, as he says, "the character of the art involved." He writes: "The importance of Mary Chesnut's work, of course, lies not in autobiography, fortuitous self-revelations, or opportunities for editorial detective work. She is remembered only for the vivid picture she left of a society in the throes of its life-and-death struggle, its moment of high drama in world history. . . . The enduring value of the work, crude and unfinished as it is, lies in the life and reality with which it endows people and events and with which it evokes the chaos and complexity of a war."[7]

For clarity and ease, Woodward adopts the practice in his introduction of referring to Chesnut's 1880s version as a "book" and to the 1860s version as a "journal." His quandary over what finally to call this text is reflected in the title he gave it: *Mary Chesnut's Civil War.* Clearly, he values it chiefly as a source of information about the times, not as a literary creation in which a woman creates a self/herself by way of recounting her story of the Civil War. And yet there is some recognition of the literary and autobiographical purposes in that title: *Mary Chesnut's Civil War.*

By and large autobiography has been regarded, at least until post-structuralist and feminist theoretical revisions, as the prose form least susceptible to the craft of the literary artist, especially so for those auto-biographical works that aim to depict faithfully the facts and events of the life witnessed. Here the writer appears to be at the mercy of the record, rather than the maker of it, subservient to the chronicle of events that is to be told. For this reason scholars prior to the 1980s typically sought to differentiate autobiography from diary or memoir or journal, naming as *autobiography* what they regarded as the more crafted and serious form, in which the development of the self is the chief object of attention, and naming as memoir the less deliberate, less artistic form, in which the persons and events surrounding the self are witnessed, interpreted, and recorded.

For example, Karl J. Weintraub (1975) insists upon the distinction between autobiography as a reflection upon the inward realm of experience and memoir as a record of the external realm of fact. He argues that "real autobiography" is dominated by self-consciousness, that it is most valuable when it focuses upon the character or personality of the self. Weintraub writes that, by contrast, "the diary, the letter, the chronicle, the annal have their value because they are but momentary interpretations of life; the premium for them lies in the function of faithful recording and not in the function of assigning long-range meaning." He concludes that "autobiography and diary do not mix well."[8]

Elizabeth Bruss (1976) is not so doctrinaire as Weintraub; she locates the significance of autobiography in the acts of writing and reading, that is, in the expectations or assumptions a writer or reader of a particular speech community brings to such acts. Unlike Weintraub, she does not advance guidelines for differentiating kinds of personal narrative to establish a hierarchy of autobiographical status. In fact, she finds "no intrinsically autobiographical form," although she does observe that the information and events reported in connection with the autobiographer are asserted as "true" and are expected to be regarded as true by the reader, who is free to "check up" on them. Cautioning against elaborate theorizing about autobiography, Bruss calls for a close reading of the "clues" provided by the text for insights into the author's intentions and psyche.[9]

A similar position had been advanced earlier by James Olney

(1972). He defines autobiography as, "intentionally or not, a monument of the self as it is becoming, a metaphor of the self at the summary moment of composition."[10] Perhaps the most influential statement asserting that psychological and aesthetic patterns should be the focus of autobiographical study, not facticity, was that of Georges Gusdorf (1956). Gusdorf held that the "literary, artistic function" of autobiography is "of greater importance than the historic objective function," that, in fact, "autobiography is not possible in a cultural landscape where consciousness of self does not, properly speaking, exist."[11] In important respects, Gusdorf anticipates Weintraub in defining autobiography as a sustained, self-reflective, self-analytical narrative.

I cite these works from the 1970s and earlier to suggest the relative agreement among scholars, even among those with differing approaches and points of emphasis, that the forms and intentions of autobiography are signifiable, knowable, and located in a stable text. But then, of course, the floodgates of feminist and poststructuralist theoretical writings opened. In the past two decades there have been hundreds of articles and books written in this country, not to mention in Europe, by scholars of history, language and literature, communications, and the behavioral sciences on theories of writing and reading autobiography. And whereas before the 1980s there were virtually no Anglo-American studies devoted specifically to female autobiographers, or even general studies of autobiography that included women to any significant degree, there have been at least a dozen such books and many more articles published since then. In a 1992 article Marjanne E. Gooze counts up and discusses a group of ten monographs and essay collections appearing in the 1980s that focus upon theories and practices of interpreting women's autobiographies.[12] These include well-known collections edited by Estelle Jelinek, Domna Stanton, Leonore Hoffman and Margo Culley, Sidonie Smith, Shari Benstock, Bella Brodzki and Celeste Schenck, as well as monographs by Carolyn Heilbrun and Francoise Lionnet.

At present, I see no indication of waning interest or closure in the theorizing of autobiography. There does seem to be an expanding consensus that facticity is an illusion in autobiographies as in other writings—"Don't be naive and read a personal narrative as a source of 'facts,'" readers are constantly reminded, and yet everyone seems to go right ahead and presume, as Elizabeth Bruss predicted, some referentiality to "truth."[13] But there is no consensus so far I can discern about the nature of autobiographical subjectivity, that is, about the nature of the self, or subject, as constructed in personal narrative, nor is there agreement about the definition of the genre of autobiography, that is, about the kind of text the personal narrative is and the way in which it should or can be read. The ambiguities about text and self must nonetheless be confronted by literary scholars and historians at every turn of their reading and commentary upon life writings, and their theoretical stance will of course dispose them to find factual, empirical information or psychological tracings of identity or aesthetic form or whatever.

The consequence of this sometimes murky theorizing for the matter I am discussing, the reading of southern women's autobiographies, is this: most life writings by southern women are not "real" autobiographies by Weintraub's definition, nor are they aesthetically significant autobiographies by Gusdorf's definition. The characteristic approach for a female writer of the nineteenth-century South, as well as for most of the twentieth century, as indeed for most women elsewhere, has not been studied attention to and analysis of the self. Such an overt display of self would have been regarded as immodest, egotistical, and above all unladylike, thereby attracting hostile reaction and dismissal from many of the very audience one seeks to address. Understandably, we find instead texts that focus attention not on the self but on the selves and events that surround the writer, and most typically in forms we call diary, journal, memoir, daybook, letters—those fragmented, discontinuous "lower" forms. Even in sustained, lengthy narratives, such as that of Mary Hamilton or even of such a public figure as Mississippian Belle Kearney in *A Slaveholder's Daughter* (1900), the focus is not upon the individual or autonomous self but upon a relational self that emerges indirectly from the author's account of others.

Mary Chesnut, for example, was adamant and explicit about her intention not to write about herself. In June 1883 she wrote in a letter to Varina Howell Davis, Jefferson Davis's wife: "How I wish you could read over my journal. I have been two years overlooking it—copying—leaving myself out. You must see it—before it goes to print—but that may not be just now. I mean the printing—for I must overhaul it again—and again." [14] Two instances of Chesnut's deleting herself from the book occur in the March 1861 passages. After a vigorous description of the preceding evening, when the drawing room had been filled with judges, governors, senators, generals, and congressmen, she turned to some thoughts of her husband and herself and then to her writing. Her original notation was abrupt, expressing embarrassment, and was later scratched. Woodward restores the deletions: "What nonsense I write here. However, this journal is intended to be *objective*. My subjective days are over. No more silent eating into my own heart, making my own misery. [She stops here.] I think this journal will be disadvantageous for me, for I spend the time now like a spider, spinning my own entrails instead of reading, as my habit *was* at all spare moments." [15]

In another deleted passage she writes: "I wonder if other women shed as bitter tears as I. They scald my cheeks and blister my heart. Yet Edward Boykin wondered and marveled at my elasticity—was I always so bright and happy, did ever woman possess such a disposition, life was one continued festival, etc., etc., etc., etc. Much they know of me—or my power to hide trouble—much trouble." [16]

In *A Slaveholder's Daughter,* Belle Kearney similarly submerges much of the feeling, desiring, judging self in her portraits of her father, family, friends, and in accounts of prohibition and suffragist activities.[17] William Andrews finds Kearney's suppression of her radically reformist self and her failure to expose explicitly the oppression of the patriarchy to be an act of bad faith. In his view, both Booker T. Washington, speaking as the "New Negro," and Belle Kearney, as the "New Woman," tried "to have it both ways." They wanted "to reform the patriarchal order, while appealing to the patriarch for sanction to do so." [18] Washington's and Kearney's books are acts of politics as well of self-expression. One might argue that their autobiographical stance is that of political moderation, rather than moral confusion or cowardice. What concerns me more, however, is a finding of failure in Kearney's autobiography to separate the self from the compromising, relational web of family affiliations and friendships. Her refusal or inability to posit a clearly defined separate self, an autonomous and ideologically consistent self, is an attribute she shares with contemporaneous and indeed with most prior and subsequent southern women autobiographers.

Mary Chesnut, Belle Kearney, Susan Dabney Smedes in *Memorials of a Southern Planter,*[19] no less than Mary Hamilton, explicitly derive identity from fathers or husbands and define selfhood—or construct their subjectivity—in relation to family, community, church, and local polity. Even Harriet Jacobs in *Incidents in the Life of a Slave Girl,* exposing as she does the abuse and oppression she suffered in the South and North during the antebellum period, constructs an identity that is interwoven not only with her family but with her oppressors and the white Victorian standard bearers whose judgment of women rested largely upon sexual purity. We could say of her, too, that indirectly, through the form of the sentimental novel that she employs, and directly, in her presentation of a self characterized as Linda Brent in the autobiography, she appeals for patriarchal sanction of the reforms she implicitly urges upon the patriarchs.[20]

Susan Stanford Friedman observes that "the individualistic concept of the autobiographical self raises serious theoretical problems for critics who recognize that the self, self-creation, and self-consciousness are profoundly different for women, minorities, and many non-Western peoples." She argues that "from both an ideological and psychological perspective . . . individualistic paradigms of the self ignore the role of collective and relational identities in the individuation process of women and minorities." Positing individualism as a prerequisite for autobiography in the manner, say, of Gusdorf, Weintraub, or even Bruss, Friedman regards as a "reflection of privilege, one that excludes from the canons of autobiography those writers who have been denied by history the illusion of individualism."[21] But she also asserts, and I agree with her, that the sense of collective or relational identity that women express is clearly as much a compensating strength as a lack.

I would also maintain that southernness disposes both male and female autobiographers to experience and express a relational rather more than an individualistic sense of self. Bertram Wyatt-Brown's study of southern honor and Steven Stowe's study of patterns of intimacy and power in the nineteenth-century South both point toward the social, relational origins of southern identity.[22] In her work on twentieth-century southern women's autobiographical and fictional writing, Lucinda MacKethan similarly identifies a sense of self that is grounded in social relationships. She outlines attributes of regionality that constitute "a southern way of seeing," which she finds exemplified by the subjects of her study, Ellen Glasgow, Zora Neale Hurston, and Eudora Welty. This southern way of seeing comprises, "first, respect for family as the heart of social order; next, the symbolization of the home as the locus of all inheritable values; third, the tension between hate and love for the father, who in the culture holds the power to define, to validate, to circumscribe, and to disinherit; and finally, acceptance of memory as the primary means of knowing."[23] The family, the home, the dominant male order—that is, a web of personal, relational affiliations—these are chief components of the lives typically depicted by female autobiographers and by southerners. Even professional writers like Glasgow, Hurston, and Welty, who have cultivated a distinctive voice and style, reflect these patterns, as MacKethan shows. Reading their texts calls upon the reader to engage selves that dissolve into other selves, protagonists who sometimes seem nearly invisible, and narrators who resist forthright expression, expressing intentions indirectly, even obliquely, but narrators who often demonstrate an acute political sense of the uses of language for winning approval of others and for influencing others' actions.

Reading the southern women's journals recently edited by Michael O'Brien, one comes to see how even in the case of so affluent and educated a woman as Elizabeth Ruffin, sister of the agricultural reformer Edmund Ruffin, or of Jane Caroline North, a quintessential belle of South Carolina, a woman sought public esteem and self-worth through social affiliations, not through independent, competitive mastery. Although Elizabeth Ruffin might voice some ambivalence about the circumscribed role of the lady, she and the other diarists find so much support and pleasure in the association with other women that they decide on balance they have the preferable lot in a strictly gendered world. "Oh! the disadvantages we labor under, in not possessing the agreeable independence with the men," Ruffin writes, "'tis shameful, that all the superiority, authority and freedom in all things should by partial nature all be thrown in their scale; 'tis bad to be a woman in some things, but preferable in others, 'tho you may crow over me, and glory in the unlimited sphere of your actions and operations, I envy you not and would not change with you to-day."[24]

For Ann Lewis Hardeman, a woman of deep Christian faith who at forty-six assumed the care of her dead sister's six children, her role as a surrogate mother in a domestic network of heavy family obligations constitutes her world, utterly dominating her life and imagination, as O'Brien observes. In a typical entry, that of Sunday, July 10, 1859, she writes:

> Our dear James arrived with his uncle W. from Oxford where he had spent the last 4 yrs. to complete his term at College—having left Sept. 8th 1855—I do not hesitate to say that he has in every respect fulfilled the expectations of his *entire* family—May he be watched over by the

eye that never slumbers and in whose hands the balances of life will be properly adjusted—may he ever watch with a vigilant eye over the conduct of life of his *dear sisters* and supply the place of Mother and Father to them. Our dear Oscar we expect to part with in a few weeks for Oxford. On Saturday 16th Dear A.G.S. and family spent the day with us—Mr. Purnell came out to breakfast and went fishing with the boys and returned home to Brandon—in the evening 19th Tuesday. My dear brother returned from Sonora in health though much fatigued—brought Henry over—and left a fine growing crop and all well—and satisfied and contented.[25]

In these diaries, as in the journal of Chesnut or the narrative of Harriet Jacobs or the autobiography of Belle Kearney, one reads personal writing that constructs the female self as connected in limitless ways with others. This self may be a contingent, uncertain, anxious being, especially when subjected to judgments according to male values of dominance and hierarchy; but the female self can also mirror great strength and resilience, supported precisely by the web of connections that constrain and define her identity. Nancy Chodorow, a theorist of psychoanalytical feminism, has proposed an analysis of the development of the female self in Western societies that is frequently applied to the study of women's autobiographies. She observes that the consequence of our child-rearing practices is that "girls grow up with a sense of continuity and similarity to their mother, a relational connection with the world," whereas boys, who must construct a gendered self by being different from their mothers, construct selfhood upon separation and difference.[26] Chodorow's theory of difference has been sharply questioned, however, by Katha Pollitt and others, who point out that the manifestation of a relational or an autonomous self may be attributed as reasonably to differences in economic and social positions as to some universal effects of child rearing.[27]

Whatever position one takes regarding the origin of socialization patterns that influence females to seek selfhood in affiliation rather than separateness, there are few other literary examples that so authoritatively validate and express women's relational connection with the world as clearly as the autobiographies of southern women. The pattern is continuous from the antebellum period very nearly to the present. One may note somewhat more forceful expressions of autonomy in women who have founded professional writing careers upon an authoritative voice or an uncommon self—women such as Glasgow or Hurston—or among younger women who have directly experienced the contemporary women's movement with its deliberate questioning of society's repression of female voice and power, but the insistent pattern of southern female experience, even among exceptional autobiographers, corresponds more closely to Mary Hamilton's *Trials of the Earth* than to, say, Lillian Smith's independent, self-focused, and reflective *Killers of the Dream* (1949) or Katharine Du Pre Lumpkin's *The Making of a Southerner* (1947).

Mary Hamilton opens her narrative with the dominant father ("In the early 1880s my father brought his family from Missouri down into the wild country of Arkansas that was just beginning to settle up"), and on the second page turns to her meeting Frank Hamilton, whom on page five she marries. The printed text of nearly 250 pages gives a chronicle of Mary as wife, mother, sister, and as friend and neighbor to a passing array of frontier settlers in the Mississippi Delta of the turn of the century. Her narrative is filled with events and includes her emotional responses to them, but she focuses her story on her husband's identity and on the consequence for her children of having had Frank Hamilton for a father.

The Mary Hamilton who prevails over so many trials of the earth is a facilitator for the lives of others. She marries Frank to secure food and shelter for her siblings, fulfilling a promise she had made to her dying mother: "Everything and everybody was trying to crowd me into a marriage I didn't want. As I look back, I believe I loved him even then; but I was young and had a will and dreams of my own. I was eighteen that May. . . . I remembered my promise to my mother and determined to do my best to make the home Frank had talked to my mother about wanting as near perfect as I could. We were married that day."[28] The unity that Mary Hamilton imposes upon this chronicle is not an unfolding pattern of selfhood—how she came to be who and what she was at age sixty-five—but rather the drama of Frank's identity—his mysterious English background, a six-hundred-year-old name, an aristocratic bearing discernible beneath the lumber man exterior, an extraordinary inheritance of distinctive golden curly hair passed to a daughter, and so on. The Cinderella paradigm that provides the skeleton plot of the narrative may owe as much to the editor Helen Davis as to Mary Hamilton, but the opening transcription bears the mark of a wife whose self is inextricably tied to that of her husband: "To my husband's people / whoever they are, / and wherever they may be."

Davis, who explains her editor's work as partly motivated by her own need to help put food on the table for her husband and children— she submitted the manuscript in a writer's competition sponsored by Little, Brown in 1933—concludes her preface to the autobiography by effacing her role as editor and asserting the mystery of Frank Hamilton's ancestry as the central focus of Mary's life: "I want to reassure the reader that my presence does not enter the book. I have not touched her style, or embellished her material. It is a direct and simple autobiography. Deep in her heart I think there remains a wistful, unadmitted hope that the book if published may fall into the hands of someone who will be able to tell her children the full identity of the man who was their father. For that mystery has remained the abiding tragedy of her life and theirs."[29]

A woman who was nearly a contemporary of Mary Hamilton but who differed from her in class and education, who was married but had no children, who lived most of her adult life outside the South, writes an autobiography that is nonetheless in many ways strikingly like *Trials of the Earth.* Mary Craig Kimbrough Sinclair, born in 1882 to a wealthy, influential family in Greenwood, Mississippi, a family who maintained a large summer home near that of Varina Howell Davis (Mrs. Jefferson Davis) on the Mississippi Gulf Coast, published her autobiography in 1957 at the age of seventy-five, four years before she died. *Southern Belle,* subtitled "A Personal Story of a Crusader's Wife," begins with a brief introduction written ostensibly by her crusader-husband, Upton Sinclair: "This is the story of a Southern belle, told by a real one. There may be those who will smile at this statement, thinking that all the charm and romance the term implies were just the imaginings of weavers of fiction. But there were many Southern belles and many men fell in love with them. Many men loved the one who lives in this book."[30]

And so the reader's first image of Craig Sinclair is of a woman distinguished by the men who have loved her. The reader may smile at the situational irony here—an elderly woman of achievement whose central identity is defined as "southern belle"—but there are even more dramatic ironies to emerge in Craig Sinclair's private account of the composition of the introduction. In a letter to her brother, Hunter Kimbrough, at the time she was completing final revisions of the book, she wrote:

> Crown [the publisher] asked U. [Upton] to write an introduction to my book—wants it to show that it is authentic story as he does not want to use Upton's name on outside of book (wants to feature Southern Belle—not crusader, I guess). Says he wants the title "Southern Belle" by Mary Craig Sinclair, not Mrs. U.S.
>
> I wrote the introduction as Upton's effort to write it featured our "radical" crusader![31]

Among the Sinclair papers there are many other examples of Craig Sinclair's direct involvement in the literary career of Upton Sinclair, but one could hardly imagine a more ironic and subversive undermining of her self-presentation as a southern belle and the self-effacing wife of a celebrated muckraker than the revelation that she herself wrote the "husbandly" introduction to her own autobiography.

In the early years of her marriage (1913–25), Craig Sinclair moved a great distance in geography and attitude from her mother, a woman who had stumped Mississippi opposing women's suffrage and had tirelessly supported the activities of the United Daughters of the Confederacy. Nonetheless, for all her involvement in progressive and socialist activities that had come with her marriage to Upton Sinclair and her life in California, Craig Sinclair constructs her self in print as an exemplar of southern ladyhood. She writes a 407-page autobiography managing to omit most dates, conceal her age, and deflect the reader's sense of her as a developing, growing person over a span of many years in favor of a presentation of herself as an ever-youthful but fully mature woman from late adolescence onward. The self she presents to her readers is Craig Kimbrough, the intelligent, high-spirited daughter, and Craig Sinclair, the efficient business manager and homemaker, a wife who assists her writer-husband as secretary, editor, even ghost writer for manuscripts published under his name, a wife who manages the financing that makes possible the political campaigns and social crusades of her husband, but a woman who is first and forever in her own eyes, Mrs. Upton Sinclair. This is the story of the making of a belle whose destiny from the beginning was wifehood. Her triumph was in marrying an estimable public figure whose career she shared, promoted, and celebrated. Despite all the misgivings of her family and friends at her marrying a *divorced* man, she triumphs, marrying a man who not only measured up but whose measure she significantly heightened. She constructs an autobiography to demonstrate her success as a belle and a wife—and trusts the reader to see beyond both to a woman of intelligence who also deployed her literary and managerial abilities with considerable success.

More recently, Virginia Foster Durr in her 1985 autobiography, *Outside the Magic Circle,* depicts a girlhood self formed in the bosom of her Alabama family, much like that of Craig Sinclair, a youthful self largely oblivious to social injustice but who as the wife of Clifford Durr living in Washington during the New Deal era comes to question many of the southern values she had grown up with, especially the race-bound ones. Her commitment to social justice in the 1950s and 1960s becomes then an extension of her growing sense of American, and especially southern, society as an extended kinship group, in which persons may justifiably lay claim to her loyalty and care by virtue of their having been left outside the circle.[32]

Among the autobiographers I have discussed are some notable omissions: Ellen Glasgow and Zora Neale Hurston, Lillian Smith and Lillian Hellman, Katherine Anne Porter, Eudora Welty—the preeminent women of letters in the twentieth-century South. To a degree, these women are exceptions to the relational autobiographers I have been considering. They are professional writers, successful, memorable ones precisely because they have constructed distinctive voices, separate selves in their writings. In his recent study of their autobiographical works, Will Brantley does in fact conclude his commentary with the observation that the "one thread . . . central to an understanding" of the self-writing of these women is "their shared independence, their need to define themselves as intense individualists."[33]

And yet the independent, individualistic selves that these professional writers depict in their autobiographies are constructed, it may be argued, upon a female legacy of affiliation and shared identity with others. Ellen Glasgow concludes *The Woman Within* with a ringing declaration of her freedom, but the qualifications she attaches to the declaration are unmistakable: "Only on the surface of things have I ever trod the beaten path. So long as I could keep from hurting anyone else, I have lived, as completely as it was possible, the life of my choice."[34] In *One Writer's Beginnings* Eudora Welty locates the emotional origins of her individualistic self in her parents, particularly noting the streak of independence she attributes to her mother. The evidence of Welty's strong sure sense of self lies in her capacity to absorb the values of the parents and not be overwhelmed by them. She acknowledges having had a "sheltered life," but insists it has also been a daring one, daring because subjected to emotional scrutiny and analysis.[35] Even Hurston, who tells her reader in no uncertain terms that she does not "have much of a herd instinct," nonetheless concludes *Dust Tracks on a Road* with a life scorecard that reflects self-satisfaction and self-realization measured by relationships with others: "I feel that I have lived. I have the joy and pain of strong friendships. I have served and been served. I have made enemies of which I am not ashamed. I have been faithless, and then I have been faithful and steadfast until the blood ran down into my shoes. I have loved unselfishly with all the ardor of a strong heart, and I have hated with all the power of my soul. What waits for me in the future? I do not know."[36]

To be sure, these writers all speak of the satisfactions their work has brought them, but rarely do they characterize it as a willed alternative to connection. Rosemary Daniell in her 1980 autobiography, *Fatal Flowers,* is an exception, seeing her choices as starkly opposed and devastating: to be "damned by self-expression *or* passivity—in one case, with the loss of love, in the other, with the loss of self."[37] In reading a variety of autobiographies written over two centuries, however, one more typically finds the condition remarked by Elizabeth Fox-Genovese: that "southern women, black and white, have wrestled with the claims of individualism and community in their self-representations, but they have not normally seen those claims as incompatible."[38] Indeed, most have identified a direct line of attachment with the past, giving them a female legacy of caring affiliations with others, especially family, and a persistent streak of independence. Nowhere is this dual, and sometimes conflicted, allegiance both to one's southern place and family and to a vision of an independent, explorative selfhood more determinedly expressed than in two recent autobiographies by academic women who grew up in the South. Gayle Graham Yates, a professor of American Studies at the University of Minnesota, writes of having lived outside her native Mississippi for over a quarter of a century, and yet her research in American cultural history, no less than her personal quest for self-understanding, leads her "home," where an enriched, revitalized subjectivity is made possible through an imaginative reconstructing (remembering) of her original connections with place and family.[39]

Like Yates, Margaret Jones Bolsterli reflects a pattern of early disillusionment with her southern roots because of the racial injustice she saw and could not effectively change. She, too, as a young adult leaves her southern home, but she later returns to teach at the University of Arkansas and focus her research on southern cultural history. She concludes *Born in the Delta* with an affirmation of her connection to place and to the younger generation of southerners in her university classes: "I left the South because I felt powerless to do anything about a situation that I found unbearable. I returned feeling that it was time to put my shoulder to a wheel now free to turn. . . . I can only hope that my teaching has the same effect on some of my students that my high school English teacher's had on me. It may be a drop in the bucket, but it's my drop and, as I finally came to understand, my bucket."[40]

A southern childhood contemporaneous with that of Yates and of Bolsterli likewise forms the emotional grounding in *Womenfolks,* a narrative of growing up in Hot Springs, Arkansas, during the 1940s and 1950s. In this autobiography, Shirley Abbott vividly defines the southern feminine culture out of which a self—a Shirley Abbott self—has been fashioned. Seeing her maternal ancestors as representative of this culture, she describes them: "Independent almost from birth. They knew how to make do in harsh circumstances, and even in clement surroundings they maintained a stubborn equilibrium with their menfolks. To a degree that infuriated me and eventually drove me away from them, they gritted their teeth and were selfless, made sacrifices, and gave in. I am not like them. Yet I am of them, mindful of their legacy wherever I go."[41]

As self-conscious autobiographer, Abbott probes the cultural values and personal psychic labors that together produce such texts as *Womenfolks, Mississippi Mind,* or *Born in the Delta.* She writes forcefully of the necessity—and cost—of asserting the self, of leaving family, revisiting and reinterpreting childhood memories, finding a new place, pointedly inserting herself into the world. Abbott doubtless reflects a southern female consciousness informed by many liberalizing social forces of the past fifty years, as do Yates and Bolsterli. And yet in her mindfulness of legacy, her capacity both to take care and to have her say, she continues in the line of many earlier southern women autobiographers. Reading the life writings of these women, one discovers a rich cultural record of the constraints and tensions attending upon an effort to maintain connection with community and family while enacting a self that struggles to locate a separate life and find a personal voice.

Notes

1. Mary Hamilton, *Trials of the Earth: The Autobiography of Mary Hamilton,* ed. Helen Dick Davis (Jackson: Univ. Press of Mississippi, 1992), xvii.

2. Ibid., xvii–xix.

3. Ibid., xix.

4. See esp. Elizabeth Fox-Genovese, "Between Individualism and Community: Autobiographies of Southern Women," in *Located Lives: Place and Idea in Southern Autobiography,* ed. J. Bill Berry (Athens: Univ. of Georgia Press, 1990), 20–38.

5. Edmund Wilson, *Patriotic Gore: Studies in the Literature of the American Civil War* (New York: Oxford Univ. Press, 1962), 279–80.

6. C. Vann Woodward, ed., *Mary Chesnut's Civil War* (New Haven: Yale Univ. Press, 1989), xvi.

7. Ibid., xxvii.

8. Karl J. Weintraub, "Autobiography and Historical Consciousness," *Critical Inquiry* 1 (1975): 827.

9. Elizabeth Bruss, *Autobiographical Acts: The Changing Situation of a Literary Genre* (Baltimore: Johns Hopkins Univ. Press, 1976), ch. 1.

10. James Olney, *Metaphors of Self: The Meaning of Autobiography* (Princeton: Princeton Univ. Press, 1972), 35.

11. Georges Gusdorf, "Conditions and Limits of Autobiography," in *Autobiography: Essays Theoretical and Critical,* ed. James Olney (Princeton: Princeton Univ. Press, 1980), 43, 30.

12. Marjanne E. Gooze, "The Definitions of Self and Form in Feminist Autobiography Theory," *Women's Studies* 21 (1992): 411–29. For brief but helpful overviews of current theories of female selfhood and the problematical nature of autobiographical "truthtelling," see Shari Benstock, "The Female Self Engendered: Autobiographical Writing and Theories of Selfhood," *Women's Studies* 20 (1991): 5–13, and Sidonie Smith, "Construing Truths in Lying Mouths: Truthtelling in Women's Autobiography," *Studies in the Literary Imagination* 23 (1990): 145–63.

13. Bruss, *Autobiographical Acts,* 10–11.

14. Chesnut, *Mary Chesnut's Civil War,* 197.

15. Ibid., 23.

16. Ibid., 29.

17. Belle Kearney, *A Slaveholder's Daughter* (1900; rpt. New York: Negro Univ. Press, 1969).

18. William L. Andrews, "Booker T. Washington, Belle Kearney, and the Southern Patriarchy," in *Home Ground: Southern Autobiography,* ed. J. Bill Berry (Columbia: Univ. of Missouri Press, 1991), 91.

19. Susan Dabney Smedes, *Memorials of a Southern Planter* (1887; rpt. Jackson: Univ. Press of Mississippi, 1981).

20. Harriet Jacobs, *Incidents in the Life of a Slave Girl,* ed. Jean Fagan Yellin (1861; rpt. Cambridge: Harvard Univ. Press, 1987).

21. Susan Stanford Friedman, "Women's Autobiographical Selves: Theory and Practice," in *The Private Self,* ed. Shari Benstock (Chapel Hill: Univ. of North Carolina Press, 1988), 35, 39.

22. See Bertram Wyatt-Brown, *Southern Honor: Ethics and Behavior in the Old South* (New York: Oxford Univ. Press, 1982), and Steven Stowe, *Intimacy and Power in the Old South: Ritual in the Lives of the Planters* (Baltimore: Johns Hopkins Univ. Press, 1987).

23. Lucinda H. MacKethan, *Daughters of Time: Creating Woman's Voice in Southern Story* (Athens: Univ. of Georgia Press, 1990), 10.

24. Elizabeth Ruffin, in *An Evening When Alone: Four Journals of Single Women in the South, 1827–67,* ed. Michael O'Brien (Charlottesville: Univ. Press of Virginia, 1993), 10.

25. Ann Lewis Hardeman, in *An Evening When Alone,* ed. O'Brien, 283.

26. Nancy J. Chodorow, *Feminism and Psychoanalytic Theory* (New Haven: Yale Univ. Press, 1989), 110.

27. Katha Pollitt, *Reasonable Creatures: Essays on Women and Feminism* (New York: Knopf, 1994), 48.

28. Hamilton, *Trials of the Earth,* 7.

29. Helen Dick Davis, ed., in Hamilton, *Trials of the Earth,* xx.

30. Mary Craig Sinclair, *Southern Belle* (New York: Crown, 1957), vii.

31. Mary Craig Sinclair to Hunter Kimbrough, 18 May 1957. Copy of letter provided to author by Hunter Kimbrough, December 1979. The major archival collection of Mary Craig and Upton Sinclair papers is held by the University of Indiana, Bloomington.

32. Virginia Foster Durr, *Outside the Magic Circle: The Autobiography of Virginia Foster Durr,* ed. Hollinger F. Barnard (New York: Simon & Schuster Touchstone, 1987).

33. Will Brantley, *Feminine Sense in Southern Memoir* (Jackson: Univ. Press of Mississippi, 1993), 241.

34. Ellen Glasgow, *The Woman Within* (New York: Harcourt, Brace, 1954), 296.

35. Eudora Welty, *One Writer's Beginnings* (Cambridge: Harvard Univ. Press, 1984), 104.

36. Zora Neale Hurston, *Dust Tracks on a Road* (1942; rpt. New York: Harper Perennial, 1991), 255.

37. Rosemary Daniell, *Fatal Flowers: On Sin, Sex, and Suicide in the Deep South* (New York: Holt, Rinehart and Winston, 1980), 85.

38. Fox-Genovese, "Between Individualism and Community," 36.

39. Gayle Graham Yates, *Mississippi Mind: A Personal Cultural History of an American State* (Knoxville: Univ. of Tennessee Press, 1990), see esp. 1–52, 247 ff.

40. Margaret Jones Bolsterli, *Born in the Delta: Reflections on the Making of a Southern White Sensibility* (Knoxville: Univ. of Tennessee Press, 1991), 131–32.

41. Shirley Abbott, *Womenfolks: Growing Up down South* (New Haven: Ticknor and Fields, 1983), 18.

Slavery, Race, and the Figure of the Tragic Mulatta; or, The Ghost of Southern History in the Writing of African-American Women

ELIZABETH FOX-GENOVESE

*I am afraid that I am destined to die at my post. I have no special
friends in the North, and no home but this in the South.
I am homeless and alone.*
— FRANCES ELLEN WATKINS HARPER, *Iola Leroy;
or, Shadows Uplifted* (1892)

*I loved history as a child, until some clear-eyed young Negro pointed
out, quite rightly, that there was no place in the American past I
could go and be free.*
— SHERLEY ANNE WILLIAMS, *Dessa Rose* (1986)

*Sadness was overtaking Lena's feeling of fear. She wanted to tell
Rachel, "I'm just a little girl. I don't want to hear all of this. I don't
want to know all this. Please don't tell me any more." But
Rachel just looked at the child's big brown eyes welling up with
tears and slipped inside her head and thoughts again.
"Child," she said softly. "Do you know how long I been waiting for
somebody like you to come along so I can tell them all of this, so I
can share some of this. You t'in I'm not gonna tell you now I
got you here on my beach?"*
— TINA MCELROY ANSA, *Baby of the Family* (1989)

*Everybody knew what she was called, but nobody anywhere knew
her name. Disremembered and unaccounted for, she cannot be lost
because no one is looking for her, and even if they were, how can
they call her if they don't know her name? Although she has*

claim, she is not claimed. . . .
It was not a story to pass on. . . .
So they forgot her. Like an unpleasant dream during a
troubling sleep. . . .
This was not a story to pass on.
—TONI MORRISON, *Beloved* (1987)

I

THE WRITINGS of African-American women writers abound with the ghosts and memories of a southern history that anchors their own and their people's experience even as it challenges their ability to represent their own and their foremothers' sense of self. Like the Russian peasants' proverbial rat, southern history has stuck in the throat of African-American women writers, who can neither swallow it nor spit it out. Toni Morrison's novel *Beloved* poignantly reminds us of the difficulty. How—in what voice—may a woman tell of women's experience of slavery? How may she represent the worst toll that slavery exacted from enslaved mothers and their children? Morrison represents those difficulties through the figure of a ghost, Beloved, that embodies the residue of what cannot be told. As the ghost of the murdered, "crawling already?" baby, Beloved dances through the pages of the text yet ultimately remains disremembered and unaccounted for. No one is even looking for her. Murdered by her own mother, she cannot rest and must, like all disremembered slave children, devote herself to (as Baby Suggs puts it) "worrying someone's house into evil." Baby Suggs knows that there is "not a house in the country ain't packed to its rafters with some dead Negro's grief," and she tells Sethe to consider herself lucky that "this ghost is a baby," not an adult man.[1]

Like Baby Suggs, Sethe knows that memories—rememories—persist, even if you do not remember them yourself. What she does remember "is a picture floating around out there outside my head," and even if "I don't think it, even if I die, the picture of what I did, or knew, or saw is still out there. Right in the place where it happened" (36). Those thought pictures, she tells her daughter, Denver, lie in wait, and one day you bump into one of them. You may think that the thought that enters your mind belongs to you, but it is really "a rememory that belongs to somebody else" (36). Thus, even a picture of events that are "all over—over and done with"—will, if you go and stand in the place where the events occurred, "always be there for you, waiting for you" (36). Even if Sethe does not think the thought picture, even if she dies, it will remain out there, waiting for someone to bump into it. Worse, as *Beloved* suggests, the most painful thought pictures do not remain bound to the place in which the events occurred, but migrate, permeating the entire country so that there is no place where one can escape them.

Even in Ohio, a free state, Sethe might suddenly find herself "remembering something she had forgotten she knew. Something privately shameful that seeped into a slit in her mind right behind the slap on her face and the circled cross" (61). Beloved's fingers massaging her neck remind her of Baby Suggs's fingers, which had eased the pain when "her spirits fell down under the weight of the things she remembered and those she did not" (98). However bad the things Sethe remembers, she knows the things she does not remember are worse. Fleetingly, the touch of Beloved's fingers seems exactly like those of the baby's ghost, but she shoves the "tiny disturbance" of that thought aside in the conviction that what now matters is to have Paul D in her life—that their shared trust and rememory will heal the wounds. "Her story was bearable because it was his as well—to tell, to refine and tell again. The things neither knew about the other—the things neither had word-shapes for—well, it would come in time: where they led him off to sucking iron; the perfect death of her crawling-already? baby" (99).

Throughout *Beloved*, Morrison reminds us that the sharing of rememories and the healing of wounds do not unfold as smoothly as Sethe hopes. The stories are not easy to tell, refine, and retell. Even when, haltingly, imperfectly, they have been told and a fragment of trust established, the powerful temptation to forget abides. Beloved, the ghost, is not claimed, for hers was not a story to pass on. And, ultimately, the significance of the forgetting of that story supersedes the importance of the original event, so that the forgetting itself becomes a story that cannot be passed on. The easy part of Beloved's story, which is also inescapably Sethe's story, indicted the horrible cost of slavery for African-American slaves; the difficult part, as Morrison does not flinch from acknowledging, implicated the slaves themselves.[2] For the transformation of slaves from passive victims—mere objects—into active resisters of their own dehumanization necessarily invoked their accountability for their actions, however desperate, however constrained. The true price of their humanity lay in the scarring acknowledgment of their responsibility—that is, in their willingness to claim the story of slavery as their own subjective experience, to claim southern history as their own.

The pain of that history has decisively complicated the challenge of claiming it as one's own, insidiously tempting its survivors into a manichaean vision of good and evil in which innocent victims confront evil oppressors. The manichaean vision has, since the nineteenth century, been fueled by the abolitionist fervor that condemned slavery as an unmitigated evil. But recognition of the injustice and the crimes of slavery as a social system does not tell us much about the character and humanity of those who participated in it. Even when we allow for the propensity of a social system to shape its participants, we are left with the knowledge that the experience of oppression does not inevitably transform fallible men and women into saints, any more than the exercise of domination inevitably transforms decent men and women into monsters.

These complexities and ambiguities have weighed heavily on black and white authors alike, but they have especially weighed upon the imaginations of black women writers who have been most likely to attempt to capture the personal experience of slave women and their female descendants. Both blacks and whites have recognized the experience of slave women as, in some essential way, emblematic of the system as a whole. Sexually vulnerable as women, slave women were if anything more vulnerable to tragedy as mothers whose children might, at any time, be wrested from them. Indeed, from the perspective of the black community, the greatest crime of slavery seems to have been the separation of families, especially the separation of mothers and children. Slaveholders' sexual access to slave women ranked a close and closely related second but was never taken fully to equal the separation of mother and child, at least in part because African cultures did not place the same weight as middle-class Anglo-American culture on women's premarital chastity. In the too frequent cases in which the separation was forcefully perpetrated by sale, the results were devastating but could at least be attributed to the malevolence of an external force. But what if it were perpetrated by the mother herself through running away, suicide, or infanticide?

If a slave woman's separation from her child might raise troubling questions, how much more so might her sexual relations with a white man? Instances of rape assuredly abounded, but so did instances of mutual consent and even love, as well as everything in between. Should writers represent slave women only as victims of rape, they would underscore the brutality of slavery, but would, by the same token, implicitly deny the special attractiveness of the individual woman: they would reduce her to a random object of the man's quest for power or his lust. We should not find it difficult to understand that black women writers might seek to endow their heroines with the charms and complexities of conventional white heroines and might even enjoy representing men who preferred a black woman to her white rivals, all the more since this choice, as the word *rival* implies, establishes the black woman as the white woman's equal. Many black women writers have resolved the tension between these two options by turning to the trope of the tragic mulatta—the beautiful woman who appears to be white, who manifests all of the personal graces fostered by freedom and privilege, but who, through the accident of a few drops of "black blood," is legally a slave.

The notion that a few drops of blood, of which the tragic mulatta manifested no external sign, could determine a woman's fate understandably chilled readers, as indeed they were intended to. Taking the drop of blood to represent the essence of a woman's identity captured the irrationality of racism and even uncomfortably evoked the concept of Original Sin—literally the sin of the parents bequeathed to the innocent child. Doubtless the certainty that readers would instinctively recoil from the injustice of an inherited destiny helps to explain the popularity of the trope among writers who sought above all to shock readers out of complacency. It is, nonetheless, worth noting that before emancipation the drop of black blood did not condemn a mulatta to slavery. Should a mulatta have had a slave father and a free mother, she would legally have been free—whether the mother was white or black. Under slavery, women—or men—were slaves because they inherited the condition from slave mothers, not because of the composition of their blood. And, as everyone knew, the probabilities were that a mulatta would have a slave mother and free father. But then, the possibility that a mulatta might result from the intimacy of a slave father and a free mother was not one that antebellum whites liked to acknowledge, and black writers have not been quick to challenge their reticence.

Since Harriet Jacobs, black women writers have consistently preferred to emphasize blood rather than slavery, even when writing about the antebellum period. They have not been alone in evoking the trope of the tragic mulatta, but they have informed it with a complexity that no black man or white woman has easily appreciated. Knowing from experience the anguish of writing the story of the slave woman from a subjective stance, they have seized upon the trope of the tragic mulatta as a way simultaneously to gain sympathy for their heroines and to remain silent about the most disturbing aspects of black women's experience. The trope has permitted them to endow their heroines with the sensibilities and personal dignity that have conventionally been attributed to white women even as it has permitted them to drive home the horrendous injustice of slavery. By inviting the identification of white readers with the tragic mulatta, black women writers have lured them into the emotional recognition that skin color counts for nothing. In effect, they are saying, "This tragic heroine, dear reader, could just as well be you." But the invitation to identification has come at the price of candor about the deepest wounds of slave women's experience. Thus, the trope of the tragic mulatta has covered over the stories that, until recently, none have felt free to pass on but that have, as in the case of Beloved, a disquieting ability to return as ghosts.

In *Dessa Rose,* Sherley Anne Williams evokes Dessa's reluctance to expose the scars around her loins where no hair would grow again and which, according to Rufel, "looked like a mutilated cat face." [3] There, hidden beneath her clothes, her history had been graven on her flesh. Considering those hidden scars, Nehemiah wonders how many others "carried a similar history writ about their privates" (21). [4] Rufel sees the scars when she inadvertently catches a glimpse of Dessa's nudity in a mirror. But Dessa refuses to discuss the part of her past to which they testify. "Even when the others spoke around the campfire, during the days of their freedom, about their trials under slavery, Dessa was silent. Their telling awoke no echoes in her mind. That part of the past lay sealed in the scars between her thighs" (59–60). Listening to Nathan's account of the travail that Dessa herself could not tell, Rufel wonders, "How did they bare such pain?" (138).

Deborah McDowell calls attention to the visual implication of "bare" in contradistinction to the internal endurance of the "bear" the reader might have expected. McDowell sees the scars of Dessa's history as "a script written in the slave master's hand and bound up in his enslaving psychosexual myths and fantasies" and her refusal to display them as "a radical act of ownership over her own body/text in a system that successfully stripped slaves' control over this, their most intimate property." In McDowell's reading, the refusal becomes "both an act of resistance (she is the repository of her own story) and a means of containing the pain by forgetting the past."[5]

Writing, like Morrison, in the 1980s, when the willingness to acknowledge both the brutality of slavery and the vitality of African-American culture ran high, Sherley Anne Williams has no qualms about representing a slave woman as physically scarred or speaking in dialect. But she holds to the notion that containment of the pain requires "forgetting the past." The recovery of African-American history, which Carter G. Woodson and W. E. B. Du Bois, among other black scholars, inaugurated early in the twentieth century and which flowered in the 1960s and 1970s, brought the horrors of slavery and the extraordinary cultural resilience of slave communities to national attention.[6] Within this context, Williams, like other black women novelists, could forsake the concern for respectability that had weighed upon earlier generations of African-American women writers and draw upon the cadences and traditions of folk culture. Yet more important, Williams, like Morrison, could attribute the most painful scars to her female protagonist. Even so, Williams does not have Dessa tell her own story, which the reader learns through the accounts of other characters. As a result, the reader learns only those parts of the story that others have learned, and the subjective story remains buried in Dessa's determined forgetting of the past. Thus does Williams suggest that continued resistance to the wounds of oppression requires resistance to history itself.

Williams's resistance to the most painful memories contrasts sharply with Morrison's determination to expose them and, thereby, to cauterize their wounds. The deteriorating social and economic condition of many black Americans during the 1980s may have tempted Williams, as it tempted others, to see an encompassing continuity between slavery and the present. This understandable discouragement had two important consequences. First, and most obviously, it prompted a rejection of confidence in the possibility of historical change on the assumption either that nothing ever changes or that the more things change, the more they stay the same. Second, it discouraged searching and candid explorations of the history of slavery on the grounds that to bare the scars of the past would be to bare those of the present. Thus, even as Williams, like other black women writers, admitted that slavery had happened to women like them, she remained reticent about the highest and most personal costs. This determined preservation of privacy, however admirable, has risked opening the door to insistent ghosts, for the repressed does have a way of returning.

Williams reflects briefly upon history in her Author's Note to *Dessa Rose,* which she claims to have based upon two specific historical incidents: the experience of a pregnant black woman who helped to lead a slave uprising, was caught, convicted, and sentenced to death, but not hanged until after the birth of her baby, and the account of a white North Carolina woman who reportedly provided sanctuary to runaway slaves. In addition, she admits to having also written in outraged response to William Styron's *Nat Turner,* which, in her view, confirms that "Afro-Americans, having survived by word of mouth—and made of that process a high art—remain at the mercy of literature and writing; often, these have betrayed us" (5). Williams leaves no doubt that the betrayal of literature and writing rests upon the betrayal of history itself, for "there was no place in the American past where I could go and be free." Slavery, she has learned, "eliminated neither heroism nor love; it provided occasions for their expression" (6). Yet her representation of slavery strips the demonstrable expressions of heroism and love of the less admirable responses that bound them to a multidimensional and credible humanity.

II

As impassable as a rain-swollen river, southern history runs like a deep dangerous current between the black American present and past. Those who would turn their eyes to an African legacy must somehow get across it; those who prefer to focus upon the recent contributions of free black communities must explain how its encompassing waters have nourished subsequent harvests. The hold of southern history has weighed as heavily upon northern as southern black women writers, for all concur that it embodies the crimes that have been perpetrated upon their people. And although they know that the North also practiced slavery and then discriminated brutally against blacks, and that the transatlantic slave traders were generally northern, they reserve a special indignation for the full-blown slave society of the South.[7]

Rarely have the historical imaginations of African-American women novelists reached back beyond 1820. The reasons why most turn to the 1850s for the seedbed of the stories they wish to tell are numerous, but high among them ranks a reluctance to focus upon a life that ended as it began under slavery. A woman protagonist who had come of age much before the 1850s would not plausibly have experienced the full fruits of post–Civil War freedom or have been young enough when she did to engage readers' imaginations. But if the personal situation of a heroine has largely dictated novelists' concern with the 1850s, other considerations have also had their say. For the 1850s could plausibly be represented as the flowering of slavery as a social system—as a designed and crafted society that self-consciously defended the bondage of the African-American people. In addition, the 1850s brought to a crescendo an abolitionist discourse that proclaimed a nonnegotiable moral line between North and South.

Antislavery and uncompromising abolitionist discourses were hardly new in the 1850s, but the Compromise of 1850, especially its Fugitive Slave Law, lent them an urgency they had previously lacked. And the outpouring of writings, fictional as well as theoretical, theological, and political, on both sides of the divide crystallized what we may call a dominant pattern of discourse. The character of the debate is familiar enough. While northern abolitionists preached the inviolability of freedom ("free soil, free labor, free men") and immorality of bondage, proslavery southerners preached the necessity for social hierarchy and the wanton cruelty of free labor. Intermingling with and enriching the abstract arguments about first principles and social systems, novelists on both sides wove a tapestry of human examples designed to show the direct consequences of the two systems for specific people.[8] This climate encouraged the publication of firsthand accounts of slavery by black writers, most of whom viewed their literary efforts as an important contribution to the abolitionist struggle. Yet the racism of many northern readers, as well as their own discretion, also encouraged them to create protagonists who met white expectations of respectability. The trope of the tragic mulatta perfectly served their purposes.

The pioneering African-American writers of the 1850s, especially the women, were latecomers to the raging discussion about their condition. William Wells Brown, who led the way with his novel *Clotel, or the President's Daughter,* set a precedent that many would follow by taking as his heroine a mulatta (the quintessential "high yaller") woman, who, betrayed and abandoned by the white planter who claimed to love her, ultimately dies.[9] Brown's role in establishing the beautiful mulatta as the exemplary black heroine has cast a long shadow and received much attention from subsequent critics. What has received less attention is his adaptation of a distinct southern pastoral mode to his own purposes.[10] To drive his point home, Brown set his novel in Virginia and attributed Clotel's parentage to none other than Thomas Jefferson, thus linking high professed political principle to the despoiling of slave women. None of Brown's female successors would follow his lead in this regard, nor even in consigning their heroines to an untimely death. But then Brown depicted Clotel as a cast-aside wife (although legally she was never married) rather than as a young girl exposed to all the horrors of random sexual exploitation. Not until the northern black woman writer Pauline Hopkins picked up Brown's story in *Hagar's Daughter* (1901) would the figure of the slave woman as forsaken wife reappear, this time with a dramatically different ending.[11]

Brown, an abolitionist who wrote primarily for northern and, especially, British readers, wrote the story of the slave woman into the fabric of southern life and discourse, not least by offering southern readers a disquieting mirror of their own professed principles. Brown firmly opposed slavery as a social system, but however broad and generous his sympathies with the great mass of slaves, he focused upon the ways in which the system most cruelly betrayed those whom it might have embraced—literally its own offspring as embodied in a beautiful, virtually white, articulate woman. He primarily evoked Clotel's delicacy, refinement, and nobility of sentiments, together with her creamy skin, to signal the hypocrisy of a society that professed to love freedom and equality. He made much of the betrayal of Clotel's womanly qualities, but always from an objective perspective. Thus, although he represented her as the novel's heroine, arguably, he did not take her as its subject.

Rather than subject, Clotel may best be understood as a figure—a distillation of discourses—that designates the condition of the tragic mulatta, which itself represents the inherent contradictions of southern society.[12] For unlike most of those who came after, Brown locates the conception of freedom (Jefferson) and the possibility of social tranquility (the garden) within the South itself. Paradoxically, by not making Clotel the center of subjectivity, he permits her a coherence of character, a freedom from soul-wrenching conflict that black women writers' protagonists frequently lack. As author and narrator, Brown offers an unapologetic and unconflicted interpretation of southern history. And since his narrative focuses directly upon his principal protagonists, whom he carefully inscribes in literate culture, the history he explores and criticizes belongs essentially to the realm of public discourse rather than to that of the memories of oral culture and the ghosts of scarred imaginations.

Brown's contemporary, Harriet Jacobs, followed his lead in directly engaging the public debate over slavery, although unlike him, Jacobs located the subjectivity of her protagonist, Linda Brent, at the center of her narrative, *Incidents in the Life of a Slave Girl*.[13] Drawing heavily upon abolitionist discourses, Jacobs followed Harriet Beecher Stowe and other antislavery women writers in emphasizing the ways in which slavery as a social system negated all social order, corrupting the integrity of domestic relations, white and black. Calling slavery an "obscene cage of birds," Linda Brent insists she can testify from "my own experience and observation, that slavery is a curse to the whites as well as to the blacks. It makes the white fathers cruel and sensual; the sons violent and licentious; it contaminates the daughters, and makes the wives wretched" (52). "As for the colored race," she continues, "it needs an abler pen than mine to describe the extremity of their sufferings, the depth of their degradation" (52). But Jacobs's use of pronouns, which juxtaposes "my" pen to "their" sufferings, dramatically, if inadvertently, betrays the conflicts that plague her attempt to bare a woman's subjective experience of slavery.

The split between "my" pen and "their" sufferings pervades Jacobs's attempt to conjoin Linda Brent's experience with the history of slavery in the South, and, in the end, she does not succeed. Casting Brent as a real woman rather than a literary figure, she cannot draw directly upon the complexities of the figure of the mulatta, although more than occasionally she appears to evoke them. Her representation of Linda Brent as a slave formally acknowledges the legal condition that governs Linda's destiny, yet her distancing of Linda from the other slaves and, indeed, from the darker blacks, very much resembles other writers' representation of free mulattas who are punished for their possession of a few invisible drops of black blood. If the history of southern

slavery is as bleak as Jacobs must paint it as being in order to justify
Linda Brent's actions—including her taking of a white lover and her
abandonment of her children—then it cannot be allowed to shape
Linda Brent's character. For if Linda Brent had indeed been marked by
slavery's evil, how could she have developed the instinctive nobility and
love of freedom that inspire her to risk everything, including life and
"virtue," to elude its grasp? Ironically, the very abolitionist beliefs that
permit Jacobs to write at all make it virtually impossible for her to
ground Linda's history in the history of the South as the abolitionists
present it. Here and there, hints of southern black history flicker in the
pages of the text, notably when she links Linda Brent's experience in
the swamp with the folklore of black oral culture. But in general, and
especially in narrative voice, she claims as much distance as possible
between Linda and the history that produced her.

Incidents in the Life of a Slave Girl contains virtually no references
to history or even to the variations in southern society. Proceeding from
the consciousness of Linda Brent, the narrative encompasses only those
incidents that her mind has encountered, whether family traditions,
cases of brutality, or random comments on proslavery religion. Jacobs's
South seems cut almost entirely from manichaean abolitionist cloth and
meshes comfortably with Orlando Patterson's conception of slavery as
social death.[14] In the measure that Jacobs pays any attention to history,
she restricts it to family history, primarily to establish a pedigree of fair
skin, literacy, respectability, and quasi freedom for herself. And in the
end, her falling off from the standards of her forebears matters considerably less than her having been reared with them in the first place.
Indeed, Jacobs seems to be suggesting that her very lapses from the
norms of middle-class respectability confirm her personification of the
fundamental ideals they embody. For, even as Linda Brent enjoins her
readers to "pity" and "pardon" her lapses from the highest standards
of womanly virtue, she reminds them that they "never knew what it is
to be a slave; to be entirely unprotected by law or custom; to have the
laws reduce you to the condition of a chattel, entirely subject to the will
of another" (55).

Such conditions make a mockery of conventional morality. Thus,
a slave woman who retains "any pride or sentiment" may well taste
"something akin to freedom" in taking a lover who is not her master,
even if he cannot be her lawful husband. Such moral principles, Linda
Brent allows, may seem like sophistry, "but the condition of a slave

confuses all principles of morality, and, in fact, renders the practice of them impossible" (55). She knows that her mother and grandmother cleaved to moral principles, but they were spared the unmediated power of a master and, by implication, did not really experience the full weight of slavery's most destructive power.

To guarantee Linda Brent's immunity to the demoralizing power of slavery, Jacobs effectively endows her with a northern history and emphasizes her grandmother and parents' possession of the skills and independence of artisans and the domestic values that flow therefrom. Slaves they may have been, but they lived largely as if they had been free. Similarly, Jacobs introduces the worst specific abuses of slavery as reports rather than as subjective experiences. Had she not, she would have had to represent Linda Brent—and by implication herself—as the victim of indiscriminate lust, and she would thereby have reduced Linda to that status of object to which the logic of chattel slavery pointed. To underscore the moral and cultural distance between Linda and her family from the mass of slaves, she represents them as speaking the purest English and the other slaves as speaking in dialect.

Harriet Jacobs's difficulty in coming to terms with southern history, above all slavery, derives from her fierce rejection of its possible consequences for slave women—for Linda Brent and, by implication, for Jacobs herself. This was not a story she could tell, much less a story to pass on. Yet the problems with her denial of its bearing permeate her narrative. If slavery does "confuse" moral principles and make their practice "impossible," then how may she, a former slave, claim basic moral decency? Tactically, Jacobs attempts to place the blame upon the slaveholders who, as a class, corrupt everything and everyone they touch. Yet this history of abuse never seems to ground Linda Brent's identity, and Jacobs consistently presents Linda Brent's lapses from northern standards of female virtue as external rather than internal to her character.

With the benefit of hindsight, we may recognize Jacobs's narrative as haunted by ghosts that never appear in the text. Avoiding bitter engagement with the specter of racism and the significance of African traditions, Jacobs, to the extent possible, adopts the perspective of her presumed abolitionist readers and refrains from offending their sensibilities. This respect for northern sensibilities leads her to minimize Linda Brent's ties to the community of black slaves, whose sufferings have etched the costs of slavery upon their persons and character. Tak-

ing northern, middle-class domesticity as a universal norm and especially reproving slavery for depriving the majority of slaves of its
benefits, she represents Linda Brent as a woman with whom her northern readers may readily identify. Jacobs takes special pains to present
Linda's desertion of her children as a violation of the tradition in which
her family reared her. On the eve of Linda's flight, her grandmother
begs her to endure a while longer if the children must be left behind.
"Nobody," she reminds Linda, "respects a mother who forsakes her
children; and if you leave them, you will never have a happy moment"
(91).

Pleas and admonitions notwithstanding, Linda persists in her
plans. Throughout the years of her hiding and after her final escape to
the North, she remains concerned about her children's fate but refuses
to accept that her first obligation is to remain with them at any cost to
herself. Jacobs never says that slavery makes it impossible for anyone
to be a good mother, but her endorsement of Linda's actions strongly
suggests that she believes it. In effect, she claims that Linda's flight, even
though it entails temporary separation from her children, is the only
way she can defend her right to be a good mother. For as Sethe tries to
explain to Paul D in *Beloved,* under slavery you could not really love
anyone at all. Pushed to the limit, Sethe kills her "crawling-already?"
baby girl rather than lose the right to be a loving mother that freedom
has provided her. But just as Paul D and the other members of the black
community shudder at Sethe's radical interpretation of the dictates of
true motherhood, so too does Linda's grandmother question Linda's
claim that only freedom will permit her to mother properly. Thus, beneath the claim that Linda is seeking her own freedom the better to
care for her children lurks the haunting possibility that she is seeking
it because slavery has so weakened family ties as to cut her innermost
identity loose from them. And beyond that possibility lurk the ghosts
of all the children who are "worrying someone's house into evil" because, as Morrison suggests, they may have had their own views of
good mothering and may have preferred to have their mother's presence
even at the cost of her self-respect.

Successful flight to the North no more solves Linda's problems than
it does Sethe's. Once there, Linda still feels that "I could never go out
to breathe God's free air without trepidation at my heart," which hardly
seems "a right state of things in any civilized country" (195). Even in
the North, she can only secure her freedom through purchase. That

purchase assures that she and her children are "as free of the power of slaveholders as are the white people of the north; and though that, according to my ideas, is not saying a great deal it is a vast improvement in *my* condition" (201). But even freedom does not realize her dream of a home of her own, much less liberate her from the pervasive shadow of racism.

Jacobs exercises great caution in expressing her reservations about northern society, which we know abounded with racism. The main complaint she makes openly concerns the extent to which southern slavery compromised northern institutions—the familiar abolitionist complaint about the long arm of the Fugitive Slave Law. But in closing the narrative with Linda Brent's still working as a servant and still lacking a home of her own, she guardedly points the way toward subsequent criticisms of the devastating economic consequences of northern racism for black people. And by ending with the consoling memory of her grandmother, she suggests that the roots of her personal history lie in the South.

III

Jacobs does not openly embrace the figure of the beautiful mulatta, but in essential respects she might just as well have. She represents Linda Brent as having more in common with educated white women than with the illiterate and abused women of the slave community. In her pages, Linda never suffers a whipping or rape, and even when she is consigned to wear modest clothing, her natural beauty does not diminish. The difficulties of escape leave scratches on Linda's hands and face (significantly, the rest of her body remains covered), but her everyday life leaves no marks. Unlike Dessa Rose, she has no physical scars to conceal or bare.

Since slave status was transmitted through the mother and since the absence of legal marriage among slaves left fathers peculiarly exposed, the transmission of history through women assumed special importance for the African-American community. Even after emancipation and the emergence of solid marriages and families, women remained privileged custodians of the history of their people under slavery. To say as much is to slight neither the sufferings of African-American men under slavery nor their centrality to African-American communities. It is simply to suggest that slavery oppressed women and men less as couples or members of coherent families than as isolated individuals who might or might not be able to establish human ties strong enough to withstand slavery's deadly tendency to atomization.

As a people, African-American slaves did withstand the worst of the atomization, notably through their creation of communities that transcended family units and that could always absorb and support those whose immediate families had been torn from them. These communities proved reliable custodians of collective memories, including those of African practices and beliefs. To these traditions they added Anglo-American Christianity and messages of political freedom that predominated in the South, interweaving all into a sustaining culture of their own design. The message of abolition contributed a new attention to individualism. For while the slaves had never needed anyone to tell them they wanted to be free, abolition's emphasis on individualism ran counter to older collective traditions. The tension between the individual and the community informed every attempt to come to terms with the southern slave experience of African Americans. For some, like Jacobs and Williams, the balance shifted in favor of the individual who had suffered unspeakable wrongs and frequently led to the refusal to "bare" the wellsprings that might expose the barer to unbearable pain.

Frances Ellen Watkins Harper and Pauline Hopkins, writing after Reconstruction, were both supremely conscious of women's responsibility to tell the history of slavery and to assess its implications for a free present and future. Both were no less conscious, during an era of vicious and institutionalized racism, of the pressing need to shift the balance toward the history of the African-American community rather than the isolate individual. Tellingly, both returned to Brown's figure of the tragic mulatta to carry the burden of that history, although unlike Brown, both allowed their mulatta heroines to triumph, pointing the way in their persons, their works, their marriages, and their offspring to a promising future for their people.

Harper and Hopkins both attended carefully to the broad historical context of their protagonists' dramas, grounding the events that followed emancipation in the slavery that came before. Hopkins, a proud New Englander to her core, had no patience with the South, notwithstanding her clear-sighted recognition of the centrality of slavery to African-American history. Harper, coming from Baltimore, shared Hopkins's harsh judgment of slavery but showed more understanding of the South as the region in which the majority of African Americans had their roots and felt at home.

Harper's *Iola Leroy*, which opens in the middle of the Civil War, plunges the reader directly into the community of slaves with a conversation between Robert Johnson and Thomas Anderson, both slaves, who, under the cover of reports on freshness of butter and fish, trade notes about the progress of the Union forces. In a few brief chapters, Harper evokes the main features of slavery and the diverse personalities of Robert, Thomas, and the other slave men she introduces. From the start the reader learns that some masters and mistresses are better than others, although even Robert's indulgent mistress regards him as a "pet"; that, notwithstanding prohibitions, the slaves have a complex network of prayer meetings; that some have learned to read although most have not; that some plan to leave and join the Union forces, whereas others feel bound by loyalties to blacks and whites to remain where they are. Deftly, Harper brings to life a small-slaveholding region of North Carolina and the textured relations and personalities of the slaves who inhabit it.[15]

With great skill, Harper simultaneously convinces the reader that her subjects, who have not been flattened by the weight of slavery, have built a rich human community and that slavery is morally and politically wrong. The differences between her and Jacobs's depiction of North Carolina slavery are subtle but arresting, primarily because of Harper's sympathy for the variety of personalities and the cultural vitality among the slaves. Judging the slaveholders harshly, she nonetheless insists that slavery did not deaden the humanity of the slaves, and she unflinchingly attributes the ultimate responsibility for slavery to the country as a whole. Slavery, she avers, "had cast such a glamour over the Nation, and so warped the consciences of men, that they failed to read aright the legible transcript of Divine retribution which was written on the shuddering earth, where the blood of God's poor children had been as water freely spilled."[16]

Significantly, the reader first glimpses Iola Leroy through the eyes of Tom, one of the local slaves, who describes her to Robert as "a mighty putty young gal," whom her owners have been selling all over the country, because "she's a reg'lar spitfire; dey can't lead nor dribe her" (38). Adoring Iola and fearing for her safety in the grip of her "reckless and selfish master, who had tried in vain to drag her down to his own level of sin and shame," Tom moves Robert to persuade the

Union commander of the local fort to secure her release and to take her as a nurse in the field hospital. The general, to whom she is taken, is astonished by her beauty and refinement. "Could it be possible that this young and beautiful girl had been a chattel, with no power to protect herself from the highest insults that lawless brutality could inflict upon innocent and defenseless womanhood?" (39). How could he take pride in his American citizenship "when any white man, no matter how coarse, cruel, or brutal, could buy or sell her for the basest purposes?" (39).

Only sixty pages into the novel does the reader learn how one as fair and unmarked by toil as Iola Leroy could indeed be a slave. Daughter of a fair-skinned slave woman and the wealthy Louisiana planter who loved, educated, and married her, Iola grew up with no knowledge of her mixed racial heritage. As a student at a New England boarding school, she treats her antislavery classmates to a spirited defense of slavery argument, cheerfully insisting that slavery could not be wrong, "for my father is a slave-holder and my mother is as good to our servants as she can be" (97). And when challenged that even the most luxurious treatment cannot outweigh the priceless good of freedom itself, she innocently counters, "Our slaves do not want their freedom. They would not take it if we gave it to them" (97–98). Only upon her father's untimely death does she come to understand the true meaning of enslavement and the subjective value of freedom. Following that death, a vicious, greedy cousin, to whom Iola's father has naively confided the secret of his wife's birth, persuades a judge to overturn the father's will and remand the mother and their children into slavery. The youngest girl mercifully dies of brain fever, the son is kept safely in school in the North, but Iola and her mother are turned over to slave traders.

With minor variations, Iola's story became the prototype for the Gothic horror of the inherent evil of slavery. One may plausibly assume that Harper herself did not necessarily view the plight of the fair-skinned woman who had been raised in the lap of luxury as slavery's worst evil. But she assuredly knew her readers and doubtless believed that to whites like the general the idea that a single drop of black blood could throw a young woman like their own daughters onto the vilest of sexual marketplaces would be infinitely more moving than the plight of a dark-skinned, illiterate laborer, male or female. Thus, when Iola's father, Eugene, tells his cousin of his plan to marry a beautiful fair-skinned mulatta woman, Marie, the cousin responds, "Don't you know that if she is as fair as a lily, beautiful as a houri, and chaste as ice, that still she is a negro? . . . One drop of negro blood in her veins curses all the rest" (67). Yet under slavery, it was the condition of enslavement, passed through the mother, that counted, whereas after emancipation, when the condition no longer existed, the drop of black blood replaced it and could be transmitted by either parent. Writing after emancipation and the beginning of Jim Crow, Harper conflates slavery and race to strengthen the impact on her audience, which had but recently been horrified by tales of the white slave trade.

Harper relied upon the moving appeal of the figure of the beautiful mulatta to bind the open racism of her day to the condition of slavery that the Civil War had purportedly destroyed—to carry the message that she feared even antislavery readers would find difficult to accept. The novel leaves no doubt that Harper's main quarrel was with the racism of the 1890s. In locating the origins of her story in slavery, she doubtless hoped to tap the wellsprings of that northern sense of moral superiority which triumphed with victory in the war. The conflation of slavery and racism permitted her, in effect, to displace some of her out-rage at bourgeois racism and say to her northern readers: this injustice, which you are so proud of yourselves for having fought against, you surely will not now tolerate in your midst.

In addition, Harper, who had a genuine feel for the strengths and vulnerabilities of the community of ordinary slaves, seems purposefully to have located the dramatic abuses of slavery in Louisiana with its special aura of mystery and corruption, thus underscoring the Gothic dimension of Iola's personal story. In contrast, she represents the slaves of North Carolina who befriend Iola as varied and engaging human beings who have suffered the debilitation of slavery but have assuredly not been crippled by it.

Pauline Hopkins, notably in *Contending Forces* and *Hagar's Daughter,* also embraces the figure of the tragic mulatta as a vehicle for expressing her passionate indictment of racism, but even more than Harper she locates the story in a broad historical canvas. *Contending Forces* opens with the arrival in Bermuda of the news of the impending British abolition of slavery.[17] Upon learning the news, Charles Mont-fort, a wealthy planter, determines to move his family and slaves to the more "congenial" climate of North Carolina, notwithstanding his determination eventually to free his own slaves. Hopkins takes his arrival in New Bern as the occasion to depict what she considers the most loathsome members of southern society: corrupt and greedy planters, overseers, and ordinary white riff-raff—stock characters who manifest the crudest possible racial and sexual attitudes.

The forces of evil swiftly wreak their jealous vengeance on Charles Montfort and his family, driving his wife Grace, whom they have charged with being a mulatta, to her death, and forcing his younger son into slavery. The older son escapes the worst only because a visiting English gentleman succeeds in buying him. Hopkins's historical object lesson apparently bears little relation to the rest of the novel, which takes place in Boston around the turn of the century, although at the end we discover that the members of the Smith family, principal participants in the main story, descend from the younger Montfort son, who had eventually made his escape.

The historical prologue nonetheless permits Hopkins to ground the novel in what she views as the distinctly sinful history of the antebellum South and thereby to link the racism of the 1890s directly to the sins of slaveholding. It also permits her to link Boston to Britain's legacy of freedom and, above all, to show that even marriage to the wealthiest of men cannot protect the woman suspected of being a mulatta. The story of Grace Montfort thus prefigures that of Sappho Clark, the beautiful mulatta who plays a central role in the novel's main plot, who at the age of fourteen had been forced into slavery and raped and who is now in Boston, supporting herself and the child who had resulted from her rape. Like Harper before her, Hopkins locates the scene of her beautiful mulatta's tragedy in Louisiana, underscoring the dangerously exotic— almost un-American and certainly un-British—aspect of slavery.

The acutely intelligent and impressively learned Hopkins understands full well that racism pervades the free capitalist North. Her articulate, genteel, light-skinned black characters all encounter difficulties in education or employment. Worse, as she underscores, their problems are being exacerbated by politicians who, while congratulating themselves on their opposition to slavery, regard racism as acceptable and even necessary to a rapidly industrializing society. At a meeting of the American Colored League to protest a recent lynching in the South, the Hon. Herbert Clapp, a northern Democrat with prosouthern sympathies, insists that the "problem is national, not sectional. The sin of slavery was the sin of the nation." Clapp tries to convince his black audience that their brothers in the South are doing well, but the North has other problems: "Here at the North the pressure is so great from the white laborer that we are forced, to some extent, to bar against the colored brother" (248).

Hopkins, who understands perfectly the nature of Clapp's arguments, will have none of them. The next speaker, Luke Sawyer, the son of a free black from Louisiana—who in telling his personal history reveals Sappho's history as well without naming her—passionately argues that "conservatism, lack of brotherly affiliation, lack of energy for the right and the power of the almighty dollar . . . are the forces which are ruining the Negro in this country" (256). Finally, Will Smith, Hopkins's hero who strikingly resembles the young W. E. B. Du Bois, speaks, presumably articulating her views.

Opening with a broadside against the South, Will avers that "to the defense of slavery in the past and the inhuman treatment of the Negro in the present, the South has consecrated her best energies. Literature, politics, theology, history have been ransacked and perverted to prove the hopeless inferiority of the Negro and the design of God that he should serve by right of color and physique" (266). But, he continues, the South has convinced none but herself and is still smarting under the "bitterer than double-distilled gall" of the federal victory (266). Now the South aims at nothing less than the disfranchisement of blacks. There are those who would deprive blacks of education on the grounds that they are incapable of absorbing and profiting from it. Yet education provides black Americans with their best hope of escaping the legacy of slavery—that is, the essential way of ridding "the Negro" of "any tendency toward vice that he may be thought to possess, and *which has been largely increased by what he has imbibed from the example and the close,* IMMORAL ASSOCIATION *which often existed between the master and the slave*" (268–69).

Historically, the responsibility for the plight and condition of the mass of black people demonstrably lies with the South. Yet the South, Will continues, "declares that she is no worse than the North, and that the North would do the same under like provocation. Perhaps so, if the offender were a Negro" (271). Human nature, after all, is everywhere the same, and "the characteristic traits of the master will be found in his dog" (272). The problem defies easy solutions and above all requires the formation of public opinion. Like the antislavery apostles of a previous generation, blacks must go out to "appeal for the justice of our cause to every civilized nation under the heavens," lifting "ourselves upward and forward . . . until 'Ethiopia shall indeed stretch forth her hand and the princes shall come out of Egypt'" (272).

In the manner of Du Bois, Hopkins weaves a complex historical and political argument especially designed to meet the needs and aspirations of elite, northern blacks.[18] In the end, the tragic mulatta remains virtually incidental to her main purposes, serving primarily to add an element of mystery and suspense to the plot. In *Hagar's Daughter,* however, the story of a beautiful mulatta returns to center stage, this time featuring the vicissitudes of a mother and daughter. As in *Contending Forces,* Hopkins begins with a historical prologue, here the secession convention in Charleston. The main action of the novel, however, unfolds in Washington during Reconstruction and focuses on the domestic consequences of slavery, especially its infinitely complex interracial sexual bonds.

The mulatta Hagar, who is not recognized for who she is throughout much of the novel, lives out the end of Clotel's story. Forsaken, like Clotel, by her white slaveholding husband, Hagar, like Clotel, throws herself into the Potomac. But, as we ultimately learn, unlike Clotel, she survives her jump into the Potomac, as does her baby daughter, Jewel, and the two (unbeknownst to Hagar) are soon reunited as mother and stepdaughter when Hagar, known throughout most of the novel as Mrs. Bowen, marries the wealthy westerner, Zenas Bowen, who has already adopted the purportedly orphaned Jewel. Bowen's election to the Senate brings the family to Washington, where much of the action of the endlessly intricate plot unfolds. The plot unites the corrupt minutiae of politics with the disastrous and interlocking influences of slavery upon domestic life. At the end, Hopkins's narrative voice summarizes the lesson: "The holy institution of marriage ignored the life of the slave, breed [*sic*] indifference in the masters to the enormity of illicit connections, with the result that the sacred family relation is weakened and finally ignored in many cases" (284). In *Hagar's Daughter,* the price of this neglect is the untimely death of Jewel, which simultaneously punishes her slaveholding father for his abandonment of his wife and child and her New England betrothed, Cuthbert Sumner, who could not face marriage to a woman with even a drop of black blood.

Sumner, much like Dr. Gresham of *Iola Leroy,* represents the flower of white New England youth and its commitment to the antislavery cause.[19] Gresham eventually overcomes his instinctive prejudice of race, although he does not win Iola, but Sumner cannot. As he tells a friend, who has been arguing that the amalgamation of the races is inevitable, "The mere thought of the grinning, toothless black hag that was her foreparent would forever rise between us" (271). He is willing "to allow the Negroes education, to see them acquire business, money, and social status within a certain environment. I am not averse even to their attaining political power" (271). More than that he cannot countenance. So, his friend counters, "this is the sum total of what Puritan New England philanthropy will allow—every privilege but the vital one of deciding a question of the commonest personal liberty which is the fundamental principle of the holy family tie" (271).

Sumner cannot be moved. Given the "ignorance, poverty and recent degradation" of black people, how can Anglo-Saxons not attempt to keep their own race as pure as possible? Sadly, his friend reminds him that there is a higher law than those of earth and predicts that Sumner may one day find that his own nature has more nobility than he suspected. By the time he does, Jewel is dead. And Hopkins has made her point that for personal liberty to flourish it must be grounded in the family.

Throughout *Hagar's Daughter*, Hopkins demonstrates that the mixture of the races has proceeded further than anyone suspects and its greatest casualty is the mulatta woman. Speaking of Aurelia Mason, another beautiful mulatta who, lacking Hagar and Jewel's advantages of family and character, has led the life of a courtesan, Sumner's secretary, Elsie Bradford, muses that although the loveliness of such women is often marvelous, their condition is too frequently deplorable.

> Beautiful almost beyond description, many of them educated and
> refined, with the best white blood of the South in their veins, they refuse
> to mate themselves with the ignorant of their own race. Socially, they
> are not recognized by the whites; they are often without money enough
> to bu[y] the barest essentials of life; honorably, they cannot procure
> sufficient means to gratify their luxurious tastes; their mothers were
> like themselves; their fathers they never knew; debauched white men are
> ever ready to take advantage of their destitution, and after living a short
> life of shame, they sink into early graves. Living, they were despised by
> whites and blacks alike; dead, they are mourned by none. (159)

Elsie Bradford, having had an illicit liaison that resulted in the birth of her son, has reason to understand something of Aurelia Mason's situation although Elsie is white, not mulatto. In using Elsie to offer the one guardedly negative, if empathetic, assessment of the beautiful mulatta, Hopkins shows the full danger and loneliness of the mulatta's situation. Yet in so doing, she shifts the emphasis in the beautiful mulatta's tragedy from the drop of black blood to the liminality of her sexual situation, thereby inviting white women to respond with "there but for the grace of God go I." Elsie's words thus subtly recast the figure of the beautiful mulatta in a way that none before Hopkins had dared. Doubtless, Hopkins was emboldened by her growing commitment to full integration, including interracial marriage, as the best way to raise the mass of blacks from the swamp into which slavery had plunged them.

For all her boldness, even Hopkins does not assign Elsie's convention-defying words to the compromised Aurelia Mason herself, much less to Hagar or Jewel. Neither she nor Harper was willing to risk a subjective expression of the greatest dangers of the beautiful mulatta's situation. Iola, Sappho, Hagar, and Jewel all remain essentially innocent, however much the forces of evil may threaten and even harm them. Even their most debasing experiences apparently leave no scar upon the purity of their souls.

IV

Notwithstanding Harper's and Hopkins's narrative deployment of the plight of the beautiful mulatta to engage the imaginations of their readers, they were ultimately more concerned with the fate of their people than the personal stories of individuals. Their politics were more national than personal: both placed their greatest faith in the responsible and creative leadership of a respectable, family-based black elite although Hopkins in her last novel also turned her attention to Africa.[20] The figure they use to dramatize their message remains effectively, indeed strikingly, silent about her own worst experiences. Like Linda Brent, Harper's and Hopkins's mulatta women do not personally tell of the worst injuries of the history they so passionately protest against, although, unlike Linda Brent, they unambiguously identify with the other members of the black community.

The figure of Aurelia Mason confirms how much they would have had to lose by breaking that silence. For Aurelia, notwithstanding some claims upon the reader's compassion, descends from and remains associated with the worst villains of the conventional antislavery melodrama—the uncouth and unfeeling slave trader. If Hopkins is correct, as we know she is, about the ubiquity of interracial sex in the antebellum South, we may assume that for every Iola Leroy or Sappho Clark there were at least two Aurelia Masons and, beyond them, countless numbers of ordinary slave women, like Margaret Walker's Vyry Dutton, whose fathers happened to be their masters.[21] Not all mulatta women were beautiful; most probably did not speak flawless English. Most, in other words, were slave women like others, except perhaps for lighter skin or straighter hair. In this respect, we should do well to ponder Hopkins's explicit evocation of the biblical Hagar, slave of Abraham and mother of his son Ishmael. In invoking the biblical precedent, Hopkins transforms it, suggesting that in her time the line that descended from Hagar was not male but female and thereby reminding her readers that women alone transmitted the condition of enslavement to their daughters.

To engage their readers' sympathy, Harper and Hopkins represented their mulatta heroines as essentially white—as elite young women who by the trick of a cruel fate were doomed by a few drops of black blood to slavery. Their texts carried the thinly veiled message that their unmerited destiny could threaten countless other unsuspecting young women. Iola Leroy and Sappho Clark ultimately choose to be black, willingly casting their fate with the African-American community. But their role within Harper's and Hopkins's texts precludes their telling the subjective story of the former slave women whose interests they represent. As figures they embody and represent a history that their mouths may never speak.[22]

The real problem is not that Iola and Sappho could not speak, but that, even through the mediation of a narrative figure, Harper and Hopkins, neither of whom had been raised a slave, could not. The wounds were too painful, the scars too raw, and, possibly, the shame too great for public exposure. So the figures of Iola, Sappho, Hagar, and Jewel were shadowed by the ghosts of Aurelia Mason and countless others who had no voice of their own. With the passage of time, especially from the 1960s, those ghosts began to press more insistently against the consciousness of their heirs. Stories that no one had wanted to remember and could pass on only privately, if at all, began, hesitantly, indirectly, to be told. A tenacious bunch, the ghosts would not down. As Tina Ansa has Rachel say to Lena, "Do you know how long I been waiting for somebody like you to come along so I can tell them all of this, so I can share some of this. You t'in I'm not gonna tell you now I got you here on my beach?" But then, only Ansa's Lena, who was born with a caul and who grows up in a tight-knit black family enmeshed in a southern black community, can begin to hear the ghosts and to absorb what Toni Morrison calls the "rememories" of the stories that could not be passed on.

Notes

1. Toni Morrison, *Beloved* (New York: Knopf-Random, 1987), 5. Subsequent references are cited parenthetically within the essay.

2. For a fuller discussion of my reading of *Beloved,* see Elizabeth Fox-Genovese, "'Unspeakable Things Unspoken': Ghosts and Memories in African-American Women's Narratives of Slavery," Elsa Goveia Lecture, published as a pamphlet (Kingston, Jamaica: N.p., 1993).

3. Sherley Anne Williams, *Dessa Rose* (New York: Morrow, 1986), 154. Subsequent references to this text are cited parenthetically within the essay.

4. For a fuller discussion of *Dessa Rose,* see Deborah E. McDowell, "Negotiating between Tenses: Witnessing Slavery after Freedom—*Dessa Rose*," in *Slavery and the Literary Imagination,* ed. Deborah E. McDowell and Arnold Rampersad (Baltimore: Johns Hopkins Univ. Press, 1989), 144–63.

5. Ibid., 154, 155.

6. Jacqueline Goggin, *Carter G. Woodson: A Life in Black History* (Baton Rouge: Louisiana State Univ. Press, 1993); David Levering Lewis, *W. E. B. Du Bois: Biography of a Race, 1868–1919* (New York: Henry Holt, 1993). For the recent history of slavery, see esp. Eugene D. Genovese, *Roll, Jordan, Roll: The World the Slaves Made* (New York: Pantheon, 1975); Lawrence Levine, *Black Culture and Black Consciousness: Afro-American Folk Thought from Slavery to Freedom* (New York: Oxford Univ. Press, 1977); Peter Kolchin, *Unfree Labor: American Slavery and Russian Serfdom* (Cambridge: Harvard Univ. Press, 1987); Elizabeth Fox-Genovese, *Within the Plantation Household: Black and White Women of the Old South* (Chapel Hill: Univ. of North Carolina Press, 1988).

7. For a very different discussion of the relation between African-American women novelists and history, see Missy Dehn Kubitschek, *Claiming the Heritage: African-American Women Novelists and History* (Jackson: Univ. Press of Mississippi, 1991).

8. Eric Foner, *Free Soil, Free Labor, Free Men: The Ideology of the Republican Party before the Civil War* (New York: Oxford Univ. Press, 1970); Elizabeth Fox-Genovese, "Stewards of Their Culture: Southern Women Novel-

ists as Social Critics," in *Stepping Out of the Shadows: Alabama Women, 1819–1990*, ed. Mary Martha Thomas (Tuscaloosa: Univ. of Alabama Press, 1995), 11–27; Elizabeth Fox-Genovese, "To Be Worthy of God's Favor: Southern Women's Defense and Critique of Slavery," Fortenbaugh Lecture, Gettysburg College, published as a pamphlet; idem, "Contested Meanings: Women and the Problem of Freedom in the Mid-Nineteenth-Century United States," *Historical Change and Human Rights: The Oxford Amnesty Lectures 1994*, ed. Olwen Hufton (New York: Basic Books, 1995), 179–216; Elizabeth Fox-Genovese and Eugene D. Genovese, "The Divine Sanction of Social Order: Religious Foundations of the Southern Slaveholders' World View," *Journal of the American Academy of Religion* 55 (summer 1987): 211–33; Jamie Stanesa, "Dialogues of Difference: Personal Identity, Social Ideology, and Regional Difference in American Women Writers, 1850–1860," Ph.D. diss., Emory University, 1993.

9. William Wells Brown, *Clotel; or, the President's Daughter* (1853; rpt. New York: Collier Books, 1975).

10. On the pastoral in southern literature, see esp. Lewis P. Simpson, *The Dispossessed Garden: Pastoral and History in Southern Literature* (Athens: Univ. of Georgia Press, 1975). See also Louis D. Rubin Jr., *The Edge of the Swamp: A Study in the Literature and Society of the Old South* (Baton Rouge: Louisiana State Univ. Press, 1989); Jan Bakker, *The Pastoral in Antebellum Southern Literature* (Baton Rouge: Louisiana State Univ. Press, 1989); Elizabeth Fox-Genovese, "The Fettered Mind: Time, Place, and the Literary Imagination of the Old South," *Georgia Historical Quarterly* 76 (1990): 622–50.

11. Pauline E. Hopkins, *Hagar's Daughter: A Story of Southern Caste Prejudice*, in *The Magazine Novels of Pauline Hopkins*, ed. Hazel V. Carby (New York: Oxford Univ. Press, 1988), 3–284. *Hagar's Daughter* was originally published in serial form in the *Colored American Magazine* 2 (Mar. and Apr. 1901); 3 (May-Oct. 1901); and 4 (Nov. and Dec. 1901, Jan. and Mar. 1902). Subsequent references to the 1988 edition are cited parenthetically within the essay.

12. Michael Kreyling, *Figures of the Hero in Southern Narrative* (Baton Rouge: Louisiana State Univ. Press, 1987).

13. Harriet A. Jacobs, *Incidents in the Life of a Slave Girl, Written by Herself*, ed. Jean Fagan Yellin (1861; rpt. Cambridge: Harvard Univ. Press, 1987). Subsequent references to this text are cited parenthetically within the essay.

14. Orlando Patterson, *Slavery and Social Death: A Comparative Study* (Cambridge: Harvard Univ. Press, 1982).

15. John Hope Franklin has explored the distinct world of free blacks in antebellum North Carolina in his *The Free Negro in North Carolina, 1790–1860* (Chapel Hill: Univ. of North Carolina Press, 1943).

16. Frances Ellen Watkins Harper, *Iola Leroy; or, Shadows Uplifted* (New York: Oxford Univ. Press, 1988), 14. Subsequent references to this text are cited parenthetically within the essay.

17. Pauline E. Hopkins, *Contending Forces: A Romance Illustrative of Negro Life North and South* (1900; rpt. New York: Oxford Univ. Press, 1988). Subsequent references to this text are cited parenthetically within the essay.

18. On domesticity in Hopkins, see Claudia Tate, *Domestic Allegories of Political Desire: The Black Heroine's Text at the Turn of the Century* (New York: Oxford Univ. Press, 1992), e.g., 149. On the young Du Bois, see Lewis, *W. E. B. Du Bois.*

19. Cuthbert Sumner bears a strong enough resemblance to Dr. Gresham, who proposes to and is rejected by Iola Leroy, to suggest that Hopkins may have been consciously glossing Harper's text. But whatever Hopkins's intentions in this regard, it seems clear that the New England man who prided himself on his antislavery liberalism while harboring an intractable racism was emerging as a trope of African-American women's fiction.

20. Pauline E. Hopkins, *Of One Blood; or, The Hidden Self,* in *The Magazine Novels of Pauline Hopkins. Of One Blood* was originally published in the *Colored American Magazine,* 1902–3. See Tate, *Domestic Allegories,* on the importance of family.

21. Margaret Walker, *Jubilee* (Boston: Houghton Mifflin, 1966).

22. For a related discussion of Iola's virtual voicelessness, see Elizabeth Ammons, *Conflicting Stories: American Women Writers at the Turn into the Twentieth Century* (New York: Oxford Univ. Press, 1992), 31.

Gender, Race, and Allen Tate's Profession of Letters in the South

Susan V. Donaldson

In a 1935 letter to fellow poet and southern *literatus* John Peale Bishop, Allen Tate noted grumpily that he had just polished off an article for the *Virginia Quarterly Review*—on a topic, he added, not of his own choosing.[1] The essay was published later that year as "The Profession of Letters in the South," and a good deal of Tate's grumpiness about writing an article he very nearly declined to do lingers on in the essay itself. "It must be confessed," he testily observed, "that the Southern tradition has left no cultural landmark so conspicuous that the people may be reminded by it constantly of what they are. We lack a tradition in the arts; more to the point, we lack a literary tradition." What southerners had instead was a "vague and feeble literature" marked by the fatal flaw of gentility and sentimentality. "If there is such a person as a Southern writer," he argued, "if there could be such a profession as letters in the South, the profession would require the speaking of unpleasant words and the violation of good literary manners."[2]

Coded into Tate's own unpleasant words was the conviction that modern southern letters should dissociate itself from the successful women writers of the nineteenth century who seemed to exemplify those good literary manners—southern writers like E. D. E. N. Southworth, Mary Virginia Terhune, Caroline Lee Hentz, Maria McIntosh, and Augusta Evans Wilson. Indeed, Tate's own contemporaries, the critic noted in "A Southern Mode of the Imagination," "called the nineteenth-century Ciceronian style 'Confederate prose,' and we avoided it more assiduously than sin. Of a Southern woman novelist of the 1860s, Augusta Evans, author of *St. Elmo*, it was said that her heroines had swallowed an unabridged dictionary."[3] But the success

492

of domestic novelists and the efforts of literary modernists to distance themselves from that tradition were not the only factors contributing to Tate's testiness. There was also the difficulty of finding a "genuine" southern literary tradition where none seemed to exist—at least none fitting the criteria of Tate's Agrarian and modernist agenda. Although the South was—at least by Tate's lights—an aristocratic, hierarchical society, one distinguished by "its comparative stability, its realistic limitation of the acquisitive impulse, its preference for human relations compared to relations economic," its literature, he complained, was marked by "the unreal union of formless revery and correct sentiment, the inflated oratory—even in private correspondence you see it witness a feeble hold upon place and time."[4]

If Tate yearned, in this essay and elsewhere, to find an image of what he thought of as the ideal southern tradition *and* writer—white, male, conservative, rooted to time and place, and unified in sensibility—he nonetheless had the integrity to acknowledge, albeit with very bad grace, the possibility that such an image would always prove chimerical or, at the very least, radically unstable. Even though the southern literary canon has traditionally been defined as white, male, and conservative—and Tate has had a large hand in defining that canon—the profession of letters in the South and its accompanying literary texts have always had a peculiarly haunted air, an aura of repressed ghosts besieging the white male writer and destabilizing his writing. Tate's testiness, in fact, might well have a good deal to do with his half-acknowledged suspicion that lying both within and without the monumentalized surface of the white patriarchal writer he earnestly sought to celebrate is a potent rival and Other—the figure of the black trickster, defined by fluidity and open possibility. This suspicion is shared by those unsatisfactory nineteenth-century writers over whom Tate grumbles, and that suspicion in turn reveals something of the radical instability underlying the tradition of southern letters that Tate inherited and helped reassemble with his fellow Fugitive-Agrarians. For even though southern literature has long been marked by its project of imposing boundaries and exclusions—and by the gender and racial anxieties prompting that project—the profession of letters in the South that Tate inherited and helped define has also been marked by the slippages, disruptions, and battles in literary texts inevitably resulting from the imposition of those boundaries.[5]

To our twentieth-century eyes the most conspicuous of those

boundaries and exclusions was the line drawn between successful white women writers and besieged white male writers in the South by both nineteenth- and twentieth-century male southern literary critics. Pro-slavery apologist George Fitzhugh was not alone when he breezily declared, "Poetry and painting requires [*sic*] boldness, originality, and inventiveness. The ladies are too modest to practice these qualities, and only become coarse when they attempt to be bold. Sappho is an exception, but Sappho, we suspect, was a myth or a man."[6] Any woman who dared to venture into this exclusively male territory, as Anne Goodwyn Jones has amply documented, was all too likely to be dismissed, in one southern editor's words, as *"une femme incomprise*—a woman out of her sphere, an anomaly, an imperfection."[7]

The literary circle associated with *Russell's Magazine* in late 1850s Charleston—including novelist William Gilmore Simms and poets Henry Timrod and Paul Hamilton Hayne—was particularly quick to voice their disdain for the popular women writers of the period and to lament what appeared to be the consequences for native sons. If Timrod, Hayne, and Simms had failed to receive their proper due in public acclaim, the editors of *Russell's* complained, it was at least partly because the average reader was all too ready to confuse "the false with the true, the nonsense of newspaper 'Floras' and 'Matildas,' with whatever is grand or beautiful in the works of acknowledged genius."[8] Twenty years later Paul Hamilton Hayne was still querulously concerned about prominent southern women writers whom he designated "The Fungous School." They are, he declared, "the worst enemies of the intellectual and repute of their section." If "the exceptional reader" dared to offer a criticism of "a literary *lioness*" associated with this "school," he complained, "all her adherents male and female, the whole body of her enthusiastic '*claquenes*' will descend upon the disagreeable critic."[9]

The urgency of these pronouncements is understandable if one takes into consideration the conspicuous presence of white southern women writers in the nineteenth-century world of letters. As Jay B. Hubbell once observed, women professional writers in the South of the 1840s and 1850s were very probably more numerous than male writers living by their pens. After all, the literary profession was one of the few "respectable" occupations open to white women in the years before the Civil War.[10] Probably "the most widely read novelist in the nineteenth century," according to Nina Baym, was E. D. E. N. Southworth, who resorted to writing in desperation after being abandoned by her husband and eventually produced about fifty novels.[11] In 1904, after her death, the *Washington Star* declared that for a while Southworth was making $6,000 a year on her fiction, "probably not an exaggerated figure," historian Mary Kelley observes. Kelley estimates that by 1867 Southworth was probably earning almost $4,000 just from her contract with the *New York Ledger* for her stories and novels.[12]

This sort of success was not lost on writers like Henry Timrod, William Gilmore Simms, and Paul Hamilton Hayne, who periodically vented their spleen against "newspaper 'Floras' and 'Matildas'" in words remarkably similar to Nathaniel Hawthorne's famous lamentation about that "damn'd mob of scribbling women" so successful in American letters in the 1850s and 1860s, some of whom were these very southerners. But if complaints about "scribbling women" remind us of the common ground shared by southerners and northerners, we would also do well to heed the especially strong hold that the white patriarchal family had on southern culture and on southern literary men throughout the nineteenth and early twentieth century. Allen Tate himself asked in "The Profession of Letters in the South": "Where else in the modern world is the patriarchal family still innocent of the rise and power of other forms of society?"[13] This familial model, as historians like Eugene Genovese, Elizabeth Fox-Genovese, Bertram Wyatt-Brown, Steven Stowe, Catherine Clinton, Jean Friedman, and Deborah Gray White have argued, stressed male authority and female and black subordination and as such reinforced gender distinctions that were probably more extreme in the South than elsewhere in Victorian America.[14]

Indeed, young white men of the elite class in the antebellum South, Bertram Wyatt-Brown argues, were brought up to be acutely aware of the social hierarchy in which they lived, to defer to their elders and betters and to assume the proper posture of superiority to their inferiors. They were, moreover, encouraged at an early age to be aggressive, active, competitive, quick to anger and quick to fight. Theirs was, after all, an honorific society where masculine identity was dependent partly upon the proper subordination of inferiors, like blacks and women, and partly upon the regard of male cohorts.[15]

Strangely enough, though, status and even gender identity were never quite a sure thing for white men in the antebellum South, where personal and social standing rested largely on the good opinion of one's fellows. If white men were to maintain their position among men and above women and black slaves, they had to prove their mettle over and over again, in duels and in appallingly brutal, eye-gouging brawls that Elliott Gorn has documented in such vivid detail.[16] The pressure to assert one's manhood seemed particularly heavy to white male authors like Simms and Hayne, for they were acutely aware how "frivolous," as Drew Gilpin Faust points out, their literary occupation appeared to southern society.[17] No one, as a matter of fact, was more blunt about the plight of the white male writer in the South than Hayne—unless, of course, it was Simms, long given to incessant complaints about the region's neglect of its artists. "A more unfortunate home for an artist (whatever his degree!) could not be found in the broad circle of Christendom," Hayne wrote in 1860. "The people are intensely provincial, narrow-minded, and I must add—*ignorant*. Literature they despise. Poetry they look upon as the feeble pastime of minds too effeminate to seek manly employment."[18]

If any occupation seemed more manly in contrast, it was that of the political orator who is able to "awe, master, and bind down his audience by the forces of a speed vigorous as the grasp of a Cyclops, and burning as the core of Etna," as the editors of *Russell's* suggested in tones evoking professional envy.[19] Indeed, the writers linked with *Russell's Magazine* were all too aware that oratory and politics were more likely than literature to attract the young men of their region. "Every youth of independent fortune, who is also possessed of cleverness, thinks it his duty—his *mission*—to adopt some party-badge, to fight under some political banner," the inaugural issue of the Charleston journal noted in 1857. "The notion of confining his ambition to the limited routine of a scholar's or author's life, he would dismiss as ridiculous and degrading."[20] It was, in fact, something of a commonplace to distinguish between political oratory and poetry in implicitly gendered terms, as William and Mary law professor Thomas Roderick Dew did in describing the decline of political eloquence in Augustan Rome: "The bold and manly voice of eloquence was hushed. The high and lofty spirit of the republic was tamed down to a sickly and disgusting servility. The age of poetry came when that of eloquence and philosophy was past."[21]

Dew's reference to servility here is telling, for the metaphor of slavery carried a wealth of ambiguous associations for white male writers who found themselves closely allied with the proslavery cause—and their numbers grew significantly in the 1850s, as Drew Gilpin Faust tells us and as we learn from the pages of the *Southern Literary Messenger* and *Russell's Magazine*.[22] After the publication of Harriet Beecher Stowe's *Uncle Tom's Cabin* white southern writers felt compelled to link the notion of a peculiarly southern literature to the defense of the peculiar institution. By 1856 the *Southern Literary Messenger* had made a plea to white southern writers to provide "the united basis of a *slavery literature*, so to speak," partly in reaction to the huge success of Harriet Beecher Stowe's *Uncle Tom's Cabin*.[23] A few years later the editors of *Russell's Magazine*, probably Henry Timrod in particular, voiced their agreement: "There are truths underlying the relations of master and slave; there are meanings beneath that union of the utmost freedom with a healthy conservatism, which, growing out of these relations, is characteristic of Southern thought, of which poetry may avail herself not only to vindicate one system to the eyes of the world, but to convey lessons which shall take root in the hearts of all mankind."[24]

What those truths of the relations of master and slave were remained to be seen, for just as compelling as the imperative to defend slavery, to define southern literature as slavery literature, was the horrifying possibility that the makers of slavery literature were themselves slaves, as writers like Simms, Timrod, and Hayne nervously speculated again and again. They might fulminate against their political and literary opponents as "slaves of English and Northern opinions, and . . . slaves of the conventional schools of the eighteenth century," as Timrod did in the pages of *Russell's Magazine;* but they remained haunted by their own suspicion that they could be perceived not as masters but as slaves—to regional audiences indifferent to poetry and art, to a profession increasingly defined as "feminine," to pressures to assert and reassert their manhood, and above all to the demands of a slave society that awarded public recognition only to those writers who threw their energies into the defense of the region's peculiar institution. Timrod, for one, noted nervously in the same essay castigating the "slaves of English and Northern opinions" that "prejudice" in the South quite simply reduces poetry "into a mere servant of our pleasures."[25] Simms was even more quick to associate the profession of letters in the South with bondage. Charleston, he wrote in 1858, "has always treated me rather as a public enemy, to be sneered at, than as a dutiful son doing

her honor. *And I too, know it as a place of tombs.* I have buried six
dear children within its soil! Great God! What is the sort of slavery
which brings me hither!" [26]

On the face of things, such language might appear innocuous
enough because of the time-honored convention of dichotomizing slavery and freedom for rhetorical effect. Hugh Honour notes that in an
early edition of Samuel Johnson's dictionary, liberty is defined quite
simply in terms of its opposite, slavery, and throughout the eighteenth
century the term *slaves* was used to describe people subject to a tyrannical government. [27] In the hands of proslavery writers like Timrod,
Hayne, and Simms, though, slavery took on a host of disturbing, powerless, unmanning connotations. For without the good opinion of other
white southern men, writers like Simms were dangerously close to being
grouped with the South's two main subordinate groups, slaves and
white women—in short, to losing their very standing as white men in
a paternalistic, stratified society. [28]

If these writers did indeed create, as Lewis P. Simpson argues, "a
novel version of the man of letters—that is to say, the man of letters as
plantation patriarch and chattel slave master," the metaphor of slavery
to which they resorted to express their deepest fears and anxieties revealed in the truest Hegelian sense the reversibility of the master-slave
relationship. [29] Like the southern white man dependent upon the subordination of his inferiors for his status, the master or lord in Hegel's
terms defines his power and autonomy according to the sway he holds
over the inferior slave, the "dependent consciousness." But the closer
one probes that relationship, Hegel warns, the more the boundaries
between master and slave are blurred as their crucial interdependence
is exposed. "Just where the master has effectively achieved lordship,"
he declares, "he really finds that something has come about quite different from an independent consciousness. It is not an independent, but
rather a dependent consciousness that he has achieved." The lord in
effect changes places with his slave, underscoring just how radically
unstable that relationship is: "But just as lordship shows its essential
nature to be the reverse of what it wants to be, so, too, bondage will,
when completed, pass into the opposite of what it immediately is: being
a consciousness repressed within itself, it will enter into itself, and
change into real and true independence." [30]

The possibility of reversal can be detected beneath the surface of
nervous references to slavery by nineteenth-century white male south-

erners but perhaps most dramatically in the studied, resonating silence concerning the professional competitors who were probably even more threatening to their status as white southern men than white women writers—authors of slave narratives. From John Pendleton Kennedy to George Frederick Holmes, white southern men of letters were quick to deplore abolitionist agitation in general and to attack Harriet Beecher Stowe in particular, but they remained stubbornly, fiercely silent on the subject of slave narratives—except perhaps to join in the chorus of accusations accusing their writers of being frauds. Slave narratives might have been referred to obliquely as yet another example of what Kennedy called "abolitionist mischief," but they were never acknowledged as literary works by white southern commentators and certainly never claimed as *southern* literature.[31] And therein lies, perhaps, the most rigorously defined border between southern and nonsouthern literature as defined first by self-conscious writers like the *Russell's Magazine* circle and later by Allen Tate and those who followed in his footsteps: the expulsion of African Americans from the world of southern letters and their redefinition as "northern." Successful white southern women writers might have been castigated and jeered at in the pages of *Russell's* and later in the essays of the Fugitive-Agrarians, but black writers and orators on antislavery platforms were stonily and resolutely ignored.[32]

Yet as Toni Morrison has eloquently argued, blackness has helped define the hue of whiteness in American letters, and nowhere more so than in the white South, whose canonized texts fairly reverberated with the effort—often unsuccessful—to contain blackness.[33] Joan Dayan provocatively suggests that such an effort can be detected in Edgar Allan Poe's stories of "the perils of mastery and nightmares about the decay of fictions of status, the rot at the heart of the Great House."[34] It is quite possible, she argues, that Poe owed his Gothic imagination as much to slave tales of conjuring as to German romanticism.[35] It is also possible, she notes, that *The Narrative of Arthur Gordon Pym,* that overwrought novel of exploration, discovery, whiteness, and blackness, can be read as nothing so much as an effort "to mime and invert the narratives of American slavery."[36]

Much the same can be said of Thomas Nelson Page's postbellum story, "No Haid Pawn," a curious anomaly in the 1887 volume of stories *In Ole Virginia* monumentalizing the Old South.[37] Lacking the reassuring presence of a faithful ex-slave narrator like Sam in "Marse Chan," the Gothic tale is told by a white narrator who recalls an inadvertent visit in the 1850s to a supposedly haunted plantation whose former owner had been renowned for his cruelty to slaves. Before the story ends, the narrator comes face to face with what may be the headless ghost of the owner *or* one of his murdered slaves *or* an escaped slave masquerading as a ghost to protect a station on the Underground Railroad. So disturbing are these three possibilities that Page concludes the tale in an unpersuasive rush, and the story as a whole casts a dark and ominous shadow upon sunny memories of Marse Chan, "meh lady," and the time "befo' de wah."

Just as telling are the sinister women of color who punctuate, disrupt, and threaten to hijack the narratives of George Washington Cable's *The Grandissimes* and Mark Twain's *Pudd'nhead Wilson*.[38] So imposing are these figures—and so threatening to their white male protagonists—that they are eventually expelled from their respective narratives so that their white creators can in a sense regain control of the plots. The figures themselves, though, lingered on in the white southern literary imagination, in, for example, Mark Twain's famous dream of the "negro wench" who propositions and feeds the white dreamer.[39] Try as they might, white southern male writers could never quite succeed in expelling unruly blackness from their texts, and in that failure could be detected the limits of white mastery, literal and verbal.[40]

It is all the more ironic, then, that a good many black antislavery activists, many of whom were once, after all, southern slaves, exhibited precisely the sort of oratorical and masterful authority on the platform that white southern writers alternately admired and envied, and no one more so, of course, than Frederick Douglass. In *My Bondage and My Freedom*, Douglass reports with pride his success as a lecturer on antislavery platforms. "It did not entirely satisfy me to *narrate* wrongs," he recalled; "I felt like *denouncing* them." And so effective were those denunciations that his friends warned him to "have a *little* of the plantation manner of speech" when he spoke and opponents charged that so powerful a speaker could not possibly have been a slave.[41]

Ironic, too, is the best-seller status that a good many slave narratives achieved, in stark contrast to the general inattention of which the writers of *Russell's Magazine* complained. Over one hundred runaway slaves of the sixty thousand who fled to the North wrote book-length narratives of their experiences, and a number of those runaways were successful enough to become, Frances Smith Foster asserts, "professional exslaves," among them William and Ellen Craft, Henry Bibb,

Josiah Henson, Anthony Burns, Lewis and Milton Clarke, Samuel Ringgold Ward, Henry "Boy" Brown, William Wells Brown, and of course Douglass himself. Foster reports that William Wells Brown's 1847 narrative sold eight thousand copies in two years, and Moses Roper's 1839 narrative went through eleven editions. Father Josiah Henson's narrative, first issued in 1849, sold six thousand copies in three years and would eventually sell nearly one hundred thousand copies after the revelation that he served as the model for Harriet Beecher Stowe's Uncle Tom.[42] No wonder, then, that one northern white commentator felt compelled to pronounce slave narratives to be "the most remarkable productions of the age."[43]

Most ironic of all, of course, was the highly masculine character of the most popular slave narratives, a masculinity often allying itself quite explicitly with white northern definitions of manhood—with autonomy, self-reliance, evangelical values, and hard work—and in direct contrast to white southern masculinity. As Foster notes, "The number of slave narratives published by men far exceeds those published by women, and thus the slave's self-portrayal is dominated by male features."[44] The archetypal story of the runaway slave became that of the solitary male fleeing the South and its restrictions for the freedom of the North, and explicit in that plot was a repudiation of all the boundaries and restrictions defining southern society and its constructions of white and black manhood.

Douglass's autobiographical writings in particular appear to offer an explicit repudiation of white southern masculinity—its tyrannical authority, its propensity for cruelty, and its susceptibility to erratic passion and intemperate behavior. But if Douglass strove to define his own sense of manhood in contrast to that of slaveholding manhood, he was not above taunting white southern men with the possibility of direct competition—in effect tweaking his opponent's nose or voicing a challenge in the time-honored fashion of white male duels in the South. Such a challenge is palpably present in the famous fight scene with Covey the slavebreaker, where Douglas makes his famous pronouncement: "You have seen how a man was made a slave; you shall see how a slave was made a man."[45] And such too was the extraordinary challenge that he delivered in the "Letter to his Old Master," appended to the 1855 version of his autobiography. For in that letter Douglass asked with startling and calculating directness how his former master would respond to Douglass's stealing away of Auld's daughter Amanda, placing her in the bonds of slavery, submitting her to the physical abuse suffered all too often by slaves, and finally exposing her to sexual exploitation.[46]

As several commentators have argued, Douglass's notion of manhood replicates to a deeply disturbing degree the very kind of masterful white masculinity he ostensibly rejects, and not just in the slave's drive toward mastery.[47] Deborah McDowell among others has noted in Douglass's work "an implied equation of masculinity with subjectivity and textuality." Throughout his narratives, she stresses, "'slave' is conflated with 'male.'" McDowell has noted as well the disturbing narrative patterns of complicity that link Douglass to the very slaveholders he excoriates—his near-exclusion of women and their contributions to his escape from slavery from the 1845 narrative in particular and his voyeuristic descriptions of women under the whip. Most disturbing of all, McDowell asserts, is Douglass's implicit but unmistakable allegiance to the very dynamics of power under which he himself has suffered. Pondering the passage in which Douglass relates his surreptitious and diligent efforts to copy the letters in his young Master Thomas's copybook, McDowell observes: "In its allegiance to the dialectics of dominance and subordination, Douglass's *Narrative* is, and not surprisingly so, a by-product of Master Tommy's copybook, especially in its gendered division of power relations."[48]

African-American women, in short, did not exist in Douglass's story, as they largely did not exist in the stories told by white male writers of the nineteenth century—except perhaps as disturbing specters and shadows darkening the white literary imagination, like Palmyre the Philosophe in Cable's *The Grandissimes*. It is with a good deal of justification, then, that Diane Roberts flatly observes, "Black women stand for the suppressed history of the South."[49] To tell their story was to articulate, in Hortense Spillers's words, "the tale writ between the lines and in the not-quite spaces of an American domesticity."[50] Barred from white southern notions of womanhood stressing fragility and purity, demonized as sexually voracious, and occluded from defining slave narratives like Douglass's autobiographies, the southern African-American woman found herself telling a story that required the unearthing of buried histories and untold tales and the disrupting of boundaries long characteristic of southern letters. Indeed, to a striking degree, the stories told by writers like Frances Ellen Watkins Harper and Pauline Hopkins were of women, like the eponymous heroine in

Iola Leroy and the mysterious Sappho Clark in *Contending Forces,* whose own narratives were premised on the breaking of long and death-dealing silences.

It was the necessity of breaking those silences, of disrupting the boundaries requiring those silences, that the formidable Anna Julia Cooper, born into slavery in 1858, addressed with verve and barely controlled rage in her 1892 volume, *A Voice from the South.* "One muffled strain in the Silent South, a jarring chord and a vague and un-comprehended cadenza has been and still is the Negro," Cooper de-clared at the beginning of the volume. "And of that muffled chord, the one mute and voiceless note has been the sadly expectant Black Woman,

> An infant crying in the night,
> An infant crying for the light;
> And with *no language—but a cry.*"

The "other side" of the South, Cooper asserted, had not been repre-sented in southern letters, nor would that representation be complete until the black woman found her voice. In her now-famous clarion call, she maintained, "Only the BLACK WOMAN can say 'when and where I enter, in the quiet, undisputed dignity of my womanhood, without vio-lence and without suing or special patronage, then and there the whole *Negro race enters with me.*'" [51]

It was, I think, precisely that "other side" finding articulation, frag-menting, complicating, and multiplying regional identity and literature, that so worried Allen Tate and his fellows a generation or so later when they were exploring the possibility of defining themselves as southern men of letters. [52] For however unsatisfactory Tate and his comrades saw nineteenth-century southern literature—a tradition that Tate himself rather significantly referred to as "the Charming Lady"—the Fugitive-Agrarians of Nashville and Vanderbilt University insisted upon seeing the nineteenth-century South itself as a sort of unified and stalwart male sensibility, in the best Eliotesque tradition, that by definition could not exist in the modern age. [53] "I can think of no better image for what the South was before 1860, and for what it largely still was until about 1914," Tate wrote in "A Southern Mode of the Imagination," "than that of the old gentleman in Kentucky who sat every afternoon in his front yard under an old sugar tree, reading Cicero's Letters to Atticus. When the hands suckering the tobacco in the adjoining field needed orders, he kept his place in the book with his forefinger, walked out into the field, gave the orders, and then returned to his reading under the shade of the tree. He was also a lawyer, and occasionally he went to his office, which was over the feed store in the county seat, a village with a population of about four hundred people." [54]

It was largely this image of the white male southerner that would lure the very different and rather quarrelsome contributors to the 1930 Agrarian manifesto *I'll Take My Stand*. For Tate's early mentor and colleague John Crowe Ransom in particular, the Old South offered a genuine, organic community, like those lost in the European past, in which little or no distinction was made between labor and leisure, belief and action, property and identity, individual and society. [55] For Tate himself, the Old South offered the last stronghold of a unified sensibility on the North American continent. "The Southern mind was simple," he declared, "not top-heavy with learning it had no need of, unintellectual, and composed; it was personal and dramatic, rather than abstract and metaphysical; and it was sensuous because it lived close to a natural scene of great variety and interest." [56]

Hence it was in the name of that unified white male sensibility that Tate in particular felt compelled to excoriate southern writers like Ellen Glasgow and James Branch Cabell, who appeared far too open to the possibilities of regional heterogeneity for his taste. [57] According to his newly awakened Agrarian sense of the importance of cultural unity, Tate wrote his friend Donald Davidson in 1929, Glasgow and Cabell in particular were dangerous "*because* they have a mixed thesis—, i.e., mixed of old Southern and Progress—*because* their intelligences are split into contradictory values, they are bad novelists." And as if to clinch the argument, he added, "all great, or really good writers, must have a simply homogeneous sense of values, which incidentally are the kind of values we wish to restore." [58]

Suspect too, both Tate and his comrade John Crowe Ransom argued, was the flowering of Charleston letters in the 1920s, one largely dominated, significantly enough, by women. Charleston writers, Ransom loftily proclaimed, were mere practitioners of "local color"—a coded dismissal of women writers whose subjects were regarded as insufficiently monumental or historical to meet Agrarian standards. Obliquely but firmly, Ransom declared that writers like Josephine

Pinckney, Beatrice Ravenel, and Julia Peterkin were not at one with their community. "So the Charleston novels," he concluded in a obscure but deft turn of logic, "are not Charleston in spirit, but may be construed somewhat indirectly as witnesses to Charleston's decay." [59]

Equally reprehensible, Ransom added, were the contaminating liberal sentiments of writers like T. S. Stribling, whose "mildly defamatory stories about Tennessee and Alabama" could hardly be construed as truly "southern" in spirit. To expose the conditions of southern life and its problems with caste, Ransom suggested, was to write in a distinctly "foreign" vein. Such an "invasion" of liberalism in literature, he noted, could only be categorized as "an importation," the result of "alien" and "foreign" influences. [60]

Above all, Tate and his fellows insisted, there was no room for African Americans in the world of southern letters they were busily inventing in the 1930s and 1940s. By the early 1930s Tate had resolutely allied himself with a white supremacist notion of southern regional identity largely in keeping with what historian Ulrich B. Phillips had identified as the "central theme of southern history"—the determination to keep the South a white man's country. [61] "I argue it this way," Tate maintained in an essay titled "A View of the Whole South"; "the white race seems determined to rule the Negro race in its midst; I belong to the white race; therefore I intend to support white rule. Lynching is a symptom of weak, inefficient rule; but you can't destroy lynching by *fiat* or social agitation; lynching will disappear when the white race is satisfied that its supremacy will not be questioned in social crises." [62] As if to underscore the point, Tate even went as far in the early 1930s as to sabotage the efforts of a young white instructor in Vanderbilt's English Department to hold an interracial party in honor of James Weldon Johnson, a new faculty member at Fisk University, and poet Langston Hughes. Energetic as always, Tate let loose a barrage of protest letters to Vanderbilt's English Department and even one New York magazine, declaring that he would meet Hughes and Johnson in New York or in Europe but not in the South. [63]

To a great extent, in fact, the efforts of Tate and his fellow Fugitive-Agrarians to define southern literature in the late 1920s, 1930s, and 1940s can be read as an exercise in exclusions and boundary-making, and one detects in that exercise an implicit agenda strikingly similar to the determination of the *Russell's Magazine* circle to protect and consolidate the masculinity of the white male southern writer. Tellingly,

Tate himself found his own exemplar of the twentieth-century southern man of letters, exiled from tradition and estranged from modernity, in the Trojan hero Aeneas. Marooned "by the Potomac," Aeneas in the 1933 poem "Aeneas at Washington" ponders his losses and his sense of alienation:

> Stuck in the wet mire
> Four thousand leagues from the ninth buried city
> I thought of Troy, what we had built her for.[64]

It was this self-image that defined in the writings of Tate and his fellows the perimeters of the modern southern writer, white, male, conservative, pondering the weighty losses of history; and this image became the implicit criterion by which other writers were judged "southern" or "nonsouthern."

The result was a southern literary canon cast largely in the self-image of the Fugitive-Agrarians. Perhaps even more to the point, they were perceived as such by those who stood on the periphery. The lone woman often linked with the Fugitives in the early 1920s, Laura Riding Gottschalk, earnestly tried to assume the title of "a Fugitive brother," but she also found her second-class status among the men who called themselves "the brethren" nothing short of infuriating. In a blistering letter to Donald Davidson upbraiding him for a review of her work, Riding wrote: "Is it just Southern or masculine nastiness or *timidity:* That you do not do me the *honour* of comparing me with MEN? Can't you take up anything better for me than Edna Millay & Sara Teasdale—what the hell do you mean any way by using phrases such as 'after a woman's fashion' about work like mine. It isn't just the vulgarity of it but the hypocrisy of it: because all along you fellows at least pretended that you were dealing with at least an equal."[65] Others were more muted in their criticism. At a 1935 conference on southern and southwestern writers organized by Robert Penn Warren and Cleanth Brooks, then the editors of *Southern Review,* Ford Madox Ford, often hailed as an honorary Agrarian, noted wonderingly: "I am surprised that you had no women to address this meeting, like Caroline Gordon and Elizabeth Madox Roberts."[66]

Even Caroline Gordon herself, married to Allen Tate and a self-consciously southern author in her own right, tended to think of the

Fugitive-Agrarian circle as a men's club. To her they were "the boys" and "the Nashville brethren."[67] And however fond she might be of the "brethren," she was acutely aware that she and other women writers were never really considered members of the inner circle. Indeed, she suspected at times that her work was not given the same serious regard as that of male southern writers. Having a story turned down by Cleanth Brooks at the *Southern Review* was likely to send her into a brooding rage, and when her longtime friend Katherine Anne Porter received similar treatment from John Crowe Ransom at the *Kenyon Review*, Gordon was quick to commiserate. "He can't bear for women to be serious about their art," she told Porter.[68]

But if Tate and his brethren were largely successful in excluding women from the self-image they wielded to delineate the boundaries of modern southern letters, they also tended to find that image itself disturbing the more they pondered it—and in ways that resembled all too readily the uneasiness underlying the metaphor of slavery used by the *Russell's Magazine* circle generations before. The closer Tate himself looked at that unified male sensibility in the past, at the features of the squire under the sugar tree or those of "Aeneas at Washington," the less and less recognizable those lineaments appeared. It was perhaps for this reason that he eventually discarded the biography of Robert E. Lee that he began in 1930.[69] No one, of course, could have better *appeared* to have represented the kind of masculinity for which Tate himself yearned than Robert E. Lee. "When he acted or spoke the whole Lee was present," Tate observed in his manuscript, "and there is left to us none of the revealing evidence of a man who existed in parts through which we may see their relations and the imperfect fashion in which they work together. Lee had no parts, from the day he was born: he was born a perfect specimen of human integration."[70] But to Andrew Lytle Tate complained: "The longer I've contemplated the venerable features of Lee, the more I've hated him. It is as if I had married a beautiful girl, perfect in figure, pure in all those physical attributes that seem to clothe purity of character, and then had found when she had undressed that the hidden places were corrupt and diseased." Significantly, he added that in Lee one sees "under the surface an abyss, and it is to this that I do not want to give a name."[71]

For years, in fact, that abyss seemed to take on the features of Edgar Allan Poe, the figure that Tate once called "this dark demon in the glass."[72] However much Tate might yearn on some level for the unified male sensibility that Lee appeared to embody, when he himself looked into the glass he saw, as he hinted in several essays on Poe, the dark features of the solitary, deracinated male self walled off from tradition and community that Poe represented for him. This was the persona that Tate periodically assumed—often in spite of himself—in such famous meditations upon southern history as "Ode to the Confederate Dead"—that is, the modern male writer attracted to the unity of the past and tradition and knowingly, utterly estranged from it. "If the trappings of Poe's nightmare strike us as tawdry," Tate warned in his famous essay "Our Cousin, Mr. Poe," "we had better look to our own." Indeed, Poe's plight was also that of Tate and his fellows, barred from tradition and the world of unity for which they longed. "He is so close to me," Tate concluded in that essay, "that I am sometimes tempted to enter the mists of pre-American genealogy to find out whether he may not actually be my cousin." [73]

There was also the possibility, though, that the abyss figured for Tate the slippage between master and slave also haunting the writers of the *Russell's Magazine* circle. Cataloguing the artistic deficiencies of the region in "The Profession of Letters in the South," Tate noted uneasily: "The Negro slave was a barrier between the ruling class and the soil." More to the point, he added: "The white man got nothing from the Negro, no profound image of himself in terms of the soil." Such was the gap lying between white master and black slave, he mused, that "we could graft no new life upon the Negro; he was too different, too alien." In a word, he concluded, "Black slavery could not nurture the white man in his own image." [74] Yet there remained the dark demon in the glass, sometimes taking on the lineaments of Poe—and sometimes taking on the features of black masculinity, undergirding and competing with white southern masculinity. [75]

In those features were all the slippages, the fluidity, the disruption of boundaries, that Tate and his colleagues feared, and those slippages could be both terrifying *and* empowering for African-American writers who found themselves implicitly quarreling with the Fugitive-Agrarians and their version of the profession of letters in the South. Richard Wright, for one, might have fled the South precisely to avoid stepping into that dark reflection, into "the roles that the white race had mapped out" for such as him, into "the role of a non-man." [76] But one can also discern in those dark features the array of black male tricksters with which southern black masculinity, as probed by scholars of black folklore like Lawrence Levine and John W. Roberts, came to be associated—the conjurer, the bad man, the "moral hard men" like John Henry and Joe Louis, men who triumphed, Levine tells us, "not by breaking the laws of the larger society but by smashing its expectations and stereotypes, by insisting that their lives transcend the traditional model and roles established for them and their people by the white majority." [77] One can discern as well the glittering, destructive weaponry of "signifying" wielded by these tricksters, disrupting the hierarchies, categories, and boundaries of southern white male discourse by underscoring the multiplicity of possible meaning. [78]

It is, in a sense, these features of the dark demon in the glass that Ralph Ellison celebrates in *Invisible Man*'s multiple-mirrored portrait of black masculinity—a celebration rooted as much in its subversive response to the image of the traditional white male southerner that Tate and the Agrarians anxiously tried to foster as in the richness of African-American culture itself. The novel's narrator discovers a bewildering and fluid range of choices available to black men—Trueblood the bluesman, Bledsoe the tyrant, Peter Wheatstraw the "Devil's only son-in-law," Lucius Brockway the modern Brer Rabbit, Clifton the activist, and Ras the Destroyer. Above all, he discovers the zoot suiters in the subway, "men out of time, who would soon be gone and forgotten. . . . But who knew . . . who knew but that they were the saviors, the true leaders, the bearers of something precious? The stewards of something uncomfortable, burdensome, which they hated because, living outside the realm of history, there was no one to applaud their value and they themselves failed to understand it." [79]

In the end, the fluid, quicksilver identity of the zoot suiters becomes that of the narrator, rendered invisible by the blindness of whites and now capable of turning that invisibility to his advantage. "Being invisible and without substance, a disembodied voice, as it were, what else could I do?" the narrator asks—and here his words, speaking from the depths of white fantasies of blackness, eerily evoke the dark demon in the glass, the reflection that Tate the white male southerner sees and only reluctantly acknowledges. "What else but try to tell you what was really happening when your eyes were looking through?" the narrator concludes. "And it is this which frightens me: Who knows but that, on the lower frequencies, I speak for you?" [80]

What words more uncannily evoke the fluidity and the slippages that Tate's profession of letters in the South so desperately strove to suppress, with only partial success? Other voices would contest Tate's version of southern letters—Sterling Brown in his angry denunciation of *I'll Take My Stand,* Lillian Smith in her pointed repudiation of Agrarian politics, Zora Neale Hurston in her retrieval of black folklore from white collectors, Caroline Gordon, Eudora Welty, and Katherine Anne Porter in their female critiques of regional memory and tradition.[81] But none would more eloquently voice Tate's own fears and anxieties—and those of southern literary history—than the concluding words of *Invisible Man,* speaking from the depths of New York City.

Tate himself, though, was honest enough to face on occasion those fears and their revealing fissures in southern letters—and perhaps most unflinchingly in his most self-consciously "southern" texts. The traditional South that he painted in his own contribution to the 1930 Agrarian manifesto was, as Paul Conkin and Richard Gray have emphasized, radically divided against itself—a feudal society without a feudal philosophy, a traditional society without a traditional literature.[82] And the lures of tradition—and its definitions of masculinity—as Tate himself reveals in essay and poems, lay precisely in its miragelike aura, in the ever-lengthening distance between tradition and the deracinated, uncertain, radically solitary modern male.

Even more pointed was the complicated relationship of Tate's white protagonist George Posey and his half brother, the slave Yellow Jim, in Tate's only novel, *The Fathers.* George sells his half brother to buy a fine horse and make an impressive show before other white male southerners and his future wife at a jousting tournament, and in that act lies, the novel implies, white southern society's doom. Among the consequences will be Jim's sense of betrayal, the accusation of rape later leveled against the slave, and the destruction of two women supposedly under George's protection. Thinking back to "the gentleman's tilt" where George first made his appearance on that horse, the novel's narrator, Lacy Buchan, has a momentary hallucination revealing as well as any other passage in Tate's work, or in southern literature, for that matter, the Hegelian master-slave relationship: "I saw Brother George charging down the course, his lance perfectly balanced; only I saw him sadly astride, not Queen Susie, but the man Yellow Jim whose face was as white as his master's. And they ran over a child in white, but they left her there, and it was all over in a minute, and the tournament had been won."[83]

Lacy's hallucination serves, in a sense, as an apt and fleeting figure of the power dynamics of southern literary history, dynamics inherited by Tate from the nineteenth century and confirmed in the shape he himself bestowed upon the profession of letters in the South. A white man is forever linked in conflict with a black man, a contest determining the masculinity of each. And the centrality of that contest necessitates the marginalization of anything remotely subordinate and feminine, including white and black women. In later years Tate would very nearly admit as much—in a late poem called "The Swimmers," tracing the connection to be made between the birth of his own poetic vision and the discovery of a black man's lynched body, and in a 1960s review of a book by his old comrade-in-arms Donald Davidson.[84] Pondering Davidson's nostalgic vision of the lost southern past, Tate noted sadly: "Mr. Davidson's Old South has always seemed to me to leave about half of the Old South out of account: the half, or third, or whatever the figures were, that included the Negro."[85] The words said as much about his own notion of southern letters as they did about Davidson's writing. Among other things, they were words acknowledging finally the cacophony of voices that Tate's version of the profession of letters in the South had tried—and ultimately failed—to suppress.

Notes

An earlier version of this essay, which has since been extensively revised, appeared as "Gender and the Profession of Letters in the South," in *Rewriting the South: History and Fiction*, ed. Lothar Hönnighausen and Valeria Gennaro Lerda (Tübingen: Francke Verlag, 1993). Permission to reprint the revised version of the essay is gratefully acknowledged. In addition, I would like to thank Colleen Kennedy, Anne Goodwyn Jones, and Judith Sensibar for their cogent criticisms of early versions of this essay. I would also like to extend general thanks to Katherine Hemple Prown and Alexandra Peña, with whom I have shared fruitful discussions on women writers and the Southern Literary Renaissance. Their work on Flannery O'Connor and Caroline Gordon, respectively, has helped me clarify my own ideas on gender and racial issues in modern southern literature and criticism.

    1. Allen Tate to John Peale Bishop, 9 March 1935, in *The Republic of Letters in America: The Correspondence of John Peale Bishop and Allen Tate,*

ed. Thomas Daniel Young and John J. Hindle (Lexington: Univ. Press of Kentucky, 1981), 113.

2. Allen Tate, "The Profession of Letters in the South," *Essays of Four Decades* (Chicago: Swallow Press, 1968), 520, 525, 530.

3. Allen Tate, "A Southern Mode of the Imagination," *Essays of Four Decades,* 579.

4. Tate, "The Profession of Letters," 527, 526.

5. Paul Bové argues that southern literary histories have "submerged all of the political struggles enacted within literary and critical practices" ("Agriculture and Academe: America's Southern Question," *Boundary 2* 14, no. 3 [1986]: 172).

6. George Fitzhugh, *Sociology for the South; or, The Failure of Free Society* (Richmond: A. Morris, 1854), 218.

7. "Women Artists," *Southern Review* (Baltimore) 5 (Apr. 1867): 318. See also Anne Goodwyn Jones, *Tomorrow Is Another Day: The Woman Writer in the South, 1859–1936* (Baton Rouge: Louisiana State Univ. Press, 1981), 3–50.

8. "Editor's Table," *Russell's Magazine* 1 (1857): 559.

9. Paul Hamilton Hayne, "Literature at the South: The Fungous School," *Southern Magazine* 14 (1872): 651, 652.

10. Jay B. Hubbell, *The South in American Literature, 1607–1900* (Durham: Duke Univ. Press, 1954), 603, 604.

11. Nina Baym, "Melodramas of Beset Manhood: How Theories of American Fiction Exclude Women Authors," *American Quarterly* 33 (1981): 124.

12. Mary Kelley, *Public Woman, Public Stage: Literary Domesticity in Nineteenth-Century America* (New York: Oxford Univ. Press, 1984), 22.

13. Tate, "The Profession of Letters," 521.

14. Steven M. Stowe, *Intimacy and Power in the Old South: Ritual in the Lives of the Planters* (Baltimore: Johns Hopkins Univ. Press, 1987), xvii. See also Eugene Genovese, *Roll, Jordan, Roll: The World the Slaves Made* (New York: Pantheon, 1974); Elizabeth Fox-Genovese, *Within the Plantation Household: Black and White Women of the Old South* (Chapel Hill: Univ. of North Carolina Press, 1988); Catherine Clinton, *The Plantation Mistress: Women's World in the Old South* (New York: Pantheon, 1982); Jean E. Friedman, *The Enclosed Garden: Women and Community in the Evangelical South, 1830–1900* (Chapel Hill: Univ. of North Carolina Press, 1985); Deborah Gray White, *"Ar'n't I a Woman?" Female Slaves in the Plantation South* (New York: Norton, 1985); *In Joy and Sorrow: Women, Family, and Marriage in the Victorian South,* ed. Carol Bleser (New York: Oxford Univ. Press, 1991); and Bertram Wyatt-Brown, *Southern Honor: Ethics and Behavior in the Old South* (New York: Oxford Univ. Press, 1982).

15. See in particular Wyatt-Brown, *Southern Honor,* 149–75. See also Ted

Ownby, *Subduing Satan: Religion, Recreation, and Manhood in the Rural South, 1865–1920* (Chapel Hill: Univ. of North Carolina Press, 1990); Elliott J. Gorn, " 'Gouge and Bite, Pull Hair and Scratch': The Social Significance of Fighting in the Southern Backcountry," *American Historical Review* 90 (1985): 18–43; and *Meanings for Manhood: Constructions of Masculinity in Victorian America,* ed. Mark C. Carnes and Clyde Griffen (Chicago: Univ. of Chicago Press, 1990).

16. Gorn, " 'Gouge and Bite,' " 39; Kenneth S. Greenberg, "The Nose, the Lie, and the Duel in the Antebellum South," *American Historical Review* 95 (1990): 62; and Ownby, *Subduing Satan,* 21–99.

17. Drew Gilpin Faust, *A Sacred Circle: The Dilemma of the Intellectual in the Old South, 1840–1860* (Baltimore: Johns Hopkins Univ. Press, 1977), x. Faust in particular notes that the concerns of literary men in the antebellum period appeared to be "very close to those of the century's ideal woman"— that is, the valuing of "culture," "sensibility," and emotional sensitivity (40).

18. Qtd. in Introduction, *A Man of Letters in the Nineteenth-Century South: Selected Letters of Paul Hamilton Hayne,* ed. Rayburn S. Moore (Baton Rouge: Louisiana State Univ. Press, 1982), 15.

19. "Editor's Table," *Russell's Magazine,* 3 (May 1858): 181. Lewis P. Simpson notes: "But the figure of the unlanded clergyman or printer or lawyer on the whole counted for less in the southern than in the northern colonies. The man of power in the South was represented in figures like William Fitzhugh and Robert Carter" (*Mind and the Civil War: A Meditation on Lost Causes* [Baton Rouge: Louisiana State Univ. Press, 1989], 18). To this statement we might add Elliott Gorn's insight about the power of words in the antebellum South: "In a culture that valued oral skills, the verbal battle itself—the contest over who best controlled the power of words—was a real quest for domination" (" 'Gouge and Bite,' " 28).

20. "Editor's Table," *Russell's Magazine* 1 (Apr. 1857): 88–89.

21. Thomas Roderick Dew, "Republicanism and Literature," *All Clever Men Who Make Their Way: Critical Discourse in the Old South,* ed. Michael O'Brien (Fayetteville: Univ. of Arkansas Press, 1982), 131.

22. Drew Gilpin Faust, "The Peculiar South Revisited," *Southern Stories: Slaveholders in Peace and War* (Columbia: Univ. of Missouri Press, 1992), 12; idem, "A Southern Stewardship: The Intellectual and the Proslavery Argument," *American Quarterly* 31 (1979): 63.

23. W.R.A., "The Duty of Southern Authors," *Southern Literary Messenger* 23 (1856): 245.

24. "Literature in the South," *Russell's Magazine* 5 (Aug. 1859): 389.

25. Ibid., 393, 391.

26. Qtd. in Hubbell, *The South in American Literature,* 580.

27. Hugh Honour, *The Image of the Black in Western Art: From the Rev-*

olution to World War I, Slaves and Liberators, vol. 1 (Cambridge: Harvard Univ. Press, 1989), 78, 51.

28. Significantly, Bertram Wyatt-Brown has argued: "Outside the fields of social commentary, law, and political theory, intellectuality was considered effete and pretentious, a sentiment that was to hobble southern men of letters for much of southern history. This was so because writing and thinking were isolating endeavors. Such activity was dangerously free of public scrutiny" ("The Evolution of Heroes' Honor in the Southern Literary Tradition," in *The Evolution of Southern Culture,* ed. Numan V. Bartley [Athens: Univ. of Georgia Press, 1988], 110). Noting the conjunction of race and gender in the antebellum period, Deborah Gray White has observed: "In the antebellum South . . . ideas about women went hand in hand with ideas about race. Women and Blacks were the foundation on which Southern white males built their patriarchal regime" (*"Ar'n't I a Woman?"* 58).

29. Simpson, *Mind and the Civil War,* 17–18.

30. G. W. F. Hegel, *The Phenomenology of Mind,* trans. and introd. J. B. Baillie, 2d ed. (London: Allen & Unwin, 1977), 236–37. See also Simpson's discussion in *Mind and the American Civil War,* 28.

31. Qtd. in Charles H. Bohner, *John Pendleton Kennedy: Gentleman from Baltimore* (Baltimore: Johns Hopkins Univ. Press, 1961), 187.

32. The standard white southern commentary on slave narratives appears to be summed up by white historian U. B. Phillips, who declared that most slave narratives "were issued with so much abolitionist editing that as a class their authenticity is doubtful" (*Life and Labor in the Old South* [Boston: Little, Brown, 1929], 219). Henry Louis Gates Jr., though, has suggested that slave narratives "spawned their formal antithesis, the Confederate romance" (*Figures in Black: Words, Signs, and the "Racial" Self* [New York: Oxford Univ. Press, 1987], 50).

33. Morrison declares: "Africanism is the vehicle by which the American self knows itself as not enslaved, but free; not repulsive, but desirable; not helpless, but licensed and powerful; not history-less, but historical; not damned, but innocent; not a blind accident of evolution, but a progressive fulfillment of destiny" (*Playing in the Dark: Whiteness and the Literary Imagination,* William E. Massey Lectures in American Civilization 1990 [Cambridge: Harvard Univ. Press, 1992], 52).

34. Joan Dayan, "Romance and Race," in *The Columbia History of the American Novel,* ed. Emory Elliott (New York: Columbia Univ. Press, 1991), 93.

35. Joan Dayan, "Amorous Bondage: Poe, Ladies, and Slaves," in *Subjects and Citizens: Nation, Race, and Gender from Oroonoko to Anita Hill,* ed. Michael Moon and Cathy N. Davidson (Durham: Duke Univ. Press, 1995), 135.

36. Dayan, "Romance and Race," 107.

37. See in general Thomas Nelson Page, *In Ole Virginia; or Marse Chan and Other Stories* (New York: Scribners, 1893). See also a brief reading of "No Haid Pawn" by Louis D. Rubin Jr. in "The Other Side of Slavery: Thomas Nelson Page's 'No Haid Pawn,'" *Studies in the Literary Imagination* 7, no. 1 (1974): 95–99.

38. See in general George Washington Cable, *The Grandissimes,* introd. Michael Kreyling (New York: Penguin, 1988) and Mark Twain, *Pudd'nhead Wilson and Those Extraordinary Twins: Authoritative Texts, Textual Introduction and Tables of Variants Criticism* (New York: Norton, 1980).

39. See, for example, Susan Gillman's discussion of this dream sequence in *Dark Twins: Imposture and Identity in Mark Twain's America* (Chicago: Univ. of Chicago Press, 1989), 50–52.

40. Eric J. Sundquist discusses the problem of unstable gender relations and the competition between black and white men in the postbellum South in *To Wake the Nations: Race in the Making of American Literature* (Cambridge: Harvard Univ. Press, 1993), 416–18, 425–28.

41. Frederick Douglass, *My Bondage and My Freedom,* in *Autobiographies* (New York: Library of America, 1994), 367. See also Frances Smith Foster, *Witnessing Slavery: The Development of Ante-Bellum Slave Narratives* (1979; rpt. Madison: Univ. of Wisconsin Press, 1994), 56.

42. Henry Louis Gates Jr., Introduction, *The Classic Slave Narratives,* ed. Gates (New York: Penguin-Mentor, 1987), ix; Foster, *Witnessing Slavery,* 146, 149, 22.

43. Ephraim Peabody, "Narratives of Fugitive Slaves," in *Critical Essays on Frederick Douglass,* ed. William Andrews (Boston: G. K. Hall, 1991), 24.

44. Foster, *Witnessing Slavery,* xli.

45. Frederick Douglass, *Narrative of the Life of Frederick Douglass, an American Slave,* in *Autobiographies,* 60.

46. Frederick Douglass, "Letter to His Old Master: To My Old Master, Thomas Auld," *My Bondage and My Freedom,* 417–18.

47. See, for example, Lucinda MacKethan, "Metaphors of Mastery in the Slave Narratives," in *The Art of Slave Narrative: Original Essays in Criticism and Theory,* ed. John Sekora and Darwin T. Turner (Macomb: Western Illinois Press, 1982), 56.

48. Deborah McDowell, "In the First Place: Making Frederick Douglass and the Afro-American Narrative Tradition," in *Critical Essays on Frederick Douglass,* 200, 203, 206. See also Valerie Smith, *Self-Discovery and Authority in Afro-American Narrative* (Cambridge: Harvard Univ. Press, 1987), 34.

49. Diane Roberts, *The Myth of Aunt Jemima: Representations of Race and Region* (New York: Routledge, 1994), 166.

50. Hortense J. Spillers, "Mama's Baby, Papa's Maybe: An American Grammar Book," *Diacritics* 17, no. 2 (1987): 77.

51. Anna Julia Cooper, *A Voice from the South,* introd. Mary Helen Washington (New York: Oxford Univ. Press, 1988), ii, iii, 31.

52. See, for example, Michael O'Brien's remarks on "the myth of Southern unity" in *The Idea of the American South, 1920–1941* (Baltimore: Johns Hopkins Univ. Press, 1979), 225 and passim.

53. See Allen Tate, "Last Days of the Charming Lady," *Nation* 28 Oct. 1925: 485–86.

54. Allen Tate, "A Southern Mode of the Imagination," 589.

55. John Crowe Ransom, "Reconstructed but Unregenerate," in *I'll Take My Stand: The South and the Agrarian Tradition,* by Twelve Southerners, introd. Louis D. Rubin Jr. (Baton Rouge: Louisiana State Univ. Press, 1977), 14.

56. Allen Tate, "Remarks on the Southern Religion," in *I'll Take My Stand,* 171–72.

57. See Michael O'Brien's discussion of Tate's notion of unity in "The Last Theologians," in *Rethinking the South: Essays in Intellectual History* (Baltimore: Johns Hopkins Univ. Press, 1988), 412.

58. Allen Tate to Donald Davidson, 12 Dec. 1929, in *The Literary Correspondence of Donald Davidson and Allen Tate,* ed. John Tyree Fain and Thomas Daniel Young (Athens: Univ. of Georgia Press, 1974), 245, 246.

59. John Crowe Ransom, "Modern with the Southern Accent," *Virginia Quarterly Review* 11 (1935): 187, 188.

60. Ibid., 194.

61. See in general Ulrich B. Phillips, "The Central Theme of Southern History," *American Historical Review* 24 (1928): 30–43.

62. Allen Tate, "A View of the Whole South," *American Review* 2 (1934): 424.

63. David Levering Lewis, *When Harlem Was in Vogue* (New York: Knopf, 1981), 269–70.

64. Allen Tate, "Aeneas at Washington," *Collected Poems, 1919–1976* (New York: Farrar, Straus, Giroux, 1977), 69.

65. Laura Riding to Donald Davidson, undated [1920s?], Donald Davidson Papers, the Fugitive Collection, the Jean and Alexander Heard Library, Vanderbilt University. Permission to quote from the Davidson papers is gratefully acknowledged.

66. Qtd. in Thomas W. Cutrer, "Conference on Literature and Reading in the South and Southwest, 1935," *Southern Review,* n.s. 21 (1985): 299.

67. *The Southern Mandarins: Letters of Caroline Gordon to Sally Wood, 1924–1937,* ed. Sally Wood (Baton Rouge: Louisiana State Univ. Press, 1984), 64, 60.

68. Qtd. in Ann Waldron, *Close Connections: Caroline Gordon and the Southern Renascence* (New York: Putnam, 1987), 199.

69. Allen Tate, note on envelope, Robert E. Lee manuscript, in Folder 6,

box 2 of the Allen Tate Papers, Manuscript Division, Department of Rare Books and Special Collections, Princeton University Libraries. Cited with permission of the Princeton University Libraries and Helen Tate. For good discussions of Tate's ambivalent feelings about Lee, see O'Brien, *The Idea of the American South*, 150; and Michael Kreyling, *Figures of the Hero in Southern Narrative* (Baton Rouge: Louisiana State Univ. Press, 1987), 111–24.

70. Tate, Robert E. Lee manuscript, 30–31, in Folder 6, box 2, Tate Papers.

71. Allen Tate to Andrew Lytle, 16 July 1931, *The Lytle-Tate Letters: The Correspondence of Andrew Lytle and Allen Tate*, ed. Thomas Daniel Young and Elizabeth Sarcone (Jackson: Univ. Press of Mississippi, 1987), 46, 47.

72. Tate uses the phrase in "Our Cousin, Mr. Poe," *Essays of Four Decades*, 387.

73. Ibid., 399, 400.

74. Tate, "The Profession of Letters," 525, 526.

75. Eric Lott, for instance, suggests that the notion "of dominant codes of masculinity in the United States was (and still is) partly negotiated through an imaginary black interlocutor." More specifically, he notes that "white male fantasies of black men undergird the subject positions white men grow up to occupy" (*Love and Theft: Blackface Minstrelsy and the American Working Class* [New York: Oxford Univ. Press, 1993], 53).

76. Richard Wright, *Black Boy (American Hunger)*, in *Later Works* (New York: Library of America, 1991), 188, 233.

77. Lawrence C. Levine, *Black Culture and Black Consciousness: Afro-American Folk Thought from Slavery to Freedom* (New York: Oxford Univ. Press, 1977), 420. See also John W. Roberts, *From Trickster to Bad Men: The Black Folk Hero in Slavery and Freedom* (Philadelphia: Univ. of Pennsylvania Press, 1989), 94, 103, 202–5.

78. See, for example, Claudia Mitchell-Kernan, "Signifying," in *Mother Wit from the Laughing Barrel: Readings in the Interpretation of Afro-American Folklore*, ed. Alan Dundes (1973; rpt. New York: Garland, 1981), 310–28, and Henry Louis Gates Jr., *The Signifying Monkey: A Theory of Afro-American Literary Criticism* (New York: Oxford Univ. Press, 1988).

79. Ralph Ellison, *Invisible Man* (New York: Random House, 1952), 134, 333.

80. Ibid., 439.

81. See, for example, Sterling Brown, "The Literary Scene: Chronicle and Comment," *Opportunity* 9 (1931): 20, and "Unhistoric History," *Journal of Negro History* 15 (1930): 134. See also Lillian Smith, *Killers of the Dream* (New York: Norton, 1949), 224–25; Zora Neale Hurston, *Mules and Men* (New York: HarperPerennial, 1990); Caroline Gordon, *Penhally* (1931; rpt. New York: Cooper Square Publishers, 1971); Eudora Welty, *The Collected*

Stories (New York: Harcourt Brace Jovanovich, 1980); and Katherine Anne Porter, *The Collected Stories* (New York: Harvest/Harcourt Brace Jovanovich, 1979).

82. Paul Conkin, *The Southern Agrarians* (Knoxville: Univ. of Tennessee Press, 1988), 70, 73; Richard Gray, *Writing the South: Ideas of an American Region* (New York: Cambridge Univ. Press, 1986), 134, 138.

83. Allen Tate, *The Fathers and Other Fiction,* introd. Thomas Daniel Young (Baton Rouge: Louisiana State Univ. Press, 1977), 227.

84. See Allen Tate, "The Swimmers," *Collected Poems,* 134–37.

85. Allen Tate, "The Gaze, Past, the Glance Present: Forty Years after *The Fugitive,*" *Memoirs and Opinions, 1926–1974* (Chicago: Swallow Press, 1975), 37–38.

Contributors

SUSAN V. DONALDSON teaches American literature and American Studies at the College of William and Mary. She is the editor of a special double issue of the *Faulkner Journal* on Faulkner and sexuality (1995) and has published many essays on Faulkner, Eudora Welty, Walker Percy, Ellen Douglas, and southern literature and culture in general. Her current projects include two book-length studies nearing completion: one on the politics of storytelling and memory in modern southern writing and painting and the other on the late nineteenth-century American novel.

ELIZABETH FOX-GENOVESE is the Eleonore Raoul Professor of the Humanities at Emory University and writes widely on women's literature, history, and contemporary issues. Her books include *"Feminism Is Not the Story of My Life": How Today's Feminist Elite Has Lost Touch with the Real Concerns of Women* (1996); *Feminism without Illusions: A Critique of Individualism* (1991); and *Within the Plantation Household: Black and White Women of the Old South* (1988).

CAROLINE GEBHARD, assistant professor of English at Tuskegee University, received her Ph.D from the University of Virginia in 1991. Specializing in American Studies, she has published essays on nineteenth-century women writers. Recent work includes an article on Harriet Beecher Stowe and an essay on the representation of Creek Indians at the Horseshoe Bend National Park. She is currently writing a book on Paul Laurence Dunbar and Alice Dunbar-Nelson.

MINROSE GWIN is professor of English at the University of New Mexico and author of *Black and White Women of the Old South: The Peculiar Sisterhood in American Literature* (1985) and *The Feminine and Faulkner: Reading (Beyond) Sexual Difference* (1990).

She is editor of *A Woman's Civil War* by Cornelia McDonald (1992) and coeditor of *Literatures of the American South* (forthcoming). She is currently working on a book on contemporary women's writing and spatial theory.

ANNE GOODWYN JONES's interest in gender and the American South can be traced to her childhood and adolescence, during which her traditional Virginia-born parents struggled endlessly to make a southern lady out of a budding Chapel Hill liberal. Her first book, *Tomorrow Is Another Day: The Woman Writer in the South, 1859–1936* (1981; 1995) will shortly be joined by *Theory and the Good Old Boys: Manhood and the Southern Renaissance*. In between she has written and spoken often about gender and the South. She next plans to complete her study of women in the South, *Faulkner's Daughters*. In 1996–97 she taught at Chiba University in Japan.

CATHERINE GUNTHER KODAT is assistant professor of English and American Studies at Hamilton College. Besides southern literature and African-American literature, her teaching and research interests include American literature of the 1950s and ballet. Her essay on William Faulkner and Toni Morrison, "A Postmodern *Absalom, Absalom!*, a Modern *Beloved*: The Dialectic of Form," appears in the University Press of Mississippi collection *Unflinching Gaze: Morrison and Faulkner Re-Envisioned* (1997).

JANE LANDERS is assistant professor of history and a member of the Center for Latin American and Iberian Studies at Vanderbilt University. She is the editor of *Against the Odds: Free Blacks in the Slave Societies of the Americas* (1996) and coeditor of *The African American Heritage of Florida* (1995) and has published essays on the African history of the Hispanic Southeast and of the circum-Caribbean in the *American Historical Review*, the *New West Indian Guide*, and *Slavery and Abolition*. Her forthcoming book, *Across the Southern Border: Black Society in Spanish Florida*, will be published by the University of Illinois Press.

DAVID LEVERENZ is a professor of English at the University of Florida. His publications include *Manhood and the American Renaissance*

(1989), *The Language of Puritan Feeling* (1980), and various articles and essays. From 1969 to 1985 he taught at Rutgers University, where he chaired the English department at Livingston College and thought of the South as a foreign country. When he and his wife decided to move to Florida, their oldest daughter said, "You had to choose the one state with less status than New Jersey."

LUCINDA H. MACKETHAN is Alumni Distinguished Professor of English at North Carolina State University. She is the author of *Daughters of Time: Creating Woman's Voice in Southern Story* (1990), and, most recently, articles on Morrison and Faulkner, on the plantation tradition, and on race in the urban fiction of Flannery O'Connor. She is completing a study entitled *Reading Women and Slavery in Nineteenth-Century Southern Literature* and, with Joseph Flora, a reference work, *The Companion to Southern Literature*.

DEBORAH E. MCDOWELL is professor of English at the University of Virginia, where she teaches courses in African-American literature. She is the coeditor with Arnold Rampersad of *Slavery and the Literary Imagination* (1989), founding editor of the Beacon Black Women Writers Series, period editor of the *Norton Anthology of African American Literature* (1997), and author, among others, of *"The Changing Same": Black Women's Literature, Criticism, and Theory* (1995) and *Leaving Pipe Shop: Memories of Kin* (1996).

MICHAEL O'BRIEN is Phillip R. Shriver Professor of History at Miami University (Ohio) and Senior Mellon Scholar in American History at the University of Cambridge. He has written mostly on the history of southern intellectual culture. His books include *The Idea of the American South, 1920–1941* (1979), *A Character of Hugh Legaré* (1985), and *Rethinking the South* (1988). He has also edited several works, notably, *An Evening When Alone: Four Journals of Single Women in the South, 1827–67* (1993).

TED OWNBY is associate professor of history and southern studies at the University of Mississippi. He is author of *Subduing Satan: Recreation, Religion, and Manhood in the Rural South, 1865–1920* (1990) and editor of *Black and White: Cultural Interaction in the Antebellum South* (1993). He is completing a study of consumer culture in Mississippi history and is pursuing a study of ideas of manhood in the recent South. He lives with family, dog, and album collection in Byhalia, Mississippi.

NOEL POLK is professor of English at the University of Southern Mississippi. He has published and lectured widely in this country, Europe, Japan, and the former Soviet Union on William Faulkner and Eudora Welty. He is the editor of the "New, Corrected" texts of Faulkner for the Library of America and Vintage International. Most recent publications include *Children of the Dark House* (1996) and *Eudora Welty: A Bibliography of Her Work* (1993).

PEGGY W. PRENSHAW holds the Fred C. Frey Chair in Southern Studies in the English Department at Louisiana State University. She is general editor of the Literary Conversations series (University Press of Mississippi) and has edited series volumes on Eudora Welty (1984 and 1996) and Elizabeth Spencer (1991). Her monographs and edited collections include *Elizabeth Spencer* (1985), *Women Writers of the Contemporary South* (1984), and *Eudora Welty: Critical Essays* (1979). She is a former editor of the *Southern Quarterly*.

STEVEN M. STOWE, an associate professor of history at Indiana University, Bloomington, received his Ph.D. from SUNY, Stony Brook, where he worked with William R. Taylor. He is the author of *Intimacy and Power in the Old South* (1987) and currently is working on a study of the experience of illness and the work of doctoring in the American South.

MARY TITUS is associate professor of English at Saint Olaf College. She enjoys writing about race and gender in southern literature and is currently engaged in a study of race, gender, and material culture in late nineteenth- and early twentieth-century American literature.

ANNE BRADFORD WARNER is associate professor of English at Spelman College. Her work has appeared in the *Southern Quarterly*, the *Hollins Critic*, and *Perspectives on Contemporary Literature*. She has published several articles on Harriet Jacobs and is currently writing a book-length project on Harriet Jacobs and the Rochester Circle.

BERTRAM WYATT-BROWN, Richard J. Milbauer Professor of History at the University of Florida, has published, among other works, *Lewis Tappan and the Evangelical War against Slavery* (1969), soon to be reissued; *Southern Honor: Ethics and Behavior in the Old South* (1982), a finalist for the Pulitzer and the American Book awards; *The House of Percy: Honor, Melancholy, and Imagination in a Southern Family* (1994); and *The Literary Percys: Gender, Family History and the Southern Imagination* (1994). His book reviews have appeared in the *New York Review of Books*, the *London Review of Books*, *Wilson Quarterly*, *Commentary*, and other journals. "The Mask of Obedience" won the ABC-Clio Award in 1990.

RICHARD YARBOROUGH is associate professor of English and African-American Studies at UCLA. A coeditor of the *Heath Anthology of American Literature* (1990) and the *Norton Anthology of African American Literature* (1997), he also directs Northeastern University's Library of Black Literature reprint series. He is currently working on a book on early black fiction.

PATRICIA YAEGER is the editor of *The Geography of Identity* (1996), coeditor of *Nationalisms and Sexualities* (1992), and author of *Honey-Mad Women: Emancipatory Strategies in Women's Writing* (1988). Her next book is *Dirt and Desire: The Grotesque in Southern Women's Fiction*. She teaches at the University of Michigan.

Selected Name and Title Index